# The Essential Guide to Public Procurement



Public procurement, the strategic process governments use to efficiently and ethically acquire goods and services, is a critical administrative function. And yet, few who practice or teach government contracting have received much formal training in the theories, tactics, and techniques of public procurement. *The Essential Guide to Public Procurement* is designed for all those who "fall into" procurement with little formal training: academic instructors teaching procurement courses without specialized backgrounds, students in Public Administration programs seeking to understand government contracting, researchers exploring this interdisciplinary field, and practitioners at all levels of government who manage over $10 trillion allocated annually in global procurement spending.

Each chapter combines academic research with practitioner insights, capturing key elements of the procurement process. Teaching cases developed in partnership with professional organizations like NIGP and NASPO make it an invaluable resource for both classroom instruction and professional development. Covering essential topics including strategic frameworks, regulations, procurement processes, and contract management, the book offers a thorough and up-to-date overview of the theoretical and practical perspectives that drive and govern procurement activities. In each chapter, authors examine the context and objectives of public procurement, the rules and institutions that shape government contracts, and the phases of the procurement process, equipping readers with the necessary knowledge to design and manage high-performing contracts. The book further identifies strategies to align procurement with broader public policy goals, including social impact and sustainability, and provides in-class activities to facilitate student learning. By bridging theory and real-world cases, *The Essential Guide to Public Procurement* equips practitioners, educators, and policymakers with the tools to navigate the complexities of government contracting and partnership management.

**Ana-Maria Dimand** is Assistant Professor in the Askew School of Public Administration and Policy, Florida State University, and Global Research Affiliate with the Sustainable Purchasing Research Initiative at American University, USA. Her extensive professional experience includes serving as Head of the Public Procurement Office and a legal advisor for the National Trade Registry in Bucharest, Romania. Dr. Dimand's research spans public management, government contracting, innovation, sustainability, and collaborative governance.

**Benjamin M. Brunjes** is Associate Professor in the Daniel J. Evans School of Public Policy and Governance at the University of Washington, USA. He studies how to design and implement complex forms of modern governance, including contracts, grants, and collaborative networks. Dr. Brunjes has served as Policy Fellow with the US Small Business Administration. His research has been published in *Public Administration Review*, *Journal of Public Administration Research and Theory*, and *Nonprofit and Voluntary Sector Quarterly*, among others.

**Andrea S. Patrucco** is an Assistant Professor of Supply Chain Management in the Department of Marketing and Logistics at the Florida International University College of Business, and currently Editor in Chief of the *Journal of Purchasing and Supply Management*. His research interests are in the field of management of buyer-supplier relationships in both the private and public sectors. He is one of the academic leaders of the International Research Study on Public Procurement Research group, and he actively collaborates with government organizations in the United States, such as the National Association of State Procurement Officers and the National Institute of Government Purchasing. His research has been published in several academic journals such as the *Journal of Supply Chain Management*, *Journal of Business Logistics*, *International Journal of Operations and Production Management*, *International Journal of Production Economics*, *Public Administration Review* and the *Journal of Purchasing and Supply Management*.

"An essential resource for public procurement professionals, this book bridges theory and practice, making it invaluable for education and application. It aligns with NIGP's mission, raising awareness in academia and inspiring future leaders. I plan to integrate it into our curriculum and ensure accessibility for our members."

**Todd Slater**, *NIGP: The Institute for Public Procurement, United States.*

"This is an excellent resource for students, practitioners, and academics interested in public procurement that has been edited by a powerhouse team of scholars. It masterfully blends together cutting edge topics in the theory and practice of public procurement, written by leading experts in key subject areas. I suspect this will be an excellent desk reference for many years to come."

**Steven Carnovale**, *Florida Atlantic University, United States.*

"*The Essential Guide to Public Procurement* is a welcome addition to the contracting literature. This book provides powerful conceptual frameworks for understanding how to maximize value from procurement along with practical approaches and tools. It is thorough, comprehensive, and accessible."

**Trevor Brown**, *Ohio State University, United States.*

"Professors Dimand, Brunjes and Patrucco have compiled a diverse set of contributions on the analysis and practice of public procurement, addressing well-established theoretical approaches and modern techniques that may prove useful in improving the efficiency and effectiveness of public procurement. It is interesting and useful for both researchers and practitioners."

**Germà Bel**, *University of Barcelona, Spain.*

"Teaching public procurement is one of the most important tasks for public affairs education worldwide. This book provides, in one place, an introduction to key theories and practical cases, making it an indispensable resource for teachers and students of public procurement."

**Ole Helby Petersen**, *Roskilde University, Denmark.*

"This book is an excellent resource for educators and public procurement professionals alike. Written by scholars specializing in public procurement, it offers an extensive overview of contemporary trends and foundational theories, making it a must-have resource. This comprehensive guide and the included case studies make it a worthy addition to any professional collection."

**Matthew Oyer**, *National Association of State Procurement Officials (NASPO), United States.*

"This book is an excellent resource for both public procurement practitioners and educators. By integrating real-world cases, it brings needed attention to public procurement and highlights its growing importance in today's complex and volatile environment. It offers valuable insights for understanding, teaching, and improving procurement practices in both public and policy settings."

**Wendy Tate**, *University of Tennessee, Knoxville, United States.*

# The Essential Guide to Public Procurement

## Bridging Theory and Practice

Edited by Ana-Maria Dimand, Benjamin M. Brunjes, and Andrea S. Patrucco

Routledge
Taylor & Francis Group
NEW YORK AND LONDON

Designed cover image: enisaksoy, Getty Images

First published 2026
by Routledge
605 Third Avenue, New York, NY 10158

and by Routledge
4 Park Square, Milton Park, Abingdon, Oxon OX14 4RN

*Routledge is an imprint of the Taylor & Francis Group, an informa business*



For Product Safety Concerns and Information please contact our EU representative GPSR@taylorandfrancis.com. Taylor & Francis Verlag GmbH, Kaufingerstraße 24, 80331 München, Germany.



*Library of Congress Cataloging-in-Publication Data*
Names: Dimand, Ana-Maria editor | Brunjes, Benjamin M. editor | Patrucco, Andrea S. editor
Title: The essential guide to public procurement : bridging theory and practice /
edited by Ana-Maria Dimand, Benjamin M. Brunjes and Andrea S. Patrucco.
Description: New York, NY : Routledge, 2026. |
Collection of essays by Christopher L. Atkinson and others. |
Includes bibliographical references and index.
Identifiers: LCCN 2025029121 | ISBN 9781032936048 hbk |
ISBN 9781032935966 pbk | ISBN 9781003566670 ebk
Subjects: LCSH: Government purchasing
Classification: LCC JF1525.P85 E87 2026
LC record available at https://lccn.loc.gov/2025029121

ISBN: 978-1-032-93604-8 (hbk)
ISBN: 978-1-032-93596-6 (pbk)
ISBN: 978-1-003-56667-0 (ebk)

DOI: 10.4324/9781003566670

Typeset in Sabon
by Newgen Publishing UK

Access the Support Material: www.routledge.com/9781032935966

# Contents

# Figures

# Tables

# Boxes

# Contributors

**Sawsan Abutabenjeh** is an Associate Professor of Public Policy and Administration in the Department of Government and Society at United Arab Emirates University. Her teaching and research focus on public management, procurement and contracting, supply chain management, public finance and budgeting, advanced research methods and design, and innovation policies..

**Barbara Allen** is Associate Professor of Public Management and Policy at Victoria University of Wellington – Te Herenga Waka, New Zealand.

**Lachezar G. Anguelov** is Member of the Faculty at The Evergreen State College.

**Christopher L. Atkinson** is Associate Professor in the Public Administration program at the University of West Florida in Pensacola, Florida, USA.

**Anisti Barrett**, a Durham County Management Fellow, graduated with her Master of Public Administration from North Carolina Central University College of Arts, Social Sciences and Humanities and is dedicated to advancing equity through public service, community development, and law.

**Shirley-Ann Augustin Behravesh** is an Assistant Professor of Sustainable Enterprise in Arizona State University's Thunderbird School of Global Management.

**Benjamin M. Brunjes** is Associate Professor in the Daniel J. Evans School of Public Policy and Governance at the University of Washington, USA.

**Carter B. Casady** is Senior Research Engineer in the Center for Sustainable Development and Global Competitiveness at Stanford University and non-resident Senior Fellow in the Center for Transportation Public-Private Partnership Policy at George Mason University.

**Yifan Chen** is an Associate Professor at Shanghai Jiao Tong University's School of International and Public Affairs.

**Nicole Darnall** is a Professor and the Arlene R. and Robert P. Kogod Eminent Scholar Chair in Sustainability at American University with appointments in the Kogod School of Business and the School of Public Affairs. She is also Director of AU's Sustainable Procurement Research Initiative.

**Luitzen de Boer** is Professor at the Department of Industrial Economics and Technology Management of NTNU in Norway.

**Michael Essig** holds Chair for Purchasing and Supply Management at Bundeswehr University Munich. He is Director of the Working Field Procurement including the Research Group for Law and Management of Public Procurement, the Defence Acquisition and Supply Management (DASM) Research Group as well as the Industrial Procurement Research Group.

**Sarah Eyaa** is Associate Professor and Head of School of Business at Excelsia University College, in New South Wales, Australia.

**Daniel Finkenstadt** is a professional military officer and previously Assistant Professor in the Naval Postgraduate School (NPS) Department of Defense Management offering courses in Enterprise Sourcing.

**Anthony Flynn** is Senior Lecturer in Purchasing and Supply Management at Atlantic Technological University.

**Stephanie Francis Grimbert** is Assistant Professor at the University of Deusto in San Sebastian (Spain) and Affiliated Member of CIRCLE at Lund University (Sweden).

**Andreas H. Glas** is PD Dr. in the Working Field Procurement and Supply Management at Bundeswehr University Munich and Managing Director of the Defence Acquisition & Supply Management Research Group.

**Sofia Gonzalez De Aguinaga** is a lead researcher on modern slavery in business supply chains based at the British Institute of International and Comparative Law with teaching experience at King's College London and the University of Liverpool.

**Heonuk Ha** is a Postdoctoral Research Associate at the Institute for Social Research, University of Michigan. His research examines American political institutions and public management, with a particular focus on government spending and AI governance.

**Moutaz Haddara** is Professor of Information Systems at Kristiania University College, Oslo, Norway; Adjunct Professor at SP Jain School of Global Management; TIAS School for Business and Society, Utrecht, Netherlands; University of South-Eastern Norway; and the American University in Cairo, in Egypt.

**Robert Handfield** is Bank of America University Distinguished Professor of Supply Chain Management at North Carolina State University, and Executive Director of the Supply Chain Resource Cooperative.

**Tamara Harden** is a Supply Technician with the Department of the Navy at Naval Air Station Pensacola. Formerly a Senior Procurement Specialist for the Escambia County School District, she has extensive experience in logistics, supply chain, and warehouse management in both federal and local government sectors.

**Timothy Hawkins** is currently Professor with the Department of Supply Chain Management, University of North Texas, Denton, TX, USA.

**Zachary Huitink** is Associate Teaching Professor, the inaugural Meredith Professorship Faculty Fellow in Online Learning, and the Birkhead-Burkhead Professor of Teaching Excellence through 2027.

**Josh Klika** is "Procurement Jedi" who holds a Certified Professional Public Buyer (CPPB) through the Universal Public Procurement Certification Council (UPPCC), a NIGP Certified Procurement Professional (NIGP-CPP) certification, and a Lean Six Sigma Green Belt (LSSGB) through the University of Washington.

**Marius Langseth** is AssociateProfessor at Kristiania University College and Associate Professor II at the Department of Industrial Economics and Technology Management at the Norwegian University of Science and Technology, Norway.

**Keunyoung (Eli) Lee** is an Assistant Professor in the Department of Public Administration and Policy at American University. His research focuses on how agency resources and political environments shape the attitudes and behavior of public employees. He is particularly interested in the role of agency reputation in influencing organizational outcomes and employee decision-making.

**Kayla Le** is completing her master's in Public Administration at Arizona State University's School of Public Affairs.

**Deanna Malatesta** is Associate Professor of Public Affairs at the O'Neill School of Public and Environmental Affairs, Indiana University.

**Carrie Mathes** is Procurement Manager for Orange County Government in Florida.

**Darin Matthews** is currently the chief procurement officer for Cal Poly State University in San Luis Obispo, CA.

**Clifford McCue** is Tenured Professor of Public Administration at Florida Atlantic University, Boca Raton, Florida.

**Jon Mikel Zabala-Iturriagagoitia** is Associate Professor at the University of Deusto in San Sebastian (Spain).

**Zulay Millan** currently serves as Assistant Manager of Procurement for Orange County, Florida.

**Godfrey Mugurusi** is Associate Professor of Logistics and Supply Chain Management, and Deputy Leader for Research at the Department of Industrial Economics and Technology management at Gjøvik, Norwegian University of Science and Technology, Norway. ..

**Arunachalam Narayanan** is Associate Professor of Analytics at G. Brint Ryan College of Business at University of North Texas.

**Suman Niranjan** is currently Assistant Professor of Logistics with the G. Brint Ryan College of Business, University of North Texas, Denton, TX, USA.

**Andrea S. Patrucco** is Assistant Professor of Supply Chain Management in the Department of Marketing and Logistics at the Florida International University College of Business, USA.

**Charles Penrod** is Professor for the Legal Studies Pre-Law Program at the University of West Florida.

**Bob Perkins** is a 30-year government procurement professional. Bob works as Procurement Director for Ada County and has served in this role since 2010.

**Eric Prier** is Tenured Professor of Political Economy at Florida Atlantic University, Boca Raton, Florida.

**Rene G. Rendon** is Professor of Acquisition Management at the U.S. Naval Postgraduate School where he teaches in the graduate degree programs in Defense Contract Management. Additionally, he conducts research in defense acquisition and contract management for the Department of Defense.

**William (Bill) Resh** is Chair and Professor of Public Management and Policy at the Andrew Young School of Policy Studies at Georgia State University in Atlanta. He is the Director of AYS's Civic Leadership Education and Research (CLEAR) Center. His work on the political economy of civil service and civil service labor markets has garnered several awards, including from the Academy of Management, the American Society for Public Administration, and the American Political Science Association.

**Evelyn Rodriguez-Plesa** is Assistant Professor in the School of Public Administration at the University of Central Florida (UCF).

**Jens K. Roehrich** is Professor of Supply Chain Innovation at the University of Bath, School of Management, UK.

**Fredo Schotanus** holds Chair of Public Procurement, Utrecht University's School of Economics in the Netherlands. He is also part of the management team of the Utrecht University Centre for Public Procurement (UUCePP).

**Thomas Sherman**, a global leader in infrastructure and risk management, has led power and energy projects worldwide, created P3 training programs for AIAI, and previously served as acting director of Virginia's Department of Transportation, where his leadership earned awards for innovation in contract management.

**Craig Smith** is Associate Professor in the School of Government and Public Policy at the University of Arizona.

**Brooke Smith** is City Recorder for Murray City, Utah, and is passionate about fostering positive community impact and promoting the responsible and ethical use of AI.

**Klaas Stek** combines an assistant professorship in Purchasing and Supply Management with managing the European Lab for Innovative Purchasing and Supply (EL-IPS) at the University of Twente (UT) in the Netherlands and coordinating a master course in Purchasing Management at the University of Twente for Industrial Engineering Management students.

**Justin M. Stritch** is Professor and Director of the Gerald G. Fox MPA Program at the University of North Carolina at Charlotte.

**Tünde Tátrai** is an economist and lawyer and works as Full Professor at the Corvinus University of Budapest, Institute of Operations and Decisions.

**Martina Trusgnach** works in the Central Responsible Procurement Group at the Greater London Authority Group, leading on ethical public procurement. She has a PhD in public procurement and human rights from the University of Greenwich.

**Helen Walker** is Chair of Operations and Supply Management at Cardiff Business School.

**Zhaohui Wu** is Professor and Toomey Faculty Fellow in the College of Business at Oregon State University in Corvallis, Oregon.

**Christopher R. Yukins** serves as Lynn David Research Professor of Government Procurement Law at the George Washington University Law School in Washington, DC, where he has taught since 2002.

# 1 Public Procurement Essentials

## An Introduction

*Benjamin M. Brunjes, Ana-Maria Dimand and Andrea S. Patrucco*

Many books begin with an introduction attempting to convince readers that the topic covered is of the utmost importance. Of course, we will get to that, as we do believe that carefully designed and well-managed public procurement is critical, both for the successful operation of modern governments and for the long-term sustainability of nations in the 21st century. But that is not why we initially conceived of this book.

This book is designed to address another common problem, both in the academy and in practice: many people who are engaged in the study, education, and implementation of public procurement entered the field by accident and with little formal training.

Around the world, we have professors and instructors who teach public procurement without having taken a class or written a paper on the topic. Sure, they might have encountered passing references to procurement in classes on political science (it's pork!), public administration (it's excessive!), management (it's hard!), or finance (it's expensive!). But not many professors have taken dedicated academic courses about public procurement. According to a recent survey, fewer than 50 universities worldwide even offer classes on public procurement.[1] Though some social scientists may have run into references to procurement in their scholarly pursuits, few are engaged in rigorous research on public procurement and government contracts.[2] To make matters worse, public procurement is taught in both public administration (or policy) schools and business schools, which each adopt decidedly different perspectives on what matters – just like governments and contractors often want vastly different things from contracts. Nonetheless, professors with peripheral knowledge and experience often step up to the lectern to teach students about public procurement. Some may occasionally even speak to news media to offer their expert opinions.

Similarly, many practitioners have little formal training. Writing about his experience entering the procurement field, Nick Jenkinson[3] states that "procurement wasn't a lifelong dream; like many, I kind of fell into it." Though Nick works in the private sector, his "many" includes a slew of public procurement officials. Surveys of children[4] indicate they are most interested in becoming social media influencers, doctors, nurses, athletes, musicians, actors, lawyers, veterinarians, soldiers, police officers, teachers, astronauts, and firefighters. Public procurement is not even mentioned as a possible career to explore! And yet, in 2024, approximately 500,000 people in the United States work for the government in public procurement roles, designing and managing contracts for public organizations at all levels – around 2 percent of all government employees. If that ratio holds for governments around the world, then more than 10 million people are currently working in public sector procurement jobs. Very few of them thought that they would be working on government contracts, and given the scarcity of academic programs, even fewer have received much education (aside from on-the-job training) about how to effectively perform the work they are assigned.

DOI: 10.4324/9781003566670-1

We get it. To be honest, none of us set out to study public procurement either. We wanted to be international business magnates, political scientists, and public servants. Well, on second thought, given those interests, it may not be that surprising that we somehow ended up studying government contracts – but we certainly did not grow up dreaming of careers in procurement.

We know that procurement is often perceived as relatively tedious, repetitive, and dry. Two of us work in policy schools. When we tell people that we teach public policy, we see their eyes light up – they are ready to talk about climate change, healthcare, technology, immigration, transportation, and so many other exciting, top-of-the-news topics. Then they ask us what we study. Government contracting and public procurement, we say, to their almost guaranteed dismay. We have seen more eyes glaze over when talking about our research than most philosophers.[5] The other one of us works at a business school, where public procurement is often seen as a lesser form of general procurement and logistics management – processes that are supposed to be made as efficient as possible. Public procurement is almost not worth studying as it is hampered by endless regulation and competing public values. Where is the profit in that?

Despite our accidental entry into public procurement, we have been among the fortunate few to take rigorous coursework in graduate school. We have learned the theories, the literature, and the practical applications. We have gone on to teach our own classes on public procurement to a range of students, including undergraduates, executives, and graduate students in public administration and business. And, to the general consternation of many around us, we have gone so far as to publish scholarly papers on the topic. In short, we have chosen to dedicate our professional careers to studying public procurement and educating people on the design and management of government contracts. We have chosen to stay, mostly because we think public procurement is more important than many people realize.

Government contracting is a practical field operating at the intersection of finance, management, policy, and politics. It involves the allocation of staggering sums for a diverse range of purposes. Contractors supply, support, and aid in the implementation of nearly every government program around the world. They work in social services, healthcare, national defense, public safety, environmental policy, transportation, and more. Contractors support government teams doing more ordinary work as well: human resources, financial management, facilities administration, and information technology. Paul Light (2018) has described contractors as a hidden workforce or shadow bureaucracy, wielding important power but operating largely unseen and unrecognized. This mysterious cadre of supporting actors is identified, vetted, and managed through the processes of public procurement.

We think that the people who teach, study, and implement public procurement should have a resource to help make sense of what is going on, from the basic motivations for contracting out to the nitty-gritty details of delivering complex procurements. This book compiles the academic literature on public procurement to offer practical insights into how to conceive of, design, and manage government contracts in the 21st century. Each chapter is designed to (a) summarize many of the key findings from academic research on public procurement, (b) offer insights for practitioners about how to manage the procurement process, (c) identify emerging issues that both practitioners and scholars should follow, and (d) provide teaching materials for instructors who are tasked with teaching a class that might be somewhat outside their area of expertise (including teaching cases). The book marries theory and practice in a way that is both useful for instructors taking on public procurement (for a week or for an entire course) and insightful for practitioners hoping to learn more about the strategies and tactics of public procurement.

This has been no small task. As both academics and practitioners tend to "fall into" public procurement, the resulting field has struggled to form a coherent identity. Academic studies have propagated across a range of disciplines, contexts, and theoretical perspectives (Trammell et al. 2020). Practitioners may identify with their agency or their previous experience more than their current role in public procurement (Steinfeld, Prier, and McCue 2015). The field can seem like a collection of accidental participants who have a very limited day-to-day impact.

Yet, procurement is one of the most important governmental activities. According to recent estimates, government contracts account for 12–15 percent of global GDP, or more than $10 trillion per year (Organisation for Economic Co-Operation and Development (OECD) 2023). Public agencies procure goods and services from nearly every marketplace, ranging from simple things, like office supplies, structure repair, and lawn care, to highly complex needs, such as submarines, IT systems, and management consulting. Contractors are involved in the design, management, and delivery of nearly every government program in many nations around the world (Dudley and Bogaevskaya 2006). As a result, government contracts are key sources of revenue for many different types of firms, meaning that public procurement spending is a critical and strategic part of most marketplaces (Patrucco et al. 2024). And governments are increasingly reliant on contractors to successfully deliver public programs. In the United States some localities have contracted out nearly every public service (Prager 2008). Though many recognize the importance of government funding for large firms (such as in the defense and consulting industries), public procurement is also a critical source of funding for small businesses. Government investment is a key factor in the incubation and success of small firms across many contexts, goods, and services (Lalkaka 2003; Preuss 2011; Shepard 2013). At the local level, nonprofits are also highly reliant on government contracts, particularly to support work on healthcare and social services (Anguelov and Brunjes 2023). That is, public procurement is important and highly influential for almost every economic sector and in many nations.

See – we told you we'd get to a bigger picture justification. Though government contracts are not everywhere, like chemistry or physics, they are very important for most government programs' day-to-day design and management. And it involves spending a lot of money. But, as we have established, few faculty and practitioners have comprehensive knowledge of public procurement – there are not many people who know the basics, and those that do are often limited in their knowledge to academic or practitioner perspectives.

## 1.1 Approach of the Book: Procurement as a Core Government Process

This book is an edited guide composed of knowledge co-created by scholars and practitioners specializing in public procurement across many disciplines. We have assembled a collection of chapters from some of the most knowledgeable and respected public procurement and government contracting scholars in the world. The authors include experienced researchers, junior scholars, and doctoral students, all of whom contribute uniquely valuable perspectives. To ensure the chapters are not purely academic, we have partnered these scholars with public procurement officials, specialists, and other practitioners. The resulting chapters bridge theory and practice across key areas of public procurement, including theoretical frameworks, regulations, procurement processes, contract management, essential skills, and emerging trends.

Procurement refers to the processes organizations (governments or companies) use to acquire goods, services, and works from third parties to meet operational and developmental needs. Procurement typically encompasses several key stages: identifying needs, planning and budgeting, drafting specifications, conducting the tendering process, evaluating bids (proposals), awarding contracts, and managing their execution. Each of these stages is vital to the success of public procurement, forming the backbone of the system explored in this guide.

The steps of the public procurement process interact with an intricate ecosystem of regulatory, institutional, strategic, and operational elements. Organizational goals, public values, and market conditions shape this ecosystem. Across markets and countries, public procurement methods, terminology, and regulatory frameworks vary widely, reflecting unique demands. Common methods include Requests for Proposals (RFPs) for complex purchases and Requests for Quotations (RFQs) for simpler, cost-driven acquisitions. Other approaches, such as open bidding, direct purchases, and long-term contracts (e.g., framework agreements) further highlight the diversity and adaptability of procurement practices.

The guide's structure reflects the complexity of public procurement as both a process and an ecosystem. Figure 1.1 illustrates the fundamentals of the procurement process as well as the complex environment that surrounds and informs government decisions. Subsequent chapters explore these themes. This conceptual roadmap highlights the interplay between stages of public and broader contextual, strategic, and practical considerations that influence outcomes.

## 1.2 Detailed Overview of the Book

The guide includes 23 chapters, spanning four primary sections. Each chapter offers insights across the public procurement cycle, facilitating a deep and far-reaching understanding of government contracting. Key areas covered include the following:

1. **Theoretical perspectives** that motivate contracting out and guide public procurement activities.
2. **Contextual goals and influences,** including rules, institutions, values, and objectives shaping government contracts.
3. **A review of the procurement process,** shedding light on designing and managing high-performing contracts.
4. **Innovative procurement modalities** and their applications in addressing emerging challenges like sustainability and technology adoption.
5. **Strategies for using procurement** to advance secondary policy goals, such as social equity, sustainability, and innovation.
6. **Practical resources for teaching and learning,** including case studies and in-class activities.

### *1.2.1 Section 1: Theoretical Perspectives: Making Sense of Public Procurement*

First, the book introduces theoretical perspectives to help make sense of public procurement: agency theory, transaction cost economics, and resource dependency theory. These are the three primary theories that have dominated scholarship on contracting and procurement for much of the past 50 years. Each chapter offers insights into the basic principles of each theory, facilitating an understanding of the core tenets and explaining how to apply these models to practical purchasing and contract management.

In Chapter 2, Christopher L. Atkinson presents the basics of contract theory and the inherent tensions created when principals hire agents to work on their behalf. This includes a discussion of the basic institutional arrangements of contracting, information asymmetries, and behavioral expectations of the principal and the agent applied to the public

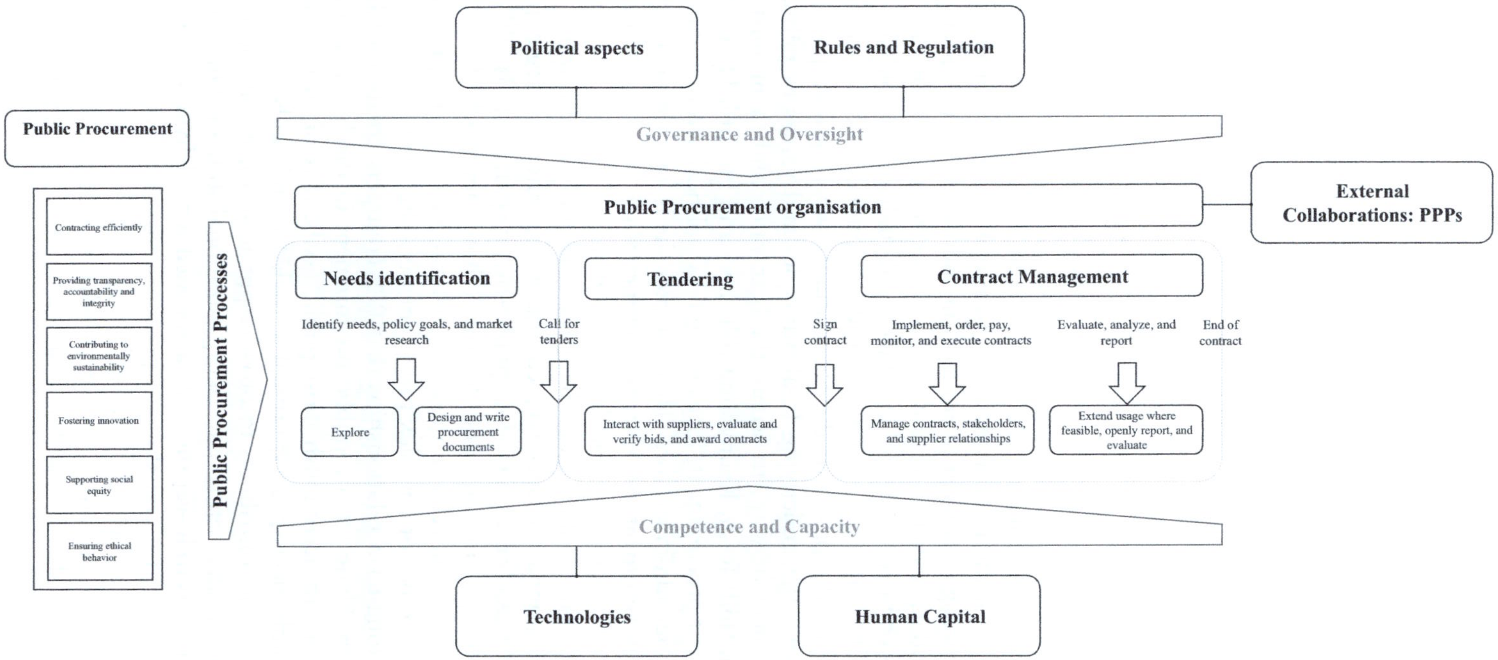


*Figure 1.1* The public procurement ecosystem.
*Source*: Original creation.

sector. In Chapter 3, Zach Huitink introduces transaction cost economics as applied to contractual relationships. Huitink notes that contracts necessarily create hidden costs that influence how organizations perceive contract opportunities. The chapter explains *ex-ante* and *ex-post* transaction costs and how they might affect the design and management of contracts. Despite the dominance of agency theory and transaction cost economics in the literature, there are other theories that matter for our understanding of public procurement. In Chapter 4, Deanna Malatesta and Craig Smith offer an alternative view of contracts and procurement, characterizing the interactions they create as a set of power relationships. This chapter discusses why and how organizations seek resources, what resource-seeking means for power dynamics between organizations, and how resource dependencies can influence the terms and performance of government contracts.

### *1.2.2 Section 2: The Context and Goals of Public Procurement*

The next section of the book addresses the context and goals of public procurement, situating contracts in the complex context of laws, politics, cross-sectoral pressures, public values, and ethics. Public procurement occurs at the nexus of many forces influencing contracting officials. This section of the book is designed to prepare readers for the various external factors that influence government contracts, including political and legal constraints, the influence of budget-makers and lobbyists, the strategic goals of public procurement programs and their competing values, and the ethical challenges of public procurement.

In Chapter 5, Christopher R. Yukins introduces public procurement law, rules, and regulations, discussing the basics of the legal context where public procurement occurs. This chapter identifies the underlying legal principles and values of public procurement, including an assessment of ways to secure the best value and maintain transparency. In Chapter 6, William (Bill) Resh, Keunyoung (Eli) Lee, and Heonuk Ha explain the role of politics in government procurement, focusing on how political actors and institutions affect the choices of contract administrators. Their chapter sheds light on the mutual dependence across branches of government and sectors, offering insights into operating effectively in a politically charged environment. Though public procurement happens in political systems, the day-to-day management of contracts happens inside public organizations.

From an organizational perspective, contracts are often strategic partnerships. In Chapter 7, Carter B. Casady et al. introduce public–private partnerships (PPP), distinguishing them from other types of contracts and describing how they work. The chapter discusses the benefits and risks associated with these longer-term contracts and provides insights into how to manage these types of complex procurements. This includes structuring incentives and managing the long-term relationships that PPP contracts create. In Chapter 8, Helen Walker and Anthony Flynn situate public procurement in the broader context of public organization strategy. To accomplish most public goals, it is often necessary to contract out, as private organizations possess critical knowledge and skills. This chapter explains how public procurement contributes to broader public sector goals and how to structure procurement systems as an essential part of organizational strategy. One powerful rationale for public procurement is to lower the costs associated with delivering government services while accessing the expertise and skills of private sector partners. In Chapter 9, Sawsan Abutabenjeh and Rene G. Rendon introduce the idea of efficiency, explain how it is achieved through markets and competition, and describe what it means in the context of public purchasing. The chapter will discuss building and maintaining an efficient procurement system and measuring efficiency in practice.

Other public values (aside from efficiency) are also critical in public procurement. Contracts are increasingly used to advance social equity and ensure sustainable production methods. In Chapter 10, Justin M. Stritch, Yifan Chen, Nicole Darnall, Shirley-Ann Augustin Behravesh, and Kayla Li describe the rise of sustainable, or green, public procurement. They define sustainable procurement, give examples of how this approach is changing procurement in practice, and offer insights into how to instill a commitment to green public procurement. In Chapter 11, Evelyn Rodriguez-Plesa and Anisti Barrett introduce the equity mission of public procurement, which is one of the most established and successful ways public funds have been consistently allocated to socially disadvantaged groups. The chapter discusses set-aside programs, preference policies, and other forms of social equity programs designed to encourage market participation for and public investment in disadvantaged or preferred groups. Procurement is also designed to spur partnerships with ethical and innovative organizations. In Chapter 12, Stephanie Francis Grimbert and Jon Mikel Zabala-Iturriagagoitia present public procurement as a tool to create a potential market for innovative products and services. Used strategically, public procurement can help governments become more innovative, improve productivity, and promote inclusiveness. The chapter defines the different types of procurement innovation and identifies principles to promote innovation through procurement. In Chapter 13, Sofia Gonzalez De Aguinaga and Martina Trusgnach address the ethical stewardship of public dollars when purchasing from nongovernmental actors. Beginning with a discussion of the ethical challenges and commitments of public procurement officers, the chapter offers practical advice on how to present and overcome procurement ethics problems, including how to ensure process transparency, reduce corruption, and retain impartiality in procurement decisions. One of the strategies to ensure ethical procurement is to share data on procurement activities openly and transparently. In Chapter 14, Clifford McCue, Eric Prier, and Tünde Tátrai introduce transparency as an accountability mechanism and offer insights into the benefits and drawbacks of transparency programs. The chapter discusses possibilities and problems with designing and implementing effective transparency programs and offers other solutions to promote procurement accountability.

### *1.2.3 Section 3: The Contracting Cycle: Managing the Public Procurement Process*

The third section of this book describes the practical steps required to manage public procurement and government contracts. Beginning with a look at the procurement function within public organizations, the section also investigates contract design, the solicitation and proposal evaluation process, performance management. Designed to be a practical guide on how to make sense of and manage procurement at each major step, this section imparts the skills and knowledge necessary to manage a contract from initiation to conclusion. In Chapter 15, Darin Matthews examines the characteristics of an effective public procurement organization, including the position of procurement in the organizational chart, the relationship of procurement with other agencies, the pros and cons of different organizational models (e.g., centralized vs. decentralized), and characteristics of the procurement workforce, in terms of roles, responsibilities, and specialization. This chapter includes important insights on how to structure and manage the people and partnerships that are so critical to public procurement.

Public procurement begins with the decision to contract out. Once governments elect to buy a good or service, contracting officials begin to design a contract. In Chapter 16, Jens K. Roehrich introduces the actions taken early in the procurement process and how they might influence the rest of a contract's lifecycle. Beginning with how a contract is designed, this chapter includes information on requirements generation, how to leverage market competition, the different financial structures and incentives, and more. In addition, it presents approaches for managing the relationship with suppliers throughout the contract lifecycle. In Chapter 17, Fredo Schotanus and Luitzen de Boer describe how to manage the solicitation process, including the different methods that can be used to solicit bids and proposals, strategies for advertising and marketing the contract, good practices for communicating with vendors, ways to evaluate proposals, and procedures for selecting winners. The chapter also discusses the ethical obligations of public managers as they navigate solicitation, a time when a range of unexpected pressures may seek to influence decision-making.

All these early steps – structuring an effective organization, designing a contract, and carefully evaluating proposals – are conducted in the hope that the contractor will perform well. In Chapter 18, Lachezar G. Anguelov and Benjamin M. Brunjes identify different strategies that can be used to inspire good performance. They link performance to the other elements of contract management, introduce the importance of relationships, discuss the benefits and drawbacks of different performance arise approaches, and outline strategies for correcting performance problems should they occur. Robert Handfield, Zhaohui Wu, and Daniel Finkenstadt add a logistics perspective in Chapter 19, discussing how public procurement matters across supply chains using the case of the United States. Looking at federal and state procurement, Handfield argues that public investments are increasingly important for performance across industries, while underscoring the importance of knowledge of supply chain and logistic management techniques for successful government contracting.

### *1.2.4 Section 4: Technologies and Skills in Government Contracting and Public Procurement*

The final section of the book covers recent developments in public procurement, including emerging technologies such as e-procurement, artificial intelligence (AI), and additive manufacturing. The section concludes with a discussion of interpersonal procurement skills, including relationship building and effective communication. This section offers information about how technologies are changing public procurement, the biases that these technologies may create, and the continued importance of human connection in contracting.

The first three chapters in this section address emerging technologies. In Chapter 20, Barbara Allen introduces e-procurement, including the rationale for using software tools and the efficiency benefits associated with electronic purchasing. The chapter also discusses how e-procurement might contribute to or detract from the attainment of procurement goals and public values. In Chapter 21, Godfrey Mugurusi, Marius Langseth, Sarah Eyaa, and Moutaz Haddara address digitalization and the use of AI in public procurement. They discuss the role of blockchain and machine learning approaches from around the world, defining these terms and showing how they are currently being applied to manage government contracts. Chapter 22, by Andreas H. Glas and Michael Essig, discusses the use of two interrelated technologies: "Digital Twin" and "Additive Manufacturing." Both technologies bridge the gap between the "physical" world with hardware products and the "digital" world where we can easily create and improve data- and software-driven products. This chapter summarizes and informs the reader about practical applications, using applied examples. All these chapters also address some of the biases and problems that software, AI, and other advanced tools might introduce to public procurement.

In the final chapter of the book, Klaas Stek presents an analysis of the core competencies required in public procurement today. He explores how contracting officials can develop soft skills such as creativity, inventiveness, and strategic thinking. This chapter identifies exercises that can enhance learning and equip future procurement professionals with the soft skills required to meet the evolving demands of public organizations.

For most chapters, the authors and editors have worked closely with practitioners to develop associated teaching cases. In this, we have benefitted greatly from the expertise and partnership of NIGP: The Institute for Public Procurement and the National Association of State Procurement Officials (NASPO). We are indebted to these practitioners for their insightful contributions. These cases are appended to each chapter, supported by teaching tips (available online), serving as a critical component of this text. After all, we are trying to bridge the gap between theory and practice. These cases give you the chance to connect the ideas from each chapter to the day-to-day problems that public contract managers confront.

As stated at the outset of this chapter, we believe that public procurement is critical in modern governments. In this book, we aim to address the gaps in knowledge and training for those studying, teaching, and practicing public procurement, while also emphasizing the field's importance. Public procurement is a vital yet underappreciated aspect of governance, touching nearly every sector of the economy and shaping the outcomes of countless public programs. By providing a comprehensive resource that integrates theory and practice, this book equips readers with the tools needed to effectively navigate the complexities of government contracting. We hope to inspire greater academic focus on public procurement while empowering practitioners to achieve better outcomes in their work. Whether you are an instructor, student, researcher, or practitioner, this book is designed to provide insights, strategies, and materials to deepen your understanding and enhance your work. You might be here by accident – we know we are. But the work you're doing is very important, no matter what your role is in public procurement. Public procurement and government contracting deserve the attention and expertise this book cultivates. Welcome to the journey – let's begin.

## Notes

1 In a forthcoming paper, some of the preeminent minds in public administration have taken stock. Brown, Brogaard, Petersen, and Potoski (2025) identified only 26 such courses across the globe.

2 See Trammell, E., Abutabenjeh, S., & Dimand, A. M. (2020). A review of public administration research: where does public procurement fit in? *International Journal of Public Administration*, *43*(8), 655–667 for an assessment of just how popular public procurement research truly is.

3 You can read all about Nick's journey to a procurement career in his blog post here: www.procurious.com/procurement-news/accidental-procurement-career?

4 This survey was conducted by YouGov – there are others that tell a similar story. You can see their findings here: https://today.yougov.com/technology/articles/39997-influencer-dream-jobs-among-us-teens

5 We actually love philosophy and political theory, as you'll see in this book. But there is some evidence that college students look on philosophy as the most impenetrable of subjects. Check it out here: https://cah.ucf.edu/fpr/article/why-is-so-much-philosophy-so-tedious/

## References

Anguelov, L. G., & Brunjes, B. M. (2023). A replication of "contracting out: for what? With whom?". *Public Administration*, *101*(3), 1163–1197.

Brogaard, L., Brown, T., Petersen, O. H., & Potoski, M. (2025). Human resources for public sector contracting: An education and training perspective for formal and relational management. *International Journal of Commerce and Contracting*, 29768829251369390.

Dudley, L., & Bogaevskaya, A. (2006). Contracting as Policy: Worldwide implications. *Privatization and market development: Global movements in public policy ideas*, 36–62. Edward Elgar Publishing.

Lalkaka, R. (2003). Business incubators in developing countries: Characteristics and performance. *International Journal of Entrepreneurship and Innovation Management*, *3*(1–2), 31–55.

Light, P. C. (2018). *The government-industrial complex: The true size of the federal government, 1984–2018*. Oxford University Press.

Organisation for Economic Co-Operation and Development (OECD). (2023). *Public procurement*. OECD. Retrieved from www.oecd.org/gov/public-procurement/

Patrucco, A. S., Kauppi, K., Di Mauro, C., & Schotanus, F. (2024). Enhancing strategic public procurement: A public service logic perspective. *Public Management Review*, 1–21. https://doi.org/10.1080/14719037.2024.2411630

Prager, J. (2008). Contract city Redux: Weston, Florida, as the ultimate new public management. *Public Administration Review*, *68*, 167–180. https://doi.org/10.1111/j.1540-6210.2007.00846.x

Preuss, L. (2011). On the contribution of public procurement to entrepreneurship and small business policy. *Entrepreneurship & Regional Development*, *23*(9–10), 787–814.

Shepard, J. M. (2013). Small business incubators in the USA: A historical review and preliminary research findings. *Journal of Knowledge-Based Innovation in China*, *5*(3), 213–233.

Steinfeld, J. M., Prier, E., & McCue, C. (2015). Public procurement and the BLS: Operationalizing occupational duties. *International Journal of Public Sector Management*, *28*(7), 510–527.

Trammell, E., Abutabenjeh, S., & Dimand, A. M. (2020). A review of public administration research: Where does public procurement fit in? *International Journal of Public Administration*, *43*(8), 655–667.

Section 1

# Theoretical Perspectives

## Making Sense of Public Procurement

# 2 Contract and Agency Theories

*Christopher L. Atkinson and Charles Penrod*

## 2.1 Introduction

A knowledge of contract and agency theory is an indispensable part of a public procurement professional's toolkit. This chapter explores contract and agency theories. Theory draws on facts and understanding to explain or describe phenomena and can help us prepare for what might happen in given contexts so that we can make better, if not optimal, choices. Theory in public procurement is a help to understanding why actors involved in contracting behave as they do and may also assist students in the field in avoiding pitfalls and hazards posed by practice. Because theory assists with explaining, predicting, and interpreting (White, 2005), theory and its application can help one make sense of this increasingly complex and challenging, yet essential and rewarding, part of the public sector enterprise.

This chapter focuses on various theoretical sources that inform contracting scholarship and practice in public contracting; while theory is a recurrent theme in this volume, generally speaking, this chapter seeks to provide a survey of theory and application to public procurement. The first section highlights major contributions to public choice and social choice theory, followed by a discussion on the theoretical foundation of competition in public procurement. The next section explores agency theory, including a detailed discussion of the law of agency, agency authority, and information asymmetry. More recent issues highlighted in the literature are contemplated, including applications of transaction cost theory, incentive theory, and incomplete contract theory. The following section presents practical applications of theory in the public administration workspace, focusing on behavioral aspects. This chapter concludes with a case study.

## 2.2 Summary of Literature

### *2.2.1 Public Choice and Social Choice Theory*

Individual interests and rights are essential to the founding conceptions of the American republic. John Locke suggested property rights as primary natural rights, the allowance of which was integral to the usefulness of society (Locke, 1952, orig. 1689). Hobbes, Locke, and Rousseau all noted the need for a social contract to allow for society to emerge from a "brutish" primordial state. Rousseau had a more positive view of human nature, in that self-interested action was not the rule of human nature but an exception and should only occur where society benefits (Munger, 2013). Locke and Hobbes, pessimistically or realistically – depending on how one considers it – saw people as more self-interested. In Locke's way of thinking, autonomy is essential to justifying society (Munger, 2013). Because contract and agency theory considers parties in contracts and business decisions that are primarily, even necessarily, self-interested, this section considers a theoretical foundation from

DOI: 10.4324/9781003566670-3

this perspective. These activities are emblematic of rational choice, meaning "purposeful or goal-oriented behavior, subject to constraints" (Munger, 2013, p. 40).

Reed, Curtis, and Lovrich offered an ideal type of rationality in public decision-making: "American democracy mandates that public organizations base their policy decisions on a rational analysis of causal relations between the policy and the underlying behavior that is the object of the policy" (2020, p. 316). There are clear expectations in public administration generally, and in public contracting in particular, that officials act in a manner that is rule-bound, predictable, rational, and well-documented. Businesses typically would not deign to put their resources at risk, so the government must guard against making decisions in an illogical and uninformed way, lest they unnerve would-be partners and reduce or eliminate their potential vendor pool.

This noted, some public officials might rationally be "advancing their own ideological interests" as a goal removed from addressing the public policy consideration in focus (Reed, Curtis, & Lovrich, 2020, p. 325). This should come as little shock to anyone who has worked in a public or private organization. All individuals have self-interests, and all choices are essentially individual ones since organizations, governments, and businesses do not, as entities, make choices – their leaders do (Reksulak, Razzolini, & Shughart, 2013). Public choice is basically a market theory, invoking "individual choice as the basis for organizational…actions, individuals' preferences as expressions of individual choices, rules to facilitate and assure order…[and] satisficing" (Farazmand, 2002, p. 35).

Those in power, representing the majority, do well to remember that a small increase in value for their group may result in large drops in value for underserved groups. Supposedly, rational people understand this, which is why there is reason to question whether the voting public or its elected officials are all that rational (Rowley, 2013). Farazmand (2002) rightfully calls out officials' behavior, potentially at public cost, and the inability of some underserved segments of the population to make their own self-interested choices in this decision context as shortfalls of public choice theory. This is important for public procurement because public choices for contracts essentially represent the public. The government's buying habits are not simply a matter of obtaining needed goods and services but also plainly send an economic message (as in buying from local or small businesses) and a social message (that the government is acting as a good steward of the public's money). Poor behavior by officials undermines public trust, which can be especially notable in public procurement contexts.

Like public choice theory, social choice theory is related to rational choice theory. Paul E. Johnson wrote that "Social choice theory investigates procedures that attempt to 'amalgamate' or 'blend' the preferences of the many into a social ranking of alternatives" (1998, p. 1). It is assumed in social choice theory that citizens have a role to play in societal decision-making. However, especially relevant to social choice theory is Arrow's impossibility theorem, which suggests that "there is no social preference function (sometimes will say social choice procedure to break up the monotony) that meets some apparently minimal (and seemingly easy to meet) criteria of democratic decision making" (Johnson, 1998, p. 13). The resulting system does not represent the will of the people (Ingham, 2019). As with public choice above, social choice does suggest some connection with public procurement, but unlike public procurement, the problem of public contracting for social choice is that given selection criteria, choices on the award are made. Preferences may be included among ranking criteria or even responsiveness criteria in procurement, but it would be difficult to amalgamate the choices of a broad coalition of people into a contract award on matters of, for example, technical merit or adherence to specifications.

### *2.2.2 Competition*

The notion is often posited that competition has significant benefits for public sector contracting, including cost savings, innovation, and accountability for contractors because they can theoretically be replaced by other rival contractors. However, Brunjes (2021), challenging market-based wisdom, demonstrated that competitive sourcing can result in costlier contracts, with some subject to early termination. The root of agency theory and expectations of a business-like government, as in New Public Management (which suggests that government should be more business-like, with customers instead of citizens), does not always hold in the very different context of public sector procurement.

Comments about the negative aspects of reducing vendor pools above notwithstanding, there are benefits and disadvantages for the government keeping a limited pool of vendors. One positive is the value of buyer–seller relationships (Brunjes, 2021). Another is the ability of the government to draw "informational rents from sellers," but this is primarily when the form of procurement is negotiation rather than auction-based (Kang & Miller, 2022, p. 1495). Simply put, the government would often rather negotiate because there is a benefit in doing so than simply put out a fixed-price solicitation with open bidding. The result is that there are a great many contracting opportunities with only one responding firm (Atkinson, 2020; Atkinson, McCue & Prier, 2023; Kang & Miller, 2022). This may create a resource dependency situation, though, with the government being in a dependent position due to a lack of suppliers (Malatesta & Smith, 2011), limiting its ability to negotiate. Contracting approaches that are less open create the opportunity for bid-rigging (Deng, Tian, Ding, & Boase, 2003). Personal connections increase the likelihood of contract awards, which can be beneficial, but the contracts are likely to stop when there is a change in government contracting personnel (Chen, Levy, Martin, & Shalev, 2021). If this sounds arbitrary, it should be noted that public procurement, like the rest of government, is full of human beings, prone to greatness as well as error.

As a related matter, public sector contracting programs may include socio-economic criteria for contracting; the literature notes that there are different perspectives on this activity, rooted in theory, that public contracts steered toward underserved businesses can help improve capacity and reduce bias and/or the increased regulation of such a system leads to rent-seeking, among other unintended consequences (Lewis, 2017).

### *2.2.3 Agency Theory*

It is important to understand agency theory because the problems with public sector efficiency are due in some part to the context of constraints and pressures that affect the sector, but also to agency problems (Bartel & Harrison, 2005). These can be addressed if there is an awareness and readiness to deal with such issues. Agency theory involves interactions between principal and agent; in this relationship, the agent acts on behalf of the principal, performing delegated activities and including a level of delegated authority to make decisions (Rod, 2011). Extending the legal discussion above, "the entity participating in the principal-agent relationship can be an individual person, entire groups of people, the state administration or an enterprise. Each party may have different (more precise, fuller) information on the subject of the relationship" (Chrisidu-Budnik & Przedańska, 2017, p. 154).

Principals and agents may have different priorities and goals; not every agent is conscientious, nor is every principal trusting of agents. Principals and agents pursue agendas that are self-interested (Atkinson & Fulton, 2013). Some principals wish to constrain the activities of agents in harsh, micromanaging ways (Rod, 2011), assuming that agents have the potential to take unfair advantage of the situation for their benefit (McCue & Prier, 2008). Agent actions have consequences for themselves and the people that they serve; while people are self-serving, this does not necessarily mean that they are liars – only that they want to maximize benefit for themselves (McCue & Prier, 2008). Agents may not consider all stakeholders in a procurement scenario (King & Sekerka, 2017), narrowing their field of vision toward suboptimal outcomes.

In public procurement, the application of principal–agent relationships can be seen in a variety of ways. A county or city administrator could micromanage a purchasing director or give him or her great latitude to implement the procurement code as written and with significant discretion for those areas that require it. A purchasing director can be supportive of his or her agents or blame them for problems when they occur to avoid issues with elected officials. Agents may have good communication with their purchasing directors, or they may withhold information that is difficult to share until a problem threatens to spin out of control.

There can be differences in expectations and outcomes for information gathering between the two parties – for example, gathering too much or too little information, being pessimistic, or failing to share information; the differing beliefs and perspectives between principals and agents might increase costs (Iossa & Martimort, 2015). With major changes, such as the introduction of new systems, monitoring is needed, as is confidence in outcomes and addressing instances of goal incompatibility (Sharma & Gupta, 2019). Mistrust between principals and agents can limit innovation and reduce the potential for added value (Parrado & Reynaers, 2020).

Principals are keen to see improvements in performance and a reduction of potential blame for themselves, so performance-based approaches might be tempting. However, these approaches can present issues with the undermining of accountability in multilayered relationships (Gordon, Morris, & Steinfeld, 2019). Principals may be amenable to public–private partnership approaches to deal with identified goal conflict; they may see the approach as a means of passing risk and removing themselves from direct responsibility for program outcomes when expectations are not met by the private sector partner (Zwalf, 2022). Budget constraints demand principal–agent solutions, but these solutions may lead to outcomes that are less than optimal for appropriation/technical efficiency (Levaggi, 1999).

### *2.2.4 The Law of Agency*

An agency relationship is the power of one individual to represent another individual or business and bind them to contracts with third parties. Agency relationships are especially important in the business world since an individual must act to bind a business – the business cannot bind itself. Agency relationships can also occur between two individuals as well.

Section 1.01 of *The Restatement of the Law of Agency*, a scholarly overview of the law, defines agency as

> the fiduciary relationship that arises when one person (a "principal") manifests assent to another person (an "agent") that the agent shall act on the principal's behalf and subject to the principal's control, and the agent manifests assent or otherwise consents so to act.
>
> (DeMottt, 2006)

This is a quasi-contractual relationship predicated on the consent of the parties to enter the relationship. An agency relationship can only be formed when there is a mutual agreement to form such a relationship.

There are generally three parties in an agency relationship. The first is the "principal," which is the party being bound. In a business transaction, the principal is the corporation that is binding itself to a contract with another party. In public administration, the principal is the government entity.

The second party is the "agent." The agent is the representative of the principal who actually "makes the deal." The acts of the agent do not bind the agent – instead, the acts of the agent bind the principal. When we say the agent "binds" the principal, what we really mean is that the agent has the power to enter into a valid and enforceable contract under which the corporation, or government entity, is obligated to perform. A purchasing agent might enter into a contract on behalf of their federal agency, and the contract is between the federal agency and the vendor rather than between the agent and the vendor.

The last part is called a "third party." The third party is the person or business that officially enters into the contract with the principal. This could be a vendor or contractor in a government procurement scenario mentioned above.

### *2.2.5 Agency Authority*

An agent can have one of three types of agent authority that allows the agent to bind the principal. They are express authority, implied authority, and apparent authority.

The first two (express and implied authority) are known as actual authority. Section 2.01 of *The Restatement of the Law of Agency* (DeMott, 2006) describes actual authority in this way:

> An agent acts with actual authority when, at the time of taking action that has legal consequences for the principal, the agent reasonably believes, in accordance with the principal's manifestations to the agent, that the principal wishes the agent so to act.

Express authority is fairly straightforward. Express authority is explicit, written consent from the principal to allow a particular agent to act on the principal's behalf. Express authority is usually required to be in writing. The terms of the written agreement cover the extent to which the agent can bind the principal. If there is no scope listed in the express authority written agreement, the agent has the power to act in any reasonable way on behalf of the government entity.

A primary example of express authority is the granting of a warrant or other authority to contract on behalf of a governmental entity for purchases up to a certain threshold. A similar example is the issuance of a purchasing card, which is an express agreement to the extent that a cardholder may purchase and use the card as authorized by the principal but is acting on behalf of the entity in doing so. Another common type of express authority is a power of attorney agreement. A power of attorney agreement gives the agent the power to sign documents, pay bills, and enter into binding and legal contracts. Often, power of attorney contracts are used for persons who have become unable to care for themselves, but they can also apply to persons who have gone overseas and simply do not have the ability to take care of day-to-day financial issues, as may be the case in a public enterprise when an executive, administrator, or the head of a department is unavailable, and actions must be taken in their absence.

Next, an agent can have implied authority. A public administration example would be a county administrator being able to sign off on a contract on behalf of a county commission as part of being a county's CEO. This is especially notable in emergency scenarios, when a commission may not be able to formally meet, but swift action must be taken. For example, let's say that the county commission is unavailable during a holiday vacation, and there is a public emergency that requires immediate contracting to avoid loss of life and property. The county administrator may be able to act on an emergency basis, given implied authority, to act where the commission would otherwise have had to meet and take direct action.

Lastly, an agent can have apparent authority. Importantly, apparent authority is *not* actual authority. Apparent authority exists when the principal creates the impression that there is an agency relationship but in fact there is not one. The principal must create that impression and not the agent. When an agent has apparent authority, the principal is typically bound by the contracts agreed to by the agent, despite the fact that the principal did not authorize that agent to act. There may be limitations dependent on context. For example, contracting officer authority is clearly delineated in U.S. Federal government regulations (FAR 1.602-1), and at this level, there are limits on claims of apparent authority (see Federal Crop Ins. Corp. v. Merrill, 332 U.S. 380 (1947)).

### *2.2.6 Application: Example of Authority in Action*

As an application of this principle, assume that a partnership is owned by two brothers, Mike and Kevin. One of the brothers has a 19-year-old son named Tom. Tom is not part of the business and is not employed there, but he often goes to the office to visit his dad. One day, a city government customer for their business calls the partnership and asks to speak to one of the owners. Mike gets on the phone and tells the customer that he is too busy but that he can speak to his son Tom, who knows the family business well. Tom and the customer talk, and Tom agreed to sell 100 car tires to the customer at a discounted rate of 50 percent of the usual cost. Even though Tom had no actual authority from the partnership, he does have apparent authority. Mike indicated to the city government customer that Tom could act on behalf of the partnership by telling him to talk to Tom. Notice it was Mike's actions that led the customer to believe he could transact business with Tom. Since Tom, therefore, had apparent authority, the contract is binding.

Apparent authority only applies to the third party that is led to believe that Tom is an actual agent. Under the hypothetical above, if a second customer (whether public or private sector) calls Tom directly and asks for 100 car tires, there is no apparent authority since Mike did not tell this second customer to talk to Tom.

Also, it is very important to understand that if the agent leads a third party to believe he is an agent, without any input from the principal, there is no apparent authority. Apparent authority is only created by an act of the principal that leads the third party to believe that the agent is an actual agent. Note, however, that the principal does have the power to "ratify" such contracts, meaning that the principal can opt to bind herself to that contract if she chooses. The third party cannot force the principal to abide by the contract, however.

### *2.2.7 Duty of Loyalty*

Just like partners in a partnership, an agent has a duty of loyalty to the principal. Agents cannot engage in self-dealing with the principal. For example, a purchasing agent selling surplus computer equipment cannot buy the property that the principal is selling – the purchasing agent only has the power to sell that property to other potential buyers. And, just as with partners, an agent cannot take a business opportunity for themselves that was originally intended to be introduced to the principal. For example, if a property is being offered for sale to a city to be acquired as public land, it would be inappropriate for an employee of the city to try to purchase it for himself or herself.

### *2.2.8 Tort Liability*

Principals are liable for the torts (acts that harm others) committed by agents when the agent is actually acting as an agent. This is called vicarious liability. Even though the principal may be completely unaware that the agent has done a wrongful act, the principal remains liable if the agent was acting on behalf of the principal at the time the act was done.

This most often occurs with employees. An employee is a type of agent with their employer. An employee who causes damage or harms another person while on the job makes the employer liable for all the damage caused. For example, assume that a truck driver is employed by a trucking company and gets into an accident while hauling lumber from one place to another. The accident causes the driver of the other vehicle to have serious injuries. The employer is liable for the injuries suffered since the employee was on the job at the time of the accident. If the employee is not on the job at the time of the accident, there is no vicarious liability. For example, if the employee is going home after work and gets into an accident, the employer, as the principal, is not liable for any accident that occurs at that time.

On the other hand, a principal is not liable for an intentional act that causes injury to another. For example, if an employee punches another employee in the face during a fight, the employer is not liable for any injuries that occur. A fight is an intentional act, and the punch was not a negligent accident. In those cases, the injured person can only sue the employee. There is one exception to this – if the intentional act was committed to help further the employer's business, the employer is liable. For the fistfight, there is no way that benefits the business. On the other hand, assume that a county park employs a security crew whose job it is to control unruly crowds and potentially physically throw people out if they become rowdy at an event. If the security crew restrains a customer too roughly and causes injury, the county would be liable since the security crew is being employed to use intentional force on customers.

### *2.2.9 Information Asymmetry and Uncertainty*

The notion that all parties have the same level of information in a contractual situation was challenged by Arrow (1971) and Akerlof (1970). Agency theory evidences considerable potential for information asymmetry, "the principal's inability to observe the agent's effort," yielding the so-called principal–agent problem (Vallury & Leonard, 2022, p. 222), or where the principal has information that the agent does not (Kauppi & van Raaij, 2015). This can have destabilizing results for organizations (King & Sekerka, 2017). Ideally, all parties in a solicitation/contracting environment have the information needed to determine their best position and contract in a way that benefits all parties. This requires some equivalence of information upon which to make decisions among all parties. Some information may be available to certain parties and not others. The government may have information vendors do not have, or vice versa (Chen, Levy, Martin, & Shalev, 2021). Information asymmetry is an externality that can affect optimization in the contracting process, resulting in inefficiencies and potentially even contract failure, where a buyer of a good or service cannot adequately discern its quality.

Generally, bids (auctions) are thought to be more transparent and objective than their negotiated counterparts; however, this does not completely remove the potential for bid rigging or situations where information about sealed bids is given to preferred vendors, allowing them to respond with a winning bid of their own (Arozamena & Weinschelbaum, 2009).

A contrasting view, following from concerns raised about cost increases and inefficiencies arising from incomplete specifications, is that the issue is not one of information asymmetry but of uncertainty on the part of both buyers and sellers due to incomplete or failed design, changes to the project, and unexpected conditions (Tadelis, 2012).

An example of information asymmetry and uncertainty is the government purchasing of public-health-related products during the global COVID-19 pandemic. COVID-19 presented a crisis that should have been potentially knowable to government agencies, but governments evidenced limited preparedness in response to the threat. Decisions were made with respect to pandemic stockpiles, including inefficiencies in procurement and distribution, which undermined public health readiness. Given the uncertainty, public organizations were pushed to make decisions with inadequate information under time constraints, lest they fail spectacularly in inescapably public forums. Organizations better able to manage and analyze information handled the pandemic better than those with inadequate infrastructures (Philips, Roehrich, & Kapletia, 2023).

Having considered agency theory, we now turn our attention to other theories relevant to public procurement, including public choice and social choice theory.

## 2.3 Emerging Issues

Because public procurement is an emerging field, application of theory within the field is necessarily emergent. As an example, transaction cost theory questions the existence of Adam Smith's theory of an invisible hand (1759) guiding society, with rich people chasing after their desires, resulting in free markets that yield societal benefits for all without trying to do so. Because externalities (Coase, 1960) and market failures exist, there is a need for governments, firms, and contractual relationships to reduce what would otherwise be substantial transaction costs. Transaction cost theory deals with this by creating a system where parties are discouraged from opportunistic behavior and encouraged to fulfill contractual obligations (Brousseau & Glachant, 2002). Transaction costs, as suggested by Coase (1937) and Williamson (1985), are "all sort of costs incurred by both the ex-ante (negotiation or writing costs) and ex-post (renegotiation, arbitration costs)," extended by Malin and Martimort to include all *impediments* (Malin & Martimort, 2002, p. 164). Transaction cost theory is not new, but certain applications, including empirical studies, remain emergent, and there are opportunities to apply transaction cost theory to public procurement scenarios, as seen elsewhere in this volume.

Incentive theory posits that "economic agents are endowed with substantial... rationality, that they possess complete information concerning the structure of the issues they confront along with unlimited computational abilities, and that they have a complete and ordered preference set" (Brousseau & Glachant, 2002, p. 8). In this scenario, the principal engages in an incentivization scheme to either encourage principal-aligned behavior in the agent or to get the agent to provide information that the principal does not have (Brousseau & Glachant, 2002).

Aligned with incentive theory, procurement officers utilize a variety of incentives, formal and informal, to encourage contractors to meet their obligations in a timely fashion (Girth, 2016). A government agent with vendor relationships may benefit from improved communication and responsiveness, and this may, in turn, benefit the principal. Incentive theory is informed by context, and with advances in artificial intelligence, building artificial intelligence (AI) systems that understand both customer- and client-side needs poses interesting research opportunities (Merrick & Shafi, 2013); this likely would extend to government procurement systems and clients.

Incomplete contracting theory points out that it is not always possible for authorities to judge what is happening in contracting activity, particularly in the efficiency of action in contracting negotiations and adjustments. Forecasts (ex-ante) can be quite different than realities (ex-post) (Brousseau & Glachant, 2002). Incomplete contracts are the result of an environment where contracts include variables that are not knowable. Incomplete contracts are materially defective in some way, but if they are defective, why do principals or agents accept them? Some benefits may have been received, but the situation may speak to a lack of capacity or simply the boundedness of the abilities and knowledge of the players involved (Simon, 1955). Neither the government nor the contractor can know or plan for all contingencies. If either side had perfect knowledge, they could write perfect contracts, but instead, the public is frequently left with contracts that focus too much on cost or features rather than a balance of the two.

An example of the above that is raised in the literature is the notion of a correctional facility, where the government contracts for a private sector firm to build and run a prison but does not stipulate quality or investment. The result is that the private sector firm will seek to optimize and reduce costs rather than provide prisoners with a high standard of care, which may then result in safety issues within the facility. The requirements would have to be perfectly stipulated to avoid the moral hazard of weighing profits over care and benefits to the prisoners (Aghion & Holden, 2011). Opportunities for further research in incomplete contracting theory as an emerging area of study abound for a variety of reasons, not least of which is the difference that separates public and private sector responsibility – to stakeholders and citizens versus shareholders.

We might also consider how theory informs emerging issues related to public procurement. Artificial intelligence has been of great interest to the public procurement community in its potential to evaluate responses to solicitations, automate document creation, and perform research, but there are questions to be asked about the responsibility government agencies have for the content of the AI-generated material. In terms of accountability, the government agency is responsible for the material the moment it is used in an official capacity, which means that the contracting officer remains responsible for the function within the procurement system. Yet, there is the potential that a contracting officer, overworked and over-reliant on AI, may pay too little attention to what is being generated, only to be held responsible for the failures of an oversimplified computer model, which has not grasped the essential nuances of the project in question. AI does not replace contracting officers; AI might assist the contracting process (Trenchfield, 2023), but turning over public sector contracting to AI would be worrisome at best. Uploading materials that are protected into AI systems would be problematic for a variety of reasons, not least of which is that the uploaded material might be drawn upon for further responses by the AI apparatus.

Government procurement professionals have not historically seen themselves as focusing on carrying out broad segments of governmental missions, but the procurement role has nonetheless spread and become intertwined with other agency roles and responsibilities. Contracting officers may find themselves considering how best to support sustainability and climate initiatives, as well as matters of equality of opportunity for disadvantaged businesses and inclusiveness for small businesses, while making decisions that must respect the financial bottom line and make sense from a business perspective. The contracting officer is in a powerful but precarious position, capable of achieving great ends for the public good. But, he or she must do so in an increasingly challenging environment, where balancing interests is quite difficult, if not practically impossible. Small business development, economic development, and climate change are not new or even emerging issues, but again, public procurement's role in responding to them is emerging and may prove to be key in resolving serious issues that plague governments and communities.

Finally, the nature of work itself is changing, with contractual arrangements shifting from long-term to gig-type work and freelancing. Understanding issues related to workers' rights and working arrangements, and the nature of the work product and ownership of same, is essential to being successful. Issues related to telework continue to be important considerations for employees (Atkinson, 2022), and this will likely persist as technology makes the virtual world of work just as vital and essential as in-person activities.

Consider, for example, that the work of public procurement is increasingly performed in a virtual environment, online, with access to vast databases of information and vendors. Having a presence in a physical office may be needed only sporadically to accept physical submissions of documents, to address projects with secret classifications, or to meet with clients where an online meeting would not otherwise suffice. Flexible work schedules can make working with headquarters and field offices or with businesses across a nation or around the world easier while also allowing for improved work–life balance for public employees. The modern procurement professional has become acclimated to working in the online workplace, responding professionally to internal and external customers efficiently and effectively, largely but not entirely, as a result of the COVID-19 pandemic and the technological and infrastructure challenges that occurred during this period. While much harm was done by COVID-19, the resilience gained from improved technological capacity, evidenced through the ability to conduct public procurement as telework, has been an achievement.

## 2.4 Practical Applications

### *2.4.1 Behavioral Aspects*

While there are a variety of practical applications that could potentially be shared in this chapter, the principal–agent relationship suggests that behavioral aspects may prove to be some of the more interesting factors that inform the unique and challenging public procurement context. This is also an appropriate consideration, given behavioral ties to public sector corruption, which often involves procurement. From behavioral contract theory, we must be aware that people working within a contracting system might be overconfident, mistakenly believing that they know more than they do (Simon, 1955) and that they have a pure focus on profit or value enhancement (Kőszegi, 2014). The literature also suggests that the procurement environment is perplexing, with purchasing officers defending their processes and activities in a context that demands efficiency, but also several types of accountabilities – within the organization, to internal relationships, and even to vendors (Bromberg, 2016). Another possibility is that they are numbed by this difficult operating context, leading to decisions that can have scandalous results (Atkinson & Fulton, 2013), further reducing public trust.

Shapiro (2005) suggested that principals are risk-neutral, with many options available to them, but agents are risk-averse, having not diversified. From an economics perspective, the arrangements in the hypothetical organization are matters of contract and expectation, but in reality, it is actually quite difficult to quantify uncertainty, or the behaviors of people acting in a less-than-rational manner, or at least in a manner that does not reflect their organization-based interests alone. Agents might become numbed to their operating context and prone to ethical fading (Atkinson & Fulton, 2013).

A problem with systems that are supposedly transparent and objective in reviewing criteria is that they may still be biased due to favoritism, specifically award rules and criteria for entry into procurement consideration (Decarolis & Giorgiantonio, 2014). Titl and Geys

(2019) found in a Czech Republic case that vendor fortunes may rise and fall with their political contributions. Brogaard and colleagues noted that well-connected businesses tend to win with a low bid and then renegotiate contracts more in their favor (2021), with change orders to increase contract values. This calls into question approaches that look only at initial award and bid amounts as supposedly objective and transparent indicators and reminds us that indicators of corruption can be hard to track.

One may reason that the government may have an aversion to further contracting with firms accused or guilty of fraud. Heese and Perez-Cavazo (2019) found that, in the case of firms found guilty of fraud, this is somewhat true in that the amount of contracting is reduced. For firms accused of fraud it was found that there was no reduction in their contracting activity, though the government did shift its procurement approach from cost-plus to fixed-price contracting (2019). Still, this begs an important question: In one sense, firms (like people) are innocent until proven guilty, but in another sense, the market is supposedly full of contractors interested in government work, so why continue with suspect contractors when there is no requirement to do so? This might call into question government purchasing behavior and the importance of existing relationships (Kang & Miller, 2022), all while underscoring the difficulty firms have with breaking into public sector contracting.

Another example where public procurement is potentially subject to extra-process influence is corporate social responsibility (CSR), with increases in CSR associated with greater government contracting activity. This may be because of a presumed alignment with public–private achievement of societal benefits or just a gut-level response to virtue signaling, which may overcome information asymmetry and help to differentiate a firm in a crowded, competitive field (Flammer, 2018).

It is important to remember when addressing theoretical issues of procurement behavior that human beings are involved. The potential for human beings and public service is likely not in rules, an imperfect "growing edge of consciousness" that fails to account for all situations, but in personal responsibility (McSwite, 2011, p. 186). The ambiguity of context in the public sector is inescapable, and so trust, through responsibility and relationships, may allow a way forward.

## References


Aghion, P., & Holden, R. (2011). Incomplete contracts and the theory of the firm: What have we learned over the past 25 years? *Journal of Economic Perspectives, 25*(2), 181–197. https://pubs.aeaweb.org/doi/pdfplus/10.1257/jep.25.2.181

Akerlof, G. A. (1970). The market for lemons: Quality, uncertainty and the market mechanism. *Quarterly Journal of Economics, 84*, 488–500.

Arozamena, L., & Weinschelbaum, F. (2009). The effect of corruption on bidding behavior in first-price auctions. *European Economic Review, 53*, 645–657.

Arrow, K. J. (1971). *Essays in the Theory of Risk*. North-Holland.

Atkinson, C. L. (2020). Full and open competition in public procurement: Values and ethics in contracting opportunity. *International Journal of Public Administration, 43*(13), 1169–1182.

Atkinson, C. L. (2022). A review of telework in the COVID-19 pandemic: Lessons learned for work-life balance? *COVID, 2*, 1405–1416. https://doi.org/10.3390/covid2100101

Atkinson, C. L., McCue, C., & Prier, E. (2023). Full and open competition in public procurement: A noble lie. *International Journal of Procurement Management, 17*(2), 204–228.

Atkinson, M. M., & Fulton, M. (2013). Understanding public sector ethics: Beyond agency theory in Canada's sponsorship scandal. *International Public Management Journal, 16*(3), 386–412.

Bartel, A. P., & Harrison, A. E. (2005). Ownership versus environment: Disentangling the sources of public-sector inefficiency. *The Review of Economics and Statistics, 87*(1), 135–147. http://dx.doi.org/10.1162/0034653053327595

Brogaard, J., Denes, M., & Duchin, R. (2021). Political influence and the renegotiation of government contracts, *The Review of Financial Studies, 34*(6), 3095–3137. https://doi.org/10.1093/rfs/hhaa093

Bromberg, D. E. (2016). Gatekeepers: How procurement personnel guard against hybrid accountability. *Public Organization Review, 16*, 549–560.

Brousseau, E., & Glachant, J. (2002). The economics of contracts and the renewal of economics. In E. Brousseau & J. Glachant (eds.), *The Economics of Contracts – Theories and Applications*, 3–30. Cambridge University Press.

Brunjes, B. M. (2021). Your competitive side is calling: An analysis of Florida contract performance. *Public Administration Review, 82*(1), 83–101.

Chen, T., Levy, H., Martin, X., & Shalev, R. (2021). Buying products from whom you know: Personal connections and information asymmetry in supply chain relationships. *Review of Accounting Studies, 26*, 1492–1531.

Chrisidu-Budnik, A., & Przedańska, J. (2017). The agency theory approach to the public procurement system. *Wroclaw Review of Law, Administration & Economics, 7*(1), 154–165.

Coase, R. H. (1937). The nature of the firm. *Economica, 4*, 386–405.

Coase, R. H. (1960). The problem of social cost. *Journal of Law and Economics, 3*, 1–44.

Decarolis, F., & Giorgiantonio, C. (2014). Favouritism and inefficiency in procurement: evidence from public works in Italy. In F. Decarolis & M. Frey (eds.), *Public Procurement's Place in the World. Central Issues in Contemporary Economic Theory and Policy*, 155–183. Palgrave Macmillan. https://link.springer.com/chapter/10.1057/9781137430649_7

DeMott, D. A. (2006). *Restatement of the Law of Agency*, 3rd ed. American Law Institute.

Deng, X., Tian, Q., Ding, S., & Boase, B. (2003). Transparency in the procurement of public works. *Public Money and Management, 23*(3), 155–162.

Farazmand, A. (2002). Organization theory: From pre-classical to contemporary and critical theories – An overview and appraisal. In A. Farazmand (ed.), *Modern Organizations: Theory and Practice*, 2nd ed., 19–62. Praeger.

Flammer, C. (2018). Competing for government procurement contracts: The role of corporate social responsibility. *Strategic Management Journal, 39*(5), 1299–1324.

Girth, A. M. (2016). Incentives in third-party governance: Management practices and accountability implications. *Public Administration Review, 77*(3), 433–444.

Gordon, M. D., Morris, J. C., & Steinfeld, J. (2019). Deepwater or troubled water? Principal–agent theory and performance-based contracting in the Coast Guard's Deepwater Modernization Program. *International Journal of Public Administration, 42*(4), 298–309.

Heese, J., & Perez-Cavazos, G. (2019). Fraud allegations and government contracting. *Journal of Accounting Research, 57*(3), 675–719.

Ingham, S. (2019). Why Arrow's theorem matters for political theory even if preference cycles never occur. *Public Choice, 179*, 97–111. https://doi.org/10.1007/s11127-018-0521-9

Iossa, E., & Martimort, D. (2015). Pessimistic information gathering. *Games and Economic Behavior, 91*, 75–96.

Johnson, P. E. (1998). *Social Choice: Theory and Research*. SAGE Publications, Inc.

Kang, K., & Miller, R. A. (2022). Winning by default: Why is there so little competition in government procurement? *The Review of Economic Studies, 89*(3), 1495–1556.

Kauppi, K., & van Raaij, E. M. (2015). Opportunism and honest incompetence—Seeking explanations for noncompliance in public procurement. *Journal of Public Administration Research and Theory, 25*(3), 953–979. https://doi.org/10.1093/jopart/mut081

King, D. R., & Sekerka, L. E. (2017). Managing competing interests: A review of ethics in military procurement. *Public Integrity, 19*(5), 444–468.

Kőszegi, B. (2014). Behavioral contract theory. *Journal of Economic Literature, 52*(4), 1075–1118.

Levaggi, R. (1999). Optimal procurement contracts under a binding budget constraint. *Public Choice, 101* (1/2), 23–37.

Lewis, G. H. (2017). Effects of federal socioeconomic contracting preferences. *Small Business Economics, 49*, 763–783.

Locke, J. (1952, orig. 1689). Concerning civil government, second essay. In R. M. Hutchins (ed.), *Great Books of the Western World*, 35, 25–81. Encyclopædia Britannica.

Malatesta, D., & Smith, C. R. (2011). Resource dependence, alternative supply sources, and the design of formal contracts. *Public Administration Review, 71*(4), 608–617.

Malin, E., & Martimort, D. (2002). Transaction costs and incentive theory. In E. Brousseau & J. Glachant (eds.), *The Economics of Contracts – Theories and Applications*, 159–179. Cambridge University Press.

McCue, C., & Prier, E. (2008). Using agency theory to model cooperative public purchasing. *Journal of Public Procurement, 8*(1), 1–35.

McSwite, O.C. (2011). The good, the bad, and the neurotic: A psychoanalytic perspective on the impossibility of administrative ethics. In M. M. Harmon & O. C. McSwite (eds.), *Whenever Two or More are Gathered: Relationship as the Heart of Ethical Discourse,* 173–189. University of Alabama Press.

Merrick, K. E., & Shafi, K. (2013) A game theoretic framework for incentive-based models of intrinsic motivation in artificial systems. *Frontiers in Psychology, 4*, 791. https://doi.org/10.3389/fpsyg.2013.00791

Parrado, S., & Reynaers, A.-M. (2020). Agents never become stewards: Explaining the lack of innovation in public–private partnerships. *International Review of Administrative Sciences, 86*(3), 427–443. https://doi.org/10.1177/0020852318785024

Phillips, W., Roehrich, J. K., & Kapletia, D. (2023). Responding to information asymmetry in crisis situations: innovation in the time of the COVID-19 pandemic. *Public Management Review, 25*(1), 175–198.

Reed, R., Curtis, C., & Lovrich, N. P. (2020). Does democracy entail an obligation to make rational policy decisions? The muddling through vs. bounded rationality debate through a Lockean and Madisonian Lens. *Public Integrity, 22*(4), 316–329. https://doi.org/10.1080/10999922.2018.1518557

Reksulak, M., Razzolini, L., & Shughart, W. F. (2013). Individual choice and collective choice: an overview. In W. F. Shughart II, L. Razzolini, & M. Reksulak (eds.), *The Elgar Companion to Public Choice, Second Edition*, 3–11. Edward Elgar Publishing. https://doi.org/10.4337/9781849806039.00010

Rod, M. R. (2011). Government/business relations: An agency-theory perspective on the procurement of market research. *International Journal of Procurement Management, 4*(1), 108–120.

Rowley, C. K. (2013). Public choice: the origins and development of a research program. In W. F. Shughart II, L. Razzolini, & M. Reksulak (eds.), *The Elgar Companion to Public Choice, Second Edition*, 12–38. Edward Elgar Publishing. https://doi.org/10.4337/9781849806039.00011

Shapiro, S. P. (2005). Agency theory. *Annual Review of Sociology, 31*, 263–284. https://doi.org/10.1146/annurev.soc.31.041304.122159

Sharma, N., & Gupta, S. (2019). An investigation of IT-intervention adoption in public distribution system: A stakeholder and agency theory perspective. *Information Development, 35*(2), 203–219. https://doi.org/10.1177/0266666917736714

Simon, H. A. (1955). A behavioral model of rational choice. *Quarterly Journal of Economics, 69*, 99–118.

Smith, A. (1759). The theory of moral sentiments. https://web.archive.org/web/20070927202818/www.adamsmith.org/smith/tms/tms-index.htm

Tadelis, S. (2012). Public procurement design: Lessons from the private sector. *International Journal of Industrial Organization, 30*, 297–302.

Titl, V., & Geys, B. (2019). Political donations and the allocation of public procurement contracts. *European Economic Review, 111*, 443–458. https://doi.org/10.1016/j.euroecorev.2018.11.004

Trenchfield, A. (2023). AI isn't likely to take your job, at least for the foreseeable future. But it certainly is going to change it. *CM Magazine*. https://ncmahq.org/Web/Shared_Content/CM-Magazine/CM-Magazine-February-2023/AI-Is-Coming-For-Contracting.aspx

Vallury, S., & Leonard, B. (2022). Canals, climate, and corruption: The provisioning of public infrastructure under certainty. *Economics & Politics, 34*, 221–252.

White, J. M. (2005). *Advancing Family Theories*. Sage Publications.

Williamson, O. E. (1985). *The Economic Institutions of Capitalism: Firms, Markets, Relational Contracting*. The Free Press.

Zwalf, S. (2022). Managing goal conflict. The case of agency theory in the policy settings for public–private partnerships; a perspective on citizen and government interests. *Annals of Public and Cooperative Economics, 93*(4), 913–930.

### *Case Study (Developed by Christopher L. Atkinson and Charles Penrod)*

A purchasing agent in a county is working on a contract for towing services. Tow truck services are under the county's small business threshold of $300,000 per year, so the contract is automatically reserved for small businesses. Among available tow truck operators, there are three ostensibly small businesses available. The purchasing agent solicits the project, accepts the bids, and makes an award to the lowest bidder but receives a protest from one of the other bidders. The second-ranked bidder complains that the awarded bidder is not actually a small business and that they are far too large to be a small business. The purchasing agent investigates and finds that the awarded vendor (who had the contract for the past three years) is indeed too large to be a small business and was, in fact, not eligible at any point in the past five years. The agent's supervisor had awarded the previous contract to the vendor with no protest and was promoted within the organization as a strong supporter of small businesses in the county.

The agent investigates the other two vendors and finds out that they, too, are too large to be considered small businesses, despite the fact that all three had offered themselves to the county as meeting small business eligibility criteria.

What theories help explain what is going on here? Was the agent right to investigate all three? What should happen to these vendors? Can you offer any comment on the previous supervisor's potential thinking? Should anything happen to the supervisor for awarding a contract to an ineligible vendor?

# 3 Transaction Cost Economics and Public Procurement

*Zachary Huitink*

## 3.1 Fundamentals of Transaction Cost Economics

Transaction cost economics (TCE) is a rich and vibrant theory that has progressed considerably over time (Williamson 2010), though the fundamentals remain the same.

To start, let's consider what we mean by "transaction" costs, as well as the basics of TCE theory.

### *3.1.1 What Are Transaction Costs?*

For procurement purposes, think of transaction costs as the administrative and procedural costs of defining government's need for a good or service, and then acquiring it by searching for potential suppliers; soliciting their interest; evaluating offers; specifying and awarding a contract; and managing it post-award. These are "the costs of organizing and governing the exchange" (Peters, Brown, and Potoski 2023, 624) and are in addition to direct production costs reflected in a product's[1] purchase price (Riordan and Williamson 1985).

### *3.1.2 What Are the Basics of Transaction Cost Economics?*

TCE theory has five basic building blocks.

1. *TCE treats the transaction as the unit of analysis.* Economic theories concern a range of actors and issues, from individuals and households to firms, markets, and the economy writ large. TCE focuses on *transactions*—on the structure and conduct of individual exchanges between buyers and sellers (Commons 1931; Coase 1937, 1960). In public procurement, the relevant concerns may include whether government should purchase a product or produce it internally—the classic "make-or-buy" decision—as well as the kind of contract it should use if it elects to buy rather than make.
2. *TCE assumes "bounded rationality."* Compared to the rational choice model, where actors have stable, complete, well-ordered preferences over different options, along with full information and processing capacity to make optimal decisions (Arrow 1959); TCE assumes *bounded rationality*. Actors cannot process all the information relevant to a given transaction, nor fully anticipate the contingencies they may face in the future. Accordingly, rather than maximize, they "satisfice," selecting something "good enough" from a smaller handful of choices instead of the optimal one from a comprehensive set (Simon 1947, 1956). In public procurement, government may not be able to fully specify its needs or every desired feature of the product it wants to buy. Likewise, in making a purchase, it might select from a small, discrete set of contract design options (Bajari and Tadelis 2001) and may not be able to fully specify relevant terms and conditions of the

DOI: 10.4324/9781003566670-4

exchange—whichever contract it uses will be "inherently incomplete" (Williamson 1981, 553; see also Grossman and Hart 1986; Hart and Moore 2008).

3. *TCE emphasizes the risks of opportunism.* Beyond the more commonly understood notion of self-interest, TCE emphasizes *opportunism*—"self-interest seeking with guile" (Williamson 1993, 97). Of course, buyers and sellers need not (and, generally, should not) approach one another with reflexive suspicion—constructive relationships can be essential to sound procurement practice (Poppo and Zenger 2002; Van Slyke 2003, 2007; Bertelli and Smith 2010)—and transactions are not inevitably bound to fail because of the parties' baser motives. TCE simply insists on acknowledging and within reason planning for adverse scenarios. For instance, buyers and sellers might exploit gaps and ambiguities in incomplete contracts, as well as power imbalances that could arise in situations of lock-in, where a party cannot easily or cheaply exit a transaction and may be subject to "hold-up" problems (Klein, Crawford, and Alchian 1978). In public procurement, this may mean a seller takes advantage of its position as one of a few suppliers (or perhaps the only supplier) of the product government wants to buy. Similarly, government may take advantage of the seller, as one of a few buyers (or perhaps the only buyer) available. TCE is concerned with how procurement approaches can safeguard against these hazards, as well as use different tools to build constructive partnerships and manage risk.
4. *TCE holds that we can systematically compare and contrast transactions.* No two transactions are alike. TCE, however, posits that we can compare and contrast even highly diverse ones along common dimensions, and that variation along them has important implications for both the risks and costs of exchange and the arrangements used to facilitate it. Key transaction attributes include (among others) *uncertainty*, *asset specificity*, and *frequency* (Williamson 1979). Respectively, how well do the parties understand the product and the circumstances surrounding the transaction (uncertainty)? To what extent must they commit resources (people, technology, and so on) to it that cannot be used as valuably for other purposes if the transaction goes wrong (asset specificity)? And how often will the buyer and seller interact—is this transaction a one-off exchange, or part of a longer-term relationship (frequency)? These conditions inform procurement choices, starting with the make-or-buy decision and extending to important aspects of contract design, management, and implementation. In public procurement, government's decision to produce a good or service itself, or turn to markets, may depend importantly on the ease or difficulty with which it can define its needs, as well as the extent to which meeting them requires investments in specialized physical, technical, and human resources, as well as long- or short-term relationships.
5. *TCE posits that exchanges are structured to minimize transaction costs.* Like any good theory, TCE is built on careful development and testing of certain hypotheses. Central among them is *efficient alignment*—that buyers and sellers match transaction attributes with exchange approaches to minimize the costs of working with one another (Williamson 1991). In short, classical TCE theory proposes that simpler arrangements (e.g., spot market exchanges or simple contracting) will be used given less uncertainty, less asset specificity, and less frequency, but more elaborate arrangements (e.g., more involved contracting, or internalizing the transaction by bringing the seller within the buyer's organization, as in an employer–employee relationship) will be used when these conditions are more pronounced. In public procurement, government may buy simple products—goods and services easy to describe and produce—using short contracts with outside organizations like private firms but may use more extensive contracting arrangements, or internally produce, more complex products (Brown and Potoski 2003; Hefetz and Warner 2012; Brown, Potoski, and Van Slyke 2010, 2015, 2016).

## 3.2 A Modest (and Partial) Review of the Transaction Cost Economics Literature

With TCE's fundamentals in mind, let's chart the theory's origins and select applications in public procurement.[2]

### *3.2.1 The Origins of Transaction Cost Economics*

TCE starts with a puzzle: If markets are such an ideal way to allocate resources, why do so many economic activities occur in organizations (that is, *outside* a market setting)?

In a now famous 1937 paper, *The Nature of the Firm*, a young British economist named Ronald Coase proposed an answer: *Market-based exchange can be costly*.

Of course, markets can (and do) handle innumerable transactions every day, including many that do not require a written contract at all. For sufficiently simple purchases and sales, "the buyer and seller can forgo writing things down because the terms of exchange are implicitly understood" (Kim and Brown 2012, 689). Others, though, may require establishing a formalized agreement, and Coase argued that the "costs of negotiating and concluding [these agreements] on a market [basis] must be taken into account" (Coase 1937, 391). In these cases, the parties could save on such costs by forming an organization. This simple yet fundamental insight (along with later work on transaction costs and bargaining approaches to problems like noise and pollution) would win Coase a Nobel Prize in economics.

### *3.2.2 Defining Transaction Cost Concepts and Extending the Analysis*

Pathbreaking though it was, not every economist took to Coase's argument. Absent more concrete definition, some argued it constituted a circular explanation for real-world institutional arrangements (see, e.g., Fischer (1977), who argued any structure we observe could be explained ex-post simply by referencing "transaction costs"; see also Rindfleisch (2020) for relevant intellectual history).

Throughout a research career that would lay the foundation for modern TCE scholarship (as well as garner him a Nobel Prize of his own, shared in 2009 with political scientist Elinor Ostrom), the economist Oliver Williamson set out to rectify this deficiency.

Surveying the full scope of Williamson's contributions is far beyond the scope of this review, though as Rindfleisch (2020) argues, "the key ideas are captured well in a 1979 article in the *Journal of Law and Economics* titled 'The Governance of Contractual Relations' " (Rindfleisch 2020, 89). Following Williamson's analytical approach, the article defines and differentiates transactions in conceptual terms—arguing that transaction costs stem from uncertainty, asset specificity, and frequency—and extends Coase by treating markets and firms as endpoints on a spectrum that also includes intermediate approaches like complex long-term contracts (Rindfleisch 2020). As Rindfleisch puts it, the essence of Williamson's argument is as follows:

> transactions that require a substantial degree of specific assets, occur frequently, and/or face a high degree of future uncertainty have higher [transaction] costs due to the fact that [buyers and sellers] have limits to their rationality and may act opportunistically.
> (Rindfleisch 2020, 89)

In other words, Williamson claims that markets can readily accommodate simple, one-off, non-asset specific transactions, but actors will adopt more formalized mechanisms to support their exchange as these conditions change. Especially as asset specificity and frequency increase, the "non-standardized nature of…transactions makes primary reliance on markets…hazardous, while their recurrent nature permits the cost of specialized governance structures to be recovered" (Williamson 1979, 250). Thus, as transactions become complex, more intricate structures for governing them would be both (i) *necessary* to safeguard against the risks present in a situation where specialized investments leave actors intertwined and unable to easily leave or replace their counterparty, as well as strategically positioned to exploit one another for individual rather than mutual gain; and (ii) *economical*, in that the prospective value from repeated rather than one-off exchange could justify the costs of a more complex administrative arrangement to manage it. This could be a long-term buyer–supplier contract with elaborate provisions for price and quantity adjustment, as well as other measures to adapt the transaction to unforeseen circumstances and guard against opportunistic behavior. It could also be "internal organization"—where one actor acquires the other and brings it within its own boundaries (Coase 1937; Williamson 1971, 1975, 1979).[3]

Throughout his research, Williamson, his collaborators, and numerous other scholars showed TCE's applicability in many different situations and cases. Beyond a simple theory of the firm, TCE could apply "…more generally to any situation where a contractual arrangement of some kind is used to organize activities involving various stakeholders with only partially overlapping objectives" (Ketokivi and Mahoney 2017).

Such is a very apt description of public procurement. Let's consider just a few places where TCE might apply to it.

### *3.2.3 Transaction Cost Economics and Public Procurement: The Make-or-Buy Decision*

As all public procurement starts with the decision to produce or purchase a product, this is an especially fitting place to harness TCE. Like other organizations, government agencies must choose how they will deliver goods and services to the public—they must also navigate the make-or-buy decision. Policy may dictate the approach—the U.S. federal government, for example, contracts for simple widely sold products—but at other times, governments have more choices.

Local governments in particular face an array of demands and responsibilities, from collecting trash and plowing snow to providing for public safety and playing important roles in areas like infrastructure, social services, and economic development. A stream of research suggests their decisions to follow transaction cost logic.

*Transaction attributes are associated with local government service delivery decisions.* In an analysis of services delivered by U.S. local governments, Brown and Potoski (2003) show that public services' transaction-cost-relevant characteristics are associated with chosen delivery approaches. Across five such approaches—internal production (direct delivery), joint delivery, and contracting with, respectively, a private for-profit, a nonprofit, or another government—the authors find governments are more likely to internally produce services that are more difficult to define and measure (a corollary of uncertainty). Their results do not show service delivery being especially responsive to asset specificity—at least for modest increases in a service's specialized investment requirements—but interestingly, they do find that governments may turn more to other governments when delivering highly asset specific services. As they argue, "highly asset specific services may seem like prime candidates for internal delivery" (Brown & Potoski 2003, 444), though this approach may exceed local fiscal capacity. Rather than turning to private firms with more ability to raise the necessary capital, however, it appears that "governments take steps to reduce the risk of opportunism, by contracting with other [government entities in these cases]" (Brown and Potoski 2003, 458–449). Accordingly, "asset specificity [still] affect[s] governments' service production decisions" (Brown and Potoski 2003, 459).

*At the same time, context is important to consider when assessing service delivery decisions.* In a comparable follow-on paper using larger, more updated, and more detailed data on U.S. local government service delivery across four modes—public delivery, intergovernmental cooperation, and contracting with a for-profit or a nonprofit—Hefetz and Warner (2012) produce distinct findings with a mix of transaction- and non-transaction-cost interpretations. Following Brown and Potoski, as well as other related work (e.g., Levin and Tadelis 2010), they consider service-specific characteristics like asset specificity, and incorporate what they call contract management difficulty. In addition, they consider the relationship between service delivery decisions and two other variables of interest: market competition (number of sellers available to supply a service) and citizen interest (low to high public interest in a service's delivery process). Their results suggest that asset specificity is less important in public service delivery decisions, though governments are more prone to use intergovernmental cooperation when delivering services more difficult to manage on a contract basis. They also find governments are more likely to use for-profit service providers in more competitive markets but less in situations of high public interest. Finally, they show that geography—metropolitan versus suburban versus rural areas—is significantly associated with service delivery. As they state, "...these results suggest the need to expand earlier theoretical models based primarily on service characteristics and give more attention to place and market characteristics" (Hefetz and Warner 2012, 303). In other words, while service-driven transaction costs may matter, context is important.

*The make-or-buy decision is therefore more nuanced in the public sector.* Extending this line of research further, Brown, Potoski, and Van Slyke (2015) focus specifically on hybrid service delivery modes, arguing that the make-or-buy decision is better treated as "make-buy-or-mix." Combining data similar to Hefetz and Warner with additional sources, they assess how service characteristics, markets, and related considerations such as the type of seller in a transaction (public, private, or nonprofit) influence use of direct government, contracting out, and hybrid modes in U.S. local government service delivery. The hybrid modes they consider include "bilateral mixed" delivery (splitting responsibilities with a single private, nonprofit, or other government organization), as well as "multilateral mixed" delivery (splitting responsibilities with multiple organizations simultaneously). Their analysis shows transaction cost considerations are associated with hybrid governance choices. Governments in their data set rely to a meaningful extent on mixed delivery, generally, and are more likely to mix responsibilities with private firms when delivering simpler services requiring less specialized investments, but nonprofits or governments when delivering more complex services requiring more specialized investments. Here as well, opportunism risks may be part of the story, meaning government turns to partners it deems less likely to pursue their own gains (and more likely to work cooperatively) as a transaction unfolds. Recent research at the U.S. federal level points to a similar pattern. For example, in a study of 25,000 contracts undertaken over a decade (2005–2015), Brunjes (2024) found agencies are more likely to engage nonprofits for complex work otherwise requiring more monitoring and safeguarding.

### *3.2.3 Transaction Cost Economics and Public Procurement: Complex Contracting*

The logic of the make-or-buy decision notwithstanding, governments often find themselves needing to purchase complex goods and services a pure TCE analysis would recommend producing internally. Fortunately, though, the theory can still guide decision-making and management in these "complex contracting" cases.

Here, looking at individual agencies and service delivery decisions can be a helpful complement to assessing such decision-making in larger samples across government as-a-whole. When tasked with contracting for complex products rather than producing them, what does an individual mission-driven organization like a government agency do?

In an in-depth case study moving the analysis from the local to the national level, Brown, Potoski, and Van Slyke (2009, 2010, 2013) assessed complex contracting by the United States Coast Guard (USCG). By law, the Coast Guard performs 11 statutory missions, from maritime law enforcement and environmental protection to drug interdiction, search and rescue, national security support, and even ice breaking in the polar regions. Based on a case study assessing USCG's procurement of an upgraded fleet of sea, air, and communication systems, a highly complex 24 billion dollar (USD) project called Deepwater, the three factors can aid in overcoming challenges such as high product uncertainty and extensive specialized investment requirements: rules, relationships, and mutual understanding.

*First, it is important to set clear rules, though rules come in different types and government may not always focus on the right ones.* Appropriate rules and processes can counteract some of the transaction costs and risks inherent in more challenging transactions. However, whereas many in public procurement might try to counteract complex contracting problems by specifying the product in ever greater detail—writing extensive product rules (or requirements) to define the attributes, features, and functionality in more and more minute ways and aiming to force "a complex product into [looking] like [a] simple [one]" (Brown, Potoski, and Van Slyke 2018, 743)—the costs associated with doing so can be prohibitive. Especially for complex products, other rules, including exchange and governance rules like choosing the right compensation method (also known as contract type), setting an appropriate contract length, and incorporating design features such as which parties have decision-making rights in different contingencies, can create the incentives and flexibility necessary to accommodate transaction complexity and promote cooperation. Others have also emphasized the importance of thoughtfully allocating decision rights (e.g., assigning rights to make product- or exchange-related choices based on knowledge and expertise) in order to manage contracts (see, e.g., Malatesta and Smith 2015).

*Second, building constructive relationships is valuable.* Rules are important, of course, though based on their case findings, Brown, Potoski, and Van Slyke stress building amicable relationships since there may be many circumstances where a contract does not give the parties clear guidance on how to proceed. In addition, as others (e.g., Girth 2014) argue, using rules could be impractical or administratively burdensome, and relationships can substitute for formal rules in resolving unforeseen challenges (Poppo and Zenger 2002; Bertelli and Smith 2010). Among other approaches discussed further below, the government's experience with Deepwater suggests building in opportunities for repeated interaction and efforts to establish credibility, trust, and goodwill between buyers and sellers. Recent research reinforces and extends these findings, emphasizing conditions like trust, communication, and shared norms, and linking them to different aspects of relationship quality (see, e.g., Chuang et al. 2020). Indeed, these findings are coalescing around an area of scholarship and practice called formal relational contracting, where (rather than relying heavily on rules) buyers and sellers commit, upfront, to establishing a sound working relationship. They may invest considerable time in getting to know one another's values, goals, and work processes; specifying principles (e.g., respect and cooperation) that underpin their relationship in the front end of contract documents; co-locate personnel managing the contract; and establish processes for communication and expeditious dispute resolution (see Frydlinger, Hart, and Vitasek 2019).

*Third, both rules and relationships can be bolstered by mutual understanding.* Brown, Potoski, and Van Slyke find that mutual understanding is an important enabler of success in complex contracting, and their case findings suggest parties should invest time and energy in developing clarity about one another's views, obligations, and responses under different transaction contingencies. Otherwise, even well-conceived approaches to conveying product expectations and measuring and managing performance can go awry. Indeed, buyers and sellers can operate for considerable periods of time under the impression they are acting in line with another's expectations, only to become mired in confusion and conflict down the road. Specific approaches to building mutual understanding will also be discussed further below, though in the USCG case, the sheer complexity of the products to be procured and the highly incomplete nature of the contract made it especially important for the parties to develop clarity about product expectations, decision-making approaches, and other aspects of the exchange. Challenges in this regard created numerous impediments to success.

### *3.2.4 Transaction Cost Economics and Public Procurement: Contract Design and Management*

Acknowledging that effective procurement depends on a variety of factors—it is not strictly a matter of further and further fine-tuning the contract—"success is [in important part] about getting [key] rules right" (Brown, Potoski, and Van Slyke 2018, 743). Here, too, TCE has been leveraged, shedding useful light on key contract design decisions. In a study of U.S. federal contracting across multiple agencies, Brown and Kim (2012) identify three features especially important in contract design—type, length, and value—each of which can be assessed from a TCE perspective.

*Contract type—how will the seller be paid?* Among the most widely discussed contract design features is type—how a seller will be paid for the goods and services it provides to the government. Here, public procurement rules and regulations often afford managers a "menu" of options, though practically speaking the "vast majority [used] are variants of simple fixed-price (FP) and cost-plus (C+) contracts" (Bajari and Tadelis 2001, 387). A fixed price contract sets a fixed price for the good or service to be purchased, thus placing risk on the seller if production exceeds budgeted costs. By contrast, a cost-plus contract and related variants, like time and materials (T&M), place risk on the buyer, as rather than paying a fixed price, the seller is compensated based on input costs (along with, e.g., a fee, in the case of "cost-plus") even if they grow beyond initial expectations (Brown, Potoski, and Van Slyke 2016).

As Bajari and Tadelis (2001) argue, the reason many real-world contracts feature one or another of these two broadly distinct approaches is that while contract design is often framed as a matter of dealing with asymmetric information and suggesting multiple different compensation methods to the seller as a screening device (the idea being that the seller's preference will reveal valuable information to the buyer), other conditions tend to be more important in procurement practice. In particular, choices over contract type may be more a matter of "uncertainty about many important design changes that occur after the contract is signed and production begins, such as design failures, unanticipated site and environmental conditions, and changes in regulatory requirements" (Bajari and Tadelis 2001, 388). In other words, transaction attributes like uncertainty create costs, risks, and adjustment challenges that may bear more centrally on decisions about contract type. Given conditions like high uncertainty, using a cost-plus contract may be helpful in that it makes renegotiation (for change orders and contract adjustments) less friction prone (Bajari and Tadelis

2001). By contrast, a fixed price contract may be more costly and challenging to renegotiate at later points in the transaction. Thus, from a TCE perspective, procuring a more complex product (where uncertainty may be more prevalent) may warrant using a cost-plus-type contract, whereas a fixed price contract may be more feasible for a simpler product. And, rather than fine-tuning compensation, buyers may invest more in other upfront design, specification, and management activities to deal with complex product and transaction risks, such as "competitive bidding, reputation, and bonding [to protect against default]" (Bajari and Tadelis 2001, 388).

Kim and Brown (2012) offer some evidence in support of this claim, finding that U.S. federal agencies working on civilian, defense, and homeland security missions rely more on cost-plus-type contracts when purchasing more complex products. In their analysis, for example, cost-plus contracting is more common for computer system services (being used up to 66% of the time by one of the agencies covered in their data set), whereas fixed price contracting is more common for other, simpler goods and services (e.g., landscaping and waste collection).

*Contract length—what is the period of performance?* In addition to compensation, contracts can incorporate different periods of performance to produce and deliver the purchased good or service. Of course, for any given contract length may be a function of transaction-, product-, and context-specific conditions, though Kim and Brown (2012, 689) argue that "when a product can be produced quickly—as is often the case with a simple product—the contract term can be short," whereas a more complex product may require a longer period of time, or even make it difficult to establish a fixed length in the first place. Subject to rules and regulatory constraints, contract lengths in these cases may be set for longer periods (e.g., multiple years, rather than a single year), or "specify a base period (e.g., one year) with a limited set of 'options' that can be exercised to extend the contract (e.g., three additional one-year options)" (Kim and Brown 2012, 689–690). Thus, this design feature may also be based on transaction cost considerations—more uncertainty and (consequently) more transaction costs common with complex products may warrant greater length or incorporation of more extension options, whereas lower costs and simpler products may allow for shorter lengths. As we will discuss below, though, in practice exercising extension options should be "conditions-based"—exercised for meeting bona fide product, performance, and service expectations—rather than simply being renewed as a matter of routine.

*Contract value—what is the contract's worth in total compensation?* Like length, a contract's precise value will ultimately be transaction-specific, though it "is partly a result of contract type and length" (Kim and Brown 2012, 690). In addition to fixed price contracts and shorter terms, simpler products for which production and delivery entail fewer transaction costs may be of smaller initial value, though, here as well "A short-term, fixed-price contract starts to resemble a more open-ended, cost-[plus] contract as contract options are exercised, or as the original base contract is modified to add time and value without rebidding or renegotiating the compensation terms" (Brown and Kim 2012, 690). Thus, the appropriate value is in part a function of complementary design choices that can be (and, in practice, at least partly are) made with transaction cost considerations in mind.

## 3.3 Emerging Issues in Transaction Cost Economics

Building on a now extensive theoretical and empirical foundation, TCE research and thinking continue to evolve. For public procurement, recent advances in understanding *ex-ante* versus *ex-post* transaction costs, as well as the transaction costs and management implications unique to working with government, warrant particular attention.

*Ex-ante and ex-post transaction costs.* As we have seen, TCE is especially concerned with the costs and organizational implications of opportunism risk. Existing research focuses in particular on "*ex post* hazard costs"—on specific risks and costs that come after two parties enter a transaction and initiate their work in earnest (Benaroch et al. 2016, 58). Of course, though, transaction costs arise *before* as well as after a buyer and seller establish an agreement. Classic TCE theory may otherwise prescribe using more elaborate governance approaches to safeguard against *ex-post* opportunism, but these approaches may come with more costs *ex-ante*. In public procurement, writing a more comprehensive contract and investing more extensively in upfront contract management efforts (e.g., market research, solicitation, evaluation, and select aspects of contract drafting) could mitigate the risk of breakdowns as work unfolds post-award, though government must incur additional expense upfront. Here, what should government do? In practice, what *does* it do? Does it follow TCE's typical prescriptions—for instance, use a more detailed contract—or forgo the ex-ante expense (thereby accepting the risk ex-post, or opting to mitigate it in some other way)?

Recent research paints at least part of the picture. For example, leveraging particularly thorough data collected by Danish local authorities, Petersen et al. (2019) fill an important gap by producing estimates of just how much governments spend ex-ante to (in part) mitigate risk ex-post. As they observe, there "has been very little research measuring governments' actual transaction cost spending…[or assessing] whether governments adjust spending in response to transaction attributes that can threaten contract outcomes" (Petersen et al. 2019, 642). Drawing on data that reflects the expenses governments incur to identify suppliers and establish contracts with agreeable terms, they find that ex-ante spending varies meaningfully across over 20 different product categories, accounting for a considerably lower percentage of aggregate contract value given a simpler product (e.g., 0.2% in the case of basic, widely sold services), but a higher value given a more complex product (e.g., 7.6% in the case of information and communications technology). They also find higher ex-ante spending given higher fiscal capacity—local governments with larger tax bases and more resources may spend more upfront—and lesser ex-ante spending given contracts for products purchased in the past, as well for larger contracts. Thus, they argue, both product-specific purchasing experience and volume purchasing can save on upfront transaction cost expenditures. Building on their efforts, future research could examine ex-ante (as well as ex-post) transaction cost spending in deeper detail, such as by disaggregating total spending into spending on specific contract and transaction risk management activities, as well as further describing and characterizing these activities operationally—the purposes they serve and the kinds of risks they address.

*Transaction costs unique to working with government.* TCE scholarship focuses considerably on how product and market characteristics generate transaction costs, and, in a public procurement context, is especially concerned with the extent to which government bears these costs. Of course, though, *both* parties to an exchange (the buyer *and* the seller) bear transaction costs and risks, and each may work to mitigate them. Petersen, Potoski, and Brown (2022) find that, like government buyers, non-government sellers also take steps to manage transaction-related risks. Turning again to the information-rich Danish procurement context, they find that, like local public authorities, businesses also expend resources pre- and post-contract award to address transaction risks and the extent of their spending follows a TCE logic. For example, they find that businesses report spending less on transaction management when selling simpler products to government (e.g., about 2.26% of aggregate contract value for cleaning services), but more when selling more complex products (e.g., about 9.5% of aggregate contract value for information technology, and almost 15%

for consulting and advisory services). In addition, more experience selling to government reduces transaction cost spending, and ex-ante spending appears to be less variable than ex-post spending (as transaction procedures may be standardized ex-ante, though more situation- and transaction-specific ex-post).

In a follow-on study (Petersen, Potoski, and Brown 2023), these authors also ask whether selling to government entails transaction costs over and above those incurred in exchanges with non-government customers. While acknowledging commonalities in selling to government and non-government buyers, they make several arguments for why doing business with government can make transaction management uniquely costly. For instance, political overseers may require agency buyers gather substantially more information about individual procurements—thus raising sellers' documentation and reporting costs—and the public procurement process may also include more steps and compliance procedures intended to achieve a broader array of socioeconomic goals than may be the case when selling to a private buyer. The challenge, however, is that in reality every exchange still remains unique. So, simply comparing a seller's contract management spending across two transactions where a government and a non-government buyer purchase the same product (under even similar circumstances) may not yield valid conclusions, as we lack the counterfactual necessary to make a credible causal inference about how the buyer's identity effects the seller's costs (Holland 1986). Petersen, Brown, and Potoski overcome this challenge by using the experimental method. In a survey of Danish firms, they give sellers prompts describing the exact same transaction—the same product and exchange circumstances—but alter the buyer's identity to be a non-government customer in the control group and a government customer in the treatment group. They ask survey respondents to estimate their transaction cost spending as a percentage of aggregate contract value (using the prompt to present a common monetary value for the kinds of contracting they studied—construction, consulting, and information technology) and found that respondents reported (on average) approximately 34% higher transaction cost spending when selling to a government customer than a non-government customer, with higher costs concentrated especially in post-award monitoring and enforcement-related activities (producing mandated performance reports, rectifying product deficiencies, and resolving disputes). As they argue, "the organizational form of the exchange partner significantly influences private firms' estimated transaction cost expenditures" (Petersen, Potoski, and Brown 2023, 633). The value of this work lies in emphasizing sellers transaction costs, carefully applying the experimental method to understand how they vary across different types of buyers, and creating a number of directions for future research and practice. Of course, it would be helpful to extend the approach to other procurement contexts and product categories—do the findings hold up when considering purchasing in other countries and jurisdictions, as well as other types of products and markets? It would also be helpful to generate additional implications for procurement practice and education. For instance, the authors argue that select aspects of public procurement processes may raise transaction costs but also serve important societal functions. Accordingly, the idea is not to eliminate every procurement rule or procedural requirement that per se increases costs, but to assess costs and benefits.

## 3.4 Practical Applications of Transaction Cost Economics in the Public Procurement Process

TCE theory offers numerous practical insights for public procurement, informing decision-making and management across the procurement process.

- *Government is in the best position to buy when products are simple and markets are thick.* When government can more readily and cheaply specify both what it wants and the terms and conditions under which it is willing to purchase it—and when production does not require significant relationship-specific investments—buying a product rather than making it may constitute a good choice. This is especially the case when markets are thick: When there are multiple sellers and meaningful competition that can drive down prices and encourage performance and quality.

- *Given appropriate capacity, government should consider making more complex products, especially in thin markets.* Government may wish to make more complex products, since both greater difficulty in specifying product attributes and exchange terms as well as higher lock-in risk (from relationship-specific investments) could otherwise leave it more vulnerable. Its contract could be considerably less complete, and it could be more intertwined with an incumbent seller prone to exploit contractual ambiguities or unforeseen circumstances.
- *If required to buy a complex product, government should develop and implement a multi-part strategy that identifies and uses appropriate procurement tactics to mitigation transaction risks and costs.* Instead of striving to turn a complex product into a simple one by specifying product attributes in ever greater detail—a costly and potentially infeasible approach—government can utilize a variety of tactics. In particular:
  - *Separate the product into component parts, making some and buying others, or, if buying all of them, cultivate redundant capacity on the seller side.* To the extent the product can be broken up into discrete parts, government could retain responsibility for producing some and contract for others or award contracts to multiple outside suppliers each responsible for certain parts. Similarly, it could retain multiple sources of supply, with each seller holding a contract to produce the whole product at different times, for different service populations, or in different areas of operation.
  - *Incorporate select product design features that retain residual competition and prevent lock-in risk.* In addition to breaking up or unbundling contracts in one of the ways discussed above, government could incorporate specific design features that "create and maintain competitive environments" (Kendall 2013, 6). Using modularity and open-source interfaces in design, or acquiring the rights to technical data, design specifications, or other intellectual property can prevent lock-in. Of course, these are also significant valuable assets to the seller, and depending on the circumstances, acquiring them may not be options. Accordingly, considering unbundling contracts can still be helpful here, too, as a means of cultivating competition.
  - *Choose contracting approaches—types, lengths, and other features—that account appropriately for transaction costs and risks.* Simple contracting practices—such as a fixed price and short-term—may befit simple products, though as with sourcing (i.e., make-or-buy) decisions, TCE can inform design choices tailored to the product and circumstances. As more complex products may be more challenging to specify and price and take more time and effort to design, produce, and deliver, government may elect to use a more flexible contract type in these cases. For example, it could use a cost-plus or T&M contract to accommodate higher uncertainty and more unforeseen developments (Bajari and Tadelis 2001). It could also make the contract longer, or incorporate contingent renewal options, to extend the term if the seller meets certain obligations and benchmarks. Likewise, it could adjust practices as product knowledge increases and uncertainty decreases, such as by using cost-plus contracts earlier on, but shifting to fixed price once production and delivery are well understood.
  - *Build strong, productive relationships with sellers, as well as clarity and credibility over the terms of exchange.* Government can also address transaction costs and risks through building sound working relationships and mutual understanding with

sellers (Brown, Potoski, and Van Slyke 2010; Brunjes 2020). Here, TCE points us to contracts as not only formalized agreements but as relationships—an idea manifest in the relational contracting approach (Williamson 1979; see also Macauly 1963; Macneil 1974; Baker, Gibbons, and Murphy 2002). Rather than treating the contract as a rigid instrument, it should be seen as a reference point to support a broader, constructive working relationship between the parties involved (Hart and Moore 2008). Toward this end, public procurement managers can focus on relationship management. Especially when procuring complex products, they can build in opportunities for repetition, again breaking a larger project or production and delivery process into component parts and building up a strong relationship through cooperative execution of each part over time (Axelrod 1984; Brown, Potoski, and Van Slyke 2018). Early success in this process—what psychologist and group formation expert Bruce Tuckman called "achieving early wins"—can promote cohesion and more effective work between individuals and groups (Tuckman 1965), or "a what's in it for 'we' mentality" (Frydlinger, Hart, and Vitasek 2019). Likewise, procurement managers can establish mutual understanding—what relational contract scholars formally refer to as *clarity* (Gibbons and Henderson 2012)—by defining key terms, obligations, and conditions under which certain actions will or will not be taken or deemed acceptable in a contracting relationship, and credibility by following through with appropriate action (awards, sanctions, or adjustments as needed).

## Notes

1 Unless otherwise specified, this chapter uses "product" as a generic term for goods or services.
2 For more in-depth reviews, see, e.g., Cuypers et al. (2021).
3 Williamson treats uncertainty separately, though he argues it can (among other consequences) amplify the effects highly asset specific investment requirements have on transactions, and further push the parties to use more intricate exchange mechanisms. In essence, higher uncertainty makes it harder to account for relevant contingencies buyers and sellers may encounter in the future, meaning "contractual gaps will be larger and [the necessity] for adaptation will increase…" (Williamson 1979, 254). In these cases, especially, the parties to an exchange may elect to organize internally, as it makes them most able to adjust to unforeseen or unexpected problems over time.

## References

Arrow, K.J. (1959). "Rational Choice Functions and Orderings." *Economica*, 26(102): 121–127.
Axelrod, R. (1984). *The Evolution of Cooperation*. New York, NY: Basic Books.
Bajari, P., & Tadelis, S. (2001). "Incentives versus Transaction Costs: A Theory of Procurement Contracts." *RAND Journal of Economics*, 32(3): 387–407.
Baker, G., Gibbons, R., & Murphy, K.J. (2002). "Relational Contracts and the Theory of the Firm." *Quarterly Journal of Economics*, 117(1): 39–84.
Benaroch, M., Lichenstein, Y., & Fink, L. (2016). "Contract Design Choices and the Balance of Ex Ante and Ex Post Transaction Costs in Software Development Outsourcing." *MIS Quarterly*, 40(1): 57–82.
Bertelli, A.M., & Smith, C.R. (2010). "Relational Contracting and Network Management." *Journal of Public Administration Research and Theory*, 20(i1): i21–i40.
Brown, T., & Kim, Y.M. (2012). "The Importance of Contract Design." *Public Administration Review*, 72(5): 687–696.
Brown, T., & Potoski, M. (2003). "Transaction Costs and Institutional Explanations for Government Service Production Decisions." *Journal of Public Administration Research and Theory*, 13(4): 441–468.

Brown, T., Potoski, M., & Van Slyke, D. (2009). *The Challenge of Contracting for Large Complex Projects: A Case Study of the Coast Guard's Deepwater Program*. Washington, DC: IBM Center for the Business of Government.

Brown, T., Potoski, M., & Van Slyke, D. (2010). "Contracting for Complex Products." *Journal of Public Administration Research and Theory*, 20(1): i41–i58.

Brown, T., Potoski, M., & Van Slyke, D. (2013). *Complex Contracting: Government Purchasing in the Wake of the U.S. Coast Guard's Deepwater Program*. New York: Cambridge University Press.

Brown, T., Potoski, M., & Van Slyke, D. (2015). "The Impact of Transaction Costs on the Use of Mixed Service Delivery by Local Governments." *Journal of Strategic Contracting and Negotiation*, 1(4): 239–267.

Brown, T., Potoski, M., & Van Slyke, D. (2016). "Managing Complex Contracts: A Theoretical Approach." *Journal of Public Administration Research and Theory*, 26(2): 294–308.

Brown, T., Potoski, M., & Van Slyke, D. (2018). "Complex Contracting: Management Challenges and Solutions." *Public Administration Review*, 78(5): 739–747.

Brunjes, B. (2020). "Competition and Federal Contractor Performance." *Journal of Public Administration Research and Theory*, 30(2): 202–219.

Brunjes, B. (2024). "Partners or Providers? An Analysis of Nonprofit Federal Contractor Performance." *Nonprofit and Voluntary Sector Quarterly*, 53(2): 428–461.

Chuang, E., McBeath, B., Carnochan, S., & Austin, M.J. (2020). "Relational Mechanisms in Complex Contracting: Factors Associated with Private Managers' Satisfaction with and Commitment to the Contract Relationship." *Journal of Public Administration Research and Theory*, 30(2): 257–274.

Coase, R.H. (1937). "The Nature of the Firm." *Economica*, 4(16): 386–405.

Coase, R.H. (1960). "The Problem of Social Cost." *The Journal of Law and Economics*, 3: 1–44.

Commons, J.R. (1931). "Institutional Economics." *American Economic Review*, 21(4): 648–657.

Cuypers, I.R.P., Hennart, J.F., Silverman, B.S., & Gokhan, E. (2021). "Transaction Cost Theory: Past Progress, Present Challenges, and Suggestions for the Future." *Academy of Management Review*, 15(1): 111–150.

Fischer, S. (1977). "Long-Term Contracting, Sticky Prices, and Monetary Policy: A Comment." Rational Expectations, and the Optimal Money Supply Rule. *Journal of Monetary Economics*, 3(3): 317–323.

Frydlinger, D., Hart, O., & Vitasek, K. (2019). "A New Approach to Contracts." *Harvard Business Review*, 97(5):116–123.

Gibbons, R., & Henderson, R. (2012). "Relational Contracts and Organizational Capabilities." *Organization Science*, 23(5): 1350–1364.

Girth, A. (2014). "A Closer Look at Contract Accountability: Exploring the Determinants of Sanctions for Unsatisfactory Contract Performance." *Journal of Public Administration Research and Theory*, 24(2): 317–348.

Grossman, S.J., & Hart, O.D. (1986). "The Costs and Benefits of Ownership: A Theory of Vertical and Lateral Integration." *Journal of Political Economy*, 94(4): 691–719.

Hart, O.D., & Moore J. (2008). "Contracts as Reference Points." *Quarterly Journal of Economics*, 123(1): 1–48.

Hefetz, A., & Warner, M. (2012). "Contracting or Public Delivery? The Importance of Service, Market, and Management Characteristics." *Journal of Public Administration Research and Theory*, 22(2): 289–317.

Holland, P. (1986). "Statistics and Causal Inference." *Journal of the American Statistical Association*, 81(396): 945–960.

Kendall, F. (2013, July–August 2013). "What Lies Ahead." *Defense AT&L Magazine*.

Ketokivi, M., & Mahoney, J.T. (2017). "Transaction Cost Economics as a Theory of the Firm, Management, and Governance," in *Oxford Research Encyclopedia of Business and Management*. Oxford, UK: Oxford University Press.

Kim, Y.W., & Brown, T. (2012). "The Importance of Contract Design." *Public Administration Review*, 72(5): 687–696.

Klein, B., Crawford, R.G., & Alchian, A.A. (1978). "Vertical Integration, Appropriable Rents, and the Competitive Contracting Process." *The Journal of Law and Economics*, 21(2): 297–326.

Levin, J., & Tadelis, S. (2010). "Contracting for Government Services: Theory and Evidence from U.S. Cities." *Journal of Industrial Economics*, 58(3): 507–541.

Macauly, S. (1963). "Non-Contractual Relations in Business: A Preliminary Study." *American Sociological Review*, 28(1): 55–67.

Macneil, I.R. (1974). "The Many Futures of Contract." *Southern California Law Review*, 47: 691–816.

Malatesta, D.M., & Smith, C.R. (2015). "Deciding Who's in Charge: Factors Driving the Choice of Decision Rights in Professional Service Contracts." *International Journal of Commerce and Contracting*, 1(1): 65–84.

Petersen, O.H., Baekkeskov, E., Potoski, M., & Brown, T. (2019). "Measuring and Managing Ex Ante and Ex Post Transaction Costs in Public Sector Contracting." *Public Administration Review*, 79(5): 641–650.

Petersen, O.H., Potoski, M., & Brown, T. (2022). "Businesses' Transaction Costs When Contracting with Governments: The Impact of Product Complexity and Public Contract Management Experience." *International Public Management Journal*, 25(5): 741–766

Petersen, O.H., Potoski, M., & Brown, T. (2023). "Same Product, Different Price: Experimental evidence on transaction cost expenditures of selling to governments and firms." *Public Administration Review*, 83(3): 627–638.

Poppo, L., & Zenger, T. (2002). "Do Formal Contracts and Relational Governance Function as Substitutes or Complements?" *Strategic Management Journal*, 23: 707–725.

Potoski, M., Petersen, O.H., & Brown, T. (2023). "Same Product, Different Price: Experimental Evidence on the Transaction Cost Expenditures of Selling to Governments and Firms." *Public Administration Review*, 83: 623–368.

Rindfleisch, A. (2020). "Transaction Cost Theory: Past, Present, and Future." *AMS Review*, 10: 85–97.

Riordan, M.H., & Williamson, O.E. (1985). "Asset Specificity and Economic Organization." *International Journal of Industrial Organization*, 3(4): 365–378.

Simon, H. (1947). *Administrative Behavior: A Study of Decision-Making Processes in Organizations*. New York, NY: Macmillan.

Simon, H. (1956). "Rational Choice and the Structure of the Environment." *Psychological Review*, 63(2): 129–138.

Tuckman, B.W. (1965). "Developmental Sequence in Small Groups." *Psychological Bulletin*, 63(6): 384–399.

Van Slyke, D. (2003). "The Mythology of Privatization in Contracting for Social Services." *Public Administration Review*, 63(3): 296–315.

Van Slyke, D. (2007). "Agents or Stewards? Using Theory to Understand the Government-Nonprofit Social Service Contracting Relationship." *Journal of Public Administration Research and Theory*, 17(2): 157–187.

Williamson, O.E. (1971). "The Vertical Integration of Production: Market Failure Considerations." *American Economic Review*, 61(2): 112–123.

Williamson, O.E. (1975). *Markets and Hierarchies: Analysis and Antitrust Implications*. New York, NY: Macmillan Publishers.

Williamson, O.E. (1979). "Transaction-Cost Economics: The Governance of Contractual Relations." *The Journal of Law and Economics*, 22(2): 233–261.

Williamson, O.E. (1981). "The Economics of Organization: The Transaction Cost Approach." *American Journal of Sociology*, 87(3): 548–577.

Williamson, O.E. (1991). "Comparative Economic Organization: The Analysis of Discrete Structural Alternatives." *Administrative Science Quarterly*, 36(2): 269–296.

Williamson, O.E. (1993). "Opportunism and Its Critics." *Managerial and Decision Economics*, 14(2): 97–107.

Williamson, O.E. (2010). "Transaction Cost Economics: The Natural Progression." *American Economic Review*, 100(3): 673–690.

### *Case Study: Make-Or-Buy in the Department of Green Infrastructure (Developed by Zachary Huitink)*

The Department of Green Infrastructure (DGI) serves a densely populated urban municipality with significant environmental challenges. The city faces recurring issues with flooding, particularly in low-lying neighborhoods, due to aging infrastructure and increased rainfall from climate change. These neighborhoods are home to vulnerable populations, making effective flood control a high priority for both equity and compliance with federal mandates. In response to recent legislation, DGI is required to implement an advanced stormwater filtration system that meets stringent environmental standards while reducing flooding risks. The system must filter contaminants effectively, support large volumes of runoff, and integrate seamlessly with the city's varied terrain and existing infrastructure.

DGI has limited in-house expertise in designing and managing projects involving advanced technology. Past procurement efforts primarily focused on relatively simple green infrastructure solutions, such as tree planting initiatives and permeable pavements. While successful, these projects encountered unforeseen challenges, including higher-than-expected costs for materials and delays caused by incomplete project specifications. A market assessment for the filtration system identified only three suppliers capable of delivering the necessary technology. Each supplier offers proprietary solutions, requiring significant upfront investments and long-term maintenance contracts. These proprietary designs are also highly tailored, raising concerns about adaptability for future projects and the potential for lock-in with a single supplier.

DGI leadership faces the following decisions:

1. Should the agency make the filtration system in-house or buy it from the market?
2. If opting to buy, should DGI use a fixed price contract or a more flexible arrangement such as a cost-plus contract?
3. How detailed should the contract be in specifying technical attributes, timelines, and responsibilities?
4. Given the limited number of potential suppliers, how can DGI safeguard against opportunism while building a productive relationship with the vendor?

### Challenges in Applying Transaction Cost Economics (TCE)

DGI's leadership recognizes the relevance of transaction cost economics (TCE) in guiding their procurement strategy. However, applying the theory to their context reveals the following challenges:

1. Uncertainty: The filtration system's complexity means its performance and costs cannot be fully anticipated.
2. Asset Specificity: The system will require substantial site-specific adaptations and long-term maintenance, making it difficult to switch suppliers.
3. Frequency: This is a one-off project, but its success will determine whether similar systems are deployed citywide in the future.

### Teaching Objectives

This case allows students to explore how TCE concepts such as bounded rationality, opportunism, and efficient alignment can inform DGI's procurement choices. Specifically, the case highlights as follows:

1. The trade-offs between making and buying under conditions of high asset specificity and market uncertainty.
2. The role of contract design in addressing transaction risks, including how contract type, length, and provisions can be tailored to the transaction's characteristics.
3. Strategies for mitigating opportunism and fostering collaboration in thin markets.

### Discussion Questions

1. How should DGI approach the make-or-buy decision for the stormwater filtration system?
2. If DGI decides to buy, what type of contract (e.g., fixed price versus cost-plus) would best address the risks of uncertainty and asset specificity?
3. What strategies can DGI use to mitigate opportunism, given the thin supplier market?
4. How might DGI build a constructive relationship with the vendor while safeguarding public interests?

# 4 Advancing Resource Dependence Theory

## Navigating Power Dynamics to Improve Public Procurement

*Deanna Malatesta and Craig Smith*

### 4.1 Introduction

Public organizations often rely on external vendors to acquire the goods and services needed to achieve their goals. Public managers, responsible for safeguarding the public interest and managing public finances, have a duty to optimize the value obtained through procurement. This optimization goes beyond considering only initial costs; it also involves evaluating factors such as quality, vendor trustworthiness, and the power dynamics that result from these exchanges. A trustworthy vendor consistently adheres to contract terms, avoids exerting undue influence, and refrains from taking advantage of unforeseen circumstances that may arise.

Resource dependence theory (RDT), rooted in foundational studies by Emerson (1962) and Pfeffer and Salancik (1978), provides valuable insights into the power dynamics that emerge in external dependencies. Organizations that control vital resources typically wield significant power, which can lead to behaviors that undermine contract agreements, such as reducing quality or failing to meet delivery deadlines. This complex landscape is further complicated by the uncertainties inherent in our ever-changing environment, which magnify the risks associated with vendor relationships. Managers operating in rapidly changing technological environments, for example, face ambiguity about the perceived state of uncertainty, its effect, and how to respond (see Milliken 1987). RDT uniquely emphasizes managers' roles and their strategic responses to power dynamics influenced by uncertainty, setting it apart from other organizational and firm theories. These managerial challenges are particularly apparent for public managers engaged in public procurement and contracting.

This chapter aims to explore the relevance of RDT to procurement, with a specific focus on how the theory sheds light on the risks stemming from power imbalances and dependencies. One of the primary objectives is to clarify the reasons behind the emergence of power dynamics in contract relationships. An additional section delves into emerging issues, explaining how recent scholarship under the concept of "formal relational contracts" can enhance our comprehension of the role of relational norms in fostering improved working relationships and aligning the interests of parties, especially in uncertain circumstances (Hart 2017; Hart and Moore 2007; Frydlinger et al. 2019; Hart et al. 2024; Hart and Halonen-Akatwijuka 2024; Vitasek et al. 2020).

In a constantly changing and volatile context, relational norms become crucial guides for behavior between interdependent organizations. These norms, which include Ian Macneil's (1978, 1980) idea of the "restraint of power," shape expectations and responsibilities, forming the basis for sustainable, long-term contractual relationships. Finally, a section on practical insights translates theoretical and research developments into actionable lessons for practitioners in public procurement.

DOI: 10.4324/9781003566670-5

## 4.2 Summary of the Literature on Resource Dependence Theory

"Resource dependence was originally developed to provide an alternative perspective to economic theories… .and to understand precisely the type of inter-organizational relations that have played such a large role in recent market failures" (Pfeffer 2003, xxv). Building on earlier work of George Homans (1958), Peter Blau (1964), and Richard Emerson (1962), this perspective holds three core principles. First, organizations are not self-sufficient and therefore they obtain resources they need from their environment, which is to say from other organizations. Thus, the fundamental driver behind organizational partnerships is the acquisition of essential resources that enable survival and expansion (Pfeffer and Leong 1977; Pfeffer and Salancik 1978).

Understanding organizational boundaries and the broader environment is vital in RDT studies. Internal activities and behaviors that the organization can control lie within its boundaries. External activities, beyond an organization's control, constitute its environment. Seen in this light, the environment becomes a network of multiple organizations, a web of dependencies. Second, organizations can adopt strategies to enhance their autonomy, crucial for survival and mission pursuit. Successfully sourcing resources from their surroundings grants them long-term influence, power, and stability. Third, power (not rationality or efficiency) is key to understanding an organization's internal and external actions.

Power and dependence operate in an inverse relationship: the power of Organization A over Organization B is related to how dependent Organization B is on Organization A's resources. Further, power is not zero-sum or one-way; Organization A and B can each have power over each other, making them interdependent. In this dynamic, the organization that controls vital resources wields greater power, leaving the organization reliant on those resources susceptible to influence.

RDT stands out from other approaches, such as transaction cost economics, due to its focus on power dynamics and a meticulous description of the specific tactics organizations can employ. Power dynamics play a crucial role in shaping public procurement processes and outcomes, and understanding these dynamics is essential for both academics and practitioners in the field.

To put RDT in practical terms, consider a city council looking to procure waste management services. Although waste management might seem relatively simple, it can be viewed as specialized, positioning the city in a new dependency relationship with service providers. In such a scenario, the city may have less negotiating leverage on contract terms. Acknowledging that all exchanges have implications for power and dependence, RDT prescribes an important lesson for procurement officials: select the approach that enables your organization to reduce uncertainty and dependence while maximizing autonomy.

### *4.2.1 The Role of the Public Manager*

In RDT, a public manager's role is central to managing organizational dependencies on external resources. Public managers must identify critical dependencies, assess the extent and implications of these dependencies, and strategize to mitigate them. This involves diversifying the resource base, which refers to the variety and sources of essential inputs such as financial assets, materials, technology, and human capital that an organization relies on. By diversifying these resources, developing in-house capabilities, or forming strategic alliances, public managers can secure essential resources, thereby reducing vulnerability and enhancing bargaining power. Effective relationship management with external entities, such as suppliers and regulatory bodies, is also a key managerial responsibility. This ensures a stable supply of resources while maintaining organizational autonomy. Additionally, managers must align organizational strategies and structures with the external resource environment, adapting to its demands and constraints. Proactive monitoring of the external environment for changes affecting resource availability is crucial. This enables the organization to anticipate shifts and adapt accordingly, maintaining resource stability.

In the context of public procurement, managerial discretion is also essential for balancing regulatory compliance with the practicalities of diverse procurement scenarios. This discretion enables managers to interpret and apply policies in context-specific ways, ensuring adaptability and flexibility in procurement processes. It is particularly crucial in areas such as supplier selection and contract negotiation, where managers assess both quantifiable factors and qualitative aspects such as supplier reliability and potential for long-term partnerships.

### *4.2.2 Mapping the Resource Environment from a Power Perspective*

Understanding the resource environment is the first step in managing organizational dependencies effectively. Mapping this environment involves identifying how resources, power, and influence are distributed. In this regard, RDT emphasizes three key environmental factors: concentration, munificence, and interconnectedness. Concentration indicates how power and authority are distributed in the environment. For instance, in a highly concentrated environment, a few large firms may dominate a market, influencing organizational responses and strategies. Conversely, in a decentralized setting with power spread across many entities, organizations might adopt more collaborative or competitive approaches. Munificence relates to the availability or scarcity of critical resources. An example of this is in industries like technology, where rapid innovation and abundant investment opportunities represent a munificent environment, impacting an organization's power or dependence. In contrast, in a resource-scarce sector such as rare minerals mining, organizations might face intense competition and dependence on limited suppliers. Knowing how much there is of a resource, or the richness of the resource, is critical to better understanding the environment and the organization's relative power or dependence. Interconnectedness, the third factor, describes the extent of an organization's integration into a broader network. This can be seen in sectors like healthcare, where interconnectedness through partnerships and alliances can lead to interdependence or power imbalances, depending on an organization's centrality within the network, or its importance and influence relative to others in the network. Each of these factors – concentration, munificence, and interconnectedness – plays a vital role in shaping organizational behavior and strategy within their respective environments. These factors collectively influence one organization's dependence on another and by extension, the supplier organization's ability to leverage power and influence. To continue the example, if the city council has multiple waste management companies to choose from (high munificence), its dependency decreases. Similarly, if these companies are reliant on the city council for contracts (high interconnectedness), the council gains negotiating power. Finally, decentralized authority (low concentration) may provide more room to negotiate favorable terms. By grasping these nuances, procurement practitioners can better navigate complex relationships and negotiate contracts that are both equitable and beneficial.

One prominent manifestation of power in public procurement is the influence exerted by suppliers.[1] Unlike the previous example where the city manager has multiple suppliers to choose from (resource munificence), sometimes a single or limited set of suppliers wields considerable power. In a sole-sourced contract, the problem is most obvious. The power dynamic is often skewed in favor of the supplier who has been selected without a competitive bidding process. The supplier holds a position of power and advantage in this scenario.

During negotiations, a dominant supplier may selectively share information or misrepresent facts to manipulate the contract's terms. For instance, they might provide incomplete or misleading data during negotiations to secure more favorable conditions. A dominant supplier may also exploit the power imbalance by imposing unfavorable terms.

### *4.2.3 Emergence of Supplier Power*

Power dynamics in public procurement can significantly impact the efficiency and fairness of the process. Yet, even when there is identifiable market competition at the outset, for example, when multiple organizations submit bids to supply a good or service, supplier dominance can still occur. To be sure, once the government selects a supplier, that supplier effectively becomes the sole supplier during the life of the contract and the procurement officer should be alert to power tactics. The absence of competition during the life of the contract creates a risk of opportunistic behavior on the part of the supplier. The supplier may be less motivated to provide high-quality goods or services or to meet deadlines, knowing that there are no alternative options (in the short term or long term) for the procuring organization. In long-term contracts, a dominant supplier may frequently propose changes or modifications to the contract's terms and conditions. This could involve altering delivery schedules, pricing structures, or quality standards to their advantage. Additionally, a dominant supplier might employ delay tactics, intentionally slowing down the contract's progress to gain leverage. In general, the more the government depends on the supplier, the more leverage the supplier has over the government. In developing countries plagued by corruption, power and influence can significantly distort procurement processes. Individuals or groups wielding political, economic, or social clout often manipulate procurement decisions, favoring vendors through favoritism or bribery rather than merit. This leads to a lack of transparency and accountability, resulting in the procurement of inferior goods or services at inflated costs. Such practices, exacerbated by weaker regulatory frameworks in these countries, not only hinder economic development but also perpetuate inequality, as only the well-connected or influential can access and benefit from procurement opportunities. Consequently, this corruption in procurement undermines trust in public institutions and impedes fair and effective governance (Diagana and Diagne 2013).

In sum, power dynamics in public procurement, particularly when suppliers are in a position of power and/or the dynamics are distorted by political interference and corruption, should be a source of concern for public managers. Public managers must first recognize potential dependencies and then consider strategies to alleviate such imbalances over time. The concentration of power can limit competition, raise prices, and hinder innovation, affecting the efficiency and effectiveness of public procurement. Public managers, responsible for safeguarding the public interest and managing public finances, should be attentive to these tactics and their potential consequences.

### *4.2.4 Recognizing Environmental Volatility*

Changes in the environment can also alter power dynamics and make public organizations more vulnerable. For example, in economic downturns smaller suppliers may struggle to survive, leading to industry consolidation. Dominant suppliers with greater financial resilience are more likely to weather economic crises and may further solidify their position vis-à-vis other suppliers. Global supply chain disruptions such as those that occurred during the COVID-19 pandemic can have significant impacts on resource availability and may make public organizations more vulnerable to dominant suppliers. As another example, regulatory changes may impose more stringent requirements or standards on certain products or services, which may limit the number of suppliers capable of meeting these new standards. Dominant suppliers that are already compliant may gain an advantage. In response to these shifting dynamics, public procurement officials must be vigilant and adaptable. Balancing the need to compete with the need to preserve relationships becomes even more crucial in such contexts. Transparency in procurement processes is essential to maintain trust and mitigate perceptions of favoritism. A principle-based approach, focusing on fairness, integrity, and value for money, ensures that competition upholds ethical standards.

Focusing on long-term relationships is also vital, especially during economic downturns when public organizations face their own budget constraints and may prioritize stability and reliability over seeking new suppliers. This tendency can reinforce existing relationships with dominant suppliers, but it's important to maintain a competitive environment. Providing feedback to unsuccessful bidders and using frameworks and pre-qualification systems can help attract more competition and level the playing field. Moreover, public organizations should consider the long-term implications of their procurement decisions. While dominant suppliers might offer stability, relying too heavily on them can lead to a lack of competition and innovation. Encouraging a diverse supplier base and fostering new entrants can mitigate this risk.

In summary, the changing environment requires public procurement officials to be alert and flexible. Balancing competition with relationship preservation, focusing on transparency, adhering to principles, and fostering long-term partnerships are key strategies. These approaches help public organizations navigate the complexities of power dynamics and environmental changes, ensuring effective and ethical procurement practices.

- **Sole (or Limited) Source:** Suppliers that have a unique or scarce resource hold more power in procurement negotiations. If a particular supplier is the sole provider of a critical product or service, it may wield considerable influence over the public organization in need of the product or service.
- **Power Plays over Time:** Procurement officers must do more than simply identify the potential for supplier dominance in the early stages of procurement, such as during the Request for Proposals (RFP) phase or supplier selection. They should be aware that a chosen supplier will be the sole provider throughout the contract's duration, making them vulnerable to opportunistic behavior.
- **Environmental Uncertainties:** Changes in the external environment, such as economic downturns, global supply chain disruptions, regulatory changes, and budget constraints can affect resource availability and make public organizations more vulnerable to dominant suppliers.

### *4.2.5 Traditional RDT Strategies*

RDT responses to power asymmetry and dependence typically fall into three generalized strategies: mergers, cooptation, and alliances (see Malatesta and Smith 2014). In the public sector, mergers can occur when government agencies combine to streamline services and manage interdependence around critical resources. For instance, the creation of the Department of Homeland Security (DHS) in 2003 merged several agencies, such as the United States Customs Service and the Immigration and Naturalization Service, to enhance national security and reduce potential bureaucratic competition (Harrigan and Newman 1990). Cooptation, on the other hand, is a strategy that requires less coordination. For example, DHS might include representatives from state and local governments or private sector security experts in advisory roles. This provides a bridging mechanism for valuable resources without a complete merging of organizations (Provan 1980; Mizruchi 1996).

Forming alliances is arguably the most common strategy employed by public managers and the most germane to our discussion here. Alliances involve agreements between two or more organizations to pursue joint objectives through coordination of activities or sharing of knowledge or resources (Scott and Davis 2007, 206–7). Unlike mergers, alliances offer considerable flexibility since many dependencies may be short-term in nature. Managers entering formal, binding contracts, particularly those that are long-term, are establishing an alliance from the RDT perspective. For example, DHS frequently forms partnerships with other federal agencies, such as the Federal Bureau of Investigation (FBI) and the Central Intelligence Agency (CIA), to share intelligence and resources, mitigating dependence on a single entity. Within this domain, organizations can design contracts to protect against abuses of power as well as encourage the development of a stable supply of potential vendors. Yet formal contracts, no matter how elegant in design, are limited instruments for mitigating power asymmetry and dependence. Organizational scholars from across the social sciences are increasingly acknowledging the importance of relational norms in such alliances. Frydlinger et al. (2019) call this "A New Approach to Contracts." In the next section, we discuss the role of relational norms in RDT and the implications for public procurement officials.

## 4.3 Emerging Issues – Focus on Relational Norms

At its core, RDT focuses on power imbalances across organizations. In public procurement there are several formal mechanisms to shield against abuses of power, starting with a transparent bidding process and including fair opportunities for potential competitors. Once a supplier is chosen, the formal contract document becomes the main mechanism to hedge against opportunistic behaviors. A carefully crafted formal agreement can mitigate abuses of power. The contract can incentivize the right behaviors, for example, by clarifying responsibilities and specifying penalties if obligations are not met. However, a fundamental challenge in constraining power stems from the fact that contracting parties cannot predict the future when they initiate their contractual relationship. This limitation significantly impacts their ability to control power dynamics. Indeed, no matter how well-defined the procurement process, how precise the contractual terms, or how robust the enforcement mechanisms, inherent constraints arise due to human cognitive limitations and the inability to predict the future. This constraint is often referred to as "bounded rationality," as coined by Herbert Simon (1972). Acknowledging this reality, numerous scholars refer to formal contracts as inherently incomplete and have proposed solutions to address what has been referred to as the "incomplete contracting problem" (e.g., Hart 2017; Tirole 1999).

To put this point in practical terms, consider a simple procurement scenario where a public school district contracts with a local supplier to provide classroom desks. While the contract specifies the quantity, quality, and delivery schedule of the desks, it cannot anticipate unexpected events like a sudden increase in the demand for desks due to unexpected student enrollment growth. The problem of unanticipated changes can be even more challenging in a complex procurement, for example, when a government agency enters into an agreement with a construction company to build a new highway. While the contract may outline specific project milestones and quality standards, its drafters cannot foresee every event or contingency that may arise during the construction phase. Therefore, the parties must navigate unforeseen challenges and adapt to changing circumstances as the project unfolds. In such cases, the contract may lack provisions to address these unanticipated changes, leaving the door open for abuses of power.

Oliver Hart and his colleagues are at the forefront of addressing the "incomplete contracting problem" (Hart 2017; Hart and Moore 2007; see also Frydlinger et al. 2019). Hart's research primarily explores the influence of ownership structures and contractual arrangements on governance and the delineation of firm boundaries. His recent studies delve into improving contract design (2022; see also Hart and Halonen-Akatwijuka 2024; Vitasek et al. 2020), preventing adversarial relationships (Frydlinger et al. 2020), and addressing the social responsibilities of businesses (Hart et al. 2024). These scholars build on the work of Ian Macneil, a prominent legal scholar, who has made significant contributions to our understanding of contract law by introducing the concept of social and relational norms. Macneil (1978) proposed that relational norms, such as trust, equity, and solidarity, serve as constraints on the exercise of power. These norms guide parties in their interactions and discourage the misuse of power to the detriment of the relationship (see also Macualay 1963). In addition, Macneil argued that relational contracts often involve balancing power between parties. This balance is achieved through mutual dependence, trust, and shared goals. Thus, parties can collaborate to maintain an equilibrium that benefits both sides. Macneil also highlighted that power dynamics can change over the course of a contractual relationship. Parties may gain or lose power based on their performance, adherence to the contract, or changes in external circumstances. This dynamic nature of power requires ongoing attention in relational contracts.

It is important to note that formal contract design need not be viewed in isolation from the development of relational norms. Indeed, contracting scholars highlight the potential complementary nature of relational contracts and incomplete formal contracts. Klein (1996) has argued that the use of formal (incomplete) contracts to structure a relationship in its early stages creates incentives for the mitigation of opportunism that become elements of trust between parties as the relationship matures. Baker, Gibbons, and Murphy (1994) show that failing to contractually specify easily identifiable elements of the exchange increases the incentive for short-term opportunism and hampers the prospects of long-term cooperation. Using data from firms engaged in information service exchanges, Poppo and Zenger (2002) find empirical support for the complementary nature of formal and relational contracts.

In summary, relational norms provide a framework for behavior in contractual relationships that goes beyond the strict terms of a contract. They encourage parties to prioritize cooperation, trust, and the long-term health of the relationship. By promoting ethical behavior and a commitment to fairness, relational norms mitigate power imbalances and foster more equitable and sustainable contractual relationships. This aligns with the principles of RDT, which emphasizes the strategic management of dependencies to minimize power asymmetries. Integrating relational norms into RDT strategies can enhance cooperation and stability in inter-organizational relationships, further supporting the goal of reducing uncertainty and dependence while maximizing autonomy. Table 4.1 describes how relational norms can guide behavior and address power imbalances.

### 4.4 Practical Applications

Combining the lessons from RDT with the insights from Ian Macneil (1978, 1980) and recent scholarship on social and relational norms (Hart 2022, 2024; Hart and Halonen-Akatwijuka 2024; Vitasek et al. 2020) provides valuable guidance for practitioners engaged in public procurement. Below we provide a set of recommendations to help practitioners identify how power and interdependence can impact decision-making and

*Table 4.1* Relational norms at work

| | |
|---|---|
| **Trust and Mutual Respect** | When trust and mutual respect are in place, parties are more likely to act in good faith, reducing the potential for one party to misuse its power. Trust encourages cooperation and a willingness to work together for mutually beneficial outcomes. |
| **Commitment to Long-Term Relationships** | Parties who value the relationship beyond the immediate transaction are more likely to consider the consequences of power misuse on the overall relationship. They are motivated to maintain the relationship's health and stability. Yet public managers must balance this with the need to develop a viable pool of potential suppliers to encourage sufficient competition. |
| **Open and Honest Communication** | When parties are transparent about their needs, expectations, and concerns, it becomes easier to address power imbalances constructively. Open dialogue can lead to mutually agreed-upon solutions that consider both parties' interests. |
| **Equity and Fairness** | Relational norms emphasize parties guided by equity and fairness are less likely to exploit their power advantage to the detriment of the other party. Fair treatment is seen as a fundamental aspect of maintaining a positive relationship. |
| **Conflict Resolution** | Parties are encouraged to address disputes or disagreements through constructive means, such as negotiation or mediation, rather than resorting to coercive tactics based on power differentials. |
| **Shared Goals and Values** | When both parties are aligned in terms of their objectives, power imbalances are less likely to result in adversarial behavior and more likely to work collaboratively to achieve their shared goals. |
| **Balancing Formal and Informal Controls** | While formal contracts have their place, informal mechanisms such as reputation and relational trust also guide behavior and help balance power dynamics. |
| **Conflict Avoidance** | Parties influenced by relational norms are generally motivated to avoid conflicts that could harm the relationship. This motivation acts as a deterrent to the misuse of power, as parties recognize that conflicts can undermine trust and cooperation. |

*Source*: Original creation.

outcomes, but also how the development and promotion of relational norms can help attenuate such disparities by increasing trust between the parties. The list is not meant to be exhaustive, but rather to capture some of the most important aspects of each theoretical approach in language that is consistent with public procurement and makes sense to practitioners.

- **Diversify Supplier Relationships:** Acknowledge the interdependence between your organization and its suppliers, as highlighted by RDT, and avoid overreliance on a single supplier by diversifying your supplier base and scoping the RFP to encourage more bidders for the product or service, considering the criticality of the resource, as well as the appropriate length of the contract term, which should be long enough to secure needed resources but short enough to incentivize quality and foster trustworthiness. These strategies reduce the risk of vulnerability to the potential misuse of power by a dominant supplier.
- **Assess Power Dynamics:** Conduct regular assessments of power dynamics within your procurement relationships. Identify suppliers with significant control over critical resources (munificence) and consider the potential for power abuse. Be prepared to address imbalances when they arise.

- **Use Contracts Strategically:** Apply the principles of RDT and relational contracting to contract design. Create contracts that not only outline terms and conditions but also address power asymmetry and resource dependencies. Incorporate provisions to build trust, such as opportunities for shared decision-making, and include mechanisms for dispute resolution.
- **Cultivate Relational Norms:** Embrace relational norms emphasized by Ian Macneil, such as trust, mutual respect, and commitment, in your procurement relationships. This involves establishing shared expectations in the earliest stages of contract design and incentivizing behaviors that guide interactions over time. Foster positive, long-term partnerships with suppliers based on these norms, as they can help mitigate power imbalances and enhance cooperation.
- **Promote Transparency:** Transparency is crucial in public procurement. Ensure that your procurement processes are transparent and open to scrutiny. This promotes fairness, accountability, and trust, reducing the potential for power misuse.
- **Advocate for Ethical Practices:** Advocate for ethical practices in procurement. Encourage suppliers to adhere to ethical standards in their interactions with your organization. Ethical behavior can contribute to healthier and more equitable procurement relationships.
- **Seek Legal and Regulatory Safeguards:** Be aware of relevant legal and regulatory frameworks that govern public procurement. Utilize these safeguards to protect your organization's interests and ensure compliance with ethical and legal standards.
- **Build Supplier Relationships:** Invest in building and maintaining strong relationships with suppliers. Regular communication and collaboration can strengthen trust and cooperation, reducing the likelihood of power misuse. For example, managers should consider the need to maintain a diversified pool of potential suppliers by providing practical feedback to unsuccessful bidders and institutionalizing a pre-qualification system.
- **Plan for Contingencies:** Monitor changes in the external environment, such as regulatory updates or shifts in market conditions, as relationships are often challenged by uncertainty. Develop contingency plans for addressing power imbalances or disruptions in the supply chain. Operate from the position that it is not a matter of *if* such disruptions occur, but rather *when*. Having strategies in place for such situations can help your organization respond effectively.

## Note

1 This chapter focuses on the use of power and influence by suppliers. Importantly, undue power and opportunism can also manifest on the part of government. Public officials and those responsible for procurement decisions wield considerable authority, and their personal preferences, biases, or even corruption can significantly impact the procurement process. This influence can manifest through the selection of suppliers based on personal relationships rather than objective criteria, favoritism toward certain companies, or even the manipulation of procurement procedures to achieve a predetermined outcome.

## References

Baker, G., Gibbons, R., & Murphy, K. J. (1994). Subjective performance measures in optimal incentive contracts. *Quarterly Journal of Economics, 109*(4), 1125–1156. https://doi.org/10.2307/2118358

Blau, P. M. (1964). Justice in social exchange. *Sociological Inquiry, 34*(2), 193–206. https://doi.org/10.1111/j.1475-682X.1964.tb00583.x

Diagana, O., & Diagne, M. (2023, June 13). Corruption is a global problem for development. To fight it, we all have a role to play. *La Tribune Afrique*. World Bank Op-Ed. [Published in French.]

Emerson, R. M. (1962). Power-dependence relations. *American Sociological Review, 27*(1), 31–40. https://doi.org/10.2307/2089716

Frydlinger, D., Hart, O., & Vitasek, K. (2019, September–October). A new approach to contracts. *Harvard Business Review.*

Frydlinger, D., Hart, O., & Vitasek, K. (2020, October 8). An innovative way to prevent adversarial supplier relationships. *Harvard Business Review.*

Harrigan, K. R., & Newman, W. H. (1990). Bases of interorganization cooperation: Propensity, power, and persistence. *Journal of Management Studies, 27*(4), 417–434. https://doi.org/10.1111/j.1467-6486.1990.tb00255.x

Hart, O. (2017). Incomplete contracts and control. *American Economic Review, 107*(7), 1731–1752. https://doi.org/10.1257/aer.107.7.1731

Hart, O., & Halonen-Akatwijuka, M. (2024). *More is less: Why parties may deliberately write incomplete contracts.* Cambridge Elements in Law, Economics, and Politics. Cambridge University Press.

Hart, O., & Moore, J. (2007). Incomplete contracts and ownership: Some new thoughts. *American Economic Review, 97*(2), 182–186. https://doi.org/10.1257/aer.97.2.182

Hart, O., Thesmar, D., & Zingales, L. (2024, January). Private sanctions. *Economic Policy*, 203–268. https://doi.org/10.1093/epolic/eiad041

Homans, G. C. (1958). Social behavior as exchange. *American Journal of Sociology, 63*(6), 597–606. https://doi.org/10.1086/222355

Klein, B. (1996). Why 'hold-ups' occur: The self-enforcing range of contractual relationships. *Economic Inquiry, 34*(3), 444–463. https://doi.org/10.1111/j.1465-7295.1996.tb01388.x

Macaulay, S. (1963). Non-contractual relations in business: A preliminary study. *American Sociological Review, 28*(1), 55–67. https://doi.org/10.2307/2090458

Macneil, I. R. (1978). Contracts: Adjustment of long-term economic relations under classical, neoclassical, and relational contract law. *Northwestern University Law Review, 72*(6), 854–905.

Macneil, I. R. (1980). *The new social contract: An inquiry into modern contractual relations.* Yale University Press. https://doi.org/10.2307/1288310

Malatesta, D., & Smith, C. R. (2014). Lessons from resource dependence theory for contemporary public and nonprofit management. *Public Administration Review, 74*(1), 14–25. https://doi.org/10.1111/puar.12181

Milliken, F. J. (1987). Three types of perceived uncertainty about the environment: State, effect, and response uncertainty. *The Academy of Management Review, 12*(1), 133–143. https://doi.org/10.2307/257999

Mizruchi, M. S. (1996). What do interlocks do? An analysis, critique, and assessment of research on interlocking directorates. *Annual Review of Sociology, 22*, 271–298.

Pfeffer, J. (2003). Introduction to the classic edition. In J. Pfeffer & G. R. Salancik (Eds.), *The external control of organizations: A resource dependence perspective* (Classic ed.) (pp. xi–xxix). Stanford University Press.

Pfeffer, J., Leong, A., & Strehl, K. (1977). Paradigm development and particularism: Journal publication in three scientific disciplines. *Social Forces, 55*(4), 938–951. https://doi.org/10.1093/sf/55.4.938

Pfeffer, J., & Salancik, G. R. (1978). *The external control of organizations: A resource dependence perspective*. Harper & Row.

Poppo, L., & Zenger, T. (2002). Do formal contracts and relational governance function as substitutes or complements? *Strategic Management Journal, 23*(8), 707–725. https://doi.org/10.1002/smj.249

Provan, K. G. (1980). Board power and organizational effectiveness among human service agencies. *The Academy of Management Journal, 23*(2), 221–236. / www.jstor.org/stable/255428

Scott, R., & Davis, G. (2007). *Organizations and organizing: Rational, natural, and open systems perspectives*. Routledge.

Simon, H. (1972). Theories of bounded rationality. In C. B. McGuire & R. Radner (Eds.), *Decision and organization* (pp. 161–176). Elsevier.

Tirole, J. (1999). Incomplete contracts: Where do we stand? *Econometrica, 67*(4), 741–781. https://doi.org/10.1111/1468-0262.00052

Vitasek, K., Winn, J. K., & Nickel, T. E. (2020). The vested way: A model of formal relational contracts. *University of the Pacific Law Review, 52*(1), 125–140.

***Case Study: Navigating Power Dynamics in Contractual Relationship (Developed by Deanna Malatesta and Craig Smith)***

**Case Title: "Vermont's Technology Procurement Challenge"**

Vermont's Health Care Administration, a large government agency responsible for managing public healthcare services, has embarked on a significant digital transformation initiative. This initiative aims to procure a comprehensive electronic health records (EHR) system from a prominent technology provider, TechHealth Solutions (THS). As one of the few reputable vendors with the expertise and capacity to provide this specialized solution, THS holds a dominant position in the market. This dynamic influences the agency's strategy, as they navigate a vendor landscape where choices are limited.

The EHR system is critical for improving patient care, data management, and administrative efficiency within the agency. Given the scarcity of highly qualified vendors, Vermont's Health Care Administration must establish a robust partnership with THS, ensuring that both parties can share resources and knowledge effectively. This relationship will be vital in maintaining the system's efficacy and responsiveness to evolving healthcare needs over the ten-year contract period.

The agency plans to enter into a ten-year contract with THS that will rely on the vendor's essential technological resources, including the EHR software, ongoing technical support, and system updates. By securing these resources from a well-established provider like THS, Vermont's Health Care Administration aims to create a resilient and innovative healthcare infrastructure, capable of adapting to future challenges and opportunities within the public health sector.

**Discussion Questions**

Part 1.
In small groups, analyze the case from a resource dependence perspective (30 min).

- Identify the key resources needed by the agency.
- Describe the potential contract relationship in terms of munificence, concentration and interconnectedness.
- Assess the power dynamics between the organization and the supplier. How does the case exemplify the concepts of resource dependence, negotiation, and power dynamics within the context of public procurement?
- What are the potential risks and challenges the agency might face in this resource-dependent procurement scenario?
- Discuss how the supplier's control over these resources and its expertise might influence the relationship.
- If you had to define the scope, purpose, and goals of the relationship in a few sentences to place in the formal contract, what would it say?
- What strategies can the agency employ to manage resource dependence effectively, ensuring a stable supply of THS expertise and compliance with federal regulations?

Present the analysis to class.

Part 2.
Reconvene in groups. Revisit the case study and consider how the application of relational norms might address the power imbalances identified in Part 1. (30 minutes)

- Considering the interests of both the agency and the supplier, develop a shared vision by discussing and documenting the desired outcomes and objectives the parties aim to achieve through the contract.
- What specific strategies do you recommend to foster trust, transparency, and cooperation during contract negotiations?
- What strategies do you recommend to keep the parties aligned throughout the life of the contract? Specifically, how will you foster trust, transparency, and cooperation as the relationship evolves and circumstances change?

Present the analysis to class.

Section 2

# The Context and Goals of Procurement

# 5 Public Procurement Law

*Christopher R. Yukins*

## 5.1 Introduction

Public procurement law – sometimes called "government contracts" law in the United States – is a rapidly globalizing discipline. Governments around the world spend trillions of dollars on public procurement every year, estimated to total roughly 12 percent of the world's economic output (Organisation for Economic Co-Operation and Development (OECD), 2023, p. 7). To ease and regularize that massive public spending, many governments have adopted updated public procurement laws (World Bank, no date), often drafted by using model laws such as the United Nations' *Model Law on Public Procurement* (United Nations Commission on International Trade Law (UNCITRAL), 2014b) or (in the United States) the American Bar Association's *Model Procurement Code for State and Local Procurement* (MPC) (American Bar Association (ABA), 2000). These public procurement laws are remarkably uniform, generally not because of close coordination among the drafters but because the laws meet a common problem: how to reduce risks and optimize procurement outcomes while addressing the dysfunctions inevitable in a public system where officials can be indifferent (or even corrupt) and privately motivated actors – the contractors – play an integral role (Yukins, 2010).

Because the risks addressed in public procurement law arise uniquely out of a *public function*, driven by special public policy imperatives, public procurement law often differs from *private supply chain management*, though the two disciplines offer important comparative lessons. Public procurement law can also differ from nation to nation, or even town to town, based upon differences in administrative habits, legal traditions, social norms, economic structures, and political perspectives (Cibinic et al., 2023, ch.16).

All that said, public procurement is sufficiently *uniform* around the world to be understood as a unified discipline. This chapter will review the key elements of procurement laws around the world, drawing on examples from different countries. The chapter will address the following issues:

- *Contract formation*: Many of the most challenging issues in public procurement law arise during the formation stage, in part because this stage – unlike contract administration, after award – attracts so many public policy concerns. As a result, public contract formation has some very unique aspects:
  - *Planning:* The planning needed for public procurement can be thought of mechanically – a series of required steps, outlined for example in Part 7 of the Federal Acquisition Regulation (FAR) (available at acquisition.gov/far), to prepare for a competition. More lies below the surface, though, as the discussion below will show. Public procurement planning generally occurs out of view, within an agency, and so is

DOI: 10.4324/9781003566670-7

largely immune from accountability measures, such as *bid challenges* (or "protests"), by which private parties can demand accountability for public officials who fail to follow procurement rules. Planning is also an important first step in *market research*, something that public procurement officials must undertake because they are often unprepared for a sophisticated private market.

- *Competition:* Like planning, the competitive process can be read as a mechanical set of steps through a highly structured process – for example, awarding using (1) *sole-source*; (2) *lowest price* (often done through a process called "*open tendering*," or (in the United States) "*sealed bidding*"); (3) a more modern version of open tendering, *electronic reverse auctions*; (4) *multilateral competitive negotiations* (called "*competitive dialogue*" outside the United States); or (5) *catalogue contracts* (often called "*indefinite-delivery/indefinite-quantity*" ("*IDIQ*") contracts in the United States, and "*framework agreements*" in most systems elsewhere) (Albano & Nicholas, 2016). As the discussion below will show, however, the choice of competitive method is much more nuanced than the regulatory structure suggests – competition affords public officials more opportunities to learn about the market but must also be shaped to contain corruption, accomplish best value, and accommodate a rapidly evolving marketplace.
- *Vendor qualification*: Every public procurement award has three essential elements – *price*, *technical conformity* with the solicitation, and a determination that the awardee contractor is *qualified* (or "*responsible*" in the U.S. system). Vendor qualification (and conversely, vendor *exclusion* from a procurement) can be viewed quite mechanically, as something akin to supply chain management in the public sector – an assessment of the *performance* and *reputational* risks posed by a prospective contractor. In the public sector, however, public policy concerns ranging from geopolitics to socio-economic preferences to global warming can crowd into the qualification decision; as a result, issues of qualification and exclusion tend to dominate modern discussions of procurement reform.

- ***Anti-corruption:*** For those inside the public procurement community, anti-corruption issues overlap in many ways with issues of *contract formation* and *administration*. This is because effective anti-corruption strategies can be used to mitigate the principal–agent issues which undermine contract formation and administration (see Figure 5.1). Thus, for example, criminal prohibitions against bribery can discourage contracting officials (the "agents" of the governing "principal") from taking bribes that would otherwise distort their decision-making and bring them to buy inferior goods. Similarly, anti-fraud laws can deter contractors ("sub-agents" to the contracting officials) from delivering cheap and defective goods and thus mitigate contractors' selfish desire to maximize profits and exploit the gaps in oversight left by indifferent contracting officials. Anti-corruption efforts in procurement are not always about "corruption" in the classic sense – misuse of public power for private ends (Transparency International, no date). Anti-corruption efforts also can reinforce systemic protections to ensure that governments purchase best value, to the benefit of the citizens who rely on what a government buys.
- ***Contract administration:*** Unlike contract formation, rules regarding the *administration* of public contracts often parallel those in the private sector, though with slightly different allocations of risk between the government and its contractor.[1] Allocations of risk differ in public contracting partly because of the unique nature of a government as a contracting partner: the government, unlike a private trading partner, is almost never a competitor of its contractor, so the law often imposes heavier burdens and expectations on the government as a contracting partner. (In private commercial law, in contrast,

courts may be reluctant to impose special risks or burdens on one of the parties if it is not clear whether doing so will upset the competitive, market-based balance between the parties.) At the same time, public contract administration is skewed by *how* those risks are allocated – typically through standard clauses, which may have been developed by the government over many years (even centuries) and which judges must apply carefully to ensure that the government does not unfairly exploit its position as the contract-writer.

- ***Bid protests and disputes:*** For professionals in public procurement, *bid protests* (the U.S. term; internationally they are often known as "*bid challenges*" or "*remedies*") and *disputes* (typically regarding claims that arise during contract performance) are a central part of their work. Depending on the local law, bid protests can be brought before a court, an independent agency and/or the purchasing agency itself (UNCITRAL, 2014b, ch. VIII). Bid protests allow a disappointed bidder to bring failures in the process (including corruption) to the attention of the government, with the hope of reopening the competition and (again depending on the local law) potentially other remedies. The bid challenge process reinforces competitors' sense that they have been treated fairly in the system and so encourages more robust competition in the future. By challenging mistakes in the procurement process, bid protesters help ensure accountability and transparency – in essence, they are highly motivated whistleblowers – and they serve as a "red flag" for system failure (Yukins & Drabkin, 2022). *Disputes*, in contrast, are typically less confrontational, and often involve contractor claims for additional costs or time as a result of changes that arise during the administration of an awarded contract.
- ***Trade agreements:*** The chapter will briefly review international trade agreements, including the World Trade Organization's "Agreement on Government Procurement," known colloquially as the "Government Procurement Agreement" or "GPA" (World Trade Organization (WTO), 2012). Even though some governments (such as the United States) may treat their obligations under these trade agreements less seriously, the trade agreements are a valuable bridge between nations – and so a place to discern *best practices* emerging internationally.

The following parts of this chapter will address these key concepts. Section 5.2 will review the literature in the field so that scholars, practitioners, and students can identify accessible and useful resources which review these concepts. Section 5.3 will discuss critical emerging issues, focusing on issues of *environmental sustainability*. Section 5.4 will offer practical applications, including insights into risk management and compliance – probably the most common issues encountered in practice. This chapter will offer a case study and a mock contractor compliance plan which could be used for teaching purposes. The supporting materials for this chapter, available online, proffer teaching tips, with a focus on resources that help illuminate emerging issues in the field.

## 5.2 Summary of the Literature

### *5.2.1 Contract Formation*

Any discussion of public procurement law ideally should begin with Steven Schooner's *Desiderata* – a 2002 piece in the United Kingdom's *Public Procurement Law Review* which mapped out the key attributes desired of any procurement system, including of course transparency, competition, and integrity, and also including other important elements such as socioeconomic goals (what Steven Schooner called "wealth redistribution") (Schooner, 2002). Steven Schooner (a fellow faculty member at George Washington University Law School (GW Law School)) is himself an excellent example of the evolution of the procurement law field: when he wrote the *Desiderata* piece in 2002, he focused more on the mechanics of procurement, but in later years his scholarship has shifted to emphasize global warming and sustainability (Schooner, 2021).

The leading book on public contract formation in the U.S. federal system is *Formation of Government Contracts* (Cibinic et al., 2023), one of the cornerstone texts of the government procurement law program at GW Law School. Because that text seeks to canvass all the leading authorities in federal procurement law, it is quite dense. But Chapter 16 of the *Formation* text (the last chapter) may be useful for those new to U.S. procurement – it offers a comparative perspective on each of the topics of the previous chapters, drawing on international examples to illustrate how different procurement systems often take very similar approaches to common problems.

Another, even more accessible resource is Danielle Conway's *State and Local Government Procurement* (2012). The text offers a very useful introduction to basic concepts in U.S. public contract formation. While the text is nominally a state-and-local guide, Dean Conway was steeped in U.S. federal procurement as well, and her book can be used to understand public contract formation issues generally in the United States. Educators also may want to consider *State and Local Procurement: A Practical Guide* (National Association of State Procurement Officials (NASPO), 2024), which is published by the National Association of State Procurement Officials and offers a handy, step-by-step guide to public procurement at the state-and-local levels in the United States.

Another accessible resource is the *Guide to Enactment of the UNCITRAL Model Law on Public Procurement* which accompanies the United Nations Commission on International Trade Law (UNCITRAL) Model Law on Public Procurement (UNCITRAL, 2014a). While the 400-page *Guide* is ostensibly merely a concordance for the model law, in fact it was quite consciously prepared by the UNCITRAL Secretariat to serve as a guide for those learning about procurement. The *Guide* is a typical UN document – the voice is often passive and technical, and the text has almost no citations – but the *Guide* does do a very good job of explaining the rudiments of international best practices in procurement, and in describing the policy considerations that drive different approaches to procurement.

### *5.2.2 Anti-Corruption*

While a good procurement system is defended by effective anti-corruption legal functions, such as bid protests (challenges), debarments, criminal prosecutions, and corporate compliance, those functions often can best be understood as systemic corrections – as strategies to check the principal–agent problems endemic to procurement (see Figure 5.1) (Yukins, 2010, p.65), per the principal–agent model proposed by Michael Jensen and William Meckling in their landmark 1976 article (Jensen & Meckling, 1976). Although their principal–agent model was used to explain the dynamics of a corporation, not procurement, the rule has proven remarkably useful in understanding public procurement as well (Trepte, 2004, p.70).

One starting point for this approach is the OECD's monograph, *Managing Risks in the Public Procurement of Goods, Services and Infrastructure* (OECD, 2023). The OECD publication was quietly revolutionary, for the OECD report made it plain that public procurement, like private supply chain management, really can be seen as a *risk management* function. In that light, anti-corruption efforts can be understood (and taught) as systems for managing risk, including the risk that contracting officials will exploit their positions as agents to extract corrupt rents from the procurement system.

This makes it much easier to understand anti-corruption strategies in public procurement because each strategy has different costs and benefits as a risk-reduction device.

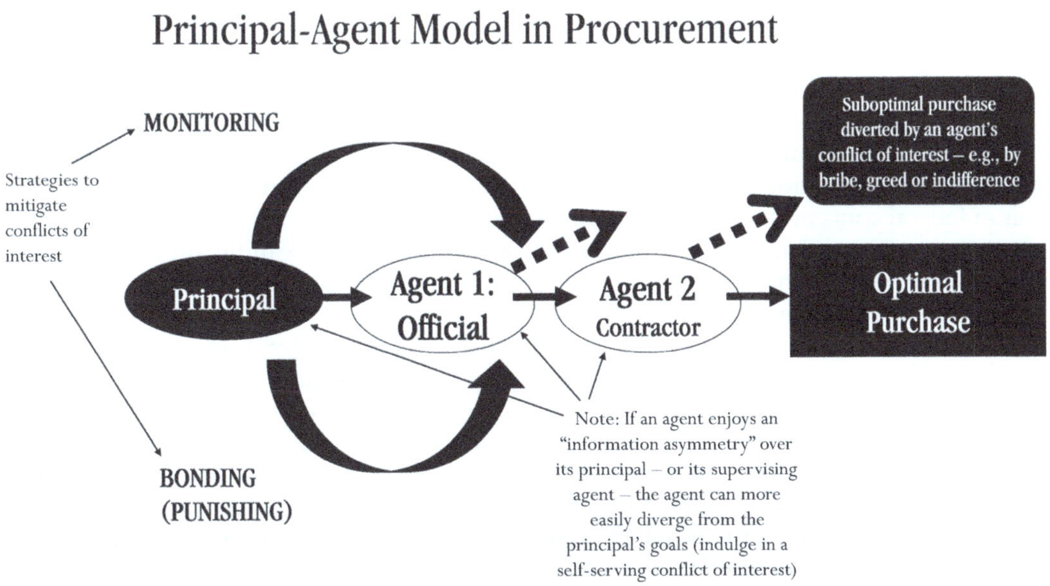


*Figure 5.1* The principal–agent model in procurement.
*Source*: Original creation.

Criminal prosecutions, for example, can be extremely effective in deterring corrupt rent-seeking behavior, but they are disconnected from the subtle risks that can undo a procurement system. A prosecutor may help send a corrupt contracting official to prison, in other words, without necessarily fixing the systemic failures that facilitated that corruption in the first place.

Because corruption problems in public procurement are so often traceable to principal–agent issues, many of the most common anti-corruption strategies can be described (as Jensen and Meckling did) as "monitoring" (oversight) or "bonding" (which translates into sanctioning in the procurement context). Because information technology has made monitoring increasingly easy, but sanctions can jar a procurement system in unpredictable ways, popular guidance such as the OECD's *Preventing Corruption in Public Procurement* tend to focus first on transparency and auditing as anti-corruption strategies (OECD, 2016).

The practical problem is that monitoring alone is not enough – sanctions may be necessary as well. As Jensen and Meckling and others have explained in elaborating on the principal–agent theory, there are concomitant problems, for example of information asymmetry. Because agents can best exploit their positions when they hold more information than their principals, in the public procurement context a corrupt contractor might enjoy and exploit an informational advantage over its bureaucratic overseers, making monitoring ineffective and sanctions imperative (Eisenhardt, 1989; Yukins, 2010, p.66). To parse these elements of the principal–agent problem in procurement, one can identify a particular anti-corruption strategy – debarment, for example, which excludes a corrupt contractor from a procurement system – and then explore what sorts of agency problems that strategy resolves.

Another important anti-corruption strategy is fighting fraud. The United States has one of the most effective anti-fraud laws in the world, the False Claims Act, which was originally passed to redress massive fraud by contractors during the Civil War. In one recent year, the U.S. government recovered more than $2.68 billion in settlements and judgments from civil cases involving fraud and false claims (U.S. Department of Justice, 2024). The Justice Department publishes a somewhat legalistic "primer" on the False Claims Act (U.S. Department of Justice, 2022), and the Congressional Research Service has produced a monograph which, though still closely footnoted, is more suitable for the lay reader (Congressional Research Service, 2021).

Under the False Claims Act, a whistleblower (known as a "relator") – who can be almost anyone with information on the fraud and is often a contractor's former employee – can bring suit in federal court in the name of the government, claiming fraud. After reviewing the suit the government can join the case (and often does), or the relator can pursue the suit alone. The contractor that committed fraud may be forced to pay treble (triple) damages and penalties (which often amount to millions of dollars) if it acted "recklessly" (i.e., proceeded in the face of a known risk of fraud) – a looser "knowledge" (or "*scienter*") requirement than the typical common law standard for fraud. If the suit is successful, the relator/whistleblower will be rewarded with a substantial share of the government's recovery by the court (Boese & Baruch, 2024). Taken together, these core elements of the False Claims Act – suit brought by an incentivized and empowered whistleblower, a low knowledge requirement, and severe penalties – make the False Claims Act a formidable anti-corruption tool.

Although contractor fraud is not corruption in the classic sense (contractor fraud is a private act, not a misuse of public power), in practice the False Claims Act *does* redress public misconduct when a fraud action against a contractor fills the oversight gap left by an indolent contracting official. The False Claims Act thus fits neatly into a broader understanding of "anti-corruption" in procurement: an effort to optimize outcomes by remedying common structural defects in the procurement system.

To identify (and parse) these various anti-corruption strategies, one resource is the United Nations Office of Drugs and Crimes (UNODC) monograph, *Guidebook on Anti-Corruption in Public Procurement and the Management of Public Finances* (United Nations Office of Drugs and Crimes (UNODC), 2013). While the *Guidebook* is anchored in Article 9 of the UN Convention Against Corruption, which focuses on a relatively limited range of anti-corruption strategies, the *Guidebook* goes beyond Article 9 to take a broader view of the risks and remedies relating to corruption in procurement.

A final (and new) anti-corruption resource is the *Routledge Handbook of Public Procurement Corruption*, edited by Sope Williams (Stellenbosch University) and GW Law's Jessica Tillipman (Williams & Tillipman, 2024). The *Handbook* presents chapters focused on anti-corruption efforts in a number of different countries – an excellent starting point for students' comparative research – and essays on issues which transcend national boundaries, such as emerging challenges in the use of artificial intelligence, and in responding to natural disasters and emergencies.

### *5.2.3 Contract Administration*

Unlike *formations* of public contracts, the body of literature relating to public contracting *administration* is uneven and incomplete, for reasons theoretical, practical, and political. The *theoretical* problem is that there has been almost no attempt to apply any unifying theories to contract administration – no effort, for example, to identify the unique patterns of risk allocation which set public contract administration apart from private contracting. (The U.S. government, for instance, is regularly held to much higher standards of good faith and fair dealing than a private party; this contorts the law of public contract administration, but there has been little written on *why* the government is such a different sort of contracting party.) The resulting *practical* problem is that because there is no clear *theoretical* or *principled* barrier between commercial and public contract administration – unlike public contract *formation*, which is so clearly divided from private contracting by a different set of principles or "desiderata" – the published works (like many jurisdictions' court decisions) tend to lump public and private contract administration together. There is also a *political* aspect to this blurred barrier between public and private contract administration: because governments naturally have a stronger interest in how public contracts are *formed* since that process defines political and social outcomes, it is hardly surprising that governments (and the literature) treat contract *administration* as something of a forgotten stepchild of public procurement.

One solution is to study the rules of public contract *administration* in detail, to identify patterns of risk allocation between the public and private parties that can be explained only by recognizing the unique role of government as a contracting party. Probably the leading text in U.S. procurement on legal issues in contract performance is *Administration of Government Contracts*, by John Cibinic, Jr., James F. Nagle, Ralph C. Nash, Jr. (Cibinic et al., 2016) – the sister text to the *Formation* text discussed above. That text carries the additional benefit of James Nagle's insights into the history of U.S. procurement. James Nagle has generously placed his multi-volume history of U.S. federal procurement into the public domain, and it is available through the GW Law School website (Nagle, 2012).

Another approach is to focus on a particular standard provision of contract law and compare the private and public law versions. The acceptance provision (Section 2-606) of Article 2 of the Uniform Commercial Code (UCC) on sales of goods, for example, can be compared to the FAR Subpart 46.5, Acceptance. The UCC provision is much more liberal and allows for implied acceptance; the government provision, in contrast, requires a formal acceptance, generally in writing by an authorized official. The difference can be confirmed by looking to the World Bank's prescribed general terms for purchases of goods – a commercial-type provision which allows for implied acceptance in paragraph 6 (World Bank Group, 2021). A final point of comparison in this example would be to FAR 52.212-4, the standard clause used for purchasing *commercial* products under the FAR; while that clause takes a more classically commercial approach, it still reserves to the government "the right to inspect or test any supplies or services that have been tendered for acceptance." To make sense of these differing approaches, in this example one might ask students to compare (1) the accountability needed for legitimacy in government procurement, (2) the need for flexibility in the commercial marketplace, and (3) a government's (or public institution's) incentives to offer more flexible terms when entering that commercial marketplace.

### *5.2.4 Bid Protests and Disputes*

Because public procurement systems around the world have evolved bid challenge ("bid protest") systems to allow disappointed bidders to raise challenges, there is a relatively rich literature assessing bid challenges and their purposes. Post-award disputes, in contrast, tend to be more specific to a given procurement system – in fact, they may simply be shunted to a country's traditional commercial courts. As a result, bid challenges offer a richer pedagogical opportunity.

Probably the best element-by-element assessment of bid challenges was done by Daniel Gordon, who played a pivotal role in making the U.S. Government Accountability Office a leading forum for bid challenges, and who was a pioneer in comparative public procurement law during his time at GW Law School. Daniel Gordon's (2006) piece for the *Public Contract Law Journal* reviewed the essential elements of any bid protest system, and explained the trade-offs that must be made in constructing an effective and efficient bid challenge system (Gordon, 2006).

Daniel Gordon's piece noted the multiple *purposes* of a bid challenge system – a question worth exploring with students. In a 2022 report for the Department of Defense, David Drabkin (a senior member of the U.S. procurement community) and the author explored that issue further. They argued that bid challenges have *two* purposes, noted above: the first (and obvious) one is to provide recourse to disappointed bidders to encourage robust competition, and the second is to create a "red flag" system warning of system failures (Yukins & Drabkin, 2022). The latter point is a useful discussion point with students – for example, if protesters serve as "whistleblowers" raising a "red flag," how can governments incentivize those protesters (whistleblowers), and who should serve as "whistleblowers" – only bidders, or any taxpayer (which is the case in some procurement systems in the U.S. states)? Bid protests, by allowing outsiders to challenge an administrative process, open fertile ground for discussions of accountability and process, and of efficient ways to address failures in a government structure.

### *5.2.5 Trade Agreements*

The most comprehensive text on trade issues in public procurement is Jean Heilman Grier's *The International Procurement System: Liberalization and Protectionism* (2022). For many years – critical years in the development of trade agreements in procurement – Jean Grier served as the lead negotiator on government procurement for the Office of the U.S. Trade Representative. In that role she gained first-hand insights on how the trade regime surrounding procurement has evolved since World War II. Her text discusses the mechanics of trade agreements and contrasts the liberalization brought by the trade agreements (often at the urging of the United States) with the more recent protectionism in U.S. policy. Jean Grier also publishes an excellent blog on the latest issues in trade and procurement (required reading for many in the procurement community), *Perspectives on Trade*, available through her consultancy's website, djaghe.com.

While Jean Grier's book offers a very useful overview on trade topics in public procurement, Sue Arrowsmith (Professor Emerita of Public Procurement Law and Policy at the University of Nottingham) and Robert Anderson (who previously headed the public procurement efforts at the World Trade Organization) have published a series of more detailed assessments of particular topics in trade. Together they edited *The WTO Regime on Government Procurement: Challenge and Reform*, a collection of essays by leading experts on topics ranging from environmental sustainability to competition law (Arrowsmith & Anderson, 2011). For students undertaking in-depth research in procurement law and international trade, this text is an important starting point.

## 5.3 Emerging Issues

Probably the most important issues emerging in public procurement law have to do with *sustainability*. The topic itself has many meanings. In Europe and across most of the world, "sustainable procurement" includes *environmentally* sustainable procurement (sometimes called "green procurement"), *social justice* in procurement, and *economically* sustainable procurement which reinforces the economic strength of the procuring jurisdiction. In the U.S. government, in contrast, "sustainable procurement" tends to mean *environmentally* sustainable procurement only – social justice and economic issues are addressed in federal procurement, but under their own regulatory regimes (for example through preferences for small businesses, and "Buy American" preferences).

The need for *environmentally sustainable* procurement is obvious, as Steven Schooner and others have pointed out (Schooner, 2021). The United Nations publishes a very comprehensive resource page, *The Causes and Effects of Climate Change* (United Nations, no date), which is a good starting point for understanding why climate change is occurring, and what the likely impacts will be. That page links to resources on "Net Zero," the goal of "zeroing-out" net greenhouse gas emissions, a goal which has been adopted by over 140 nations. That "net zero" goal is the cornerstone to many governments' "green procurement" initiatives.

"Green public procurement" strategies can be grouped into at least five different categories (see Figure 5.2) (Schooner, 2021; Andhov & Yukins, 2024):

- Using *procurement planning* to steer procurement toward more environmentally sound solutions. Planning is an important part of a 2024 federal rule (89 Fed. Reg. 30212 (Apr. 2024)) which called for contracting officials to make "maximum practicable" use of environmentally sustainable products. (That rule, like most U.S. government initiatives in green procurement, may be reversed during President Donald Trump's administration, given his opposition to environmental sustainability.)
- Focusing on *contractor qualification* to encourage vendors to chronicle, and reduce, the greenhouse gas emissions attributable to their goods and services; contractors which fail to assess their greenhouse gas emissions may be excluded from procurements under this strategy. The danger here is the unpredictability of this strategy; without more information on *which* vendors might be disqualified, this strategy risks excluding vitally important vendors in a government's supply chain.
- Looking to *eco-labels*, which are technical standards used to endorse products or services that are more environmentally friendly. One practical problem is that eco-labels differ from market to market and so can raise barriers to cross-border trade.
- Incorporating environmental data (the volume of carbon emissions, for example, attributable to one type of aircraft versus another) into *evaluations* for procurement awards. A threshold problem here is the sheer lack of commercially available data regarding vendors' goods and services; this helps explain, then, why governments have used contractor *qualification* (discussed above) as an incentive to spur contractors to gather and present data on their greenhouse gas emissions.
- *Life-cycle costs*: The costs of green procurement may be much lower if the *life-cycle costs* of sustainable products and services are taken into account. Traditionally, government focused only on the purchase price of a good or service in making award decisions. Increasingly, though, governments are weighing the costs of a product (including environmental costs) over its entire life-cycle. This approach, while prudent, raises concerns

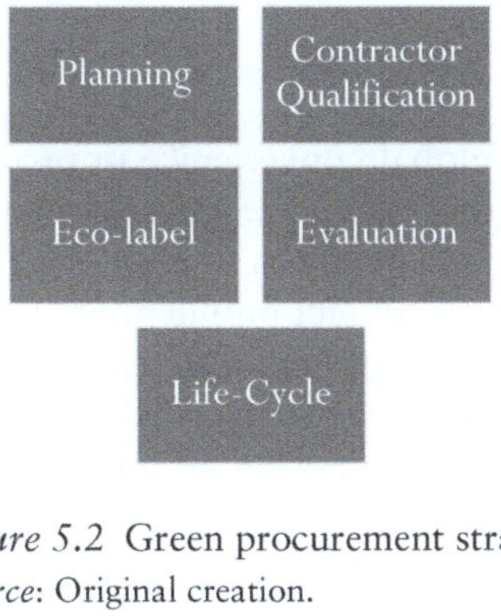


*Figure 5.2* Green procurement strategies.
*Source*: Original creation.

about market barriers if governments adopt life-cycle cost assessments which favor particular goods (or services) over others.

These and other "green procurement" initiatives were discussed in a recorded webinar, with supporting materials available online (GW Law, 2024). The webinar centered on a catalogue (produced jointly by the U.S. government and the European Commission) of "green procurement" strategies adopted in the European Union and the United States (U.S.-EU Trade & Technology Council, 2024).

One common theme across all these strategies is the need for *training*, both among officials and members of industry. Although *cost* can be an important factor in determining which strategy will succeed (in part because of cost concerns, for example, Congress stalled a proposed rule which would have disqualified contractors that did not chronicle their greenhouse gas emissions) (Yukins, 2024), the sheer complexity of "green procurement" means that reforms may be stalled by misunderstanding, no matter how urgent it is to address global warming.

While "green procurement" is a relatively new topic, *economic* sustainability has been a well-established part of procurement for many years. Probably the most common strategy for boosting the economy of the purchasing government is through *domestic preferences* – a "Buy American" preference, for example, for goods purchased by the federal government. Those trade preferences can be staggeringly complex in application (Yukins & Green, 2018). As a threshold matter, there is an open question whether in practice domestic preferences may cause a net economic loss. For example, a 2017 Victoria University (Australia) study, which drew on macroeconomic data regularly used by the U.S. government itself, concluded that on balance "Buy American" requirements cost over 300,000 U.S. jobs (Dixon et al., 2017).

*Social justice* initiatives in procurement – the third type of "sustainable" public procurement – can be equally controversial. Preferences afforded to racial, gender, or ethnic groups have long been a part of public procurement (McCrudden, 2007) but have also attracted bitter criticism for being divisive or unfair. It remains unclear what impact the Supreme Court's 2023 decision in *Students for Fair Admissions v. Harvard*, which primarily addressed affirmative action in U.S. higher education admissions, will have on public procurement. Much more clear, however, is the second Trump administration's dislike for some procurement preferences. What is worth emphasizing for now is *how* social justice initiatives are implemented in public procurement. As Article 2 of the UNCITRAL model public procurement law stresses, socioeconomic preferences cannot be imposed on an individual official's whim but must be codified in law (UNCITRAL, 2014b) – an important assurance of a deliberative process which lends legitimacy to social justice initiatives in procurement.

## 5.4 Practical Applications

To make sense of the themes outlined above, including the global convergence in procurement rules, as noted it is useful to stress the central role that *risk management* plays in public procurement. While public procurement law is often presented as a branch of administrative law, which seeks to order and constrain agency actions, in fact public procurement law (certainly in the United States, where it dates back to the Continental Army) *predates* the administrative state which grew up in the United States in the twentieth century (Yukins, 2017). While administrative law imposes checks and balances on agencies' action, procurement law is much more instrumental – procurement law seeks to optimize outcomes, largely by controlling predictable risks in the procurement process (such as bribery, over-pricing, or officials' indifference). Both practically and theoretically, therefore, to understand procurement law it makes sense to see it as a form of risk management – and not to assume that it falls squarely into administrative law's norms and structures.

This was precisely the approach taken by the OECD in its June 2023 report, *Managing Risks in the Public Procurement of Goods, Services and Infrastructure* (OECD, 2023). The OECD report was focused not on procurement *law*, but more broadly on the need to deal with public procurement as an integrated exercise in the management of risks. But the OECD's insight – that public procurement, like supply chain management in the private sector, is centered on risk management – makes it much easier to connect doctrine to practice in public procurement law.

The law surrounding *contractor compliance* is a good example. Taken in isolation, compliance – remedial measures taken by contractors to contain the risk of legal non-compliance – can seem to be just another anti-corruption tool. But that does not explain why compliance rules are essentially identical around the world, as shown in Table 5.1.

As the Justice Department and the U.S. Securities and Exchange Commission have noted (and as the Table 5.1 reflects), after corporate compliance standards were published by the U.S. Sentencing Commission in the United States in the 1990s (U.S. Sentencing Commission, 2024), legal systems around the world have adopted essentially the same requirements for corporate compliance (U.S. Department of Justice & U.S. Securities and Exchange Commission, 2020, p.58).

How to explain these converging compliance standards, which (per FAR 52.203-13 and Article 57 of the European Procurement Directive, 2014/24/EU) have been adopted for public contractors as well? The answer appears to lie in risk management. As the OECD explained in its 2023 report, risk management calls for the steps reported in Figure 5.3 (OECD, 2023, p.14):

Taken in perspective, these elements of risk management align elegantly with a contractor's compliance system. The first elements of a compliance system, standards (a corporate code of conduct) and internal procedures, give a firm a benchmark against which to *identify* risks (breaches of law, for example, or bribes to government customers). A "knowledgeable leadership" allows the leaders of the firm to *assess* any violations – to direct the risk assessment, in other words, from a coordinating position in leadership. Excluding risky personnel (past felons, for example) is a form of *risk treatment*. Training is a form of *risk reduction*, for it ensures employees understand the firm's intolerance for specified risks. Establishing a hotline for employees to report violations is a means of *risk identification*. Monitoring and evaluating the system's effectiveness are an integral part of *risk monitoring*. Disciplining

*Table 5.1* Characteristics of corporate compliance systems

| *Characteristics of Corporate Compliance System* | *U.S. Sentencing Commission* | *France* | *United Kingdom* | *Mexico* |
|---|---|---|---|---|
| **Standards and procedures** | Yes | Yes | Yes | Yes |
| **Knowledgeable leadership** | Yes | Yes | Yes | Yes |
| **Excluding risky personnel** | Yes | Yes | Yes | Yes |
| **Training** | Yes | Yes | Yes | Yes |
| **Monitor system, evaluate system, establish hotline** | Yes | Yes | Yes | Yes |
| **Incentives and discipline** | Yes | Yes | Yes | Yes |
| **Adjust program to risk** | Yes | Yes | Yes | Yes |

*Source*: Original creation.

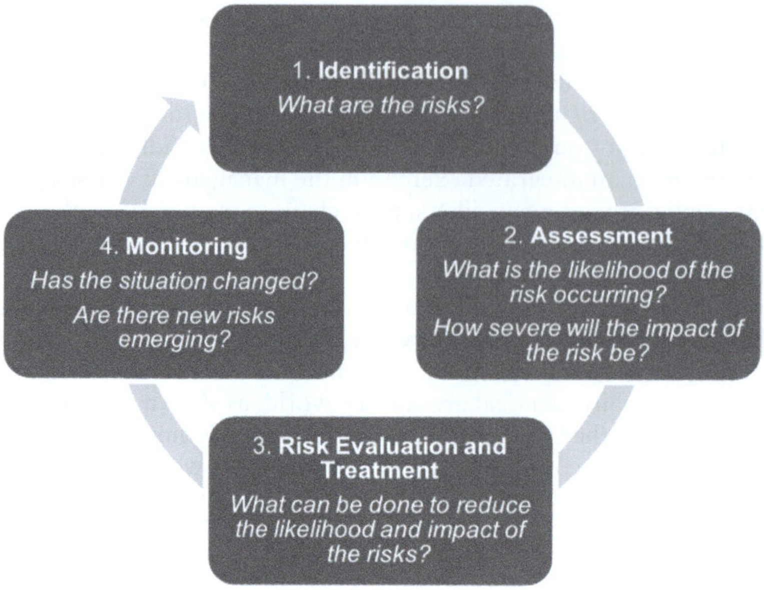


*Figure 5.3* Risk management and public procurement.
*Source*: Original creation.

employees who violate the law (and incentivizing those who do not) are *risk treatment* strategies, and modulating the resources spent on compliance based on the scope of risk (intensifying compliance efforts when entering a corruption-prone industry, for example) is a natural part of *risk monitoring*. Every element in a compliance system thus aligns with risk management; put differently, common *legal* requirements for corporate compliance systems around the world can be seen as practical operating rules for common risk-management systems, in different countries and markets but with a common approach.

Having shown that risk management readily explains common approaches to compliance around the world (a point explored in the case study below), the question is how risk management might explain other areas of procurement law. "Green public procurement," for example, can be seen as an array of tools – from planning to technical evaluations – to control the risk of global warming. *Which* risk management tool (which "green procurement" strategy) to deploy turns on many factors, including cost, stakeholder attitudes, and the political climate – all of which highlight the very public nature of risk management in public procurement. Understanding public procurement law as a means of dynamic risk management demystifies the topic and arguably sets procurement law apart from drier topics of public administration.

## Note

1 Compare, though, Professor Joshua Schwartz (George Washington University Law School), who argued the opposite: drawing extensively on his prior work in the area, he argued that federal public contract *formations* law is much closer to its commercial counterpart, and public contract *performance* (or *administration*) law is very different from the commercial law of contract performance. *See* Joshua I. Schwartz, *The Centrality of Military Procurement: Explaining the Exceptionalist Character of United States Federal Public Procurement Law* (2004) (unpublished), available at

https://scholarship.law.gwu.edu/cgi/viewcontent.cgi?article=2024&context=faculty_publication. Neither approach is necessarily right or wrong; the point is that in the classroom the laws of public contract *formation* and *administration* can be distinguished in part by pointing to their similarities (what Professor Schwartz called "congruence") and differences ("exceptionalism") compared to commercial law, as Section III.C. below discusses in more detail.

## References

Albano, G.L. & Nicholas, C. (2016). *The Law and Economics of Framework Agreements: Designing Flexible Solutions for Public Procurement*. Cambridge: Cambridge University Press.

American Bar Association (2000). *Model Procurement Code for State and Local Procurement*. ABA. Available at: https://publicprocurementinternational.com/wp-content/uploads/2019/04/2000-ABA-Model-Procurement-Code.pdf (Accessed: 20 May 2024).

Andhov, M. & Yukins, C. (2024). 'Feature Comment: A Transatlantic Analysis of EU And U.S. Strategies in "Green Procurement"'. 66 Gov. Contractor ¶ 60. Available at: https://publicprocurementinternational.com/wp-content/uploads/2024/03/GOVTCONT_66_10_60-AS-PUBLISHED-Andhov-Yukins.pdf (Accessed: 21 May 2024).

Arrowsmith, S. & Anderson, R. (2011). *The WTO Regime on Government Procurement: Challenge and Reform*. Cambridge, United Kingdom: Cambridge University Press.

Boese, J. & Baruch, D. (2024). *Civil False Claims and Qui Tam Actions*. 5th edn. New York: Wolters Kluwer.

Cibinic, J., Nash, R.C., & Nagle, J. (2016). *Administration of Government Contracts*. 5th edn. New York: Wolters Kluwer.

Cibinic, J., Nash, R.C., Yukins, C.R., & Castellano, N.E. (2023). *Formation of Government Contracts*. 5th edn. New York: Wolters Kluwer.

Congressional Research Service (2021). *Qui Tam: The False Claims Act and Related Federal Statutes*. Washington, DC: Congressional Research Service.

Conway, D.M. (2012). *State and Local Government Procurement*. Chicago: American Bar Association.

Dixon, B., Rimmer, M.T., & Waschik, R. (2017). 'Macro, industry and regional effects of eliminating Buy America(n) programs: USAGE simulations'. Melbourne: Centre of Policy Studies/IMPACT Centre, Victoria University. Available at: vuir.vu.edu.au/36340/1/g-271.pdf (Accessed: 21 May 2024).

Eisenhardt, K.M. (1989). 'Agency Theory: An Assessment and Review'. *The Academy of Management Review*, 14, 57.

George Washington University Law School (GW Law School) (2024). 'Webinar: Joint U.S.-EU Catalogue of Best Practices on Green Public Procurement'. Available at: https://publicprocurementinternational.com/webinar-joint-us-eu-green-procurement/ (Accessed: 21 May 2024).

Gordon, D.I. (2006). 'Constructing a Bid Protest Process: Choices Every Procurement Challenge System Must Make'. *Public Contract Law Journal*, 35, 427. Available at: https://scholarship.law.gwu.edu/faculty_publications/604/ (Accessed: 21 May 2024).

Grier, J.H. (2022). *The International Procurement System: Liberalization and Protectionism*. Washington, DC: Dalston Press.

Jensen, M.C. & Meckling, W.H. (1976). 'Theory of the Firm: Managerial Behavior, Agency Costs and Ownership Structure'. *Journal of Financial Economics*, 3, 305. Available at: http://papers.ssrn.com/abstract=94043 (Accessed: 20 May 2024).

McCrudden, C. (2007). *Buying Social Justice: Equality, Government Procurement and Legal Change*. Oxford: Oxford University Press.

Nagle, J. (2012). *A History of Government Contracting*. 3d edn. Washington: Government Training LLC. Available at: https://scholarship.law.gwu.edu/history_gov_contracting/ (Accessed: 21 May 2024).

National Association of State Procurement Officials (NASPO) (2024). *State and Local Procurement: A Practical Guide*. 4th edn. Lexington, Kentucky: NASPO.

Organisation for Economic Co-Operation and Development (OECD) (2023). *Managing Risks in the Public Procurement of Goods, Services and Infrastructure*. OECD Public Governance Policy Papers,

No. 33. Paris: OECD Publishing. Available at: https://doi.org/10.1787/45667d2f-en. (Accessed: 20 May 2024).

Organisation for Economic Co-Operation and Development (OECD) (2016). *Preventing Corruption in Public Procurement.* Paris: OECD. Available at: www.oecd.org/gov/ethics/Corruption-016Public-Procurement-Brochure.pdf (Accessed: 21 May 2024).

Schooner, S. (2002). 'Desiderata: Objectives for a System of Government Contract Law'. *Public Procurement Law Review*, 11, 103. Available at: https://ssrn.com/abstract=304620 or http://dx.doi.org/10.2139/ssrn.304620 (Accessed: 20 May 2024).

Schooner, S. (2021). 'No Time to Waste: Embracing Sustainable Procurement to Mitigate the Accelerating Climate Crisis'. *Contract Management*, 61(12), 24. Available at: https://ssrn.com/abstract=3980915 (Accessed: 20 May 2024).

Schwartz, J. (2004) (unpublished). 'The Centrality of Military Procurement: Explaining the Exceptionalist Character of United States Federal Public Procurement Law'. Available at: https://scholarship.law.gwu.edu/cgi/viewcontent.cgi?article=2024&context=faculty_publication (Accessed: 31 Oct 2024).

Transparency International (no date). What Is Corruption?. www.transparency.org/en/what-is-corruption (Accessed: 20 May 2024).

Trepte, P. (2004). *Regulating Procurement: Understanding the Ends and Means of Public Procurement Regulation.* Oxford: Oxford University Press.

U.S. Department of Justice (2022). 'The False Claims Act: A Primer'. Available at: www.justice.gov/sites/default/files/civil/legacy/2011/04/22/C-FRAUDS_FCA_Primer.pdf (Accessed: 19 May 2024).

U.S. Department of Justice (2024). 'The False Claims Act'. Available at: www.justice.gov/civil/false-claims-act (Accessed: 19 May 2024).

U.S. Department of Justice & U.S. Securities and Exchange Commission (2020). *FCPA: Resource Guide.* Available at: www.justice.gov/criminal/criminal-fraud/file/1292051/dl?inline (Accessed: 21 May 2024).

U.S.-EU Trade & Technology Council (2024). *Joint U.S.-EU Catalogue of Best Practices on Green Public Procurement.* Available at: https://publicprocurementinternational.com/wp-content/uploads/2024/04/EU-US-TTC6_Annex_GPP-Best-Practices.pdf (Accessed: 21 May 2024).

U.S. Sentencing Commission (2024). *Sentencing Guidelines*, ch. 8, Sentencing of Corporations. Available at: www.ussc.gov/guidelines/2023-guidelines-manual/annotated-2023-chapter-8 (Accessed: 21 May 2024).

UN Commission on International Trade Law (UNCITRAL) (2014a). *Guide to Enactment of the UNCITRAL Model Law on Public Procurement.* New York: United Nations. Available at: https://uncitral.un.org/sites/uncitral.un.org/files/media-documents/uncitral/en/guide-enactment-model-law-public-procurement-e.pdf (Accessed: 20 May 2024).

UN Commission on International Trade Law (UNCITRAL) (2014b). *Model Law on Public Procurement.* New York: United Nations. Available at: https://uncitral.un.org/sites/uncitral.un.org/files/media-documents/uncitral/en/2011-model-law-on-public-procurement-e.pdf (Accessed: 20 May 2024).

UN Office of Drugs and Crime (UNODC) (2013). *Guidebook on Anti-Corruption in Public Procurement and the Management of Public Finances.* Vienna: United Nations. Available at: www.unodc.org/documents/corruption/Publications/2013/Guidebook_on_anti-corruption_in_public_procurement_and_the_management_of_public_finances.pdf (Accessed: 21 May 2024).

United Nations (no date). 'The Causes and Effects of Climate Change'. Available at: www.un.org/en/climatechange/science/causes-effects-climate-change (Accessed: 21 May 2024).

Williams, S. & Tillipman, J., eds. (2024). *Routledge Handbook of Public Procurement Corruption.* New York: Routledge.

World Bank (no date). *Global Public Procurement Database.* Available at: www.worldbank.org/en/topic/governance/brief/global-public-procurement-database (Accessed: 20 May 2024).

World Bank Group (2021). 'Purchase Order – General Terms and Conditions – Goods and Services' (Aug. 2021). Available at: https://thedocs.worldbank.org/en/doc/9b94d4733c75f93830230e2307fce684-0180012021/original/WBG-PO-GTC-Goods-and-Services-English-2021.pdf (Accessed: 21 May 2024).

World Trade Organization (WTO) (2012). *Agreement on Government Procurement 2012 and Related WTO Legal Texts*. Geneva: WTO. Available at: www.wto.org/english/docs_e/legal_e/rev-gpr-94_01_e.pdf (Accessed: 20 May 2024).

Yukins, C.R. (2010). 'A Versatile Prism: Assessing Procurement Law Through the Principal-Agent Model'. *Public Contract Law Journal*, 40(1), 63. Available at: https://ssrn.com/abstract=1776295 (Accessed: 20 May 2024).

Yukins, C.R. (2017). 'The U.S. Federal Procurement System: An Introduction', 2017 UrT 69. Available at: https://ssrn.com/abstract=3063559 (Accessed: 21 May 2024).

Yukins, C.R. (2024). National Defense Authorization Act for Fiscal Year 2024: Key Procurement Provisions—Study Guide, 'Environmental Sustainability'. Available at: https://publicprocurementinternational.com/national-defense-authorization-act-for-fiscal-year-2024-key-procurement-provisions/#Environmental_Sustainability (Accessed 1 December 2025).

Yukins, C.R. & Drabkin, D.A. (2022). *DoD Bid Protests*. Washington, DC: Acquisition Innovation Research Center. Available at https://apps.dtic.mil/sti/trecms/pdf/AD1198392.pdf (Accessed: 20 May 2024).

Yukins, C.R. & Green, A. (2018). 'International Trade Agreements and U.S. Procurement Law', in *The Contractor's Guide to International Procurement*, Felix, E.L. & Peterson, M., eds. Chicago: American Bar Association. Available at: https://ssrn.com/abstract=3443244 or http://dx.doi.org/10.2139/ssrn.3443244 (Accessed 21 May 2024).

## *Case Study (Developed by Christopher R. Yukins)*

This case study asks students to develop, and critically assess, a corporate compliance plan. This is a very useful exercise, as almost anyone involved in public procurement (or in regulated industries in general) is likely to help prepare and/or evaluate a corporate compliance plan during the course of his or her career, and the requirements for compliance plans are strikingly uniform around the world.

### Introduction:

This case study offers practical illustrations of the concepts discussed above, including anti-corruption, risk management, and sustainability. It is a classroom exercise: several students (the "corporate" team) will prepare the different elements of a contractor's compliance program (here focused on a relatively narrow problem of compliance), while other students (the "government" team) will review and challenge the adequacy of the proposed approach. Each team should be conscious of the performance and reputational risks that it faces – and that the other team faces. This is very much a real-world problem, as companies around the world prepare compliance programs every day, and government officials (such as contracting officers, anti-corruption investigators, and prosecutors) must assess and comment upon those compliance efforts.

### Background Facts:

In 2024 (the last full year of the Biden administration) the U.S. government published a final rule calling for agencies to make "maximum practicable" use of environmentally sustainable products and services, generally as identified by "eco-labels" recommended by the U.S. Environmental Protection Agency (EPA) (George Washington (GW) University Law, 2024). The fictional company at the heart of this exercise, U.S. Contractor, Inc. (USCI), has long sold tens of millions of dollars in office furniture to the federal government. Now USCI wants to be prepared if its government customers require "sustainable" furniture in future solicitations (as the final rule anticipated). USCI senior management is concerned, however, that USCI salespeople, eager to meet quarterly sales targets, may simply paste an EPA-endorsed eco-label (even if the product does not qualify for the label) onto the furniture sold to the U.S. government. If that occurs and the misconduct is discovered, USCI faces potential contract termination, debarment, adverse past performance ratings in future competitions, and fraud liability under the False Claims Act. If found liable for falsely claiming that its products are environmentally "sustainable," USCI also faces possible exclusion in other public procurement markets, such as in the Member States of the European Union under Article 57 of EU procurement directive 2014/24/EU.

Because this exercise involves eco-labels used in a public procurement, for context it is helpful to understand how an eco-label was used under the federal rule. (Note: Although in the U.S. government this rule issued under the Biden administration faced reversal during the second Trump administration, eco-labels are used in procurement systems around the world.)

- The goal, as noted, is for the customer agency to purchase sustainable products and services to the "maximum practicable" extent.
- The definition of sustainable products and services at FAR 2.101 and in the clause published with the rule, FAR 52.223-23, specified that products and services must meet the EPA Recommendations of Specifications, Standards, and Ecolabels (EPA Recommendations). The EPA website at www.epa.gov/greenerproducts/recommendations-specifications-standards-and-ecolabels-federal-purchasing provided a search functionality to allow users to search for EPA recommended specifications, standards, and eco-labels.
  - That EPA website listed far fewer eco-labels for furniture than, for example, a more comprehensive listing of furniture eco-labels worldwide, at www.ecolabelindex.com/ecolabels/?st=category,furniture. What effect could this have had on competition?
  - The students should examine one or more eco-labels for furniture that were recommended by the EPA. Taking this closer look, do the eco-labels focus narrowly on the chief policy goal in environmental sustainability – reducing global greenhouse gas emissions – or do the eco-labels look to other environmental qualities associated with the furniture?
  - Is there any way to tell if the eco-labels recommended by the EPA were developed in accordance with the standards set out in Article 43 of EU Procurement Directive 2014/24/EU? These are demanding standards, derived in part from precedents of the Court of Justice for the European Union, which could be used to assess many technical requirements – not just eco-labels:
    - Are the label requirements "linked to the subject-matter of the contract" and are they appropriate to define the furniture's characteristics?
    - Are the label requirements based on "objectively verifiable and non-discriminatory criteria?"
    - Were the labels established "in an open and transparent procedure in which all relevant stakeholders, including government bodies, consumers, social partners, manufacturers, distributors and non-governmental organizations, [could] participate?"

  - Were the labels (and the criteria for achieving a label) accessible to any interested party?
  - Were the label requirements set by a third party over which a company applying for the label could not exercise a decisive influence?
- What would a furniture manufacturer have to do to qualify for the eco-label at issue? Would the furniture maker register its products with the eco-label provider, for example?

Taking all of the issues listed above into account, and looking to the various "green procurement" strategies summarized in Section 5.3, students may wish to assess whether eco-labels are, in fact, the best way to reduce global warming. If not, why would governments place such a strong emphasis on eco-labels as a "green public procurement" strategy – why not use other strategies, such as demanding that a manufacturer state the greenhouse gas emissions attributable to its product, or excluding vendors that do not report data regarding the greenhouse gas emissions attributable to their products? These policy questions help put the accompanying compliance exercise into context, for these policy questions help shape the compliance system that a company would put in place to meet green procurement requirements.

# 6 Understanding the Political Dynamics of Public Procurement

*William (Bill) Resh, Keunyoung (Eli) Lee and Heonuk Ha*

## 6.1 Introduction

### *6.1.1 The Distributive Politics of Public Procurement*

#### *6.1.1.1 Act of Selecting "Who Gets What, When, and How"*

Politics is comprehensively described as the legalized distribution of public goods or the act of selecting "who gets what, when, and how" (Lasswell, 1936; Easton, 1965). Since bureaucracy (or bureaucrats) are often tasked with decisions on how to allocate public goods, scholars attest that they participate in "politics of the first order" (Meier, 1993). A number of studies indicate that public administrators engage in political conduct, with public procurement not exempt from this phenomenon as the term "procurement" refers to the process by which the government utilizes supplies and services for its own "direct benefit or use" (Huber & Shipan, 2002; Schooner, 2002; Berry, Burden, & Howell, 2010). If we acknowledge Waldo's (1946, 2017) precept that the allocation of resources is neither wholly technical work nor a value-neutral activity (Waldo, 1946/2017), then it follows that we acknowledge as much in the area of public procurement.

For public agencies, the influence of politics can be both overt and subtle. The choices made by public administrators are notably influenced by political actors and institutions. Evidence from several studies in political science shows that partisanship plays a significant role in how the executive branch allocates spending in the form of grants, contingent liabilities, and other forms of administrative outlays. This work collectively highlights the complexity of the political economy in which bureaucrats—delegated with discretion over allocational decisions—operate, and it underscores the need for a nuanced understanding of how political dynamics within the institutional environment can affect the distribution of public resources.

### *6.1.2 The Legal Authority of U.S. Federal Agencies in the Federal Contract Process*

U.S. federal government contracting has increased exponentially over the last three decades, reaching $694.2 billion in Fiscal Year 2022,[1] which constituted 10% of total federal expenditures. Consequently, the role of contracting agencies and officials has gained increasing significance in the procurement process (see Figure 6.1). In the federal contract procurement process, the activities of federal agencies are principally governed by the Federal Acquisition Regulations (FAR) and associated legislation like the Competition in Contracting Act (CICA) of 1984. Nonetheless, federal agencies wield a great degree of discretionary authority in selecting contract recipients with the expectation that they are responsible for stimulating market interest and competition among private actors and

DOI: 10.4324/9781003566670-8

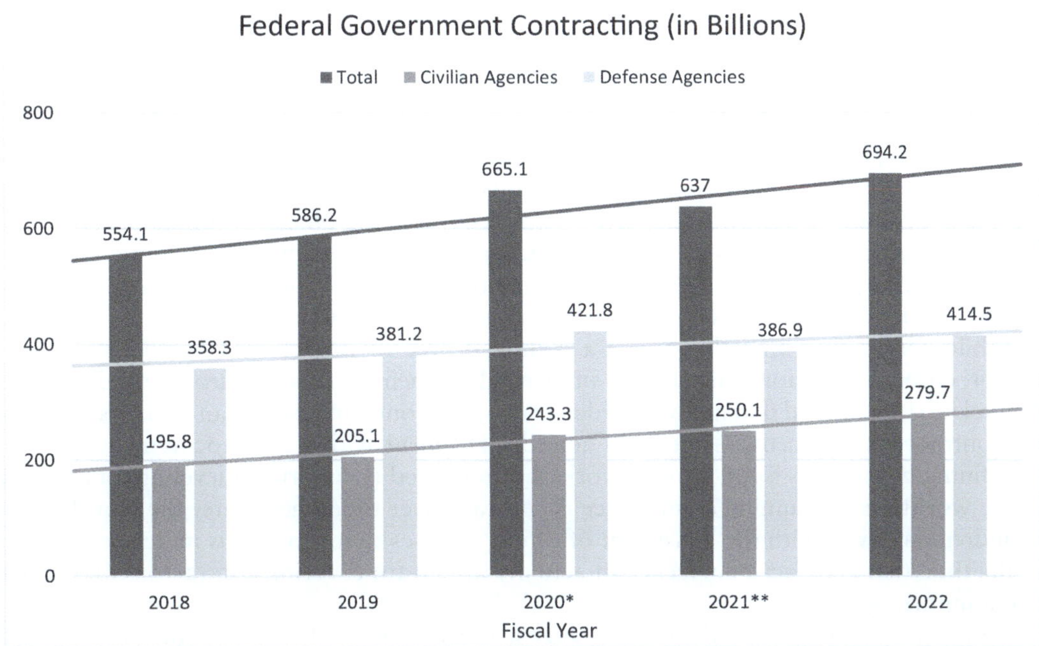


*Figure 6.1* Federal government contracting trends: FY 2018–2022.

*Notes*:
*FY 2020: Increase attributing to treat COVID-19.
**FY 2021: Decrease after adjusting for inflation.

*Source*: Original creation, data taken from U.S. General Service Administration's Federal Procurement Data System.

making selections among those actors, in contrast to (for instance) formula grants or other types of federal outlays.

The federal contracting process is generally executed in accordance with the principles of full and open competitive bidding, as stipulated by CICA. However, there are several circumstances that allow for deviations from this standard procedure. These include (1) exclusive availability of goods or services from a single source; (2) instances of unusual and compelling urgency; (3) the need to maintain an industrial base; (4) obligations arising from international agreements; (5) statutory authorization or the acquisition of brand-name items for resale; (6) national security considerations; and (7) contracts deemed essential for the public interest (Schooner, 2002). Furthermore, federal agencies have the discretionary authority to employ "Simplified Acquisition Procedures (SAP)" for certain types of contracts involving goods or services priced below $150,000, as well as for other commercial goods and services valued at less than $6.5 million (Schooner, 2002). Consequently, federal agencies have room for discretionary authority and responsibility, not only in selecting participating firms but also in maintaining or terminating ongoing contracts. As well, regardless of the manner of competition, agencies retain discretion in selecting the winning bid. Additionally, federal agencies possess expanded responsibility and discretion to rescind solicitations during periods of fiscal uncertainty (Manuel & Lunder, 2012).

Federal agencies are equipped with an array of legal instruments to either ensure satisfactory contract performance by a contractor or, when justified, to hold a contractor accountable for lapses in performance or misconduct based on the federal procurement statutes and

FAR, such as (1) corrective actions, (2) incentive fees, (3) performance and payment surety bonds, (4) liquidated damages, (5) contract termination for default, (6) contractor performance evaluations, (7) suspension and debarment, and (8) civil fraud enforcement (Carpenter & Ruane, 2018). Federal agencies have the discretion to employ various tools to enhance contract performance, contingent upon the specific types and objectives of the contract in question.

Specifically, specialized standards ("definitive criteria") are often incorporated into agency solicitations for particular types of acquisitions. In this context, the role of contracting officers is pivotal. Before awarding any contract, contracting officers evaluate the responsibility of potential contractors by scrutinizing information either submitted by the contractors or otherwise acquired by the agency. Consequently, contracting officers within each agency wield considerable discretionary authority in this process (Manuel, 2011).

While contracting officials possess a certain degree of discretionary authority in federal procurement, performance is also influenced by their working environment. Resh and Marvel (2012) contend that an overburdened task environment restricts an agency's capacity for contract management, resulting in goal displacement within the procurement process. In defining capacity as a function of workload, one need not ascribe a level of competence to the workforce. Assuming competence is constant over time, the greater the workload at an individual level (with the constraint of time) proposes that capacity is merely a function of the time that contract managers can actually attend to, ensuring contractor compliance and minimizing shirking.

Under that standard, as Figure 6.2 shows, the U.S. federal government has lost capacity in its contract management functions over the course of recent years. From the 110th Congress (2007–2008) to the 116th Congress (2020–2021), the number of contracts per federal employee in a contract management position in the federal government (job series 1102 and 1106 as determined by the U.S. Office of Personnel Management) has increased from an average of at least 150 contracts per contract management employee (per year) to over 300 contracts per year in the 27 largest agencies/departments. This is a conservative measure as it excludes outliers among agencies that measure over 1000 contracts per contract manager in a given year.

As Resh and Marvel's (2012) work demonstrates, perverse outcomes and favoritism can increase as a function of lower capacity. They find that agencies with lower levels of contract management capacity tend to exploit loopholes in a program intended to encourage agencies to award a proportion of contracts to small business competitors owned by people representative of traditionally marginalized populations (Resh & Marvel, 2012). Other work by Warren (2014) shows that diminished contract management capacity leads to decreased reliance on competitive acquisition procedures, decreases in firm-fixed-price contracts, and increases in the risk of renegotiation and associated costs.

Many countries have implemented similar procurement systems to the U.S. system. However, other countries employ more centralized procurement systems, such as the United Kingdom and South Korea. In the United Kingdom, the procurement system operates under the framework of several regulations, including the Public Contracts Regulations 2015, Utilities Contracts Regulations 2016, Concession Contracts Regulations 2016, and the Public Procurement (Amendments, Repeals, and Revocations) Regulations 2016. The UK system adheres to the principle of full competition while also allocating a certain proportion of contracts to small and medium-sized enterprises (SMEs) to promote equality. In contrast to the U.S. system, which grants discretionary authority to individual agencies in the procurement process, the U.K. system entrusts centralized power to the Crown Commercial Service (CCS) to manage and oversee the procurement process.[2]

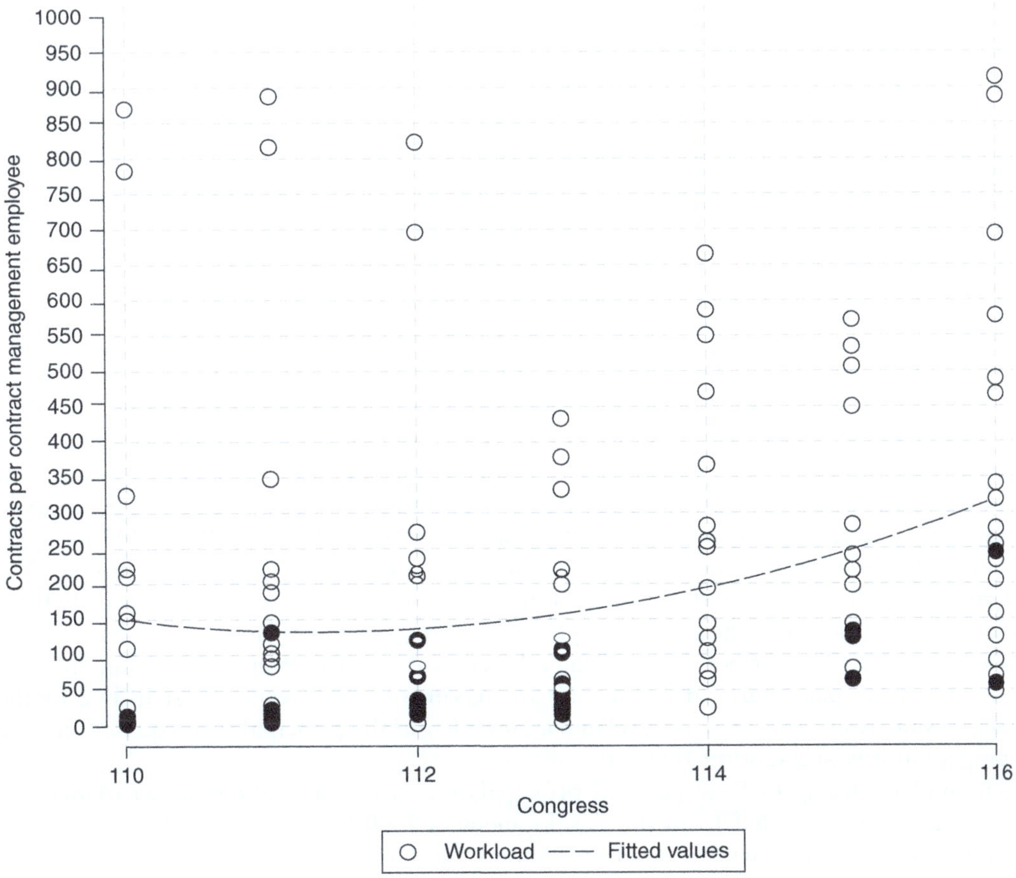


*Figure 6.2* Contracts per contract management employee in the U.S. federal government by congress.
*Source*: Original creation, data taken from the U.S. General Service Administration's Federal Procurement Data System and the U.S. Office of Personnel Management's Electronic Human Resources Initiative.

South Korea's procurement system is governed by a comprehensive set of regulations, including the Acts on Contracts to which the State is Party (ACSP) and the Government Procurement Act (GPAT) (Kim, 2000).[3] Furthermore, South Korea has implemented various set-aside contracts to facilitate collaborative growth with small businesses. It also offers diverse educational programs aimed at supporting small and female-owned businesses, particularly those located in rural areas. In a manner akin to the UK's system, South Korea's procurement system emphasizes efficiency by adopting a centralized procurement system, and the central government agency, Supply Administration ("*Jodalchung*"), plays a central role in the procurement process. This office is responsible for overseeing contracts, managing public property, and collaborating with local governments to ensure the smooth operation of the procurement system.

Nonetheless, centralization is no panacea for preventing the incursion of politics into contracting decisions. Indeed, centralized decision-making in executive branch operations has been generally shown to be more politically charged than that of decentralized decision-making among career civil servants (Resh, 2019). In the next section, we demonstrate how contractors can become key constituents to the reelection concerns of democratically elected officials. In doing so, we argue that they can potentially circumvent traditional principal–agent accountability mechanisms to exacerbate dilemmas of agency loss, such as moral hazard and adverse selection.

## 6.2 Literature Review

### *6.2.1 Principal–Agent Theory: Exploring Delegation and Control in a Political–Economic Context*

If a bureaucrat participates in the public procurement process with discretionary authority, as shown above, the pertinent question arises: By what mechanisms are the bureaucratic activities controlled and checked? And what underpins their authority to do so? To engage with this inquiry, principal–agent theory (PAT) has been harnessed in the study of bureaucratic delegation, furnishing a conceptual framework to examine the equilibrium that balances the extent of control over and delegation to public bureaucratic institutions.

Many researchers who apply PAT to bureaucratic delegation postulate that elected leaders or their institutions are like "principals" in a contract. They hire bureaucratic "agents" to carry out their plans (as shown in Figure 6.3). This theory is based on economic conceits about contracts and the costs involved in those transactions (Resh & Zook, 2018). Thus, making a contract with the right incentives is key to keeping these agents accountable. The inherent concern in such models is one of agency loss—i.e., that an agent will drift from the intended delegation. There are two primary sources of agency loss: moral hazard and adverse selection. The former is due to the inherent self-interest of the agent being different than that of the principal and the pursuit of maximizing that self-interest in lieu of the principal's interests. The latter comes from an inability of the principal to adequately choose a competent or well-intentioned agent.

The understanding of how political principals seek to control the conduct of bureaucratic agents has benefited from the development of PAT (Miller, 2005). Indeed, despite assumptions to the contrary, most research shows that bureaucrats demonstrate responsiveness to their political principals, with most of the emphasis from political science employing the principal–agent framework on the relationship between agencies and Congress (McCubbins et al., 1989; Wood & Waterman, 1993; Epstein & O'Halloran, 1999). Indeed, recent work has taken a critical look at the assumptions proffered in earlier applications of the model to the concept of bureaucratic delegation and concluded that the propensity for principal moral hazard (and not agency loss) is a far higher likelihood in bureaucratic–political relations (Miller & Whitford, 2016). One reason is that delegations are built for long-term commitments that span election cycles where principals change their preferences either by pressures from constituents or by outright replacement.

### *6.2.2 Utilizing Principal–Agent Theory in Procurement: The Role of Transaction Costs*

The United States allocates more than a quarter of its budget toward procuring goods and services from external non-public sector suppliers, usually establishing contracts between governmental bodies and private enterprises (Organization for Economic Cooperation and Development (OECD), 2017). Considerable variation exists among federal programs in relation to the degree of effective discretion delegated by Congress to implementing agencies for fund allocation (Stein & Bickers, 1997). The initiation of the formal procurement process commences when a federal agency makes the determination to acquire a specific commodity or service. Program officials take the lead in initiating this process, collaborating with contracting officers who facilitate the procurement endeavors. During this process, at the heart of the political–economic paradigm lies the premise that a non-neutral bureaucracy might be subject to governance by elected representatives (principals). However, statutes principals may enact could present limited flexibility for effecting minor modifications, even when their intention is to exert influence over agents' decisions. Should these alterations be undertaken for overtly political reasons, the potential hazard of violating the Hatch Act looms. Following its revision in 1993, the Act imposed constraints upon the majority of government personnel, proscribing their engagement in disrupting electoral processes or soliciting political endorsement in exchange for preferential treatment (Maskell, 1998; see also Resh et al., 2022).

In theory, contracting officers, whether operating within their primary agency or externally in agencies tasked with the acquisition of goods or services, significantly mitigate transaction costs when consistently selecting contractors over successive years. In this case, bureaucratic agencies are not only "*agents*" but also "*principals*" to the contractor(s) (see Figure 6.3). This efficiency stems from their accumulated familiarity with entities vying for agency contracts. Such intimate knowledge uniquely positions them to evaluate the strengths and weaknesses of bids, thereby streamlining the decision-making process. Public employees, possessing inherent knowledge of the historical performance and capabilities of competing businesses, can navigate the complexities of the selection process with more efficacy. This enhanced understanding not only expedites bid assessments but also reinforces the agency's capacity to make informed decisions rooted in a comprehensive grasp of each contractor's track record. Consequently, this expertise results in reduced information search costs, elevated decision quality, and a more streamlined contracting procedure. These advantages contribute to the diminished transaction costs when awarding contracts to familiar yet qualified contractors in consecutive years, which may reduce information asymmetry between the agency and contractor and subsequently lowering associated uncertainties and potential risks.

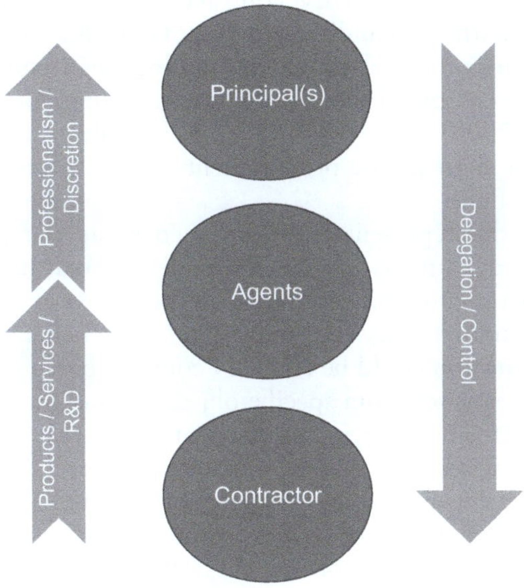


*Figure 6.3* Schematic representation for easy understanding of PAT.
*Source*: Original creation.

## 6.3 Emerging Issue: Contracting Reality in Politics

In the previous section, we theoretically examined the logic behind delegation and control, as well as how bureaucrats influence distributive politics by using traditional applications of PAT to bureaucratic delegation. However, as we mentioned above, recent work has criticized the top–down orientation of PAT with its focus on agency loss and bureaucratic moral hazard. This work has argued that principal moral hazard is just as, if not more, likely in these delegations due to the changing preferences of political principals as a function of the election cycle. Therefore, in this section, we aim to focus on the actual landscape of public procurement that explores how and why principal moral hazard may be proliferated by an extended delegation chain from political principal to bureaucratic agent to contracted agent. By doing so, we hope to provide a more comprehensive understanding of the intricate landscape of public procurement.

### *6.3.1 Principal–Agent Theory in Public Procurement: Understanding Two-Way Stream*

Faced with resource constraints and overburdened task environments, agencies find themselves under mounting stress to manage their contract portfolios effectively (Resh & Marvel, 2012). Interestingly, while the number of federal employees has remained fairly constant since the 1960s, the financial responsibilities shouldered by each have increased nearly fivefold—a trend attributed to the government's burgeoning reliance on external vendors, both for profit and nonprofit (DiIulio, 2014; Light, 2018). Light (2018) reveals a ratio of four contractors for each federal worker, and although less studied, similar outsourcing patterns emerge at state and local government levels (Verkuil, 2017). The escalating transfer of governmental responsibilities to the private sector calls for a nuanced, comprehensive analysis to understand its complexities (Verkuil, 2017). As a seemingly inevitable outcome of these challenges, agencies have turned to external expertise, not merely for specialized tasks but even for their own contract oversight functions. While this strategy alleviates immediate pressures, it has the subtle effect of obscuring the demarcation between governmental bodies and contractors. A case in point is a defense contracting agency where a notable proportion of procurement specialists (the very individuals responsible for contract oversight) were, in fact, outsourced contractors themselves. Compounding this trend, the government's online database, which serves as a critical tool for contract tracking, has also been managed by an external entity (Stier, 2009). This evolving landscape illustrates the intricate and interconnected dynamics of modern public procurement, wherein the traditional roles and boundaries are increasingly fluid.

Also, while PAT traditionally portrays the representatives (or agency) as the principal, with contractors acting as agents, this dynamic is not strictly unidirectional. In fact, contractors not only serve as agents who execute the directives of their governmental principals, but they also wield considerable influence as key stakeholders and benefactors in the political landscape. The dynamic in question could be labeled "contract patronage," wherein a patron leverages patronage as a means to attain specific objectives and, in reciprocation, anticipates a measure of allegiance from the recipient or client (Bearfield, 2009). This relationship challenges the conventional wisdom of PAT by introducing a layer of reciprocity and influence. Therefore, the relationship between principals and agents in public procurement is better understood as a two-way stream of influence and obligation rather than a one-sided hierarchy. This begs the question (in terms of PAT): if contracting firms represent important constituencies to political principals while also being putative agents to the bureaucratic principals with whom they've contracted, then in which direction is moral hazard most likely promulgated?

### *6.3.2 Agency's Survival Tool: Implicit Compliance with Principals*

Agencies, while allotted financial resources by legislative bodies, operate under a balance of power where adherence to political will is often nuanced yet unmistakable. Agencies understand that procurement is not merely a logistical endeavor but also a means to demonstrate alignment with principals' priorities and objectives. To survive in a political landscape, agencies adopt what is known as "anticipatory exchange," a predictive strategy wherein they allocate resources in a manner that would likely meet with the principal's approval (see Hudak, 2014; Bertelli & Grose, 2009; Nagel, 1976). This not just ensures compliance with the principals' wishes but also fortifies the agency's standing in future appropriations and legislations. In other words, such action will strategically position them for favorable treatment in future budget cycles and policy discussions.

Agency behaviors in procurement processes take the form of "soft compliance," where an agency may opt for awarding contracts to firms or sectors that are politically aligned with the prevailing congressional sentiment, a practice that gains prominence, especially in battleground states (Gordon, 2011; Hudak, 2014; Dahlstrom et al., 2021). Witko (2011) shows that firms contributing more substantially to campaign funds were more likely to receive a greater number of contracts post-election. However, the study also emphasized that a firm's reputation and prior contracting experience were significant determinants in the allocation of contracts (Witko, 2011). Moreover, during election seasons, agencies may deliberately issue more non-competitive contracts to firms that hold political clout, thereby serving the twin objectives of streamlining the procurement process and appeasing political allies. This is why Arnold (1979) argued that these decisions often serve as a nod to past support and an invitation for future backing. As agencies fine-tune their procurement strategies to reflect the complex electoral calculus, they ensure their own operational needs while maintaining ostensible neutrality and compliance.

More recent scholarship extends this model to consider not just the direction of allocation but also the targeted recipients or even specific categories of funding (Berry et al., 2010; Bickers & Stein, 2000). Gordon (2011) disclosed that during the G.W. Bush administration, the President engaged in the particularistic allocation of federal contracts, targeting Republican congressional districts through the political appointees of the General Services Administration (GSA). Dahlstrom and the team (2021) found that when there is a change in the administration, there is a notable turnover in contract recipients who mirror the new political landscape. In this light, the complexity of the procurement process serves as both a tool and a theater for political strategy, where agencies juggle the need for administrative efficiency with the imperative of maintaining political relevance.

Of course, as Boland and Goodsell (2021, p.1) argue, there are considerable constraints on the ability of political actors to influence contract decisions:

> even when bureaucrats are susceptible to political influence, bureaucrats have little discretion to inject political bias into contracting outcomes because their contracting actions are bounded by regulators (e.g., Office of Management and Budget [OMB], GAO, Office of Federal Procurement Policy, Federal Acquisitions Institute) enforcing procurement rules (e.g., Competition in Contracting Act of 1984, Federal Acquisition Regulations, National Defense Authorization Act) designed to minimize bureaucratic contracting discretion and political bias in contracting outcomes.

Given these constraints, it is likely that contract market fluctuations driven by political dynamics will be marginal. Still, contracting decisions are a function of both vertical and horizontal demands placed on the organization in terms of both the preferences of political principals (vertical) and the exigent operational needs of the organization (horizontal) (Cooper, 2003). The logic follows that legislators of both partisan stripes want contracts brought to their jurisdictions, as contracts bring jobs and projects that are more evident to constituents who may not directly benefit from the outlay. The mechanisms of political influence are several, but many are not directly observable including direct communications from the legislator to agency offices.

For instance, a Senator (or her staff) might simply introduce firms to agencies and help explain how their products or services meet the agency's needs. This both gives the agency new viable contractors and signals to agencies what the Senator wants. Yet, from an operational perspective, a contract award decision should be made based on the contractor's capacity to fulfill the implementation prerogatives of an agency, not on the partisan or ideological preferences of a community in which its performance takes place. At the same time, it is feasible that these two characteristics (capacity and political desirability) are endogenous. A political principal can influence a contract decision through their privileged access to an agency's strategic deliberations, thereby advantaging certain firms while remaining compliant with statutes and regulations such as FAR and the CICA, higher authorities within the agencies, as well as by the investigative agencies external to the buying agency. Indeed, recent evidence suggests that when bureaucrats do have discretion over contracts, political bias is evident (at least marginally) (Dahlstrom et al. 2021; Boland and Goodsell 2021; Fazekas et al. 2023).[4]

#### *6.3.3 Contract Patronage: Politicization/Favoritism in Procurement*

In the complex landscape of public procurement, the intrusion of political considerations regarding contracts adds layers of complexity to the application of PAT to bureaucratic delegation. Although PAT would suggest a straightforward chain of command and decision-making, real-world instances of favoritism significantly complicate this picture. A range of academic studies indicates that political factors such as electoral geography (Berry, Burden, & Howell, 2010), the flow of political donations (Titl & Geys, 2019), or political ideology (Bertelli & Grose, 2009) can influence the allocation of public resources. Within the United States, this politicization is not a monolithic phenomenon but varies widely depending on the specific federal regulations governing individual agencies and the internal dynamics of these agencies themselves (Selin, 2015).

Anderson and Potoski (2016) illuminate the role of organizational structure in federal agencies' grant allocation decisions. They demonstrate that agencies more insulated from political pressures are less responsive to spending demands from members of Congress and the President. Specifically, the agency's internal structure, particularly its personnel composition, significantly affects its susceptibility to politicization. Agencies heavily staffed by political appointees—typically situated at higher echelons of the organizational hierarchy—are more likely to be responsive to the needs and whims of the ruling party or the President (Hudak, 2014). These appointees often pursue initiatives that enhance the electoral prospects of the party in power, even if it means departing from best practices in procurement. In contrast, agencies primarily composed of career civil servants, who are insulated from electoral politics and make decisions based on merit and long-term public service considerations, are less likely to exhibit favoritism in procurement processes (Lewis, 2008). The two categories of employees, therefore, embody contrasting motivations and susceptibilities to political influences, which directly or indirectly shape their engagement in procurement activities. For example, Zarit's research (2018) revealed that decision-making units within agency hierarchies display varying degrees of vulnerability to political pressures in relation to funding allocations for U.S. federal procurements. Building upon this notion, scholars have ascertained that low-risk government procurement agreements exhibit a stronger association with decentralized decision-making processes within the middle and lower tiers of agency hierarchies, as opposed to the more centralized approach at the top echelons, where political influence tends to be most pronounced (Krause & Zarit, 2022). The authors contend that when government contracting risk is low, procurement agreements are more likely to be managed at lower managerial and field office levels within an agency, while riskier government contracts tend to be centralized at the executive office level rather than dispersed across non-executive levels.

Further insights into the politicization of procurement are provided by a burgeoning body of academic literature examining the distributive consequences of policy formulation. For example, studies have demonstrated that presidential administrations often direct economic resources to strategically important counties, particularly during election years (Kriner & Reeves, 2015). This strategic allocation often involves political appointees as critical facilitators. Moreover, the degree of "agency insulation"—the extent to which agencies can operate independent of political pressures—has been identified as a key factor in determining how funds are allocated (Berry & Gersen, 2017). Agencies that permit more direct political oversight are observed to show greater partisan responsiveness in their spending decisions. These agencies often use less competitive methods of contract allocation, such as non-competitive solicitations and sole-source contracts, often aligning themselves strategically with both the President and influential members of Congress in these decisions (Berry & Fowler, 2018). This suggests that the structure and personnel composition of agencies play a pivotal role in shaping the extent and nature of politicization and favoritism in public procurement.

### *6.3.4 Contractors as Constituents: Influential Supporters of Politicians*

The involvement of contractors in public procurement has long been viewed with caution and scrutiny. As early as 1818, Secretary of War John C. Calhoun expressed concern about the inherent vulnerabilities associated with depending on contractors for critical military operations. Contractors, he noted, were not directly accountable to military norms but were driven by their own profit-maximizing objectives. This perspective gains additional nuance in modern times, where contractual relationships go beyond mere transactional exchanges to involve deeply embedded ties between contractors and the government. Verkuil's (2017) assessment confirms this by highlighting how contractors gain a "privileged" status through competitive renewals based on their past performance. Though this may lead to operational efficiency, it raises questions about the true effectiveness of a system that increasingly resembles a closed-loop feedback mechanism, safeguarding the interests of a select few.

Contractors today serve not just as providers of goods and services but also as potent political entities. Their influence extends beyond mere service delivery to shaping policy decisions, effectively becoming constituents with vested interests. They leverage historical performance and network ties to exert influence on intermediary selection and other key decision-making processes. This raises two notable issues: adverse selection, where agencies may be inclined to choose contractors based on these historical ties rather than objective metrics, and moral hazard, where contractors, knowing they are almost indispensable, may take higher risks or slacken performance. The interdependence between contractors and government agencies takes on even more nuanced contours when the role of campaign contributions and lobbying is factored into the equation. The influence here becomes cyclical, reinforcing itself through successive transactions and policy decisions.

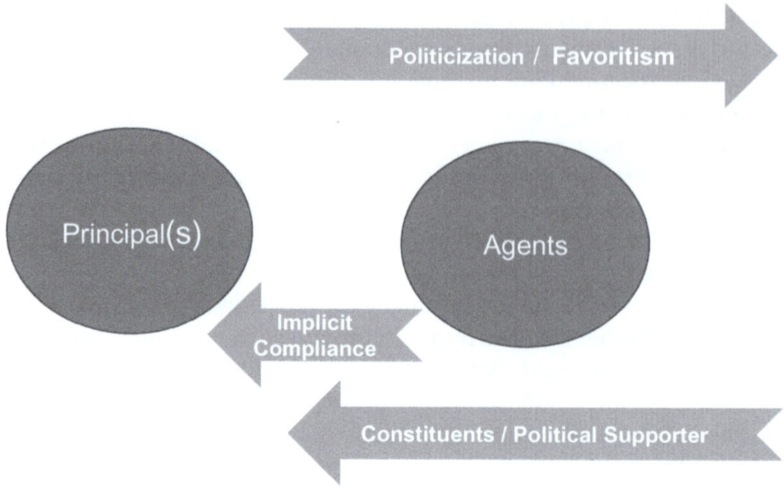


*Figure 6.4* Schematic representation for easy understanding of reality—two-way stream.
*Source*: Original creation.

The increasing presence of contractors in political contributions and lobbying efforts adds an opaque layer of complexity to public procurement. While lobbying and campaign finance may not be disclosed fully, they provide an undercurrent of influence that, although tacit, is palpable. Ahmed's (2019) study underscores the potential impact of this phenomenon, revealing that these contributions could be directed toward committees responsible for budgetary allocations affecting the contractor's revenue streams. These intricate relationships between contractors and political entities blur the lines between service delivery and policy influence, making contractors not just external agents but critical constituents in the political ecosystem. As such, they serve as complex figures straddling the domains of public service and political power, thus making the dynamics of public procurement a subject that demands multifaceted scrutiny (Figure 6.4).

## 6.4 Practical Implications: Integrating the Public Values for Effective Accountability in Private Operations

The intended goal of government contracting and procurement is to encourage market competition in the provision of goods and services required by the government. This competition is anticipated to drive efficiency improvements that the government would be unable to achieve independently. However, due to the involvement of politics, skepticism of the objectivity of market discipline manifests in myriad ways, including inflated costs associated with government programs, augmented instances of noncompliance with governmental directives, catalyzed corruption, decelerated innovation in policy-making, and an overall erosion of the very bedrock upon which government functions (Kaufman, 1981; Golden, 2000). All of this can escalate into a significant challenge undermining trust and accountability within the critical sphere of the public procurement process, involving the government and its bureaucracy. In this section, we will explore the public ethics and attitudes that public servants should uphold and foster to safeguard democratic values.

### *6.4.1 Values and Ethics: Enhancing Trust in Governance through Contract Professionalism*

A pervasive lack of trust in governmental institutions stands as one of the most formidable hurdles encountered by the public sector (Kettl, 2017). Drawing from Robert Putnam's notion of social capital, this widespread lack of trust adds to the challenges faced by governments, making their tasks more demanding and resource-intensive (and reducing more societal capital). Consequently, the earlier critique that mainly focused on the somewhat limited responsiveness seen in bureaucratic democratic engagement has expanded to consider other routes for achieving responsiveness. This change aligns with a deeper exploration of the supportive environment needed to effectively put these approaches into action.

To enhance the trust of the government, scholars propose the importance of enhancing the professionalism of public employees (Dooling & Potter, 2022; Miller & Whitford, 2016; Curry, 2016). According to Miller and Whitford (2016), bureaucrats may play a significant role in checks and balances between branches and can even restrain the influence from outside. Authors stated that public officials' professionalism prevents Congress members' personal interests and/or partisan bias from destroying democratic calls (Miller & Whitford, 2016). Because elected politicians cannot always be relied upon to achieve sound governance or protect the public good, authors suggested that bureaucrats assess politicians' actions in view of their professional norms and identities and anticipate their goals. Thus, the professionalism of officials will act as an effective political strategy for reacting to their political beliefs in a manner that permits the agency to shape and evolve in the bureaucracy's correct path, resulting in bureaucracies works that are "*above politics*" (Miller & Whitford, 2016). Such professionalism of public officials not only contributes to enhancing agency trust but also bestows various benefits upon these officials, creating a cycle of mutual reinforcement. In Curry's book "*Government Contracting—Promises and Perils*," the author (2016) elucidates that when public employees uphold ethical contracting standards (akin to professionalism in the contracting context), various benefits accrue to individuals. These benefits encompass sustained opportunities for career advancement within the government, an enhanced personal and professional reputation (including within family circles), preserved compensation, and the maintenance of personal freedom and self-assurance (pp.62–63).

Indeed, the very vision of the Federal Acquisition System, as stated in the FAR is "for the Federal Acquisition System is to deliver on a timely basis the best value product or service to the customer, while maintaining the public's trust and fulfilling public policy objectives." There have been extensive administrative and legislative interventions to enhance professionalism in procurement across defense and security agencies, for instance, including the Defense Acquisition Workforce Improvement Act, hiring and pay flexibilities to attract adequate talent to these professions, the Defense Acquisition Workforce Development Fund, and strategic planning for the acquisition workforce. These four tools aim to enhance the training, recruitment, and retention of acquisition personnel by, respectively, establishing (1) professional development requirements, (2) monetary incentives and accelerated hiring, (3) dedicated funding for workforce improvement efforts, and (4) formal strategies to shape and improve the acquisition workforce. The OFPP has similar initiatives for the contracting workforces of civilian agencies (e.g., the establishment of the Federal Acquisition Institute (FAI), the Federal Acquisition Certification in Contracting (FAC-C), and certification in Program Management (FAC-PM)).

### *6.4.2 Honing Skills: Establishing Reliable Public–Private Partnerships (PPPs) for Effective Procurement*

Eggers and Kettl (2023) suggest that elevating trust within the public sector hinges on a highly professional public sector that embraces PPPs ("bridgebuilding"). Frequently, the government engages private and nonprofit entities as intermediaries within its operational framework. This involvement is facilitated through the government's utilization of steering mechanisms, such as grants and contracts, with the overarching aim of collectively pursuing public objectives. While certain scenarios position the government as a pivotal player at the core of this ecosystem, the crucial facet for ensuring robust accountability within private endeavors pivots on a shift in perspective of who is ultimately responsible for outcomes. This shift entails moving beyond the dichotomy of choosing between private or public entities to deliver services and instead focuses on the intricate orchestration and effective management of all sectors to optimize collective societal outcomes.

Through such cross-sectoral collaborations, administrators can effectively scrutinize and counteract instances of non-objective processes, which are susceptible to influence from corruption or political considerations that arguably are not pursuing public values. These collaborations foster a comprehensive evaluation of the intricate network of intermediaries that significantly contribute to the delivery of government services and the formation of public perspectives. In the contemporary landscape, governmental functions are intricately entwined within networks of service providers. These collaborative undertakings between government bodies and multifaceted entities encompass not only contractors but also additional layers of government and private sector stakeholders. Consequently, the issue of trust in government transcends individual citizens and encompasses a wide array of stakeholders. Simultaneously, this intricate web of relationships mandates the preservation of mutual trust between governmental entities and their constituents (Resh, Sidikki, and McConnell, 2014).

Egger and Kettl (2023) posit that the mechanisms of transparency and accountability, indeed, have struggled to keep pace with the intricacies of the interplay between public and private actors. Any participant in this multifaceted process who fails to uphold the principles of trustworthiness can undermine the broader image of both government and service providers. Thus, Eggers and Kettl (2023) propose that nurturing trust necessitates the establishment of a uniform standard of accountability and transparency across the entirety of this intricate network of stakeholders.[5] A well-executed network structure holds the potential to fortify trust in government services, which can foster confidence in these services and mitigate instances of moral hazard in its many directions.

## Notes

1 A Snapshot: Government-Wide Contracting 2022: https://gaoinnovations.gov/Federal_Government_Contracting/www.gao.gov/blog/snapshot-government-wide-contracting-fy-2021-interactive-dashboardwww.gao.gov/blog/snapshot-government-wide-contracting-fy-2020-infographic#:~:text=In%20fiscal%20year%202020%2C%20the,things%20related%20to%20COVID%2D19.
www.gao.gov/blog/snapshot-government-wide-contracting-fy-2019-infographic
www.gao.gov/blog/2019/05/28/federal-government-contracting-for-fiscal-year-2018-infographic

2 United Kingdom's Guidance for Public procurement policy: www.gov.uk/guidance/public-sector-procurement-policy

3 South Korea's Public Procurement Act: www.law.go.kr/%EB%B2%95%EB%A0%B9/%EC%A1%B0%EB%8B%AC%EC%82%AC%EC%97%85%EC%97%90%EA%B4%80%ED%95%9C%EB%B2%95%EB%A5%A0

4 Yet, the extent to which that discretion is salient to a bureaucrat is as important as the zone available to them. In other words, the creep of political pressure into a bureaucrat's use of discretion will depend on both the agency as an institution and the process by which the contracting has been approved. At times, businesses have made capital investments with relative assurance of long-term funding. Others are absorbing larger risks. As well, scale will matter (i.e., small versus large

contracts). Hence, one needs to think carefully about the level (and locus) of administrative discretion when thinking about the decision processes that a bureaucrat (or their agency) uses when determining contract awards.

5 As an illustration, in the context of fostering effective collaboration through public–private partnerships, Eggers and Kettl (2023) advocate a multitude of strategies, including the establishment of a robust performance data framework. The authors highlight the significance of delineating explicit deliverables and reporting stipulations, which necessitate rigorous oversight to identify potential lapses in milestone achievements and deviations from intended initiatives (p.180).

## References


Ahmed, H. (2019). *How Private Prisons Are Profiting Under the Trump Administration*. Washington, DC: Center for American Progress.

Anderson, S.E. & Potoski, M. (2016). Agency structure and the distribution of federal spending. *Journal of Public Administration Research and Theory*, *26*(3), 461–474.

Arnold, R.D. (1979). *Congress and the Bureaucracy: A Theory of Influence* (Vol. 28). Yale University Press.

Bearfield, D.A. (2009). What is patronage? A critical reexamination. *Public Administration Review*, *69*(1), 64–76.

Berry, C.R. & Fowler, A. (2018). Congressional committees, legislative influence, and the hegemony of chairs. *Journal of Public Economics*, *158*, 1–11.

Berry, C.R. & Gersen, J.E. (2017). Agency design and political control. *Yale Law Journal*, *126*, 1002.

Berry, C.R., Burden, B.C. & Howell, W.G. (2010). The president and the distribution of federal spending. *American Political Science Review*, *104*(4), 783–799.

Bertelli, A.M. & Grose, C.R. (2009). Secretaries of pork? A new theory of distributive public policy. *The Journal of Politics*, *71*(3), 926–945.

Bickers, K.N. & Stein, R.M. (2000). The congressional pork barrel in a Republican era. *The Journal of Politics*, *62*(4), 1070–1086.

Carpenter, D.H. & Ruane, K.A. (2018). Selected Legal Tools for Maintaining Government Contractor Accountability (Report No. R45322). Congressional Research Service.

Cooper, P.J. (2003). *Governing by Contract: Challenges and Opportunities for Public Managers*. Washington, DC: CQ Press.

Dahlström, C., Fazekas, M. & Lewis, D.E. (2021). Partisan procurement: Contracting with the United States federal government, 2003–2015. *American Journal of Political Science*, *65*(3), 652–669.

Dooling, B.C.E. & Potter, R.A. (2022). Contractors in Rulemaking (draft report to the Admin. Conf. of the U.S.). Link: www.acus.gov/sites/default/files/documents/Contractors%20in%20Rulemaking%20Draft%20Report%202022.03.17.pdf

Easton, D. (1965). *A Systems Analysis of Political Life*. New York: Wiley.

Eggers, W.D. & Kettl, D.F. (2023). Bridgebuilding for a new vision of government. *Leader to Leader*, *2023*(109), 13–18.

Epstein, D. & O'Halloran, S. (1999). Asymmetric information, delegation, and the structure of policy-making. *Journal of Theoretical Politics*, *11*(1), 37–56.

Golden, M.M.. (2000). *What Motivates Bureaucrats? Politics and Administration during the Reagan Years*. New York: Columbia University Press. https://doi.org/10.7312/gold10696 Retrieved from www.jstor.org/stable/10.7312/gold10696

Gordon, S. (2011). Politicizing agency spending authority: Lessons from a Bush-era scandal. *American Political Science Review*, *105*, 717–734.

Huber, J.D. & Shipan, C.R. (2002). *Deliberate Discretion?: The Institutional Foundations of Bureaucratic Autonomy*. Cambridge: Cambridge University Press.

Hudak, J. (2014). *Presidential Pork: White House Influence over the Distribution of Federal Grants*. Washington, DC: Brookings Institution Press.

Kaufman, H. (1981). Fear of bureaucracy: A raging pandemic. *Public Administration Review*, *41*(1), 1–9. https://doi.org/10.2307/975718

Kettl, D.F. (2017). *Can governments earn our trust?*. Hoboken, New Jersey: John Wiley & Sons.

Kim, K. (2000). Institutional diagnosis and remedies of government procurement system in South Korea: In search of effective governance. *International Review of Public Administration*, *5*(2), 99–114.

Krause, G.A. & Zarit, M. (2022). Selling out? Contingent politicization and contracting risk in US Federal Procurements, 2001–2016. *Journal of Political Institutions and Political Economy*, *2*(4), 509–535.

Kriner, D.L. & Reeves, A. (2015). *The Particularistic President: Executive Branch Politics and Political Inequality*. Cambridge: Cambridge University Press.

Lasswell, H. (1936). *Politics: Who Gets, What, When, How?* New York. Whittlesey House, McGraw-Hill Book Co.

Lewis, D.E. (2008). *The Politics of Presidential Appointments: Political Control and Bureaucratic Performance*. Princeton, New Jersey: Princeton University Press.

Light, P.C. (2018). *The Government-Industrial Complex: The True Size of the Federal Government, 1984–2018*. New York: Oxford University Press.

Manuel, K.M. & Lunder, E.K. (2012). Government Procurement in Times of Fiscal Uncertainty. Congressional Research Service, Library of Congress.

Manuel, K.M. (2011). *Responsibility Determinations Under the Federal Acquisition Regulation (FAR): Legal Standards and Procedures*. Collingdale, Pennsylvania: DIANE Publishing.

Maskell, J. (1998). *"Hatch Act" and Other Restrictions in Federal Law on Political Activities of Government Employees*. Congressional Research Service, the Library of Congress.

McCubbins, M.D., Noll, R.G. & Weingast, B.R. (1989). Structure and process, politics and policy: Administrative arrangements and the political control of agencies. *Virginia Law Review*, *75*, 431.

Meier, K.J. (1993). *Politics and the Bureaucracy: Policy Making in the Fourth Branch of Government*. Pacific Grove, CA: Brooks/Cole Publishing.

Miller, G.J. & Whitford, A.B. (2016). *Above Politics*. Cambridge, UK: Cambridge University Press.

Miller, G.J. (2005). The political evolution of principal-agent models. *Annual Review of Political Science*, *8*, 203–225.

Organization for Economic Cooperation and Development (OECD) (2017). Government at a Glance. Paris: OECD Publishing.

Resh, W., Siddiki, S. and McConnell, W.R. (2014), Network centrality of government actors. *Review of Policy Research*, *31*, 584–609. https://doi.org/10.1111/ropr.12101

Resh, W.G. & Marvel, J.D. (2012). Loopholes to load-shed: Contract management capacity, representative bureaucracy, and goal displacement in federal procurement decisions. *International Public Management Journal*, *15*(4), 525–547.

Resh, W.G. & Zook, H.L. (2018). Public administration as a function of executive and legislative power. In *Handbook of American Public Administration*. Northampton, Massachusetts: Edward Elgar Publishing.

Resh, W.G. (2019). The disarticulation of the administrative state (and public administration). *Administration & Society*, *51*(3), 347–370.

Resh, W.G., Napolio, N.G., & Lee, E. (2022). The pivotal and distributive politics of senate-confirmed appointee vacancies. *Presidential Studies Quarterly*, *52*(1), 60–83.

Schooner, S.L. (2002). Desiderata: Objectives for a system of government contract law. *Public Procurement Law Review*, *11*, 103.

Selin, J.L. (2015). What makes an agency independent? *American Journal of Political Science*, *59*(4), 971–987. https://doi.org/10.1111/ajps.12161

Stein, R.M. & Bickers, K.N. (1997). *Perpetuating the Pork Barrel: Policy Subsystems and American Democracy*. Cambridge, UK: Cambridge University Press.

Stier, M. (2009, February 4). Federal contracting system in serious disrepair. *Washington Post*. www.washingtonpost.com/wp-dyn/content/article/2009/02/04/AR2009020402605.html

Verkuil, P.R. (2017). *Valuing Bureaucracy: The Case for Professional Government*: Cambridge, UK: Cambridge University Press.

Waldo, D. (1946/2017). *The Administrative State: A Study of the Political Theory of American Public Administration*. Abingdon, UK: Routledge.

Wood, B.D. & Waterman, R.W. (1993). The dynamics of political-bureaucratic adaptation. *American Journal of Political Science*, *37*(2), 497–528.
Zarit, M. (2018) *Lost in Translation: How Bureaucratic Hierarchies Limit Presidential Control Over Distributive Policymaking in US Federal Agencies* (Doctoral dissertation, University of Pittsburgh).

### *Case Study: The Flawed Procurement Process: A Case of JEDI Contract and the U.S. Department of Defense (Developed by Suman Niranjan, Arunachalam Narayanan, Timothy G. Hawkins)*

#### Background

The JEDI (Joint Enterprise Defense Infrastructure) contract began as a U.S. Department of Defense (DoD) initiative launched in 2017 to modernize its outdated technology systems (Miller, 2018). It aimed to consolidate and enhance military cloud computing capabilities, enabling improved data processing, AI integration, and rapid decision-making support for military operations worldwide. The $10 billion, decade-long project attracted significant interest from major IT firms in the United States. U.S. Representatives Womack and Cole, on October 22, 2018, sent a letter to the DoD Office of the Inspector General requesting an investigation into the processes used to develop the Request for Proposal (RFP), especially regarding the influence of certain high-ranking DoD officials with significant connections to Amazon (Department of Defense Inspector General (DoD IG), 2020). Microsoft ultimately secured the contract in 2019, beating Amazon, which led to bid protests alleging political influence during the procurement process (Figuenick, 2022). Also, the reliance of DoD on one company for such a large-scale IT makeover needed to be revised. These protests led to significant delays in the project's implementation. Recognizing the evolving technological landscape and the need for a more flexible approach, the DoD canceled the JEDI contract in July 2021. Subsequently, the DoD introduced the Joint Warfighting Cloud Capability (JWCC) as a replacement.

#### The Protest: Amazon versus Microsoft

In 2018, the DoD announced its $10 billion JEDI contract to overhaul cloud computing infrastructure. While initially expected to be a straightforward competition, it became a highly controversial procurement case. Amazon Web Services (AWS) and Microsoft Azure emerged as frontrunners, with AWS widely considered the favorite due to its technical expertise, market share, and experience. However, in October 2019, Microsoft was awarded the contract (McKinnon, 2019). AWS contested the decision, citing unfairness and bias, especially pointing to former DoD official Anthony DeMartino's ties to Oracle, raising questions about conflicts of interest (Parloff, 2020). AWS's protest delayed the contract's implementation, leading the U.S. Court of Federal Claims to identify issues with the DoD's evaluation process, further halting progress. In 2021, facing prolonged legal battles and evolving technological needs, the DoD canceled the JEDI contract and opted for a multi-cloud strategy through the JWCC, involving AWS, Microsoft, and other vendors to enhance competition and diversify capabilities.

The JEDI case highlighted the flaws in procurement practices for high-stakes government contracts. Political interference, alleged favoritism, and transparency concerns necessitated judicial review and delayed DoD's modernization efforts. Intended initially to consolidate cloud capability from over 500 providers into 1, JEDI's single-source structure placed the project within reach of only two firms due to its scale and expertise requirements (Freedberg, 2020; Miller, 2018). This "winner-take-all" model posed the risk of technological path dependencies, compelling major firms to protest fiercely. The decision to split contracts underscored the benefits of multi-vendor strategies, avoiding stifled competition and promoting innovation. While not new, this approach echoes broader public procurement practices, as seen in multi-billion dollar contracts awarded by the Defense Logistics Agency to providers like Cardinal Health and Owens & Minor (Whooley, 2019).

### Delays of Awarding the Contract and Avoidance

The delay and cancellation of the JEDI contract caused significant setbacks for the DoD, slowing its IT modernization and integration of advanced cloud technology, including artificial intelligence and big data capabilities essential for military operations. Although the early stages of the contract validated buyer authority, with the Government Accountability Office (GAO) finding the RFP fair (Government Accountability Office (GAO), 2018), subsequent legal battles and political controversies derailed progress. The U.S. Court of Federal Claims dismissed Oracle's 2020 lawsuit, aligning with the DoD's determination that no conflicts of interest existed, and a DoD Inspector General investigation primarily supported buyer authority and regulatory adherence (DoD IG, 2020). However, these findings failed to quell external pressures from media scrutiny, lobbyists, and members of Congress, who raised concerns of misconduct, implicating even the President and former Secretaries of Defense. Allegations by former Secretary of Defense Mattis of Presidential directives to "screw Bezos out of that $10 billion contract" (Miller, 2019) fueled public distrust. However, evidence was limited due to White House non-cooperation (DoD IG, 2020).

The legal battle between Amazon and Microsoft, driven by allegations of political interference and bias, delayed modernization efforts, increased costs, and diverted essential resources. This erosion of trust in government procurement processes strained relationships with key tech companies and highlighted the fragility of major technology projects. In response, the DoD's creation of the JWCC program marked a shift to a multi-vendor approach to enhance competition and flexibility. The JEDI case underscores the challenges and high stakes in government technology procurement, emphasizing the need for transparent, efficient processes to promote timely innovation while avoiding political and external subversion.

### Path Forward and Current Situation

The DoD has progressed with the JWCC, awarding contracts to AWS, Google, Microsoft, and Oracle. JWCC, structured as a multiple-award contract, aims to deliver cloud services across all classification levels, from headquarters to tactical environments, ensuring global accessibility, robust security, elastic computing capabilities, and advanced analytics. Unlike the single-vendor approach of JEDI, JWCC's flexible, multi-vendor strategy offers more resilient and mission-tailored services, streamlining cloud service acquisition to meet military operational speed and needs. This shift raises critical questions about resilience and flexibility: How does the multi-vendor strategy of JWCC differ from JEDI's single-vendor approach in these areas, and what implications does this have for government technology projects? Furthermore, what lessons from the JEDI contract can help promote transparency and fairness in future procurement processes? Finally, how can a deeper understanding of the political dynamics involved in such large-scale contracts prevent similar delays and controversies? As of August 2024, the DoD has issued numerous task orders under JWCC, totaling nearly $1 billion (Harper, 2024), reflecting the DoD's continued commitment to adapting cloud solutions for complex military demands while learning from past experiences to enhance fairness, transparency, and operational agility.

***References***

Boland, M., & Godsell, D. (2021). Bureaucratic Discretion and Contracting Outcomes. *Accounting, Organizations and Society*, 88, 101173.

Curry, W. S. (2016). *Government Contracting: Promises and Perils*. Routledge.

Department of Defense Inspector General (2020, April 13). Report on the Joint Enterprise Defense Infrastructure (JEDI) Cloud Procurement, Report No. DODIG-2020-079.

DiIulio, J. (2014). *Bring Back the Bureaucrats: Why More Federal Workers Will Lead to Better (and Smaller!) Government*. Templeton Foundation Press.

Fazekas, M., Ferrali, R., & Wachs, B. (2023). Agency Independence, Campaign Contributions, and Favoritism in US Federal Government Contracting. *Journal of Public Administration Research and Theory*, 33(2), 262–278. https://doi.org/10.1093/jopart/muac026

Figuenick III, D. J. (2022). Billions, and Billions, and Billions: Recent Administrations, Cronyism, and the Need for Greater Independence in Contract Awards. *Public Contract Law Journal*, 51(4), 599–622.

Freedburg, S. J. (2020, May 4). Experts Debate: Should JEDI Cloud Be Saved? *Breaking Defense*, accessed on August 2, 2024, at https://breakingdefense.com/2020/05/experts-debate-should-jedi-cloud-be-saved/

Government Accountability Office (2018, November 14). GAO Statement on Oracle Bid Protest. Press Release, accessed on August 2, 2024, at www.gao.gov/press-release/gao-statement-oracle-bid-protest

Harper, J. (2024, August 7). *Pentagon awards nearly $1B in JWCC task orders*. DefenseScoop. https://defensescoop.com/2024/08/07/pentagon-awards-nearly-1b-jwcc-task-orders/

McKinnon, J. (2019, October 25). Pentagon picks Microsoft for JEDI Cloud-Computing contract over Amazon. *The Wall Street Journal*. Retrieved November 8, 2024, from www.wsj.com/articles/pentagon-picksmicrosoft-for-jedi-cloud-computing-contract-over-amazon-11572045221

Miller, R. (2018, September 15). Why the Pentagon's $10 billion JEDI deal has cloud companies going nuts. *TechCrunch*. Retrieved November 8, 2024, from https://techcrunch.com/2018/09/15/why-the-pentagons-10-billion-jedi-deal-has-cloud-companies-going-nuts/

Miller, R. (2019, October 18). Even after Microsoft wins, JEDI saga could drag on. *TechCrunch*accessed on July 7, 2023, at https://techcrunch.com/2019/10/28/even-after-microsoft-wins-jedi-saga-could-drag-on/

Nagel, J. H. (1972). *The Descriptive Analysis of Power*. Yale University.

Parloff, R. (2020, April 20). Amazon's lawsuit over a $10 billion Pentagon contract lays out disturbing allegations against Trump. Yahoo Finance. Retrieved November 8, 2024, from https://shorturl.at/QT7he

Titl, V., & Geys, B. (2019). Political Donations and the Allocation of Public Procurement Contracts. *European Economic Review*, 111, 443–458.

Warren, P. L. (2014). Contracting Officer Workload, Incomplete Contracting, and Contractual Terms. *The RAND Journal of Economics*, 45(2), 395–421.

Whooley, S. (2019, November 8). *DoD awards billions in contracts to Cardinal Health, Owens & Minor*. MassDevice. www.massdevice.com/dod-awards-contracts-to-cardinal-health-owens-minor/

# 7 Procuring Public–Private Partnerships (PPPs)

*Carter B. Casady, Thomas Sherman and Benjamin M. Brunjes*

## 7.1 Introduction

Around the world, infrastructure projects remain politically contentious, complex, and challenging to deliver. The distinct phases of project lifecycles—from planning and design to construction and operations—often carry high degrees of "broken agency", whereby decisions in one phase of the project impose unexpected costs across work stages (Casady et al., 2020). "Broken agency" refers to the ways that complex infrastructure projects fragment responsibility for the successful completion of a project. Traditional approaches to managing these complex projects include Design-Build (DB) and Construction Manager/General Contractor (CMGC) schemes, where project managers are hired during the design phase to enhance the likelihood of success and to control costs. Project managers encounter an age-old problem: the parties involved in infrastructure projects are self-interested. Each party focuses on completing their own sub-section of the work, rather than thinking about the bigger-picture success of the overall project. Self-interested actors often make decisions that create costs that are borne by other organizations or the general public in subsequent phases of the project. For example, consider a project to develop a new stormwater system in a local community. An architecture firm might focus exclusively on structural design, ignoring things like resource availability and environmental impact. Upon confronting the plans, construction firms might have to extend timelines to locate and build with the materials listed. An environmental impact assessment might reveal ecological harm, which may require new designs, different materials, or even new locations for the work to be done. By narrowly focusing on their part of the project, each actor accidentally creates problems for the others, while also making it harder to complete the whole project successfully. Due to the complexity of the design and phased implementation of infrastructure projects, it can be difficult to reduce these unexpected costs.

Despite their widespread use, traditional methods of procuring infrastructure services, such as DB or CMGC, may be ineffective for the development of infrastructure projects. In particular, traditional procurement methods can lead to overly conservative contract designs (Levitt, Ashley, and Logcher 1980), the costly and time-consuming exploration of contract specifications through change orders (Henisz, Levitt, and Richard Scott 2012), the over-estimation of project benefits and underestimation of potential costs (Flyvbjerg, Holm, and Buhl 2002), and government favoritism for building new infrastructure over investments in maintenance and renewals (Bennon, Julie, and Levitt 2017; Casady and Geddes 2020). These shortcomings of traditional public procurement are particularly pronounced for large, complex megaprojects that require substantial capital investment and sophisticated management strategies. As infrastructure needs grow more complex, such as with efforts to fight climate change or integrate systems of systems, traditional methods are becoming

DOI: 10.4324/9781003566670-9

increasingly obsolete. In recent years, governments have developed a new and innovative approach to improve the chances of successful infrastructure development: public–private partnerships (PPPs).

Across the spectrum of infrastructure development options, PPPs serve as a promising alternative to address challenges of "broken agency", offering unique opportunities for innovation and efficiency. PPPs bring together the strengths of the public and private sectors through collaborative efforts that leverage private sector expertise, efficiency, and capital to deliver public infrastructure projects that might otherwise be unfeasible. PPPs integrate multiple phases of development, implementation, and operation under a single contractual agreement. This approach contrasts with traditional procurement, where these stages are often managed and contracted separately. By bundling various stages of the project lifecycle (Casady and Geddes 2019), this approach not only distributes risks and rewards more equitably but also fosters a culture of innovation and efficiency, leading to better schedule delivery and higher quality outcomes (Casady, Verweij, and van Meerkerk 2022). Contracts ranging from Design-Build-Finance (DBF) to Design-Build-Finance-Operate-Maintain (DBFOM) and concession agreements illustrate the range of possible PPP arrangements (Auriol and Picard 2013). However, in practice, PPPs are not a panacea for the shortcomings of traditional infrastructure provision. The planning, procurement, and execution of PPPs is very challenging and complex (Guasch, Laffont, and Straub 2008) because "the idea of partnership [within PPPs] is often introduced without much reflection on the need to reorganize policy-making processes and to adjust existing institutional structures" (Teisman and Klijn 2002, 197). Greve and Hodge (2010, 156) astutely point out that:

> PPPs present challenges to the traditional forms of public administration in terms of the complexity of the deals and the number of actors involved; the government's capacity to steer; the choice between governance forms; possible strategic behavior by the private-sector organizations; and the duration of contracts which makes evaluation difficult.

As a result, over the last 30 years, public sector experiences with PPPs have been mixed. Despite documented performance advantages (see, e.g., Verweij, van Meerkerk, and Casady 2022a, 2022b), "there have been multiple, highly publicized cases of public opposition to the private provision of infrastructure and large numbers of contract renegotiations and cancellations" (Jooste and Scott 2012, 150; see also Gifford et al. 2024). With PPPs, there are also the associated challenges of potential corruption, lack of transparency, and the need for careful planning and contract management (Vecchi et al. 2022; Casady 2021).

Taken together, PPP procurement is a complex endeavor, requiring legitimacy, trust, and capacity to be successful (Casady 2024). Both academics and practitioners are likely to encounter PPPs in their field over the coming years, as resource-strapped public organizations work to find ways to tackle the wicked problems of the 21st century. Therefore, the goal for the remainder of this chapter is to (1) outline what we know about PPP procurement from the extant academic literature, (2) describe how PPP procurement is conducted in practice, and (3) highlight emerging issues in the field. Overall, the chapter will help readers understand why and how PPPs are being implemented and offer insights into how to manage PPPs more effectively.

## 7.2 Literature on PPP Procurement

Academic scholarship on PPP procurement covers many different aspects of design and implementation. Some of the most important areas of study focus on (1) enabling legislation,

(2) value-for-money (VfM) assessments, and (3) transaction costs/tendering durations. These areas address how PPPs have been integrated into political and regulatory systems, compare the impact of PPP investments to other approaches, and identify some of the most important considerations for successful PPP implementation.

### *7.2.1 PPP-Enabling Legislation*

For many scholars and practitioners, PPP-enabling legislation is the cornerstone of effective PPP implementation. The enactment of PPP legal frameworks tends to be particularly important because these laws create "a general sense ... that a given policy decision has been formulated in acceptable ways, through justifiable procedures" (see, e.g., Hult and Walcott 1990, 63–67). Such legislation establishes the formal basis for public–private collaboration by setting out the legal, institutional, and procedural environment in which PPPs operate. When done correctly, these frameworks help clearly define roles, responsibilities, and obligations for all stakeholders involved, thereby promoting transparency, accountability, and good governance (Brinkerhoff and Brinkerhoff 2011).

Supportive legal frameworks ensure that governments can standardize procurement procedures, reduce ambiguity, and foster trust among potential private partners. Standardization is especially critical for reducing the learning curve for both public agencies and private firms, which might otherwise face significant barriers due to varying or unclear requirements across jurisdictions. By building these frameworks (Tvarnø 2006), governments not only create a more predictable and stable environment for investment but also signal their commitment to fostering long-term partnerships. This is why the codification of PPP legislation is often viewed as a necessary condition for PPP market development (Casady 2021) and a key driver of additional private investment (Albalate, Bel, and Geddes 2020).

Well-designed PPP legislation can enhance accountability mechanisms. Clear legal frameworks mandate robust reporting, monitoring, and evaluation systems, ensuring that both public agencies and private partners adhere to agreed-upon performance standards (Shaoul, Stafford, and Stapleton 2012). These mechanisms are crucial for maintaining public trust, particularly in contexts where skepticism about private involvement in public services runs high (Abdullah and Khadaroo 2020). By embedding such safeguards in legislation, governments can reduce risks of corruption, favoritism, or inefficiency that could otherwise undermine the success of PPPs.

Examples of successful PPP-enabling legislation illustrate the transformative power of a strong legal framework. For instance, the United Kingdom's Private Finance Initiative (PFI) in the 1990s laid the foundation for one of the most extensive PPP markets globally. The PFI legislation established clear procurement processes, risk allocation mechanisms, and evaluation criteria, enabling the government to attract significant private investment into public infrastructure projects (Dixon, Pottinger, and Jordan 2005). Similarly, Australia's National PPP Guidelines provide a standardized approach to assessing, procuring, and managing PPPs across different states, ensuring consistency while allowing for jurisdictional flexibility (Johnston and Gudergan 2007).

However, developing effective PPP legislation is not without its challenges. Governments must navigate political opposition, which often arises from concerns about privatization, loss of public control, or potential inequities in service delivery (Rwelamila, Fewings, and Henjewele 2015). The effectiveness of PPP-enabling legislation depends on how well it balances flexibility and standardization. While standardization helps reduce uncertainty, excessive rigidity can stifle innovation and limit the adaptability of PPP contracts to project-specific needs (van den Hurk and Verhoest 2016). Overly prescriptive legislation may prevent public and private partners from negotiating customized solutions that account for unique local conditions or emerging challenges during project implementation.

### 7.2.2 *Value-for-Money (VfM)*

When choosing PPPs, another oft-cited reason to use this procurement approach is VfM. VfM assessments evaluate the economic viability and efficiency of PPP projects, serving as a critical tool for determining whether a PPP offers better returns on investment compared to traditional procurement methods. These assessments compare key factors such as life-cycle costs, risk allocation, and service quality, which are essential for understanding the full implications of a procurement decision. By considering not just upfront costs but also the long-term costs and benefits of infrastructure projects, VfM analyses provide a comprehensive view of economic efficiency.

Studies have consistently demonstrated that PPPs often deliver better VfM by leveraging private sector expertise, fostering innovation, and improving risk management practices. For example, private sector involvement frequently leads to better life-cycle costing, wherein decisions made during the design and construction phases optimize maintenance and operational costs over the project's lifespan (Grimsey and Lewis 2007). Additionally, the transfer of risks—such as construction delays, cost overruns, or operational inefficiencies—to private partners incentivizes them to perform efficiently, potentially reducing the overall costs borne by the public sector (Tallaki and Bracci 2021).

Numerous early studies have highlighted the potential of PPPs to deliver superior VfM. For instance, a 2003 report by the United Kingdom's National Audit Office (NAO) demonstrated that PPPs often achieve significant cost savings and efficiency gains compared to traditional procurement. More recent research has further affirmed these performance advantages, with studies such as Verweij, van Meerkerk, and Casady (2022a) identifying measurable improvements in delivery timelines and quality outcomes in PPP projects.

However, the practice of VfM analysis has not been without criticism. Critics argue that VfM analyses are fraught with methodological and practical challenges. For instance, Grimsey and Lewis (2005) and Morallos and Amekudzi (2008) point out that assumptions underlying VfM calculations—such as discount rates, risk premiums, and long-term revenue projections—are often highly subjective and prone to bias. These assumptions can skew results in favor of PPPs, even in cases where traditional procurement might offer better outcomes. Similarly, Petersen (2019) highlights the lack of standardized methodologies for conducting VfM assessments, making it difficult to compare results across jurisdictions or project types.

Some scholars, such as Moore and Vining (2023), go further in questioning whether VfM evaluations are being conducted appropriately at all. They argue that VfM assessments often prioritize financial metrics at the expense of broader social and environmental considerations, such as equity, accessibility, and sustainability. These omissions can lead to procurement decisions that are economically efficient in the narrow sense but fail to deliver on the broader objectives of public infrastructure projects. Evidence on the accuracy of VfM assessments remains contested, partly due to the inherent complexity of quantifying all relevant costs and benefits (Lonsdale 2000). VfM analyses often also fail to capture the dynamic nature of PPPs, where outcomes may evolve over the decades-long lifespan of a typical project (Morallos and Amekudzi 2008).

Real-world cases illustrate the contested nature of VfM assessments. For example, in the procurement of a large toll road in Australia, the VfM analysis faced scrutiny for overestimating traffic volumes and underestimating maintenance costs, leading to financial challenges for both the public sector and private investors (Quayle 2021). Similarly, in the United Kingdom, the VfM justification for some PFI projects was criticized for relying on overly optimistic risk transfer assumptions, which ultimately failed to materialize as planned (National Audit Office (NAO) 2023; Sherratt, Sherratt, and Ivory 2020).

### *7.2.3 PPP Transaction Costs*

Finally, transaction costs are critical factors for PPP projects. Like other types of purchases, PPPs must go through the public procurement process. The procurement phase of PPPs typically involves substantial transaction costs, whereby the sponsoring organization (usually a government agency) must organize the tender process, assess bids, and negotiate the final contract with a preferred bidder. As discussed in Chapter 3, each of these steps is costly for public organizations. Due to the complexity of PPP projects, governments routinely take on high costs in defining requirements, assessing proposals, and negotiating terms with the winning partner.

Likewise, consortiums of private firms angling to win these PPP contracts may also incur substantial costs when preparing their bids. The most important among these is the marshaling of resources to submit a competitive proposal *ex ante* (before a contract is signed). Firms may need to build new facilities, hire additional personnel, and reallocate human capital to write and refine the proposal itself. These are not small investments. Klein, So, and Shin (1996) indicate transaction costs are 3–5% of project costs in developed markets and 10–12% in developing markets. Similarly, Välilä (2005) notes ex-ante transaction costs represent about 12% of a project's capital value (7% for the public sector/winning bidder and the remaining 5% associated with the costs of failed bids. Moreover, Sanchez Solino and Gago de Santos (2010) assert that transaction costs account for 10% and 3% of the capital value in negotiated and open procedures, respectively. Participating in government marketplaces, even for potentially large and profitable projects like PPPs, is expensive and risky for private partners.

Many *ex ante* costs arise as a function of tendering duration (the length of time it takes to find and negotiate a contract). Reeves, Palcic, and Flannery (2015), Reeves et al. (2017), Casady et al. (2019), and Palcic et al. (2022) have all analyzed the determinants of PPP tendering periods in different jurisdictions, both in isolation and comparatively. Factors such as project size (i.e., capital value), project sector, procurement authority, and the timing of contract notice tend to influence procurement duration, with the long tendering periods found in the housing, health, and defense sectors. PPP projects have longer tendering periods relative to traditional procurements (Ahadzi and Bowles 2004), which makes sense due to the complexity of the work and the long-term nature of the relationship PPPs initiate (Kolpakov and Anguelov 2018). While this is often attributed to the complex nature of procurement under PPP (Casady et al. 2019), any higher upfront transaction costs associated with these procurements are expected to be offset by long-term value and efficiency gains (see VfM discussion).

Both parties also incur transaction costs *ex post* (or, after the project has begun), as the work done on PPPs is difficult to fully specify. There will be unanticipated developments in nearly every PPP, as they tend to be among the most complex contracts that governments write (Klijn and Koppenjan 2016). For example, PPPs for the development of toll fast lanes on highways (where the private partner shares in both the development costs and the profits reaped from driver payments) include aspects related to construction, information technology, and public safety. Effectively blending these competing goals among the unexpected developments that can arise during the early stages of construction and piloting is a complex and costly process. Operations may become easier over time, but defining and measuring performance can be challenging throughout a complex contract (Brown, Potoski, and Van Slyke 2013; Soomro and Zhang 2016).

Overall, the literature emphasizes the significance of thorough analysis and strategic planning in PPP procurement. By conducting comprehensive feasibility studies, considering alternative procurement options, and involving stakeholders in the decision-making process, governments are expected to optimize PPP project outcomes. Effective procurement practices, such as competitive tendering and transparent evaluation criteria, help ensure that PPPs are awarded to the most qualified and capable private partners, delivering the best value for public funds. The next section outlines in more detail how such steps are carried out in practice.

## 7.3 PPP Procurement in Practice

### *7.3.1 Authorizing Legislation*

As discussed earlier, effective PPP procurement begins with strong authorizing legislation. Model legislation should encompass key provisions such as clear definitions of PPPs, the scope of permissible projects, and the roles and responsibilities of public and private entities. Well-crafted legislation serves as the foundation for a robust PPP framework, ensuring transparency, accountability, and adaptability. It is important to bridge the gap between law and practice by establishing detailed procedures that facilitate smooth implementation while accommodating evolving project needs and innovations.

For example, the United Kingdom's PFI established a framework that clearly delineated procurement processes, evaluation criteria, and risk-sharing mechanisms. Similarly, Australia's National PPP Guidelines standardized practices across jurisdictions while allowing flexibility for local conditions. These examples illustrate how authorizing legislation provides a predictable environment for both public agencies and private investors, fostering trust and encouraging participation.

In addition to legislation, comprehensive guidelines and manuals, such as the *World Bank PPP Reference Guide Version 3*, the *EPEC Guide to Public–Private Partnerships*, the *FHWA P3 Toolkit*, and the *UK Green Book*, play a critical role in operationalizing PPP frameworks. These resources offer best practices for standardizing procurement processes, managing stakeholder expectations, and promoting consistent execution.

However, guidelines must strike a balance between standardization and flexibility. While standardization reduces uncertainty and streamlines processes, excessive rigidity can hinder the customization of contracts to meet project-specific requirements. Flexible guidelines allow public and private partners to address unique challenges, adapt to innovations, and incorporate lessons learned from prior projects. For instance, tailoring risk-sharing arrangements or performance benchmarks to the needs of individual projects ensures that both parties can effectively manage their responsibilities.

Developing and maintaining these frameworks and guidelines is considered a best practice in PPP procurement. They not only legitimize the PPP model but also serve as essential tools for stakeholder management, ensuring that all parties—public officials, private investors, and community stakeholders—clearly understand their roles, responsibilities, and expectations. By fostering this alignment, governments can enhance the success and sustainability of PPP projects while building public confidence in the procurement process.

### *7.3.2 Project Development and Due Diligence Analyses*

For the different phases of PPP project delivery—screening, development, procurement, and implementation—meticulous planning and due diligence are essential. Effective project development begins with a meaningful screening process that evaluates potential projects for PPP suitability. A comprehensive screening report includes detailed project descriptions, feasibility studies (technical, financial, and environmental), and risk assessments. For example, a transportation PPP might include demand forecasts, environmental impact assessments, and financial models comparing traditional procurement with the PPP approach. Objective criteria and third-party reviews are critical for ensuring the process remains impartial and robust.

While thorough screenings are indispensable, governments may also benefit from quick, high-level assessments to identify early-stage project suitability. These preliminary evaluations can save resources by filtering out projects unlikely to succeed as PPPs before engaging in more detailed analysis. Clear project descriptions are vital at this stage, outlining the purpose, goals, and objectives of the project in a manner that aligns with stakeholder interests and is supported by relevant data.

Key performance indicators (KPIs) are integral to performance-based PPP contracts. These metrics define success and may include targets for demand risk, service quality, and cost efficiency. While public and private sectors prioritize different KPIs, aligning these metrics ensures that all stakeholders have a shared understanding of project expectations. For instance, public agencies may focus on social equity and accessibility, while private partners emphasize financial returns and operational efficiency.

Accurate cost and revenue estimations are equally crucial. To protect the public sector from underestimation risks, mechanisms such as independent audits and contingency reserves should be incorporated. Similarly, a robust risk register developed collaboratively by public and private sectors can identify, allocate, and manage risks effectively. Innovative risk management practices, such as using digital tools for real-time monitoring or structuring risk-sharing agreements that adapt to unforeseen circumstances, can further enhance efficiency and resilience.

### *7.3.3 Evaluation and Analysis*

Quantitative and qualitative screenings, such as benefit–cost analysis (BCA), are critical for evaluating the value and impact of potential PPP projects. BCA examines whether the benefits of a project outweigh its costs, considering factors like economic growth, environmental sustainability, and social equity. Complementing BCA, VfM assessments compare PPPs to traditional procurement models, evaluating criteria such as life-cycle costs, risk transfer, and service quality. While VfM is a cornerstone of PPP decision-making, it should not be the sole determinant. Instead, a comprehensive business case that integrates multiple delivery options, constraints, and qualitative factors ensures a holistic approach.

For instance, in the development of a major healthcare facility, a business case might evaluate both traditional procurement and PPP models, considering not only financial metrics but also the project's ability to meet long-term healthcare needs. This justification process ensures the chosen model aligns with the public interest and optimizes resource use.

Determining technical and financial terms in PPP contracts requires detailed negotiations and the development of term sheets and appendices. These documents must balance clarity with adaptability, ensuring that contracts remain enforceable while allowing for adjustments as conditions evolve. Flexibility is particularly important when reviewing unsolicited proposals, as innovative solutions from private firms can enhance project outcomes if effectively integrated into existing frameworks. To manage stakeholder risks, governments should establish clear guidelines for engagement, transparency, and dispute resolution.

### *7.3.4 Beginning the Procurement Phase*

Formally initiating the procurement process requires a well-defined strategy that prepares public agencies for success. This preparation often includes engaging external advisors with expertise in PPP procurement to guide the agency in structuring contracts, assessing market conditions, and aligning project objectives with stakeholder needs. Requests for Information (RFIs) and market-sounding processes are useful tools for gathering industry insights and gauging private sector interest, helping to refine procurement strategies.

Stakeholder management and communication are particularly critical during this phase. Proactive engagement with community groups, private firms, and other stakeholders ensures that potential concerns are addressed early, building trust and fostering collaboration. Deciding between a one-stage or two-stage procurement process depends on factors such as project complexity, cost, and timeline. A one-stage process may be faster and less costly but can limit competitive tension and due diligence. In contrast, the two-stage process, often favored in PPPs, begins with a request for qualifications (RFQ) to shortlist bidders based on predefined criteria. This is followed by a Request for Proposals (RFPs), which involves detailed submissions from shortlisted bidders.

Draft and final RFPs often include one-on-one negotiations with potential bidders, allowing for the consideration of alternative technical and financial concepts. Writing a clear and feasible RFP is crucial to attracting high-quality bids. For example, an RFP for a highway project should specify technical standards, maintenance requirements, and expected traffic volumes while leaving room for innovative solutions from bidders. Conducting readiness assessments before issuing an RFP ensures that the project is well-prepared and that the procurement process can proceed smoothly.

### *7.3.5 Final Negotiations and Project Implementation*

Achieving commercial and financial close represents a significant milestone in the PPP lifecycle. Once a preferred bidder is selected, the selection and award processes transition into final negotiations to finalize contract terms. Independent audit reviews are often conducted at this stage to ensure transparency and accountability. Managing contingent liabilities—such as risks retained by the public sector—requires careful oversight to prevent unforeseen financial burdens.

During project implementation, early works validate the project's scope and feasibility. Adjustments to project agreements may be necessary to address changes in circumstances, such as design modifications or unexpected risks. These adjustments often involve revisiting risk transfer mechanisms, which can significantly impact the underlying transaction's financial and operational balance. For instance, if a project faces unforeseen construction delays, renegotiating timelines and penalties may be necessary to protect both parties' interests.

Independent construction reviews and quality assurance processes are vital to maintaining project standards. These reviews typically focus on compliance with technical specifications, safety standards, and environmental regulations. Benchmarking the project against alternative delivery models, such as DB or CMGC, provides valuable insights for continuous improvement. For example, a periodic comparison of PPP outcomes with traditional procurement metrics can help refine VfM assessments and ensure that the project continues to deliver its intended benefits.

## 7.4 Emerging Issues in PPP Procurement

As practitioners grapple with the complexities of procuring PPPs, the landscape of PPP procurement is also undergoing significant evolution, influenced by emerging issues that are reshaping traditional approaches. One key aspect of this evolution is the rethinking of risk allocation, especially the movement toward more collaborative PPP models such as progressive PPPs and pre-development agreements. These models are purported to foster greater cooperation and shared responsibility between public and private partners, ultimately enhancing project outcomes. According to Casady and Garvin (2022), these agreements try to develop assets that are more "fit-for-purpose" by jointly engaging in project design, risk allocation, and pricing. However, such an approach also creates uncertainty for investors, loss of competitive tension, exposure to heightened legal challenges and disputes, and reduced multi-advisor involvement, raising the potential for anti-competitive practices, compliance issues, and extended timelines that lead to escalated costs. Currently, the concept of progressive PPPs is gaining traction in North America, particularly in the United States and Canada, where several high-profile projects are adopting this model.

At the same time, an increasing trend of PPP contract cancellations, particularly in the United States, highlights the need for a deeper understanding of the underlying causes. Within the context of broader procurement failures (see, e.g., Casady, Petersen, and Brogaard 2023), new development strategies, like project development agreements (PDAs), are being trialed to mitigate such risks. Financial challenges, changes in political priorities, and unanticipated project complexities are often the primary factors contributing to these cancellations. Addressing these issues will require robust feasibility studies, stakeholder engagement, and more flexible contracting mechanisms.

On this last point, the PPP industry is pushing to move beyond lump-sum fixed-price contracts toward more flexible and adaptive contracting methods, especially in response to long-standing issues with contract renegotiations (García and Casady 2024). Target cost contracts and alliancing are examples of other approaches that emphasize collaborative problem-solving and shared incentives, reducing adversarial relationships and fostering project success. There is interest among practitioners to incorporate elements of these more collaborative models into PPPs to improve project delivery by lowering transaction costs and limiting downside exposure to overruns and delays.

The future of PPP procurement will see increased emphasis on sustainability (Li et al. 2024), technological integration, and resilience (Casady et al., 2024), aligning infrastructure development with broader societal goals. By addressing these emerging issues and leveraging innovative procurement methods, the field of PPP procurement can continue to adapt and evolve, ensuring that public infrastructure needs are being met. The involvement of both practitioners and academics is crucial to this evaluation of dynamic PPP procurement processes.

## References


Abdullah, A. and Khadaroo, I., 2020. The trust-control nexus in public private partnership (PPP) contracts. *Journal of Accounting and Public Policy*, 39(6), p. 106768.

Ahadzi, M. and Bowles, G., 2004. Public–private partnerships and contract negotiations: an empirical study. *Construction Management and Economics*, 22(9), pp. 967–978.

Albalate, D., Bel, G. and Geddes, R.R., 2020. Do public-private-partnership-enabling laws increase private investment in transportation infrastructure?. *The Journal of Law and Economics*, 63(1), pp. 43–70.

Auriol, E. and Picard, P.M., 2013. A theory of BOT concession contracts. *Journal of Economic Behavior & Organization*, 89, pp. 187–209.

Bennon, M., Julie, K. M., and Levitt, R. E., 2017. U.S. Infrastructure Gap(S): Federal Policy and Local Public Institutions. doi:10.2139/ssrn.3036650

Brinkerhoff, D. W. and. Brinkerhoff, J. M., 2011. Public–private partnerships: Perspectives on purposes, publicness, and good governance. *Public Administration and Development* 31(1), pp. 2–14.

Brown, T.L., Potoski, M. and Van Slyke, D.M., 2013. *Complex contracting*. Cambridge University Press.

Casady, C.B., 2021. Examining the institutional drivers of public-private partnership (PPP) market performance: A fuzzy set qualitative comparative analysis (fsQCA). *Public Management Review*, 23(7), pp. 981–1005.

Casady, C.B., 2024. A time differencing qualitative comparative analysis (QCA) of public-private partnership (PPP) market maturity. *Public Management Review*, 26(5), pp. 1360–1382.

Casady, C.B., Cepparulo, A. and Giuriato, L., 2024. Public-private partnerships for low-carbon, climate-resilient infrastructure: Insights from the literature. Journal of Cleaner Production, 470, p.143338.

Abutabenjeh, S., Dimand, A. M., & Tao, J. 2023. Determinants of the success of cooperative public procurement. *Public Performance & Management Review*, 46(2): 391–417.

Casady, C.B., Eriksson, K., Levitt, R.E., & Scott, W.R. 2020. (Re) defining public-private partnerships (PPPs) in the new public governance (NPG) paradigm: an institutional maturity perspective. *Public Management Review*, 22(2), pp. 161–183.

Casady, C., Flannery, D., Geddes, R.R., Palcic, D., and Reeves, E., 2019. Understanding PPP tendering periods in Canada: A duration analysis. *Public Performance & Management Review*, 42(6), pp. 1259–1278.

Casady, C.B. and Geddes, R.R., 2019. Private participation in US infrastructure: the role of regional PPP units. In *Public-Private-Partnerships for Infrastructure Development: Finance, Stakeholder Alignment, Governance*, edited by R. E. Levitt, W. R. Scott, and M. Garvin, pp. 224–242. Cheltenham: Edward Elgar.

Casady, C.B. and Geddes, R.R., 2020. Asset recycling for social infrastructure in the United States. *Public Works Management & Policy*, 25(3), pp. 281–297.

Casady, C.B., Petersen, O.H., and Brogaard, L., 2023. Public procurement failure: The role of transaction costs and government capacity in procurement cancellations. *Public Management Review*, pp. 1–28. www.tandfonline.com/doi/full/10.1080/14719037.2023.2231945#abstract

Casady, C.B., Verweij, S., and van Meerkerk, I., 2022. Conclusions about the performance advantage of PPP. In *Assessing the Performance Advantage of Public-Private Partnerships: A Comparative Perspective*, edited by S. Verweij, I. van Meerkerk, and C. B. Casady, pp. 206–228. Cheltenham: Edward Elgar.

Dixon, T., Pottinger, G., and Jordan, A., 2005. Lessons from the private finance initiative in the UK: Benefits, problems and critical success factors. *Journal of Property Investment & Finance*, 23(5), pp. 412–423.

Flyvbjerg, B., Holm, M.S., and Buhl, S., 2002. Underestimating costs in public works projects: Error or lie?. *Journal of the American Planning Association*, 68(3), pp. 279–295.

García, L.C. and Casady, C.B., 2024. Reviewing the efficacy of flexible contracts: A reassessment of the least present value of revenue (LPVR) model for public-private partnerships (PPPs). *Journal of Management in Engineering*, 40(1), p. 05023010.

Gifford, J.L., Bolaños, L.A., Daito, N., and Casady, C.B., 2024. What triggers public-private partnership (PPP) renegotiations in the United States? *Public Management Review*, 26(6), pp. 1583–1609.

Greve, C. and G. Hodge., 2010. Public-private partnerships and public governance challenges. In *New Public Governance?: Emerging Perspectives on the Theory and Practice of Public Governance*, edited by S. P. Osborne, pp. 149–162. Abingdon: Routledge.

Grimsey, D. and Lewis, M., 2007. Public private partnerships and public procurement. *Agenda: A Journal of Policy Analysis and Reform*, 14(2), pp. 171–188.

Grimsey, D. and Lewis, M.K., 2005, December. Are public private partnerships value for money?: Evaluating alternative approaches and comparing academic and practitioner views. *Accounting Forum*, 29(4), pp. 345–378.

Guasch, J. L., Laffont, J.-J., and Straub, S., 2008. Renegotiation of concession contracts in Latin America: Evidence from the water and transport sectors. *International Journal of Industrial Organization*, 26(2), pp. 421–442.

Henisz, W.J., Levitt, R.E., and Scott, W.R., 2012. Toward a unified theory of project governance: Economic, sociological and psychological supports for relational contracting. *Engineering Project Organization Journal*, 2(1–2), pp. 37–55.

Hult, K.M. and. Walcott, C.E., 1990. *Governing Public Organizations: Politics, Structures, and Institutional Design*. Pacific Grove, CA: Brooks/Cole Pub.

Johnston, J. and Gudergan, S.P., 2007. Governance of public—Private partnerships: Lessons learnt from an Australian case?. *International Review of Administrative Sciences*, 73(4), pp. 569–582.

Jooste, S.F. and Richard Scott, W., 2012. The public–private partnership enabling field: Evidence from three cases. *Administration & Society*, 44(2), pp. 149–182. doi:10.1177/0095399711413868

Klein, M., So, J., and Shin, B., 1996. Transaction costs in private infrastructure projects – are they too high? In *Public Policy for the Private Sector*, note no. 95. Washington, DC: World Bank.

Klijn, E.H. and Koppenjan, J., 2016. The impact of contract characteristics on the performance of public–private partnerships (PPPs). *Public Money & Management*, 36(6), pp. 455–462.

Kolpakov, A. and Anguelov, L.G., 2018. Decision-making approaches to contracting out. *Journal of Strategic Contracting and Negotiation*, 4(3), pp. 148–166.

Levitt, R.E., Ashley, D.B., and Logcher, R.D., 1980. Allocating risk and incentive in construction. *Journal of the Construction Division*, 106(3), pp. 297–305.

Li, J., Liu, B., Wang, D., and Casady, C.B. 2024. The effects of contractual and relational governance on public-private partnership sustainability. Public Administration.

Lonsdale, J., 2000. Developments in value-for-money audit methods: Impacts and implications. *International Review of Administrative Sciences*, 66(1), pp. 73–89.

Moore, M.A. and Vining, A.R., 2023. PPP performance evaluation: the social welfare goal, principal–agent theory and political economy. *Policy Sciences*, 56(2), pp. 267–299.

Morallos, D. and Amekudzi, A., 2008. The state of the practice of value for money analysis in comparing public private partnerships to traditional procurements. *Public Works Management & Policy*, 13(2), pp. 114–125.

National Audit Office (NAO). 2003. PFI: Construction performance, report by the comptroller and auditor general. London: HMSO.

Palcic, D., Reeves, E., Flannery, D., and Geddes, R.R., 2022. Public-private partnership tendering periods: An international comparative analysis. *Journal of Economic Policy Reform*, 25(2), pp. 156–172.

Petersen, O. H., 2019. Evaluating the costs, quality, and value for money of infrastructure public-private partnerships: a systematic literature review. *Annals of Public and Cooperative Economics*, 90(2), pp. 227–244.

Quayle, A., 2021. The infrastructure king and the PPP tunnel. *Accounting, Auditing & Accountability Journal*, 34(1), pp. 246–251.

Reeves, E., Palcic, D., and Flannery, D., 2015. PPP procurement in Ireland: An analysis of tendering periods. *Local Government Studies*, 41(3), pp. 379–400.

Reeves, E., Palcic, D., Flannery, D., and Geddes, R. R., 2017. The determinants of tendering periods for PPP procurement in the UK: An empirical analysis. *Applied Economics*, 49(11), pp. 1071–1082.

Rwelamila, P.D., Fewings, P., and Henjewele, C., 2015. Addressing the missing link in PPP projects: What constitutes the public?. *Journal of Management in Engineering*, 31(5), p. 04014085.

Sanchez Solino, A. and Gago de Santos, P., 2010. Transaction costs in transport public-private partnerships: Comparing procurement procedures. *Transport Reviews*, 30(3), pp. 389–406.

Shaoul, J., Stafford, A., and Stapleton, P., 2012. Accountability and corporate governance of public private partnerships. *Critical Perspectives on Accounting*, 23(3), pp. 213–229.

Sherratt, F., Sherratt, S., and Ivory, C., 2020. Challenging complacency in construction management research: The case of PPPs. *Construction Management and Economics*, 38(12), pp. 1086–1100.

Soomro, M.A. and Zhang, X., 2016. Evaluation of the functions of public sector partners in transportation public-private partnerships failures. *Journal of Management in Engineering*, 32(1), p. 04015027.

Tallaki, M. and Bracci, E., 2021. Risk allocation, transfer and management in public–private partnership and private finance initiatives: A systematic literature review. *International Journal of Public Sector Management*, 34(7), pp. 709–731.

Teisman, G. R. and Klijn, E., 2002. Partnership arrangements: Governmental rhetoric or governance scheme? *Public Administration Review* 62(2), pp. 197–205.
Tvarnø, C.D., 2006. Denmark: Public-private partnerships from a Danish perspective. *Public Procurement Law Review*, 15, pp. 98–108.
Välilä, T., 2005. How expensive are cost savings? On the economics of public-private partnerships. *EIB Papers*, 10(1), pp. 95–119.
van den Hurk, M. and Verhoest, K., 2016. The challenge of using standard contracts in public–private partnerships. *Public Management Review*, 18(2), pp. 278–299.
Vecchi, V., Cusumano, N., Casady, C.B., Gatti, S., and Borgonovo, E., 2022. Addressing adverse selection in public-private partnership (PPP) procurement: An agent-based approach. *Public Works Management & Policy*, 27(4), pp. 371–395.
Verweij, S. van Meerkerk, I., and Casady, C.B. (Eds.) 2022a. *Assessing the Performance Advantage of Public Private Partnerships: A Comparative Perspective*. Cheltenham: Edward Elgar Publishing.
Verweij, S., van Meerkerk, I., and Casady, C.B. 2022b. The performance advantage of public-private partnerships: does it exist or not? In *Assessing the Performance Advantage of Public-Private Partnerships: A Comparative Perspective*, edited by S. Verweij, I. van Meerkerk, and C. B. Casady, pp.1–26. Cheltenham: Edward Elgar.

## *Case Study: The Riverbend Stormwater Management Project (Developed by Carter B. Casady, Thomas Sherman, and Benjamin M. Brunjes)*

### Case Details

The Riverbend Metropolitan Region is experiencing rapid urbanization, leading to significant challenges in managing stormwater runoff. Increased impermeable surfaces, such as roads and buildings, have caused frequent flooding, water quality degradation, and ecological disruption in the nearby Riverbend Basin. To address these issues, the regional government proposed the Riverbend Stormwater Management Project, a multi-phase infrastructure initiative aimed at controlling runoff, improving water quality, and restoring the community's ecosystem.

The project includes the construction of green infrastructure, such as retention basins, bioswales, and permeable pavements, alongside traditional gray infrastructure like culverts and drainage systems. Given the scale and complexity of the initiative, traditional public procurement approaches faced criticism for delays, cost overruns, and piecemeal implementation. Instead, the regional government decided to explore a public–private partnership (PPP) model to integrate planning, construction, and maintenance under a single contract.

A private consortium, StormTech Solutions, submitted a proposal for a Design-Build-Finance-Operate-Maintain (DBFOM) contract. The proposal promised innovative stormwater management techniques, including smart sensors to monitor runoff and AI-driven water flow optimization. The consortium also pledged to use sustainable materials and align the project with regional climate resilience goals.

While the PPP model offered potential benefits, such as transferring risks and leveraging private sector expertise, public opposition emerged. Environmental groups expressed concerns about the transparency of the contract and the potential for private profit to outweigh public interest. Local contractors worried they would be excluded from the bidding process, and some residents feared increased stormwater fees. Additionally, during negotiations, disagreements arose over risk allocation, particularly around long-term maintenance responsibilities and performance metrics.

After months of deliberation, the regional government approved the PPP contract with StormTech Solutions, including specific performance-based incentives and penalties to ensure accountability. Construction is set to begin, but the project remains under intense scrutiny. Policymakers and practitioners alike are watching Riverbend to see whether the PPP model can deliver on its promise of innovation, efficiency, and public value in stormwater management.

**Discussion Questions**

*Analyzing the PPP Model*

- What are the primary advantages and disadvantages of using a PPP model for the Riverbend Stormwater Management Project?
- How does the DBFOM structure address or fail to address the challenges of traditional procurement in this context?

*Risk Allocation*

- What risks are being transferred to the private partner, and which risks remain with the public sector? Are these allocations appropriate?
- How could disagreements over long-term maintenance responsibilities have been mitigated during contract negotiations?

*Stakeholder Management*

- How should the regional government engage stakeholders, including environmental groups, local contractors, and residents, to build trust and support for the project?
- What strategies can be implemented to ensure transparency and public accountability throughout the project lifecycle?

*Performance and Sustainability:*

- How can performance metrics be designed to balance private sector profitability with public interest and sustainability goals?
- What innovative solutions or technologies could further enhance the project's outcomes?

# 8 Public Procurement Strategy

*Helen Walker and Anthony Flynn*

## 8.1 Introduction

In common parlance, a strategy is understood as a plan intended to achieve a set of objectives. We all follow strategies, consciously or otherwise, in our professional and personal lives. We may have a strategy for getting fit, finding a new home or raising our kids. Academics have defined strategy as a particular course of action that a firm takes over the long-term, which is aimed at delivering a competitive advantage against their rivals (Mintzberg, 1978; Porter, 1979). Strategy implies several things here: a plan of action, mobilisation of resources, goal orientation, and a long-term perspective. Originally associated with military planning, strategy has become central to studying organisations over the last half century. Strategy is not only about organisations, however. We can also examine strategy in relation to supply chains, for instance, or how a country tries to co-ordinate areas like enterprise development, healthcare provision, or the procurement of products and services.

Turning to our topic of interest, what does strategy mean in a public procurement context? Essentially, it is about managing public procurement over the long-term to achieve desired outcomes. At this juncture, we need to define public procurement. Public procurement is the process by which public-sector organisations purchase products and services or commission infrastructural works (including construction, repair, and maintenance) from external third parties (OECD, 2023). A public procurement strategy, therefore, is a long-term plan of action for how public-sector organisations secure supplies from the marketplace with a particular set of outcomes in mind. What outcomes are we talking about here? Well, firstly public-sector organisations want to acquire the right products and services on the most favourable economic terms. Thereafter, they might want to purchase goods and services in a way that supports small- and medium-sized enterprise (SME) suppliers, protects the natural environment, promotes diversity, equity, and inclusion (DEI) throughout society, and encourages suppliers to be innovative in proposing solutions to public-sector challenges.

Discussing procurement alongside strategy is a relatively recent trend among academics and practitioners. Procurement traditionally had low status in the organisational hierarchy and was not recognised as a value-creating function (Reck and Long, 1988; Ellram and Carr, 1994). Instead, it was seen as a back-office, administrative function and of lesser value than marketing, sales, finance, and product design. While this is still the case in some organisations, there is acceptance in theory and industry practice that the procurement function can boost economic, social, and environmental performance (Glas et al., 2018; Guarnieri et al., 2019). This is what people mean when they say that procurement is "strategic". In order for procurement to be "strategic", firms must have a plan or "strategy" that guides their actions towards the achievement of performance outcomes over the long-term. Of course, not every act of public purchasing is strategic. Non-critical items like office

DOI: 10.4324/9781003566670-10

stationery and cleaning supplies can be purchased in a routinised, automated way. The chapter will elaborate on this point in the Supply Strategy section.

As with private-sector organisations, it is now expected that public-sector organisations will have a procurement strategy. Procurement strategies are not only used to guide organisational action but also to signal to stakeholders like suppliers, taxpayers, and elected officials how procurement will be managed. For procurement to be strategic, it must support and be consistent with organisational objectives. An example is procurement supporting the delivery of essential local authority services like waste collection and water treatment to residents in a convenient, cost effective, and environmentally friendly way. Policies are often adopted to help execute procurement strategies. Typical public procurement policies include the requirement for procurers to obtain at least three quotations from suppliers to ensure value for money (VfM), a desire to partner with local suppliers, and only purchasing electrical appliances that meet minimum energy efficiency standards.

When discussing public procurement strategies, it is important to be aware that what happens at organisational level is heavily influenced by what happens at national or international level. In most countries, the central government sets out a strategic direction for public procurement in terms of its aims and objectives. Individual public-sector organisations like local authorities, universities, and hospitals formulate their procurement strategies within this context. For instance, the EU encourages public-sector organisations throughout its 27 Member States to "buy green" and "buy social" (European Commission, 2016, 2021). In other words, it wants to see public procurement used to help mitigate climate change and promote social inclusion. Many public-sector organisations have incorporated these concerns into their procurement strategies and everyday practices. We see this when organisations opt for energy from renewable sources, purchase products made from recycled materials, and award contracts to not-for-profit suppliers who employ disabled workers, among other initiatives.

*Question for reflection: Can you think of any other ways in which public procurement can be used to help mitigate climate change and promote social inclusion?*

The chapter proceeds as follows. The next section elaborates on key concepts from strategy and public procurement. The aim is to give readers further insight into public procurement strategies and how thinking on them has evolved. Thereafter, it looks at emerging issues in public procurement such as goal conflict, e.g., minimising upfront purchase costs versus buying "green" products, professionalisation, and technological change. Here readers are encouraged to critically reflect on what these issues mean for public procurement strategies. The following section addresses five factors that managers and policy makers should consider when creating a new public procurement strategy. The chapter concludes with a mini case study that highlights poor practice in public procurement in the UK in the 2000s and what changes were made to transform it into something more strategic and value-adding.

## 8.2 Summary of the Literature

Distinctions can be made between strategy, supply strategy, and public procurement strategy, as well as what strategy means in the public sector versus the private sector. We set out these distinctions in Figure 8.1, where we show strategy in the public and private sectors side by side. In the public sector, at the top are the overarching (inter)national strategies and policies set by government(s). Below them, each public-sector organisation will develop its own strategy. On the bottom row, each organisation may develop public

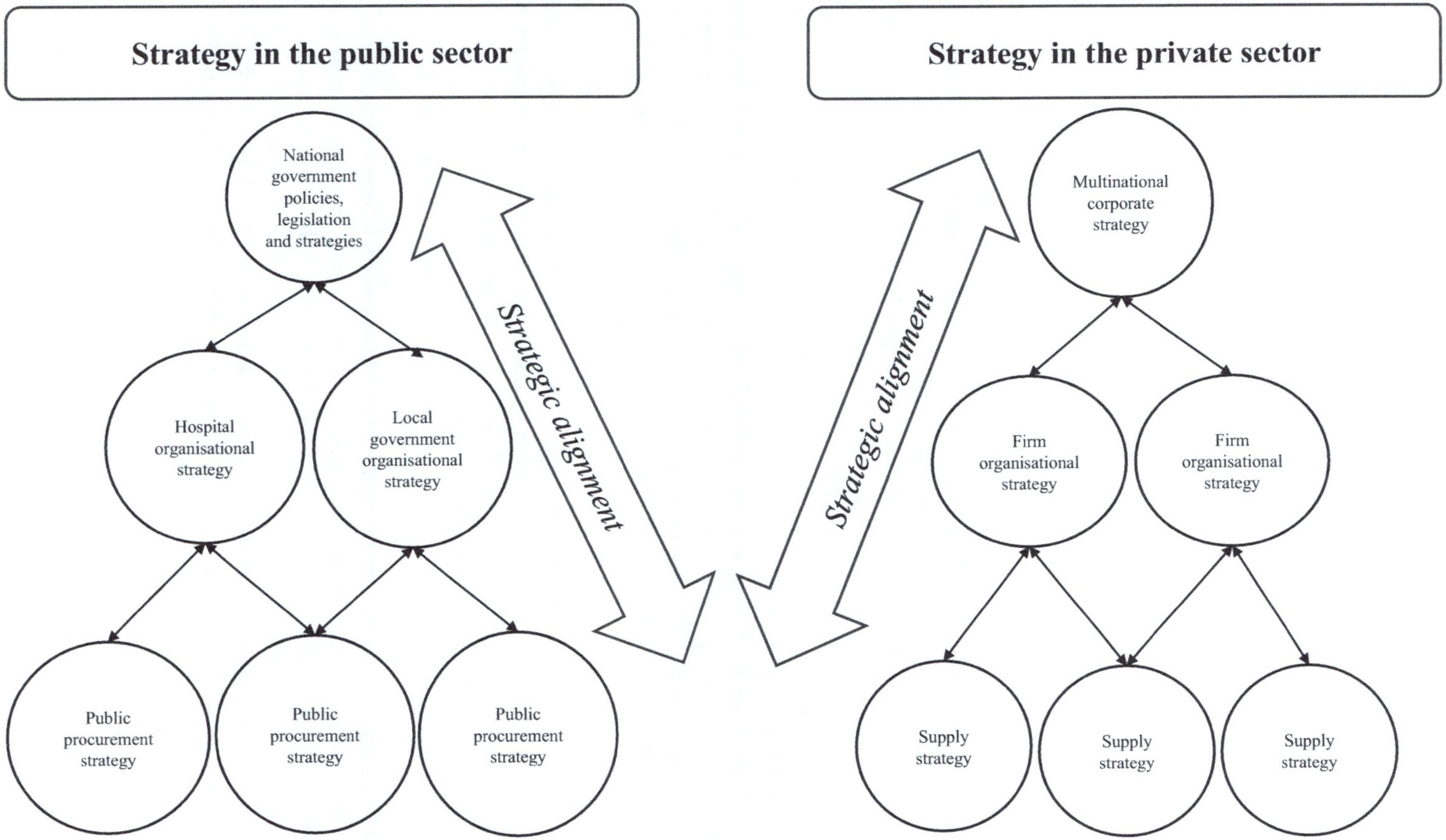


*Figure 8.1* Distinguishing between overarching strategy, organisational strategy, supply strategy and public procurement strategy in the public and private sectors.

*Source*: Original creation.

procurement strategies. In the private sector, there might be an overarching strategy of a multi-national corporation. Below that, each firm will develop a corporate strategy. Below that, firms may develop supply strategies. These strategies at the bottom level are called procurement strategy in the public sector, and supply strategy in the private sector, but these terms essentially mean the same things, which is securing products and services from external providers. Of course, how the public and private sectors manage this process is different. In both sectoral contexts, there is ideally strategic alignment between strategies at different levels. We discuss these different sorts of strategies in the literature reviewed below.

### *8.2.1 Strategy*

Strategy grew as an area of management and business practice and research in the 1970s, focusing on how private firms can develop business strategies to achieve competitive advantage. It has been variously defined by key authors in the business field. Mintzberg (1978) defines a strategy as "a pattern in a stream of decisions" (p. 934) and distinguished between intended strategies, i.e., what the firm sets out to achieve and realised strategies, i.e., what the firm actually achieves. Mintzberg and Waters (1985) later differentiated between planned and emergent strategies. Planned strategies make sense when there is a high degree of stability and predictability in an organisation's operating environment. Planned strategies make less sense in dynamic environments where there is instability and unpredictable events. In such circumstances, organisations rely on emergent strategies that adjust to changes in the marketplace and wider society (Mintzberg and Waters, 1985).

Taking a different angle, Porter suggested that "the essence of strategy formulation is coping with competition" (p. 137) (Porter, 1979) and included the bargaining power of buyers and suppliers in the five forces that influence competition and shape a business strategy (Porter, 1980). This was one of the earliest acknowledgments in the mainstream business literature of the importance of the buyer and supplier context in influencing strategy. Porter (1985) subsequently went on to delineate three generic corporate strategies, which are (i) cost leadership, (ii) differentiation based on quality, innovation, or brand, and (iii) a focus on niche markets. Other authors have described business strategies to achieve competitive advantage in terms of the core competences of the firm (Prahalad & Hamel, 1990), the dynamic capabilities of the firm to respond to a changing environment (Teece, Pisano, & Shuen, 1997), and the unique resources available to a firm (Barney, 1991).

The term "strategic alignment" refers to aligning a firm's overarching strategy or mission with other internal strategies or objectives, such as a firm's supply strategy (Cousins, 2005) or environmental strategy (Wu, Wu, Chen, & Goh, 2014). The different levels and functions of the organisation must be synchronised, reinforce one another, and be coherent if the strategy is to be successful. A mismatch between a firm's corporate-level strategy and its business unit or functional strategies would lead to a dysfunctional organisation and a reduction in performance. Strategic alignment can also mean aligning a firm's strategy with external or environmental factors such as supply chain structures (Stavrulaki & Davis, 2010), product uncertainties (Lee, 2002), and the marketing strategies of supply chain partners (Green, Whitten, & Inman, 2012). Organisations should therefore be mindful of external as well as internal fit when formulating their strategic plans. An organisational strategy that is inconsistent with the actions of its commercial partners and stakeholders will be ineffective.

### *8.2.2 Supply Strategy*

Supply strategy, which has tended to focus on the private sector, has been described as "how organisations arrange and conduct themselves within modern economic environments, in order to satisfy markets in the long and short terms" (Harland, Lamming, & Cousins, 1999). We add to this by stating that it involves organisations planning their approach to engaging with the supply marketplace, managing supplier relationships and securing inputs, products, and supplies necessary for them to operate as a commercial entity. There is both an external and internal aspect to supply strategy. As well as engaging with the external supply marketplace, organisations should liaise with their own internal departments to match their needs with supplier capabilities. As per Porter's (1985) generic types, supply strategies can aim for cost leadership through relentless focus on minimising the price paid for products and services. Alternatively, supply strategies can aim for differentiation by emphasising attributes like quality or innovation when deciding what to buy and whom to buy from.

Authors have focused on different issues in discussing supply strategies to achieve competitive advantage. Kraljic wrote an influential article on how purchasing must become supply management and suggested different supply strategies depending on the extent to which products or services impact on profit and represent a supply risk (Kraljic, 1983). To illustrate, the supply strategy for low profit impact, low risk products should prioritise efficient and automated purchasing processes, not unlike the cost leadership approach. Here we could be talking about products like stationery or catering supplies. By contrast, the supply strategy for high-profit impact, high-risk products should prioritise long-term partnerships between buying and supplying firms, which is similar to the differentiation approach. Here we could be talking about the development of a new IT system or the design and development of an electric battery for a car brand. The key point is that the different categories of products and services a firm needs from the marketplace may require different sourcing strategies (Figure 8.2).

*Question for reflection: Taking an industry with which you are familiar, can you identify products/services that firms typically buy that are (i) low profit impact and low supply risk and (ii) high-profit impact and high risk?*

Along similar lines to Kraljic (1983), several authors have developed typologies to help practitioners identify appropriate supply strategies, often simplifying the choices to two supply chain dimensions (Figure 8.2). Fisher (1997) asked what is the right supply chain for your product, distinguishing between functional and innovative products, and efficient and responsive supply chains. Lee (2002) suggested that choosing the appropriate supply strategy depends on supply uncertainty (stable or evolving) and demand uncertainty (functional or innovative products). For example, a product with a stable demand and a reliable source of supply does not need the same amount of time or effort as one with a highly unpredictable demand and an unreliable source of supply. Even in recent years, studies have debated and adapted Kraljic's portfolio model, showing its enduring influence upon supply strategy (Corsini, De Bernardi, Gusmerotti, & Frey, 2024).

### *8.2.3 Public Procurement Strategy*

The public and private sectors differ in strategy conceptualisation and strategic alignment (Hawkins, Gravier, & Powley, 2011; Patrucco, Moretto, Ronchi, & Luzzini, 2019).

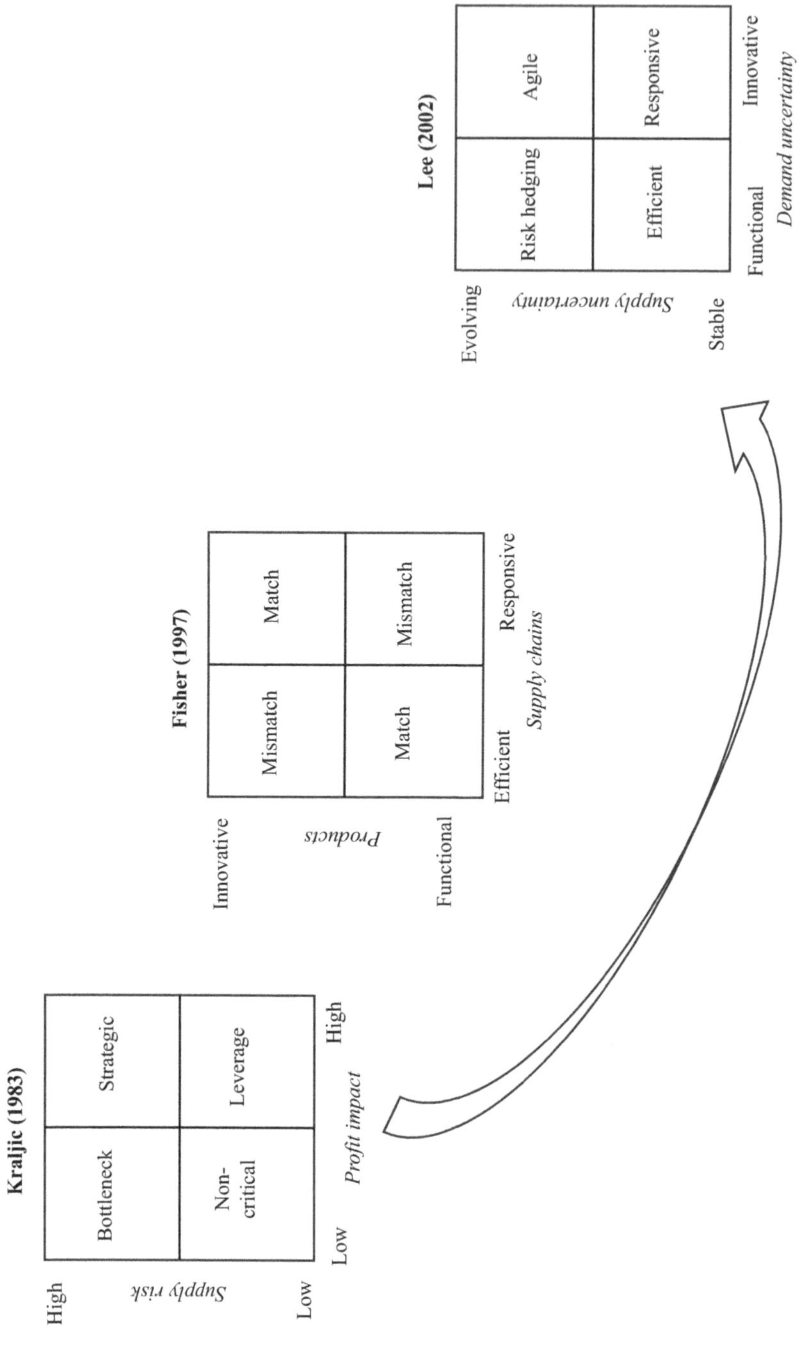


*Figure 8.2* Kraljic's portfolio model for supply strategy, and some examples of variations on the 2×2 model.
*Source:* Original creation.

Private-sector firms often see strategy formulation as a means of achieving competitive advantage, looking at ways to differentiate the firm from its competitors and maximise profit for shareholders, increase market share, or improve customer satisfaction, amongst other goals (Porter, 1979, 1985). Public-sector organisations, by contrast, have a broader remit, as they do not answer to shareholders, but act in the interests of citizens, taxpayers, society, and the environment. Furthermore, public-sector organisations do not exist to make a profit. Strategic management for them is not about competitive advantage in the marketplace. Remember, public-sector organisations do not have competitors. Instead, their priority is to deliver public and social services within budget while trying to support societal wellbeing. It is important to remember that the public sector is not a homogeneous entity. It contains many different types of organisations, including local government authorities, hospitals, schools, universities, utility and transport companies, central government departments, state agencies, defence agencies, and others besides. Strategic procurement will mean something different depending on the type of the public-sector organisation in question.

How governments spend money on goods and services can have a significant strategic impact. Public procurement represents, on average, 12 per cent of GDP and 29 per cent of government expenditure in OECD member countries (OECD, 2023). To put these percentages in perspective, the UK spends approximately £250 billion per annum buying goods and services. The corresponding figures for the US and the European Union are $1800 billion and €2 trillion, respectively. Identifying cost saving opportunities in public procurement is a direct and uncontroversial way for governments to control expenditure and free up money for investment elsewhere. Not surprisingly, public procurement strategies almost always involve obtaining VfM from the supply marketplace irrespective of country or context. India's General Financial Rules oblige public-sector organisations to strive for efficiency and economy when buying products and services (Government of India, 2017), while recent public procurement reforms instituted in the UK and South Africa cite VfM as an overriding priority for government authorities (UK Government, 2022; South African Government, 2023).

A second strategic aspect of government procurement relates to service provision. Decisions taken by public buyers over what to buy and who to buy from have a direct bearing on the quality and effectiveness of public service delivery, end-users' experiences of these services, and even the terms and conditions of those working in public-sector supply chains (Jaehrling, 2015). The trend across developed countries has been to outsource public and social services in areas like transport, social care, waste collection, and criminal justice. This elevates the strategic importance of public procurement because it assumes increased responsibility for service delivery. It also means that public procurement accounts for a higher percentage of total government spend. As such, how external service providers are selected, what they are asked to do, and the way in which the relationship between them and the public-sector organisation is managed has wide ranging economic, environmental, and societal implications, especially for high-profit impact, high-risk supply requirements.

As well as financial considerations and service quality, another strategic aspect of public procurement relates to the pursuit of socio-economic and environmental outcomes. Governments are increasingly interested in how they can leverage public procurement spending in such ways. What does this mean in practice? For a start, it means directing business opportunities towards SMEs and start-up firms to help them grow, professionalise, and create more jobs (Flynn, 2018). SMEs are under-represented as public-sector suppliers in many countries, which is not a good outcome for SMEs, public-sector organisations, or the economy. It also means designing public contract competitions in ways that allow suppliers to propose innovative solutions to public-sector challenges (Uyarra & Flanagan, 2010). Doing so not only enhances the quality of public services and saves money but also encourages innovation by industry.

Notably, the European Commission sees strategic public procurement as comprising three pillars: environmental protection, social justice, and innovation. Essentially, governments want to use their procurement budgets, which are sizeable, to support objectives like reducing social inequality and transitioning to net zero carbon emissions. Viewed in this way, public procurement is a tool that governments can use to address contemporary challenges. Examples can be found of construction contracts that require firms to create apprenticeships for school leavers as part of the terms and conditions (McCrudden, 2004; Wontner, Walker, Harris, & Lynch, 2020), while some countries, e.g., the US, Canada, Australia, and South Africa, reserve a proportion of public contracts for ethnic minority or indigenous owned firms (see, for example, South Africa Government, 2023). In an environmental sense, we see the strategic use of public procurement when public-sector organisations purchase electric vehicles, e.g., buses, vans to minimise their carbon footprint, source organic or locally produced food, and use "green" energy sources.

As noted in the Introduction, public procurement strategy can be formulated at international, national, regional/state/province, local, and organisational levels. Table 8.1 shows a range of public procurement strategies from these different levels. There are similarities between public procurement objectives at different levels, with phrases such as "value for money", "efficiency", and "open competition" occurring frequently. However, some differences are also apparent. Broadly speaking, the higher the level, the more likely that the strategies will focus on outcomes such as fostering competition in the supply marketplace, achieving VfM, and maintaining regulatory compliance. Public procurement strategies at lower levels are more concerned with how purchasing decisions affect local communities, SMEs, and service users. Sometimes strategies at different levels are in alignment, and sometimes they are in tension. We will discuss these tensions in the Emerging Issues section further on in the chapter.

#### *8.2.4 Public Procurement Strategy Research: Adopting Different Theories*

Academic studies of public procurement strategy have been growing over the years, and below we consider how scholars have approached framing and understanding it better. Researchers have used different theories to investigate the factors that affect public procurement strategy. Theories provide a lens to look at something and help make sense of it. Theories often have their origins in different disciplines, and the original authors may have proposed the theory many years ago (e.g., The economist Ronald Coase put forward his theory of transaction cost economics in 1937, see Table 8.2). Such "classic" theories have an enduring interest for researchers, as they can often be helpful in shedding light on the factors that influence organisations, and have been adopted in many research studies in the purchasing and supply field (Walker, Chicksand, Radnor, & Watson, 2015).

Table 8.2 focuses on two example disciplines, Economics and Strategic Management. These disciplines traditionally explore the economic and market forces that affect private sector organisations. However, some "classic" theories from these disciplines have been applied in public procurement research. In Table 8.2, we illustrate this by giving the discipline, the original authors of the theory, providing an example of how the theory might give insights into how public-sector organisations procure from suppliers and include some example studies that apply the theory in a public procurement context. For example, institutional theory has its origins in the Strategic Management discipline and was developed

*Table 8.1* Examples of public procurement strategies at different levels

| *Level* | *Example organisation and link* | *Example quote* | *Objectives* |
|---|---|---|---|
| International | World Trade Organisation<br>WTO I What is the WTO? – What we do | "The WTO agreements e.g., Government Procurement Agreement (GPA) cover goods, services and intellectual property. They include… individual countries' commitments to lower customs tariffs and other trade barriers, and to open and keep open services markets". | Open markets |
| | United Nations Development Business, Africa<br>A call for African businesses to join global public procurement market I Africa Renewal (un.org) | "The (UNDB) platform supports transparent and inclusive public procurement… aiming to encourage women-owned businesses to engage in international development projects. For small and medium-sized enterprises, UNDB keeps them apprised of any sub-contracting opportunities". | Transparency<br>Inclusivity<br>Women-owned businesses<br>SMEs |
| International Regional | European Union<br>Public tenders and contracts I European Union (europa.eu) | "EU law sets out minimum public procurement rules to safeguard the core principles of transparency, equal treatment, open competition, and sound procedural management. This creates a competitive, open and well-regulated procurement market to support growth in jobs and investments in the EU". | Transparency<br>Equal treatment<br>Open competition<br>Open markets |
| | International Development Bank<br>IDB I IDB approves the use of public procurement systems in eight Latin American and Caribbean Countries (iadb.org) | "IDB approves the use of public procurement systems in eight Latin American and Caribbean Countries… The impact of these efforts… include(es) market access .. and reducing transaction costs". | Open markets<br>Transaction costs |
| National | UK Government<br>The Procurement Act – a summary guide to the provisions – GOV. UK (www.gov.uk) | "The reforms … will place value for money, public benefit, transparency and integrity at the heart of our procurement system; they will modernise and unify our systems and processes; and they will get tough on the poor performers and fraudsters". | Value for money<br>Public benefit<br>Transparency<br>Integrity<br>Procedures |

(*Continued*)

*Table 8.1* (Continued)

| *Level* | *Example organisation and link* | *Example quote* | *Objectives* |
|---|---|---|---|
| | Ministry of Finance, South Africa Government | The new Public Procurement Act introduces uniform norms and standards for all procuring institutions to implement, which cover value for money, ethical conduct, efficient processes, dispute resolution, economic development, etcetera. It also creates a preferential procurement framework to support certain enterprise categories. | Value for money<br>Ethical conduct<br>Efficient process<br>Economic development<br>Preferential programmes |
| Federal | Office of Federal Procurement Policy, USA<br>The Office of Federal Procurement Policy I OMB I The White House | "The Office of Federal Procurement Policy (OFPP)… provides overall direction for government-wide procurement policies, regulations and procedures and to promote economy, efficiency, and effectiveness in acquisition processes". (NB: Affirmative action for disabled ex-service personnel, women-owned firms and ethnic minority-owned firms are federal goals and apply to federal contracts. Each US state has its own set of procurement policies underneath these federal goals.) | Economy<br>Efficiency<br>Effectiveness<br>Procedures<br>Affirmative action |
| | Federal Public Policy and Support Service, Belgium<br>BOSA–eProcurement (publicprocurement.be) | "Our e-procurement platform, provided by the Federal Public Policy and Support Service, is designed to make public procurement in Belgium more efficient, transparent and accessible to all". | Efficiency<br>Transparency<br>Accessible to all |
| Regional/State/Province | Northern Ireland<br>NI Public Procurement Policy document (finance-ni.gov.uk) | "Here are 12 guiding principles to govern the administration of public procurement: Accountability, Competitive Supply, Consistency, Effectiveness, Efficiency, Fair-dealing, Integration, Integrity, Informed Decision-making, Legality, Responsiveness, Transparency". | Accountability<br>Efficiency<br>Effectiveness<br>Fair dealing<br>Transparency etc. |
| | Procurement Division, Department of General Services, California Government, USA<br>About Procurement (ca.gov) | "The Procurement Division (PD) … sponsors the Small Business Council; participates in the Disabled Veterans Business Enterprise Council; and provides innovative purchasing methods that save taxpayers' dollars, integrating quality solutions to meet customers' needs". | SMEs, disabled veterans<br>Innovation<br>Value for money<br>Effectiveness |

*Table 8.1* (Continued)

| *Level* | *Example organisation and link* | *Example quote* | *Objectives* |
|---|---|---|---|
| Local | City of Melbourne Procurement Policy (melbourne.vic.gov.au) | "The policy enables Council and Council employees to:<br>• Meet legislative requirements enables compliance with the Act.<br>• Deliver best value outcomes effectively procuring items while delivering best value to the Council and benefits to the municipal community.<br>• Ensure ethical conduct, accountability and transparency procurement must be conducted ethically and to the highest standard of integrity.<br>• Manage risk management factors and ensure continuity of supply appropriate risk management must be considered to ensure continuity of supply of goods and services to Council". | Legislation<br>Value for money<br>Community benefits<br>Ethical<br>Accountable<br>Transparency<br>Integrity<br>Risk management |
| | East of England NHS Collaborative Procurement Hub, UK (eoecph.nhs.uk) | "Our aim is to help members to reduce risk whilst improving the quality and efficiency of patient care and driving healthcare innovation. The Hub assists members to … deliver cash-releasing savings and added-value benefits that can be seen throughout entire organisations". | Innovation<br>Service delivery<br>Risk management<br>Value of money |
| Organisational | United Nations Procurement Division<br>About the UN Procurement Division (UNPD) \| UN Procurement Division | "The Procurement Division … provides responsive, effective, and quality procurement services …, while achieving best value for money and ensuring a competitive, fair and transparent process in accordance with established regulations, rules and procedures". | Value for money competitive fair<br>Transparent procedures |
| | Paris 2024, Olympic Games, France<br>Innovating to purchase for a purpose – Paris 2024 | "we (have) … five commitments namely reducing carbon impacts, spurring the circular economy, working with social enterprises, integrating the long-term unemployed and people with disabilities, and creating value in local areas by encouraging small and large businesses to join forces in consortiums". | Carbon impacts<br>Circular economy<br>Social enterprises<br>Long-term unemployed<br>SMEs |

Source: Original creation.

*Table 8.2* Different theories adopted to investigate public procurement

| *Discipline origins* | *Classic theory* | *Original authors* | *What the theory might tell us in a public procurement context* | *Example studies* |
|---|---|---|---|---|
| Economics | Transaction cost economics theory | Coase (1937) | Public-sector organisations try to minimise transaction costs with their suppliers | Abutabenjeh et al. (2023), Rodrigues and Reis (2023), and Rokkan and Haugland (2022) |
| | Principal-agent theory/Agency theory | Jensen and Meckling (1976) | Public-sector organisations (principal) rely on suppliers (agent) to deliver services | Kauppi and van Raaij (2015) and Wang et al. (2020) |
| | Resource based view theory | Barney (1991) | Public-sector resources, whether internal e.g., procurement expertise or external e.g., supplier capabilities can enhance organisational performance | Flynn (2017) |
| | Dynamic capabilities theory | Teece et al. (1997) | Public-sector organisations need to develop capabilities to adapt to changing supply environments | Akenroye et al. (2020) |
| Strategic Management | Stakeholder theory | Freeman (1984) | Public-sector organisations need to take account of different stakeholder interests (their own, suppliers, end users, politicians, taxpayers etc.) | Johnson and Klassen (2022) and Rodrigues and Reis (2023) |
| | Resource dependency theory | Pfeffer and Salancik (2003) | Public-sector organisations depend on suppliers for essential resources within reciprocal relationships | Genovese et al. (2022) and Wontner et al. (2020) |
| | Institutional theory | DiMaggio and Powell (1983) | Institutional forces (e.g., from government) shape how public-sector organisations approach public procurement strategy | Meehan et al. (2016) and Raj et al. (2020) |

*Source*: Original creation.

originally for a private-sector setting. It considers the institutional pressures acting on organisations (DiMaggio & Powell, 1983). These pressures are termed mimetic (e.g., pressure to "mimic" other organisations), coercive (e.g., pressure to follow legislation), and normative (e.g., pressure from professional bodies). Researchers in public-sector settings have often considered how national government exerts coercive pressure on public-sector organisations through policies and legislation, and which has an influence on their procurement strategies.

Whilst different theories from different disciplines have been adopted to conduct research in public procurement (Flynn & Davies, 2014; Koala & Steinfeld, 2018), there is not one particular theory that stands out or dominates. However, it seems certain that researchers will continue to adopt classic theories or develop conceptual models (like Kraljic, 1983), because such advances help to make sense of the factors that affect public procurement strategy.

## 8.3 Emerging Issues

There are several emerging issues around public procurement strategy. We focus on three of the main ones in this section of the chapter. They are (i) strategic tensions between different procurement objectives, (ii) human capital for procurement, and (iii) technology in the management of procurement.

### *8.3.1 Strategic Tensions*

Achieving VfM is not always compatible with socio-economic and environmental objectives in public procurement. VfM is interpreted in practice as achieving the best price for the products and services required by an organisation (Loader, 2013). However, pursuing socio-economic and environmental objectives may result in organisations having to incur a price premium. The upfront purchase price of electric vehicles used for public transport is greater than petrol or diesel engine vehicles despite their environmental benefits. Likewise, purchasing Fair Trade products will be more expensive than purchasing products that are not certified according to international labour and human rights standards. As another example, expecting contractors to create apprenticeships for school leavers will invariably add to the final cost of the project. The essential point is that trade-offs may have to be made between cost savings and sustainability-related outcomes in public procurement. One solution is for the public sector to take a longer-term view of VfM if it is serious about using procurement to achieve social and environmental outcomes. This is easier said than done if public finances are constrained and public-sector organisations are under pressure to identify cost savings in the short-term.

There are also tensions between public procurement strategies at different levels. Table 8.1 explained how international accords on public procurement like the WTO's Government Procurement Agreement are designed to foster open competition and end protectionism. However, this is problematic if countries want to use public procurement to favour domestic firms. Tensions also exist between regional and local procurement strategies. Collaborative regional procurement, which involves organisations like universities or local authorities from the same region combining their purchasing requirements to exploit economies of scale, can produce cost savings (Bakker, Walker, Schotanus, & Harland, 2008). However, it may also undermine any attempt to facilitate increased SME participation in public procurement. This is because it creates relatively large contracts that SMEs will find difficult to manage. Thus, collaborative procurement succeeds in achieving one strategic objective of public procurement, i.e., VfM, at the expense of another, i.e., strengthening the SME population (Loader, 2013).

A further tension exists between social inclusion and efficiency in public procurement. In the interests of social inclusion, some countries make special provision for small and/or indigenous suppliers. South Africa's Public Procurement Act 2023 is one such example (South Africa Government, 2023). It stipulates that large public contracts should be divided into lots in the interests of Black-owned SME participation. The upside of dividing contracts into lots is that SMEs are in a position to bid for and win public contracts, which ultimately benefits the domestic economy, diversifies public-sector supply chains, and supports the DEI agenda. The downside is that it can result in inefficiencies. There will be an additional administrative cost to the public sector when a single large contract is divided into multiple smaller contracts. Moreover, setting aside public contracts for disadvantaged groups can mean that the public sector ends up paying more for products and services than it would have done under conditions of open competition.

### *8.3.2 Human Capital*

Besides tensions in public procurement strategies, there are several other emerging issues to consider. One is the human capital that lies behind public procurement. The ultimate success of any organisational strategy depends on the capabilities of those responsible for implementing it. When we talk about strategic public procurement, the assumption is that there are trained professionals capable of achieving VfM while also remaining attentive to social and environmental outcomes. Yet the reality is somewhat different. Public procurement suffers from under-professionalisation, whether measured by staff numbers or qualifications (OECD, 2023). This reduces the probability that it will be managed strategically. In response, some countries have started to prioritise upskilling for public buyers or hire in expertise from the private sector (OECD, 2023). Others are creating specialist category teams to manage public contract competitions on behalf of the entire public sector. The UK has shifted towards this structure over the last decade by creating specialist teams in categories as diverse as IT consumables and legal services. The objective is to maximise VfM, ensure consistency in product and service quality, and align procurement spend with national social and environmental priorities.

### *8.3.3 Technology*

Another emerging issue is technology in the management of procurement. Technology is an enabler of organisational strategies, and public procurement strategies are no exception. In other words, they depend on technology to succeed. Low levels of technology adoption have traditionally characterised the public sector, which is one reason why public procurement was more operational than strategic (McCue and Roman, 2012). However, progress has been made in recent years to exploit technology as part of a strategic approach to public procurement. One area where this is evident is in the migration of public tendering online. Dedicated online sites like the EU's Tenders Electronic Daily (TED) or India's Central Public Procurement Portal allow firms to search and apply for hundreds of thousands of public contracts. From a public-sector perspective, this increases the visibility of available contracts and draws in more bids. More bids, in turn, should translate into better VfM. The digitalisation of procurement introduces administrative efficiencies for both public buyers and suppliers, which is to be welcomed. It also generates data insights, e.g., number of bids received, average bid price, and location of bidders. Public-sector organisations can use this data to set performance targets and shape future procurement strategies.

Looking beyond digitalisation of the procurement process, artificial intelligence (AI) has the potential to transform public procurement. As one example, machine learning (ML) can be used to review vast amounts of historic purchasing data in order to predict future purchasing requirements at organisational level and above. Likewise, natural language processing (NLP) can be used to write contracts or interpret existing contracts, while e-invoicing software is already being used to screen and authorise requests for supplier payments. These AI-assisted developments will, in the first instance, reduce the resources needed to manage public procurement, making it less manual. Freed-up staff could be deployed to value-adding activities like researching new products and services or nurturing relationships with key suppliers. AI-assisted developments will also allow public buyers to make evidence-based decisions on demand forecasting and supplier selection in ways not currently possible. Again, this will support the strategic management of public procurement.

*Question for reflection: Can you think of any other emerging issues of relevance to public procurement besides the three mentioned here?*

## 8.4 Practical Applications

In this section we examine the practical aspects of devising and implementing public procurement strategies. While not an exhaustive treatment, it nonetheless highlights five key considerations for practitioners (see Figure 8.3). These are (i) stakeholder involvement, (ii) strategic alignment, (iii) resource provision, (iv) performance measurement, and (v) resilience.

### *8.4.1 Stakeholder Involvement*

One of the first steps in formulating any strategy is involving stakeholders from inside and outside the organisation. It is recommended that procurement directors communicate with and involve key stakeholders from the outset. The input of internal stakeholders like buyers, end-users, and financial controllers increases the likelihood that the procurement strategy is fit for purpose. For example, buyers will be able to tell management whether there is sufficient supplier capacity to justify a "buy local" strategy for food products; IT staff can advise if it is practical for the organisation to implement e-invoicing as part of a proposed e-procurement strategy, etcetera. Involving internal stakeholders not only leads to informed strategy making. It also secures buy-in from those responsible for strategy implementation on an everyday basis. Many strategies fail because of low buy-in from staff at operational level, as McCue and Roman (2012) showed in the case of digital transitions in public procurement. External stakeholders should also be involved in formulating procurement strategies for the very same reasons, e.g., co-designing social care services alongside health professionals, patients, and the external contractors, as shown in Figure 8.4.

### *8.4.2 Strategic Alignment*

Earlier in the chapter we discussed how procurement strategies should be aligned with overarching and organisational objectives (Figure 8.1). Procurement directors must be able to articulate how their procurement strategy will strengthen organisational strategy. This requires being able to identify overarching government or specific organisational objectives that the procurement function will support, whether to do with the effectiveness of service delivery, VfM, or social and environmental agendas. Directors need to think not only about vertical alignment between procurement strategies and organisational strategies

*Figure 8.3* Factors relevant to public procurement strategizing.
*Source*: Original creation.

but also horizontal alignment. Is the procurement strategy consistent with the service operations strategy, for instance, or the digital transformation strategy? As mentioned in discussing stakeholder involvement, it is advisable to engage with other departments to ensure compatibility between procurement and other organisational functions. The same principle applies to external fit. Directions should ask themselves if the proposed procurement strategy is in line with industry and supply market trends. In contemplating a "green" procurement strategy, for instance, is there evidence that suppliers are able to provide eco-friendly products and services?

### *8.4.3 Resource Provision*

Formulating and implementing procurement strategies is resource intensive, requiring additional human capital, finance, and technology. Organisations must prepare for it and budget accordingly. In terms of human capital, directors should assess if the existing complement of staff can implement the new procurement strategy. Do staff have the technical and subject-specific knowledge to source innovative products and services from the supply marketplace if innovation is part of the new procurement strategy? If not, training and mentoring will be required. A new strategic direction for procurement often means recruiting staff or collaborating with external consultants to assist with the change process, which has cost implications. New IT systems to help procurement seamlessly connect with internal users and external providers is a common feature of strategic re-organisation. The time, effort, and money involved in rolling out IT procurement systems should not be under-estimated. The introduction of a new strategy might also necessitate changes to the structure of the procurement function as regards roles, responsibilities, and reporting obligations. For the strategy to work, procurement may have to become centralised.

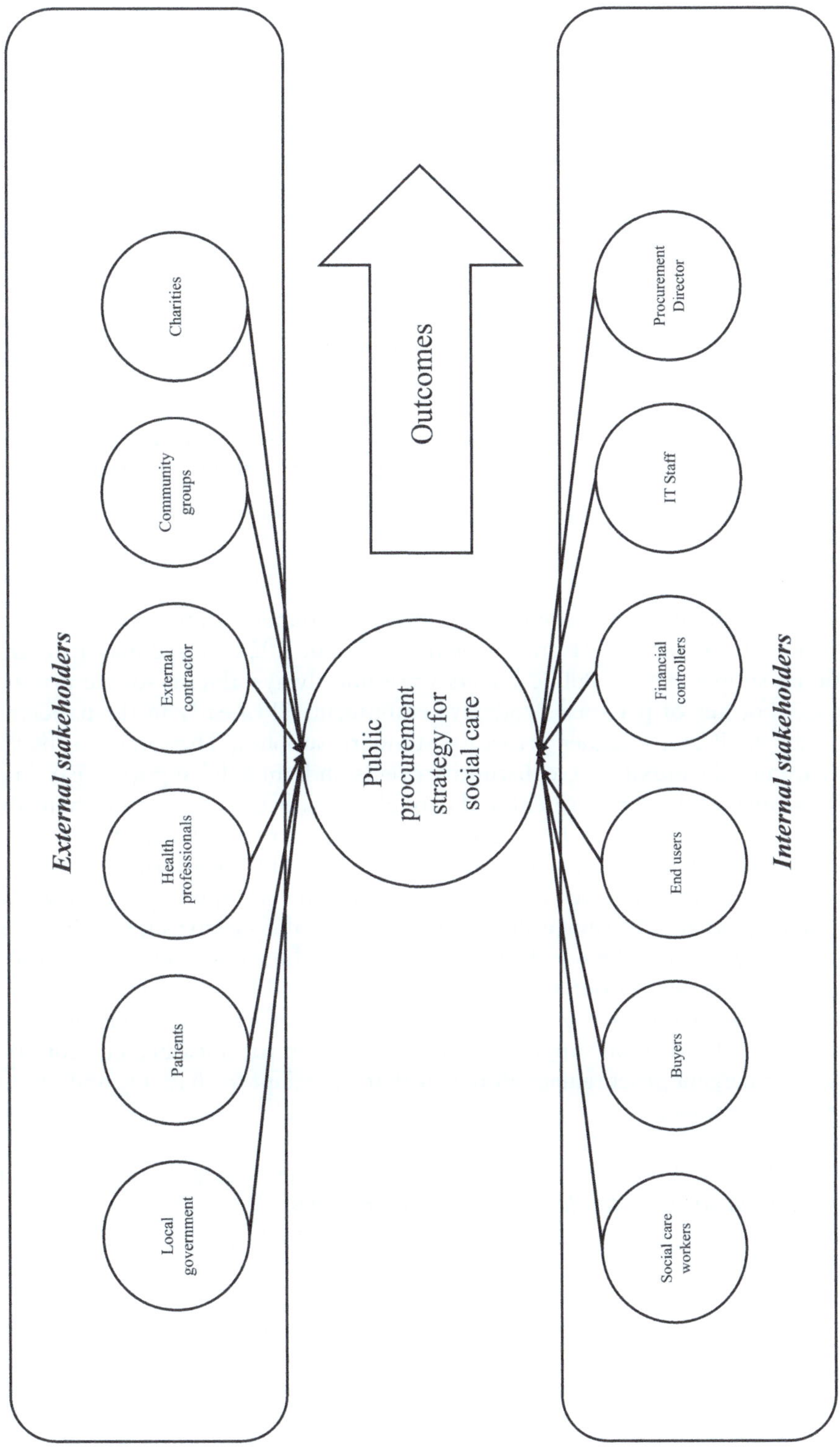


*Figure 8.4* Stakeholders that could be consulted for a social care services procurement strategy.
*Source:* Original creation.

#### *8.4.4 Performance Measurement*

Strategy, as stated earlier, is a plan of action aimed at achieving a desired set of outcomes. Being able to measure progress against those intended outcomes is integral to strategic management. Without measurement, there is no way of accurately determining if the strategy was a success. In the case of public procurement strategies, directors must define their targets and be able to operationalise, measure, and report on them. Typical procurement outcomes include cost savings on products and services purchased, shorter procurement cycle times, increased on-time delivery rates, better quality products or services, higher end-user satisfaction levels, and environmental improvements. Quantitative indicators will be required for each target. Examples of indicators for environmental improvements include the percentage of energy purchased from renewable sources and the percentage of paper certified by the Forest Stewardship Council (FSC). At the outset of any new procurement strategy, it is advisable to baseline current performance. Baselining allows you to determine if the new strategy is yielding a positive, neutral, or negative effect. Thereafter, the procurement function starts to collect and analyse performance data on a rolling basis. Adjustments to the procurement strategy will be required if the results are below expectations.

#### *8.4.5 Resilience*

Another factor that should be considered for public procurement strategies is resilience. The Covid-19 pandemic in 2020–2021 and the war in Ukraine 2022 caused major disruptions to international supply chains. Public buyers were not always able to source products as required (e.g., shortage of personal protective equipment (PPE) early in the pandemic) or else had to pay significantly higher prices for standard supplies. The same can be said of geo-political events like Brexit. These disruptive events underline the importance of building procurement strategies that are resilient and capable of withstanding supply chain shocks. What does this mean in practice? First, procurement directors should start mapping their supply chains and risk-assess product lines against possible disruptions. Contingency planning comes next. This involves weighing up options if the supply of a product or service line is interrupted and devising a Plan B. De-risking public-sector supply chains is also part of resilience. Questions like whether it is possible for the public sector to localise more of the supply chain or even insource services should be asked here. Mintzberg and Waters (1985) made the distinction between planned and emergent strategies four decades ago. Given volatility in international supply chains, the public sector must become comfortable with the idea of emergent procurement strategies that can adapt to changing and oftentimes unfavourable circumstances.

*Question for reflection: Are there any other factors that practitioners should consider when devising and implementing public procurement strategies?*

## Note

1 Dynamic purchasing systems (DPS) are similar to framework agreements. The main difference is that DPS are open-ended and suppliers can apply to join at any time. Framework agreements are for a fixed period of time and new suppliers cannot join once the framework agreement has started.

## References


Akenroye, T. O., Owens, J. D., Elbaz, J., & Durowoju, O. A. 2020. Dynamic capabilities for SME participation in public procurement. *Business Process Management Journal*, 26(4): 857–888.

Bakker, E., Walker, H., Schotanus, F., & Harland, C. 2008. Choosing an organizational form: The case of collaborative procurement initiatives. *International Journal of Procurement Management*, 1(3): 297–317.

Barney, J. 1991. Firm resources and sustained competitive advantage. *Journal of Management*, 17(1): 99–120.

Cabinet Office. 2010. *Efficiency Review by Sir Philip Green*. UK Government. Retrieved 30/10/2025 from https://assets.publishing.service.gov.uk/media/5a78f0be40f0b62b22cbe018/sirphilipgreenreview.pdf

Coase, R. H. 1937. The nature of the firm. *Economica*, 4(November): 386–405.

Corsini, F., De Bernardi, C., Gusmerotti, N. M., & Frey, M. 2024. Introducing the circular assessment of suppliers (CAoS) tool: A Kraljic matrix-based tool to facilitate circular procurement in private organizations. *Journal of Cleaner Production*, 452: 142085.

Cousins, P. D. 2005. The alignment of appropriate firm and supply strategies for competitive advantage. *International Journal of Operations & Production Management*, 25(5–6): 403–428.

DiMaggio, P. J., & Powell, W. 1983. The iron cage revisited: Institutional isomorphism and collective rationality in organizational fields. *American Sociological Review*, 48: 147–160.

Ellram, L. M., & Carr, A. S. 1994. Strategic purchasing: A history and review of the literature. *International Journal of Purchasing and Materials Management*, 30(1): 9–19.

European Commission. 2016. *Buying green! A handbook on green public procurement*. Publications Office of the European Union. Retrieved 30/10/2025 from https://green-forum.ec.europa.eu/document/download/ca687d70-bdb9-4a8b-82ea-2ab05958a8d2_en?filename=EMAS%20-%20Buying%20Green%20Handbook.pdf

European Commission. 2021. *Buying social: A guide to taking account of social considerations in puplic Procurement*. Publications Office of the European Union. Retrieved 30/10/2025 from https://commission.europa.eu/funding-tenders/tools-public-buyers/social-procurement_en

Fisher, M. 1997. What is the right supply chain for your product? *Harvard Business Review*, 75(2): 105–116.

Flynn, A. 2017. Re-thinking SME disadvantage in public procurement. *Journal of Small Business and Enterprise Development*, 24(4): 991–1008.

Flynn, A. 2018. Measuring procurement performance in Europe. *Journal of Public Procurement*, 18(1): 2–13.

Flynn, A., & Davies, P. 2014. Theory in public procurement research. *Journal of Public Procurement*, 14(2): 139–180.

Freeman, R. E. 1984. *Strategic management: A stakeholder approach*. Marshfield, MA: Pitman.

Genovese, A., Morris, J., Koh, S. C. L., & Acquaye, A. 2022. An investigation into design and performance of supply chains for public procurement projects. *Production Planning & Control*, 33(9–10): 811–830.

Glas, A. H., Gaus, J., & Essig, M. (2018). Effects of governance structures on sustainability-oriented supplier behaviour: analysis of national action plans and their effects in public procurement. *International Journal of Business Environment*, 10(1): 75–94.

Government of India. (2017). *General financial rules*. Government of India. Retrieved 30/10/2025 from https://doe.gov.in/files/circulars_document/FInal_GFR_upto_31_07_2024.pdf

Green, K. W., Whitten, D., & Inman, R. A. 2012. Aligning marketing strategies throughout the supply chain to enhance performance. *Industrial Marketing Management*, 41(6): 1008–1018.

Guarnieri, P., & Gomes, R. C. (2019). Can public procurement be strategic? A future agenda proposition. *Journal of Public Procurement*, 19(4): 295–321.

Harland, C. M., Lamming, R. C., & Cousins, P. D. 1999. Developing the concept of supply strategy. *International Journal of Operations and Production Management*, 19(7): 650–674.

Hawkins, T. G., Gravier, M. J., & Powley, E. H. 2011. Public versus private sector procurement ethics and strategy: What each sector can learn from the other. *Journal of Business Ethics*, 103(4): 567–586.

Jaehrling, K. 2015. The state as a 'socially responsible customer'? Public procurement between market-making and market-embedding. *European Journal of Industrial Relation*, 21(2): 149–164.

Jensen, M. C., & Meckling, W. H. 1976. Theory of firm-managerial behaviour, agency costs and ownership structure. *Journal of Financial Economics*, 3: 305–360.

Johnson, P. F., & Klassen, R. D. 2022. New directions for research in green public procurement: The challenge of inter-stakeholder tensions. *Cleaner Logistics and Supply Chain*, 3, 100017.

Kauppi, K., & van Raaij, E. M. 2015. Opportunism and honest incompetence-seeking explanations for noncompliance in public procurement. *Journal of Public Administration Research and Theory*, 25(3): 953–979.

Koala, K., & Steinfeld, J. 2018. Theory building in public procurement. *Journal of Public Procurement*, 18(4): 282–305.

Kraljic, P. 1983, Sept–Oct. Purchasing must become supply management. *Harvard Business Review*: 109–117.

Lee, H. L. 2002. Aligning supply chain strategies with product uncertainties. *California Management Review*, 44(3): 105–119.

Loader, K. 2013. Is public procurement a successful small business support policy? A review of the evidence. *Environment and Planning C: Government and Policy*, 31(1): 39–55.

McCrudden, C. 2004. Using public procurement to achieve social outcomes. *Natural Resources Forum*, 28(4): 257–267.

McCue, C., & Roman, A. V. (2012). E-procurement: Myth or reality? *Journal of Public Procurement*, 12(2): 221–248.

Meehan, J., Ludbrook, M. N., & Mason, C. J. 2016. Collaborative public procurement: Institutional explanations of legitimised resistance. *Journal of Purchasing and Supply Management*, 22(3): 160–170.

Mintzberg, H. 1978. Patterns in strategy formation. *Management Science*, 24(9): 934–948.

Mintzberg, H., & Waters, J. A. 1985. Of strategies, deliberate and emergent. *Strategic Management Journal*, 6(3): 257–272.

OECD. 2023. Public Procurement, Vol. 2023.

Patrucco, A. S., Moretto, A., Ronchi, S., & Luzzini, D. 2019. Organisational choices in public procurement: What can public management learn from the private sector? *Local Government Studies*, 45(6): 977–1000.

Pfeffer, J., & Salancik, G. R. 2003. *The external control of organizations: A resource dependence perspective*. Stanford: Stanford Business Books.

Porter, M. E. 1979. How competitive forces shape strategy. *Harvard Business Review*, 57(2): 137–145.

Porter, M. E. 1980. *Competitive strategy: Techniques for analysing industries and competitors*. New York: Free Press.

Porter, M. E. 1985. *Competitive advantage: Creating and sustaining superior performance*. New York: Free Press.

Prahalad, C. K., & Hamel, G. 1990. The core competence of the corporation. *Harvard Business Review*, 68(3): 79–91.

Raj, A., Agrahari, A., & Srivastava, S. K. (2020). Do pressures foster sustainable public procurement? An empirical investigation comparing developed and developing economies. *Journal of Cleaner Production*, 266, 122055.

Reck, R. F., & Long, B. G. (1988). Purchasing: A competitive weapon. *Journal of Purchasing and Materials Management*, 24(3): 2–8.

Rodrigues, B. C., & Reis, P. R. D. (2023). Internal stakeholders and public procurement performance in the perspective of stakeholders' and transaction costs theories. *Cadernos Gestao Publica E Cidadania*, 28, p. e88342.

Rokkan, A. I., & Haugland, S. A. 2022. A transaction cost approach for public procurement. *Journal of Business & Industrial Marketing*, 37(2): 341–352.

South African Government. (2023). *Public Procurement Bill*. South African Government. Retrieved 30/10/2025 from www.gov.za/sites/default/files/gcis_document/202312/b18b2023publicprocurement.pdf

Stavrulaki, E., & Davis, M. 2010. Aligning products with supply chain processes and strategy. *International Journal of Logistics Management*, 21(1): 127–151.

Teece, D. J., Pisano, G., & Shuen, A. 1997. Dynamic capabilities and strategic management. *Strategic Management Journal*, 18(7): 509–533.

UK Government. 2022. *Common Framework for Public Procurement*. UK Government. Retrieved 30/10/2025 from https://assets.publishing.service.gov.uk/media/61eea44b8fa8f505985ef499/common-framework-public-procurement-jan-2022.pdf

Uyarra, E., & Flanagan, K. 2010. Understanding the Innovation Impacts of Public Procurement. *European Planning Studies*, 18(1): 123–143.

Walker, H., Chicksand, D., Radnor, Z., & Watson, G. 2015. Theoretical perspectives in operations management: An analysis of the literature. *International Journal of Operations & Production Management*, 35(8): 1182–1206.

Wang, C. H., Qiao, Y. H., & Li, X. M. 2020. A systems approach for green public procurement implementation. *Journal of Public Procurement*, 20(3): 287–311.

Wontner, K. L., Walker, H., Harris, I., & Lynch, J. 2020. Maximising "Community Benefits" in public procurement: tensions and trade-offs. *International Journal of Operations & Production Management*, 40(12): 1909–1939.

Wu, T. H., Wu, Y. C. J., Chen, Y. M. J., & Goh, M. 2014. Aligning supply chain strategy with corporate environmental strategy: A contingency approach. *International Journal of Production Economics*, 147: 220–229.

### *Case Study: How Not to Manage Public Procurement (Developed by Helen Walker and Anthony Flynn)*

In 2010 the UK government commissioned Sir Philip Green, a self-made entrepreneur and founder of one of the UK's most successful high-street fashion retail chains, to lead a review into central government procurement. The backdrop to the review was the 2008 international financial crisis, which squeezed public finances and sent the UK government searching for ways to reduce spending and cut waste across the public sector. Public procurement was identified as one area where cost savings were achievable if inefficiencies could be ironed out and a strategic approach put in place for managing major supply contracts.

The Efficiency Review (Cabinet Office, 2010) that Sir Philip Green produced did not pull any punches. It laid bare inefficient, wasteful spending practices and a lack of professionalism and strategic thinking in how central government departments transacted with the supply marketplace. Among the issues identified were above average market prices paid for standard products and services, variations in price paid for the same products and services across government departments, no co-ordination among government departments when purchasing the same commodity items, and inflexible contracts that disadvantaged the buyer. Overall, the Efficiency Review found that central government departments were failing to exploit purchasing economies of scale, not leveraging their favourable credit rating and managing procurement unprofessionally.

The consequences of these procurement failings were significant. Central government departments were over-spending by hundreds of millions of pounds at a time when budgetary cutbacks were being introduced and public services were being pared back. The examples provided in the Efficiency Review (2010) speak for themselves. In one case, government departments were paying between 15 and 80 per cent higher than the average market price for leaflet printing. Given that total spend on printing was approximately £100 million annually at the time, such differentials meant millions of pounds wasted. In another case, government departments were paying anywhere between £8–73 pounds for a box of printing paper and £86–398 pounds for printer cartridges. There was no logical explanation for why these differentials should exist in the procurement of office supplies.

From the Efficiency Review it emerged that there was no attempt to centralise and aggregate the procurement of standard items used across central government departments. Each department was acting as an individual buyer. This meant two things. First, they were not exploiting purchasing economies of scale. By aggregating their purchasing requirements, central governments would be in a much stronger position to extract bulk discounts from suppliers. Second, multiple contracts existed with suppliers when one single contract was advisable. Having multiple contracts is administratively inefficient and uses time and labour that could be deployed for value-adding activities in public procurement. Illustrative of this problem, there were 68 individual mobile phone contracts across central government departments totalling over £20 million with just one supplier. A single contract would mean financial savings in two ways: a reduction in the purchase price by exploiting purchasing economies of scale and a simultaneous reduction in contract administration costs.

A lack of procurement co-ordination across departments was not the only problem. Departments had inaccurate or missing procurement data, leading to no transparency or accountability over what was purchased and how much was spent. It also made planning and target setting very difficult. Under-professionalisation was also in evidence. The individuals and teams with responsibility for procurement did not instil confidence that they had the commercial expertise or product-specific knowledge to achieve value for money (VfM). The procurement approach taken was transactional rather than strategic, and suppliers were getting the better part of the deal. Coupled with under-professionalisation was the absence of incentives to drive down procurement costs. Each department was allocated an annual budget. If they did not use up the budget, it would be reduced in the next financial year. This meant that there was no incentive to achieve savings by taking a more strategic approach to procurement.

Amid the various shortcomings and problems, the Efficiency Review showed what was possible if a strategic approach to procurement was embraced by the central government departments. When the procurement of gas and electricity was centralised and brought under the control of a team of category experts, a cumulative saving of £500 million was realised over four years. A similar approach taken with the procurement of other major category items for central government like mobile phone services, office supplies, travel, catering, facilities management, and property leasing could reasonably be expected to deliver comparable savings without any deterioration in product or service quality. In this way, public procurement starts to play a strategic role in central government.

As a postscript to the case, the UK has since centralised the procurement of its main services and supply categories. Category specialists in the Crown Commercial Services (CCS) engage with the supply marketplace on behalf of all UK public-sector organisations and qualify suppliers onto framework agreements and dynamic purchasing systems (DPS[1]). Suppliers must meet minimum product or service standards and be competitive in their pricing to be admitted onto a framework agreement or DPS. Individual public-sector organisations from throughout the UK can request a quotation from participants listed on the framework agreement or DPS in the knowledge that the supplier has been vetted, the product or service meets approved quality standards, and the price is competitive.

Leveraging economies of scale in this way is becoming the default procurement strategy in the UK and other developed economies. Importantly, it is delivering better VfM. It is also resulting in improved consistency in the quality of products purchased by the public sector through centralised framework agreements and DPS. Several changes to procurement have enabled this approach. These include centralised category management, recruitment of outside expertise, and enhanced spend analysis and data capture. While not all procurement is covered by centrally managed agreements and professionalisation still has to improve, the UK has made measurable progress over the last decade towards strategic, co-ordinated, and cost-effective procurement.

### Discussion Questions

1. Examine the main causes of inefficiency in UK central government procurement, which were identified by the Efficiency Review (2010).
2. Discuss why the causes of inefficiency identified in central government procurement in this case study are less likely to happen in private sector procurement.
3. Assess the benefits and potential drawbacks of centrally managing procurement in the UK or in any other country.

# 9 Efficiency in Public Procurement

*Sawsan Abutabenjeh and Rene G. Rendon*

## 9.1 Introduction

Public sector contracting emphasizes three values, namely efficiency, accountability, and equity (Abutabenjeh et al., 2022; 2023). In addition to these values, price, effectiveness, responsiveness, and responsibility are other critical factors in contracting (Cooper, 2022, p. 5). While simultaneously striving to harmonize multiple values and adhere to various rules and regulations, public procurement also aims for greater efficiency (Kloot & Martin, 2000; Schapper et al., 2006). Although determining a balance among these values is a challenge, nonetheless, procurement systems are designed to encourage competition and strive to minimize administrative costs while exercising integrity, fairness, and transparency in fulfilling public policy objectives (Brunjes et al., 2023; Kumar et al., 2015). This chapter discusses efficiency in public procurement price and process as a cost-saving mechanism to justify contracting in the public sector context. There are multiple approaches through public procurement that can enhance/boost efficiency (Jovanovic et al., 2013). This chapter narrows its focus to (1) summarizing the relevant literature and research on the topic of procurement and efficiency (2) reporting the latest methods and practical approaches to increasing efficiency within public procurement. It is likely that additional methods/ways/strategies exist which fall outside the scope of this chapter. Identifying which public procurement practices, tools, and policies contribute to increased efficiency presents a complex challenge. The chapter is organized into three sections: first, it provides a summary of the existing literature; second, it discusses emerging issues and their practical applications; and finally, it includes a teaching case study for further exploration.

## 9.2 Public Procurement Efficiency: Literature Review

The literature has various definitions, applications, dimensions, and interpretations of the concept of efficiency. The term efficiency is frequently employed to signify the level of output achieved in relation to the resources invested or utilized per unit (Cooper, 2022). Researchers, scholars, public authorities, and agencies around the world looked at the concept of efficiency in public procurement (Milosavljević et al., 2019). In public procurement and contracting, efficiency refers to reducing administrative costs and procurement administrative lead time to maximize the value of taxpayers' money during the procurement process (National Contract Management Association [NCMA], 2022). Achieving efficiency in the public procurement cycle can manifest in terms of price or process or both.

Efficiency in price can be achieved by innovative procurement practices to lower cost and foster a more competitive supplier environment, partnerships, and other collaborative

DOI: 10.4324/9781003566670-11

arrangements, which can lead to "more efficient and cost-effective project delivery, ultimately benefiting the competitive landscape" and managing suppliers relationships post contract award to sustain competitive market conditions over the long term (Caldwell et al., 2005; Davies, 2023).

Efficiency in the procurement process requires minimizing administrative costs and red tape costs, reducing the elapsed time taken during the procurement, and reallocating resources toward more complex procurement processes (Kumar et al., 2015; Panayiotou et al., 2004). This efficiency can be evaluated using both subjective and objective measures. For example, the European Commission regularly performs a six-item Single Market Scoreboard analysis, encouraging European countries to adopt more efficient procurement processes. While this initiative aims to save money and promote a competitive, sustainable economy, the measures used in the analysis rely heavily on expert judgment, incorporating subjective weights and thresholds that can influence the outcomes. To address the subjectivity, scholars have constructed several methodologies that leverage the additive aggregation method. These methodologies employ objective, albeit biased, weights, such as the I-distance (Išljamović et al., 2015) and Composite I-distance Indicator (CIDI) (Milosavljević et al., 2019).

Even though scholars and researchers have explored several methods to enhance procurement efficiency, here, we specifically narrow the focus to three approaches aimed at enhancing the efficiency of the procurement cycle. First, the impact of collaborative public procurement is examined, highlighting how collaboration among entities can improve efficiency and value. Second, the focus shifts to various practices and strategies that elevate efficiency within public procurement, showcasing innovative approaches to optimize processes. Additionally, the role of control and audit systems in optimizing procurement efficiency is explored, emphasizing the importance of oversight and accountability in ensuring that procurement activities are both effective and efficient. Finally, emerging issues and practical applications for increasing efficiency in public procurement are discussed.

### *9.2.1 The Impact of Public Procurement Collaboration on Efficiency*

Extant literature advances the importance of collaboration for enhancing efficiency (Lopes & Farias, 2020; Feiock, 2013; Abutabenjeh et al., 2023). In addition to enhancing efficiency, collaboration is useful for pooling financial and human resources, sharing information and knowledge and best practices, and building legitimacy (Selviaridis et al., 2023).

Such collaboration efforts can occur internally among government entities and departments within the same organization or externally with private or nonprofit organizations. The efficacy of internal collaboration in enhancing procurement efficiency is illustrated through the adoption of United States federal government procurement policies that allow for interagency contracting methods. Through the use of interagency contracts, federal government agencies can leverage other federal agencies' existing contracts for the procurement of needed supplies or services (Federal Acquisition Regulation, 2024). As federal government agencies enhance collaborative efforts among themselves, they then become more aware of the existence of current contracts by other agencies, and the opportunity to leverage those contracts is made possible. Using another agency's already-existing contracts alleviates the need to initiate new contracts and thus increases efficiencies in government procurement. Leveraging other current existing federal government contracts also results in lower prices paid for products and services. Additionally, when government agencies collaborate, specifically by sharing procurement data such as products and services procured, delivery methods, names of contractors, contract periods, and contract pricing, there are efficiencies to be gained in reducing procurement timelines and prices. This data sharing and collaboration allow for a more strategic approach to procurement (Rendon, 2005).

External collaboration between government agencies and private or nonprofit organizations can enhance procurement efficiency as demonstrated in the use of Other Transaction Agreements (Dunn, 2021). These agreements give government agencies the flexibility necessary to adopt and incorporate business practices that reflect industry standards in its contract instruments. As government and industry collaborate on developing emergent technology solutions for government requirements, the resulting collaborative efforts result in more efficient procurement of these technologies using these flexible contract instruments. The use of flexible contract instruments not only increases efficiencies but also results in lower prices paid for products and services.

Moreover, collaboration between government entities and suppliers or vendors is instrumental in achieving efficient public procurement (local and regional inter-organizational collaborative networks). The use of Partnership Intermediary Agreements (PIA) in which government agencies can engage with academia and industry to accelerate technology transfer for needed government solutions provides an example of external collaboration (Pena et al., 2020). Collaboration between the government and academia using these partnership agreements provides the government a more efficient approach to transfer technology to the private sector (Pena et al., 2020).

### *9.2.2 Tools to Elevate Efficiency in Public Procurement*

Several studies have suggested a range of practices and tools to enhance efficiency in public procurement. Among these, the public procurement performance measurement system (PP-PMS) addresses various performance areas, including cost, quality, time, compliance, innovation, and sustainability. It proposes that the procurement function should be recognized as strategic within public institutions for such systems to be effectively implemented (Patrucco et al., 2016). This approach replaces the traditional PMSs that focus on the financial aspect of the contracts. Milosavljević et al. (2019) critiqued the subjective approaches to measure efficiency of PP, specifically the EU's Single Market Scoreboard, and suggested the use of the CIDI methodology. By analyzing data from 30 European countries, CIDI ranks them based on several indicators: competitiveness, transparency, and procedural comprehensiveness. This methodology provides a more accurate and fairer comparison of public performance across countries. Focusing on social needs and expectations, Pysmenna et al. (2019) provided a step-by-step system for public procurement performance assessment, including establishing criteria for an ideal participant, developing observation matrices for tenderers' proposals, and determining the vector-standard characteristics of the most economically advantageous proposal. In addition to the above-mentioned tools, Wondimu et al. (2018) showed that employing practices related to Early Contractor Involvement (ECI) can enhance the adoption of innovative, efficient, and value-added solutions. The U.S. Navy Procurement Performance Management Assessment Program (PPMAP) is another example of a tool to enhance efficiency in public procurement practices. The PPMAP was designed to create internal audit controls on the procurement processes and practices within Navy contracting organizations. The Navy relies on the PPMAP program as its primary method of validating the extent of sound contracting practices that occur throughout the Navy procurement organizations. The Navy's PPMAP program identifies and enhances procurement efficiencies by encouraging and assisting its contracting organizations in making continuous improvements in all phases of their acquisition processes to ensure compliance with statutes and policies and by leveraging best practices/processes and "lessons learned" across the spectrum of Navy contracting organizations (Office of the Secretary of the Navy, 2019).

Research conducted by World Commerce & Contracting (WorldCC) shows that poor contracting processes and practices cost the average organization an equivalent of 9.15% of its annual revenue in the form of increased costs, missed savings, and loss revenues (International Association of Contract and Commercial Management [IACCM], 2013). WorldCC (formerly known as International Association for Commerce and Contract Management [IACCM]) is a professional association of commerce and contract management professionals with over 70,000 members across 180 countries and 20,000 organizations. It is a global not-for-profit association promoting standards and raising capabilities in commercial practice (World Commerce & Contracting [WorldCC], 2024).

The Contract Management Maturity Model (CMMM), which is used to assess the process maturity level of an organization's contract management processes, is another example of a tool to increase efficiencies in public procurement. The CMMM assesses an organization's contract management processes using a five-level framework representing five levels of maturity. These maturity levels consist of Ad Hoc, Basic, Structured, Integrated, and Optimized. This range of maturity levels is based on the extent that the organization's processes are documented, established, mandated, integrated with other functional areas, and continuously measured and improved. The maturity levels are aligned across the six contract management process areas of Procurement Planning, Solicitation Planning, Solicitation, Source Selection, Contract Administration, and Contract Closeout. The CMMM can be used to not only assess an organization's process capability but also can be used to benchmark its process capability with those of other contracting agencies. Benchmarking can be effective in measuring and improving contracting process capability and procurement efficiency throughout an organization. In one case study, CMMM was applied to U.S. Navy procurement organizations and the results indicated that, generally, post-award contracting processes have a lower level of process maturity compared to the pre-award phase activities. The results of this Navy case study have been benchmarked with CMMM assessments on the Army and Air Force (Rendon, 2015).

### *9.2.3 The Role of Control and Audit Systems in Optimizing Procurement Efficiency*

Audits on procurement contracts are performed by all government agencies at all levels (Abutabenjeh and Rendon, 2023) because the agencies are responsible for spending taxpayer money to buy products and services in efficient and effective ways. A variety of audit reports, transparency measures, and independent verifications are crucial for providing accountability for stakeholders and third parties who cannot monitor the internal operations of agencies and organizations. Based on the monitoring theory, top management, government agencies, and creditors place high value standards on audit reports and monitoring systems because of their efficiency in monitoring inconsistencies and errors in control processes (Abutabenjeh & Rendon, 2023). Using Chile as a case, Celhay et al. (2024) found that monitoring performance can reduce overspending, particularly when managers can observe buyer performance. This implies that the efficiency of buyers is largely influenced by external motivations.

Internal control and audit systems also play a significant role in increasing public procurement efficiencies. For example, the U.S. Department of Defense (DoD) Inspector General (IG) conducts audits and investigations on various aspects of the DoD operations and processes in order to assess compliance with statutes, regulations, and policies related to acquisition and contracting. These policies include complying with competition in awarding contracts, providing procurement opportunities for small and minority businesses, and negotiating fair and reasonable prices. An example of this type of oversight is the recent DoD IG audit of DoD use of the government purchase card (GPS) in response to the Coronavirus–2019 pandemic (Department of Defense Inspector General [DoD IG], 2024a). The objective of this audit was to determine whether cardholders used GPCs to support the DoD's response COVID-19 pandemic in accordance with federal and DoD policies. The audit found that "DoD cardholders made COVID-19 contingency operation purchases that did not always support the DoD's response to the COVID-19 pandemic and did not maintain appropriate supporting documentation for purchases in accordance with Federal and DoD policies" (DoD IG, 2024a, p. i). In another DoD IG report on the use and oversight of cost-plus award fee (CPAF) contracts, the IG found that DoD contracting officials made overpayments of at least $872,309 on two contracts and an improper payment of $1,978,267 on a third contract. CPAF contracts are contracts that provide for the reimbursement to the contractor for all allowable, allocable, and reasonable costs of performing the contract. In addition, these contracts provide for the payment of an award fee if the contractor meets additional performance criteria that had been identified by the government in the contract (Rendon & Snider, 2019). The IG also found that contracting officials inappropriately obligated $2.2 million (DoD IG, 2024b).

Additionally, each service department (e.g. Army, Air Force, and Navy) conducts internal audits on its contracting organizations to ensure those contract management processes are performed in accordance with public policy. An example is the Navy Audit Service audit report on the Contract Closeout Procedures at Naval Facilities Engineering Systems Command (Naval Audit Service, 2023). Contract closeout procedures are those administrative procedures performed by the procurement agency after a contract for products and services is physically completed (all deliverables have been made and accepted) and the final payment has been made to the contractor (Rendon & Snider, 2019). Using these internal control audits the organizations can determine how effective the procurement internal controls are, thus identifying any noncompliance issues as well as inefficient processes that may be resulting in fraud, waste, or mismanagement. Conducting internal audits and improving the effectiveness of procurement internal controls will not only increase procurement efficiency, but also lower costs paid for products and services by eliminating contract overpayments, improper payments, and inappropriate funding obligations (Rendon & Rendon, 2016).

The European Union has established rules that mark a significant evolution in its approach to public procurement, seeking to modernize and simplify the procurement process (Medeiros, 2014). The impact of Directive 2014/24/EU on public procurement is evident in its role of enhancing procurement practices, implementing control and audit mechanisms, and driving efficiency across the European Union (Medeiros, 2014; Kozik & Karasińska-Jaśkowiec, 2016; Andhov, 2020). Using a survey conducted in Russia in 2020, the majority of procurers and suppliers agreed that the objectives of optimal regulation of public procurement are to achieve procurement efficiency and to minimize corruption (Balaeva, 2022).

## 9.3 Emerging Issues and Practical Applications

Practical applications for increasing efficiencies in public procurement will be discussed in this section of the chapter. The focus will be primarily on contracting policies that are established in United States federal government procurement policies. Additionally, the chapter touches upon how Artificial Intelligence Initiatives play a crucial role in advancing the efficiency of procurement processes. Finally, this section examines the role of common standards in increasing workforce competency and organizational capability as an approach to achieving procurement efficiency.

### *9.3.1 Contracting Policies*

The United States federal government establishes policies for the planning, awarding, and administering of federal government contracts. These public procurement policies provide for more efficiency in the federal government contracting processes throughout the contract life cycle. These policies allow for more efficient contracting methods such as use of government procurement cards and simplified acquisition procedures for the purchase of low cost products and services (Federal Acquisition Regulation, 2024). These policies support reducing administrative costs, thus improving opportunities for small businesses, small disadvantaged businesses, women-owned businesses, veteran-owned businesses, and service-disabled veteran-owned small businesses to obtain a fair proportion of government contracts. Further, the policies are meant to promote efficiency and economy in contracting and avoid unnecessary burdens for agencies and contractors.

Another public policy that provides for more efficiency in government contracting is the approach used for procuring commercial (i.e., non-developmental) products and services (Federal Acquisition Regulation, 2024). These policies provide for a more streamlined procurement approach that more closely resembles those of the commercial marketplace and encourages the acquisition of commercial products and commercial services by the federal government. As the government increases its procurement of commercial products and services, as opposed to procuring developmental products, the benefits of price competition are realized and this results in lower prices paid for these products.

The U.S. federal government also provides for more efficiency in government contracting by allowing the use of contract options (Federal Acquisition Regulation, 2024). Contract options allow the government to purchase additional products or services called for in an existing contract. Using contract options when in the best interest of the government results in a timelier and streamlined approach for procuring additional products or services on contracts with periods of performance greater than a single year. These federal acquisition policies also provide for efficient contracting through the use of interagency contracting methods, which allows federal government agencies to leverage other agency's existing contracts for the procurement of needed supplies or services.

Another U.S. federal government policy that has significantly increased the efficiencies of federal contracting is the use of indefinite delivery, multiple award contracts. These contract instruments allow for the award of indefinite delivery/indefinite quantity (ID/IQ) multiple award contracts, which provides for the procurement of an indefinite quantity of supplies or services at various times over a fixed period of performance (Federal Acquisition Regulation, 2024). There is a multiple-award (i.e., contract awards to multiple contractors) preference for ID/IQ contracts, which provides for a more efficient, streamlined, and timelier approach for the contractors to compete for the delivery orders or task orders of those contracts. The use of multiple award ID/IQ contracts allows the benefits of price competition, and this results in the potential for lower prices paid for the products and services.

An example of improving efficiency in the U.S. federal government is the U.S. General Services Administration (GSA) Federal Strategic Sourcing Initiative (FSSI). Strategic sourcing is the structured and collaborative process of critically analyzing an organization's spending patterns to better leverage its purchasing power, reduce costs, and improve overall performance. Some of the goals of the GSA FSSI program is to strategically source across federal agencies, establish mechanisms to increase total cost savings, value, and socioeconomic participation, and collaborate with industry to develop optimal solutions. The FSSI program consists of commodity solutions for building maintenance and operations, maintenance repair facility supplies, wireless solutions, and office supplies (GSA, 2024).

The U.S. federal government's push for more agile, innovative, and efficient contracting approaches has resulted in other Congressional procurement authorities. These authorities are established by U.S. Congressional direction and only for specifically authorized agencies.

An example of a Congressionally authorized contracting method is the use of Other Transaction Authority (OTA) contracts. The Other Transaction (OT) authorities provide agile, innovative, and efficient contracting procedures that give government agencies the flexibility to tailor commercial business practices reflecting industry standards and best practices into its award instruments (Dunn, 2021). This increased contracting efficiency results in the government getting access to state-of-the-art technology solutions from its contractors. OT contracts also encourage flexible, quicker, and less expensive project design and execution as it broadens the industrial base available to the government (Dunn, 2021). OT contracts have been successfully used in procuring research and development effort, developing prototype systems, and for production items (Dunn, 2021).

Another example of a specialized Congressional authorization is the use of PIA. A PIA is "an agreement between a DoD entity and a partnership intermediary". A partnership intermediary is defined as an "agency of State or local government, or nonprofit entity owned, chartered by, funded, or operated on behalf of the State or local government" (Pena et al., 2020, p. iii). The partnership intermediary assists, counsels, advises, evaluates, or otherwise cooperates with small business firms and institutions of higher education that need or can make demonstrably productive use of technology-related assistance from a federal laboratory (Pena, 2020). PIAs are used by government labs to increase the likelihood of success in convincing higher education to make use of technology-related assistance from a government lab and to facilitate technology transfer to the private sector (Cameron & Rendon, in press). These special Congressional authorities allow agencies to establish PIAs. For example, they allow agencies to award partnership intermediaries to federal labs that are owned, leased, or otherwise used by a federal agency and funded by the federal government, whether operated by the government or by a contractor (Pena et al., 2020).

### *9.3.2 Artificial Intelligence Initiatives*

The government's push for efficiency in public procurement has also included a focus on the application of artificial intelligence (AI) to government contracting processes. AI "involves the development of computer systems able to perform tasks that normally require human intelligence, such as visual perception, speech recognition, decision-making, and translation between languages". The applications of AI have resulted in organizations "modernizing operations, increasing efficiency, reducing costs, and providing more accurate and timely services" (Trenchfield, 2023, p. 20). AI, to include robotic process automation (RPA), and machine learning (ML) have been applied to the phases within the contract life cycle. Although a separate chapter in this book is devoted to the application of AI in public procurement, here we provide brief examples on how AI has been applied to each of the contract life cycle phases.

During the pre-award life cycle phase, an example of the application of RPA to government contracting is the U.S. Army's contractor determination of responsibility assistant bot (DORA) that searches government databases and pulls information about vendors and creates reports for contracting officers to use in making contractor responsibility determinations prior to contract awards. The use of this RPA application reduces the time to pull this information from an hour, when performed manually, to less than five minutes. The Army's DORA bot was modeled on the Internal Revenue Service (IRS) procurement office Contractor Responsibility Bot. An award life cycle phase application of AI to government contracting is from the Department of Homeland Security (DHS) Procurement Innovation Lab (PIL) AI for Past Performance Project. The PIL applied AI to help contracting professionals analyze contractor past performance information during the contract source selection process. The AI solution was able to identify which records in the Contractor Performance Assessment Reporting System (CPARS) contain the information most relevant to a specific source selection. A post award contract life cycle application of AI is when the Health and Human Services (HHS) Department combined block chain, AI, RPA, and ML to develop the Accelerate tool that analyzed contracts and identified discrepancies in prices paid for the same goods across the HHS. The tool discovered more than 200 contracts with the same contractor with significant price variation across the department. HHS entered discussions with the contractor and was able to modify the contract to achieve significant cost avoidance (Trenchfield, 2023, pp. 19–21).

### *9.3.3 Procurement Common Standards*

Another approach to increasing efficiency in public procurement and contract management is through the establishment and adoption of third-party accredited industry standards. An example of this is the National Contract Management Association (NCMA) Contract Management Standard (CMS). The CMS is a consensus-based American National Standard (ANS) approved by the American National Standards Institute (ANSI) (ANS number: ANSI/NCMA ASD 1-2019 [R2022]).

The CMS defines key contract management concepts and processes and serves as the foundation and framework for the NCMA Contract Management Body of Knowledge (CMBOK) (NCMA, 2023, p. 1). The CMS is applicable to all acquisitions, grants, leases, orders, procurements, purchases, subcontracts, and any other types of legally enforceable contracts—from credit card purchases to major system acquisitions. Additionally, the CMS is applicable to any organization that works with any type of contract (e.g., government [federal, state, and local], industry [business-to-business, business-to-government, large business, midsize business, small business], and subcontractors [all tiers]). Furthermore, the CMS can be applied by any organization developing public procurement and contract management training courses and programs or education courses and curricula (e.g., schools, colleges, training providers, and professional associations) (Cleven et al., 2024).

At the U.S. federal government level, the NCMA CMS has been adopted by federal civilian agencies as well as defense agencies as the contracting competency model for training their contracting workforce (Tenaglia, 2021; Field, 2023). Thus, all of the federal government executive agencies have adopted the NCMA CMS in its contracting competency model and the basis for its contracting workforce training (Cleven et al., 2024).

At the state government level, the North Carolina state procurement organization has adopted the CMS as the basis for its training curriculum. North Carolina's Department of Administration (DOA), Division of Purchase & Contract (P&C) established its first-ever state certification program in 2019 through the North Carolina Procurement Academy (NCPA) as part of a legislative mandate. The North Carolina Contract Manager (NCCM) certification is a requirement for all state employees responsible for awarding contracts or monitoring contract compliance (Cleven et al., 2024).

Within the industry sector, industry partners such as Leidos, The FedPROPEL Institute, Lockheed Martin, Federal Publications Seminars, SMX, Bidscale, and BMRA have adopted the CMS (NCMA, 2024). Some industry partners have adopted the CMS as part of their hiring and training frameworks by incorporating the CMS into corporate policies and procedures as a quality assurance guide for their contracting teams. Other industry partners are using the CMS as the basis for developing internal training for their contract departments. They are also committed to using the terminology of the CMS in their job requisitions, training, and internal processes. This adoption supports the NCMA initiative of establishing one common language for the contract management profession. Finally, Bidscale has licensed the CMS and is building into their Contract Lifecycle Management (CLM) software as an optional workflow (Cleven et al., 2024).

Within academia, higher education institutions are also adopting the CMS in their procurement and contract management curricula. For example, the University of California, Irvine, Division of Continuing Education has aligned its Contract Management Certificate with the competencies established in the CMS. The University of Maryland Global Campus MS in Acquisition and Contract Management and the Webster University's Procurement and Contract Management for Information Technology Management program have also aligned their curricula to the competencies based on the CMS (Cleven et al., 2024).

> The U.S. Naval Postgraduate School's graduate degree programs in contract management, both resident and distance learning, have adopted the CMBOK and CMS in their graduate curricula and aligned the curricula with the competencies established in the NCMA Contract Management Body of Knowledge (CMBOK) and the Contract Management Standard (CMS). The curriculum supports preparation for the NCMA professional certification examinations including the Certified Federal Contract Manager (CFCM) and the Certified Professional Contract Manager (CPCM).
>
> (Naval Postgraduate School [NPS], 2025, p. 72, 88)

When government, industry, and academia adopt the CMS, it does so through common language to form an intuitive learning infrastructure that increases individual competence and organizational capability. This learning infrastructure not only increases the understanding of oneself (e.g., vision, mission, and goals) but also increases the mutual understanding of others who successfully execute the CMS. Without this mutual infrastructure, limitations, misalignments, and performance risks are increased. When contract management terminology, practices, policies, and processes are interpreted consistently, the likelihood of reaching agreement on matters relating to contract intent, interpretation, and performance is increased (Cleven et al., 2024). Additionally, when government and industry adopt the CMS, the skills and experience gained from each sector are valuable to the other sector as well. The common and repeated use of a consensus-based standard will improve productivity, increase efficiency, and reduce cost (NCMA, 2023, p. 1). For example, when contract management professionals, both buyers and sellers, speak a common language based on the CMS, the government and industry workforce have marketability through the transfer of skills (Williams, 2024) and this will help organizations improve productivity, increase efficiency, and reduce cost.

## Notes

1 NASPO, "Chapter 17: Cooperative Purchasing," in *State and Local Government Procurement: A Practical Guide* (Plantation, FL: J. Ross Publishing, 2024), 255–256.

2 NASPO ValuePoint. "About NASPO Value Point Cooperative Contracts," accessed March 8, 2024, www.naspovaluepoint.org/cooperative-contracts/

3 NASPO ValuePoint. "Ask ValuePoint," accessed March 8, 2024, www.naspovaluepoint.org/faqs/

4 NASPO ValuePoint. "Explore Contract Portfolios" NASPO ValuePoint, accessed March 8, 2024, www.naspovaluepoint.org/portfolios/?sortBy=name&sortByDir=asc#list
5 NASPO, "Chapter 17: Cooperative Purchasing," in *State and Local Government Procurement: A Practical Guide* (Plantation, FL: J. Ross Publishing, 2024), 255–256.
6 National Association of State Procurement Professionals (NASPO). "About Us," NASPO, accessed March 8, 2024, www.naspo.org/about/about-naspo/

## References

Abutabenjeh, S., Dimand, A. M., & Tao, J. (2023). Determinants of the success of cooperative public procurement. *Public Performance & Management Review*, *46*(2), 391–417.

Abutabenjeh, S., Dimand, A. N., Trammell, E., & Ahmadu, A. (2022). Assessing gender and diversity in public procurement research and practice. *International Journal of Public Administration, 46*(10), 728–739. https://doi.org/10.1080/01900692.2021.2013258.

Abutabenjeh, S., & Rendon, R.G. (2023). Procurement and contract management deficiencies: Analysis of state audit reports. *International Journal of Public Sector Performance Management*, *11*(1), 81–107.

Andhov, M., Caranta, R., Stoffel, T., Grandia, J., Janssen, W. A., Vornicu, R., ..., & Wiesbrock, A. (2020). Sustainability through Public Procurement: The Way Forward–Reform Proposals.

Balaeva, O., Rodionova, Y., Yakovlev, A., & Tkachenko, A. (2022). Public procurement efficiency as perceived by market participants: The case of Russia. *International Journal of Public Administration*, *45*(16), 1156–1167.

Brunjes, B., Abutabenjeh, S., Anguelov, L., Dimand, A. M., & Rodriguez-Plesa, E. (2023). Future Directions for Research in Public Procurement and Contract Management. In *Research handbook on public financial management*. K.D. Dzigbede & W.B. Hildreth (Eds.). Edward Elgar Publishing (pp. 341–367).

Caldwell, N., Walker, H., Harland, C., Knight, L., Zheng, J., & Wakeley, T. (2005). Promoting competitive markets: The role of public procurement. *Journal of Purchasing and Supply Management*, *11*(5–6), 242–251.

Cameron, A. & Rendon, R. G. (in press). Effective practices in the use of partnership intermediary agreements: A case study of the U.S. Air Force. *Journal of Contract Management*.

Celhay, P. A., Gertler, P., Olivares, M., & Undurraga, R. (2024). *How Managers Can Use Purchaser Performance Information to Improve Procurement Efficiency* (No. w32141). National Bureau of Economic Research.

Cleven, J., Rendon, R. G., & Wilkinson, J. (2024). Professional association impact on training, academia, and professional development: The case for contract management. *Journal of Contract Management*, *18*, 39–63. National Contract Management Association.

Cooper, P. J. (2002). *Governing by contract: Challenges and opportunities for public managers*. CQ Press.

Davies, G. (2023). *Lessons learned: Competition in public procurement*. National Audit Office. Retrieved from: www.nao.org.uk/wp-content/uploads/2023/07/lessons-learned-competition-in-public-procurement-summary.pdf

Department of Defense Inspector General (DoD IG). (2024a). Audit of DoD Use of the Government Purchase Card in Response to the Coronavirus Disease–2019 Pandemic. Report No. DODIG-2024-045.

Department of Defense Inspector General (DoD IG). (2024b). Audit of the DoD's Oversight of Cost-Plus-Award-Fee Contracts. Report No. DODIG-2024-055.

Dunn, R. L. (2021). *Guide to other transactions authority*. Strategic Institute for Innovation in Government Contracting.

Federal Acquisition Regulation (FAR) (2024). Federal Acquisition Regulation (FAR), 48 C.F.R. ch. 1 (2025). Available online at: www.acquisition.gov/browse/index/far

Feiock, R. C. (2013). The institutional collective action framework. *Policy Studies Journal*, *41*(3), 397–425.

Field, L. A. (2023). Federal Acquisition Certification in Contracting (FAC-C) Modernization (Memorandum). Executive Office of the President, Office of Management and Budget, Office of Federal Procurement Policy. www.whitehouse.gov/wp-content/uploads/2023/01/FAC-C-Modernization-Memorandum-19-Jan-2023.pdf

GSA (2024). U.S. General Services Administration. Available online at www.gsa.gov/buy-through-us/purchasing-programs/federal-strategic-sourcing-initiative

International Association of Contract and Commercial Management (2013, September 2013). The Value of Contract Management Return on Investment Survey Results.

Išljamović, S., Jeremić, V., Petrović, N., & Radojičić, Z. (2015). Colouring the socio-economic development into green: I-distance framework for countries' welfare evaluation. *Quality & Quantity*, *49*, 617–629.

Jovanovic, P., Joksimovic, N. Z., & Milosavljevic, M. (2013). The efficiency of public procurement centralization: Empirical evidence from Serbian local self-governments. *Lex Localis*, *11*(4), 883.

Kloot, L., & Martin, J. (2000). Strategic performance management: A balanced approach to performance management issues in local government. *Management Accounting Research*, *11*(2), 231–251.

Kozik, R., & Karasińska-Jaśkowiec, I. (2016). Green public procurement–legal base and instruments supporting sustainable development in the construction industry in Poland. *E3S Web of Conferences*, *10*, 00044. EDP Sciences.

Kumar, A., Nair, A., & Piecha, J. (2015). Measuring efficiency in international public procurement. *Journal of Public Procurement*, *15*(3), 365–389.

Lopes, A. V., & Farias, J. S. (2020). How can governance support collaborative innovation in the public sector? A systematic review of the literature. *International Review of Administrative Sciences*, *88*(1), 114–130.

Medeiros, R. (2014). The new Directive 2014/24/EU on Public Procurement: A First Overview. In *2nd European Conference on e-Public Procurement*, Portugal.

Milosavljević, M., Dobrota, M., & Milanović, N. (2019). A new approach to the evaluation of public procurement efficiency among European countries. *European Review*, *27*(2), 246–259.

National Contract Management Association (NCMA). (2022). *Contract management body of knowledge (CMBOK)* (7th edition). NCMA.

National Contract Management Association (NCMA). (2023). The Contract Management Standard (ANSI/NCMA ASD 1–2019 [R2022]). www.ncmahq.org/Web/Web/Standards---Practices/Contract-Management-Standard-Publication.aspx

National Contract Management Association (NCMA). (2024). National Contract Management Association. www.ncmahq.org/

Naval Audit Service. (2023). Contract Closeout Procedures at Naval Facilities Engineering Systems Command. Naval Audit Service, Report N2024-0002.

Naval Postgraduate School (NPS). (2025). Academic Catalog. https://nps.edu/web/registrar/academic-catalog

Office of the Secretary of the Navy. (2019, May 14). Organic Department of the Navy Procurement System Oversight and Management (SECNAVINST 4200.37A). Department of the Navy. https://apps.dtic.mil/sti/pdfs/AD1127102.pdf

Panayiotou, N. A., Gayialis, S. P., & Tatsiopoulos, I. P. (2004). An e-procurement system for governmental purchasing. *International Journal of Production Economics*, *90*(1), 79–102.

Patrucco, A. S., Luzzini, D., & Ronchi, S. (2016). Evaluating the effectiveness of public procurement performance management systems in local governments. *Local Government Studies*, *42*(5), 739–761.

Peña, V., Mandelbaum, J., Babou, T., & Cavanaugh, C. (2020). *Opportunities to advance Department of Defense technology transfer with partnership intermediary agreements*. Institute for Defense Analyses.

Pysmenna, M., Pohribna, N., & Kalnytska, M. (2019). Assessment system of the public procurement efficiency. *Baltic Journal of Economic Studies*, *5*(5), 136–144.

Rendon, J. M., & Rendon, R. G. (2016). Procurement fraud in the US Department of Defense: Implications for contracting processes and internal controls. *Managerial Auditing Journal*, *31*(6/7), 748–767.

Rendon, R. G. (2005). Commodity sourcing strategies: Processes, best practices, and defense initiatives. *Journal of Contract Management*, *3*(1), 7–20.
Rendon, R. G. (2015). Benchmarking contract management process maturity: A case study of the US Navy. *Benchmarking: An International Journal*, *22*(7), 1481–1508.
Rendon, R. G., & Snider, K. F. (Eds.). (2019). *Management of defense acquisition projects*. American Institute of Aeronautics and Astronautics.
Schapper, P., Veiga Malta, J. N., & Gilbert, D. L. (2006). An analytical framework for the management and reform of public procurement. *Journal of Public Procurement*, *6*(1), 1–26.
Selviaridis, K., Luzzini, D., & Mena, C. (2023). How strategic public procurement creates social value: Evidence from UK anchor institutions. *Public Management Review*, 1–29. https://doi.org/10.1080/14719037.2023.2277814
Tenaglia, J. M. (2021). Restructuring of the Certification Program for the Contracting Functional Area (Memorandum). www.acq.osd.mil/dpap/policy/policyvault/USA000182-21-DPC.pdf
Trenchfield, A. (2023). Artificial intelligence is coming for contracting. *Contract Management*, *63*(2), 18–23. National Contract Management Association.
Williams, S. (2024, January). Common language adopters are elevating the profession. *Contract Management*, *64*(1), 24–29. National Contract Management Association.
Wondimu, P. A., Lohne, J., & Laedre, O. (2018). Competitive dialogue in Norwegian public infrastructure projects. *Journal of Construction Engineering and Management*, *144*(10). https://doi.org/10.1061/(asce)co.1943-7862.0001540
World Commerce & Contracting (WorldCC). (2024). Your Global Hub for Commercial & Contract Management. www.worldcc.com/

## *Case Study: Turning Around a Failing Procurement Department (Developed by Sawsan Abutabenjeh and Rene G. Rendon)*

### Background

Mr. Allen Montogramy is the new procurement director for a state procurement department located in the midwestern United States. The state has a population of 11 million and approximately 50,000 full-time employees. Allen reports directly to the director of the Department of Administration. The state procurement department's mission is to provide supplies and services to state agencies in an effective and efficient manner that ensures both the appropriate expenditure of taxpayer dollars and the uninterrupted provision of supplies and services.

### Problem Statement

Unfortunately, the department is currently not meeting mission objectives. The newly hired procurement director is faced with improving the department's procurement processes, policies, and personnel so it can increase procurement operation efficiency and begin to achieve its mission objectives. The department is specifically plagued with problems related to management, contracting, and internal controls. Each of these issues is detailed in the three sections below.

#### *Management Problems*

1. The state has not established any education, training, or experience requirements for the recruitment, hiring, or retention of procurement personnel.
2. The procurement department does not provide any contract management training or competency development for its procurement personnel.

3. The procurement department has no established contracting policies or processes required for use by the procurement personnel.
4. The procurement department does not conduct any contracting process assessments or personnel performance reviews.
5. The procurement department has not established a best practice or lessons learned program to help improve future procurements.
6. The procurement department does not provide any training to companies interested in doing business with the state. The procurement department has not established a contractor guidebook to help contractors in doing business with the state.
7. The procurement department does not provide any training to its state customers in need of procured products or services.

*Contracting Problems*

1. State procurement personnel are not conducting due diligence in pre-award, award, and post-award contracting activities. This has led to the awarding of the deficient contracts to non-performing contractors, and the procurement of supplies and services that fail to meet the needs of state agencies.
2. Contracts are awarded late and deliveries are always behind schedule.
3. Contractors are not meeting cost, schedule, and performance objects of the contract.
4. Companies that are being awarded contracts are not qualified to perform the required work.
5. The procurement department's customers are not satisfied with the performance of the procurement department.
6. The procurement department has established only one contracting method that is used regardless of the estimated dollar amount or the type of product or service that is being procured.
7. The procurement department's contracts have total periods of performance of only one year and the contracts expire at the end of the year even though the required product or service is needed for multiple years. This forces contract re-competitions every year.
8. The procurement department's contracts are awarded to only one company even though the requirement quantity is large enough that it can be met by multiple companies working on separate contracts.
9. Many of the department's procurement activities are manual using simple software solutions such as word processing and spreadsheets. None of the procurement activities are automated.

*Internal Control Problems*

1. The procurement department's contracts have been found to be non-compliant with state statutes and policies.
2. The procurement department's procurement processes and activities have not been reviewed by an independent state audit agency.
3. The procurement department's award contracts and related contract files do not get reviewed on a periodic basis by an independent state audit agency.
4. The procurement department lacks adequate documentation and procedures that lead to missing procurement records for audits.

**Discussion Questions**

1. As the newly hired procurement director, what system can you use to assess your department's procurement performance? How would such a system be established?
2. What tool(s) can be used to assess your department's contracting process capability?
3. How can the director establish a system of internal controls and audits to ensure department procurement practices comply with state procurement laws and codes?
4. What resources are available to the procurement director for establishing polices, processes, and practices for the departments' contract life cycle activities?
5. How can the department establish procurement policies and processes to reflect the type of product/service being procured?
6. How can the department establish procurement policies and processes to reflect the dollar value of the expected procurement?
7. What contract instruments can be used to extend the period of performance of awarded contracts without having to re-compete contracts?
8. What contracting approach can be used to leverage multiple contractors working on similar effort to meet the mission requirement?
9. How can the director apply artificial intelligence (AI) solutions to the contract life cycle activities?
10. What resources are available to the director to use in providing training to the procurement workforce, department customers, as well as to the state's contractor workforce?

*Case Study: Cooperative Procurement: NASPO ValuePoint (Developed by NASPO)*

National Association of State Procurement Officials (NASPO) ValuePoint is the cooperative contracting program division of the NASPO that uses the unique the Lead State™ model, which allows states to leverage their spending through a single solicitation to obtain favorable contract terms and competitive pricing for states and public entities. NASPO ValuePoint's emphasis on best value pricing, reliability, transparency, and favorable terms makes it a valuable tool for public governance by enabling states to streamline procurement processes, save resources, and secure high-quality contracts for public entities.

Unique to NASPO ValuePoint, the Lead State™ model allows NASPO ValuePoint to aggregate the demand of public entities and then support a lead state in developing the solicitation, facilitation of the competitive evaluation, and award with the assistance of a multistate sourcing team.[1]

These sourcing teams bring together procurement and subject matter experts from state and other government procurement professionals around the nation. The resulting NASPO ValuePoint contracts allow public entities to purchase from these contracts with various benefits, such as lower costs and contractual protections. Additionally, contractors benefit from limiting the expense of repetitive bid preparations, and the process benefits taxpayers through improved transparency and reliability.

All states, US Territories, and the District of Columbia are eligible to use NASPO ValuePoint contracts. Within each state, the State Procurement Official, in accordance with its own state statutes, determines if the state is eligible, whether it will use each NASPO ValuePoint contract, and which entities within its state may use each NASPO ValuePoint contract.[2] These entities can include state agencies, higher education institutions, and political subdivisions. Additionally, in some states, non-profit organizations are eligible.

NASPO ValuePoint cooperative contracts facilitate billions of dollars in annual spend. There are no costs or fees for public entities to use NASPO ValuePoint contracts.[3] Instead, a small fee is collected from the supplier. This fee helps fund NASPO operations, provide professional development training opportunities to public entities nationally, and reimburse costs to the states or public entities related to their development and administration of the solicitations and agreements. In 2024, NASPO ValuePoint offered more than 70 contract portfolios ranging from Women, Infant , and Children (WIC) infant formula to Cloud Solutions.[4]

NASPO ValuePoint staff support state and public entity staff by[5]:

- Performing market and technical research in the industry marketplace to determine commodity and service opportunities to benefit governmental purchasing
- Utilizing analytics and metrics on current portfolios to determine the next steps and improvement in any re-solicitations
- Providing technical and procurement expertise and support Lead States™ and sourcing teams
- Identifying and supporting volunteer sourcing teams
- Collecting and managing administrative purchasing fees from participating suppliers
- Providing ongoing education to Lead States™ and Teams
- Conducting supplier development and training programs to assist in understanding government procurement and/or NASPO ValuePoint Cooperatives

As a nonprofit association, NASPO is dedicated to advancing public procurement through leadership, excellence, and integrity. It is made up of the directors of the central purchasing offices in each of the 50 states, the District of Columbia, and the territories of the United States.[6] NASPO is an organization that seeks to help its members achieve success as public procurement leaders through the promotion of best practices, education, professional development, research, and innovative procurement strategies. NASPO's educational resources are widely available through Procurement U, with numerous professional development opportunities, training, and career advancement resources. These resources support procurement professionals nationally in achieving the Certified Public Procurement Officer (CPPO) and Certified Professional Public Buyer (CPPB) certifications. NASPO also sponsors multiple conferences, events, and webinars throughout the year for its members, public entities, and the supplier community.

### Discussion Questions

How does the Lead State™ model used by NASPO ValuePoint enhance efficiency, transparency, and cost savings in public procurement compared to traditional decentralized procurement approaches?

What governance and accountability challenges might arise when multiple states and public entities rely on cooperative contracts, and how could these challenges be mitigated?

Considering NASPO ValuePoint's funding structure (supplier-paid fees and no cost to public entities), what are the potential advantages and risks of this model for maintaining fairness, sustainability, and trust in the cooperative procurement process?

# 10 Sustainable Public Procurement

*Justin M. Stritch, Yifan Chen, Nicole Darnall, Shirley-Ann Augustin-Behravesh and Kayla Le*

## 10.1 Introduction

Public procurement accounts for 13–20 percent of global gross domestic product annually (World Bank Group, 2020). Purchased items range from chemicals to electronics to office materials and many other products and services that are required to provide public goods and services. Collectively, these purchases generate significant environmental and social impacts, risks, and costs and account for 92 percent of an organization's total greenhouse gas (GHG) emissions (Carbon Disclosure Project (CDP), 2021) and 40 percent of global GHG emissions (Labutong and Hoen, 2018).

The tremendous purchasing power of governments, coupled with the sustainability impacts associated with their procurements, presents an immense opportunity to affect global sustainability outcomes. The United Nations and other international governance bodies, such as the World Bank and the Organisation for Economic Co-operation and Development, have identified sustainable public procurement (SPP) as a critical climate solution and a way to improve multiple societal objectives, including pursuing social equity among historically disadvantaged groups (Fernandez et al., 2013; Dimand and Cheng, 2023; Stritch et al., 2020; United Nations Environment Programme (UNEP), 2022). Additionally, research organizations, such as the Sustainable Procurement Research Initiative, and professional organizations, including the Sustainable Purchasing Leadership Council and the International City/County Management Association, are increasingly endorsing SPP as a tool for governments to achieve their sustainability goals (Hafsa et al., 2021b).

**SPP** is a process employed by public authorities to improve societal and environmental outcomes while stimulating the production of more sustainable products and services through procurement practices (Li and Geiser, 2005; Darnall et al., 2022a). The underlying objective of SPP is to enhance the overall well-being of society (Dimand and Cheng, 2023; Behravesh et al., 2022) by integrating sustainable development principles across all stages of the procurement process, from sourcing to purchasing and supply chain management.

Additionally, by aligning procurement processes with sustainability principles, governments can improve their operational efficiencies while reducing risks posed by climate change and other global threats (Stritch et al., 2020; Behravesh et al., 2022). For instance, by procuring energy-efficient streetlights, the City of Phoenix (United States) saved over $1 million per year in energy costs and reduced its overall carbon emissions (Darnall et al., 2018b).

While the focus of this chapter is on key elements of SPP in practice, SPP research has been informed by a range of theoretical perspectives. Institutional theories and perspectives are instructive for understanding the role of policies, stakeholders, and organizations in the

DOI: 10.4324/9781003566670-12

adoption and implementation of SPP (e.g., Brammer and Walker, 2011; Raj et al., 2020), as well as theories on the diffusion of innovation (e.g., Rolfstram et al., 2011; Dimand, 2022). Theories of leadership and organizational culture (e.g., Etse et al., 2022), organization structures and technology (e.g., Chen et al., 2022), and theories of the individual (e.g., Grandia et al., 2015) have also generated important insights into the different aspects of SPP implementation. However, the goal of this chapter is not to develop nor extend these theoretical perspectives. Instead, we synthesize this diverse, complex, and growing literature to help students and practitioners understand what SPP is in practice and the factors that facilitate its adoption and implementation, as well as the barriers or challenges they will need to consider.

In the next section, we review the literature to define SPP and discuss factors that are associated with SPP adoption and implementation success. We focus on seven facilitators that are widely discussed in SPP literature and draw from a wide range of U.S. and international examples. We want to note that while we discuss these items as facilitators, their absence may also present barriers to implementation depending on the local context.

## 10.2 Summary of the Literature – Factors Supporting SPP Success

**Purchasing criteria** are the characteristics by which goods and services are evaluated in the procurement process. Traditionally, products and services have been judged by criteria such as cost and quality. SPP introduces environmental and social criteria into the public procurement process (Walker and Phillips, 2009; Walker and Brammer, 2009; Coggburn and Rahm, 2005) either formally, by way of SPP policies such as ordinances, executive orders, resolutions, and administrative directives, or less formally when governments append SPP to related policies or plans (Hsueh et al., 2020). **Environmental criteria** are the characteristics used to evaluate and select suppliers and products based on their environmental impacts, such as energy efficiency, waste reduction, or carbon footprint. These criteria are often added to a government's existing sustainability plan or energy conservation policy (Darnall et al., 2017b, 2018a; Hsueh et al., 2020). Environmental criteria may also include reducing broader environmental impacts such as minimizing consumption, GHG emissions, solid waste, and toxic chemicals. For instance, as part of its broader sustainability plan, a government may introduce procurement criteria that reduce its packaging and waste, assess its vendor's environmental performance, encourage more environmentally friendly products, or reduce carbon impacts associated with the transport of goods (Islam et al., 2017). Often the term "green" is associated with these characteristics.

Related to the social aspects of SPP, **social criteria** are the characteristics used to evaluate and select suppliers and products based on opportunities to enhance or improve social equity, diversity, working conditions, and human rights (Alkadry et al., 2019; Behravesh et al., 2022; Cheng and Ali, 2023). They may also seek to increase community involvement and support community economic development by focusing on buying from small-scale suppliers (Carter and Rogers, 2008; Romzek and Johnston, 2005; Walker and Brammer, 2009). Other social criteria may advance social equality in economic development through purchasing preferences given to women-owned businesses (McCrudden and Doreen, 2007; Furneaux and Barraket, 2014), veteran-owned businesses (McGrann, 2014), and minority-owned businesses (Stritch et al., 2020; Hawkins et al., 2018).

Regardless of whether a government emphasizes environmental sustainability, social sustainability or both, SPP requires system-wide changes to traditional procurement processes. These changes often involve new regulatory and internal support structures, training, and different ways of engaging with vendors and other stakeholders (Behravesh et al., 2022).

### *10.2.1 National/State Sustainability Commitment and Regulation*

About 19 percent of national governments have instituted regulations for mandatory SPP. **Mandatory SPP** consists of regulation that requires compliance with set SPP standards (UNEP, 2022). These higher level sustainability commitments can help bring focus to SPP as a sustainability solution and help to garner resources and attention to facilitate successful implementation. For example, in its national plan, Australia has established national climate emission reduction goals to reduce its carbon emissions by 26–28 percent by 2030. By establishing these national goals, states within Australia have begun considering creative sustainability approaches, including SPP. For example, New South Wales, Australia's southeast state, requires its local governments to emphasize the procurement of low-emission products (Lingegård et al., 2021). These requirements provide clear focus from higher level support, which helps mobilize actions and shift internal cultures in lower levels of government (Wierzbicki et al., 2022).

Mandatory SPP relies on regulations to create strong incentives that encourage SPP across the organization, because expectations are formalized and employees can be held accountable for implementation (UNEP, 2022). For instance, within the U.S., an Executive Order in the Commonwealth of Massachusetts requires all state agencies to mitigate the negative sustainability impacts of their purchases. This requirement has provided the Commonwealth with a pathway to dedicate resources toward SPP training and education. Today, Massachusetts is recognized as a state leader in advancing SPP. At the local level, the City of Tempe, Arizona (U.S.), reports that its departments have prioritized SPP because it is endorsed by a City Council directive (Behravesh et al., 2022).

National and regional mandatory sustainability regulations can also provide motivation for local governments to adopt SPP, even if it is not required. For instance, in 2001, Japan passed a law requiring all national agencies and all prefectural governments to develop SPP policies. Because of the mandatory requirements at the national and prefectural level, 700 local governments developed SPP policies of their own (Darnall et al., 2018a).

In contrast, **voluntary SPP** consists of general guidance to include certain sustainability criteria in procurement but does not require any specific action. Voluntary SPP can elevate SPP as an organization goal or an objective to consider but lacks the same monitoring, incentives, and resources that come with a mandatory SPP. This can lead to inconsistent implementation while sending only a weak signal to markets about the importance of producing sustainable products and services (Wierzbicki et al., 2022).

### *10.2.2 Value Procurement*

When government emphasizes sustainability attributes associated with a purchase (over the product's purchase price), it is more likely to implement SPP successfully because it pays greater attention to the economic, environmental, and social equity impacts of its procurement activities (Casier and Ruete, 2020). By doing so, procurement managers are incentivized to deliver social benefits to a wider range of stakeholders and reduce environmental harms. **Value procurement** focuses on the total life cycle cost of procuring a good or service and is a more accurate assessment of the true cost of goods and services (Busellato et al., 2021; Swanson et al., 2022). By contrast, the most common criterion used for procuring goods and services is purchase price, which tends to exclude social and environmental costs that are associated with product sourcing, use, and disposal (Swanson et al., 2022).

**Life cycle cost** is the full cost (social, environmental, and economic) of a product over its entire life, including costs for research and development, testing, production, operation, maintenance, and disposal (França et al., 2021). For instance, the United Kingdom's 2012 Social Value Act requires the government to "explicitly evaluate social value when awarding most major contracts." Similarly, the executive authority of the Australian Capital Territory (ACT), one of the territories of Australia, which also governs all local government affairs, requires its departments and local governments to pursue value for money procurement. Factors to be considered in procurement include existing government policies, whole-of-life costs, design for the environment, environmental labels, environmental performance, and demand management opportunities (Andhov et al. 2025).

### *10.2.3 Internal SPP Leaders and Champions*

Management research has long recognized the importance of leaders and champions as drivers of cultural changes and implementation of new organizational practices, routines, and norms related to SPP (Pruess and Walker 2011; Roman 2017). An **SPP champion** is a leader that helps build momentum for SPP across the organization by translating the vision for SPP into actions, words, and commitments in a way that inspires and empowers others to act (Behravesh et al., 2022; Sönnichsen and Clement, 2020). Because of their legitimacy among their peers and support from higher level management, champions influence others around them (Hoffman, 2000) and are an essential part of SPP implementation.

One example of how SPP champions help facilitate SPP is seen in the City of Tempe (U.S.). When the city implemented its 2019 Climate Action Plan, the Director of Purchasing believed that SPP might be a means by which the city could meet its climate goals. He became the central champion for exploring SPP and developing a shared set of SPP beliefs, values, and activities across the city (Behravesh et al., 2022). His ideas were reinforced by the city's Director of Sustainability and Resilience and its Deputy Mayor, both of whom were strong advocates for sustainability across the city (Behravesh et al., 2022). As a consequence of his advocacy, in 2020, the City of Tempe voted on and approved its SPP policy, which is now an integral component of the city's climate action plan.

### *10.2.4 SPP Training and Education*

In addition to leaders and champions, the broader base of employees also plays a critical role in SPP implementation, and a lack of knowledge and skills is a limiting factor in effective SPP implementation (UNEP, 2022; Grandia and Voncken, 2019). In many instances, despite having a formal policy, organizations fail to invest in employee training and education when managers and leaders fail to see the full value of SPP (Swanson et al., 2022). **SPP training and education** occur when organizations dedicate time and resources to create a shared understanding about the importance of sustainability and how the procurement process can be leveraged to advance sustainability goals. SPP training and education include short workshops and certification programs offered through professional associations. They are critical mechanisms for employees to understand the concepts and practical applications of SPP and are vital first steps toward empowering them to act and ensuring they are positioned to implement SPP successfully and reinforce a culture of sustainability (Swanson et al., 2022). Trained and educated staff play a critical role in shaping an organization's adoption and implementation of sustainability innovations, since they tend to have a stronger understanding of organizational issues based on their daily interactions (Hasu et al., 2011).

### *10.2.5 SPP Criteria and Performance Measurement*

**SPP criteria** define what product characteristics must be met in order for a procurement contract or a product to meet the organization's expectation of being "sustainable." Formal SPP criteria reduce ambiguity for procurement managers. Example criteria include requiring that procured products be produced with no child labor, meet minimum expectations for energy or water efficiency, and ensure that vendors have a climate risk mitigation plan (Zhang et al., 2018). Having clear SPP criteria reduces the chance of procuring products that are less sustainable. Clear criteria also provide vendors with transparent expectations of what is needed to do business with the government and incentives to address their sustainability impacts. As an example, Poland has adopted a National Plan for Sustainable Procurement, which sets clear SPP criteria. These criteria were used to create a catalog of products and services that meet minimum sustainability expectations (Ministerstwo Rozwoju i Technologii, 2022), which have increased procurement managers' confidence about implementing SPP (Lewis and Machlowska, 2022).

**Performance measurement** refers to the process of collecting and tracking outcome data. Organizations manage what they measure, and those that track their SPP spending are more likely to elevate the importance of SPP in their organizational routines and practices (Darnall et al., 2017a). By tracking sustainable procurement spending, organizations are better positioned to reduce costs related to energy, water, fuel, and other expenditures and reward employees who are making strides to meet the organization's SPP goals (Darnall et al., 2017a). The Commonwealth of Massachusetts is one example. It has embedded SPP performance tracking within its electronic procurement (or e-procurement) systems. Using spreadsheets and data visualization software, the Commonwealth is able to produce informative reports about their SPP performance that can be assessed over time. Performance measurement approaches such as these create opportunities to develop goals and targets around SPP and more appropriately recognize departments and employees who are meeting or exceeding (or failing to meet) SPP expectations.

### *10.2.6 Information Management and E-Procurement*

While setting criteria and measuring performance are important, it is also important to consider the systems that are needed to implement these criteria and ensure that performance is monitored and measured. Well-organized, user-friendly information systems ensure procurement personnel have access to product information. Even for simple decisions, information is vital to effective decision-making. Product **ecolabels/certifications** are particularly important SPP information (Darnall et al., 2017a). Ecolabeled products generally bear a recognizable label or seal that indicates to procurement officers specific information about the product's sustainability attributes (Darnall and Aragón-Correa, 2014). Because they are externally verified, ecolabels increase the credibility of a vendor's sustainability claims (Darnall et al., 2023). In order to access this information, organizations often rely on online SPP **product catalogs**, which are digital platforms or databases that provide searchable information about sustainable products and services.

However, sustainable product information is often lacking for many governments. For instance, in the U.S., less than half of local governments reported that they have access to environmental information that is critical to SPP decisions (Darnall et al., 2017a). Such information includes access to product ecolabels/certifications and online databases of sustainable products and services.

**E-procurement systems** are digital platforms or software solutions that automate and streamline the procurement process (Chen et al., 2022). They are another way to effectively integrate sustainability information into purchasing and can radically reduce the costs of seeking sustainable goods and services for purchasing managers. This is done by customizing standard e-procurement systems to include sustainability criteria and dashboards to track sustainability performance (UNEP, 2022). By integrating SPP into e-procurement, organizations have the potential to raise the profile of sustainable products or services so that they become the default decision during purchasing. Because purchasing information is maintained in an integrated electronic system, organizations can more easily track their sustainable spend, monitor SPP progress, and incentivize sustainable purchasing behavior (Swanson et al., 2022).

In addition to e-procurement systems that provide product information, more complex tools are available that can be used to calculate different product risks. An example is Sweden's online "risk analysis service" and "Life Cycle Costing" tools, which have helped inform procurement managers about a product's environmental and social impacts that are accrued over its lifetime. **Life cycle cost tools** enable procurers to quickly estimate the lifetime costs (and savings) associated with multiple products (Lewis and Machlowska, 2022) and help facilitate SPP implementation success.

### *10.2.7 Vendor Collaboration*

**Vendors** are entities that sell goods or services. Also "suppliers" or "sellers," vendors can be useful partners in facilitating an organization's SPP success because they can educate purchasers about their product options (Behravesh et al., 2022). At the local level, municipalities that report having greater SPP implementation success tend to work closely with their vendors and regard them as collaborators and important allies during the implementation of their SPP (Darnall et al., 2017a). Examples of governments that strongly encourage vendor collaboration include the Netherlands, which has created "Green Deals" that enable public and private actors to form coalitions and actively collaborate (Lingegård et al., 2021, p. 9). The interactions facilitate critical information exchanges between the two groups so that they can discover innovative ways to meet their sustainability goals. Additionally, the European Union encourages market consultations with vendors prior to developing a tender and in every stage of the procurement process (before, during, and after the tender), as long as transparency, equal treatment of all suppliers, and other conditions are satisfied (European Union, 2014). These collaborations support governments by providing critical information that informs SPP opportunities that may otherwise not be discovered.

## 10.3 Important Themes and Emergent Issues

While the previous section provides an overview of current literature on the factors that are associated with SPP adoption and implementation success, there are a number of emergent issues both driving and shaping how public organizations enact SPP and the considerable challenges and barriers they must work to confront.

### *10.3.1 Shifts in the Regulatory Environment*

As noted in the previous section, broader environmental regulations are drivers of both SPP adoption and implementation (Walker et al., 2008; Behravesh et al., 2022). However, recent regulatory shifts related to addressing climate change are accelerating this focus (Lăzăroiu et al., 2020). Early SPP efforts focused on recycled products and reducing the use of toxic materials. These were often consistent with local policies and ordinances regarding recycling and discarding toxic materials. As other environmental policies and regulations influenced early SPP efforts, there has been an increasing regulatory shift toward a greater emphasis on carbon and GHG reductions, which serves as an impetus for increased SPP engagement on these issues (Lăzăroiu et al., 2020). Moving forward, these are likely to be areas where governments will need to dedicate additional capacity in their SPP programs. Furthermore, the greater international focus stemming from the **United Nations Paris Climate Agreement,** a legally binding treaty aimed at mitigating climate change, will likely lead to more national governments making SPP mandatory in order to reduce their overall carbon footprint.

### *10.3.2 Fragmentation of Procurement and Purchasing Processes*

Government procurement reflects a wide array of processes, actors, and information technology (IT) systems (Chen et al., 2022). From a request for quotes or proposals to the processing of payment to a vendor, there are often multiple groups of people and different systems utilized. **Centralized procurement systems** are those in which a single group or department conducts all procurements for the organization. In **decentralized procurement systems,** individuals in different departments have the ability to procure goods and services. In many local governments, procurement and purchasing often occur in hybrid procurement systems (McCue and Pitze, 2000; Dimitri et al., 2006). In **hybrid procurement systems,** some types of procurement are centralized, while others are decentralized. For example, procurements such as those that exceed a particular cost threshold and require certain technical specifications might be led by the finance department or individuals who procure as their main job responsibilities. In contrast, other purchases for low-cost items (e.g., office and cleaning supplies) might be completed by individuals who purchase on behalf of a unit through catalogs and pre-existing vendor contracts but for whom purchasing is only a minor part of their job (Stritch et al., 2020; Chen et al., 2022). The fragmented and often decentralized nature of procurement adds multiple layers of complexity for SPP policy implementation, and environmental considerations have to be embedded and prioritized in the work among a wide range of actors.

This creates several challenges. First, given that procurement might only be a small part of some individuals' jobs, it can be challenging to increase the saliency of sustainability criteria across all relevant employees. One solution may be to utilize technologies such as e-procurement systems and online product catalogs to shape the choice architecture that purchasers confront, presenting or limiting choices to environmentally preferred options (Walker and Brammer, 2012). However, a second challenge is that purchasers are generally not the end users of the product or service. The purchaser is thus discouraged from taking on the risk associated with purchasing a product or service that is unproven, even if it is more sustainable.

### *10.3.3 Challenges with Advanced Data Tracking and Integrating IT Infrastructure*

Related to the often decentralized and fragmented nature of many procurement processes, data tracking and integration have emerged as a challenge for governments seeking to integrate SPP into their existing procurement practices. For example, information regarding the environmental performance of products might not be linked with the procurement system. Additionally, in many instances, procurement practitioners note that data collected regarding the sustainability performance of products and services are often not used to inform decision-making rather are aggregated and presented *after* the fact. Data are collected, and reports are generated, but in a way that is disconnected from the procurement process.

In instances where data are collected, they often are not integrated across different digital systems, which prevents them from being considered during the procurement process (Darnall et al., 2024). One reason relates to governments' continued reliance on **legacy digital technology systems**, or outdated software and hardware systems, which pose barriers to converting sustainability data to other formats or the applications and are not easily upgraded (Irani et al., 2023). Additionally, data integration would likely cause considerable disruption for users. Shifting the mindset of individuals and organizations to regard such data as an input rather than an output of their SPPs is critical for organizations to consider as they seek to embed SPP in their procurement systems.

An additional issue regarding SPP data is that governments are often dependent on the vendors themselves for information about the sustainability impacts associated with their business and their products. This can create a lack of standardized metrics and reporting that requires considerable effort to transform into usable data structures. While ecolabels and third-party certifications are useful, they vary significantly, with some being more robust than others, which makes them incomparable and not always reliable (Darnall and Aragón-Correa, 2014; Darnall et al., 2017b). With more than 450 ecolabels in the market, expecting purchasing managers to manually verify each of them is impossible. Within the U.S., the Environmental Protection Agency has developed recommendations for standards and ecolabels to help purchasers identify and procure more sustainable products and services (U.S. Environmental Protection Agency (USEPA), 2023); however, this guidance does not encompass the full range of available ecolabels in the market.

Given the complexity of this landscape, considerable opportunities exist for governments to utilize technologies and third-party application program interfaces that independently verify the sustainability impacts of the products and services they wish to purchase. Additionally, artificial intelligence technologies offer enormous promise to integrate sustainability considerations into contracting and procurement practices while creating new opportunities for SPP (Caldera et al., 2022).

#### *10.3.4 Multiple Priorities in the Procurement Process*

With respect to elevating SPP as a priority within an organization's procurement process, several opportunities exist. First, it is critical to note that historically procurement has been leveraged to advance a number of social goals (Stritch et al., 2020; Dimand and Cheng, 2023). For instance, governments at all levels have used procurement to support minority-owned business, women-owned business, veteran-owned business, or locally owned business preference policies (Darnall et al., 2018b). While such policies are important to social sustainability, in many instances, they are inconsistent with each other and environmental sustainability (Liao et al., 2019; Chen et al., 2022). Competing goals are further complicated when some policies are mandatory, while others are voluntary. Indeed, identifying ways to integrate social goals within the broader context of sustainability is critical in moving beyond seeing these goals as an "either/or" proposition.

As noted previously, elevating SPP as a priority in organizations is costly. While taking into account a product's life cycle costs has reshaped procurement thinking to some extent, the upfront cost and initial purchase price of products and services remain important considerations in public procurement (Keulemans and Van de Walle, 2017; Walker et al., 2008). Additionally, investment of any public resources toward meeting sustainability goals is often met with political opposition. Although value procurement can save budget resources in the long term, it often involves a higher initial purchase price, which can be a major issue when the budgets are limited (Brammer and Walker, 2011). Moving forward, it will be important for governments managing these political discussions to rely on the best practices of other governments who have successfully advanced the value procurement discussion.

#### *10.3.5 Rules and Limits to Engaging Vendors and Suppliers*

The previous section illustrates how SPP can be enhanced by collaborating with vendors. Vendors are important sources of information on both the environmental performance and impacts of different products and services, and often have more information regarding goods and services available on the market (Behravesh et al., 2022). This access to information helps reduce market uncertainty about the sustainability attributes of procured products and services. However, many governments, including the U.S., are less eager to promote **vendor collaboration**, which involves cooperative relationships between a government and its vendors (e.g., communication, information sharing) aimed at achieving shared goals and mutual benefits (Erridge and Nondi, 1994; Caldwell et al., 2005). Reluctance is due in part to regulatory safeguards against corruption and the misuse of taxpayer money, which generally requires public purchasers to keep an arm's length distance from vendors (Behravesh et al., 2022). These safeguards tend to reduce the public sector's discretion in vendor selection, while increasing accountability expectations (Schotanus and Telgen, 2007). Increased regulations around vendor selection also mean that procurement managers must be cautious of (or, in some settings, avoid) collaborations with vendors and contractors (Erridge and Nondi, 1994; Caldwell et al., 2005). Yet, U.S. governments, especially those at the local level, which respect these boundaries while seeking creative ways to engage their vendors, report greater SPP implementation success (Darnall et al., 2017a).

## 10.4 Conclusion

Governments have tremendous purchasing power. This fact, coupled with the sustainability impacts associated with their procurement, presents an immense opportunity to affect global sustainability outcomes. This chapter provides readers with an introduction to the literature, including the key factors associated with SPP success as well as emerging issues and challenges. In Appendix 1, we provide a teaching case to allow students to implement key concepts from the chapter. We describe a local government official responsible for exploring SPP in their community. After the description of the organization, we ask a series of questions to help you consider the various challenges and opportunities faced by decision makers tasked with implementing SPP.

## 10.5 Glossary

**Centralized procurement systems** are those in which a single group or department conducts all procurements for the organization.

**Decentralized procurement systems** allow for individuals in different departments to have the ability to conduct procurement.

**E-procurement systems**, or electronic procurement systems, are digital platforms or software solutions that automate and streamline the procurement process.

**Ecolabels** are recognizable labels or seals that indicate to procurement officers specific information about the product's sustainability attributes.

**Environmental criteria** are the characteristics used to evaluate and select suppliers and products based on their environmental impacts, such as energy efficiency, waste reduction, or carbon footprint.

**Hybrid procurement systems** are present when some types of procurements are centralized while others are decentralized.

**Legacy digital technology systems**, or outdated software and hardware systems, pose barriers to converting sustainability data to other digital formats or applications and are not easily upgraded.

**Life cycle cost** is the full cost (social, environmental, and economic) of a product over its entire life, including costs for research and development, testing, production, operation, maintenance, and disposal.

**Life cycle cost tools** enable procurers to quickly estimate the lifetime costs (and savings) associated with multiple products.

**Mandatory SPP** consists of regulation that requires compliance with set SPP policy standards.

**Performance measurement** refers to a process of collecting and tracking data on an activity.

**Purchasing criteria** are the characteristics by which goods and services are evaluated in the procurement process.

**Social criteria** are the characteristics used to evaluate and select suppliers and products based on their opportunities for improved social equity, diversity, working conditions, and human rights.

**SPP** is a process employed by public authorities to improve societal and environmental outcomes while stimulating the production of more sustainable products and services through procurement practices.

**SPP champion** is a leader that helps build momentum for SPP across the organization by translating the vision for SPP in actions, words, and commitments in a way that inspires and empowers others to act.

**SPP criteria** define what product characteristics must be met in order for a procurement contract or a product to meet the organization's expectation of being sustainable.

**SPP training and education** occur when organizations dedicate time and resources to create a shared understanding about the importance of sustainability and how the procurement process can be leveraged to advance sustainability goals.

**SPP product catalogs** are digital platforms or databases that provide searchable information about sustainable products and services.

**United Nations Paris Climate Agreement** is a legally binding treaty aimed at mitigating climate change.

**Value procurement** focuses on the total life cycle cost of procuring a good or service and provides a more accurate assessment of the true cost of goods and services.

**Vendors** are entities that sell goods or services.

**Vendor collaboration** involves cooperative relationships between a government and its vendors (e.g., communication, information sharing) aimed at achieving shared goals and mutual benefits.

**Voluntary SPP** consists of general guidance to include certain sustainability criteria in procurement but does not require any specific action.

## References

Alkadry, M. G., Trammell, E., and Dimand, A. M. (2019). The power of public procurement: social equity and sustainability as externalities and as deliberate policy tools. *International Journal of Procurement Management* 12(3), 336–362.

Andhov, M., Darnall, N., Andhov, A. (2025). Leveraging AI for sustainable public procurement: Opportunities and challenges. *Frontiers in Sustainability* 6. https://doi.org/10.3389/frsus.2025.1603214

Behravesh, S.-A., Darnall, N., and Bretschneider, S. (2022). A framework for understanding sustainable public purchasing. *Journal of Cleaner Production* 376, 134122. https://doi.org/10.1016/j.jclepro.2022.134122

Brammer, S., and Walker, H. (2011). Sustainable procurement in the public sector: an international comparative study. *International Journal of Operations & Production Management*, 31(4), 452–476.

Busellato, N., Drentin, R. and Kishore, S. (2021, February 25). *The Hidden Source of Value: Procurement*. New York: McKinsey & Company.

Caldera, S., Mohamed, S., and Feng, Y. (2022). Evaluating the COVID-19 impacts on sustainable procurement: experiences from the Australian built environment sector. *Sustainability*, 14(7), 4163.

Caldwell, N., Walker, H., Harland, C., Knight, L., Zheng, J., and Wakeley, T. (2005). Promoting competitive markets: the role of public procurement. *Journal of Purchasing and Supply Management* 11(5), 242–251.

Carbon Disclosure Project (CDP). (2021). Transparency to Transformation: A Chain Reaction. CDP Global Supply Chain Report. Available at: https://cdn.cdp.net/cdp-production/cms/reports/documents/000/006/106/original/CDP_SC_Report_2021.pdf

Carter, C. R., and Rogers, D. S. (2008). A framework of sustainable supply chain management: moving toward new theory. *International Journal of Physical Distribution and Logistics Management* 22(2), 195–219.

Casier, L., and Ruete, M. (2020). *Toward Strategic Public Procurement in Latin America and the Caribbean*. Washington, DC: Organization of American States and the International Institute for Sustainable Development.

Chen, Y., Bretschneider, S., Stritch, J. M., Darnall, N., and Hsueh, L. (2022). E-procurement system adoption in local governments: the role of procurement complexity and organizational structure. *Public Management Review* 24(6), 903–925.

Cheng, S., and Ali, S. (2023). A tiered pathway toward sustainability: the role of public administrators in advancing social equity in US local governments. *Public Administration Review* 83(4), 878–894.

Coggburn, J. D., and Rahm, D. (2005). Environmentally preferable purchasing: who is doing what in the United States? *Journal of Public Procurement* 5(1), 23.

Darnall, N., and Aragón-Correa, J. A. (2014). Can ecolabels influence firms' sustainability strategy and stakeholder behaviors? *Organization & Environment* 27(4), 319–327.

Darnall, N., Arimura, T., Miyamoto, T., Stritch, J. M., Bretschneider, S., and Hsueh, L. (2018a). *Advancing Green Purchasing in Japanese Municipalities*. Arizona State University's Sustainable Purchasing Research Initiative and Waseda University's Research Institute for Environmental Economics and Management, Phoenix. https://doi.org/ 10.13140/RG.2.2.13769.77925

Darnall, N., Hsueh, L., Stritch, J. M., and Bretschneider, S. (2018b). Environmental purchasing in the City of Phoenix. In *Handbook of Sustainability: Case Studies and Practical Solutions*, vol. 26, Garren, S. J., Brinkman, R. (eds.). London: Palgrave Macmillan, pp. 485–502. https://doi.org/10.1007/978-3-319-71389-2

Darnall, N., Iatridis, K., Kesidou, E., and Snelson-Powell, A. (2023). Penalty zones in international sustainability standards: where sustainability doesn't pay. *Journal of Management Studies*. https://doi.org/10.1111/joms.12975

Darnall, N., Ji, H., and Potoski, M. (2017b). Institutional design of ecolabels: sponsorship signals rule strength. *Regulation & Governance* 11(4), 438–450.

Darnall, N., Stritch, J. M., Bretschneider, S., Hsueh, L., Duscha, M., Iles, J., No, W., Suarez, J., and Burwell, C. (2017a). *Advancing Green Purchasing in Local Governments*. Phoenix: Arizona State University, Center for Organization Research and Design, Sustainable Purchasing Research Initiative. https://doi.org/10.13140/RG.2.2.13106.50884

Darnall, N., Stritch, J. M., Chen, Y., Fox, A., Swanson, J., Adell, A., and Wierzbicki, A. (2022a). Introduction. *Sustainable Public Procurement: 2022 Global Review, Part I*. Chapter 1, pp. 1–6. Paris: United Nations Environment Programme.

Darnall, N., Stritch, J. M., Chen, Y., Fox, A., Swanson, J., Adell, A., and Wierzbicki, A. (2022b). *Sustainable Procurement in Local Governments. 2022 Global Review of Sustainable Public Procurement. Executive Summary*. Paris: United Nations Environment Programme.

Darnall, N., Stritch, J. M., Singh, A., and Behravesh, S.-A. (2024). *Advancing Sustainable Public Procurement through Digital Technologies*. Paper submitted for presentation at the Academy of Management Research Conference, Chicago, IL.

Dimand, A. M. (2022). Determinants of local government innovation: the case of green public procurement in the United States. *International Journal of Public Sector Management* 35(5), 584–602.

Dimand, A. M., and Cheng, S. (2023). Bottom-up innovation adoption of green public procurement in the United States. *Local Government Studies* 49(6), 1359–1385.

Dimitri, N., Dini, F., and Piga, G. (2006). When should procurement be centralized. In *Handbook of Procurement*, Dimitri, N., Piga, G., Spagnolo, G. (eds.). Cambridge: Cambridge University Press, pp. 47–81.

Erridge, A., and Nondi, R. (1994). Public procurement, competition and partnership. *European Journal of Purchasing Supply Management* 1(3), 169–179.

Etse, D., McMurray, A., and Muenjohn, N. (2022). The effect of regulation on sustainable procurement: organisational leadership and culture as mediators. *Journal of Business Ethics*, 177(2), 305–325.

European Union. (2014). Directive 2014/24/EU of the European Parliament of the Council of 26 February 2014 on public procurement and repealing Directive 2004/18/EC, Article 40. https://eur-lex.europa.eu/legal-content/EN/TXT/PDF/?uri=CELEX:32014L0024 (Accessed 28 June 2024).

Fernandez, S., Malatesta, D., and Smith, C. R. (2013). Race, gender, and government contracting: different explanations or new prospects for theory? *Public Administration Review* 73(1), 109–120.

França, W. T., Barros, M. V., Salvador, R., Carlos de Francisco, A., Moreira, T., and Moro Piekarski, C. (2021). Integrating life cycle assessment and life cycle cost: a review of environmental-economic studies. *International Journal of Life Cycle Assessment* 26, 244–274.

Furneaux, C., and Barraket, J. (2014). Purchasing social good (s): a definition and typology of social procurement. *Public Money Management* 34(4), 265–272.

Grandia, J., Steijn, B., and Kuipers, B. (2015). It is not easy being green: increasing sustainable public procurement behaviour. *Innovation: The European Journal of Social Science Research* 28(3), 243–260.

Grandia, J., and Voncken, D. (2019). Sustainable public procurement: the impact of ability, motivation, and opportunity on the implementation of different types of sustainable public procurement. *Sustainability* 11(19), 5215.

Hafsa, F., Darnall, N., and Bretschneider, S. (2021b). Social procurement: addressing a critical void in public procurement. *Public Administration Review* 18(5), 818–834. https://doi.org/10.1111/puar.13438

Hasu, M., Saari, E., and Mattelmäki, T. (2011). Bringing the employee back in: integrating user-driven and employee-driven innovation in the public sector. In *User-Based Innovation in Services*, Sundbo, J. and Toivonen, M. (eds.). Cheltenham: Edward Elgar Publishing Limited, pp. 251–280.

Hawkins, T., Gravier, M., and Randall, W. S. (2018). Socio-economic sourcing: benefits of small business set-asides in public procurement. *Journal of Public Procurement* 18(3), 217–239.

Hoffman, A. (2000). *Competitive Environmental Strategy: A Guide to the Changing Business Landscape*. Washington, DC: Island Press.

Irani, Z., Abril, R. M., Weerakkody, V., Omar, A., and Sivarajah, U. (2023). The impact of legacy systems on digital transformation in European public administration: Lesson learned from a multi case analysis. *Government Information Quarterly*, 40(1), 101784.

Islam, M., Turki, A., Murad, M., and Karim, A. (2017). Do sustainable procurement practices improve organizational performance? *Sustainability* 9(12), 2281.

Keulemans, S., and Van de Walle, S. (2017). Cost-effectiveness, domestic favouritism and sustainability in public procurement: a comparative study of public preferences. *International Journal of Public Sector Management* 30(4), 328–341.

Labutong, N., and Hoen, V. (2018, 18 May). How can companies address their scope 3 greenhouse gas emissions? *Science-Based Targets*. https://sciencebasedtargets.org/blog/how-can-companies-address-their-scope-3-greenhouse-gas-emissions

Lăzăroiu, G., Ionescu, L., Uță, C., Hurloiu, I., Andronie, M., and Dijmărescu, I. (2020). Environmentally responsible behavior and sustainability policy adoption in green public procurement. *Sustainability*, 12(5), 2110. https://doi.org/10.3390/su12052110

Lewis, A. N., and Machlowska, M. (2022). *Decarbonizing the EU's Road and Construction Sectors through Green Public Procurement: The Case of Sweden and the Netherlands*. Sweden: *Stockholm Environment Institute*.

Li, L., and Geiser, K. (2005). Environmentally responsible public procurement (ERPP) and its implications for integrated product policy (IPP). *Journal of Cleaner Production* 13(7), 705–715.

Liao, L., Warner, M. E., and Homsy, G. C. (2019). Sustainability's forgotten third E: what influences local government actions on social equity? *Local Environment* 24(12), 1197–1208.

Lingegård, S., Olsson, J. A., Kadefors, A., and Uppenberg, S. (2021). Sustainable public procurement in large infrastructure projects—policy implementation for carbon emission reductions. *Sustainability* 13(20), 11182.

McCrudden, C., and Doreen, M. (2007). *Corporate Social Responsibility and Public Procurement*. University of Oxford Faculty of Law Legal Studies Research Paper Series.

McCue, C. P., and Pitzer, J. T. (2000). Centralized vs. decentralized purchasing: Current trends in governmental procurement practices. *Journal of Public Budgeting, Accounting & Financial Management* 12(3), 400–420.

McGrann, Kelly. (2014). Benign neglect: Veteran-owned small business in federal procurement today. *Veterans Law Review*, 6(6), 187–212

Ministerstwo Rozwoju i Technologii. (2022). *Polityka Zakupowa Pańśtwa*. Ministerstwo Rozwoju i Technologii. www.gov.pl/web/rozwoj-technologia/polityka-zakupowa-panstwa2

Preuss, L., and Walker, H. (2011). Psychological barriers in the road to sustainable development: evidence from public sector procurement. *Public Administration* 89(2), 493–521.

Raj, A., Agrahari, A., and Srivastava, S. K. (2020). Do pressures foster sustainable public procurement? An empirical investigation comparing developed and developing economies. *Journal of Cleaner Production* 266, 122055.

Rolfstam, M., Phillips, W., and Bakker, E. (2011). Public procurement and the diffusion of innovations: exploring the role of institutions and institutional coordination. *International Journal of Public Sector Management* 24(5), 452–468.

Roman, A. V. (2017). Institutionalizing sustainability: a structural equation model of sustainable procurement in US public agencies. *Journal of Cleaner Production* 143, 1048–1059.

Romzek, B. S., and Johnston, J. M. (2005). State social services contracting: exploring the determinants of effective contract accountability. *Public Administration Review* 65(4), 436–449.

Schotanus, F., and Telgen, J. (2007). Developing a typology of organisational forms of cooperative purchasing. *Journal of Purchasing and Supply Management*, 13(1), 53–68.

Sönnichsen, S. D., and Clement, J. (2020). Review of green and sustainable public procurement: Towards circular public procurement. *Journal of Cleaner Production*, 245, 118901.

Stritch, J. M., Bretschneider, S., Darnall, N., Hsueh, L., and Chen, Y. (2020). Sustainability policy objectives, centralized decision making, and efficiency in public procurement processes in US local governments. *Sustainability* 12(17), 6934.

Swanson, J., Darnall, N., Stritch, J. M., Chen, Y., Fox, A., Adell, A., and Bres, L. (2022). *Recommendations and Conclusions. Sustainable Public Procurement: 2022 Global Review, Part I*. Chapter 4, pp. 71–79. Paris: United Nations Environment Programme.

U.S. Environmental Protection Agency (USEPA). (2023). *Recommendations of Specifications, Standards, and Ecolabels for Federal Purchasing*. Washington, DC: USEPA. www.epa.gov/greenerp roducts/recommendations-specifications-standards-and-ecolabels-federal-purchasing, last accessed 3 September 2023.

United Nations Environment Programme (UNEP). (2022). *Sustainable Public Procurement: 2022 Global Review, Part II*. Paris: United Nations Environment Programme.

Walker, H., and Brammer, S. (2009). Sustainable procurement in the UK public sector. *Supply Chain Management: An International Journal* 14(2), 127–138.

Walker, H., and Brammer, S. (2012). The relationship between sustainable procurement and e-procurement in the public sector. *International Journal of Production Economics* 140(1), 256–268.

Walker, H., Di Sisto, L., and McBain, D. (2008). Drivers and barriers to environmental supply chain management practices: lessons from the public and private sectors. *Journal of Purchasing and Supply Management* 14(1), 69–85.

Walker, H., and Phillips, W. (2009). Sustainable procurement: emerging issues. *International Journal of Procurement Management* 2(1), 41–61.

Wierzbicki. A., Stritch, J. M., Darnall, N., Chen, Y., Fox, A., Swanson, J., and Adell, A. (2022). Executive Summary. *Sustainable Public Procurement: 2022 Global Review, Part I*, pp. xi–xxiii. Paris: United Nations Environment Programme.

World Bank. (2020, March 23). *Global Public Procurement Database: Share, Compare, Improve!* Washington, DC: The World Bank.

Zhang, Y., Song, H., and Zhang, G. (2018). A review of emerging trends in global PPP research: analysis of four leading PPP journals. *Journal of Cleaner Production* 183, 631–6471.

***Case Study: Green Horizon City's Journey toward Sustainable Public Procurement (Developed by Justin M. Stritch, Yifan Chen, Nicole Darnall, Shirley-Ann Augustin Behravesh, and Kayla Le)***

## Background

Green Horizon City is a medium-sized U.S. city with a population of around 450,000. The city has been experiencing rapid growth and development. With a general operating fund exceeding $500 million annually and a large capital improvement budget, the city procures a diverse range of products and services, ranging from office supplies to large infrastructure projects. While there are some exceptions, the majority of Horizon City's seven council members recognize the profound economic, social, and environmental impacts of their purchasing decisions on the local community and beyond. That said, different council members vary in how they prioritize the environmental, social, and economic impacts of procurement and the importance of adopting a city-wide policy. Five of the seven council members have expressed an interest in exploring the possibility of adopting some type of sustainable public procurement (SPP) policy.

## Your Role

**You have been tasked with spearheading the initial examination of implementing a SPP policy in Horizon City. City Council has asked that you:**

1. Identify opportunities for Horizon City to implement a city-wide policy
2. Identify potential challenges of implementing a policy in Horizon City
3. Develop recommendations to help Horizon City develop a pathway forward

Your role places you at the heart of the city's sustainability transformation, navigating the interplay of regulatory compliance, organizational change, technological advancements, and stakeholder engagement. ***In constructing your response, consider the background information and critical questions detailed below, in addition to the overall chapter readings.***

## Procurement in Green Horizon City

Horizon City's procurement activities and processes are complex – involving a blend of centralized and decentralized decision-making that adds complexity to implementing a SPP policy across departments. Additionally, the city IT infrastructure is outdated and ill-equipped to integrate and effectively manage the data needed to track sustainability performance, a key aspect of the SPP policy.

Horizon City's SPP policy would need to align with its existing policies, which address other social objectives, such as supporting local businesses, and preferences given to veterans and women- and minority-owned businesses. Balancing these priorities will require strategic planning and coordination to ensure all goals can be met.

Engaging with vendors presents other complexities. On one hand, vendors often are knowledgeable about the availability of sustainable products and services. On the other hand, the Green Horizon City has to strike a careful balance between fostering effective vendor collaboration and adhering to regulatory safeguards designed to ensure transparent and fair tendering processes.

Amidst these complexities, most council members believe that adopting an SPP could help the city adapt and meet rapidly evolving state and national environmental regulations and standards, especially as it explores ways in which it can reduce its carbon emissions. This change in the regulatory environment requires alignment of its procurement policies to stay compliant with state and national regulations while pursuing its own sustainability goals.

### Critical Questions to Consider

As you begin your work, you are faced with several critical questions that you quickly see will inform your overall recommendations (item 3, above):

**Integrating the policy in fragmented systems**: How would you approach the integration of SPP policy within the city's complex, hybrid procurement system? What strategies would you employ to ensure consistency and effectiveness across various departments?

**Balancing priorities**: Considering the multifaceted nature of sustainable procurement goals, how would you ensure alignment among goals such as environmental sustainability, societal goals, and economic priorities?

**Vendor engagement**: How would you navigate the issue of collaborating with vendors while adhering to strict regulatory safeguards against corruption? What mechanisms would you implement to ensure transparency and integrity in these collaborations?

**Overcoming technological barriers**: Faced with the challenge of outdated IT infrastructure, what steps would you take to modernize the city's procurement systems? How would you leverage technology to enhance policy implementation and data tracking?

**Maximizing the role of SPP champions**: What actions would you take to ensure that the appointed SPP champions are effective in their roles? How would you support and empower them to drive the SPP agenda across the organization?

**Building political support**: What aspects of SPP might be used to build political support among council members as well as other external stakeholders (community groups, businesses, etc.)? What groups are likely to support an SPP policy? What groups are likely to oppose an SPP policy, and why? What arguments for SPP might shift opposition to support?

# 11 Social Equity and Economic Development through Contracting

*Evelyn Rodriguez-Plesa and Anisti Barrett*

## 11.1 Introduction

This chapter teaches students how government contracting advances social equity and promotes economic development. Economy, efficiency, effectiveness, and social equity are pillars of public administration practice. Social equity is a multidimensional and multilayered concept addressing fairness, justice, and equity across public policy and administration (National Academy of Public Administration, n.d.). Early connections of social equity to public administration are attributed to the first Minnowbrook conference, which was held in response to widespread social and political turmoil of the time (Blessett, Dodge, Edmond, Goerdel, Gooden, Headley, Riccucci, and Williams, 2019). Svara and Brunet (2005) define social equity as:

> the fair, just and equitable management of all institutions serving the public directly or by contract, and the fair, just and equitable distribution of public services, and implementation of public policy, and the commitment to promote fairness, justice, and equity in the formation of public policy.
>
> (pg. 256)

This definition promotes procedural fairness and equity in service provision and access to programs and services (Svara and Brunet, 2005).

Social equity complements other policy objectives such as economic development (Svara, Watt, and Takai, 2015). The United Nations integrates dimensions of social equity in their sustainable development goals, demonstrating interconnectedness to broader policy outcomes (e.g., United Nations Sustainable Development Goal 8, Decent Work and Economic Growth) (United Nations, n.d.). Svara et al. (2015) note, however, that social equity is not as often promoted as other dimensions of sustainability.

Social equity and economic development can also coalesce in public procurement. This chapter applies social equity and economic development to public procurement to achieve the following student learning objectives:

- Describe the rationale for social equity and economic development contracting programs.
- Explain the role of the changing market in the development of social equity and economic development contracting programs.
- Apply theoretical perspectives providing a foundation for these programs.
- Describe different ways in which government agencies implement social equity and economic development contracting programs.

DOI: 10.4324/9781003566670-13

- Describe the successes and challenges in the implementation of social equity and economic development contracting programs.

The chapter acknowledges the inherent overlap between social equity and economic development programs in public procurement and refers to this as socio-economic equity procurement throughout. The next section describes the public procurement environment, including a discussion on how the market impacts procurement and how disparities emerge. The following section summarizes the literature on socio-economic equity procurement and related theoretical perspectives. This is followed by a discussion on existing socio-economic equity procurement programs and emerging trends. Takeaways for practitioners and educators are also presented. The chapter concludes with two cases: a case about an equitable RFP of commercial food distribution to school districts in Texas by a public state agency; and, a case featuring the City of Durham, North Carolina, United States, which demonstrate how contracting promotes socio-economic equity and discusses the professional competencies needed to achieve these outcomes. While this chapter describes socio-economic equity in contracting in several contexts, it is important to note that changes in federal priorities may have shifted programmatic focus at all levels of government. The content included in this chapter was applicable and in place at the time the chapter was written and may have changed at the time of publication.

## 11.2 The Public Procurement Environment

An important element of public procurement is its environment, as it influences policies and affects decisions guiding its programs. Students should understand the context in which public procurement takes place. This section sets the stage for public procurement and explains how disparities manifest within this context.

The public procurement function is charged with the efficient use of public funds in support of an organization's operations and the delivery of goods/services. It involves understanding and analyzing market conditions to determine whether to buy or provide services with in-house resources, aligning values, and managing the governance system in contracting (Brown, Potoski, and Van Slyke, 2006; Girth, Hefetz, Johnston, and Warner, 2012; Kim and Brown, 2017; Brunjes, Abutabenjeh, Anguelov, Dimand, and Rodriguez-Plesa, 2023). Although public procurement operates in environments where priorities and preferences of stakeholders are often competing, efficiency often is the foundation for procurement decisions (Brown et al., 2006; Brunjes, 2020; Brunjes et al., 2023; Brunjes and Rodriguez-Plesa, 2023).

Competitive markets reduce the costs of goods and services, leading to a more efficient procurement for government agencies. However, these markets can also result in disparities where small and disadvantaged businesses are not able to compete for contracting opportunities. The U.S. Code of Federal Regulations (§ 124.103) defines socially disadvantaged individuals as

> those who have been subjected to racial or ethnic prejudice or cultural bias within American society because of their identities as members of groups and without regard to their individual qualities. The social disadvantage must stem from circumstances beyond their control.
>
> (Code of Federal Regulations, 2023)

Socially disadvantaged individuals may include Black Americans, Hispanic Americans, Native Americans, and Asian Americans (Code of Federal Regulations, 2023). These individuals may have faced barriers to entry or advancement in terms of education, employment, and business (Code of Federal Regulations, 2023). This definition pertains to the U.S. federal government; the same or similar definitions for social disadvantage are adopted by U.S. states and local governments.

In response to institutional and systemic barriers that hinder the ability of small and disadvantaged businesses to compete for contracting opportunities, government agencies at all levels of government use contracting and related procurement programs to promote social equity and economic development. Examples include set-aside contracts,[1] local business preference programs, vendor outreach, and facilitating business development for qualifying small and disadvantaged businesses.

There are also government programs that provide similar benefits and opportunities to other qualifying firms (i.e., service-disabled veteran-owned small businesses, women-owned businesses, and HUBZone businesses, Section 8(a) business development participants). Similar programs are implemented globally to promote equity and economic development in contracting. For example, the European Union has implemented several legislative initiatives to reduce burdens (e.g., access to capital) faced by small- and medium-sized enterprises (SMEs) (European Union, 2019). SMEs in Asia face similar challenges (e.g., access to capital, market access, skilled labor) (Yoshino and Taghizadeh-Hesary, 2016). To address these challenges, Yoshino and Taghizadeh-Hesary (2016) recommend the development of credit guarantee schemes to provide stable financing and creating support systems offering expertise on various business development areas.

## 11.3 Theories and Summary of the Literature

This section focuses on introducing key theories applied to public procurement and socio-economic equity procurement. Findings of empirical research applying these theories are also presented to demonstrate why these theories are important and how they are applied within the context of this chapter.

Public procurement and contracting operate in a politically charged environment where public law and organizational arrangements guide the process (Brown et al., 2006; Amirkhanyan, Kim, and Lambright, 2007). Market conditions also effect whether services are provided in-house or contracted out (Girth et al., 2012). Girth et al. (2012) find that direct government delivery is more prevalent when there are "few alternative providers and high impact on the public" (pg. 892). Much empirical work on public procurement and contracting has been based on economic and market theories, institutional theories, agency theories, and new public management (NPM) (Ferris and Graddy, 1986; Hood, 1991; Brown et al., 2006; Amirkhanyan et al., 2007; Petersen, Baekkeskov, Potoski, and Brown, 2019; Brunjes, 2020; Lapuente and Van de Walle, 2020; Anguelov and Brunjes, 2023; Smith, 2023). These theories contribute to the understanding of market mechanisms, make-or-buy decisions, and ex ante and ex post transaction costs involved in the contracting process, as well as challenges with the principal–agent relationship.

NPM "implies competition through marketization, either with internal markets in the public sector or contracting out to the private sector" (Lapuente and van de Walle, 2020, pg. 464). The rationale for contracting is that competition in the market is key to reducing costs and improving the quality of goods and services received (Hood, 1991). This approach calls for an increase in contracting out to trigger rivalry in the market (Hood, 1991; Brunjes, 2020). Girth et al. (2012) note that noncompetitive markets increase transaction cost and risk efficiency gains. Brunjes (2021), however, finds that competitively sourced contracts are more likely to run into performance issues such as cost overruns and early termination of their contracts.

Research resting on theories of New Public Governance (NPG) analyzes the governance structure guiding contracts (Amirkhanyan et al., 2007; Amirkhanyan, Kim, and Lambright, 2010; Casady, Eriksson, Levitt, and Scott, 2020). NPG describes the government's role in organizing, maintaining, and managing networks in complex policy environments (Casady et al., 2020). Governance in the contracting process relies on the cooperation between parties to execute contract terms and address performance issues. This is evident in relational contracting arrangements, which are best when there is a high level of uncertainty and flexibility is required (Amirkhanyan et al., 2010; Brown, Potoski, and Van Slyke, 2018). Agency–contractor relationships may also result in better contract performance (Brunjes, 2021).

### *11.3.1 Theories and Literature Applied to Socio-Economic Equity Procurement*

While economic, institutional, agency, NPM and NPG have been applied more generally to contracting research, there has been limited research conducted to provide insight into ex ante and ex post activities to examine the socio-economic implications of contracting out and its related processes. In theory, competitive markets promote efficiency. Although, we know that is not always the case (Brunjes, 2021). This focus on competitive markets does not consider the systemic issues that the market and institutional environments create. There are disparities where certain groups are unable to compete for contracting opportunities.

Most of the research examining disparities in contracting and determinants of contracting with small, disadvantaged businesses mainly examines representative bureaucracy (Smith and Fernandez, 2010; Fernandez, Malatesta, and Smith, 2012; Brunjes and Kellough, 2018; Rodriguez-Plesa, 2024) and contributes to the literature on public values (Brown et al., 2006; Reynaers, 2013; Brunjes and Rodriguez-Plesa, 2023). Research on sustainable public procurement has also provided further insight into the determinants of the implementation of the socio-economic components of sustainability in local governments in the United States (Rodriguez-Plesa, Dimand, and Alkadry, 2022). In their analysis, executive leadership support and political ideology of the community have a positive relationship with the implementation of social equity procurement activities (Rodriguez-Plesa et al., 2022). Recent literature has also used portfolio management framework theory to shed light on the factors relating to spending with small, disadvantaged businesses in times of emergencies (Dimand, Patrucco, Rodriguez-Plesa, and Hiriscau, 2023).

The theory of representative bureaucracy has been used to specifically examine social equity contracting programs such as the U.S. small, disadvantaged business certification program and Section 8(a) program (Smith and Fernandez, 2010), U.S. small, disadvantaged business program and U.S. women-owned small business program (Fernandez et al., 2012), and minority-owned business program (Brunjes and Kellough, 2018). Social equity contracting includes procurement programs that aim to achieve social and economic goals; it can also include environmental considerations (Hafsa, Darnall, and Bretschneider, 2022; Brunjes and Rodriguez-Plesa, 2023). It focuses on "what is being purchased and from whom it is being purchased" (Hafsa et al., 2022; Brunjes and Rodriguez-Plesa, 2023). Smith and Fernandez (2010) examine the relationship between female and minority representation on federal contracts awarded to small, disadvantaged businesses. They find that minority representation in senior executive levels in federal agencies relates to an increase in contracts to small, disadvantaged businesses (Smith and Fernandez, 2010). Fernandez et al. (2012) similarly find evidence that minority representation results in increased contract dollars to minority-owned businesses. However, they did not find evidence that female representation relates to increased contract dollars for women-owned businesses (Fernandez et al., 2012).

Brunjes and Kellough (2018) contribute to the research on the relationship between representative bureaucracy and contracting with small, disadvantaged businesses by examining contracting decisions at multiple administrative levels in federal agencies (i.e., program managers, management analysts, financial managers, contracting officers, procurement officers). The biggest positive effects between passive minority representation and contracting with minority-owned businesses are seen at the contracting officer level (Brunjes and Kellough, 2018). Individuals in these positions have knowledge of each contract and are heavily involved with the selection process.

Other streams of research have contributed to the debate on public values in contracting (Brown et al., 2006; Brunjes and Rodriguez-Plesa, 2023). Brown et al. (2006) note that "managers have opportunities to optimize, balance, or trade off stakeholder values" in the following contracting stages: make-or-buy stage, after deciding to contract, and after the contract is awarded (pg. 324). Reynaers (2013) notes that public values can be "threatened, safeguarded, or strengthened" in different project stages in the case of public–private partnerships (pg. 49). The same is true in other contract arrangements.

In the different contract stages, values such as efficiency and equity may be weighed against each other (Brown et al., 2006). There is also considerable discretion in the agenda setting, formulation, implementation, and evaluation components of contracting where public values influence decisions (Yang, Hsieh, and Li, 2009; Brunjes and Kellough, 2018). Kelman (2021) asserts that social equity contracting programs can limit competition and obstruct a government's ability to secure the best value. Recent research asserts that this is not the case (Brunjes and Rodriguez-Plesa, 2023; Dimand et al., 2023). In their research on examining the performance of small, disadvantaged businesses, Brunjes and Rodriguez-Plesa (2023) find that there are no significant performance differences between small, disadvantaged businesses and other firms. In some cases, small, disadvantaged firms overperform when compared to other firms. This is particularly evident when analyzing cost-ratios among firms in their sample (Brunjes and Rodriguez-Plesa, 2023). Further, Dimand et al. (2023) find that small, disadvantaged businesses can win contracts that were solicited using competitive procedures. Government agencies do not need to reduce competition to promote the participation of small, disadvantaged businesses (Dimand et al., 2023). Therefore, there does not necessarily have to be tradeoff between values of efficiency and equity. Social equity contracting programs can still achieve efficiency goals; prioritizing equity does not sacrifice efficiency.

There are several socio-economic equity procurement initiatives, policies, and programs in place at all levels of government. Most studies on this topic focus on the determinants of socio-economic equity procurement. Few studies empirically focus on performance and social and economic implications after a contract is awarded. While trends in research are projecting in this direction, further research on socio-economic equity procurement is still needed to provide additional insight into how organizational, institutional, economic, public values, and other factors affect varying socio-economic procurement policies, programs, and initiatives. Further understanding of the implications of socio-economic procurement at all levels of government is also needed. Future research should seek to separate these policies, programs, and initiatives to determine their efficacy (e.g., Brunjes and Rodriguez-Plesa, 2023 examination of SBA's Section 8(a) program).

## 11.4 Emerging Issues in Socio-Economic Equity Procurement

Legal stipulations often guide public procurement processes, particularly those related to socio-economic equity procurement. United States federal government legislation greatly influences how and to what extent socio-economic equity programs are implemented at all levels of government. The focus of this section is to present the legal context for socio-economic equity procurement programs in the United States as it was when this chapter was written. Students should be familiar with the legal stipulations and challenges affecting the implementation of these programs.

In 1953, the Small Business Act was passed by Congress mainly as a response to the challenges of the Great Depression and World War II (Federal Register, n.d.; U.S. Small Business Administration, n.d.a). This created the U.S. Small Business Administration (SBA), which is an "independent agency of the federal government to aid, counsel, assist and protect the interest of small business concerns; preserve free competitive enterprise; and maintain and strengthen the overall economy" (Grants.gov, n.d.). Public Law 95-07 amends the Small Business Act of 1953 and the Small Business Investment Act of 1958 to require agencies to set contracting goals for small businesses (Public Law 95-507, 1978). It also expands the small business program to include subcontract awards. There are SBA offices throughout the United States that serve as branches of the national organization. The local offices assist with federal contracting certifications and funding programs and connect qualifying small businesses to partner organizations, lenders, and other groups that aid small businesses so they can thrive.

Socio-economic procurement policies have been legally contested throughout history. In 1989, in the case of the *City of Richmond v. J.A. Croson Co.*, Justice O'Connor concluded that the city failed to demonstrate past discrimination in the construction industry that would authorize the use of race-based programs in contracting (O'Connor and Supreme Court of the United States, 1988). This resulted in the requirement for disparity studies to justify certain socio-economic equity procurement policies and programs. Recently, the ruling in *Ultima Servs. Corp. v. Department of Agriculture* affected the U.S. SBA's 8(a) program and how the determination of social disadvantage is made (U.S. Small Business Administration, 2023). Socio-economic equity procurement programs continue to make positive progress despite legal disputes questioning their constitutionality (U.S. Small Business Administration, 2023).

## 11.5 Trends in Socio-Economic Equity Procurement

### *11.5.1 Socio-Economic Equity Procurement Initiatives, Policies, and Programs*

There are several ways in which governments at all levels implement socio-economic equity procurement programs given legal limitations. This section highlights innovative strategies implemented by governments to achieve socio-economic goals. In this section, students are introduced to several ways in which these socio-economic equity procurement manifests in practice.

Socio-economic equity procurement programs connect to social and economic goals they were intended to achieve. Socio-economic procurement includes policies, programs, and varying initiatives to enhance access for and limit discrimination of socially disadvantaged individuals so they may be more competitive in the market and participate in government contracting opportunities. Socio-economic procurement implementation is evident in governments at all levels of governments in the United States and abroad as well.

### *11.5.2 U.S. Federal Government Socio-Economic Equity Procurement*

Initiatives by the U.S. SBA and the White House to recognize small businesses include National Small Business Week that highlights the impact of small businesses in the United

States; National Veterans Small Business Week that highlights the work of veteran, service member, and military spouse businesses; Small Business Saturday takes place the Saturday after Thanksgiving and is a day dedicated to supporting small businesses; the White House HBCU Initiative that recognizes the role of historically Black colleges and universities in providing entrepreneurs with business counseling and training; and the Equity Initiative to focus on removing the barriers and improving access to SBA services for underserved communities. The SBA also collaborates with several councils and committees to support and strengthen small and disadvantaged businesses. This includes the Council on Underserved Communities; Investment Capital Advisory Committee; Invention, Innovation, and Entrepreneurship Advisory Committee; and the National Pan-Hellenic Council (U.S. Small Business Administration, n.d.). The SBA also provides access to capital for small businesses, entrepreneurial development to new and existing small businesses, works with federal agencies to set small and disadvantaged business contracting goals, and advocates of behalf of small businesses (e.g., testifying to Congress on behalf of small businesses) (U.S. Small Business Administration, n.d.).

Contracting assistance programs provided by the SBA to support small, disadvantaged businesses include the 8(a) Business Development program, HUBZone program, Women-owned Small Business Federal contracting program, and the Service-disabled Veteran-owned Small Business program (U.S. Small Business Administration, n.d.). The Section 8(a) program is a nine-year program that provides professional and technical development and contractual assistance to qualifying small, disadvantaged businesses. The HUBZone program helps small businesses in designated urban and rural communities with their principal offices located in a HUBZone to obtain preferential access to federal contracting opportunities. The Women-owned Small Business Federal contracting program and the Service-disabled Veteran-owned Small Business program authorizes set-aside contracts for qualifying women-owned businesses and service-disabled veteran-owned small businesses. Set aside contracts are contracts that are exclusively reserved for qualifying firms. Competitive set-aside contracts for small businesses are used "when at least two small businesses could perform the work or provide the products being purchased" (U.S. Small Business Administration, n.d.). In some cases, these opportunities are only open to small businesses who participate in the SBA programs.[2]

#### *11.5.3 U.S. State Government Socio-Economic Equity Procurement*

States across the United States have similar programs in place. For example, the North Carolina Small Business Enterprise Program assists for-profit small businesses headquartered in North Carolina, whose net income does not exceed $1,500,000 and have less than 100 employees, to access contract opportunities (North Carolina Department of Administration, n.d.). The Florida Department of Transportation (FDOT) implements a "race and gender neutral program in that it aspires to achieve its approved DBE goal" (U.S. Department of Transportation Federal Highway Administration, n.d.).

#### *11.5.4 U.S. Local Government Socio-Economic Equity Procurement*

Local governments in the United States have programs and policies like those implemented at federal and state levels of government. It is worthwhile to note that some programs are implemented outside of but in coordination with or in support of agencies' procurement function. The City of Durham Underutilized Business Compliance Division, housed under the Finance Department, implements the city's Equal Business Opportunity Program (EBOP) and Small Local Business Enterprise Program (SLBE) (City of Durham, n.d.a).

To achieve the intended outcomes of the SLBE, the Underutilized Business Compliance Division recruits small, local business enterprises to participate in this program. For the EBOP, the Underutilized Business Compliance Division provides a list of certified UBEs under the North Carolina Office of Historically Underutilized Businesses (HUB), North Carolina Department of Transportation (NCDOT) as well as SBA Section 8 eligible firms (State of North Carolina Executive Order 150, 1999) to prime contractors to facilitate the process of finding certified UBEs. They also certify local businesses seeking to participate in the city's SLBE program. Additionally, the division monitors and tracks participation in the city's programs and updates the appropriate databases. They manage business development initiatives to support small, disadvantaged and small, local businesses. These programs help small, disadvantaged and small, local businesses thrive in the market and compete for contracting opportunities with the City of Durham. The EBOP and SLBE programs are further detailed in the teaching case at the end of this chapter.

The City of San Antonio's Economic Development Department coordinates with the Procurement Division to implement their Small Business Economic Development Advocacy (SBEDA) program. To ensure that their SBEDA program complies with "strict constitutional scrutiny and national best practices," they conduct regular disparity studies (City of San Antonio, 2023a). Their 2023 Disparity Study recommends that the city continue to implement race- and gender-based SBEDA program initiatives (City of San Antonio, 2023a). The City of San Antonio's Economic Development Department ensures that contracting goals are met and that small, disadvantaged businesses have fair opportunities to compete for contracting opportunities. They also work together with the South-Central Texas Regional Certification Agency to help small, disadvantaged businesses become certified as such. The City of San Antonio also partners with the Alamo Colleges District to administer their Business Empowerment Program, which includes a Small Business Bootcamp and Mentor Protégé Program (City of San Antonio, 2023). These programs aim to provide small, disadvantaged businesses with the tools and resources they need to succeed in the market and contribute to a flourishing economy.

Additional strategies implemented throughout the supply chain life cycle that can have implications on the economy and society are included as contract provisions. Living wages are essential in providing fair working conditions. In support of fair working conditions, government agencies will have a living wage ordinance applicable to government contractors. For example, Washington, DC's Living Wage Act of 2006 requires that certain contractors pay their employees living wages (Government of the District of Columbia, n.d.). Ethical sourcing certifications may also provide suppliers with a competitive edge when competing for government contracts.

### *11.5.5 Socio-Economic Equity Procurement Outside the United States*

There are several strategies government agencies may implement to stimulate the economy in addition to, or to complement, the long-standing practices implemented globally to address barriers in contracting with small, disadvantaged businesses and SMEs. For example, regional, domestic, and/or local purchasing programs aim to support local suppliers and create a sustainable supply chain. An update to the European Union's rules on public procurement "expand the definition of the 'most economically advantageous tender' … and so gives contracting authorities more leeway to consider social and environmental elements," which includes purchasing regionally (European Union, 2017). The European Union has food procurement programs in place (i.e., Strength2Food Project) aiming to use the "buying local" strategy to support domestic agriculture and local farmers (European Union, 2017).

Overall, various strategies implemented at all levels of government in the United States and globally leverage contracting to achieve social and economic outcomes. Governments use their regulatory power to mandate practices, and agencies can also implement discretionary practices (e.g., business development programming) to achieve social–economic equity. Strategies outlined in this chapter provide examples of initiatives implemented in the United States and globally at different stages of the procurement process.

## 11.6 Takeaways for Education and Practice

This chapter provides historical context for socio-economic equity procurement programs, outlines relevant empirical research and theories applied specifically in this context, and highlights varying programs at the federal, state, and local levels of government in the United States. There is inherent overlap between social equity and economic development in theory and in practice. The knowledge, skills, abilities, and competencies to effectively deliver socio-economic contracting programs apply whether practitioners implementing them are employed in economic development or procurement departments or are managers in other departments.

This chapter offers three main takeaways for education and practice. First, it is critical to understand how different public values manifest in public procurement. A dominant driver of public procurement is to maximize efficiency. It is important to demonstrate how the four pillars of public administration – economy, efficiency, effectiveness, and social equity – can be reconciled in public procurement. To accomplish this, economy, efficiency, effectiveness, and social equity need to be defined at a basic level and then connected to public procurement. Consider what each of these means separately for procurement and then how they come together in the context of this chapter. Recent empirical findings of recent research (Brunjes and Rodriguez-Plesa, 2023; Dimand et al., 2023) demonstrate how efficiency and equity are balanced in public procurement. Practical examples presented in section 11.5.1 also show how economy, efficiency, effectiveness, and social equity can be reconciled in public procurement.

Second, several factors influence decision-making in procurement. Social equity and economic development are considerations within that decision-making process. Therefore, aligning theoretical foundations with practical applications of socio-economic equity procurement is essential to prepare students and public service professionals at all levels of an organization.

Third, the historical context and current climate surrounding procurement equity programs are essential, as they facilitate an understanding of the barriers faced by varying socially and economically disadvantaged groups. A foundation in these ideas will help ensure that public sector contracting professionals are aware of strict and developing compliance requirements for these programs, which aligns with requirements for professionalization in the field. It is also important to build familiarity with the legal context surrounding social equity and economic development contracting programs. Practitioners seeking to become Certified Public Procurement Officers or Certified Professional Public Buyers need to be familiar with the procurement Body of Knowledge and proficient in procurement competencies. Exams for these certifications require that procurement officials understand the legal framework of public procurement. This domain specifically requires that they "recognize and apply requirements of supplier diversity programs and sustainable procurement initiatives" and "determine methods to ensure compliance" of the programs (Universal Public Procurement Certification Council, 2021). Social equity and economic development are important considerations for the classroom and the public procurement profession.

## Notes

1 The term set-asides is used throughout the chapter to provide one example of how some agencies will promote social equity and economic development through contracting, but this does not apply to the City of Durham which is highlighted in the teaching case at the end of the chapter.
2 These programs and initiatives were in place at the time this chapter was written and may have changed since due to changes in federal priorities.
3 This refers to participation goals, not set-aside goals. The City of Durham does not have a set aside perception in any language of contracts. The State of North Carolina does not recognize any set aside programs. The NC General Statutes only recognize good faith efforts.
4 National School Lunch Program, www.squaremeals.org/Programs/National-School-Lunch-Program.

## References

Amirkhanyan, A., Kim, H., and Lambright, K. (2007). Putting the pieces together: A comprehensive framework for understanding the decision to contract out and contractor performance. *International Journal of Public Administration,* Vol. 30, 699–725.

Amirkhanyan, A., Kim, H., and Lambright, K. (2010). Do relationships matter? Assessing the association between relationship design and contractor performance. *Public Performance & Management Review,* Vol. 34, Iss. 2, 189–220.

Anguelov, L., and Brunjes, B. (2023). A replication of "Contracting out: For What? With Whom?" *Public Administration,* Vol. 2023, Iss. 101, 1163–1197.

Blessett, B., Dodge, J., Edmond, B., Goerdel, H., Gooden, S., Headley, A., Riccucci, N., and Williams, B. (2019, December). Social equity in public administration: A call to action. *Perspectives on Public Management and Governance*, Vol. 2, Iss. 4, 283–299.

Brown, T., Potoski, M., and Van Slyke, D. (2006, May/June). Managing public service contracts: Aligning values, institutions, and markets. *Public Administration Review,* Vol. 66, Iss. 3, 323–331.

Brown, T., Potoski, M., and Van Slyke, D. (2018). Complex contracting: Management challenges and solutions. *Public Administration Review,* Vol. 78, Iss. 5, 739–747.

Brunjes, B. (2020). Competition and federal contractor performance. *Journal of Public Administration Research and Theory,* Vol. 30, Iss. 2, 202–219.

Brunjes, B. (2021). Your competitive side is calling: An analysis of Florida contract performance. *Public Administration Review,* Vol. 82, Iss. 1, 83–101.

Brunjes, B., Abutabenjeh, S., Anguelov, L., Dimand, A., and Rodriguez-Plesa, E. (2023). Future Directions for Research in Public Procurement and Contract Management. In K.D. Dzigbede & W.B. Hildreth (Eds.), *Research Handbook on Public Financial Management* (pp. 341–367). Edward Elgar Publishing (London).

Brunjes, B., and Kellough, J. (2018). Representative bureaucracy and government contracting: A further examination of evidence from federal agencies. *Journal of Public Administration Research and Theory,* Vol. 28, Iss. 4, 519–534.

Brunjes, B., and Rodriguez-Plesa, E. (2023). Equity in government contracting: Analyzing the performance of small disadvantaged businesses. *Public Administration Review.* DOI: 10.1111/puar.13704

Casady, C., Eriksson, K., Levitt, R., and Scott, R. (2020). (Re)defining public-private partnerships (PPPs) in the new public governance (NPG) paradigm: an institutional maturity perspective. *Public Management Review,* Vol. 22, Iss. 2, 161–183.

City of Durham. (2013). Article IV. Small Local Business Enterprise Program (Ord. No. 14431, 4-1-2013). Retrieved from www.durhamnc.gov/DocumentCenter/View/27072/Small-Local-Business-Enterprise-Ordinance on August 04, 2024.

City of Durham. (2023). Durham's Small Local Business Enterprise Program. Retrieved from www.durhamnc.gov/DocumentCenter/View/49970/SLBE-Information-Sheet on August 04, 2024.

City of Durham. (n.d.a). Underutilized Business Compliance Division. Retrieved from www.durhamnc.gov/4091/Underutilized-Business-Compliance-Divisi on August 3, 2024.

City of Durham. (n.d.b). Welcome to the City of Durham. Retrieved from www.durhamnc.gov/1457/Welcome-to-The-City-of-Durham on August 03, 2024.

City of Durham Code of Ordinances. (2024). Ordinance 16292. Ordinance to Revise the Equal Business Opportunity Program. Chapter 18, Contracting with the City. Article III. Equal Business Opportunity Program, § 18–51. Policy Statement. Retrieved from www.durhamnc.gov/DocumentCenter/View/55353/EBOP-Ordinance-revision on August 18, 2024.

City of San Antonio. (2023a). 2023 Disparity study. Retrieved from www.sanantonio.gov/SBO/Compliance/Disparity on September 13, 2023.

City of San Antonio. (2023b). SBEDA Compliance. Retrieved from www.sa.gov/Directory/Departments/EDD/Programs-Grants/Preference/SBEDA on September 13, 2023.

City of San Antonio. (2023c). Small Business Assistance & Programming. Retrieved from www.sa.gov/Directory/Departments/EDD#252733109-mentoring--consulting on September 13, 2023.

Code of Federal Regulations. (2023). § 124.103 Who Is Socially Disadvantaged? Retrieved from www.ecfr.gov/current/title-13/chapter-I/part-124/subpart-A/subject-group-ECFR4ef1291a4a984ab/section-124.103 on September 09, 2023.

Dimand, A.-M., Patrucco, A. S., Rodriguez-Plesa, E., and Hiriscau, A. M. (2023). Social equity in federal contracting during emergencies: A portfolio management perspective. *Public Administration Review,* Vol. 83, Iss. 5, 1319–1338. DOI: 10.1111/puar.13614

European Union. (2017). Buy Locally, Buy Quality: Sustainability in Public Food Procurement. Retrieved from https://projects.research-and-innovation.ec.europa.eu/en/projects/success-stories/all/buy-locally-buy-quality-sustainability-public-food-procurement on February 1, 2024.

European Union. (2019). EU Policy Framework on SMEs: State of Play and Challenges. Retrieved from https://cor.europa.eu/en/engage/studies/Documents/EU-SMEs/EU-policy-SMEs.pdf on September 09, 2013.

Federal Register. (n.d.). Small Business Administration. Retrieved from www.federalregister.gov/agencies/small-business-administration on September 13, 2023.

Fernandez, S., Malatesta, D., and Smith, C. (2012). Race, gender, and government contracting: Different explanations or new prospects for theory? *Public Administration Review,* Vol. 73, Iss. 1, 109–120.

Ferris, J., and Graddy, E. (1986). Contracting out: for what? With whom? *Public Administration Review,* Vol. 46, 332–244.

Girth, A., Hefetz, A., Johnston, J., and Warner, M. (2012). Outsourcing public service delivery: Manage responses in noncompetitive markets. *Public Administration Review,* Vol. 72, Iss. 6, 887–900.

Government of the District of Columbia. (n.d.). Living Wage Act Fact Sheet. Retrieved from https://does.dc.gov/sites/default/files/dc/sites/does/publication/attachments/2023%20Living%20Wage%20Fact%20Sheet.pdf on February 1, 2024.

Grants.gov. (n.d.). Small Business Administration (SBA). Retrieved from www.grants.gov/learn-grants/grant-making-agencies/small-business-administration-sba on October 21, 2025.

Hafsa, F., Darnall, N., and Bretschneider, S. (2022). Social public purchasing: Addressing a critical void in public purchasing research. *Public Administration Review*, Vol. 82, 818–834.

Hood, C. (1991). A public management for all seasons? *Public Administration,* Vol. 69, Iss. Spring 91, 3–19.

Kelman, S. J. (2021). Worries from a democrat about the Biden administration and federal procurement. *FCW the Business of Federal Technology*. Retrieved from www.nextgov.com/acquisition/2021/07/worries-from-a-democrat-about-the-biden-administration-and-federal-procurement/249769/

Kim, Y., and Brown, T. (2017, March). Autonomy versus control in procurement and contracting: The use of cost-reimbursement contracts in three US federal departments. *International Review of Administrative Sciences,* Vol. 83, Iss. 1, 41–58.

Lapuente, V., and Van de Walle, S. (2020). The effects of new public management on the quality of public services. *Governance,* Vol. 33, 461–475.

National Academy of Public Administration. (n.d.). Foster Social Equity. Retrieved from https://napawash.org/grand-challenges/foster-social-equity#:~:text=Social%20equity%E2%80%94a%20key%20pillar,a%20variety%20of%20public%20contexts on September 01, 2023.

North Carolina Department of Administration. (n.d.). NCSBE Certification. Retrieved from https://ncadmin.nc.gov/divisions/historically-underutilized-businesses-hub/hub-certification/ncsbe-certification on September 13, 2023.

O'Connor, S. D. & Supreme Court of the United States. (1988) U.S. Reports: City of Richmond v. J. A. Croson Co., 488 U.S. 469. [Periodical] Retrieved from the Library of Congress, :// www.loc.gov/item/usrep488469/ on September 13, 2023.

Petersen, O., Baekkeskov, E., Potoski, M., and Brown, T. (2019). Measuring and managing ex ante transaction costs in public sector contracting. *Public Administration Review,* Vol. 79, Iss. 5, 641–650.

Public Law 95-507. (1978). Title I – Amendments to the Small Business Investment Act of 1958. Retrieved from www.govinfo.gov/content/pkg/STATUTE-92/pdf/STATUTE-92-Pg1757.pdf on September 13, 2023.

Reynaers, A. (2013). Public values in public-private partnerships. *Public Administration Review,* Vol. 74, Iss. 1, 44–50.

Rodriguez-Plesa, E. (2024). Representative bureaucracy and local government contracting: Examining supplier diversity programs. *Public Administration Review,* 1–16. https://doi.org/10.1111/puar.13867

Rodriguez-Plesa, E., Dimand, A., and Alkadry, M. (2022). Community social capital, political values or organizational capacity? Indicators of engagement in sustainable public procurement at the local level. *Journal of Cleaner Production,* Vol. 338, Iss. 1. https://doi.org/10.1016/j.jclepro.2022.130556

Smith, S. (2023). US state government privatization: Implications for social equity and inequality? *Public Administration Review,* Vol. 83, 35–50.

Smith, C., and Fernandez, S. (2010). Equity in federal contracting: Examining the link between minority representation and federal procurement decisions. *Public Administration Review,* Vol. 70, Iss. 1, 87–96.

State of North Carolina. (1999). Executive Order 150. Support for Historically Underutilized Businesses. Retrieved from www.doa.nc.gov/documents/files/hub-hunt-1999-eo-150-pdf/open on August 18, 2024.

Svara, J., and Brunet, J. (2005). Social equity is a pillar of public administration. *Journal of Public Affairs Education,* Vol. 11, Iss. 3, 253–258.

Svara, J., Watt, T., and Takai, K. (2015). Advancing social equity as an integral dimension of sustainability in local communities. *Cityscape,* Vol. 17, Iss. 2, 139–166.

U.S. Department of Transportation Federal Highway Administration. (n.d.). Florida Disadvantaged Business Enterprise (DBE). Retrieved from https://highways.dot.gov/field-offices/florida/florida-disadvantaged-business-enterprise-dbe on October 18, 2025.

U.S. Small Business Administration. (n.d.a). SBA Initiatives. Retrieved from www.sba.gov/about-sba/organization/sba-initiatives on September 13, 2023.

U.S. Small Business Administration. (n.d.b). Organization. Retrieved from www.sba.gov/about-sba/organization on September 13, 2023.

U.S. Small Business Administration. (n.d.c). Small Disadvantaged Business. Retrieved from www.sba.gov/federal-contracting/contracting-assistance-programs/small-disadvantaged-business on September 13, 2023.

U.S. Small Business Administration. (n.d.d). Types of Contracts. Retrieved from www.sba.gov/federal-contracting/contracting-guide/types-contracts#:~:text=To%20help%20provide%20a%20level,for%20and%20win%20federal%20contracts on September 13, 2023.

U.S. Small Business Administration. (2023). SBA Releases Interim Guidance to 8(a) Program Participants in Light of Lower Court Ruling. Retrieved from www.sba.gov/article/2023/08/18/sba-releases-interim-guidance-8a-program-participants-light-lower-court-ruling on September 13, 2023.

United Nations. (n.d.). The 17 Goals. Retrieved from https://sdgs.un.org/goals on September 9, 2023.

United States Census Bureau. (2020). Durham City, North Carolina. Retrieved from https://data.census.gov/profile/Durham_city,_North_Carolina?g=160XX00US3719000 on August 03, 2024.

Universal Public Procurement Certification Council. (2021). 2021 UPPCC Body of Knowledge and Competency (BoK-C): Certified Public Procurement Buyer® (CPPB®) Certification. Retrieved from

https://staging.uppcc.org/wp-content/uploads/2024/07/2021_UPPCC_BoKC_CPPb_Crosswalk_1-1.pdf on September 13, 2023.
Yang, K., Hsieh, J., and Li, T. (2009, July/August). Contracting capacity and perceived contracting performance: Nonlinear effects and the role of time. *Public Administration Review,* Vol. 69, 681–696.
Yoshino, N., and Taghizadeh-Hesary. (2016). Major challenges facing small and medium-sized enterprises in Asia and solutions for mitigating them. *Asian Development Bank Institute.* Retrieved from www.adb.org/sites/default/files/publication/182532/adbi-wp564.pdf on February 1, 2024.

## *Case Study: Social Equity in the City of Durham (Developed by Evelyn Rodriguez-Plesa and Anisti Barrett)*

The City of Durham, North Carolina, United States, presents an exemplary case for socio-economic equity procurement in local government. This section highlights the City's Equal Business Opportunity Program (EBOP) and Small Local Business Enterprise (SLBE) Program. These programs demonstrate how local governments can incorporate social equity in economic development to encourage gainful competitiveness and participation from minority- and women-owned business enterprises (MWBEs) and local, small business enterprises in the contracting marketplace.

This teaching case directly applies to the following student learning objectives presented in this chapter.

- Describe the rationale for social equity and economic development contracting programs.
- Describe different ways in which government agencies implement social equity and economic development contracting programs.
- Describe the successes and challenges in the implementation of social equity and economic development contracting programs.

### About the City of Durham, North Carolina, United States

The City of Durham was incorporated in 1869 by the General Assembly (City of Durham, n.d.b). The city has approximately 2,600 employees (City of Durham, n.d.b) and serves about 283,506 residents (United States Census Bureau, 2020). The city has a council-manager form of government where the city manager is appointed to run the operations of the organization with policy direction from the city council. Socio-economic equity procurement programs are managed by the Finance Department's Underutilized Business Compliance Division. This section highlights the city's EBOP and SLBE Program. The EBOP and the SLBE Program are two of Durham's economic development programs aimed at improving opportunities for MWBEs and local, small business enterprises.

### Equal Business Opportunity Program (EBOP)

The City of Durham EBOP policy statement (Code of Ordinances, Chapter 18, Article III, § 18–51. Policy statement) reads as follows:

> It is the policy of the city to provide equal opportunities for city contracting for underutilized business enterprises owned by minorities and women doing

> business in the city's contracting marketplace. It is further the policy of the city to prohibit discrimination against any firm in pursuit of these opportunities, to conduct its contracting activities to prevent such discrimination, to correct the present effects of past discrimination, and to resolve complaints of discrimination.
> (City of Durham Code of Ordinances, 2024)

The EBOP aims to increase participation of MWBEs in the city contracting marketplace. Participation goals are set to hold the city accountable for the inclusion of MWBEs (City of Durham, n.d.a). Current participation goals set for minority businesses are 11% participation for construction, 8% for professional services, 7% for services, and 2% for goods. For women-owned business enterprises, participation goals are 7% for construction, 6% for professional services, 5% for services, and 4% for goods.

The EBOP goals were established following a disparity study that was completed in conjunction with Durham County in 2015. Disparity studies are conducted to determine if there are inequities or discrimination in the marketplace, particularly in procurement and contracting. Disparity studies provide legitimate, evidence-based reasons for implementing programs to correct past and present inequities faced by specific segments of the population (e.g., disadvantaged, minority, and women-owned businesses).

#### *EBOP Successes*

The EBOP is a major mechanism to achieve the city's goal of shared economic prosperity. It has been instrumental in building capacity for MWBEs. Several strategies implemented as part of EBOP have contributed to the city's achievements.

The city identified that data collection, cleaning, and refinement will improve performance and provide data to support evidence-based decisions. Ensuring that MWBE vendors are certified and coded appropriately has proven crucial for documenting participation of vendors in their programs. To improve data collection, analysis, and evaluation, the city invested in an updated enterprise resource planning (ERP) system. This enhances tracking and reporting mechanisms, which are then used to measure program outcomes.

Additionally, the City of Durham has increased capacity-development services for MWBEs by providing support with small grants to assist qualified local MWBEs. The city also partners with agencies such as the Women's Business Development Center and the Office of Economic Workforce and Development Department for grants designed for small business development and capacity building. This helps MWBEs build their capacity and increase competitiveness.

The city has also implemented a strategic solicitation plan to query successful bidders of contracts that require specialized skills or trades through an outreach plan. An outreach plan is intended to engage successful contractors and local MWBEs as well as inform MWBEs how to obtain those specialized skills or trades with the outcome of incentivizing "good faith efforts" from contractors and bridging the gaps in competitiveness for local MWBEs. To support this process, the city can implement a Minority Participation Plan requirement in city contracts to incentivize scopes of work that would normally be a specialty area. Language is included in the Request for Proposal or Request for Qualification asking how the participant can increase minority participation in this specialized area.

Another success of the EBOP program comes in the form of administrative efficiency. The organization adopts the NC HUB certification. The city validates each vendor through this database and then enters the minority- or women-owned firms as such into their own system. They also use NCDOT's certification to facilitate participation and expand what qualifies a business to count toward the city's participation goals that have been set.[3] This process eliminates duplication of certification and improves administrative efficiency.

### *EBOP Challenges*

Challenges are viewed as opportunities, and the city aims to leverage these challenges to build capacity for local MWBEs. City Manager Wanda Page noted that a challenge has been connecting local minority- and women-owned business expertise to more highly invested city services, such as capital projects. For example, the city's water and sewer department has a large capital improvement program with projects that call for highly specialized skills. To be competitive and awarded these types of contracts requires contractors to have experience and KSAs of a specialized trade. Many Durham MWBEs are small and may not have obtained the experience and/or lack those specialized trades and skills that the city's capital projects require.

Another challenge to the participation of MWBEs in the EBOP was the completion of program forms. The complexity of forms and the submission process may be a deterrent for some vendors. To address this, the city improved their forms and processes to make them more user-friendly.

Regular evaluation of the EBOP provides the city the opportunity to identify areas where processes and procedures can be adjusted to enhance program effectiveness. Efforts made in these areas aim to facilitate and increase participation and help MWBEs build their capacity. Ultimately, this should increase their competitiveness and improve their ability to participate in city contracting opportunities.

## Small Local Business Enterprise (SLBE) Program

The SLBE program is a "race and gender neutral" program that supports the inclusion of small, local business enterprises in the City of Durham's contract marketplace (City of Durham, 2023). The SLBE program was enacted through an ordinance "to increase employment opportunities for city residents and to enhance the city's tax base by promoting city contracting opportunities for small local business enterprises" (City of Durham, 2013). To participate in the SLBE program, businesses are required to apply for and receive certification from the City of Durham, wherein the city reviews a company's financial statements and time in operation as a residential business for eligibility.

### *SLBE Program Successes*

The SLBE program has proven to be an effective avenue for increasing participation from small, local businesses in the city contracting marketplace. Consistent efforts from the City of Durham to specifically develop local, small business enterprises, utilizing internal resources and robust data refinement, have been driving forces in the city's success to gain participation, track goals, and measure outcomes.

In addition, the city strives to meet vendors in the spaces they are already in to facilitate information sharing and network building. Outreach at events such as small local business expositions serves as an opportunity for the city to increase visibility and highlight their economic development programs. This has helped to gain exposure of this program and tap into Durham's "hidden jewel" – it's small businesses.

The city has also been able to maintain full retention and recertification of current vendors, in addition to observing an increase of vendors participating in the SLBE program. Overall, a revitalized focus from the City of Durham on engaging participation from small, local business enterprises and offering assistance and capacity-development services feeds into the overarching intended outcome of shared economic prosperity aimed at bridging the wealth gap in the Durham community.

#### *SLBE Program Challenges*

One challenge noted was exposure to the program. To address this, the city has focused efforts on finding creative ways to market the SLBE program. Specifically, they have enhanced their outreach to increase the city's visibility and highlight their programs. In addition to the expositions the city has participated in (see *SLBE Program Successes* section above), they are co-hosting Durham Minority Enterprise Development Week in October 2024. This will provide an opportunity to build relationships, build capacity, and gain exposure for their program.

To further build relationships with local businesses, the city distributes surveys that serve multiple purposes. First, it helps the city better cater to the needs of their local businesses. Second, it provides data needed for their capacity building and workforce development programs. Third, it provides information so they can plan future initiatives.

### Discussion Questions

1. How do the City of Durham's EBOP and SLBE programs demonstrate the role of procurement in advancing social equity and economic development, and what policy mechanisms make these programs effective?
2. What are the main challenges the City of Durham faces in connecting underutilized and small local businesses to large or specialized contracts, and what additional strategies could strengthen their competitiveness and participation?
3. How can data collection, certification coordination, and community outreach be leveraged to improve accountability, efficiency, and measurable outcomes in social equity–focused procurement programs?

### Acknowledgments

We are deeply grateful to the City Manager Wanda Page (retired), Assistant City Manager Bertha Winbush, Deputy Chief Financial Officer Sheilah Faucette, and Underutilized Business Compliance Manager Timothy Jackson from the City of Durham for their insight and participation in developing the case study for this chapter.

***Case Study: Equitable RFP of Commercial Food Distribution to School Districts in Texas by a Public State Agency (Developed by Arunachalam Narayanan, Timothy G. Hawkins, and Suman Niranjan)***

**Background**

USDA, through the National School Lunch Program (NSLP), provides free or subsidized lunch to more than 3 million children in schools and residential child care institutions.[4] The amount of food is allocated as dollars to spend based on the economic status of the student's family in the school districts. The food is procured by the USDA and sent to the state of Texas free of cost. The food products could range from a can of beans to ground beef and chicken. The product first arrives at a contracted warehouse, and if processing is needed, it is sent to a processing center and then stored at the warehouse facilities. Due to the low volume of food consumed at any given amount of time and availability of space at these school campuses, very few items are shipped directly to school. By government mandate, the distribution process has to be bid out through a Request for Proposal (RFP), where the commercial food distributors competitively bid out the regions to provide service to these schools or recipient agencies. The process is depicted in Figure 11.1.

**School Food Distribution in Texas**

The state of Texas is huge, and the population is both spread out and concentrated in some huge cities (see Figure 11.2). Also, the economic status is not uniform across

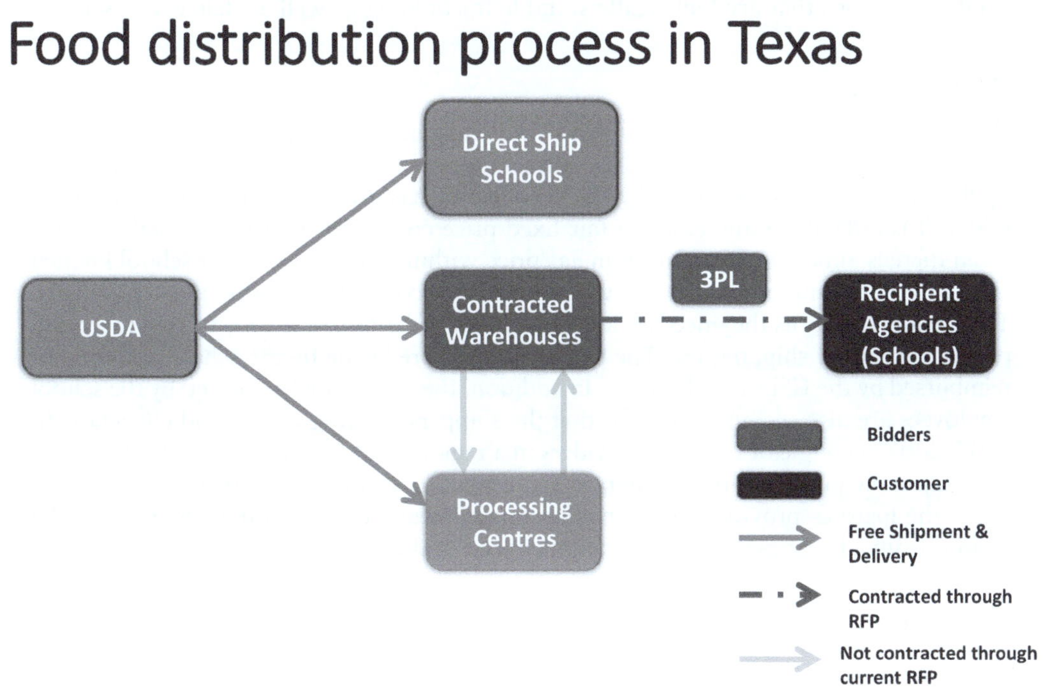


*Figure 11.1* Food distribution process in Texas.
*Source*: Original creation.

*Table 11.1* Distribution of demand across regions

| *Regions* | *Demand (No. of cases)* | *No. of schools or recipient agencies (RAs)* |
|---|---|---|
| 1 | 152,550 | 34 |
| 2 | 61,832 | 76 |
| 3 | 260,824 | 274 |
| 4 | 166,169 | 118 |
| 5 | 199,730 | 195 |
| 6 | 362,306 | 170 |
| 7 | 232,745 | 241 |
| 8 | 327,188 | 113 |
| 9 | 34,109 | 53 |
| 10 | 24,774 | 71 |
| Total | 1,822,227 | 1,345 |

*Source*: Original creation.

the large state, and the per capita need for subsidized school food is higher in regions that are not densely populated. In 2009, there were ten regions in the RFP, and they were not equitably divided. Table 11.1 provides the number of schools and their total demand in a year; we can clearly see that this is not a fair division of demand or travel distance for the logistics provider. When the RFP was bid out, there were regions with no bids, and the Texas Department of Agriculture (TDA) had to group a few regions so that they could have a logistics provider in each region. This ad hoc process was not sustainable in the long run, and some providers went bankrupt as these were operating in unprofitable regions. There was a need to creatively partition the state of Texas into equitable regions that are logistically suitable for bidding as well as delivery of service.

#### *Other Challenges*

Once a 3PL provider chooses a sliding rate schedule in the bidding process, they remain the same for the entire duration of the contract (up to four years). The rate schedule varies by the number of cases ordered by the schools but has no room for adjustment in gas prices. It is difficult to implement a fair fixed-price contract between both stakeholders when there is almost high variation in gas price within a year. Also, most school kitchen and storeroom employees are not well trained in economical procurement processes. They tend to order as they needed, and sometimes order as low as one to two cases and pay an exorbitant shipping fee. The shipment costs are borne by the school and are not reimbursed by the USDA or the TDA. In addition, the sizes of orders placed by the school employees are also inconsistent, affecting the shippers' routing ability and efficiency. In 2007–2008, a couple of logistics providers in a region went bankrupt, and the TDA had to collapse the initial ten-region map to six to make it viable for the providers. In some areas, the logistics providers were making huge profits due to inequalities between the regions from a logistics perspective (shipment size and distance).

### Looking Forward

TDA was looking to set up a sustainable RFP and rate schedule that addresses the challenge around demand distribution, gas price fluctuation, better ordering practices from schools and attracting new bidders during the solicitation process. They would have to do it in a competitive manner such that it is fair for the bidders (economic viability) as well as being cost-efficient across the various school districts.

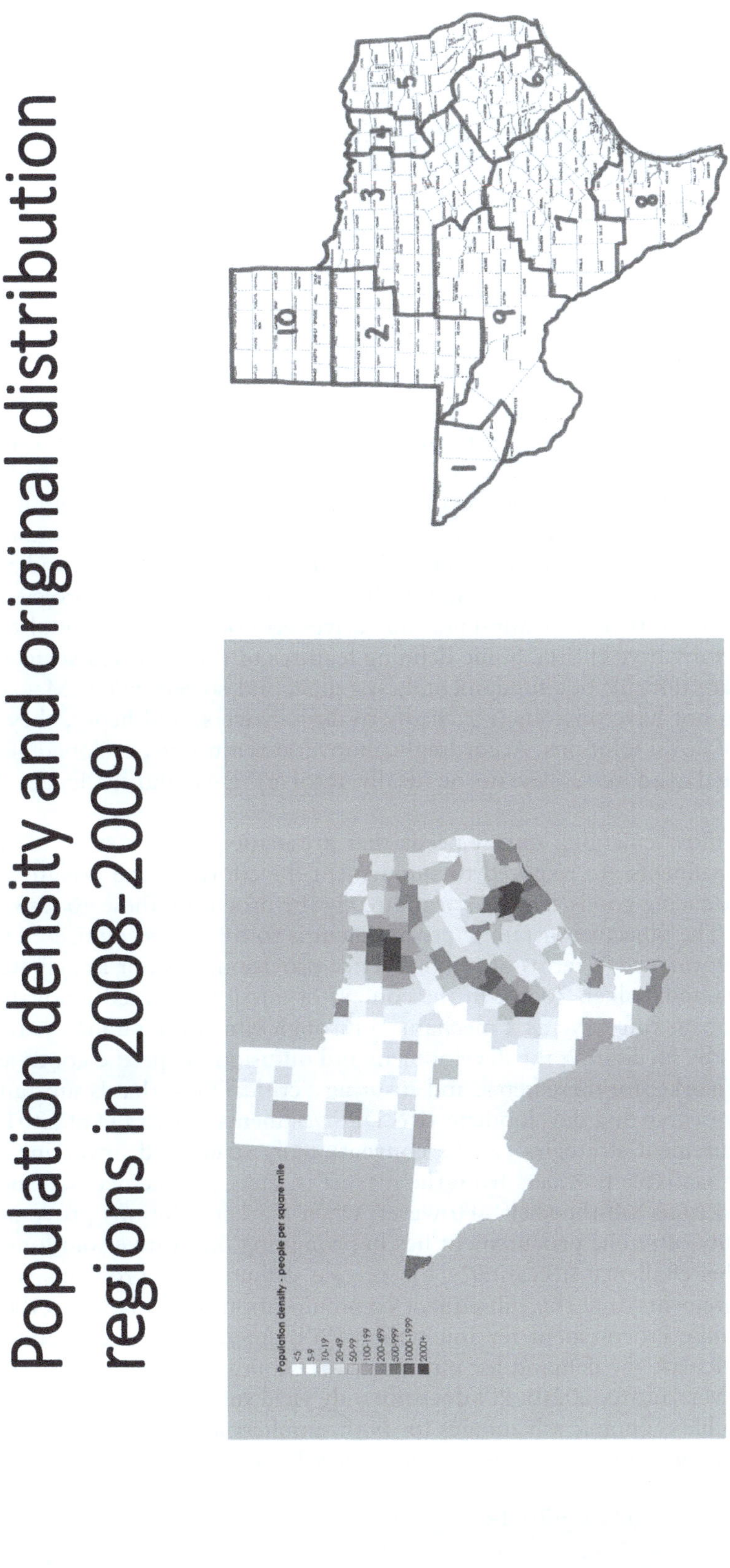


*Figure 11.2* Population density and original distribution regions in 2008–2009.
*Source:* Original creation.

# 12 Innovation in Public Procurement

*Stephanie Francis Grimbert and*
*Jon Mikel Zabala-Iturriagagoitia*

## 12.1 Introduction

Major societal challenges, such as those delineated by the United Nations Sustainable Development Goals, exert significant influence not only on the priorities and lifestyles of contemporary societies but also on the formulation and implementation of innovation policies. In fact, innovation policies have assumed a central role in fostering economic advancement, environmental sustainability, and societal transformation (Schot and Steinmueller, 2018). Therefore, there is a need to align technological and economic progress with these overarching goals, so that innovation not only drives economic growth but also contributes to global transformative efforts. Some defining features of these wicked societal challenges are that they are difficult but fundamental, systemic, and society-wide (Mazzucato et al., 2024), they do not have obvious (i.e., ready-to-use) answers, and hence, they request the development of novel solutions. Accordingly, innovations must be developed, implemented, and disseminated to address, alleviate, or, ideally, resolve these grand challenges (Mazzucato, 2018a).

To address those emerging unmet needs that are inadequately met by existing market solutions, governments are required to supplement the efforts of the private sector, either directly (by producing goods/services) or indirectly (by procuring these goods/services from private firms). The objective of public procurement is to fulfill a recognized demand while optimizing performance in terms of public service provision, cost, or anticipated functionalities (Grandia and Volker, 2023). In the context of mission-oriented innovation policies, public procurement can serve as a mechanism through which the public sector can rectify market failures by facilitating the development and diffusion of specific goods and services, expanding the market for these items, and ensuring a critical mass that is substantial enough to incentivize research and development (R&D) investments (Uyarra et al., 2014, p. 631).

Public procurement strategies can be conventionally structured, involving the acquisition of readily available products from the market to meet specific needs, a method colloquially referred to as 'off-the-shelf'. However, when market solutions prove non-existent, the responsibility of public procurement lies in prompting innovative solutions. Effectively undertaking this challenge necessitates the precise definition of problems, their translation into requirements, and the subsequent communication of the latter to the market. In this regard, Public Procurement for Innovation (PPI) emerges as a key policy instrument designed to articulate the demand for innovations, encouraging their widespread adoption and diffusion (Mazzucato, 2020). PPI does not only yield substantial social benefits but also engenders tangible economic advantages for both suppliers and their corresponding supply chains, augmenting its overall socio-economic contribution (Wesseling and Edquist, 2018).

DOI: 10.4324/9781003566670-14

The existing body of scientific research indicates that public procurement is more likely to foster innovations compared to other traditional policy instruments like R&D subsidies, a fact substantiated by numerous scholars (Rothwell and Zegvel, 1981; Geroski, 1990; Aschhoff and Sofka, 2009; Guerzoni and Raiteri, 2012). However, despite its potential, contracting authorities encounter significant challenges when attempting to implement PPI (Georghiou et al., 2014; Uyarra et al., 2014). This challenge primarily stems from entrenched routines that may have been suitable in the past but hinder the adaptation of procurement processes to the evolving demands of contemporary societies. Indeed, there is a body of evidence indicating that public procurement is often executed perfunctorily, following established patterns and routines out of habit, thereby creating an operational barrier to innovative development (Edquist and Zabala-Iturriagagoitia, 2021).

The implementation of PPI demands changes in the design of such policy interventions and requires the development of new capabilities, so as to maximize the effectiveness of this policy instrument (Loijas et al., 2024). To respond to this gap, this chapter aims to offer guidelines concerning (i) the phases in which PPI is conducted; (ii) the different ways in which PPI can be undertaken by contracting authorities; and (iii) the capabilities needed for the successful implementation of PPI. In particular, the chapter focuses on those situations in which the views on the needs to be fulfilled are convergent, but the solutions addressing them remain unknown or contested (i.e., when contracting authorities need to play a lead user role), as we believe this is the most common situation that public procurers face in the context of grand challenge mitigation, and mission-oriented policy formulation.

The remainder of the chapter is structured as follows. Section 12.2 offers a summary of the literature, highlighting the central role that PPI plays within the realm of mission-oriented innovation policies. Section 12.3 presents the various phases constituting the PPI cycle and highlights the main obstacles encountered by public procurers and contracting authorities when implementing PPI. Section 12.4 identifies the key capabilities necessary for contracting authorities to play a lead user role, highlighting the need for conducting PPI in functional terms. The chapter concludes by presenting several practical cases, tailored to nurturing these capabilities.

## 12.2 Summary of Literature

Contemporary societies are marked by their inherent uncertainty, complexity, ambiguity, volatility, and rapid pace of change (Johansen, 2009). In these contexts, the formulation of innovation policy necessitates responsiveness and capacity to adapt to evolving requirements and to offer agile solutions to rapidly changing environments (Labory and Bianchi, 2021). Achieving such adaptability mandates a holistic understanding of the challenge at hand, the specific needs demanding fulfillment, and the precise articulation of policy measures (Borrás and Edquist, 2019).

### *12.2.1 Mission-Oriented Innovation Policies*

Mission-oriented policies have emerged as a suitable strategic framework to address specific societal challenges by setting clear, ambitious goals, referred to as 'missions'. Mission-oriented policies foster a holistic understanding of the challenges to be addressed by integrating multiple stakeholders and disciplines, so as to ensure that the solutions to be developed are not only innovative but also relevant and effective in meeting societal and environmental needs (Mazzucato, 2018a). These policies have gained prominence as a way to drive transformative change in response to the complex and dynamic challenges facing contemporary societies (Hekkert et al., 2020).

Mission-oriented innovation policies exhibit three discernible characteristics (Mazzucato, 2018a, 2018b):

1. They should aim to proactively establish markets rather than merely addressing existing market deficiencies (i.e., market failures). This shift necessitates a fundamental transformation in the role of the public sector, from remedying market imperfections to instigating innovative market opportunities (Mazzucato, 2023).
2. They must provide (strategic) directionality. Their pivotal inquiry revolves around determining the trajectory of transformation to which the system (i.e., a territory, an industry) should aspire, rather than focusing on the participants involved in this transformation. In essence, governments ought to move from 'picking winners' to 'picking the willing' (Mazzucato, 2019, p. 13).
3. They must facilitate the creation of the necessary conditions for the emergence of innovation, fostering an environment of experimentation and embracing risk. This implies that public entities should stimulate the capacity of societal stakeholders to foresee innovative solutions, addressing both current challenges and anticipating future needs.

To operationalize mission-oriented innovation policies, a diverse array of instruments has been introduced (Edler and Georghiou, 2007), among which public procurement has been emphasized (Mazzucato and Wainwright, 2024). Its efficacy lies in its ability to foster innovation, promote competition, and drive the realization of targeted objectives, as highlighted by Edquist and Zabala-Iturriagagoitia (2012).

### *12.2.2 The Potential Roles of PPI within Mission-Oriented Policy*

PPI is a strategic process wherein a contracting authority formulates and places an order for a good, service, or technology that does not presently exist but is essential for addressing specific functions to solve societal, departmental, ministerial, or related problems (Edquist et al., 2015). The fundamental objective of PPI is to address unmet public, societal, and environmental needs or to mitigate challenges that are often of a global nature but may have national or local dimensions concurrently (Saussier and Tirole, 2015). It is imperative that this procurement approach leads to innovative solutions before the delivery to the contracting authority occurs. Naturally, the innovations arising from PPI must surpass the functionalities of existing products or services available at the time of the order (in case they exist). Failure to meet this criterion would lead the state to consider procuring the existing goods, as they provide a more effective solution to the targeted problem.

PPI offers multifaceted advantages. Foremost, it grants access to novel products or services for procurement by government entities, presenting an opportunity to achieve economies of scale through significant initial purchases. This early engagement can result in reduced production costs and enhanced product quality owing to learning effects related to production (Chicot and Matt, 2018). Additionally, PPI plays a critical role in shaping demand by signaling unaddressed societal needs, thereby fostering interaction between government entities (i.e., the users) and potential suppliers (i.e., the producers). PPI contracts serve as incentives for developers of innovative technologies, particularly small and medium enterprises (SMEs), some of whom might not receive support from conventional R&D subsidies (Knutsson and Thomasson, 2014). PPI can also serve to legitimize product standards, creating new markets or expanding existing ones, thereby facilitating adoption and diffusion

(Uyarra et al., 2020). Beyond these aspects, PPI offers additional benefits such as enhancing the quality of public services within optimal budget constraints, modernizing public services, and fostering the growth of start-ups and innovative SMEs (European Commission, 2021). PPI also serves as a transformative policy instrument by surmounting the institutional rigidities often associated with the public sector due to regulatory complexities (Grimbert and Zabala-Iturriagagoitia, 2023). Summing up, PPI can accelerate technological advancement, as well as the adoption and diffusion of innovations, potentially reshaping the overall industrial landscape (Neij, 2001; Bleda and Chicot, 2020).

Given the complexities behind mission-oriented innovation policies, a natural question is how to conduct PPI. Table 12.1 delineates four distinct scenarios and outlines four strategies that governments can follow to incorporate PPI as a fundamental element of mission-oriented innovation policies. These strategies are categorized based on two critical dimensions (Uyarra et al., 2020): the inherent characteristics of the problem space, and the nature of potential solutions.

In the presence of an established and acknowledged societal issue lacking a definitive solution within existing markets, it becomes imperative to engage in systematic exploration and experimentation with diverse potential solutions (see bottom left quadrant). Public procurement can serve as a strategic tool in this context, facilitating the identification and direction of innovative markets. In such scenarios, the public sector can assume the role of a *lead user*, supporting the inception of emerging markets that hold promise for broader diffusion (von Hippel, 1986). This can be achieved through the strategic implementation of functional PPI (Edquist and Zabala-Iturriagagoitia, 2021), fostering the development and dissemination of pioneering solutions.

In a second scenario, characterized by a well-defined comprehension and consensus concerning both technological priorities/possibilities and societal needs, PPI can assume a *brokering* role (see bottom right quadrant). Here, it acts as a liaison, aligning identified economic strengths with global demands. This strategic approach can be regarded as an integral component of a diffusion-centric innovation policy, facilitating the uptake and dissemination of incremental product and process innovations within established sectors. In this context, public procurement may not necessarily be innovation-driven but can adopt an 'innovation-friendly' stance.

A third scenario involves situations with vague or wicked problems and solutions that are highly uncertain or unrealistic within the constraints of existing technological and industrial capabilities (see top left quadrant). In such contexts, procurement can act as a tool to bolster

*Table 12.1* Potential roles of PPI within mission-oriented policy

| | | *Nature of the solution space* | |
|---|---|---|---|
| | | *Solution unclear or contested* | *Consensus about solutions* |
| **Nature of problem space** | **Demand poorly articulated or fragmented** | Government as a purchaser of R&D<br>Goal: increase R&D<br>Procurement mode: PCP | Government as catalyst<br>Goal: market creation<br>Procurement mode: catalytic PPI |
| | **Clearly identified and agreed upon needs** | Government as a lead user<br>Goal: boost innovation<br>Procurement mode: functional PPI | Government as broker<br>Goal: innovation diffusion<br>Procurement mode: innovation-friendly regular procurement |

*Source*: Based on Uyarra et al. (2020).

industrial R&D, addressing societal demands and *augmenting R&D investments*. To navigate these risky contexts, the implementation of pre-commercial procurement (PCP) can prove instrumental in fostering the advancement of novel technologies (Edquist and Zabala-Iturriagagoitia, 2015). PCP entails the procurement of research outcomes and constitutes a form of direct public investment in R&D (European Commission, 2006a, 2006b). It should be noted that the SBIR program (Small Business Innovation Development Act, 1982; Audretsch, 2003) represents the US equivalent to the 'European' PCP approach. Notably, PCP does not entail product development, as it does not mandate any commitment from the purchasing entity to acquire a specific product. It is essential to recognize that the research outcomes procured through PCP may subsequently evolve into product innovations upon the completion of the PCP process or phase. Importantly, in many instances, the PCP scheme could be replaced by a full-fledged R&D project. Hence, to achieve innovation outcomes, it is crucial to emphasize that PCP must be complemented by more commercially oriented or solution-driven policies. This synergy is fundamental to facilitate the integration of these technological solutions into the market landscape.

Finally, in those cases in which the demand/need may not be clearly understood, but for which there might be consensus about the potential solutions to be used, PPI can be used to *catalyze* the development of particular technologies or markets (see top right quadrant). Catalytic PPI occurs when the procuring agency takes on the role of coordinator to support the needs of end-users. In this context, the demands originate from entities external to the public realm, and hence, the goal of PPI is to acquire new products on behalf of other stakeholders (Edquist and Zabala-Iturriagagoitia, 2012).

## 12.3 Emerging Issues

In recent times, the scholarly discourse on PPI has undergone a significant transformative turn, largely attributable to the profound impact and potential inherent in this policy instrument. In this regard, Grimbert and Zabala-Iturriagagoitia (2023) contend that the transformative potential of PPI is not only related to its ability to provide a response to the ambitious goals and needs posed by mission-oriented policies, but also to its capacity to reshape the functioning of public administrations. Their understanding is related to the substantive and procedural dichotomy introduced by Demircioglu and Vivona (2021), according to which a policy instrument can have substantive effects when the results derived from it are being observed outside the public sector, and procedural effects when these results are observed inside public organizations. While existing literature extensively delves into the substantive benefits arising from PPI, the procedural dimensions, encompassing elements such as institutional frameworks, operational routines, organizational capabilities, market dialogues, and inter-organizational cooperation, remain untapped. In order to address these soft procedural dimensions, in the next two sub-sections we will introduce which are the main barriers faced by demanding and supplying organizations in PPI.

### *12.3.1 Main Barriers to PPI on Behalf of the Demanding Organizations*

In a study conducted in the UK, Uyarra et al. (2014) evidence the challenges faced by public authorities acting as demand-side actors. As reported in Figure 12.1, the most prominent obstacle is the limited engagement with procuring organizations. This limitation has direct repercussions on demand fragmentation, diminishing the efficacy of PPI in comparison to its potential effectiveness if demand could be bundled (Timmermans and Zabala-Iturriagagoitia, 2013). The second prevalent barrier experienced by public

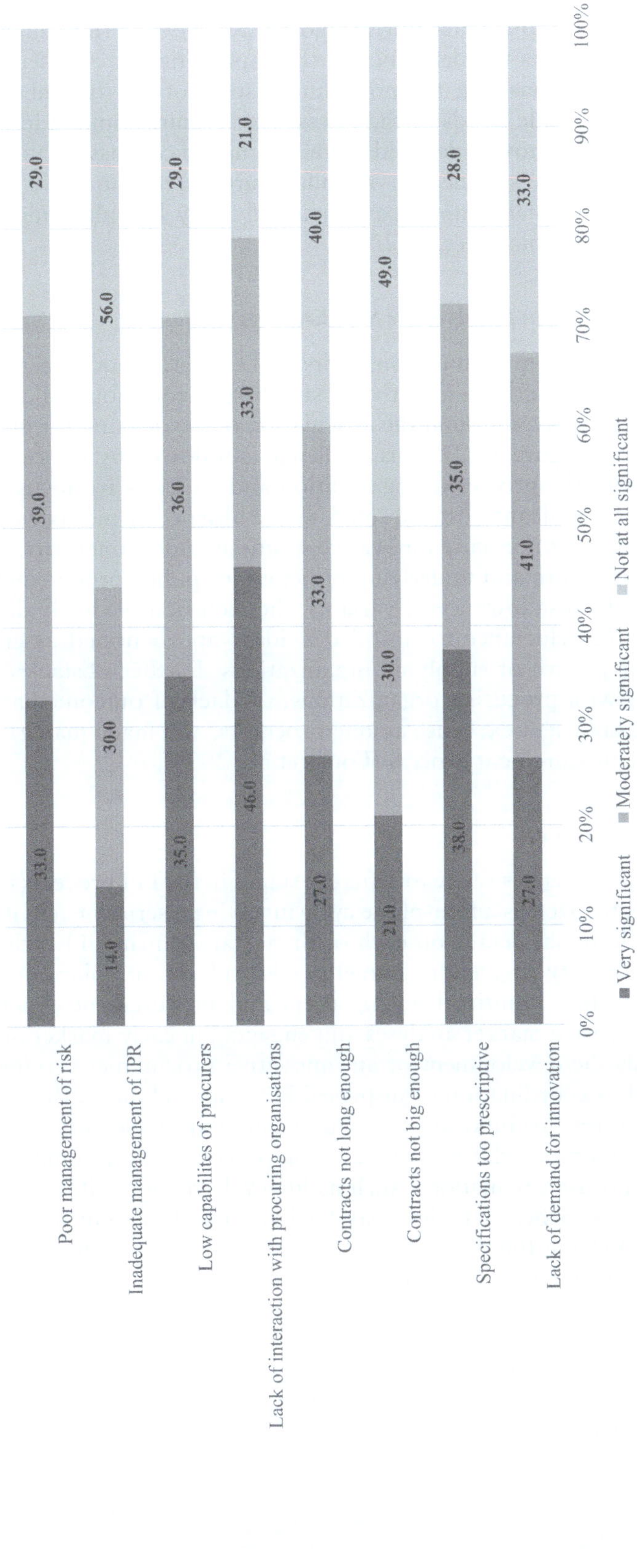


*Figure 12.1* Main barriers to PPI on behalf of demanding organizations.
*Source:* Adapted by authors, based on Uyarra et al. (2014, p. 635).

procurers deals with overly detailed and technical specifications in tender documents. To alleviate this challenge, one viable approach involves adopting functional specifications, as proposed by Edquist and Zabala-Iturriagagoitia (2021). The third major hurdle faced by contracting authorities is the deficiency in the capabilities of civil servants to procure innovative solutions, emphasizing the procedural aspect of PPI (Grimbert et al., 2024). While procuring ready-made goods at the lowest cost requires limited in-house expertise, encouraging suppliers to innovate demands higher competence (Tassabehji and Moorhouse, 2008). This underscores the significance of skilled purchasers who wield substantial influence over financial performance and operational efficiency by enhancing quality, design, and reducing lead times (Cousins et al., 2006).

### *12.3.2 Main Barriers to PPI on Behalf of the Supplier Organizations*

The previous challenges align with existing empirical evidence concerning the barriers that impact the PPI process from the perspective of suppliers (Georghiou et al., 2014). Notably, the primary difficulty revolves around the articulation of the demand for innovation within tender documents (see Figure 12.2). This challenge is followed by the capacity to initiate early interactions with the procuring organization and an excessive focus on pricing considerations. Another significant obstacle refers to the absence of mechanisms signaling the readiness and willingness to procure innovative solutions. Additional barriers are rooted in the organizational structure and underlying principles of public procurement. Specifically, constraints such as the disallowance of variants, the inclusion of overly detailed technical specifications, and the reluctance to unsolicited ideas are identified as critical obstacles to PPI from the perspective of supplying organizations. Further obstacles encompass the limited engagement with procuring organizations, the lack of outcome-based (functional) specifications, the insufficient expertise among procurers, and inadequate risk management practices during the procurement process (Loijas et al., 2024).

### *12.3.3 Stages in the PPI Process*

The aforementioned challenges relate to different stages in the PPI process (see Figure 12.3), which can be conceptualized as a four-phase cycle involving a series of activities (see Edquist et al., (2015) for additional details on each of these stages in the PPI cycle). In the initial phase, there is a necessity to identify unmet needs and absent solutions. This demands proficient communication abilities bridging users and procurement experts, along with conducting comprehensive market analyses and engaging in early market interactions. The second phase entails the development of an innovative procurement strategy. This phase mandates the seamless coordination of dispersed PPI responsibilities, the presentation of a compelling argument for pro-innovation procurement, and the definition of the associated award and evaluation criteria during the tendering process. This argumentation should be substantiated with precise calculations, such as life-cycle costing, allowing for the incorporation of functional specifications that may facilitate the development of variants to the identified need, or opening the possibility of dividing the tender into small lots that may foster the involvement of SMEs and start-ups. The third phase, centered on the execution of the PPI process, requires the suitable utilization of existing procurement procedures (i.e., open procedure, restricted procedure, competitive procedure with negotiation, competitive dialogue, negotiated procedure without prior publication, design contest, innovation partnership), technical specifications, and the definition of a strategy to deal with the intellectual property that may emanate from the initiative. Additionally, it necessitates ongoing

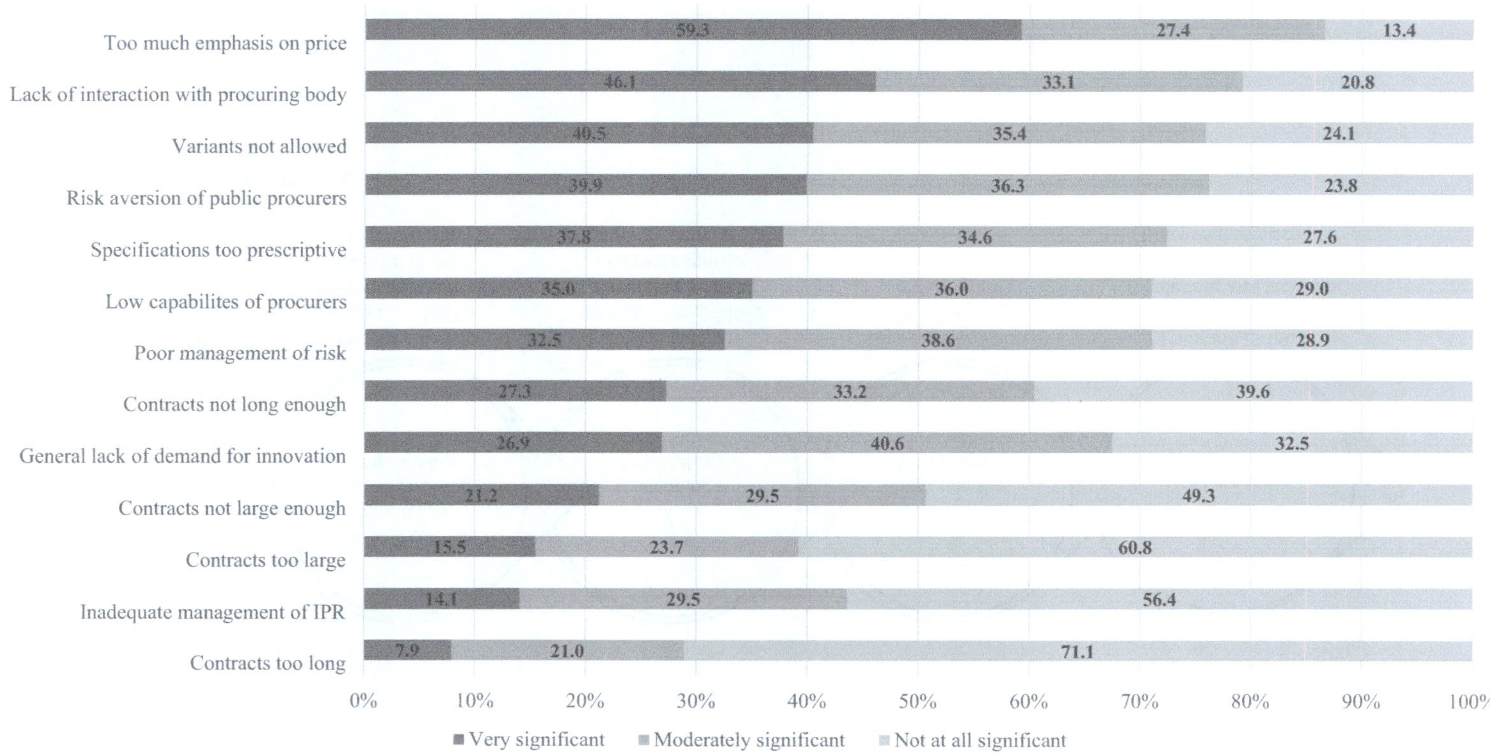


*Figure 12.2* Main barriers to PPI on behalf of supplier organizations.
*Source*: Adapted by authors, based on Georghiou et al. (2014, p. 9).

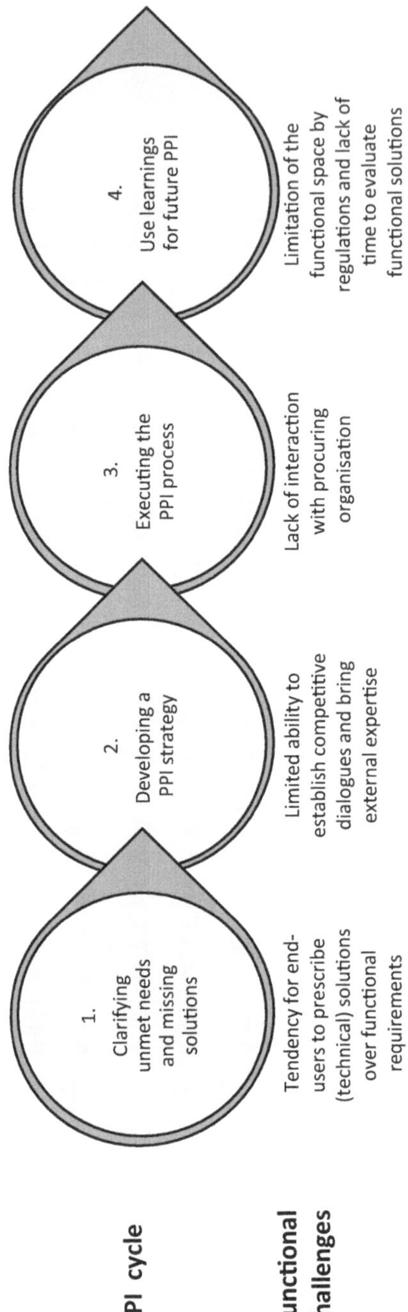


*Figure 12.3* The PPI cycle.
*Source:* Original creation.

dialogues between procurers and suppliers, so the solution being developed responds to the actual need, an activity that may be facilitated by the use of an intermediary that acts as a broker. Lastly, the fourth stage, focused on utilizing acquired knowledge for future procurements, centers on evaluating the satisfaction of the contracting authority as a final user, and assessing the extent to which the identified societal need has been effectively addressed.

Considering the PPI process outlined above, and the barriers listed in the literature on behalf of both demanding and supplying organizations, we identify a set of emerging challenges at each phase of the PPI cycle when contracting authorities need to act as lead users, which, as argued, we believe is the most common situation that public procurers face in the context of grand challenges. During phase 1, these emerging challenges include (i) the inclination of end-users to prescribe specific solutions rather than formulating functional requirements, (ii) the risk-averse behavior of public authorities, leading them to favor the certainty offered by technical requirements over functional ones, (iii) their preference for widely recognized standard products, and (iv) their lack of time or expertise to articulate comprehensive functional requirements. The primary obstacle impeding the advancement of phase 2 is related to the restricted capacity for initiating competitive dialogues and integrating external expertise. This challenge is particularly pronounced in the context of PPI, given that the solution to be procured is yet to be developed. Addressing this issue necessitates a comprehensive understanding and evaluation of the market dynamics and its potential offerings, as well as an exploration of the market's latent capabilities (Edler and Yeow, 2016). In phase 3, challenges emerge due to the lack of meaningful interaction between suppliers and procuring organizations, thereby hindering the smooth progression of the PPI process. In this regard, Roberts and Siemiatycki (2015) evidence how collaborative approaches involving diverse stakeholders are essential, since public organizations cannot be presumed to possess the entirety of the technical expertise necessary for monitoring the development of innovative solutions. Finally, in phase 4, specific challenges arise in terms of evaluating the efficacy of proposed solutions in addressing the specified requirements due to the regulatory limitations of the functional space. As a consequence, while public procurers may possess proficiency in standard procurement procedures and regulations, the evidence indicates a lack of expertise in implementing PPI processes effectively, in particular when a lead user role is required from the contracting authority (Grimbert et al., 2024).

## 12.4 Practical Applications

As previously stated, a prominent hindrance to the efficacy of PPI lies in the insufficiency of the required capabilities within the administrative domain (El-Taliawi and van der Wal, 2019; Kattel and Mazzucato, 2018; Haque et al., 2021), which is the level at which policies are implemented. Therefore, to address this gap, and departing from the procedural barriers discussed above, this section aims to identify the capabilities that can help overcome these challenges. As already argued, we will here only focus on the capabilities needed in the case that contracting authorities aim to effectively assume the role of lead users, as we consider this is the archetypical case found in the context of mission-oriented policies. However, Grimbert et al. (2024) provide a detailed analysis of the capabilities that are required in each of the four roles of contracting authorities presented in Table 12.1. Note that as delineated in Table 12.1, it might be necessary for contracting authorities to play a lead user role when the problem is clearly identified and defined, but solutions are either unclear, contested, or not available as to yet, which is exactly the context in which mission-oriented policies operate.

One of the means through which the lead user role can be articulated by contracting authorities is through the use of functional procurement.[1] Functional PPI refers to those situations in which the procuring entity sets out the desired functions or performance criteria to be achieved, rather than specifying the technical means or detailed characteristics of how those outcomes should be met (Edquist and Zabala-Iturriagagoitia, 2021). For example, procuring 'clean floors' should not be equated with the procurement of vacuum cleaners, nor should the pursuit of 'silent asphalt' be synonymous with the acquisition of noise barriers designed to block sound refraction.[2] Defining the function, such as 'clean floors' or 'silent asphalt', allows for a diverse array of potential ideas, technologies, and products, each capable of delivering enhanced value and effectiveness compared to existing solutions (Loijas et al., 2024). Consequently, using functional specifications in procurement calls serves to spur the emergence of solutions that the governing authority or unit may not have previously contemplated and, indeed, should not limit themselves to.

Functional requirements offer suppliers greater flexibility to leverage their skills and creativity, thereby expanding the potential for innovative solutions. Simultaneously, granting suppliers a broader scope for devising solutions tailored to the specified needs or functions can liberate the contracting authority's resources, enabling a more concentrated focus on its primary endeavors (i.e., ensuring the efficacy and efficiency of public services). Additionally, functional PPI may also serve as a powerful competition policy tool (Anderson and Kovacic, 2009). This mechanism operates by functional descriptions intensifying competition among diverse products aiming to fulfill identical needs or resolve identical issues.

A counterargument against the adoption of functional PPI lies in the elevated expertise demanded of the procuring authority or unit and the associated costs (Wu et al., 2015). Conducting functional PPI necessitates significant organizational performance, particularly concerning established routines and processes, as formulating functional specifications can prove more challenging than technical specifications (Grimbert et al., 2024). Nevertheless, it is also to be acknowledged that the evaluation of the final delivery may be comparatively more straightforward, given the measurable and observable adherence or deviation from functional standards (e.g., noise reduction in asphalt due to road vibrations).

Presented in Table 12.2 are the capabilities required for public procurers and contracting authorities to assume a lead user role. These capabilities are clustered according to the four phases of the PPI cycle, as depicted in Figure 12.3.

The focus of the first phase is on accurately translating unmet needs into functional requirements. This involves not only a deep understanding of the needs but also the ability to engage in creative dialogues to define the functional requirements that these solutions must meet. In this regard, early engagement with users and other stakeholders is crucial to ensure broader acceptance and support for the prospective innovative solutions. To this end, contracting authorities must also build and maintain relationships with suppliers while adhering to procurement norms of fairness and non-discrimination.

In the second stage contracting authorities need to develop a robust PPI strategy that leverages the government's market power to drive broader societal transformation. This requires a comprehensive understanding of how to integrate and balance innovation goals with other societal objectives. Authorities must also anticipate the risks (i.e., public, private, and societal) that might arise from the proposed solutions. Promoting the acceptance of these innovations among users is a critical aspect of this phase, ensuring that the solutions are not only viable but also embraced by the target audience.

The execution phase focuses on the co-generation of solutions, which often necessitates organizational changes within both the contracting authorities and the economic operators. This collaborative approach might include developing product-service systems (Alhola et al.,

*Table 12.2* Capabilities needed by a lead user type of contracting authority

| *Phases of the PPI cycle* | *Capabilities needed by a lead user type of contracting authority* |
|---|---|
| **1 Clarifying unmet needs and missing solutions** | Translation of the need into functional requirements.<br>Creative dialogues to define the function to be met (i.e., functional specifications).<br>Build supplier relationships while respecting procurement norms of fairness and non-discrimination.<br>Include users and other stakeholders in early engagement dialogues to increase acceptance of new prospective solutions. |
| **2 Developing a PPI strategy** | Understand the government's market power to drive societal transformation.<br>Integrate and balance innovation goals with other societal objectives.<br>Anticipate the current and future public, private, and societal risks associated with the developed solution.<br>Promote the acceptance of innovations among users. |
| **3 Executing the PPI process** | Co-generation of functional solutions requiring organizational changes in both contracting authorities and economic operators (e.g., Product-Service Systems).<br>Pilot testing with final users.<br>Evaluate solutions using functional performance requirements.<br>Embrace trial and error as part of the necessary experimentation.<br>Provide feedback to economic operators following the use of the functional solution leading to IPR reformulation. |
| **4 Using learnings for future PPI** | Assess the externalities created (or avoided).<br>Ensure current and future public value creation through public data sharing.<br>Forecast the weaknesses of suppliers and communicate possible corrective actions to other areas of public policy.<br>Include society in the definition of future needs. |

*Source*: Grimbert et al. (2024).

2019) and conducting pilot tests with end-users to refine the solutions. A critical part of this phase is evaluating the solutions based on their functional performance requirements and embracing trial and error as a necessary part of the innovation process. Providing feedback to economic operators post-implementation is also essential, particularly when it comes to the reformulation and management of the developed intellectual property.

The final phase emphasizes the importance of learning from the outcomes of and the procedural contribution made by the PPI process. For example, contracting authorities must assess the externalities (i.e., both positive and negative) created by the implemented solutions, internally in the public administration and in society at large. They are also responsible for ensuring that public value is created and sustained, which can be facilitated through public data sharing. Additionally, it is important to anticipate potential weaknesses in suppliers and communicate these to inform other areas of public policy. Finally, involving society in defining future needs is essential to ensure that the PPI process continues to evolve in a way that meets public expectations and needs.

## 12.5 Case Studies

In the following four sub-sections, a series of real cases are going to be presented. Each of these cases is related to one of the four stages of the PPI process, as discussed above. These cases are aimed at evidencing the capabilities used in each of the examples, so as to highlight the relevance of having in place the required capabilities.

### *12.5.1 Phase 1: Clarifying Unmet Needs and Missing Solutions*

The departing point for the first stage of the PPI cycle is the identification of the need(s). This need(s) can be either current or future and represent(s) a (current or future) problem because it negatively impacts the delivery of a service of public interest. The identification of needs requires understanding the current situation, namely, gathering data about existing solutions, identifying why these solutions do not properly address the identified need, and hence, quantifying the 'cost' of the problem and determining why innovation is needed.[3] After thoroughly assessing the current situation, the next step is to define what the new (desired) scenario would look like. This requires thinking in terms of the functions that the new solution should deliver (i.e., these functions are derived from the previously mentioned problems). The definition of the need in terms of these (functional) requirements will be presented as a statement of demand that should be promoted and disseminated to facilitate outreach to potential suppliers and other interest groups.

For example, the Austrian Mint, responsible for coin production in Austria, identified that the residual water (wastewater) generated during coin production contained elevated levels of chemicals that surpassed the legal limits. The PPI initiative included the following description of the demanded functionality: 'Cleaning up the residual water left over from the production of coins in Austria'. The tendering process was divided into the following phases:

- Analysis of the current situation, conducting thorough market research, including alternative studies to assess various technical possibilities.
- Invitation of potential suppliers and selection of the most appropriate firms based on their potential competence.
- Reception of preliminary proposals by suppliers, incorporating life-cycle cost evaluation estimates.
- Execution of practical tests, followed by analysis of the results.

Based on the previous process, the Federal Procurement Agency launched a PPI for the Austrian Mint for planning, delivery, installation, and bringing into service a wastewater treatment plant including maintenance and service.[4] As a result, suppliers were able to submit their final offers, which were then assessed according to the established criteria, which included achieving the lowest possible long-term total costs, including the energy, operating materials, and working hours of the operating staff required. The solution developed by the winning consortium led Austrian Mint to reduce its need for fresh water by 97% and saving 4 million liters of clean drinking water per year.

Preliminary market consultations with potential suppliers, end-users, experts, and other interest groups are key drivers in this demand articulation.[5] First, they are useful to announce the existence of an implicit demand not being satisfied at present (i.e., a market sounding). Second, they allow to disentangle what the state-of-the-art may be, identifying whether a solution addressing the problem may already exist (a solution that the contracting authority may not be aware of). Assuming that no solution may be sensed, open market consultations could be instrumental in asking potential bidders and experts about the extent to which the identified requirements may be satisfactorily addressed (i.e., if it is feasible to develop solutions targeting those needs). Third, open market consultations facilitate the participation of end-users and other stakeholders to increase the acceptance of the prospective solutions.

As an illustration, in 2013 the fire departments in London (UK) and Ghent (Belgium) collaborated on a joint procurement that explored the future of fire engines and support vehicles in 2050 (see Morgan et al., 2016). Fire services encounter distinctive challenges in enhancing the sustainability of their operations. The evolving climate introduces the need for diverse emergency response measures, particularly in the face of increased incidents of flooding and wildfires. To address this specific need, both contracting authorities had to interact with suppliers in the automotive sector and beyond. Preliminary research revealed 21 distinct technologies and processes with the potential to make fire engines more environmentally friendly. Each fire department selected focus areas for engaging the market, considering their relevance to their operations, innovative potential, and feasibility within the project timelines. For instance, London concentrated on telematics, while Ghent focused on designing a new secondary vehicle to support its frontline fleet.

In reaching out to telematics providers, the London Fire Brigade issued a prior information notice and a market sounding questionnaire to over 75 companies involved in telematics and information systems. Responding companies were invited to a headquarters open day, where they could present their ideas and engage in discussions with key staff and project advisors. Following a different approach, Ghent employed the concept of 'planning poker', inviting both internal users and interested companies to assess various functionalities for the proposed new vehicle. Ghent also published a prior information notice and conducted two engagement sessions with potential suppliers. Moreover, the two fire brigades collaboratively established an advisory board to assist with market engagement. The board comprised members from other brigades and technical experts with relevant sector knowledge. In February 2013, a workshop was held with the board to assess the state-of-the-art in the field and contribute to the development of documents for market engagement.

### *12.5.2 Phase 2: Developing a PPI Strategy*

An example in which PPI is systematically being used as a strategic policy instrument is the case of Galicia (Spain). Galicia started using PPI in 2009, amid the global financial crisis, by focusing on health. The Galician health service serves 95% of the Galician population and represents more than 40% of the regional budget. Since it was expected that the financial crisis was going to have a direct impact on its performance, the regional government decided to support a set of PPI initiatives leading to new healthcare processes that would allow the health service to respond to the needs of its aging population.

Since Galicia lacked prior experience in the deployment of PPI, the regional government dedicated significant efforts to institutionalize PPI, mobilizing existing expertise, supporting capacity building, and establishing new formal structures to manage PPI (see Uyarra et al., 2020). After nearly a decade of PPI development in the healthcare sector, Galicia formulated a new regional strategy with the goal of diversifying its industrial landscape. This ambitious strategy aimed to position Galicia as a hub for creating technological solutions for sustainable land management, covering areas such as forest fire prevention, control of forest and agricultural pests, coastal security, and offshore applications like fishery surveillance. It also addressed airspace-related challenges, including interoperability between manned and unmanned aircraft, issues not unique to Galicia but faced globally. With this strategy in mind, the regional government initiated the civil unmanned aerial vehicles project. Although the initiative is still ongoing, the region has successfully attracted major multinational companies in the aerospace sector and has managed to create and solidify an industrial ecosystem centered around the Galician aerospace pole.[6]

Sweden is another example in which the government has developed a national strategy where PPI plays a central role. The Swedish government took a decision to adopt a national strategy for PPI in 2016, being functional PPI an important element of that strategy. As Edquist (2019) discusses, this new strategy represents a major opportunity for Sweden to improve its public services, by using the existing funds already allocated to public procurement, which amount to 700 billion Swedish crowns (approx. €80 billion) in a different way (i.e., from the procurement of products to the procurement of functions). If 10% of the public budget used for public procurement would be oriented to stimulate innovation in the future, this would correspond to 70 billion crowns (approx. €8 billion). The public annual research budget in Sweden is about 35 billion crowns (approx. €4 billion). Sweden believes that the application of this strategy will align innovations with societal goals, leading to better needs satisfaction, to increasing the quality and the effectiveness of public services, and to fostering the competitiveness of domestic firms in international markets. It is also worth stating that Sweden has traditionally been very active in promoting the societal acceptance of innovations among its citizens, through the organization of community workshops, creating citizen platforms, and facilitating their involvement in policy processes (Grimbert and Zabala-Iturriagagoitia, 2023).

### *12.5.3 Phase 3: Executing the PPI Process*

With more than 35 specialized medical centers, and about 6,500 employees, the Vilnius University Hospital Santaros Klinikos is one of the major hospitals in Lithuania. Delivering cutting-edge healthcare services for individuals of all ages, the hospital acknowledges the challenges posed by unpredictable life-threatening emergencies, necessitating immediate specialized assistance, including complicated tracheal intubation, severe bleeding, and cardiac arrest. These emergencies require the rapid mobilization of the appropriate assistance to the site of the emergency. The Santaros Klinikos thus decided to develop a PPI project to procure a smart emergency call and response system to improve the effective management of life-threatening emergencies and patient outcomes (EcoQUIP+, 2024).

Previous attempts to find suitable solutions proved unsuccessful, highlighting a gap in the market for effective and reliable emergency response systems across European hospitals. The project team embarked on a thorough needs definition phase, publishing a statement of demand that garnered support from multiple hospitals facing similar unmet needs. The project team concluded that there was scope for the technology to be updated, with recent advances in information and communication technology having the potential to offer a smarter solution.

After an intense needs definition phase, an open market consultation ensued, drawing feedback from potential suppliers across diverse sectors such as ICT, telecommunication, and medical device manufacturing. Twelve responses from six countries, including representation from SMEs, showcased a promising market response. These meetings helped to better understand what the market was ready to propose and how much effort they were willing to invest to offer a new innovative solution.

In crafting the tender specifications to foster innovation, the team faced the challenge of balancing detailed technical requirements with the imperative for novel and effective solutions. Recognizing suppliers' preferences for detailed specifications and the need for innovation, Santaros Klinikos struck a balance by providing sufficient technical details alongside functional requirements. Clinical support emerged as a crucial element, lending credibility and momentum to the project. Stakeholder engagement, involving clinicians and technical staff, facilitated a comprehensive understanding of the current situation and the precise definition of the unmet need. Transitioning to an outcome-based approach, the team overcame initial challenges posed by a shift from detailed technical schematics, ultimately defining the requirement as 'a smart emergency communication and response solution that improves the management of life-threatening emergencies, leading to better patient outcomes and staff experience, incorporating ... a 24/7 alert pathway... a feedback mechanism... [and] data collation and analysis' (EcoQUIP+, 2024, p. 50).

The tender, launched in November 2023, employed a competitive dialogue procedure to maximize supplier flexibility and ensure the best outcome. The agreed specification encompassed both functional and non-functional requirements, emphasizing compatibility with existing systems and work practices. Evaluation criteria extended beyond price, focusing on strategic fit, quality, and implementation (with a breakdown of 50% for price, 40% for compliance with non-functional requirements, and 10% for additional functionalities).

### *12.5.4 Phase 4: Using Learnings for Future PPI*

The ultimate purpose of PPI is to address societal needs, namely, to deliver public value. In this regard, the evaluation of the effectiveness of PPI should consider the contribution of PPI to society, to industry and to the environment, also considering the value of the externalities created in each of these levels. Undoubtedly, the involvement of stakeholders in the evaluation process is critical. As regards the costs, evaluations should consider the total cost of ownership, since the cost of a product is not just its purchase price (i.e., costs associated with the operation of the product, its maintenance, and end-of-life disposal also need to be assessed). Hence, the management of PPI should consider the results of the evaluation and feed the policy formulation process in phase 1.

For instance, the procurement agency of the Dutch government (i.e., PIANOo) established an electronic platform for discussions and information exchange.[7] The goal was to leverage collective procurement intelligence, ensuring ongoing and future creation of public value through the sharing of public data. All public procurement practitioners can access this information online. The underlying idea is that sharing experiences can significantly encourage the adoption of PPI and, hence, maximize the returns of public intervention through procurement policy.

The identification of future societal needs and their translation into a strategic agenda is essential for PPI. In this regard, the application of foresight might help identify both long-term societal needs and the evolution shown by emerging technologies, which can potentially match these needs (Vecchiato and Roveda, 2014). The participation of stakeholders such as firms, trade associations, chambers of commerce, NGOs, and local communities may thus help to identify future needs, and in turn, to increase the awareness, commitment, and consensus around PPI.

As the chapter has evidenced, PPI represents a profound shift in the role of the state, transforming it from a mere regulator or facilitator to an active co-creator of public value (Mazzucato et al., 2020). This transformation is procedural in nature, as it involves the establishment of new processes that enable ongoing collaboration, experimentation, and knowledge sharing among diverse stakeholders, so as to respond to transformative goals through nurturing bottom-up experimentation and exploration. The focus on delivering public value underscores the importance of not only achieving immediate outcomes but also generating positive externalities that extend beyond the immediate scope of the procurement initiative, such as the development of capabilities within the public administration. Hence, both formative and summative evaluations are essential to comprehensively assess the effectiveness of PPI. Ultimately, by embedding formative and summative evaluations into the PPI process, policymakers can ensure that public procurement remains a dynamic and responsive policy instrument for driving innovation and delivering long-term public value.

## Notes

1 See Box 12.1 for an eventual template.
2 The term silent asphalt is used here due to a case, identified in the Netherlands, which aimed to develop a new solution to minimize noise reduction along secondary roads. The road traffic noise part of the program was managed by Rijkswaterstaat Dienst Verkeer en Scheepvaart (Centre for Transport and Navigation).
3 When considering the costs, it is important to distinguish between the costs that the problem entails for the public administration and for society, the opportunity costs, and the life-cycle costs of the potential solutions, all of which should be assessed.
4 This PPI initiative won the Public Procurement of Innovation Award in year 2015. See www.procurious.com/procurement-news/austrian-wastewater-solution-wins-procurement-innovation-award
5 Article 40 in the European Directive on public procurement (Directive 2014/24/EU) states that 'advice may be used in the planning and conduct of the procurement procedure, provided that such advice does not have the effect of distorting competition and does not result in a violation of the principles of non-discrimination and transparency'.
6 See www.civiluavsinitiative.com/
7 See https://joinup.ec.europa.eu/collection/eprocurement/document/pianoo-desk-interactive-community-public-procurement-pianoo-desk

## References

Alhola, K., Ryding, S. O., Salmenperä, H., & Busch, N. J. (2019). Exploiting the potential of public procurement: Opportunities for circular economy. *Journal of Industrial Ecology*, 23(1), 96–109.

Anderson, R. D., & Kovacic, W. E. (2009). Competition policy and international trade liberalisation: Essential complements to ensure good performance in public procurement markets. *Public Procurement Law Review*, 18(2), 67–101.

Aschhoff, B., & Sofka, W. (2009). Innovation on demand – Can public procurement drive market success of innovations? *Research Policy*, 38, 1235–1247.

Audretsch, D. B. (2003). Standing on the shoulders of midgets: The US Small Business Innovation Research program (SBIR). *Small Business Economics*, 20, 129–135.

Bleda, M., & Chicot, J. (2020). The role of public procurement in the formation of markets for innovation. *Journal of Business Research*, 107, 186–196.

Borrás, S., & Edquist, C. (2019). *Holistic Innovation Policy: Theoretical Foundations, Policy Problems and Instrument Choices*. Oxford, Oxford University Press.

Chicot, J., & Matt, M. (2018). Public procurement of innovation: A review of rationales, designs, and contributions to grand challenges. *Science and Public Policy*, 45(4), 480–492.

Cousins, P. D., Handfield, R. B., Lawson, B., & Petersen, K. J. (2006). Creating supply chain relational capital: The impact of formal and informal socialization processes. *Journal of Operations Management*, 24(6), 851–863.

Demircioglu, M. A., & Vivona, R. (2021). Positioning public procurement as a procedural tool for innovation: An empirical study. *Policy and Society*, 40(3), 379–396.

EcoQUIP+ (2024, January). *Delivering Efficiency, Quality and Sustainability in Healthcare through Innovation Procurement. A Case Study Based Report*.

Edler, J., & Georghiou, L. (2007). Public procurement and innovation—Resurrecting the demand side. *Research Policy*, 36(7), 949–963.

Edler, J., & Yeow, J. (2016). Connecting demand and supply: The role of intermediation in public procurement of innovation. *Research Policy*, 45(2), 414–426.

Edquist, C. (2019). Towards a holistic innovation policy: Can the Swedish National Innovation Council (NIC) be a role model?. *Research Policy*, 48(4), 869–879.

Edquist, C., & Zabala-Iturriagagoitia, J. M. (2012). Public procurement for innovation as mission-oriented innovation policy. *Research Policy*, 41(10), 1757–1769.

Edquist, C., & Zabala-Iturriagagoitia, J. M. (2015). Pre-commercial procurement: A demand or supply policy instrument in relation to innovation? *R&D Management*, 45(2), 147–160.

Edquist, C., Vonortas, N. S., Zabala-Iturriagagoitia, J. M., & Edler, J. (Eds.) (2015). *Public Procurement for Innovation*. Cheltenham, Edward Elgar.

Edquist, C., & Zabala-Iturriagagoitia, J. M. (2021). Functional procurement for innovation, welfare, and the environment. *Science and Public Policy*, 47(5), 595–603.

El-Taliawi, O. G., & van der Wal, Z. (2019). Developing administrative capacity: An agenda for research and practice. *Policy Design and Practice*, 2(3), 243–257.

European Commission (2006a, March). *Pre-commercial procurement. A missing link in the European innovation cycle*. European Commission.

European Commission (2006b, September). *Pre-commercial procurement. Public sector needs as a driver of innovation*. European Commission.

European Commission (2021). *Guidance on innovation procurement*. C(2021) 4320 final.

Georghiou, L., Edler, J., Uyarra, E., & Yeow, J. (2014). Policy instruments for public procurement of innovation: Choice, design and assessment. *Technological Forecasting and Social Change*, 86, 1–12.

Geroski, P.A. (1990). Innovation, technological opportunity, and market structure. *Oxford Economic Papers*, 42, 586–602.

Grandia, J., & Volker, L. (2023). *Public Procurement. Theory, Practices and Tools*. Cham, Palgrave Macmillan.

Grimbert, S. F., & Zabala-Iturriagagoitia, J. M. (2023). Public procurement as a transformative innovation policy instrument: Urban rehabilitation in Malmö. In: M.C., Sánchez-Carreira, P.J., Reis Mourão, B. Blanco-Varela (Eds.) *European Regional Policy and Development. Forgotten Regions and Spaces*. London, Routledge, pp. 169–188.

Grimbert, S. F., Zabala-Iturriagagoitia, J. M., & Valovirta, V. (2024). Transformative public procurement for innovation: Ordinary, dynamic and functional capabilities. *Public Management Review*, 1–24, in press. https://doi.org/10.1080/14719037.2024.2326079

Guerzoni, M., & Raiteri, E. (2012). *Innovative procurement and R&D subsidies: confounding effect and new empirical evidence on technological policies in a quasi-experimental setting*. Universita Di Torino, Department of Economics Working Paper Series.

Haque, M. S., Ramesh, M., de Oliveira, J. A. P., & de Avila Gomide, A. (2021). Building administrative capacity for development: Limits and prospects. *International Review of Administrative Sciences*, 87(2), 211–219.

Hekkert, M. P., Janssen, M. J., Wesseling, J. H., & Negro, S. O. (2020). Mission-oriented innovation systems. *Environmental Innovation and Societal Transitions*, 34, 76–79.

Johansen, P. (2009). HRM in changing organizational contexts. In: D. G. Collings, G. Wood (Eds.) *Human Resource Management: A Critical Approach*. London, Routledge, pp. 19–37.

Kattel, R., & Mazzucato, M. (2018). Mission-oriented innovation policy and dynamic capabilities in the public sector. *Industrial and Corporate Change*, 27(5), 787–801.

Knutsson, H., & Thomasson, A. (2014). Innovation in the public procurement process: A study of the creation of innovation-friendly public procurement. *Public Management Review*, 16(2), 242–255.

Labory, S., & Bianchi, P. (2021). Regional industrial policy in times of big disruption: Building dynamic capabilities in regions. *Regional Studies*, 55(10–11), 1829–1838.

Loijas, K., Jääskeläinen, A., & Karttunen, E. (2024). Dyadic capabilities in implementing performance-based public procurement. *Journal of Business & Industrial Marketing*, 39(13), 128–144.

Mazzucato, M. (2018a). Mission-oriented innovation policies: Challenges and opportunities. *Industrial and Corporate Change*, 27(5), 803–815.

Mazzucato, M. (2018b). *Mission-Oriented Research & Innovation in the European Union. A Problem-Solving Approach to Fuel Innovation-Led Growth*. Brussels, European Commission.

Mazzucato, M. (2019). *Governing Missions in the European Union*. Brussels, European Commission.
Mazzucato, M. (2020). *Mission-oriented public procurement: international examples*. UCL Institute for Innovation and Public Purpose, Policy Report (IIPP WP 2020–20).
Mazzucato, M. (2023). Governing the economics of the common good: From correcting market failures to shaping collective goals. *Journal of Economic Policy Reform*, 27(1), 1–24.
Mazzucato, M., Conway, R., Mazzoli, E. M., Knoll, E., & Albala, S. (2020). *Creating and measuring dynamic public value at the BBC*. UCL Institute for Innovation and Public Purpose, Policy Report (IIPP WP 2020–19).
Mazzucato, M., Spanó, E., & Doyle, S. (2024). *Leveraging procurement to advance Brazil's economic transformation agenda*. UCL Institute for Innovation and Public Purpose, Working Paper – Tuesday 23 July 2024.
Mazzucato, M., & Wainwright, D. (2024). *Mission-led procurement and market shaping: Lessons from Camden Council*. IIPP Policy Report No. 2024/06.
Morgan, D., Ochoa, A., Grana, E., & Semple, A. (2016). *Engaging the Market in Public Procurement. A Collection of Good Practice Cases*. ICLEI – Local Governments for Sustainability, European Secretariat.
Neij, L. (2001). Methods of evaluating market transformation programmes: Experience in Sweden. *Energy Policy*, 29, 67–79.
Roberts, D. J., & Siemiatycki, M. (2015). Fostering meaningful partnerships in public-private partnerships: Innovations in partnership design and process management to create value. *Environment and Planning C: Government and Policy*, 33, 780–793.
Rothwell, R., & Zegveld, W. (1981). *Industrial Innovation and Public Policy: Preparing for the 1980s and the 1990s*. Westport, Greenwood Press.
Saussier, S., & Tirole, J. (2015). Strengthening the efficiency of public procurement. *Notes du conseil d'analyse économique*, 22(3), 1–12.
Schot, J., & Steinmueller, W. E. (2018). Three frames for innovation policy: R&D, systems of innovation and transformative change. *Research Policy*, 47(9), 1554–1567.
Small Business Innovation Development Act (1982). Public Law 97-219-JULY 22, 1982.
Tassabehji, R., & Moorhouse, A. (2008). The changing role of procurement: Developing professional effectiveness. *Journal of Purchasing and Supply Management*, 14(1), 55–68.
Timmermans, B., & Zabala-Iturriagagoitia, J. M. (2013). Coordinated unbundling: A way to stimulate entrepreneurship through public procurement for innovation. *Science and Public Policy*, 40(5), 674–685.
Uyarra, E., Edler, J., Garcia-Estevez, J., Georghiou, L., & Yeow, J. (2014). Barriers to innovation through public procurement: A supplier perspective. *Technovation*, 34, 631–645.
Uyarra, E., Zabala-Iturriagagoitia, J. M., Flanagan, K., & Magro, E. (2020). Public procurement, innovation and industrial policy: Rationales, roles, capabilities and implementation. *Research Policy*, 49(1), 103844.
Vecchiato, R., & Roveda, C. (2014). Foresight for public procurement and regional innovation policy: The case of Lombardy. *Research Policy*, 43(2), 438–450.
von Hippel, E. (1986). Lead users: A source of novel product concepts. *Management Science*, 32(7), 791–805.
Wesseling, J. H., & Edquist, C. (2018). Public procurement for innovation to help meet societal challenges: A review and case study. *Science and Public Policy*, 45(4), 493–502.
Wu, X., Ramesh, M., & Howlett, M. (2015). Policy capacity: A conceptual framework for understanding policy competences and capabilities. *Policy and Society*, 34(3–4), 165–171.

**Box 12.1 The Key Elements in a Needs' Description**

**Introduction**

- Why are we challenging the market for new solutions?

**The Problem (Current Situation)**

- Describing the problem and how it is solved today (or not solved)
- Desired effects

**The Need**

- Why does this problem represent a challenge?
- Which are the technical (state-of-the-art) and legal frameworks to take into consideration?

**The Needs Matrix**

| | *Needs* | *Performance/functions* |
|---|---|---|
| #1 | Description of the need #1 (e.g., the solution has to be robust) | Description of the desired performance/function #1 (e.g., the new solution should be used in all weather conditions) |
| #2 | Description of the need #2 (e.g., the solution has to be sustainable in material use/ reuse and climate emissions) | Description of the desired performance/function #2 (e.g., the new solution should reduce emissions at least in a 50% and material use in at least 75%) |
| … | … | … |
| #n | Description of the need #n (e.g., the solution has to be self-sufficient in power) | Description of the desired performance / function #2 (e.g., the new solution should have an autonomy of at least 600 km, or 10 h of work at full power) |

# 13 Public Procurement Ethics

## A Human Rights Lens to Public Procurement

*Sofia Gonzalez De Aguinaga and Martina Trusgnach*

### 13.1 Studying Public Procurement from a Human Rights Lens

Traditionally, public procurement ethics has focused on issues such as corruption, conflict of interests, public accountability, rule of law, and a fair and impartial use of resources, but human rights are increasingly an important ethical and risk-management issue in public procurement. The climate crisis, war and conflict, displacement of populations, and the COVID-19 pandemic, exacerbate the global inequalities that increase the risk of human rights violations in global supply chains that do not only supply large corporations but also governments worldwide. In fact, a large proportion of public procurement spending goes to high-risk sectors, including construction and manufacturing.

During the COVID-19 pandemic, for instance, the Malaysian medical gloves supply chain, the world's largest manufacturers of rubber gloves, was found to employ forced labour with cases of debt bondage, excessive overtime and abusing working and living conditions. Due to the pandemic, the global demand for medical gloves increased significantly, placing further pressure on labour standards in a supply chain already facing challenging working conditions (Bhutta et al., 2021). It significantly disrupted supply chains and shifted power from buyers to suppliers, posing greater responsibilities on public buyers (Bhutta et al., 2021). Leveraging from its forced labour import bans regime (the US Tariff Act 1930), the US Customs and Border Protection banned some Malaysian medical gloves suppliers from importing their products into the US until indicators of forced labour were eliminated and recruitment fees were repaid. In the UK, however, where no such bans are in place, and without a human rights framework for managing emergency procurement, large Malaysian suppliers directly connected to the abuse were approved as suppliers of the UK's National Health Service (NHS). Public buyers followed the public procurement regulations in place at the time, but without a human rights approach, the public procurement process in the UK failed to ensure that money was spent responsibly in terms of impacts on people.

According to the Organisation for Economic Co-operation and Development (OECD), public procurement accounts for 13% of the Gross Domestic Product (GDP) in OECD countries (OECD, 2023). Therefore, the government represents a powerful buyer of works, services, and products and can play a key role in improving workers' rights in business supply chains (Martin-Ortega, 2018). This was recognised by the "Five Eyes" group (UK, US, Canada, Australia, and New Zealand) in 2018 who committed to "analyse, develop, and implement measures to identify, prevent, and reduce the risk of human trafficking in government procurement supply chains" (Home Office, 2018). Similarly, the G7 group (the US, Canada, France, Germany, Italy, Japan, and the UK) committed to respect international labour standards in their assessments of publicly funded projects in a joint statement in

DOI: 10.4324/9781003566670-15

2021 (see Department of International Trade, 2021). In the Global South, many countries such as Chile, Colombia, Peru, and Kenya have committed in their National Action Plans (NAPs) on Business and Human Rights to integrate human rights considerations into their public procurement process. There is also an increasing expectation that the State upholds human rights through its public procurement function. Recent legal changes, including in public procurement legislation, are shifting public procurement policy and practice to include human rights issues. Public buyers must be ready to navigate these, especially if modern slavery is to be eradicated by 2030 as intended by the United Nations Sustainable Development Goals (UN SDGs) in target 8.7.

The remainder of this chapter is structured in five key sections. Section 13.2 discusses the relationship between human rights and public procurement drawing from the Business and Human Rights field. Section 13.3 discusses how public procurement laws and policies at the international, supranational, and national levels are including human rights considerations. Section 13.4 discusses the six elements of the human rights due diligence (HRDD) process in the context of public procurement. Section 13.5 explores the challenges faced by public buyers in the Global North and the Global South for integrating HRDD and implementing human rights criteria in the tender cycle. Section 13.6 discusses two emerging issues that public procurement professionals should be prepared for the integration of social and environmental criteria, and the remediation of human rights abuses in public supply chains. This chapter is complemented by a case study for discussion in class that illustrates some of the key ideas explored in this chapter.

## 13.2 Business, the State, and Human Rights

*What does the Business and Human Rights field say about human rights in public procurement?*

In 2011, the UN Guiding Principles (UNGPs) on Business and Human Rights, the global standard and leading normative framework on human rights, referred for the first time to HRDD as a method for businesses to address actual and potential human rights abuses. The UNGPs defined it as an ongoing process to *identify, prevent, mitigate, and account* for adverse human rights impacts in businesses' own operations and their value chains. It differentiated it from conventional corporate due diligence by focusing on risks to people as opposed to risks to businesses. In the same year, the OECD Guidelines for Multinational Enterprises (recently updated in 2023) extended this concept to include environmental impacts.

According to the UNGPs, the HRDD process has four main components: assessing actual and potential human rights impacts, integrating and acting upon the findings, tracking responses, and communicating how impacts are addressed. Both the UNGPs and the OECD guidelines further mention the need to embed HRDD into policies and management and provide or collaborate in remediation measures, when appropriate (Pillar 3 of the UNGPs). Therefore, in this chapter we refer to six elements of the HRDD process (see Figure 13.1). We will be discussing these in detail in Section 13.4.

HRDD was originally envisioned as a *voluntary* process aimed to work as a normative transnational expectation of responsible business conduct, but it is now increasingly becoming a legal obligation. In recent years, as part of the State duty to protect against human rights abuses by business through appropriate policies, regulation, and adjudication (UNGPs, 2011) and under the assumption that HRDD is an effective method for businesses to address human rights harms, States have developed mandatory human rights

*Figure 13.1* Key elements of HRDD based on the UNGPs and the OECD guidelines.
*Source*: Original creation.

and environmental due diligence (mHREDD) laws. France, Germany, the Netherlands, Norway, Switzerland, and, more recently, the European Union, have developed mHREDD legislation that require certain large companies to undertake human rights (and environmental) due diligence and impose legal liabilities for failure to meet their obligations. They generally create a duty of care that applies to some or all internationally recognised human rights, including the International Labour Organisation's (ILO) Declaration on Fundamental Principles and Rights at Work, which include freedom of association, the effective recognition of the right to collective bargaining, and the ILO core conventions that include the elimination of forced and child labour.

But the State's human rights responsibilities are not limited to regulating business conduct as the State is also an economic actor (through State-owned enterprises and export credit agencies) and a business client. Through its public procurement function and contracting-out or outsourcing models, the State is in fact a large buyer of goods and essential works, and services from the private sector such as those related to health, infrastructure, and energy. Public procurement is thus increasingly recognised as a means through which States can meet their obligation to *respect, protect, and fulfil* human rights under International Human Rights Law (see Figure 13.2).

This means that when purchasing goods, services, and works, States must refrain from interfering with the enjoyment of human rights, protect individuals against human rights abuses, and take positive action to facilitate the enjoyment of human rights and create positive impacts on people. In 2022, the UN Working Group on Business and Human Rights referred to "human rights-based procurement" as that which captures these three international human rights obligations (United Nations Working Group on Business and Human Rights, 2022).

*Figure 13.2* Human rights duties of the State under International Human Rights Law.
*Source*: Original creation.

The UNGPs in pillar I (in principles 4, 5, and 6) establish a "State-business nexus" whereby States should take additional steps to protect against human rights abuses and promote respect for human rights when it acts as an economic actor, when it *contracts* companies to provide services that may impact on human rights, and when it conducts *commercial transactions* with companies such as those related to *procurement activities*. They also highlight the unique position of the State to "promote awareness of and respect for human rights" by those enterprises with which it conducts commercial transactions "including through the terms of contracts".

It is therefore expected that governments lead by example and cascade responsible supply chain requirements to their suppliers if they want to conduct business with the public sector. In 2017, the UK Joint Committee on Human Rights stated that *"if the Government expects businesses to take human rights issues in their supply chains seriously, it must demonstrate at least the same level of commitment in its own procurement supply chains"* (Paragraph 86). Some argue that public buyers, as organs of the State, have heightened obligations, compared to private buyers, to prevent, mitigate, and account for human rights violations in business supply chains (see Martin-Ortega, 2017).

However, most States are not yet legally obliged to report on their efforts to address human rights violations in their supply chains or to exercise HRDD in their public procurement function. For instance, most supply chain transparency legislation which requires certain entities to report on their efforts to address modern slavery does not apply to public bodies (see Box 13.1), with a few exceptions (i.e., the Australia Modern Slavery Act 2018, and the Canadian Fighting Against Forced Labour and Child Labour in Supply Chains Act 2023). mHREDD laws do not extend their requirements to undertake HRDD to public

**Box 13.1 UK Modern Slavery Act 2015**

Section 54 of the UK Modern Slavery Act 2015 requires commercial entities with a total turnover of £36 million or more to report annually on their actions to identify, prevent, and mitigate modern slavery in their supply chain. Certain public bodies who are subject to the UK Public Contracts Regulations 2015 (mostly universities and other higher education providers) fall within the scope of Section 54. Other public buyers, including purchasing consortia, local authorities, councils, and other authorities who are not covered by the legislation have been reporting voluntarily. In 2019 an Independent Review of the Modern slavery Act 2015 recommended to extend transparency in supply chain obligations (Section 54) to public sector organisations with an annual budget of £36 million, but this recommendation has not yet been actioned.

authorities either, albeit some mHREDD laws have implications on public procurement practices. For instance, under the German Due Diligence Supply Chain Act 2021 companies operating in Germany can be excluded from public procurement for up to three years if an administrative fine for non-compliance is imposed above a certain minimum level.

Changes in public procurement laws and policies are increasingly enabling and encouraging public buyers to consider human rights issues. We discuss this next.

## 13.3 Human Rights in Public Procurement Policies and Regulations

*What does the public procurement field say about human rights?*

Public procurement has traditionally focused on ensuring best value for money based on cost-efficiency, non-discrimination, and open competition. However, over the past decade, the concept of *value* in public spending has been evolving to encompass other objectives known as "complementary policy objectives" or "horizontal aims" that look to achieve strategic goals such as those related to social and environmental aspects. For instance, determining the most economically advantageous tender is no longer limited to a cost-effective approach, but it can also include environmental and social considerations. Human rights issues fall, along with a mix of other non-economic aspects, within these horizontal objectives, typically under the "sustainability" or "social" umbrellas.

According to target 17 of the UN SDG 12 on responsible consumption and production, the State should set *new objectives* and promote public procurement practices that are *sustainable*. The concept of *sustainable public procurement* extends the purpose of public procurement beyond traditional objectives to include social and environmental considerations throughout the procurement cycle (Meehan and Bryde, 2011). However, it has heavily focused on the environmental dimension, both in policy and practice. The social dimension has been captured by terms such as "*socially responsible public procurement*" or "*buying social*" which focus on achieving positive social outcomes through public procurement. For instance, the idea of delivering "*social value*" through strategic public procurement involves public buyers considering a broad range of additional social benefits that can be achieved in the delivery of public contracts, such as decent work, social inclusion, employment opportunities for disadvantaged people, opportunities for social enterprises, and gender equality. This idea of using public procurement to address social issues, such as labour standards and inequality, is however not new. Many public procurement policies in the 19th and 20th century, mostly in the US, the UK and to some extent in France, looked to address labour standards such as working hours, fair working conditions, and minimum wages (albeit not along the supply chain) in the procurement of public works (McCrudden, 2004).

The European Union Directive 2014/24/EU was the first public procurement regulatory framework in Europe to enable new non-economic objectives in the form of "sustainability criteria", namely social and environmental considerations before, during, and after tendering that contracting authorities can *voluntarily* adopt. Supported by this, international agreements such as the WTO's plurilateral Agreement on Government Procurement (GPA) and the integration of sustainable public procurement into NAPs, many countries worldwide have introduced *mandatory* and *discretionary* human rights criteria, including on modern slavery, into their policies. By implementing these criteria, public buyers are taking appropriate actions to prevent and mitigate human rights abuses in their supply chains (step 3 of the HRDD process). Table 13.1 describes these criteria and provides examples from different countries.

Most countries have identified high-risk sectors to which these human rights criteria should be implemented such as Information and Communication Technology (ICT), apparel

*Table 13.1* Human rights criteria in public procurement laws and policies worldwide

| *Criteria* | *Characteristics* | *Examples* |
|---|---|---|
| **Exclusionary criteria** | • They are used to prevent suppliers that have committed any violations of applicable social or labour law, or collective agreements, from bidding for a public contract.<br>• They generally apply to all tenders.<br>• They can be mandatory or discretionary. Mandatory exclusions generally apply to suppliers that have been convicted for human rights violations (e.g., modern slavery). | • Brazil mandates exclusion of bidders sentenced in court in the five previous years for child or forced labour (United Nations Working Group on Business and Human Rights, 2022).<br>• In the UK, modern slavery offences are listed as mandatory exclusion criteria under the Public Contracts Regulations 2015. Non-compliance with the Modern Slavery Act can be introduced as discretionary exclusion by public bodies.<br>• In the EU, the Directive 2014/24/EU on public procurement allows for mandatory exclusion for child labour and human trafficking and discretionary exclusion for violations of the ILO core conventions.<br>• The US and Western Australia have established human trafficking debarment regimes, a form of exclusion that involves removing a supplier for a specific procurement process for a period of time or from "preferred supplier" or equivalent lists. |
| **Selection criteria** | • They allow public buyers to stipulate minimum requirements in relation to human rights that must be met for a supplier to be eligible for a procurement (The Danish Institute for Human Rights, 2020).<br>• These are voluntarily implemented by public buyers and are usually set in the pre-tender stage.<br>• They can apply to direct suppliers or extend to subcontractors and include HRDD requirements.<br>• They can be used to increase corporate transparency and disclosure and be category specific. | • In Chile, a criterion for bidders is to present evidence on their labour risk-management practices.<br>• Costa Rica requests bidders to include in their offers the number and type of workers and their working hours (United Nations Working Group on Business and Human Rights, 2022).<br>• To be eligible to supply rubber gloves to the Region Stockholm, suppliers are requested to report on migrant workers in factories and to disclose policies related to forced labour and no recruitment fees (The Danish Institute for Human Rights, 2020). |

(*Continued*)

*Table 13.1* (Continued)

| *Criteria* | *Characteristics* | *Examples* |
|---|---|---|
| **Award criteria** | • They are considered by the buyer when deciding which tender to accept.<br>• They are voluntarily decided by public buyers and are usually defined in the pre-tender stage.<br>• The weighing of "sustainable" or "social criteria" varies across countries, may vary across tenders, and can have a significant impact on the awarding of contracts. | • In the UK, Public Procurement Note 06/20 establishes that a minimum of 10% weighting should be given to *social value* criteria, which can include modern slavery considerations.<br>• Chile establishes that a higher score can be given to bidders that exhibit better employment conditions and remunerations, such as salaries over the legal minimum wage and other benefits (United Nations Working Group on Business and Human Rights, 2022).<br>• In Bonn, Germany public authorities included compliance with ILO core labour standards as award criteria in a call for tenders for uniforms in 2016 and increased the weighting of social criteria from 15% to 30% between the first and second tendering of the contract, allowing bidders to win the contract even if they were not the cheapest offer (European Commission, 2020). |
| **Contract performance clauses** | • They are used to set human rights-related conditions in procurement contracts.<br>• They generally require certain steps to be taken by the supplier for the duration of the contract. For instance, they can require suppliers to exercise HRDD or manage human rights risks.<br>• Some are voluntarily applied by public buyers and others are mandatory, depending on the country.<br>• They may be category and tender specific.<br>• A breach in these clauses can lead to financial penalties, suspension, or termination of the contract or debarment. | • Copenhagen has implemented *mandatory* labour clauses focused on fair pay and labour conditions as contract performance conditions in all service and construction public contracts for contractors and subcontractors (European Commission, 2020).<br>• Norway, Australia, and the UK provide public authorities with model contact clauses that can be incorporated voluntarily by public buyers.<br>• The government of New South Wales has developed two sets of model contract clauses on modern slavery available to public buyers (GRS Model Tender Clauses). One is a heightened version for procurement requiring heightened HRDD and the other is a streamlined version for procurement requiring light, minimal, or standard HRDD. Clauses include training on modern slavery, ensuring no recruitment feed are paid by workers, ensuring safe accommodation, implementing a migrant worker standard, among others.<br>• The use of contract clauses to limit long subcontracting chains are compulsory for construction and cleaning contracts in Norway, and in for construction contracts in Finland. |
| **Suspension or termination of contracts criteria** | • Human rights criteria can be considered voluntarily for suspending or terminating a contract with a supplier. | • In the UK, public authorities can insert termination clauses for modern slavery offences in high-risk contracts but should only terminate a contract as a last resort.<br>• In the US, the Federal Acquisition Regulation (FAR) allows for public authorities to terminate a contract if they find that an entity or its subcontractors are engaged in forced labour or human trafficking.<br>• In Germany, between 2013 and 2015, and following labour clauses inspections, the authorities in Bremen imposed penalties for non-compliance to several suppliers including a suspension from public tenders for a period of 6–15 months (Jaehrling et al., 2018). |

*Source*: Original creation.

and textiles, health supplies and construction (Gonzalez De Aguinaga et al., 2022). The UK Government's own Modern Slavery Statement identified ICT hardware and electronics, construction and catering and cleaning staff as high-risk areas. The Swedish Country Councils identified textiles, surgical instruments, rubber gloves, dressings, IT, pharmaceuticals and food as high-risk categories (The Danish institute for Human Rights, 2020). Similarly, Canada issued a policy notification in 2018 that required child and forced labour considerations in the apparel supply chain. However, implementing these criteria in practice does not come without challenges, as we will discuss in Section 13.5.

Beyond the integration of human rights criteria into tenders, some governments encourage public buyers to undertake all six steps of HRDD and have issued guidelines, training, toolkits, and resources (some of which are category specific). For instance, the UK government issued in 2021 a practical guide for public bodies to undertake modern slavery due diligence in personal protective equipment supply chains. The Association of Flemish Cities and Municipalities and the City of Ghent in Belgium developed a toolbox for HRDD in the textile supply chain as part of their socially responsible workwear project in 2014. However, most public procurement policies and laws do not explicitly mandate that public buyers undertake all six steps of the HRDD process. The integration of HRDD in public procurement is discussed next.

## 13.4 Integrating HRDD into Public Procurement

*How can HRDD be integrated into public procurement?*

Applying a human rights lens to public procurement goes beyond implementing human rights criteria in the tender process. It requires public authorities to integrate all six steps of HRDD into their function in a regular basis and throughout the procurement cycle. This can take many forms depending on the procurement system and legislation in place, the resources and capabilities of public buyers, and the risk levels of specific tenders. However, an example of how HRDD may look in public procurement is illustrated in Table 13.2. In this section we discuss the six elements of HRDD and how they can be integrated into public procurement. We also highlight stakeholder engagement and exercising leverage as two cross-cutting practices that are key for integrating HRDD into public procurement.

### *13.4.1 Integrating HRDD in Procurement Policies and Risk-Management Systems*

To integrate HRDD into any organisation, it is necessary to embed it into existing policies and management systems. Doing so goes beyond standard policy statements. It requires a clear articulation of how risks will be assessed, prevented, mitigated, remedied, reported, and managed. In the public procurement context, this includes integrating HRDD into framework agreements and establishing human rights criteria (and weighting) that can be used for excluding, selecting, and awarding contracts, which we discussed in Section 13.3. It also includes establishing who would be responsible for what, the scope of HRDD expectations according to the organisation's values and resources, and contract management, monitoring and reporting practices, in a way that the policy ensures accountability and effective governance of human rights risks. Policies should also be expanded into procurement strategies or implementation plans and be communicated to bidders and suppliers.

As a risk-management process, HRDD can be integrated into exiting risk-management systems that public buyers may already have to address financial risks, fraud, corruption, or inefficiency (UNGPs, 2011). In Latin America, States have developed risk-management frameworks for assessing different types of procurement risks, mostly focused on integrity

*Table 13.2* Example of integrating HRDD into public procurement

| *HRDD steps/ procurement cycle* | *On a regular basis (not tied to a specific procurement exercise)* | *Pre-tender (preparing the tender)* | *Tender (including awarding)* | *Post-tender (contract management)* |
|---|---|---|---|---|
| 1. **Embed HRDD into policies and management** | - Develop and regularly review HRDD procurement policies, plans, and strategies.<br>- Integrate HRDD into existing management systems. | - Communicate policies to bidders and require compliance. | - Communicate policies to bidders and require compliance. | - Stakeholder engagement. |
| 2. **Identifying and assessing risk** | - Mapping supply chains.<br>- Identifying high-risk categories in portfolio.<br>- Undertaking human rights risks assessments.<br>- Training staff.<br>- Collaborative efforts.<br>- Stakeholder engagements. | - Establishing risk for a particular upcoming tender by undertaking risk assessments.<br>- Market research to introduce human rights criteria. | - Evaluating bidders on human rights criteria based on risk.<br>- Use of risk assessment tools (pre-qualification questionnaires).<br>- Verifying supplier information. | - Engaging with suppliers through regular meetings to highlight risks. |
| 3. **Taking appropriate action** (**cease, prevent, mitigate**) | - Identify leverage in existing supplier base.<br>- Prioritise contracts for further risk assessments.<br>- Engagement with suppliers and stakeholders (workers and survivors). | - Adapt tendering specifications (setting human rights criteria).<br>- Drafting human rights-related contractual clauses.<br>- Engagement with potential bidders. | - Excluding bidders according to criteria.<br>- Briefing bidders on criteria and engagement to ensure understanding (pre-award and if not done in the pre-tender stage). | - Exercising leverage (e.g., for remediation if needed).<br>- Engaging with high-risk suppliers (including to provide support or training). - Collaborative efforts.<br>- Negotiating contractual clauses (if needed). |
| 4. **Tracking effectiveness** | - Risk-based monitoring of supplier base through audits, visits, etc.<br>- Collaborative efforts.<br>- Establishing human rights-related KPIs.<br>- Engagement with stakeholders. | N/A | - Monitoring the competitiveness of the tender based on the new human rights criteria (to avoid unintended consequences). | - Monitoring compliance with contract clauses.<br>- Tracking KPIs. - Collaborative efforts.<br>- Supplier engagement for continuous improvement process. |

| | | | | |
|---|---|---|---|---|
| **5. Communicate how impacts are addressed** | - Produce annual public reports.<br>- Stakeholder engagement. | N/A | N/A | - Supplier engagement for reporting on human rights-related KPIs. |
| **6. Providing or enabling remediation** | - Remediation policies.<br>- Establishing and reviewing grievance mechanisms. | N/A | N/A | - Engage with suppliers to provide or enable remediation.<br>- Assess the connection to harm: causing, contributing, or linked to the harm to determine best action. |

*Source*: Original creation.

and environmental risks but not on human rights risks (United Nations Working Group on Business and Human Rights, 2022). The risk-management system should allow for sharing of information among public buyers. However, integrating HRDD into existing policy and management requires a paradigm shift from risks to business to risk to people and it may be necessary to make changes into the existing systems to make them fit for purpose. Therefore, it is important to understand the nature of human rights risks in global supply chains as we discuss next.

#### *13.4.1.1 Understanding Human Rights Risks in Global Supply Chains*

The threats to human rights in public supply chains are varied and fall within a spectrum from decent work to extreme forms of exploitation, including modern slavery (Box 13.2).

Understanding human rights risks in global supply chains implies recognising that these are likely to be present in almost every supply chain. This is because global supply chains are long and complex and operate within production systems and business models that create the demand for and supply of modern slavery (LeBaron et al., 2018).

It also implies taking a human rights risk-based approach. That is, to focus efforts where the most severe human rights violations are most likely to occur. In other words, based on the salience and severity of such risks. There are specific countries, sectors, and goods that are at a higher risk of human rights abuses, either because they involve vulnerable populations (such as migrants, women, children, and indigenous populations), a higher supply chain complexity, or little or absent State protections of worker's rights (e.g., in conflict situations).

The highest risks of human rights violations are often found at the lower tiers of the supply chain (usually located in the Global South) where there is less visibility and where it is most likely to find a larger number of vulnerable workers involved in informal work, unauthorised outsourcing, or subcontracting. However, modern slavery is not exclusively a problem of low- and middle-income countries. In fact, more than half of all forced labour in the world occurs within upper-middle- and high-income countries, especially in agriculture, domestic work, and construction (ILO, Walk Free and IOM, 2022). For instance, a recent study found that forced labour is prevalent (65%) in the domestic agri-food system in the US as opposed to coming from imported food products from low-income countries (Blackstone et al., 2023).

**Box 13.2 What Is Modern Slavery?**

*More than 50 million individuals are victims of modern slavery* (International Labour Organization (ILO), Walk Free and International Organization for Migration (IOM), 2022). Modern slavery is an umbrella term that covers extreme forms of exploitation including human trafficking, forced labour, debt bondage, and forced child labour. Extreme forms of exploitation include violations related to retention of wages, restrictions on freedom of association, and the right to collective bargaining. Less extreme forms of exploitation include poor, unhygienic, or unsafe working conditions, low pay, excessive working hours, discrimination, and harsh and inhumane treatment. Because labour exploitation occurs in a continuum, these can lead to more extreme forms of exploitation, such as modern slavery, and are likely to occur in parallel.

### *13.4.2 Identifying and Assessing Risk*

The first step in the HRDD process is to identify and assess actual and potential adverse human rights impacts in the supply chain (UNGPs, 2011). As illustrated in Table 13.1, public authorities should do so regularly and throughout the public procurement process. For this, public buyers need to map their supply chain, identify high-risk categories, and inherent risks in their portfolios, and carry out human rights risk assessments of actual or potential risks on rightsholders.

#### *13.4.2.1 Mapping Supply Chains*

Public buyers need to map their supply chains to identify salient modern slavery risks. Mapping the supply chain means identifying direct (tier 1) and indirect (tier 2 and beyond) suppliers of goods, works and services, where they operate, how they are structured in terms of business models, their workforce composition, their HRDD practices, among other factors. This should be undertaken on a regular basis as supply chains may change over time. For instance, a supplier may change locations from a low- to a high-risk geography. However, mapping supply chains is not an easy task and requires significant human and economic resources. We discuss these challenges in Section 13.5.

Fortunately, public buyers do not have to map all their supply chains at once. Rather, taking a risk-based approach, public buyers can focus on mapping high-risk supply chains. For instance, the Essex County Council, one of the largest in the UK, decides the scope and depth of its supply chain mapping according to whether the product category has been assessed as having a higher risk of human rights abuses. Public bodies can also start with mapping tier 1 suppliers and gradually move to tier 2 and 3 suppliers.

#### *13.4.2.2 Identifying High-Risk Categories and Inherent Risks in Procurement Portfolio*

Public buyers can use publicly available information to identify high-risk categories in their portfolio. For instance, The Global Slavery Index (2022) identifies countries at a high risk of modern slavery. At the country level, the US publishes regularly a "List of Products Produced by Forced or Indentured Child Labor" that identifies high-risk products and their source countries. Moreover, the US State Department and the NGO Verité provide US contractors and organisations with the Responsible Sourcing Tool, an online and publicly available resource that includes risk maps and reports across industries, commodities, and countries where risks of forced labour have been documented.

This information should be mapped against the procurement portfolio. For instance, Norway identifies high-risk products based on ILO studies and the government's procurement activities. In the UK, Transport for London (TfL) maps public information with its main product categories and where they are sourced from to identify inherent risks in their portfolio (see Table 13.3).

In 2021, the Canadian Government was the first to commission a risk assessment of human trafficking, forced labour, and child labour in the supply chains of goods of its central purchasing body, Public Services and Procurement Canada, as part of its efforts to implement its National Strategy to Combat Human Trafficking. This risk analysis determined which categories were at the highest risk of human rights violations and informed their approach to procurement and further actions.

Based on the inherent risks identified, public authorities can be better informed to take appropriate action, including establishing specific requirements. For instance, when

*Table 13.3* TFL's mapping of some of their main product categories in their portfolio and identification of inherent risks

| *Category* | *Country* | *Sector risk* |
|---|---|---|
| Electronic equipment | China, East Asia, Eastern Europe | Labour intensive, often low-skilled work; mining of raw materials in high-risk countries. Poor labour practices including underpayment of wages, delayed payment, or wage deductions; physical abuse; working excessive overtime; worker's visa or permit is tied to a single employer; and financial penalties for early contract termination |
| Uniforms and workwear | Bangladesh, China | Risks include gender inequality; weak protection of workers' rights; poor labour practices including excessive overtime, underpayment, or deduction of wages; |
| Batteries | Cobalt: Democratic Republic of Congo (DRC); Lithium: Chile, Bolivia, China; Nickel: Indonesia, Philippines; Tin: Bolivia; Copper: Chile; and semiconductors: China, Malaysia, Taiwan | Sourcing of minerals presents the greatest risk to human rights abuses. Political instability or conflict particularly in the DRC, weak protection of civil liberties and workers' rights, safe and healthy working conditions in mines can be poorly regulated and protected, particularly in artisanal mines. |

*Source*: Taken from TflL's Modern Slavery Statement 2023.

procuring cleaning services, public buyers may want to focus on requiring the supplier to show that workers are not charged recruitment fees, disclose the proportion of migrant workers and those being outsourced through labour agencies or subcontractors, and that the supplier takes the appropriate steps to ensure fair working practices.

#### *13.4.2.3 Undertaking Human Rights Risk Assessments*

Public authorities should undertake human rights risks assessments on their suppliers regularly. These can be prioritised according to level of spend and criticality of contracts. For example, a public authority may want to gradually undertake risks assessments of its contracts starting with their high-level spend procurements and those that are deemed more critical (either because they carry the highest cost or because they pose a higher risk). For instance, the Department of Health and Social Care in the UK undertook initial risks assessments in 2021 of its "gold" and "silver" contracts (based on criticality) and high-level spend procurements that were procured in a regular basis across all category areas and to those that were in the process of tendering or live at the moment. The following year, the UK's Department of Health and Social Care (DHSC) committed to expand its risks assessments to bronze-level contracts and lower-level spend procurements.

Some countries have tools in place to aid public buyers in their risk assessments. In the UK, public sector organisations are encouraged to use the Modern Slavery Assessment Tool (MSAT), a modern slavery risk identification and management tool, in their existing supply chains. Many organisations such as TfL ask their medium- and high-risk suppliers to complete the MSAT questionnaire. The score in the questionnaire then allows them to either give suppliers a "green status" or take further action. Similarly, LUPC has developed a supplier due diligence tool (SDDT) to assess suppliers' HRDD practices in a regular basis.

The tool screens suppliers on their policies and practices in relation to human rights, social value and the environment and flags areas for further in-depth assessment (see the London Universities Purchasing Consortium Case Study). Risk assessments should also be undertaken to bidders in specific tenders using pre-qualification questionnaires. In the UK, local authorities can use the Crown Commercial Service's Standard Selection Questionnaires (SSQs). The London Universities Purchasing Consortium (LUPC), which tenders framework agreements for a broad range of public sector buyers in the UK, has inserted tailored questions at the award stage.

The information provided by suppliers or bidders should not be taken at face value. Rather, it should be verified, especially if these operate in high-risk sectors or geographies. Verification methods can include desk-research, in-person audits, access to independently verified audit reports from online platforms such as the Supplier's Ethical Data Exchange, or collaborative initiatives such as Electronics Watch. However, public authorities should avoid relying on data-assurance platforms or purchasing consortia to manage their supply chain human rights risks. Public authorities need to understand what risks are actually being covered and managed and should seek to regularly engage with these stakeholders (Rogerson et al., 2024). Ideally, identifying and assessing risk would also involve consultation with stakeholders, including workers (UNGPs, 2011) as we will discuss in Section 13.4.7.1.

#### *13.4.3 Taking Appropriate Action (Cease, Prevent, Mitigate)*

When there is a high risk of human rights abuses, public authorities must take appropriate action to cease, prevent, or mitigate them. The appropriateness of these actions would depend on the extent to which these are proportionate to the likelihood of human rights risks occurring and their severity. It may mean for example, undertaking in-depth human rights risks assessments to contracts previously identified as high-risk. In relation to a specific tender, taking appropriate action may include adapting the human rights criteria we discussed in Section 13.3 according to the salience and severity of the risks identified for such category. For instance, including new requirements in the tender stage or add contract terms and conditions to prevent and mitigate such risks.

When thinking about taking appropriate action to cease actual human rights violations found in the supply chain, public authorities may terminate contracts with those suppliers. However, this should be a measure of last resort, after other measures have proved inefficient (UNGPs, 2011) such as when there is State-sponsored forced labour. This is because the aim of HRDD is to tackle human rights abuses as opposed to divert them elsewhere (by cutting ties with suppliers) or creating more harm than good to workers (e.g., by leaving them unemployed). Public buyers can instead engage with such suppliers and exercise their leverage to bring such violations to an end. We discuss this in Section 13.4.7.

#### ***13.4.4 Tracking Effectiveness***

Monitoring actual or potential human rights impacts is a key step in the HRDD process to ensure human rights policies and specific standards of behaviour are being implemented effectively and to drive continuous improvement (UNGPs, 2011). While audits are the most commonly used tool for monitoring suppliers, they have significant limitations for identifying human rights abuses. Therefore, it is key to combine audits with other tools to monitor suppliers, including by engaging directly with workers and their representatives (as we discuss in Section 13.4.7.1). Ideally, monitoring would be undertaken in-house, but public buyers can also outsource it. Electronics Watch for example provides monitoring services to public buyers that become affiliated and collaborated with civil society monitors in production regions to collect data directly from workers and Civil Society Organisations (CSOs) to protect the rights of workers in their electronics' supply chains.

Public authorities can also engage in collaborative monitoring as public buyers tend to purchase many of the same goods and services as each other. For instance, the Swedish County Councils pool resources to undertake audits. Each County Council contributes 40 Swedish cents (€0.04) per capita and each is responsible for auditing a specific supply chain (Electronics Watch, 2016). See Box 13.3 for an example in Sweden.

### *13.4.5 Communicating Progress*

Producing regular reports to communicate how impacts are addressed is a key element of HRDD (UNGPs, 2011). Reporting regularly increases transparency and enables communication of progress. This also contributes to keeping public authorities and their suppliers accountable. Some public authorities voluntarily report on this, but as we discussed in Sections 13.2 and 13.3, public authorities in most countries are not obliged to report on their HRDD processes as they do not fall within mHREDD legislation or modern slavery transparency legislation.

### *13.4.6 Providing for or Collaborating in Remediation*

According to international human rights law, all individuals have the right to an effective remedy for the rights violations they experience. The UNGPs in pillar 3 require companies to provide for or cooperate in remediation, but public buyers' responsibilities for providing remedy or enabling remediation have not been clearly articulated (Pesterfield & Rogerson, 2023). So far, public procurement laws, policies, and practices have focused on preventing and mitigating human rights abuses in public supply chains (Gonzalez De Aguinaga, 2022).

According to the UNGPs, if businesses are linked to the harm, they are not required to contribute to remedy but should use their leverage to ensure it is achieved. Often public procurement bodies are linked to the harm; however, public procurement bodies have rarely engaged in remediation of human rights abuses. Both, in terms of procedural remedy (having a mechanism that can receive human rights complaints and investigate and establish whether an abuse has been committed) and substantive remedies to rightsholders (including but not limited to financial and non-financial compensation).

**Box 13.3 Collaborative Monitoring in Sweden**

In Sweden, local and regional contracting authorities can sign to the Swedish SKL Kommentus Central Purchasing Body (SKI), who regularly undertakes third-party audits of suppliers under its framework agreements and monitors high-risk categories through a three-step process consisting of a supplier self-assessment, desktop audit, and on-site audit. The audit results are shared among the contracting authorities and have so far enabled a more efficient approach to audits, avoiding duplication and informing contracting authorities when undertaking risk assessments (The Danish institute for Human Rights, 2020).

In fact, the term remedy in public procurement is often used to refer to contractual remedies that can be sought by public buyers when their suppliers breach their contracts, such as sanctions, as opposed to remedy to those harmed. Public buyers have also required companies to have grievance mechanisms in place, but this may be insufficient for enabling effective remediation to rightsholders as they are not driven by the rights, needs, expectations, and priorities of those affected (Trusgnach et al., in press). Many governments have set out complaint mechanisms to address issues related to their public procurement function, but these have been limited to corruption, lack of transparency, or unlawful behaviour from public servants (e.g., Chile's Observatory *ChileCompra* and Colombia's CPA, Colombia *CompraEficiente*). The increasing expectation for public buyers to engage in remediation is discussed in Section 13.6.2.

### *13.4.7 Key Practices for Integrating HRDD into Public Procurement*

#### *13.4.7.1 Stakeholder Engagement*

Stakeholder engagement is a key element that cuts across all six stages of HRDD. It can be exercised on a regular basis and at every stage of a procurement exercise, from the pre-tender stage to contract management, as illustrated in Table 13.2.

Stakeholder engagement can be undertaken to collect and monitor data on the ground to identify, mitigate, and remediate for human rights violations. Bottom-up data, that is, from workers themselves and people with lived experience and their representatives (including trade unions, CSOs, local independent labour, and human rights organisations) is increasingly recognised as the most reliable, as workers are the best placed to report on their working conditions. In the ICT sector, public buyers can affiliate to Electronics Watch, who, through its network of local trade unions, workers' rights, and CSOs (who have a deep understanding of the country, industry, and factory dynamics, and who have established trusted relationships with workers), can provide public bodies with on the ground information.

Public authorities may also engage with potential bidders and suppliers throughout a procurement exercise. The purpose of doing so can vary widely, and the engagement can take different forms as there is no set process of it. For instance, before a tender, public buyers can conduct market engagement to understand the practices of potential bidders, and their ability to meet specific requirements, and ensure they understand the importance of human rights for public buyers. Public authorities can continue this engagement throughout the procurement cycle to ensure compliance with human rights requirements. For instance, the City of Ghent engaged in dialogue with bidders from the pre-tender stage in a tender for workwear in 2016 regarding the contract clauses for that procurement. It was reported that this engagement from the pre-tender stage all the way to contract performance was key in ensuring the contractual clauses were implemented in practice. In fact, Ghent works together with its suppliers to achieve its labour rights objectives for the entire course of the framework (European Commission, 2020).

Public buyers may also want to engage with suppliers to increase their capacity to address human rights risks after a contract has been signed, establishing long-term dialogue and collaboration. For instance, the London Universities Purchasing Consortium (LUPC) reviews the results of their SDDT tool during contract management meetings to assess and incentivise progress. For those areas where a majority of suppliers is lagging behind, training and guidance material is developed. LUPC's approach is based on the recognition that long-term collaboration with suppliers, rather than antagonistic behaviour, is more likely to bring improvements (see the London Universities Purchasing Consortium (LUPC) case study). Such continuous engagement with suppliers can increase leverage as discussed next.

#### *13.4.7.2 Exercising Leverage*

Leverage refers to the ability of an entity to influence change in the practices of another party that may cause or contribute to an adverse impact on human rights (UNGPs, 2011). As illustrated in Table 13.2, identifying and exercising leverage can be done regularly and throughout the public procurement cycle.

Exercising leverage in the post-tender stage is key to mitigate actual risks (UNGPs, 2011). For instance, during the length of the contract, public authorities can exercise leverage to resolve any issues or enable suppliers to provide remediation before considering terminating contracts. For instance, Electronics Watch engages with the ICT industry on behalf of its affiliated public buyers to provide responses to human rights abuses and bring about improvements in suppliers' practices.

It is important to identify the level of leverage a public body can have over specific contracts as this can inform the level and extent of their HRDD. For instance, the Organization for Security and Co-operation in Europe (OSCE) prioritises risks to address based on the risk of procurement categories and the level of leverage they can have on suppliers. It first identifies the product or service categories that have an increased risk and then the specific high-risk goods and services within those categories. They focus on higher spending categories within the identified high-risk sectors and complement this by looking at the leverage they can have on those suppliers. They illustrate this in a matrix that allows to visually identify those categories of goods or services where there is a high risk of human rights violations and where they may have a high ability to influence suppliers (see OSCE, 2022).

Leverage may also vary according to the duration of the contract. For instance, the longer the contract, the more opportunity there is to engage with suppliers (The Danish Institute for Human Rights, 2020) as it allows to build ongoing and long-term relationships with suppliers who would need sufficient time to change their practices and meet the new procurement requirements and to resolve or remediate any instances of human rights abuse. Leverage may also increase by collaborating with other actors, providing capacity building, and incentivising suppliers (UNGPs, 2011). In the public procurement context, this is done through collaborative procurement. That is, when public authorities work together pooling their purchasing power to increase leverage (Meehan et al., 2016).

A good example of increasing leverage through collaboration is that of the Swedish Regions. Their progressive and meaningful engagement with suppliers is considered a best practice example for increasing leverage and achieving impact on the ground. The Dell case described in Box 13.4 shows that the effectiveness of contract performance clauses is likely to increase when there is long-term engagement with suppliers and continuous work with them to develop their capacities rather than terminating relations.

## 13.5 Challenges for Integrating HRDD into Public Procurement

In practice, there are several challenges to implementing HRDD in public procurement and integrating human rights criteria into tenders. These include siloed approaches, lack of transparency and complex global supply chains, prioritising value for money, lack of resources, knowledge, and skills, insufficient or incomplete policies, challenging contexts, structural challenges, prioritisation of other social aspects, and the readiness of the market.

**Box 13.4 Increasing Leverage through Collaboration**

**The Case of the Swedish Regions and Dell**

The Swedish Country Councils engaged with Dell and Atea, the Swedish reseller of Dell, for 18 months after DanWatch reported excessive working hours, forced overtime, inadequate safety conditions and wages below the minimum wage in four Dell supplier factories in 2013. The ongoing dialogue and engagement that started in February 2014 resulted in Atea's improvement of their due diligence processes in its supply chain through the creation of a robust system and moved from a CSR report review to a detailed social audit reports and corrective action plans approach. Dell's due diligence to ensure social responsibility in its supply chain was also improved and after the long process of engagement, Dell increased its transparency and disclosed detailed audit reports, records of working hours, corrective action plans, and status reports. Although these improvements were achieved, the Stockholm County Council will continue to meet regularly with Atea for the contract's duration and, given the collaborative structure of the Swedish councils, once the contract ends the national county council network can continue its engagement with Atea through another county council. These collaborative practices increase the capacity for long-term engagement and improvements in the supply chain (Electronics Watch, 2016).

### *13.5.1 Siloed Approaches*

A key challenge for integrating HRDD into public procurement is the siloed approach that dominates in public procurement bodies. For instance, most procurement teams are not the ones responsible for defining contract performance clauses or for contract management. Often, procurement practitioners are in charge of tender drafting and evaluation, while contract managers are responsible for overseeing the execution of the contract. These silos in public procurement teams have significant implications for ensuring compliance with contract clauses. For instance, a study by the Dutch government found that public procurement buyers did not verify supplier compliance with their policies due to a lack of ownership at different administrative levels (Methven O'Brien et al., 2016). Therefore, it is important that, when these different functions exist within public authorities' structures, they streamline their actions, share knowledge, and collaborate, ensuring that actions to address human and labour rights impacts do not stop after the awarding of contracts.

### *13.5.2 Lack of Transparency and Complex Global Supply Chains*

Public authorities face challenges to identify and assess human rights risks due to a general lack of transparency and complexity in global supply chains. For instance, public buyers may struggle to map their supply chains beyond direct suppliers (tier 1) and obtain sufficient information to identify high human rights risks. Certain requirements such as those related to having human rights policies in place can be easy to collect, but more specific requirements such as those related to the supply chain may be more difficult. Often, direct suppliers may not be able (due to confidentiality clauses or non-disclosure agreements) or open to disclosing the required information. In other cases, businesses themselves may not be collecting information from their suppliers in the first place due to resource constraints. To increase transparency, public buyers may need to build trust over long-term engagements with suppliers.

### *13. 5.3 Prioritising Value for Money*

In practice, public buyers often continue prioritising value for money over social considerations. For instance, a study found that in Mexico, public authorities prioritise economic objectives over non-economic ones in road infrastructure projects, regardless of whether the public authority was contracting through traditional public works or public–private partnerships (Treviño-Lozano, 2021).

This prioritisation may be, at least partially, explained by two factors. First, there are still tensions between primary (economic and efficiency criteria) and secondary, or horizontal (social criteria) aims within law regimes (Martin-Ortega & O'Brien, 2017) that limit the implementation of social considerations in practice. For instance, a study covering mostly OECD countries found that public buyers' efforts to use human rights criteria into procurement are undermined by restrictive provisions in public procurement laws and policies that fail to effectively integrate social considerations into the procurement cycle (Methven O'Brien et al., 2016) (Box 13.5).

Second, a traditional view of value for money (prioritising lower cost) and broader value-based approaches (those including social and environmental aspects) are two contrasting logics that may hamper the adoption of human rights criteria. Studies have found, for example, that the legitimisation of (Meehan et al., 2017) and organisational inertia around (Meehan & Bryde, 2011) the long-established price-based approach hamper the adoption of value-based procurement despite willingness by stakeholders. Individual public buyers are thus likely to experience tensions between balancing cost and social value that may be difficult to reconcile (Pesterfield & Rogerson, 2023).

### *13.5.4 Lack of Resources, Knowledge, and Skills*

Another reason for poor or absent implementation of HRDD and integration of human rights criteria is that public procurement buyers tend to lack the necessary resources, knowledge, and skills to identify human rights risks, introduce human rights considerations in procurement exercises, and monitor the implementation of contract performance clauses. For instance, a study by the Centre for Research on Multinational Corporations (SOMO) found that the implementation of public procurement policies related to human rights

**Box 13.5 Legislative Tensions in the EU Directive**

An example of how legislative tensions can restrict the implementation of social criteria is the "link to subject matter" condition in the EU Directive 2014/24. Under this Directive, for contract authorities to include sustainability criteria into selection, awarding, and contract performance clauses, these must be related and proportionate to the subject matter of the contract, as unlike exclusion criteria, these are specific to each contract. This means for example, that if a public buyer is tendering for police uniforms and the contractor is a textile retailer that sources different types of gowns and uniforms from different suppliers, public buyers can only request the contractor to include human rights (and environmental) conditions in its contract with its supplier(s) of police uniforms and only in relation to those (as these are the tendered product) even if the supplier also supplies the contractor with firemen uniforms (Treviño-Lozano & Uysal, 2023).

varied substantially across public procurement authorities and that this was related to the different levels of knowledge on the impacts of labour rights violations in supply chains and on the differences in risk across sectors (SOMO, 2014). Lack of awareness and knowledge of human rights risks was also found when explaining a lack of implementation of human rights criteria in public road infrastructure works in Mexico (Treviño-Lozano, 2021). In Sweden, it was found that despite it was mandated by procurement policy, public buyers monitoring was limited due to knowledge, capacity, and resource constraints (Methven O'Brien et al., 2016).

Through collaboration, public buyers can reduce costs, administrative burden, and share good practices. Public buyers can share common tools, such as codes of labour standards or standard contract performance conditions through different types of collaboration including central purchasing bodies, framework agreements, or collective monitoring organisations. For instance, the Swedish Country Councils share standardised human and labour rights requirements for suppliers (covering a code of conduct and terms and conditions of contract) as well as monitoring resources. Similarly, Electronics Watch provides affiliated public buyers with template contracts for ICT suppliers. Public buyers can also work collaboratively through purchasing consortia, such as the London Universities Purchasing Consortium (LUPC) which tenders and manages framework agreements on behalf of public sector bodies. Below is an example of leveraging resources through collaboration.

#### *13.5.5 Unclear, Incomplete, or Inexistent Policies and Laws*

Having legal clarity into what public buyers can and cannot do is key for implementing HRDD and integrating human rights criteria into tenders. However, laws may not always provide the legal clarity that can provide public authorities with confidence to implement human rights criteria. For example, Australia's Commonwealth Procurement Rules do not provide such clarity as it does not explicitly mention forced labour, and child labour (Amanze et al., 2022). In the UK, a recent study found that there is a lack of clear direction for actively addressing modern slavery risks in public procurement as there is not a clear mandate across public institutions that focuses on action and goes beyond disclosure (Rogerson et al., 2024). Similarly, in a pilot study in the garment industry public buyers cited a lack of legal clarity as an obstacle for greater implementation of HRDD (OECD, 2022). Moreover, there is still a lack of policies governing framework agreements that explicitly include human rights considerations (United Nations Working Group on Business and Human Rights, 2022).

In Latin America it has been found that NAPs tend to focus on including human rights criteria in the selection and awarding stages, but not through the entire procurement cycle, particularly overlooking enforcement measures in the contract management phase which is likely to reduce the impact of implementing such criteria (Treviño Lozano, 2022). In Mexico it was found that one of the barriers for implementing social criteria in public works is that there are non-existent or existent but unclear or unenforced policies and laws (Treviño-Lozano, 2021).

#### *13.5.6 Challenging Contexts*

There are specific contexts in which it may be more challenging for public buyers to undertake HRDD and incorporate human rights criteria into tenders. For instance, the COVID-19 pandemic challenged the capacity of public buyers worldwide to monitor compliance with contract clauses and the emergency situation enabled public buyers to except suppliers from specific procedures (see Box 13.7).

**Box 13.6 Leveraging Resources through Collaboration**

In 2014 the City of Madison, US, in consultation with the Sweatfree Purchasing Consortium, created a collaborative "piggy-back" contract for uniforms in 2014, mainly used by Fire, Metro Transit, Police and other municipal operations agencies to eliminate unsafe and illegal working conditions in apparel factories. The contract can still be used by all City of Madison agencies, approximately 167 other local government counties, cities, town, and other public entities and agencies in the US. Each agency has the opportunity to join in the bid, which helps agencies with limited resources to participate in tenders without having to set the requirements themselves (The Danish Institute for Human Rights, 2020).

**Box 13.7 Challenging Contexts**

**COVID-19 Pandemic**

During the COVID-19 pandemic, countries worldwide experienced an overwhelming demand for personal protective equipment (PPE) such as medical gloves. In the UK, the Department for Health and Social Care established an emergency parallel supply chain for PPE and triggered Regulation 32 of the Public Contracts Regulations 2015 to enable new contracts to be urgently set up without going through the usual procurement procedure (Bhutta et al., 2021). Once in contract, limitations to in-person audits hampered the monitoring of supplier's compliance with the contract clauses established (Bhutta et al., 2021).

In Latin America, Panama issued a decree that exempted health and safety suppliers from general procedures, Colombia issued decrees to allow direct awarding and permitted acquisition in the international market, and Chile adopted fast-track purchases for those with amounts of less than 5,000 US dollars, effectively avoiding public procurement procedures for these purchases (Treviño-Lozano & Martin-Ortega, 2020).

### *13.5.7 Structural Challenges*

Implementing human rights criteria in some countries, especially in the Global South, may also be exacerbated by existing structural challenges. For instance, a study found that a barrier for socially responsible public procurement in Mexico is political opposition and corruption (Treviño-Lozano, 2021). In Latin America, public procurement contracts may be awarded directly to suppliers due to the levels of corruption, lack of transparency and accountability in these economies where the boundaries between the State and businesses are often blurred (Treviño-Lozano & Martin-Ortega, 2020). The need for a human rights-based approach to combat corruption in public procurement in African countries has also showed the link between corruption and human rights whereby corruption impairs the State duty to protect human rights. Therefore, a human rights lens would not be effectively embedded in public procurement under an institutional environment that lacks transparency, accountability, and oversight. This illustrates how human rights issues are linked to ethical public procurement principles against corruption and to those that favour transparency and integrity.

#### *13.5.8 Prioritisation of Other Sustainability or Social Aspects*

Implementing human rights criteria can also vary across countries, not only because of their different legal frameworks but also because of their different policy landscapes. As we discussed before, human rights are only one of the many issues covered under the "social" or "sustainability" criteria in public procurement legislation. Countries may, therefore, prioritise specific social issues that relate to the country's priorities, but that do not necessarily address human rights violations in global supply chains. For instance, in South Africa an important part of their procurement policy landscape is the need to empower minority groups within society which can lead them to prioritise social inclusion (Brammer & Walker, 2011). Therefore, South Africa's Preferential Procurement Policy Framework Act requires black economic empowerment and local production and content with fair wages.

#### *13.5.9 Market Readiness*

The extent to which contracting authorities include human rights criteria in specific tenders is also likely to depend on the readiness of the market, which often varies across sectors and countries. Some markets may not be ready for the implementation of human rights criteria. For instance, the Sweden's National Agency for Public Procurement launched a tender in 2015 for mobile phones with award criteria focused on conflict minerals due diligence where none of the bidders were able to report such due diligence procedures (Methven O'Brien et al., 2016). However, undertaking market research during the pre-tender stage to inform what can reasonably be required of bidders as a minimum standard can prevent the risk of setting requirements that the market is not yet ready to provide or conversely, to set requirements that are too low for such market. To test the readiness of the market, public authorities should consider issues such as how many suppliers could meet the proposed requirements, whether such number would be sufficient to keep the tender competitive, whether requirements need to be adjusted to the local context, and weather the requirements could lead to singling out one supplier or unfairly impact specific suppliers or group, such as Small and Medium Enterprises (SMEs).

Undertaking market research and stakeholder engagement from the pre-tendering phase may prepare, incentivise, and encourage markets for the introduction of human rights criteria. For instance, it can inform the ways in which these requirements can be introduced most effectively across the procurement cycle and to different products (as illustrated in the example of Germany below), whether they can be gradually introduced (as in the example of Norway below) or tailored across lots (as illustrated in the Ghent example below). See Box 13.8.

### 13.6 Looking Ahead

There are at least two areas in which public procurement professionals should be moving towards according to emerging research and practice: integrating social and environmental elements and engaging in remediation efforts.

#### *13.6.1 Integration of Social and Environmental Criteria*

So far, we have discussed HRDD in isolation from environmental impacts. Mainly because these are often discussed and addressed in silos in businesses, policy making (for instance modern slavery legislation and climate change legislation), and public procurement (see Rogerson et al., 2024). However, such separate efforts limit the extent to which these can

**Box 13.8 Tailored Approaches to Introducing Human Rights Criteria Based on Market Research**

In 2016, the Federal Ministry for Economic Cooperation and Development in Germany took a two-step approach for an ICT pilot tender based on market research on what the ICT supply chain market was able to prove in regard to human and labour rights. This study showed that effective verification of compliance with labour and social standards could not yet be provided by a broad range of bidders for the entire supply chain, given the complex supply chains in the industry, but it could for the first tier of the supply chain. As a result, the authorities used a combination of minimum criteria as binding criteria (technical specifications) for the first tier of the main subject of the tender (computers and monitors) and award criteria for the first tier of the peripheral tender (keypad and pc-mice) and for the second and further tiers of both tenders. The result was that almost all bidders complied with the minimum requirements and were incentivised to improve labour rights beyond the first tier of the supply chain (European Commission, 2020).

In Norway, the municipality of Skien decided to adopt an incremental approach to labour standards requirements in the building and construction sector building upon previous measures undertaken by the municipality. This was based on discussions with construction business organisations, who shared their main challenges, and trade unions, who recommended appropriate procurement requirements. Dialogue with social partners and stakeholders in the sector was key to set out requirements in a realistic way and ensure compliance and effective results. This approach allowed the municipality to improve labour rights whilst ensuring the level of requirements did not hamper reliable suppliers to participate (European Commission, 2020).

In 2016 the City of Ghent authorities divided the framework agreement of workwear procurement into five lots that required varying degrees of social and environmental performance. This was based on an analysis of previous public tenders in the Flanders region and a market study conducted by Ghent and the Association of Flemish Cities and Municipalities (VVSG) that showed that the market was not ready to deliver the level of social impact required to guarantee ILO labour standards and increased transparency throughout the textile supply chain. By requesting various degrees of social performance across the five lots, the city was able to increase supplier awareness on labour rights, supplier membership to the Fair Wear Foundation, supply chain transparency, and supplier engagement with third-party verification systems (European Commission, 2020).

be addressed effectively as one may be prioritised over the other when, in fact, they interact and perpetuate each other in several ways.

There is increasing evidence of the interconnectedness between human rights and environmental impacts and the need for an integrated approach. Such evidence shows that human rights violations, such as modern slavery, and environmental impacts, especially climate change, are two converging global emergencies deeply intertwined and rooted in unsustainable production and consumption practices that exacerbate existing and overlapping vulnerabilities (such as poverty and inequality), disproportionally impacting the poorest and most vulnerable. The evidence shows that the relationship is bi-directional (one can contribute to the other) and cyclical, whereby they are constantly shaping each other. For instance, environmental degradation and climate change can contribute to modern slavery by pushing people into situations where they may become vulnerable to modern slavery due to climate-induced migration or displacement. At the same time, modern slavery can contribute to environmental degradation and climate change when people in modern slavery work in activities that perpetuate biodiversity loss and environmental degradation, such as deforestation and overfishing.

Human rights violations can also be found in sectors that are not environmentally degrading, but that aim to tackle environmental issues. This is the case of the renewables sector where research is increasingly finding instances of forced labour, in particular in relation to the extraction of critical minerals for the production of solar panels or electronic vehicles (EVs) from specific geographies. In Australia, the New South Wales Anti-Slavery Commissioner, in partnership with the Clean Energy Council, is developing a code of practice to manage modern slavery risks in renewable energy value chains and public procurement buyers that purchase renewable energy, specifically photovoltaic solar power, will be expected to follow it.

Some public buyers are starting to address human rights and environmental issues together to ensure that the transition to a lower carbon economy does not negatively impact the rights of vulnerable groups. Box 13.9 provides an example. We expect more public bodies to move towards similar approaches in the near future as the concept of "just transition" gains attention by policy makers, CSOs, businesses, and investors.

### *13.6.2 Public Buyers' Engagement in Remediation*

There is an increasing expectation that public buyers, often linked to harm in global supply chains (and in some cases contributing to abuse directly), engage in the remediation of human rights abuses in their supply chains. For instance, according to The Danish Institute for Human Rights and in line with the UNGPs, purchasing bodies should consider establishing an internal grievance mechanism to provide remedy to victims in their supply chains (2020).

#### Box 13.9 Integrating Social and Environmental Criteria in the Renewables Sector

The Mayor of London is incentivising a shift to EVs and has publicly committed to ensuring that the transition to zero carbon is fair and just. For Transport for London (TfL), as part of the Greater London Authority (GLA) Group, this means working on plans to achieve the Mayor's commitment to deliver a zero-emissions bus fleet by 2030. Given the high human and rights risks associated with the supply of critical minerals needed for renewables, TfL, and other GLA bodies, joined a pilot programme by Electronics Watch on Low-Emission Vehicles in 2022, which expands on Electronics Watch's worker-driven model to address human rights abuses in the mining of minerals and production of semi-conductors necessary for batteries (TfL Modern Slavery Statement, 2023). Additionally, TfL has included contract performance clauses in its new framework agreement for the delivery of EV infrastructure (e.g., charging points) requiring progressive requirements for suppliers to improve their HRDD. The 15 year-long contracts provide TfL with great leverage for incentivising progress.

**Box 13.10 New Swedish Contract Clause on Remediation**

*Supplier shall, if supplier has caused or contributed to actual adverse impact, provide for remediation by:*

a. *in so far it is possible, restoring affected rightsholders to the situation they would be in had the adverse impact not occurred and enabling remediation that is proportionate to the significance and scale of the adverse impact;*
b. *consulting in a meaningful way with affected rightsholders or their representatives on appropriate forms of remedy;*
c. *assessing whether affected rightsholders are satisfied with the process and its outcome.*

Moreover, in 2023, Electronics Watch developed in consultation with public buyers and rightsholders the "Principles for Worker-Driven Remedy". These principles aim to provide a guiding framework for public buyers, their suppliers, worker rights organisations, and other relevant stakeholders to facilitate remedy to workers in global supply chains from the perspective of rightsholders.

More recently, in 2023, the Swedish Regions updated their shared due diligence contract requirements for suppliers and included a specific clause on human rights remedy (see Box 13.10). The clause requires not only the provision of remedy, but also meaningful engagement with the rightsholders affected by the harm, which is crucial for remedy to be effective. This is a best practice example that has emerged after years of practice of implementing HRDD and engaging with CSOs. As more public bodies become familiar with these processes, and remedy requirements are introduced in new mHREDD legislation, it is likely that similar approaches will increase, and remedy requirements in public procurement will become the norm.

## References

Amanze, M., Cahill, D., & Evans, C. (2022). Tackling Human Trafficking in Governments Supply Chains: Legal Certainty and Effectiveness Issues under the Australian Commonwealth Procurement Rules Model. *Federal Law Review*, *50*(4), 479–503. https://doi.org/10.1177/0067205X221126554

Bhutta, M., Bostock, B., Brown, J., Day, E., Hughes, A., Hurst, R., Tautrims, A., & Trueba, M. (2021). *Forced labour in the Malaysian Medical Gloves supply chain before and during the COVID-19 pandemic: Evidence, scale and solutions*. Modern Slavery & Human Rights Policy & Evidence Centre.

Blackstone, N. T., Rodríguez-Huerta, E., Battaglia, K., Jackson, B., Jackson, E., Benoit Norris, C., & Decker Sparks, J. L. (2023). Forced Labour Risk Is Pervasive in the US Land-Based Food Supply. *Nature Food*, *4*(7), 596–606. https://doi.org/10.1038/s43016-023-00794-x

Brammer, S., & Walker, H. (2011). Sustainable Procurement in the Public Sector: An International Comparative Study. *International Journal of Operations & Production Management*, *31*(4), 452–476. https://doi.org/10.1108/01443571111119551

Department for International Trade. (2021). G7 Trade Ministers' Statement on Forced Labour. News Story. UK Government. www.gov.uk/government/news/g7-trade-ministers-statement-on-forced-labour-annex-a

Electronics Watch. (2016). *Public Procurement and Human Rights Due Diligence to Achieve Respect for Labour Rights Standards in Electronics Factories: A Case Study of the Swedish County Councils and the Dell Computer Corporation*. Electronics Watch. https://electronicswatch.org/en/pub

lic-procurement-human-rights-due-diligence-a-case-study-of-the-swedish-county-councils-and-the-dell-computer-corporation-february-2016_2456642.pdf

European Commission. (2020). *Making socially responsible public procurement work: 71 good practice cases*. Publications Office. https://data.europa.eu/doi/10.2826/844552

Gonzalez De Aguinaga, S. (2022). *Effectiveness of public procurement measures at addressing modern slavery in supply chains: Evidence review*. Modern Slavery & Human Rights Policy & Evidence Centre. www.modernslaverypec.org/resources/public-procurement

Home Office. (2018). UK agrees principles for tackling modern slavery in supply chains. News Story. UK Government. www.gov.uk/government/news/uk-agrees-principles-for-tackling-modern-slavery-in-supply-chains

International Labour Organization (ILO), Walk Free, and International Organization for Migration (IOM). (2022). Global Estimates Modern Slavery. Forced Labour and Forced Marriage.

Jaehrling, K., Johnson, M., Larsen, T. P., Refslund, B., & Grimshaw, D. (2018). Tackling Precarious Work in Public Supply Chains: A Comparison of Local Government Procurement Policies in Denmark, Germany and the UK. *Work, Employment and Society*, *32*(3), 546–563. https://doi.org/10.1177/0950017018758216

LeBaron, G., Howard, N., Thibos, C., & Kyritsis, P. (2018). *Confronting root causes: Forced labour in global supply chains*. https://drive.google.com/file/d/1KX7Rcfbw4SK4nh5RQmcZ-7fZho296bg6/view?usp=embed_facebook

Martin-Ortega, O. (2017). Human Rights Risks in Global Supply Chains: Applying the UK Modern Slavery Act to the Public Sector. *Global Policy*, *8*(4), 512–521. https://doi.org/10.1111/1758-5899.12501

Martin-Ortega, O. (2018). Public Procurement as a Tool for the Protection and Promotion of Human Rights: A Study of Collaboration, Due Diligence and Leverage in the Electronics Industry. *Business and Human Rights Journal*, *3*(1), 75–95. https://doi.org/10.1017/bhj.2017.35

Martin-Ortega, O., & O'Brien, C. M. (2017). Advancing Respect for Labour Rights Globally through Public Procurement. *Politics and Governance*, *5*(4), 69–79. https://doi.org/10.17645/pag.v5i4.1073

McCrudden, C. (2004). Using Public Procurement to Achieve Social Outcomes. *Natural Resources Forum*, *28*(4), 257–267. https://doi.org/10.1111/j.1477-8947.2004.00099.x

Meehan, J., & Bryde, D. (2011). Sustainable Procurement Practice. *Business Strategy and the Environment*, *20*(2), 94–106. https://doi.org/10.1002/bse.678

Meehan, J., Ludbrook, M. N., & Mason, C. J. (2016). Collaborative Public Procurement: Institutional Explanations of Legitimised Resistance. *Journal of Purchasing and Supply Management*, *22*(3), 160–170. https://doi.org/10.1016/j.pursup.2016.03.002

Meehan, J., Menzies, L., & Michaelides, R. (2017). The Long Shadow of Public Policy; Barriers to a Value-Based Approach in Healthcare Procurement. *Journal of Purchasing and Supply Management*, *23*(4), 229–241. https://doi.org/10.1016/j.pursup.2017.05.003

Methven O'Brien, C., Vander Meulen, N., & Mehra, A. (2016). *Public procurement and human rights: A survey of twenty jurisdictions*. International Learning Lab on Public Procurement and Human Rights. www.humanrights.dk/sites/humanrights.dk/files/media/migrated/public-procurement-and-human-rights-a-survey-of-twenty-jurisdictions-final.pdf

OECD. (2023). *Public procurement performance*. OECD Public Governance Policy Papers. www.oecd.org/en/publications/public-procurement-performance_0dde73f4-en.html

OECD. (2022). *Pilot on integrating OECD due diligence into public procurement in the garment sector*. OECD.

OSCE. (2022). *Combating trafficking in human beings and labour exploitation in supply chains—Guidance for OSCE procurement—Second updated edition*. Organization for Security and Co-operation in Europe. www.osce.org/cthb/536001

Pesterfield, C., & Rogerson, M. (2023). Institutional Logics in the UK Construction Industry's Response to Modern Slavery Risk: Complementarity and Conflict. *Journal of Business Ethics*. https://doi.org/10.1007/s10551-023-05455-4

Rogerson, M., Grosvold, J., & Alves, K. (2024). *Climate change and modern slavery in public procurement*. Modern Slavery & Human Rights Policy & Evidence Centre. www.modernslaverypec.org/resources/climate-change-modern-slavery-public-procurement

SOMO. (2014). *A Review of Dutch Policy for Socially Responsible Public Procurement.* www.somo.nl/wp-content/uploads/2014/03/A-review-of-Dutch-policy-for-socially-responsible-public-procurement.pdf

Transport for London (TfL) Slavery and Human Trafficking Statement. (2022/2023). https://board.tfl.gov.uk/documents/s22829/Appendix%201%20Modern%20Slavery%20Statement%202023 24%20Draft.pdf

The Danish Institute for Human Rights. (2020). *Driving change through public procurement.* The Danish Institute for Human Rights. www.humanrights.dk/publications/driving-change-through-public-procurement

Treviño Lozano, L. (2022). Is Latin America Missing the Links Between Procurement, Sustainability and Human Rights? *Business and Human Rights Journal*, 7(3), 461–467. https://doi.org/10.1017/bhj.2022.9

Treviño-Lozano, L. (2021). Sustainable Public Procurement and Human Rights: Barriers to Deliver on Socially Sustainable Road Infrastructure Projects in Mexico. *Sustainability*, *13*(17), 9605. https://doi.org/10.3390/su13179605

Treviño-Lozano, L., & Martin-Ortega, O. (2020). *Public procurement during Covid-19 in Latin America: Challenges, responses and next steps forward.* https://gala.gre.ac.uk/id/eprint/31094/1/31094_MARTIN_ORTEGA_Public_procurement_during_Covid_19.pdf

Treviño-Lozano, L., & Uysal, E. (2023). Bridging the Gap between Corporate Sustainability Due Diligence and EU Public Procurement. *Maastricht Journal of European and Comparative Law.* https://doi.org/10.1177/1023263X231213335

Trusgnach, M., Martin-Ortega, O., & Berman, C. (2024). Towards Worker-Driven Remedy: Advancing Human and Labour Rights in Global Supply Chains. *Journal of Modern Slavery*, *9*(1), 152–178. https://slavefreetoday.org/journal_of_modern_slavery/v9i1a8-towards-worker-driven-remedy-advancing-human-and-labour-rights-in-global-supply-chains.pdf

UNGPs. (2011). *Guiding Principles on Business and Human Rights: Implementing the United Nations "Protect, Respect and Remedy" Framework.* OHCHR. www.ohchr.org/en/publications/reference-publications/guiding-principles-business-and-human-rights

United Nations Working Group on Business and Human Rights. (2022). *Integrating Human Rights in Public Procurement: A focus on Latin America and the Caribbean.* https://empresasyderechoshumanos.org/wp-content/uploads/2022/04/INFORMATION-NOTE-on-PP_LAC_EN.pdf

## *Case Study: Adopting an Internal Supplier Assurance and Contract Management Programme – The Case of LUPC's Supplier Due Diligence Tool (SDDT) (Developed by Sofia Gonzalez De Aguinaga and Martina Trusgnach in collaboration with the London Universities Purchasing Consortium)*

### Context

To effectively procure goods, services, and works, UK universities can affiliate to the UK Universities Purchasing Consortium (UKUPC) of which the London Universities Purchasing Consortium (LUPC) represents one of the six regional consortia. LUPC manages a large set of framework agreements for their almost 100 members, including universities and higher education institutions as well as not-for-profit organisations in the education, arts, science, charity, and wider public sectors, which include some county councils, the Met Office, and the Bank of England. For example, they manage laboratory equipment ICT hardware and software, estates and facilities including waste management services, and cleaning and security services. These framework agreements are available for use by all UKUPC members. LUPC deals with over 100 suppliers across these framework agreements, of which 56% are SMEs. Currently, 11 framework agreements developed by LUPC are actively used by its members.

Following their commitment to responsible procurement, as outlined in their vision and mission statements, LUPC has for a number of years established responsible procurement practices. For instance, they follow the ISO 20400 International Standard on Sustainable Public Procurement, include human rights considerations in their invitations to tender, evaluate potential suppliers for their framework agreements according to responsible and sustainable procurement criteria, and utilise the UKUPC's supplier code of conduct called sustain, which integrates modern slavery considerations. They also produced the first online training on modern slavery in the UK for CIPS in 2016 and were a founding member of Electronics Watch.

### Challenge

LUPC used a post-tender questionnaire to verify suppliers' commitment to the UKUPC's supplier code of conduct. Between 2020 and 2021, LUPC identified that its already appointed suppliers needed support to improve their practices, and that LUPC was underutilising its power to influence change and continuous improvement. LUPC saw the need, and the opportunity, to integrate within their responsible procurement process, a tool to improve the practices of suppliers post-awarding and to focus on supplier engagement, a very different approach to compliance or auditing. This tool would take the shape of a questionnaire that would rate suppliers' performance using a streetlight system and would enable the production of tailored support plans. It was also envisaged that the tool would help facilitate continuous engagement with suppliers in the contract management stage. However, the current information they were obtaining from their suppliers, and the data collected by existing third-party platforms were ill-fitted and insufficient, with many of the latter providing abstract and aggregated data at the parent company level. LUPC needed to collect in-depth and specific information about their suppliers' practices to provide the support they envisioned. This meant developing their own tool in-house.

### Action

In 2022, LUPC set itself to develop a tool to support the continuous improvement of their supplier base and manage supplier engagement, called supplier due diligence tool (SDDT). LUPC had the resources to do this, as over 10% of their budget is allocated to responsible procurement. LUPC also had the support from academics sitting in their executive board and other experts to develop the tool in-house. Developing this allowed LUPC to integrate its main priority areas within one tool: human and labour rights (explicitly including modern slavery within the SDDT questionnaire), social value, and the environment, which had not been done before. The tool was to be used as an initial screening for all its framework suppliers to flag areas where suppliers needed further improvement and where LUPC could provide further support.

The tool was piloted in 2022 with suppliers of the estates and facilities framework agreement, as informed by the risk assessments undertaken by UKUPC. They then decided to gradually roll out the tool to all their framework agreements, prioritising contracts with higher risks, and adjusting for any differences across categories. Since the pilot, and following an agile methodology, the tool has been updated a few times based on feedback from suppliers and LUPC staff, including Senior Category Managers. For instance, to avoid duplication and overburdening suppliers, LUPC decided that any third-party reports that suppliers already have can be used to input into the SDDT questionnaire, but LUPC would follow up directly with suppliers to collect any missing data necessary to provide suppliers with a tailored assessment and follow-up engagement. In 2024 the questionnaire has been expanded to include freedom of association, health and safety and a set of sustainability-related key performance indicators.

### Impact

LUPC has implemented this tool for two years, and since then, its internal expert group has carefully evaluated the evidence and information provided by 42 framework suppliers across the estates and facilities, legal supplier services, and laboratory equipment framework agreements, and has produced bespoke reports for them that include action plans (e.g., to develop policies and procedures to provide remedy when human rights abuses are discovered), and relevant online resources (e.g., reports and guidelines from various sources) that they can use. Suppliers have generally responded positively to this tool as LUPC is focusing on building an open and collaborative relationship where suppliers feel supported by the consortium, rather than policed. To measure the effectiveness of this tool in improving suppliers' practices, LUPC will soon undertake an assessment to measure the progress of those first engaged in the tool, and based on the results make further improvements to the tool and the process.

### Looking Forward

LUPC will continue to roll out this tool to the remainder of their framework agreements. LUPC is likely to face some challenges, including scalability issues or resistance from suppliers. Accepting the use of third-party reports to input into SDDT has already helped reducing resistance from some suppliers. But, LUPC is anticipating these challenges and has started thinking about automatising processes and is working on further developing trust with its supplier base through continuous engagement.

LUPC's Responsible Procurement Lead also aims to engage with category managers and embed supplier engagement into the contract management stage, so that the tailored reports provided to suppliers are discussed regularly between LUPC and the suppliers during contract management meetings. This engagement has already started. In the words of a Senior Category Manager, "responsible procurement is embedded in the very start of our ITT process ensuring that all bidders understand LUPC's absolute and unequivocable commitment to responsible procurement from the outset, and for that to develop throughout the term of the framework".

LUPC aims to use the information gathered from the SDDT to shape their training offer and to facilitate supplier improvement through its established partnerships. For instance, if modern slavery issues were reported through the SDDT tool or through follow-up dialogue with their direct suppliers, LUPC would facilitate engagement between suppliers and unseen to support remediation. In the case of the electronics category, if it was identified that suppliers needed on the ground data from their supply chain, LUPC would facilitate suppliers' engagement with Electronics Watch to run on the ground investigations and provide tailored follow-up support.

In the longer term, LUPC aims to share the reports they generate for suppliers with their membership base and to launch an online portal for suppliers and members to use to track live progress of framework agreement suppliers.

**Discussion Questions**

1. Is LUPC integrating a human-rights lens to public procurement?
2. What enabled LUPC to develop SDDT?
3. What steps of the HRDD process were involved in the development of SDDT? Which steps are involved in its implementation? Which steps are missing?
4. Does the SDDT contribute to prevent, mitigate, or remediate human rights abuses?
5. In which stages of the procurement cycle is the tool used?
6. How do you think LUPC's approach addresses human rights risk management in public supply chains?
7. How can LUPC increase trust with their supplier base and encourage greater transparency? What else could LUPC do to obtain more and better data from their suppliers?
8. What role do data platforms play in LUPC's approach? What are the implications of this for addressing modern slavery in public procurement supply chains?
9. Could LUPC's engagement with suppliers help them identifying and addressing some human rights risks more quickly? (e.g., before the framework agreements are re-negotiated).

### *Case Study: Durable Web of Corruption: The Case of "Fat Leonard" and the US Navy (Developed by Timothy G. Hawkins, Suman Niranjan, Arunachalam Narayanan)*

**Background**

US Navy ships often visit foreign ports and contract for husbanding services such as tugging, piloting, cargo drayage, security, interpreters, water taxis, repair, maintenance, waste removal, and local transportation. In 2023, the US Navy awarded 192 contracts to 23 different suppliers worth $48 million for husbanding services (U.S. Department of the Treasury, Bureau of the Fiscal Service, 2023). The "Fat Leonard" corruption occurred over seven years, beginning in 2006 (Standifer, 2017). A group of senior Navy officials conspired with Glen Marine Defense Asia (GMDA), headed by Leonard Francis, in bribery and corruption. At 6 foot 3 inches tall and 350 pounds, Francis became known as "Fat Leonard".

**Bribery**

On 17 February 2006, three Naval officers indulged in a $20,000 bar tab at a resort in Hong Kong paid for by GMDA. On 9 March 2006, Naval officers were treated to expensive food, liquor, and Cohiba cigars on a rooftop helipad in Singapore. In July 2006, a Naval officer had Francis pay for his 75-person promotion party at a hotel in Singapore. In exchange for docking the USS Blue Ridge in Hong Kong, GDMA paid for a seven-course dinner for Naval officers and their spouses at the Shangri-La hotel. In February 2007, Francis funded expensive hotels in Cebu and Singapore along with the services of sex workers. In April 2007, Francis reported one of GDMA's competitors to the Naval Criminal Investigative Service for overcharging the US Navy – information passed to Francis by a Naval Officer. In December 2007, Francis gifted a Naval officer and his wife expensive watches worth $25 thousand. Since 2008,

Francis provided hotels, meals, alcohol, cigars, sex workers, family vacations, gifts, and possibly several post-military jobs.

All of the bribery paid off for Francis. In February 2008, Francis requested proprietary invoice pricing from competitors of GDMA. In June 2008, one Naval officer influenced another to switch the husbanding service provider to GMDA for a port call in Russia. One officer sent lists of Navy admirals to Francis. Arranged port calls continued including the USS Abraham Lincoln and USS Reagan in July 2009 costing the Navy $1.5 million. In 2011, GDMA won multiple-award contracts in three of four competed regions (Whiteley et al., 2017).

### Classified Information

An enlisted sailor provided classified ship schedules to GMDA in exchange for cash, travel costs, and consumer electronics. In April 2006, Francis influenced the port-call locations of the USS Abraham Lincoln and three escort ships by sending them to Laem Chabang, Thailand, worth $2. In June 2007, Francis paid over $20,000 for Naval officers to stay at the Shangri-La Hotel in exchange for a classified list of port visits. During July to September 2007, Francis again steered a port call of the USS Kitty Hawk to Port Klang securing another $2 million contract and classified ship locations.

### The Investigations

From 2004 to 2012, 14 investigations resulted in ten criminal intelligence reports (Prine, 2017). Numerous tips were submitted to the NCIS and to the Department of Defence (DOD) hotline reporting overbilling, using the Indonesian military to harm to a competitor, and questionable invoices. The investigations resulted in an NCIS-orchestrated sting operation in San Diego, CA in 2013, at which time Francis was arrested. In sum, Francis admitted to offering bribes exceeding $500,000 to Navy personnel and cheating the US Navy out of $35 million (Baldor & Watson, 2023). A study of the case identified 1,194 alleged instances of fraud (Whiteley et al., 2017) that permeated all steps of the sourcing process. Unbeknownst to the Navy, Francis even submitted fake quotes from fictitious vendors to show that GDMA's prices were fair and reasonable. In 2015, he pleaded guilty to fraud in the US and faces up to 25 years behind bars. His contracts were terminated by the Navy and GMDS was disbarred from US government contracts. In custody, Francis managed to escape house arrest and flee to Venezuela on his way to Russia. In December 2023, the US government traded Francis in a prisoner exchange and extradited him back to the US (Vyas et al., 2023).

Fat Leonard did not act alone; it came to light that, in 2007, the "wolf pack" members signed up for covert email accounts through cooltoad.com in order to conceal their unlawful acts. As of 2022, 33 US Navy personnel have either pleaded guilty or been convicted (Walsh, 2022) of bid rigging, bribery, and conspiracy to defraud the government (Whiteley et al., 2017). Francis claimed, "Everybody was in my pocket. I had them in my palm. I was just rolling them around" (Helmore, 2022). Even an NCIS agent and a contracting officer at FISC-Singapore colluded with Francis (Whiteley et al., 2017). One retired Navy officer described Francis. "The Soviets couldn't have penetrated us better than Leonard Francis" and "At one time he had infiltrated the entire leadership line" (Helmore, 2022).

The "Fat Leonard" case is that of tacitly satisfying many of the seven deadly sins, cloaked by legitimate US government needs, and funded by the US taxpayer. Shockingly, the costs for the bribery supplies and services were incorporated into GDMA's invoices and paid by the Navy.

## Looking Forward

The extent of personnel involved in the corruption, the magnitude of the economic consequences, and the duration of the deceit raise serious questions for those responsible for ethical supply management. Instances of corruption have occurred as long as the antiquity of commercial trade, but how did the initial instances of corruption grow to an institution of corruption? In an organisation with such mature and extensive procurement statutes, case law, regulations, policies, and oversight bodies (e.g., Inspectors General, Defense Contract Audit Agency, Defense Contract Management Agency, Government Accountability Office (GAO), etc.) such as the US federal government, how can such corruption occur? How can corruption be detected? How can institutional corruption be prevented in the future?

## References

Baldor, L.C. and Watson, J. (2023, 20 December). "'Fat Leonard,' a fugitive now returning to the US, was behind one of the military's biggest scandals." *The Associated Press*. Available at: https://apnews.com/article/fat-leonard-navy-bribery-scandal-venezuela-extradition-57c07f7efdf9e0cbcaad35d04eff3b6e

Helmore, E. (2022, 11 September). "Whiskey, Kobe beef and suckling pig: inside the 'Fat Leonard' navy bribery scandal." *The Guardian*. Available at: www.theguardian.com/us-news/2022/sep/11/fat-leonard-navy-bribes-scandal-explained

Prine, C. (2017). "Dirty cop, Navy moles helped "Fat Leonard" stay ahead of the law for years." *San Diego Tribune*. Available at: www.sandiegotribune.com/military/sd-me-fat-leonard-moles-20170804-story.html

Standifer, C. (2017). "Timeline: The "Fat Leonard" Case." U.S. Naval Institute News. Retrieved from https://news.usni.org/2017/03/16/timeline-fat-leonard-case

U.S. Department of the Treasury, Bureau of the Fiscal Service (2023). USASpending.gov. Washington, DC.

Vyas, K., Radnofsky, L., Viswanatha, A., and Randazzo, S. (2023, 20 December). "'Fat Leonard' handed over to U.S. in prisoner exchange with Venezuela." *Wall Street Journal*. Available at: www.wsj.com/world/americas/fat-leonard-handed-over-to-u-s-in-sweeping-prisoner-exchange-with-venezuela-1b907786

Walsh, S. (2022, 30 June). "A Jury convicts 4 former Navy officers in 'Fat Leonard' bribery trial." *National Public Radio*. Available at: www.npr.org/2022/06/30/1108843844/a-jury-convicts-4-former-navy-officers-in-fat-leonard-bribery-trial

Whiteley, J.T., Foster, J.A., and Johnson, K.A. (2017). "Contracting for Navy Husbanding Services: An Analysis of the Fat Leonard Case." *Acquisition Research Program* NPS-CM-18-016, Naval Postgraduate School, Monterey, CA.

# 14 Transparency and Accountability in Public Procurement

*Clifford McCue, Eric Prier and Tünde Tátrai*

## 14.1 Introduction

Transparency and accountability anchor democratic regimes. Yet, according to Etzioni (2014), simply being transparent is not necessarily sufficient for citizens to be engaged with oversight of elected officials, executive officers, public administrators, and even public procurement practitioners. He contends, "many other problems cannot be effectively treated by merely releasing information and leaving it up to the public to take action" (p. 688). Therefore, democratic regimes employ costly regulations to produce accountability and actionable justifications.[1]

Holding public officials accountable for their actions and inactions implies that there is "a relationship between an actor and a forum, in which the actor has an obligation to explain and to justify his or her conduct, the forum can pose questions and pass judgement, and the actor may face consequences" (Bovens, 2007, p. 450; though see Riese, 2023 on substantive justifications for secrecy). However, the "forum" encompasses numerous competing stakeholder interests in need of resolution. According to McCue, Prier and Swanson (2015), the trade-offs between transparency, regulation, and accountability create what they coined the fraud–red tape dilemma in public procurement. To constrain corruption opportunities, mismanagement, and/or malfeasance, public procurement practitioners confront numerous rules and regulations to conform with legalistic outcomes and thereby reduce discretionary decision-making. This risk-aversion requires public procurement officials (PPOs) to follow the "rules" when balancing competing stakeholder demands.

The fraud-red tape dilemma creates an agency problem whereby the PPO is an agent who must navigate regulations across all stakeholders, operate in the "sunshine", and promote economy and efficiency (best value), while acting in the best interests of others (principals). Under this common agency situation, PPOs are agents of many often-competing principals (elected officials, department heads, vendors, media, and the public). Consequently, identifying to whom a procurement official is accountable and then specifying for what the official is to be held accountable is an ambiguous and constant balancing act.

Similar to the fraud/red tape dilemma, in the public procurement setting, there is often a delicate balance between accountability and efficiency, and navigating this balance involves trade-offs. Accountability is crucial to ensure transparency, fairness, and responsible use of public funds, while efficiency is essential to optimize resources, minimize costs, and deliver services promptly. While accountability and efficiency are both important goals, there can be inherent tensions between them. For example, stringent accountability measures, such as extensive documentation requirements, multiple oversight layers, and lengthy approval

DOI: 10.4324/9781003566670-16

processes, can potentially slow down procurement timelines and increase administrative costs, thereby hampering efficiency. This situation can also increase costs on the supply side by increasing compliance costs and lead delivery times. Conversely, efforts to streamline processes and prioritize efficiency may inadvertently compromise transparency, fairness, or compliance with regulations, potentially leading to accountability concerns. To strike an appropriate balance, public procurement systems should be carefully designed and continuously reevaluated.

This chapter provides an overview of the current state of knowledge on public procurement in terms of the relationship between transparency and accountability. It begins by identifying key concepts, scholarship, and contexts under which PPOs address procurement transparency and accountability. Finally, this chapter highlights emerging issues and practical applications and provides a case study titled "Reversely Transparent" contracts.

## 14.2 Contextualizing Transparency and Accountability in Public Procurement

According to Fox (2007), there are myriad ways to define transparency and accountability in public procurement, but for the purpose of this chapter, these two concepts are examined based on Dawson and Maricut-Akbik's (2021) procedural and substantive dimensions. Approaching both transparency and accountability in this light requires four elements: (1) how the public is informed of government procurement actions, regardless if the public uses that information or not (procedural transparency), (2) the justification of government's actions to the public relative to their procurement actions or inactions (substantive transparency), (3) how governments, including elected and appointed officials, are held accountable for their actions or inactions (structural accountability), and (4) how public officials follow the rules and regulations (procedural accountability). Table 14.1 summarizes these dimensions.

### *14.2.1 Procedural Transparency*

Governments across the globe have made admirable advances in procurement procedural transparency. Not only can the public access procurement information, but they can also readily see how a government is operating in the sunshine. Some important innovations include open procurement initiatives (most of which promote open data availability), adopting "sunshine" laws, and posting contracting opportunities and processes on the web. Each of these is discussed below.

*Table 14.1* Systematizing transparency and accountability in public procurement

| | *Procedural* | *Substantive* |
|---|---|---|
| Transparency | Mapping procurement officials' stepwise constraints: the processes by which procurement decisions are made are open to public scrutiny | Mapping procurement officials' behavioral conduct: procurement information is made readily accessible so stakeholders understand their rights and responsibilities |
| Accountability | Procurement officials justify compliance with the prevailing rules and regulations | Procurement officials explain the quality and characteristics of their decisions |

*Source*: Adapted from Deighton-Smith (2004) and Dawson and Maricut-Akbik (2021).

#### *14.2.1.1 Open Procurement Initiatives – Open Records*

Open government, which applies to procurement, is "a culture of governance that promotes the principles of transparency, integrity, accountability and stakeholders' participation in support of democracy and inclusive growth" (OECD, 2017).

According to Transparency International (TI, 2015), governments that ensure transparency throughout the entire procurement process enable "processes and decisions to be monitored and reviewed, helps ensure that decision-makers can be held accountable and also helps open public procurement to more competition" (p. 1). Therefore, transparency requires an open procurement process that is readily accessible by all stakeholders, "unless there are valid and legal reasons to keep certain information confidential" (OECD, n.d.).

The benefits of public procurement transparency include the following:

- Performance enhancement through open data that contribute to improving public procurement efficiency by providing stakeholders access to all procurement processes and decisions. Resultant cross-sector sharing of data can help identify procurement problems.
- Easier access to procurement information, rules, and regulations – all of which may contribute to developing innovative services and creating new business models.
- Social welfare improvement because society benefits from knowing how government is spending public resources via open data: this enhances collaboration, participation, and social innovation.[2]

Sweden is perhaps the first nation to grant public access to government information. In 1766, the Swedish parliament passed a constitutional amendment, which granted the press access to all official archives of the state.[3] A more recent example of providing access to government information is the Freedom of Information Act (FOIA) adopted by the U.S. federal government in 1966. According to Suzanne Piotrowski (2007, pp. 21–43), the U.S. national government was a "pioneer" in passing legislation that promoted procedural transparency by providing the public access to all documents held by executive branch agencies, and the public can request access to those documents, including procurement records, from any federal agency. Around the same time, similar legislation can be found in the various states and is often referred to as "sunshine laws".[4]

### *14.2.2 Open Meetings*

According to Chance and Locke (2008), in 1967, the Florida Legislature passed what is coined the "Sunshine Law", which mandates that, with a few exceptions, procurement meetings shall be open to the public through proper notification (prepublicity). The authors contend that most "open meetings laws contribute to a less corrupt, more efficient government and encourage more accurate news reporting" (p. 246).

Since public procurement must be conducted in a way that is transparent and respectful of the rights of the parties involved, commercial confidentiality, data protection rules, and efficiency, the following information is typically available to all in public procurement:

- Preliminary contract notices;
- Contract notices, main procedural documents;
- Contract award notices;
- Contracts concluded as a result of the procedure and any amendments thereto;
- Information and notices concerning the performance of contracts;

- Decisions on appeals relating to the procedure.

The procedure remains transparent on several levels, such as maintaining access to the bids of competitors and characteristics of the winning bid, among other things. Simultaneously, all monitoring bodies should have access to all information generated during the procedure, including sensitive information as indicated by Piotrowski and Borry (2010).

### *14.2.3 Substantive Transparency*

Promoting substantive transparency is essential to prevent corruption, encourage competition, demonstrate integrity within the procurement process, and ultimately foster trust in government procurement. Substantive transparency involves providing detailed and specific information about a process, decision, and/or action resulting from acquiring the needed goods, services, and works for government. This information should be sufficient for stakeholders to grasp the context, rationale, and implications of what is being disclosed. Deighton-Smith (2004) contends that advancements in substantive transparency include the following:

- Adoption of more public and more extensive consultation processes;
- Providing better information to support consultation;
- Increased use of independent appeals processes;
- Increasing importance of international trade rules in promoting transparency requirements; and
- Electronic access to legislation and related documentation.

In addition to providing meaningful information to all stakeholders, substantive transparency requires procedural systems and remedies that provide stakeholders opportunities to seek recourse when real or perceived violations occur. For example, the state of Arkansas' FOIA clearly states "[a]ny person who negligently violates any provisions of this [act] shall be guilty of a Class C misdemeanor", while in Idaho, the "court shall award reasonable costs and attorney fees to the prevailing party or parties, if it finds that the request or refusal to provide records was frivolously pursued". Five common ways public procurement agencies promote substantive transparency include:

- Publication of procurement data: Detailed procurement information, including solicitation documents, contract awards, and procurement plans, on publicly accessible platforms. Easy stakeholder access for the public, suppliers, and civil society organizations is key, and open data standards should be employed to ensure information is machine-readable and easily analyzed. According to Oyegoke (2012), making contracts publicly accessible helps identify potential issues and ensures compliance with the terms of the agreement.
- Transparent procurement processes: Guidelines ensuring stakeholders understand how procurement decisions are made. This includes specifying evaluation criteria and each component's weight (importance) in the decision-making process, the composition of evaluation committees, and anticipated timelines in each contractual stage.
- Public disclosure of contracts: After a contract is awarded, all contract documents shall be readily available. This includes the terms and conditions, pricing details, and any relevant amendments made during the contracting process.
- Supplier registration and prequalification: Maintaining a publicly accessible database of registered suppliers and their prequalification status should include details on supplier

qualifications, past performance, and any sanctions or disqualifications. This ensures that only qualified suppliers participate in the procurement process.
- Stakeholder engagement and consultation: Procurement agencies can actively engage with stakeholders, including civil society organizations, industry associations, and the public, at various stages of the procurement process. This can involve seeking input on procurement policies, conducting public consultations on major procurements, and encouraging feedback on procurement practices.

In addition to these methods, it's essential for public procurement agencies to have effective oversight mechanisms, such as audit and monitoring processes, to ensure compliance with transparency standards. Implementing these strategies promotes substantive transparency, enhances accountability, and fosters public trust in the procurement process.

### *14.2.4 Limitations of Transparency*

While many governments have become more transparent by providing web-based access to their procurement rules and regulations, stakeholders differ in their capacity to understand them. For example, while there is easy access to regulations governing U.S. federal government contracting (see Federal Acquisition Regulation, or FAR), FAR is over 2,000 pages long and extremely complex, and this accessibility and complexity is repeated for the European Union (EU) and most local-level procurement agencies. Given the vast amount of available information, piecing it all together is done by very few stakeholders who really understand what is occurring in practice – all of which results in less substantive transparency. For example, three European Directives[5] deal with public procurement, complemented by numerous policy documents across the EU. These highly detailed Directives are implemented by the Member States and are the subject of national rules. In fact, the specificities of national rules require the involvement of national experts in each case, which means that overall public procurement rules in Europe are diverse and complex.

Consequently, governmental transparency is necessary but not sufficient for accountability.

## 14.3 Accountability in Public Procurement

Many scholars have addressed accountability in public procurement (Arrowsmith, 2003; Oyegoke, 2012) and have generally concluded that transparency alone will not solve all public procurement issues. A good example is Coppier and Piga (2006), who argue that countries that adopt more "transparent procurement", as calculated by the share of solicitations advertised publicly, are also the ones where corruption is considered more pervasive. Nonetheless, many methods and tools can reduce corruption using available public records (Soylu et al., 2022; Tátrai and Németh, 2018).

According to the United Nations Transparency and Accountability Initiative (UNTAI), better accountability structures increase the availability and accuracy of information provided publicly, solidify oversight and ethics systems, and bolster financial management and governance practices.[6] However, secrecy may occasionally be used to protect patent information from businesses that submit bids on government contracts or during times of war and other security threats.

The UNTAI suggests that to promote procedural accountability, governments should consider the following:

- Making available internal audits and other reports, evaluations, investigations, etc.;
- Providing access to all relevant documentation related to operations and activities, including budget information and procurement activities;

- Publicizing financial disclosure policies; and
- Providing transparent administrative support costs for voluntarily funded activities.

The UNTAI also recommends that nations bolster their substantive accountability structures by the following:

- Establishing "Whistleblower Protection" policies;
- Establishing an effective Ethics Office;
- Ensuring independence of internal oversight bodies; and
- Adopting the International Public Sector Accounting Standards (IPSAS) for government financial systems.

### *14.3.1 Procedural Accountability*

In terms of accountability, PPO management of the procurement process influences public trust, and tools that help include codes of conduct, conflict of interest policies, ethical standards, whistleblower policies, effective internal and external controls, independent audits, and professional training of procurement staff.

#### *14.3.1.1 Ethics Code*

According to the Organization for Economic Cooperation and Development (OECD, n.d., pp. 1–2), clear expectations of PPO conduct can increase public confidence in procurement outcomes. In addition to transparency and accountability, behavioral standards often include serving the public interest by maintaining and strengthening trust and confidence in public institutions through professional competence, efficiency and effectiveness, and upholding legal principles. In addition, public officials are expected to make decisions and act without consideration of their private interests. Improperly using one's office for private gain is a serious breach of professional integrity and is to be avoided. Thus, legitimate use of delegated public authority requires exercising power impartially without fear or favor by considering only the merits of the matter. In other words, official decisions and actions taken are done in a fair and equitable manner that are "responsive to the legitimate interests and needs of the government, public organizations, other civil servants, and citizens in a timely manner". Moreover, this should all be done efficiently to obtain the best value in the expenditure of public funds that results in effective public management.

#### *14.3.1.2 Whistleblower Policies*

Whistleblowers provide an essential function in maintaining the integrity of the procurement process and holding anyone involved in the procurement process accountable for their actions or inactions. A whistleblower is anyone, including government employees, (sub) contractors and/or their employees, and personal services contractors who disclose fraud, corruption, malfeasance, or any illegal activity, including activities that present a danger to public health and safety.

Most whistleblower policies establish protections for anyone who reports factual violations of an established procurement rule or regulation. These protections ensure that a whistleblower is free from any form of reprisal, including taking, failing to take, or threatening to take a personnel action, such as firing, demoting, or otherwise discriminating against the whistleblower.

#### *14.3.1.3 Cone-of-Silence*

Governments protecting the integrity of the procurement process can impose a cone-of-silence on all solicitations that are publicly advertised. The cone-of-silence requires all communication with the government regarding an active solicitation by any bidders or proposers, or their representatives, to be in writing. For example, if a bidder had a substantive clarification question about a requirement identified in the solicitation document, they are required to submit the question in writing, typically, to the Chief Procurement Official (CPO). If the CPO determines that clarification is needed, an addendum is issued and posted so all bidders have equal access to the clarification. In essence, imposing a cone-of-silence prevents bidders, or anyone acting on their behalf, from attempting to influence an agency procurement decision after the solicitation is posted. This includes direct lobbying of any employee or officer of the executive or legislative branch, as well as indirect lobbying (this occurs, for example, when the bidder asks their neighbor, who happens to be the campaign director for the Mayor, to speak to the Mayor on their behalf).

The cone-of-silence typically applies to the following:

1. Publicly advertised pre-bid or proposal meetings;
2. Any proposed site inspections;
3. Emergency procurements;
4. Written or verbal contact with government attorneys or their staff;
5. Sole-source procurements;
6. Oral presentations before selection/evaluation committees and communications occurring during advertised meetings of a selection/evaluation committee;
7. Competitive negotiations;
8. Public presentations to elected or appointed officials; and
9. Contract negotiations.

#### *14.3.1.4 Oversight Bodies*

Regulatory or supervisory bodies play a central role in ensuring the integrity of procurement procedural transparency through monitoring, regulating, and enforcing contracting rules and procedures. Four common accountability methods include the following:

1. Monitoring and compliance: Conducting independent audits or investigations when necessary to assess compliance and identify any illegal activities or mismanagement;
2. Enforcement: Identifying violations and then enforcing penalties or sanctions against the offending parties;
3. Conflict resolution: Mediating and/or arbitrating disputes related to procedural matters. In fact, good specifications will normally include provisions that require mediation or arbitration prior to formal judicial consideration;
4. Reporting: Many oversight boards are required to issue periodic reports on their activities and findings – see, for example, the European Union's Single Market Scoreboard (https://single-market-scoreboard.ec.europa.eu/_en). These reports often include information on compliance, violations, enforcement actions, and recommendations for improvement.

Oversight boards are instrumental in upholding procedural transparency by creating and identifying violations and enforcing penalties via monitoring – all of which may improve procurement rules and regulations. They ensure that procedures are conducted in a transparent, accountable, and fair manner, benefiting both the governments they oversee and the public they serve.

### *14.3.2 Substantive Accountability*

Public procurement agencies promote substantive accountability through four common practices, including:

1. Full and open competition: Efficiency and effectiveness gains from government contracting can accrete from purchasing scale, thus reducing prices and enhancing the quality of goods and services purchased. This ultimately results in better value for money (VFM), since more bidders provide a wider choice for the procurement agency when awarding a contract (see, for example, Lofaro et al., 2023).
2. Conflict of interest policies: Buffington and Flynn (2004) explain how conflict of interest policies help prevent undue influence or bias in the procurement process. Staff members and suppliers involved in the procurement process are often required to disclose any real or potential conflicts and, if such a conflict exists, recuse themselves.
3. Performance monitoring and reporting: After contracts are awarded, monitoring and reporting contractor adherence to contractual terms and conditions is important. These reports are then included in the contract files and, under "sunshine" requirements, are open to public scrutiny.
4. Sanctions and penalties: If misconduct or non-compliance with contractual conditions and specifications is identified, sanctions and/or penalties may be imposed on suppliers, employees, or contractors responsible for the violations. In terms of suppliers or contractors, this could include disbarment.

By implementing these common practices and mechanisms, public procurement agencies can promote substantive accountability in their operations, thereby enhancing trust, reducing corruption, and ensuring that taxpayer funds are used efficiently and effectively.

### *14.3.3 Accountability Limitations*

Although the various instruments previously discussed are critical for promoting accountability in public procurement, there are several limitations and challenges that can impede the effectiveness of these efforts. For example, best practices suggest limiting interference (and potential engagement) of elected officials in procurement decisions, yet this may happen often, especially when one party dominates the political landscape for a long time (see Broms et al., 2019, p. 1287). Unsurprisingly, this is tied to resource constraints because many and perhaps a majority of public procurement agencies typically lack sufficient resources, professional expertise, and/or time to conduct business commensurate with best practices. This can result in inadequate oversight to identify potential remedies for contract failures. In addition, individuals responsible for oversight may lack necessary training and skills to effectively navigate complex procurement regulations and identify irregularities.

Numerous limits exist for encompassing such a multifaceted undertaking as procuring huge variation in obtaining goods, works, and services within a transparent system that should account for broad and deep variability in what is needed to produce the "public good". Public procurement involves multiple stages, goals, and stakeholders embedded within a highly regulated and complex process. This complexity can make it difficult to establish clear, noncontradictory objectives and oversight – all leading to confusion and potential gaps in accountability. And, as noted previously, this situation can be exacerbated by resource constraints and restricted procurement workforce capabilities.

## 14.4 Transparency and Accountability in Developing Nations

Public procurement transparency and accountability elements face significant hurdles in many developing nations due to a combination of institutional weaknesses, resource constraints, and sociocultural factors. For example, weak governance frameworks, inadequate legal and regulatory structures, and limited institutional capacity pose major challenges. Many developing countries lack robust procurement laws, effective oversight mechanisms, and well-established systems for monitoring and auditing procurement activities. Furthermore, a shortage of skilled procurement professionals, limited training programs, and inefficient information management systems can undermine transparency and accountability efforts. Political interference, corruption, and deep-rooted cultural norms that promote nepotism or disregard for transparency can also hinder fair and open procurement processes. Additionally, restricted access to information, limited public participation opportunities, and capacity constraints of civil society organizations and independent media can impede external scrutiny and public oversight of procurement activities.

Despite these constraints, the OECD (n.d.) highlights a number of developing nations committed to accountable procurement practices. In Argentina, the Argentina Compra – Public procurement website of the Argentinian National Public Administration ensures free access for all stakeholders to public procurement information, while Mexico is increasing transparency in public procurement through the introduction of the Open Contracting Data Standard.

Developing nations also face significant resource constraints that can hamper their ability to invest in robust public procurement systems, implement advanced technologies like e-procurement platforms, and establish comprehensive training and capacity-building programs. Financial limitations can also restrict the allocation of funds for monitoring and evaluation mechanisms, as well as the development of effective complaint and redress systems. In fragile or conflict-affected states, the challenges are further exacerbated by breakdowns in institutional structures, relaxed commitment to the rule of law, and degraded governance systems, making it even more difficult to establish and/or recover transparent and accountable procurement practices.

Process mechanisms that promote accountability and transparency in public procurement are critical for developing nations as they contribute to combating corruption, fostering economic growth and investment, ensuring effective resource allocation, improving public service delivery, and strengthening citizen trust in government institutions. Addressing the challenges and prioritizing these principles can significantly enhance the overall governance and development outcomes in these countries.

## 14.5 Emerging Issues

The latest research and practical developments suggest at least five emerging issues regarding procurement transparency and accountability, which include the following:

1. **Circular procurement and sustainable practices:** In contrast to traditional procurement emphases on cost, quality, and timeliness, circular procurement reprioritizes procurement efforts toward waste minimization and resource conservation by promoting the reuse, repair, and recycling of materials. In the face of rising economic and social costs

associated with resource depletion, intensifying political instability, and supply-chain disruptions across the globe, circular procurement is an emerging issue in public procurement that focuses on the entire lifecycle of products and services in ways that prioritize sustainability and resource efficiency through several key principles, including reuse and refurbishment rather than single-use replacement, recycling and recovery to inhibit negative environmental impacts, and innovative collaboration between suppliers, government agencies, and other stakeholders (for beginning discussions, see Xu et al., 2022; also Jones et al., 2017).

However, ensuring transparency and accountability in sustainable procurement requires tracking and verifying the environmental impact of products and services, which poses challenges in terms of data collection and verification. For example, governments may not always provide clear explanations or justifications for their procurement decisions, especially regarding why certain suppliers or green products were chosen over others. This lack of transparency can raise suspicions about favoritism or corruption.

Effective circular procurement requires collaboration with various stakeholders, including suppliers, environmental organizations, and communities. Failure to engage these stakeholders can lead to decisions that overlook important perspectives and priorities. To effectively engage with stakeholders, government procurement agencies should not only develop clear policies and guidelines that prioritize green procurement and environmental sustainability but also engage in educating the public, explaining why circular procurement is beneficial from a long-run perspective.

Unfortunately, governments may engage in greenwashing – presenting themselves as more environmentally friendly than they are in actuality – by exaggerating their green procurement efforts or misrepresenting the environmental benefits of their practices. Under these conditions, citizens, elected officials, and other stakeholders may face challenges in accessing relevant information about government procurement processes and sustainable practices. This lack of access can hinder oversight and accountability efforts. Therefore, robust monitoring and reporting mechanisms are required since it can be challenging to assess whether government green procurement goals are being achieved.

An additional transparency risk from engaging in circular procurement processes is its inherent complexity that can extensively challenge procurement practitioners and lead to stakeholder confusion due to unfamiliarity with sustainability concepts and lack of access to appropriate information. In turn, this can create market asymmetries whereby suppliers with more expertise and resources can gain greater market share and lock out smaller suppliers who can consistently match these capabilities. Moreover, these hazards are likely exacerbated in developing nations that typically have fewer resources and lighter professional procurement capabilities. Taken together, these vulnerabilities may effectively hinder stakeholder accountability by creating new challenges for understanding and evaluating public procurement decisions.

2. **Artificial Intelligence (AI)**: Advancement in technologies presents both opportunities and challenges for procurement transparency and accountability. AI has the potential to transform procurement by providing instant access to open data for journalists, researchers, and civil society that can be used to monitor, evaluate, and critique how governments are using public resources. Currently AI-powered contract analytics tools, for example, can automatically review and analyze procurement contracts to ensure compliance with regulations, identify risks, and highlight areas for improvement. AI can streamline the process of evaluating bids by automatically analyzing bid documents, assessing compliance with requirements, and identifying the most suitable bids based on predefined criteria. Additionally, AI-powered monitoring systems can track procurement transactions

in real-time, flagging potential issues or deviations from established procedures. This allows government agencies to intervene promptly, address identified areas of concern, and maintain accountability throughout the procurement process.

While AI has the potential to enhance government transparency and accountability, there are several challenges that should be addressed prior to adopting AI technology in public procurement. Currently, one of the major areas of concern is algorithmic bias. Research has shown that AI algorithms may unintentionally perpetuate or even exacerbate existing biases present in government and private datasets. For example, the situation of choosing a supplier exhibits numerous similarities with hiring an employee, and there is a large and growing literature that algorithmic bias often results in discriminatory hiring practices (see Chen, 2023). Consequently, these biases are likely to be mirrored in public procurement processes, especially if large language models are used to create the algorithms that might be utilized in supplier selection and vendor qualification. If these biases go unchecked, they can lead to unfair or discriminatory outcomes that undermine transparency and accountability.

Another area of concern is data privacy. AI systems often require access to large amounts of data, including sensitive personal information. Improper handling or misusing these data can violate citizens' privacy rights and raise concerns about government surveillance, hindering transparency efforts. AI systems may also inadvertently exclude or disadvantage marginalized groups if the training data used to develop these systems does not adequately represent their experiences or needs. This exclusion can perpetuate existing inequalities and limit the effectiveness of transparency initiatives in reaching all segments of society. Moreover, AI systems used for government transparency initiatives may be vulnerable to cyberattacks or malicious manipulation. If these systems are compromised, it can lead to the dissemination of false or misleading information, undermining public trust in government transparency efforts.

3. **Complex procurement structures**: Many governments are using increasingly complex procurement structures, such as public–private partnerships (PPPs) and outsourcing arrangements. Ensuring transparency and accountability in these arrangements can be challenging, as they involve multiple stakeholders and layers of decision-making. For example, promoting transparency and accountability in complicated public procurement structures requires a comprehensive approach, including establishing clear and comprehensive regulations and guidelines that outline transparent procedures, criteria for evaluation, and accountability mechanisms. In addition, relevant stakeholders, including government agencies, suppliers, civil society organizations, and the public, can be engaged through consultations, feedback mechanisms, and other transparency initiatives.

   However, the intricacy associated with complex procurement structures involving multiple stages, stakeholders, and regulations can make it challenging to ensure transparency and accountability at every step. Moreover, how decisions are made in blended and composite procurement structures often involves multiple actors across various departments, businesses, legal advisors, and financial institutions, leading to fragmented accountability and difficulties in coordination. Add to this the notion of information asymmetry, where disparities in information between procuring entities and suppliers may lead to unfair advantages or manipulation, and the result may be the potential for undermining transparency and fairness in the procurement process.
4. **Corruption and bribery**: Corruption and bribery remain persistent issues and present significant challenges in public procurement, undermining transparency, fairness, and

efficiency. Indeed, according to the OECD (n.d.), some of the risks to public procurement related to transparency include the following:

a. Cases of mismanagement, fraud, and corruption related to the lack of transparency and disclosure of information around public procurement processes;
b. Distorted competition in case interested suppliers do not have access to the same type of information;
c. A decrease of public confidence and trust in governments in case goods and services are poor quality, inappropriate or costly or if information on public procurement processes is lacking.

Overall, instances of corruption in public procurement erode public trust in government institutions and undermine confidence in the integrity of the procurement process. This can have long-term consequences for governance and democratic accountability. For example, corruption and bribery can distort decision-making processes, leading to the selection of suppliers based on improper considerations such as kickbacks or personal connections rather than merit or VFM, oftentimes resulting in public funds wasted on overpriced or substandard goods and services, resulting in lower quality outcomes for taxpayers.

Addressing these challenges requires a multifaceted approach, including strengthening legal and regulatory frameworks, enhancing transparency and accountability mechanisms, promoting integrity and ethical behavior, building institutional capacity, and fostering a culture of zero tolerance for corruption.

5. **Capacity building:** Adequate provision of training and capacity-building programs for procurement officials is required to enhance their understanding of transparency principles, ethical standards, and best practices in procurement management – all of which are necessary to address the four major concerns discussed above. Training programs, for example, can educate procurement officials about relevant laws, regulations, and policies governing public procurement. This knowledge helps ensure compliance with legal requirements and can raise awareness of ethical issues by promoting standards and principles such as integrity, fairness, and impartiality that are essential for maintaining transparency and accountability in procurement.

   Training programs can help procurement officials identify and mitigate risks related to corruption, fraud, and other integrity issues in procurement. By understanding potential vulnerabilities in the procurement process, officials can implement appropriate control measures to safeguard against misconduct. Coupling this with training on the use of technology, such as e-procurement systems, electronic bidding platforms, and data analytics tools, helps procurement officials learn how to leverage these technologies to enhance transparency and accountability in procurement processes.

   Overall, training plays a critical role in building the capacity of procurement officials, promoting ethical behavior, and fostering a culture of transparency and accountability in public procurement. By investing in training initiatives, governments can strengthen their procurement systems and enhance public trust in the integrity of the procurement process.

Addressing these emerging issues in public procurement transparency and accountability will require an inclusively proactive approach, including the development of new regulations and standards, investments in technology and data management, and continued collaboration between governments, industry, civil society, and international organizations to adapt to the changing landscape of procurement practices.

## 14.6 Practical Applications

How to promote transparency and accountability in public procurement? Here are some suggestions that are worth discussing with students and developing their own guidelines of conduct. This list can be extended freely, while some suggestions may be omitted, depending on the students' choice:

1. Implement open and competitive bidding processes to allow multiple suppliers to submit bids for government contracts. This ensures that contracts are awarded based on merit rather than favoritism.
2. Use e-procurement platforms that provide transparency by publishing procurement documents, bid information, and contract awards online. This allows stakeholders to track the entire procurement process.
3. Develop clear and comprehensive procurement guidelines and procedures that are easily accessible to all stakeholders. Ensure that these guidelines are consistently followed in all procurement activities.
4. Create online portals and databases where all procurement-related structured information, including contract details, supplier performance, and procurement plans, is available for public scrutiny and download.
5. Implement a system for supplier prequalification to ensure that only qualified and reputable suppliers are eligible to bid on contracts. This reduces the risk of contract failure.
6. Establish independent oversight bodies or agencies responsible for monitoring and auditing procurement processes. These bodies can investigate irregularities and ensure compliance with procurement laws and regulations.
7. Implement whistleblower protection mechanisms to encourage individuals to report corruption, fraud, or unethical practices in public procurement without fear of retaliation.
8. Regularly assess and evaluate the performance of suppliers and contractors to ensure they meet contractual obligations and quality standards. Make this information publicly available.
9. Require all procurement officials to disclose any potential conflicts of interest and establish mechanisms to manage such conflicts when they arise.
10. Ensure that the budget allocated for procurement is transparent and that it aligns with the government's overall fiscal and development goals.
11. Incorporate social and environmental responsibility criteria into procurement decisions to promote sustainable and ethical practices among suppliers.
12. Provide training and capacity-building programs for procurement officials to enhance their knowledge of procurement rules and ethical standards.
13. Require suppliers to provide performance bonds or guarantees to ensure that they fulfill their contractual obligations. These bonds can be used to compensate the government in case of default.
14. Conduct regular internal and external audits of procurement activities and publish audit reports for public review. Ensure that audit findings lead to corrective actions.
15. Involve the public and relevant stakeholders in the procurement process by seeking their input on procurement plans, priorities, and decision-making.
16. Any amendments or changes to contracts should be made transparent and subject to scrutiny to prevent hidden modifications that favor specific suppliers.
17. Continuously monitor and benchmark procurement practices against international best practices and adapt them as necessary to improve transparency and accountability.

## Notes

1 Linking transparency with accountability is not confined to democratic regimes. For example, error-free information dissemination in undemocratic regimes can shape public discussion and frame policy discourse (see Gunitsky, 2015), and while this may be thought of as transparency, it is often accompanied by informational omissions designed to lead to public misperceptions that may induce autocratic regime stability (also see Stiglitz, 2003). Indeed, Matheus and Janssen (2020) identify potential negative effects of transparency in their study of the literature.

2 European Commission (n.d.), What Is Open Data? Retrieved September 5, 2023 from https://data.europa.eu/en/dataeuropa-academy/what-open-data

3 The passage in the Swedish parliament of "His Majesty's Gracious Ordinance Relating to Freedom of Writing and of the Press" in 1766 abolished censorship of books and newspapers and required authorities to provide public access to all official records.

4 According to the Office of the Attorney General of Florida, the roots of the Sunshine Law began when the Florida legislature passed the Public Records Law in 1909 (see "The 'Sunshine' Law | My Florida Legal." www.myfloridalegal.com/open-government/the-quotsunshinequot-law (accessed August 30, 2023)).

5 Public Procurement Directives (2014) Directive 2014/24/EU of the European Parliament and of the Council of 26 February 2014 on public procurement and repealing Directive 2004/18/EC; Directive 2014/25/EU of the European Parliament and of the Council of 26 February 2014 on procurement by entities operating in the water, energy, transport, and postal services sectors and repealing Directive 2004/17/EC.

6 UNTAI did not differentiate between procedural and substantive accountability (see for example, de Fine Licht, 2014; Heald, 2012).

## References

Arrowsmith, S. (2003). Transparency in government procurement—the objectives of regulation and the boundaries of the WTO. *Journal of World Trade*, 37(2): 283–304.

Bovens, M. (2007). Analysing and assessing accountability: a conceptual framework. *European Law Journal*, 13: 447–468.

Broms, R., Dahlström, C., & Fazekas, M. (2019). Political competition and public procurement outcomes. *Comparative Political Studies*, 52(9): 1259–1292.

Buffington, K. W., and Flynn, M. (2004). *The Legal Aspects of Public Purchasing*, 2nd edition. Herndon, VA: National Institute of Governmental Purchasing.

Chance, S. F., & Locke, C. (2008). The government-in-the-sunshine law then and now: model for implementing new technologies consistent with Florida's position as leader in open government. *Florida State University Law Review*, 35(2): 245–270.

Chen, Z. (2023). Ethics and discrimination in artificial intelligence-enabled recruitment practices. *Humanities and Social Sciences Communications*, 10(567): 1–12.

Coppier, R., & Piga, G. (2006). Why do transparent public procurement and corruption go hand in hand?. *Rivista di Politica Economica*, 96(1/2): 185.

Dawson, M., and Maricut-Akbik, A. (2021). Procedural vs substantive accountability in EMU governance: between payoffs and trade-offs, *Journal of European Public Policy*, 28(11): 1707–1726.

de Fine Licht, J. (2014). Transparency actually: how transparency affects public perceptions of political decision-making. *European Political Science Review*, 6(2): 309–330.

Deighton-Smith, R. (2004). Regulatory transparency in OECD countries: overview, trends and challenges. *Australian Journal of Public Administration*, 63: 66–73.

Etzioni, A. (2014). The limits of transparency. *Public Administration Review*, 74(6): 687–688.

Fox, J. (2007) The uncertain relationship between transparency and accountability. *Development in Practice*, 17(4–5): 663–671.

Gunitsky, S. (2015). Corrupting the cyber-commons: social media as a tool of autocratic stability. *Perspectives on Politics*, 13(1): 42–54.

Heald, D. (2012). Why is transparency about public expenditure so elusive? *International Review of Administrative Sciences*, 78(1), 30–49.

Jones, M., Sohn, I. K., & Bendsen, A. L. (2017). Circular Procurement Best Practice Report. ICLEI Europe, SPP Regions (Sustainable Public Procurement Regions) Project Consortium.

Lofaro, R., Boykin, E., McCue, C., & Prier, E. (2023). Year-end spending spikes and single bid procedures: a comparative analysis of public procurement in the European Economic Area. *Public Finance and Management*, 21(2): 135–166.

Matheus, R., & Janssen, M. (2020). A systematic literature study to unravel transparency enabled by open government data: the window theory. *Public Performance & Management Review*, 43(3): 503–534.

McCue, C., Prier, E., & Swanson, D. (2015). Five dilemmas in public procurement. *Journal of Public Procurement*, 15(2): 177–207.

OECD. (2017). Recommendation of the Council on Open Government, Approved by All OECD Member Countries, OECD, Paris, https://legalinstruments.oecd.org/en/instruments/OECD-LEGAL-0438.

OECD. (n.d.). Public Procurement Toolbox. www.oecd.org/governance/procurement/toolbox/principlestools/transparency/

Oyegoke, A. S. (2012). Transparency in public procurement: a study of the European Union Directive for public works, supply and services contracts. *International Journal of Business Excellence*, 5(3): 195–219.

Piotrowski, S. J. (2007). *Governmental Transparency in the Path of Administrative Reform*. Albany, NY: State University of New York Press.

Piotrowski, S. J., & Borry, E. (2010). An analytic framework for open meetings and transparency. *Public Administration and Manag*ement, 15(1): 138–176.

Riese, D. (2023). Theorising and studying democratic secrecy. In *Executive Secrecy and Democratic Politics: Arguments and Practices in the German Bundestag*, New Perspectives in German Political Studies, ed. Dorothee Riese (pp. 19–53). Cham: Springer Nature Switzerland.

Soylu, A., Corcho, Ó., Elvesæter, B., Badenes-Olmedo, C., Yedro-Martínez, F., Kovacic, M., ..., & Roman, D. (2022). Data quality barriers for transparency in public procurement. *Information*, 13(2): 99.

Stiglitz, J. E. (2003). On liberty, the right to know, and public discourse: the role of transparency in public life. *Globalizing Rights: The Oxford Amnesty Lectures*, 1999: 115–156.

Tátrai, T., & Németh, A. (2018, June). Improving red flag instruments for public procurement. *ERA Forum*, 9 : 267–285.

Transparency International. (2015). Transparency in Public Procurement, G20 Position Paper, May 2015. www.transparency.org/files/content/activity/2015_TI_G20PositionPaper_PublicProcurement.pdf

United Nations. (n.d.). United Nations Transparency and Accountability Initiative. https://2009-2017-usun.state.gov/about/2196/6657.html.

Xu, L., Jia, F., Yan, F., & Chen, L. (2022). Circular procurement: a systematic literature review. *Journal of Cleaner Production*, 365: 132845. doi:10.1016/j.jclepro.2022.132845

### *Case Study – "Reversely Transparent" Contracts (Developed by Clifford McCue, Eric Prier, and Tünde Tátrai)*

#### The Circumstances

The CEO of a state-owned public service provider nervously summoned his colleagues. He even prepared a presentation for the occasion. The title of the presentation was "How can we benefit from public procurement?".

The colleagues looked at the manager inquisitively. They were not used to dealing with issues related to public procurement. This public service provider used to be a private company but was acquired by the state a few years ago. It is now a state-owned company and was legally required to apply the state's public procurement rules. Many colleagues remember the holidays of the previous years. Even then, internal rules were strict; at least three bids had to be requested each time, and there was a relatively high level of free purchasing, which was flexible enough to allow all employees to take home a sufficient amount of stationery for their loved ones.

Nationalization of public service companies was not new in the region, but public service providers were not used to it. The staff employed by the company had worked together for a long time; some had been with the company for more than 20 years, although younger colleagues spent considerably less time with the company, particularly in recent years, which had been helped by the re-nationalization of the company (i.e. its buy-back by the state). In any case, the legislation in the country was in place, and the public procurement market players followed it.

Public companies were also subject to stricter controls to reduce abuses. One of the key pillars of this was full disclosure of public procurement contracts. The public utility had an interest in the energy market and had a number of subsidiaries not only in the region, so its acquisition plans, major investments, and outsourcing solutions were typically not made in public, but information was kept behind closed doors. However, with the introduction of public procurement, all its procedures, their results, appeals processes and the entire contract file became available to any citizen and, of course, to its competitors, with a myriad of consequences.

#### The CEO's Explanation

The manager explained to his staff:

> *I received an analysis written by an independent consultant, in which the data of the competitors all contain estimated values, uncertain elements; we are the only ones with validated data with Datasource and a point-by-point page reference. I would like to ask who has published this data and by what right was all the information put on the Internet so that everyone has access to it?*

The legal director rose to speak, but the director waved him off.

> *I know you are going to say that this is because of public procurement. And so that we can be called to account. We have already had our declarations examined under a microscope, and the Anti-Corruption Authority found everything to be in order. So why do we need to make our most closely guarded secrets public? Give me an answer to that.*

The room was silent; no one had a viable idea. The legal director's co-counsel timidly suggested that in the future only the first pages should be scanned, or in reverse, perhaps in a format too difficult to download.

The manager broke up the meeting after a short reflection, called some lawyer friends, and then summoned the brave brainstormer and instructed him to develop an internal set of rules for the company that would meet the legal requirements but with as little transparency as possible.

### Actions Taken

The document was presented after a series of high-quality technical discussions and was then implemented as a non-public internal guideline. After a year, the members of the Public Procurement Committee met again to discuss the new internal rules and to discuss the strategic issues of public procurement in the company.

A newcomer to the company, a procurement expert, boldly took the floor and challenged in detail the company's publicity practices and then referred to an unnamed document that explicitly confirmed that the company's internal policy was to ensure a minimum level of publicity. The CEO thanked the new colleague very much for his insight, and the meeting was adjourned. The manager had a delicate matter on his hands because the contracts for the "transport of money" had expired, and the winner of the new public procurement procedure was already known, although the procedure had not yet ended; in fact, everyone knew who should win. The content of the contract was sensitive in every respect. The legal department could not justify that the data could not be disclosed for reasons of protection and security. The CEO had spoken to numerous legislators and had prepared a legislative amendment, although he did not forward it, for it would have drawn attention to the problem of the current procedure.

He produced the internal rules a year ago, which still showed in small print his comment that blank pages scanned upside down between properly scanned pages seemed the most acceptable solution to him. Finally, the majority opted for a vaguely scanned file, without an appendix, preferably with a large enough file size.

The available software was already able to handle this problem, and the only solution was to upload a document without content or context. Satisfied, he sat back and issued a verbal instruction to convert the content of the contract concerned. It took days of work. The result was a completely useless and opaque mass of information other than the cover page. The next task of the Public Procurement Committee was to make the company's Annual Procurement Plan untraceable, a job that was made easier. The experienced staff did not leave it to chance, and within a few hours they mixed up and changed the names and types of procedures. Even the CEO himself was delighted with the result.

### The Aftermath

When the year-end bonus was set, the staff of the Public Procurement Committee was given a special reward after watching the CEO's presentation on the usual comparative analysis of the market, which now included estimated figures alongside the firm's name. The young colleague who drew attention to the unlawful practice was given another important opportunity by the company – far away from the head office.

Later, in his conference presentation on the experience of public procurement for public company executives, the CEO highlighted how successfully his company has been able to align competitive market requirements and interests with current public procurement regulations. He also suggested that they would be happy to share their best practices with colleagues on effective and ethical public procurement. The CEO had to wait for the "Public Procurement Officer of the Year" award for two more years, as this was the time needed to standardize the flowerbeds around the company's sites, which the energy company wanted to contribute to sustainability.

The company has welcomed several new managers in its later years, but none of them has touched the internal rules and has continued to support the value-creating work of the Public Procurement Committee.

## Questions

1. How would you describe the procurement culture in the company?
2. What are the objectives of the new state-owned company?
3. How would you prevent the use of similar circumvention techniques as a legislator?
4. In your opinion, is the existence of a whistleblowing system in the company relevant in this case?

Section 3

# The Contracting Cycle

## Managing the Public Procurement Process

# 15 Managing the Procurement Organization

*Darin Matthews*

## 15.1 Introduction

Public procurement has a rich history, perhaps richer than many people realize. While it is difficult to pinpoint an exact date, many scholars note that it can date back some 2,800 years (Callender and Matthews, 2005). China's dealings with parts of Europe included competitive bidding, contract negotiation, and supply management. The Roman armies also performed procurement activities to support their war efforts, including the acceptance of three bids for consideration by the state (Laistner, 1966).

In more modern times, procurement has been viewed as a multi-disciplinary function that interacts with all parts of an organization. This can include key partnerships with risk management, legal, finance, and information technology.

The purpose of this chapter is to introduce some key concepts associated with public procurement and to explore the past, present, and future of this noble profession. The learning objectives for this chapter are as follows:

- Recognize the history of public procurement and its evolution to its current state.
- Describe the recent developments in public procurement including technology advancements impacting the profession.
- Differentiate the functions of strategic and tactical procurement.
- Identify ways to effectively manage the procurement workforce.

Much has been said about the impact that public procurement can have on an organization. Many years ago, Tether stressed the role of procurement is so powerful that it might be considered an implement of social change (Tether, 1977). The ability to make decisions on the purchase of goods, services, and systems is significant. It impacts not only the public agency itself but also the businesses that earn the contracts. Local suppliers and contractors can benefit greatly from the revenue generated by earning a public contract through a competitive procurement process.

In many respects it is quite like private sector procurement. Sound decisions made by procurement and supply chain managers can literally "make or break" a company. For example, negotiating a contract for a key material at a significant cost savings can improve a firm's bottom line. Therefore, procurement plays a crucial and impactful roll in both sectors.

Research has noted the distinctions between public and private sector procurement (Arlbojorn and Freytag, 2012), which are important to keep in mind. These can include the regulatory nature of public procurement, as well as the ethical codes subscribed to by many

DOI: 10.4324/9781003566670-18

in the profession. It should be noted, however, that ethical codes of conduct are provided by both the Institute for Public Procurement (NIGP), as well as the Institute for Supply Management (ISM) representing the private sector.

Of course, public procurement extends worldwide. In 2020, the Public Procurement Professional Association of India (PPPAI) was established to help improve the value-for-money proposition that procurement professionals face. It is estimated that India's annual procurement volume exceeds $700 billion US. Partners and stakeholders of PPPAI include the World Bank, the United Nations (UN), and the International Trade Centre (www.pppai.org).

Another excellent example of professional public procurement in action is the European Union (EU). The contracts awarded by EU agencies and institutions are done so through established tendering practices that promote fairness, competition, and transparency. In many ways, the EU is a global leader in public procurement best practices (https://european-union.europa.eu/live-work-study/public-contracts_en). Even prior to the global pandemic in 2020, many EU members utilized digital procurement systems. Since 2018, the Netherlands has required electronic tendering in the public sector as part of its Dutch Digitalisation Strategy (Nederland, 2021).

### 15.2 Overview of Chapter

This chapter will offer insights on how to best manage the procurement function for an organization. Despite the variety in titles for this role (which include chief procurement officer, procurement director, supply chain manager, and others), there are still some common themes that represent effective strategies and practices in procurement management (Procurious, 2015).

A survey of the existing literature aligned with public procurement will be offered. These include historical publications that have validated procurement's existence, as well as current books and journals from leading organizations in the procurement space.

As with all professions, public procurement continues to evolve. Recent developments in the sector will be noted such as the professionalization of procurement and how it has been impacted by a global pandemic. The chapter will look at the structure of the procurement organization at various levels of government. Federal, state, local, and higher education systems have similarities with procurement structures but unique aspects as well.

Finally, the strategic elements of procurement will be highlighted, along with the importance of its alignment with academia. For all procurement professionals, there are opportunities to effectively apply their knowledge and make a difference, both now and in the future.

### 15.3 Literature Review

In recent decades, public procurement has attempted to better align the profession with higher education. The world of academia is complex, but the inclusion of procurement in education is viewed by many procurement leaders as critical. Whether it is a stand-alone academic program or a required course within a business or public administration degree, public procurement truly needs a "seat at the table."

Perhaps the first book to acknowledge procurement as a profession was published in 1915 by Harry Twyford. Entitled *Purchasing: Its Economic Aspects and Proper Methods* (Twyford, 1915), it highlighted the importance of spending money judiciously. While it characterized those who worked in the field as unimaginative, it nonetheless recognized purchasing (procurement) as a bona fide profession.

The Chartered Institute of Procurement and Supply (CIPS) supports the need for procurement's inclusion within research and education. This inevitably leads to greater recognition of the profession (Nonhoff, 2017). The organization also advocates for the alignment of a procurement strategy with the mission of the organization. This is an example of the advanced maturity of procurement as a profession.

In the mid-2000s, NIGP launched a program that sought an improved partnership with higher education. Learning and Education to Advance Procurement (LEAP) paired procurement practitioners with college professors to develop a new curriculum. This effort resulted in several textbooks on procurement-related topics that are still relevant today. These include such titles as "Strategic Sourcing in the Public Sector," "Legal Aspects of Public Procurement," and "Managing Logistics and Transportation in the Public Sector" (NIGP Bookstore, www.nigp.org).

Public procurement has historically received little mention in academic journals related to public administration, financial management, and supply chain management. This changed in 2000 with the publication of the first issue of the *Journal of Public Procurement.* For the past two decades, the journal has continued to gain acceptance in academic circles by featuring articles on everything from bid protest to social responsibility. Originally published by PrAcademics Press, the Journal of Public Procurement is now offered through Emerald Publishing (www.emeraldgrouppublishing.com/journal/jopp).

Another significant publication is the *International Handbook of Public Procurement*, edited by Dr. Khi Thai of Florida Atlantic University. Published by Routledge of New York in 2009, the book offers an extensive array of topics written by procurement experts around the world. Thai was also the author of *Introduction to Public Procurement*, which was viewed as a foundational text for NIGP, particularly for practitioners new to public procurement. The book offered the generally accepted model of procurement and its three distinct phases, which are planning, sourcing, and contract management. The following figure depicts the past involvement by procurement in the sourcing phase with a call to expand their future role to all phases (Figure 15.1).

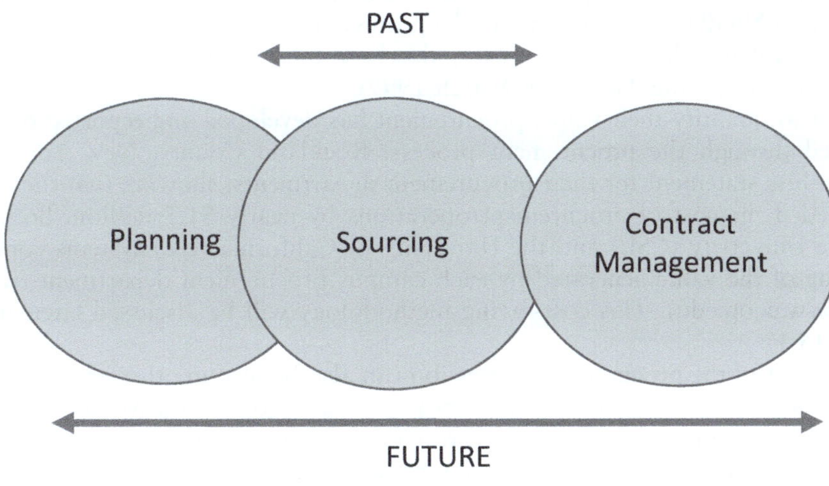


*Figure 15.1* The procurement cycle.
*Source*: Adapted from Introduction to Public Procurement, Khi Thai.

More recently, *Procurement with Purpose* was published in 2021 by Peter Smith and Mark Perara. Both authors are from the UK, and Smith is a former president of the CIPS. Through case studies and shared professional experiences, insights are shared with public procurement peers about the tremendous impact and potential the profession holds. The book focuses on sustainability and explores programs such as supplier diversity, economic impacts, and environmental causes in which procurement professionals play a key role.

Other formidable professional organizations that support the procurement profession are the National Contract Management Association (NCMA) and the National Association of Educational Procurement (NAEP). Each offers a magazine publication for its membership, contract management, and Educational Procurement Journal, respectively. NCMA is aligned with the federal procurement system in the US; so logically, its publication includes topics such as debarment, federal contract compliance, and participation goals established by the Small Business Administration (SBA). Similarly, NAEP's magazine features common challenges faced in higher education, such as inbound campus freight and sustainability goals for universities.

As a US leader within the public procurement ranks, NIGP offers several publication resources to the profession. Offering an extensive list of white papers and global best practices, NIGP continually aligns its guidance based on the current body of procurement knowledge and established best practices. Areas of focus include contract administration, procurement leadership, and policy and legislation. It should be noted that NIGP also publishes an annual salary survey for public sector procurement, as does ISM for private sector salary trends.

The China Council for the Promotion of International Trade (CCPIT) continues to promote an open and transparent system of public procurement. As a key player in international procurement markets, China looks to strengthen its collaboration with other countries and regions. According to the *Asia Times*, in 2020 over 7,000 Chinese suppliers registered to participate in the UN procurement program (Herrero, 2020).

## 15.4 Recent Developments in Procurement

In recent years, public procurement professionals have seen an increased recognition of their value. According to NIGP CEO Rick Grimm, the profession has evolved from a gatekeeper role to that of a strategic player. This shift has also been referred to as going from "controller to collaborator" (Public Purchaser, March 1999).

In an attempt to quantify their value, procurement has developed and reported on cost savings achieved through the procurement process. Rockland County, New York, has created a profit–loss statement for their procurement departments, showing that the value generated exceeded the cost of procurement operations by nearly $1.5 million. Both the California State University (CSU) and the University of California (UC) systems conduct annual reporting of the value generated by each campus procurement department (www.calstate.edu. www.ucop.edu). This cost-saving methodology will be discussed later in the chapter (Table 15.1).

The advancement of the procurement profession can also be seen in other areas, such as organizational placement. For example, the chief procurement officer for Mississippi State University holds the position of associate vice president, which in the past was simply a director. It is not unusual to see the head of procurement at a state or local agency with the title of executive director. This puts them on the same level as their peers in facilities management, information technology, and finance. The chief procurement officer (CPO) typically

*Table 15.1* P/L statement

| | |
|---|---|
| **Department Revenue** – Departmental income, surplus property sales, inter-fund revenues | $386,727 |
| **Cost Containment Activities** – Audit savings, buyer innovation, cost avoidance, energy contract savings, p-card administrative savings, price reductions (contract, PO) | $1,510,637 |
| **Revenue Generating Activities** – Revenue increases through negotiation, rebates negotiated | $86,021 |
| **Gross Profit** – Total savings and revenue generation | $1,986,385 |
| **Direct and Indirect Expenses** – Personnel services, equipment, suppliers, equipment rentals, contractual expenses | $1,473,900 |
| **Net Profit** – Contribution to bottom line | **$512,485** |

*Source*: Adapted from Rockland County, NY.

reports to the top administrative authority for an organization, which is a noticeable change from past practices.

Salaries have also become more competitive in the procurement ranks. Each year, NIGP publishes a salary survey that reports trends at all levels of government. In partnership with the University of Virginia, NIGP looks at average salary levels for various positions (buyer, procurement manager, contract analyst, etc.) based on experience, education, and professional certification. The survey also looks at geographic areas and gender to determine their impacts. According to NIGP, it is not uncommon for a chief procurement officer to earn over $100,000 in base salary (NIGP: Institute for Public Procurement, 2022). For procurement professionals in other sectors, such as retail, automotive, and food service, ISM also publishes an annual salary survey (www.ismworld.com).

Professional certification has long been a part of public procurement. Starting back in the 1960s, the Universal Public Procurement Certification Council (UPPCC) has offered the Certified Public Procurement Official (CPPO) designation, as well as the Certified Professional Public Buyer (CPPB). In 2020, NIGP launched its own certification program, the Certified Procurement Professional (NIGP-CPP). It is competency-based, meaning that candidates apply their knowledge of procurement practices in an exam rather than simply memorizing information. For UPPCC, which is also competency-based, it is known as the Body of Knowledge and Competency (BoKC).

NIGP and UPPCC offer certification programs to a national audience, with each representing generally accepted procurement practices and concepts. Conversely, many states offer certification programs that specifically apply to their own statutes and practices. The following is an example of these state-specific programs (Table 15.2).

## 15.5 Centralization vs. Decentralization

Centralization occurs when a central office retains authority over procurement activity throughout an organization. It doesn't mean that all goods and services are purchased centrally, but ultimately, all activity fall under their authority. A 2022 study by the National Association of State Procurement Officials (NASPO) notes that 77% of organizations maintain a central procurement authority. In many cases, a certain dollar threshold of authority is granted to using departments, which is referred to as delegation of authority (DOA). State and local entities, as well as colleges and universities, are seeing similar trends in centralization. In reality, every organization is a combination of centralized and decentralized procurement authority.

*Table 15.2* State certifications

| *State* | *Certification* |
|---|---|
| Florida | Florida Certified Contract Manager (FCCM) |
| New Jersey | Qualified Purchasing Agent (QPA) |
| Oklahoma | Certified Procurement Officer (CPO) |
| Oregon | Oregon Procurement Advanced Certification (OPAC) |
| Texas | Certified Texas Contract Manager (CTCM) |
| Virginia | Virginia Contracting Officer (VCO) |

*Source*: Original creation.

What is the proper balance of centralization? That is something that each entity must decide for themselves. As an example, a state procurement office might centralize all procurement over a certain bid threshold, say, $100,000. Purchases lower than that amount could be handled by other state offices. The benefits of such an arrangement are plentiful. A central procurement authority can then focus on high-dollar, complex procurements that have a significant impact. Smaller purchases can be handled by the requesting department, which allows them more control and saves them time.

Potential drawbacks of using departments having increased procurement authority include the need for oversight, accountability, and even auditing. When purchasing decisions are made by non-procurement staff, there can be a risk of restrictive specifications and supplier favoritism. Formal training, departmental outreach, and spending monitoring can certainly decrease or eliminate these risks.

## 15.6 Pandemic Impacts

Like other industries around the world, public procurement adjusted its way of doing business with the onset of a global pandemic in 2020. Traditional offices were transitioned to home-based operations, and "working remotely" became commonplace in procurement. Meetings, both internal and external, were held in a digital world through the use of video platforms such as Zoom and Teams. Procurement managers were prompted to engage their staff more frequently online, as the daily in-office interaction did not exist. Staff training and annual evaluations were also done online, requiring increased proficiency with video systems. Even after more than two years of working remotely, standard office environments included a combination of in-office and remote procurement work. These hybrid schedules were managed effectively across many industries, with some sectors requiring their remote workforces to return to the office during 2023. Zoom, a video conferencing company that became a household name during the pandemic, recently directed its workers to return to the office twice a week (Hsu, 2023). It is difficult to determine what the future holds for the procurement workforce, but it seems likely that a combination of in-office and remote work will continue.

A silver lining of the pandemic? It forced procurement leaders to embrace digital technology. Thousands of procurement offices across the country implemented electronic procurement systems in order to receive bids and proposals from their suppliers. Some systems also allow for online evaluation of proposals, which prompted an increase in collaboration between procurement and their evaluation committees. The US has not been as eager to embrace digital procurement as other countries, but the pandemic certainly increased participation. Will the US catch up to The Netherlands, which requires digital procurement for all public offices (European Union, 2024)? Only time will tell.

Many public procurement organizations expanded their role during the pandemic. Out of necessity, procurement professionals managed end-to-end supply chain needs and not merely the procurement of the supplies. In addition to increasing their involvement in warehousing and logistics, state procurement agents began working with international suppliers, import tariffs, and customs brokers (National Association of State Procurement Officials (NASPO), 2021).

## 15.7 Developing a Procurement Workforce

As previously mentioned, public procurement and academia have come a long way in their ability to work effectively together. However, there is still much work to be done in this area. Academic programs with a public procurement focus are relatively few and far between. Some notable programs include the Master Certificate in Public Procurement offered through Florida Atlantic University, School of Public Administration, and the Public Procurement Management certificate program developed by Dr. Alexandru Roman of CSU, San Bernardino. On a positive note, there are many established degree programs, both graduate and undergraduate, that include a course on public procurement. For example, Portland State University includes a Governmental Procurement course as part of its Bachelor of Science in Supply Chain Management (www.pdx.edu).

Today, there are more educational opportunities than ever before for those interested in a public procurement career. Through professional associations and institutions of higher education, training can occur that will be invaluable to the next generation of professionals. In many ways, procurement professionals have historically "fallen into" the profession. But today's generation tends to be purposeful about choosing a career in public procurement by completing relevant degree programs, completing internships, and pursuing opportunities in public service.

In addition to education and technical training, there are many characteristics that can contribute to the success of a procurement professional. Most leaders in public procurement would agree that the profession is highly dependent on relationships. Having the ability to effectively work with organizational leaders, key suppliers, and departmental users is imperative. Networking with peers within their procurement organization and colleagues from outside organizations is key to professional development (Alvarez, 2015). Additionally, skills like negotiation and strategic thinking are highly beneficial. These attributes will all play a role in the development of a world-class procurement professional.

## 15.8 Procurement in Action

At all levels of government, procurement professionals are tasked with buying the goods and services needed for their organization to operate. Whether at a large federal agency or a small rural fire department, procurement must function efficiently and effectively (Pitzer and Thai, 2009). Depending on the size and complexity of the entity, the procurement function may consist of 2 people or 20. When it comes to procurement, there is certainly not a "one size fits all." The following is a sample organizational chart.

Many organizations have procurement embedded in the finance department, while for others, it resides in a central administrative group (Figure 15.2).

Wherever the procurement function is placed in an organization, it needs to be at a comparable level as other parts of the organization that it serves. The chief procurement officer should be of a similar stature as the chief information officer, director of facilities, or budget official. This will allow them to operate effectively and with the proper authority.

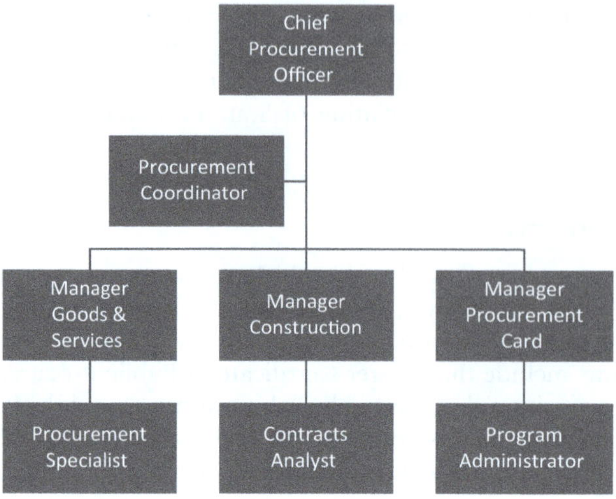


*Figure 15.2* Procurement organizational chart.
*Source*: Adapted from Portland State University www.pdx.edu.

The positive rapport that procurement professionals build with their end users should be a priority (Grilli and Webb, 2023). Establishing positive relationships that allow them to match their procurement knowledge with the expertise of the customer department will make procurement indispensable. This should be considered an ongoing effort that includes frequent participation in operational meetings and key projects. Knowing about an upcoming procurement need (and not being the last to know about it) will allow procurement professionals to add the most value.

Procurement leaders should make it a priority to be involved with the rule-making and legislative process for their organization. Whether it is at the local level through ordinance or resolution or at the state level through procurement statutes, procurement professionals can ensure the practicality of public contract regulations. Therefore, it is important that lawmakers hear from the procurement community through committee testimony and the review of legislative bills. Examples can include competitive bidding practices, local business preferences, small business set-asides, or the purchase of recycled products. Many local chapters of NIGP: The Institute for Public Procurement feature legislative committees that monitor new policies and laws that directly impact public procurement. Failure to assume such a role is an opportunity lost, as lawmakers may not have all the information needed to cast their vote. Seasoned procurement leaders need to be involved in this environment, as they can best represent the profession and their own entity. As part of its educational program, NIGP focuses on Advanced Legislation and Legal Environment for senior practitioners (www.nigp.org).

## 15.9 Procurement Practices

Regardless of whether a procurement professional is working for a federal, state, or local entity, there are many commonalities. Sound procurement procedures need to be established that meet the organization's needs and deliver value. In every entity, there are procurement regulations that must be adhered to, which a practitioner needs to be aware of. A federal procurement official will be familiar with the FAR (Federal Acquisition Regulations), while their colleague in state procurement likely knows their procurement statutes inside and out. Counties and local governments typically have public contracting codes that govern their procurement activities, along with local policies and ordinances that supplement the code (Flynn, Buffington and Pennington, 2020). These can include rules on local supplier preference, living wage requirements, and sustainable procurement policies. However, within each set of regulations, there is an opportunity for consistent procurement methods that are considered to be best practices.

The two basic approaches to public procurement are bid and request for proposal (RFP). An invitation to bid (ITB) is also referred to as a request for bid (RFB) or invitation to tender (ITT). All are based on the lowest-bid-wins methodology. If all bids received meet the requirements of the solicitation, they are responsive (NASPO, 2022). The lowest cost is then the determining factor.

The use of an RFP has gained popularity during the past two decades, with many public agencies making it their predominant solicitation method. An RFP utilizes both cost and non-cost selection criteria. When factors such as experience, expertise, and product quality are considered, the best value can be achieved (not just the lowest cost).

As part of the evolution of public procurement, entities of all types and sizes are focusing their efforts on strategic procurement. Routine duties such as purchase order (PO) issuance and low bid evaluation are being minimized as procurement professionals are considering the "big picture." They are working collaboratively with using departments to determine long-range needs and using best value procurement to achieve them. Cost minimization in the short term has shifted toward long-term value creation through strategic procurement (Hong and Kwon, 2012).

If daily procurement tasks are considered, there has also been an evolution. Procurement professionals are spending more of their time on strategic tasks and less on routine functions. The following table compares some common tactical duties with those considered more strategic (Table 15.3).

The type of procurement tasks assigned to individual staff members should be based on their level of experience and expertise. Routine and tactical duties can be performed by buyers with less experience but with the understanding they will handle strategic tasks in the future. With a strong professional development program in place, procurement staff can hone their advanced skills and advance in the organization. Organizational structures that include multiple levels of procurement positions are ideal for establishing career paths. This can include procurement assistant, procurement specialist, senior procurement specialist, and procurement supervisor.

*Table 15.3* Tactical vs. strategic procurement

| *Tactical* | *Strategic* |
|---|---|
| Issuing purchase orders (PO) | Establishing long-term agreements |
| Carrying excess inventory | Just in time (JIT) inventory management |
| Focusing on lowest cost | Focusing on best value |
| Maintaining paper files | Utilizing digital systems |
| Reporting to finance director | Reporting to administrative official |

*Source*: Original creation.

## 15.10 Procurement Talent

Successful procurement leaders realize the value of developing their procurement talent. Procurement and contract specialists must be effectively recruited and also retained. Building a high-performing team is a formidable task, but also very rewarding. In the ever-changing world of public procurement, the development of staff is critical. Today's entry-level buyers will be tomorrow's senior procurement specialists and managers.

Pairing a new staff member with an experienced peer can create an effective learning environment. By shadowing a more senior procurement specialist, staff can actually learn by doing. Leading organizations make formal mentoring arrangements a key part of their procurement operation. When these internal training efforts are coupled with professional development classes, it is a powerful combination. Organizations like NIGP, ISM, and others offer procurement-related training courses on topics that are relevant to today's professionals. These include strategic procurement planning, contract negotiation skills, and sustainable procurement strategies.

A current practice by leading public agencies in the US and Canada is the proactive engagement of end users. On a regular basis, procurement professionals meet with their departmental counterparts to discuss procurement needs and strategies. This will allow a procurement professional to develop strategies that best meet the operational needs of their customer, as well as avoid surprises or last-minute procurement requests. The engagement between procurement and using departments can be successfully achieved regardless of how assignments are made. Assigning a procurement professional to a specific commodity (i.e., technology, construction, fleet vehicles) or to a specific operating department can lend itself to an ongoing and productive partnership.

Procurement managers need to do all they can to ensure the job satisfaction of their team members. Public procurement offers many opportunities, and talented procurement professionals certainly have choices. If they are satisfied and challenged with their current role, it can create a more stable workforce. How can a manager know if their employees are satisfied? To start with, they can provide a safe environment that welcomes employee feedback. Some organizations employ 360 reviews that allow both the supervisor and employee to provide input. Employees should be able to voice their concerns and preferences on matters such as work assignments, work hours and location, and professional development. There are no guarantees that procurement staff will not consider advancement opportunities for other agencies, but providing a healthy work environment can make the decision to leave a bit tougher.

Employee motivation is another important consideration. Only by getting to know the individual employee can a manager learn what things may motivate them. It can include increased pay, challenging assignments, job titles, or public praise of their accomplishments (or a combination of these). Recent studies indicate that today's workforce is motivated by ethical leadership, inclusive work environments, and work–life balance. Procurement managers who acknowledge the importance of these things can help create a great place to work.

Both new and longstanding employees can focus their energies on negotiating and effectively monitoring contract relationships with suppliers. There is an inherent risk of failure in the complex world of public contracting (Brown and Potowski, 2003). Therefore, it is critical that this talent be developed through professional training and mentorship programs.

When a staff vacancy does occur, there are certain strategies that can help attract procurement talent to an organization. Reaching out to professional procurement organizations, such as local NIGP chapters, to advertise the position is a great start. Qualified professionals in existing professional networks can help create a diverse pool of excellent candidates. Job descriptions should be well developed and paint an accurate picture of a rewarding role in a leading organization. Having professional certification as a preferred credential is a good strategy, or the ability to obtain it within a set period after hire. Finally, if the procurement organization has gained a reputation for valuing people and providing a positive work environment, there are likely to be many who wish to join it.

## 15.11 Quantifying Procurement's Value

The value of procurement can be quantified in many ways, including the validation of cost savings achieved. While there are a variety of methods employed by public procurement offices to document cost savings, the methodology used by CSU and the UC is noteworthy. Procurement activities can achieve various types of benefits, which is the term used in the world of California higher education. The four categories of cost savings (or benefits) are cost reduction, cost avoidance, incentives, and revenue. Procurement staff at each of the campuses can enter their cost-saving achievements in a common platform. If an initial supplier proposal for software implementation is negotiated down, it would fall under the cost reduction category. When a contract renewal eligible for a 5% increase is negotiated to 3%, cost avoidance can be claimed. During the 2021/2022 fiscal year, the CSU system achieved over $63 million in financial benefit (California State University, 2022) (Table 15.4).

An area of procurement management that may be overlooked but is nonetheless critical is the management of public records requests. Florida is known as the sunshine state as much for its weather as it is for its public records law. Virtually all documents related to a procurement solicitation, purchase agreement, or contract are available for public inspection. In Article I, Section 23 of the Florida Constitution, the right for a member of the general public to have access to public records is clearly stated. Individuals have the right to inspect "all public records" related to the business of the government. While many states, including Florida, have broad laws on public records, each state has its own version. Procurement professionals across the country must be familiar with these records laws.

An area that will no doubt impact procurement in both the near and long term is artificial intelligence (AI). This tool can be relied upon by today's workforce to do comprehensive supplier research and develop effective work scopes. These are just two examples of a potentially endless list. In partnership with Amazon and its own Digital Transformation Hub, Cal Poly State University-San Luis Obispo began an AI project in 2024. Procurement

*Table 15.4* CSU cost savings methodology

| *Input* | *Definition* |
|---|---|
| **Cost Reduction** | Benefit achieved when procurement action results in total cost that is lower than baseline cost, which is supported by documentation (previous contract, historical costs, etc.) |
| **Cost Avoidance** | Benefit achieved when procurement action results in avoidance of additional costs (maintenance fees, requested price increases, etc.) |
| **Incentives** | Benefit achieved when procurement action results in new financial incentive (based on volume, transaction size, electronic payment, signing bonus, etc.) |
| **Revenue** | Benefit achieved when procurement action results in new revenue stream or revenue generating project (licensing revenue, revenue share for commercial service, etc.) |

*Source*: Adapted from California State University, www.calstate.edu.

staff and students are working together on a generative AI program that produces detailed scopes of work (SOW) for various services. Using a chatbot feature that poses a series of questions, an SOW can be generated in a professional "RFP ready" format. The project is in its infancy but looks to significantly impact the procurement process for the university (https://dxhub.calpoly.edu).

## 15.12 Sustainable Procurement Strategies

Leading organizations around the world have adopted sustainable procurement practices as part of their organizational culture (Stanley and Matthews, 2008). One of the best examples of this is the Greater London Authority (GLA) in the UK. Their policy ensures that sustainability issues are addressed in all phases of the procurement process and even addresses social issues like the reduction of drugs, slavery, and prostitution in their community (Greater London Authority (GLA), 2019). Many other organizations have formidable policies in place, including Portland State University (Oregon), King County (Washington), and Old Dominion University (Virginia).

The workforce of today embraces sustainability, as it addresses the social, economic, and environmental needs of their communities (Roman and Matthews, 2023). What better way to attract and retain a strong procurement workforce than by engaging in sustainable procurement practices? These can include the use of digital procurement systems that greatly reduce paper usage, green cleaners that do not contain harmful chemicals, and electric vehicles that do not use gasoline or produce emissions. For many organizations, it is a chance to "walk the talk" when it comes to sustainability. They engage in sustainable business practices and serve as a role model to their peers.

An example in the educational sector is the UC, Office of the President. In 2018 the ten-campus university system established a comprehensive sustainable procurement policy. In addition to the promotion of green and recycled products, UC put in place a requirement that sustainability be part of the selection criteria for any RFP over $100,000. For the most part, the policy has received acceptance from both the campus and supplier communities (www.ucop.edu).

## 15.13 Chapter Summary

Public procurement has a rich history that goes back many centuries. While historically, the profession may have been overlooked and under-appreciated, today's professionals are viewed as value-added decision-makers. They hold high-level positions throughout all types of public entities and are well respected by their peers.

A continued challenge for procurement will be a stronger collaboration with academia, which will help increase knowledge and credibility for procurement. Accredited degree programs in business and supply management areas will remain important, as well as training and certification through professional associations such as NIGP and NASPO. Procurement professionals should focus their time and energy on the strategic elements of procurement. Tactical activities should be minimized or delegated to departmental users. This can include the establishment of master agreements through a central procurement authority, with the actual purchases being handled by the end user.

Procurement managers and leaders will continue to be in demand across the globe as organizations rely heavily on procurement to achieve their goals and missions. Managers need to analyze the best practices of their peers and direct a procurement team that operates at a world-class level. Tremendous opportunities will continue to exist for those professionals willing to seek them out, including the advancement of sustainable procurement. Professional organizations around the world will offer a support and training network for the public procurement workforce that will prove to be invaluable.

## References


Alvarez, B. (2015, February 3). The 7 Traits of Successful Procurement Specialists, Coupa, Procurement. www.coupa.com

Arlbojorn, J.S. and Freytag, P.V. (2012, March 30). Public procurement vs. private purchasing: Is there any foundation for comparing and learning across the sectors? *International Journal of Public Sector Management*, Vol. 25, No. 3, pp. 203–220.

Brown, T. and Potoski, M. (2003). Managing contract performance: A transaction costs approach. *Journal of Policy Analysis and Management*, Vol. 22, No. 2, pp. 275–297.

California State University (2022). Office of the Chancellor, Procurement and Contracting, CPOA Impact Report. www.calstate.edu

Callender, G. and Matthews, D. (2005). "We've Come a Long Way", Government Procurement, Atlanta, GA: Penton Media.

European Union. (2024). Public Procurement Tenders and Contracts within the EU. https://european-union.europa.eu/live-work-study/public-contracts_en

Flynn, M., Buffington, K. and Pennington, R. (2020). *Legal Aspects of Public Procurement*, London: Routledge.

Greater London Authority (GLA). (2019). Responsible Procurement Policy. www.london.gov.uk

Grilli, B. and Webb, T. (2023). *Strategic Sourcing in the Public Sector*, London: Routledge.

Grimm, R. (1999). *A Shifting Paradigm, the Public Purchaser*, Herndon, VA: NIGP.

Herrero, A.G. (2020). Epidemic tests China's supply chain dominance, Asia Times, February 17, 2020, www.asiatimes.com, https://asiatimes.com/

Hong, P. and Kwon, H.-B. (2012) Emerging issues of procurement management: A review and prospect. *International Journal of Procurement Management*, Vol. 5, No. 4, pp. 452–469. Florida State University, College of Law, Public Records and Sunshine Laws. https://guides.law.fsu.edu/FOIA/Florida

Hsu, A. (2023, September 1). Remote work is harder to come by as companies push for return to office, National Public Radio, Business. www.npr.org

Laistner, M. L. W. (1966) Livy, the Historian. *The Greater Roman Historians*. Berkeley: University of California Press.

National Association of State Procurement Officials (NASPO). (2021). *Assessing State PPE Procurement during COVID-19: A Research Report*, Chicago, IL: National Association of State Procurement Officials.

National Association of State Procurement Officials (NASPO). (2022). Survey of State Procurement Practices Report, Lexington, KY: NASPO.

Nederland. (2021). The Dutch Digitalisation Strategy. www.nederlanddigitaal.nl/english/the-dutch-digitalisation-strategy-2021

NIGP: Institute for Public Procurement. (2022). Dictionary of Procurement Terms. www.nigp.org

Nonhoff, B. (2017, September 17). Functional excellence vs strategic alignment, Procurement, CIPS. www.cips.org/supply-management/opinion/2017/august/functional-excellence-vs-strategic-alignment/

Pitzer, J. and Thai, K. (2009). *Introduction to Public Procurement*, Herndon, VA: NIGP.

Procurious (2015, November 29). 99 Names You Can Call a Procurement Professional. www.procurious.com

Roman, A. and Matthews, D. (2020). *Public Procurement: A Guide to the Body of Knowledge through Exercises and Case Studies*, San Diego, CA: Birkdale Publishing.

Stanley, L. and Matthews, D. (2008). *Effective Supply Management Performance*, Tempe, AZ: Institute for Supply Management.

Tether, I. J. (1977). *Government Procurement and Operations*. Ballinger Publishing Company, Cambridge, MA.

Twyford, H. B. (1915). *Purchasing: Its Economic Aspects and Proper Methods*, New York: Nichols Copper Co.

## *Case Study: Orange County (Developed by Darin Matthews in collaboration with Orange County, Florida Procurement Division, Carrie Mathes and Zulay Milan)*

### Overview

Orange County (OC) is a large, local government located in Orlando, Florida with an annual budget of $6.2 billion and more than 8,000 employees in 2022. The Procurement Division is within the Administrative Services Department and has an annual spend of approximately $800 million. All goods-, services-, and construction-related contracts are handled by the Procurement Division.

### Organizational Structure

The Procurement Division is led by manager and assistant manager, who oversee the following work groups: purchasing section, contracts section, buying section, and procurement card services. There are 34 full-time equivalents (FTE) that work as procurement professionals.

### Professional Development

The professional experience of the OC procurement team varies greatly. Some have been with the agency for several years, some bring significant procurement experience from other entities, and others are relatively new to the world of public procurement.

Procurement department leaders are active in professional procurement associations and support professional development, including procurement certification. However, agency funding is limited for training classes and travel. Therefore, creativity is needed to ensure all procurement staff receive the appropriate training.

### Supplier Diversity

Both the state and county have a diverse array of qualified suppliers and contractors. OC procurement is committed to provide a fair and equitable procurement process, which is supported by the county's elected leaders.

In addition to the regulatory requirements for bid submission and subcontractor outreach, the county desires to better engage the diverse business community, including small businesses, as well as minority- and women-owned firms. Increased participation in the OC bid and RFP process is a desired outcome of procurement leadership.

### Technology Implementation

Like other Florida agencies, OC has a history of paper-based procurement, which included printed solicitation documents and the receipt of large bid and proposal packets (several copies of each). In recent years, OC procurement has implemented an electronic procurement process through a third-party software provider.

OC procurement would like to fully leverage the capabilities of the e-procurement system, ensure procurement staff are properly trained in its operation, and serve as a resource to suppliers that are not well-versed in digital procurement (or technology in general).

### Questions for Reflection and Discussion

Based on the information provided, as well as any assumptions you might make, consider the following questions regarding OC procurement. Use your own ideas and experiences as you respond, keeping in mind there are no "right or wrong" responses.

1. Do you believe the structure and placement of procurement are appropriate for the agency? Please explain why or why not?
2. How would you go about evaluating the effectiveness of procurement while you are considering the previous question (survey, peer review, spend data analysis, other research, etc.)?
3. How high should staff professional development be as an agency priority? What types of development opportunities might be most effective in your opinion?
4. Can you think of creative ways to provide development opportunities for OC staff without spending too much budget ("break the bank")?
5. How can OC procurement determine how well they are doing in the area of supplier diversity?
6. What outreach initiatives could be effective to better engage with small and diverse suppliers?
7. What would you see as the primary advantages of OC implementing a digital procurement system?
8. Can you list at least two strategies for supporting suppliers looking to do business with OC and their new e-procurement system (that they may be wary of)?
9. What other observations or suggestions would you offer for OC procurement?

# 16 Managing Procurement Contract Design, Incentives, and Relationships

*Jens K. Roehrich*

## 16.1 Introduction

Public procurement is vital for the delivery of public products, infrastructure, and services by seeking to effectively allocate public resources and funds in order to achieve value for money (Vfm), which means getting the best possible outcomes with the resources invested (Harland et al., 2021). However, public procurement can not only have an economic impact (e.g., supporting the development of small- and medium-sized enterprises – SMEs) but also meet sustainability and social value and objectives (e.g., buying eco-friendly products; skills development of workers in a deprived region; encouraging diversity and inclusion for public sector work) (Harland et al., 2019; Roehrich et al., 2024). Public procurement is a crucial tool for governments around the world to manage (limited) public resources effectively, drive economic growth, encourage competition and innovation, and achieve sustainability, social, and developmental objectives (Patrucco et al., 2017). When carried out transparently and ethically, public procurement contributes to the overall well-being of societies and economies.

Supporting public procurement in achieving and driving these crucial values and objectives are contract design and management, referring to the process of effectively setting up and administering contracts, and its related key activities such as supplier management, from initiation to closure (Roehrich et al., 2013, 2021). As argued in this chapter and in the book more widely, contract management goes far beyond a 'simple administration function', or to 'merely control suppliers'. In the context of public procurement, proper contract management includes practices such as establishing and maintaining collaboration with a myriad of key stakeholders including public, private, non-for-profit organizations, communicating objectives and coordinating activities across a network of (internal and) external actors, assessing and mitigating risks, as well as conducting vital market research and supplier assessments and negotiations (Brown and Potoski, 2005; Petersen et al., 2019; Roehrich et al., 2021). These, and other, practices are vital to contribute to better procurement outcomes, reduce risks, and increase transparency, and thus ultimately benefiting both governments and the public they serve.

Contract management in public organizations, and beyond, matters significantly for a variety of reasons. It is important for value realization as effective contract design and management ensures that the promised (economic, sustainability, and social) value from the procured goods, services, and/or works is realized (Zheng et al., 2008; Roehrich and Lewis, 2014; Roehrich et al., 2020). The various activities across the CLM process help to bridge the gap between the initial procurement objectives and the actual outcomes. Also, contracts often involve substantial financial commitments for public organizations (and by extension

DOI: 10.4324/9781003566670-19

for the public). Here, proper contract management ensures that funds are allocated and utilized efficiently, preventing cost overruns, unauthorized expenditures, and financial mismanagement. This is closely linked to the management of contractors (often suppliers from the private sector) to deliver the goods, services, and/or works as detailed in the contract and to align with legal obligations and standards (Roehrich et al., 2021). A public buyer's need to monitor supplier performance and adherence to contract terms to ensure that it receives the quality and standards it paid for. Moreover, strong relationships between the public organization and its suppliers contribute to successful outcomes, and effective contract management is vital to nurture these relationships which may then lead to better collaboration, communication, and problem-solving. If done properly, contract design and management also identify and address potential risks, mitigating their impact on timelines, budgets, and objectives. A public buyer needs to ensure clear documentation of contract-related activities including key performance indicators (KPIs). Practical examples of KPIs used in contract management might include quality of service, schedule adherence, or cost saving achieved. Given that public funds are being used to procure various work and/or services, a transparent contract management process also enhances accountability and reduces the potential for corruption or unethical behavior. Transparent and efficient contract design and management help maintain public trust by demonstrating responsible use of public funds and achieving intended results (Moretto et al., 2017). In summary, contract design and management in public organizations are essential for ensuring the successful setup and execution of contracts to achieve key values and objectives, managing risks, maintaining legal compliance, and fostering transparent and accountable practices.

This chapter serves as a starting point for readers interested to learn more about contract design and management in the context of public organizations. This chapter will particularly focus on the frontend of the contract management lifecycle. Section 16.2 provides a summary of prior studies on the importance and role of contracts and their management, before positioning a brief overview of key contract types and explaining the CLM process. Section 16.3 introduces the reader to emerging contracting themes in practice and policy when it comes to contract design and management. This section is also underlined by practical applications and case insights. The chapter concludes by briefly summarizing key points and provides further learning and teaching resources (available online) for the reader.

## 16.2 Summary of the Literature

Contracts including their design and management are crucial for public organizations to achieve their various economic, sustainability, and social values and objectives. This section outlines the role and function of contracts and contracting before providing a brief overview of key contract types and by explaining the CLM process.

### *16.2.1 Contracts and Relational Governance*

Contracts present the formal mode of governing inter-organizational (and sometimes intra-organizational) relationships by specifying the terms, conditions, as well as roles and responsibilities between two (or more) parties (Vandaele et al., 2007; Roehrich et al., 2021). Using contracts may help to nurture and manage relationships between public organizations and their various stakeholders (e.g., other public organizations, private firms, non-for-profit organizations) across countries (Roehrich et al., 2025). Contracts are important in the sense that they not only affect the performance of the focal organization but also that of its suppliers, customers, and business partners (Brunjes, 2020). More specifically, contracts interpret the relevant norms (from a legal system and industry), act as framing tools as well as outline agreed rules and responsibilities that underpin the relationship (Roehrich et al., 2020). Prior studies on contracts and contracting have emphasized the functions of control – referring to safeguarding parties against potential opportunism (Schepker et al., 2014; Kapsali et al., 2019) – and coordination – emphasizing the delineation of roles and responsibilities, communication, information sharing, and joint problem-solving activities (Schepker et al., 2014; Roehrich et al., 2023). The concept of 'contracts' (and 'contractual governance') has received ample attention by a variety of scholars from management (including, but not limited to, strategy, operations and supply chain management, public administration, marketing, and project management) over the last decades (e.g., Poppo and Zenger, 2002; Zheng et al., 2008; Cao and Lumineau, 2015; Petersen et al., 2019; Roehrich et al., 2020).

Early contracting and contractual governance studies have often adopted a transaction cost economics (TCE) perspective to explore the relationship between the transaction characteristics (e.g., uncertainty and asset specificity) and the design of a contract (Brown and Potoski, 2005; Schepker et al., 2014). These studies posited that while transactions characterized by lower uncertainty and asset specificity do often not need very detailed contracts (i.e., characterized by fewer control and coordination clauses), transactions with high uncertainty and asset specificity often lead organizations to write very detailed and lengthy contracts (i.e., more control and coordination clauses, resulting in a much longer and more detailed contract; Reuer and Ariño, 2002; Zheng et al., 2008). In parallel to early contracting studies, (management) scholars have also investigated the role of relational governance which includes trust and social norms in business relationships (Dyer and Singh, 1998; Roehrich et al., 2020). While contracts and relational governance were initially positioned as substitutes (e.g., Macaulay, 1963; Heide and John, 1992; Ghoshal and Moran, 1996), over the last two decades both governance mechanisms have started to be considered complementary in governing inter-organizational relationships (e.g., Poppo and Zenger, 2002; Zheng et al., 2008; Cao and Lumineau, 2015; Roehrich et al., 2020). Since the conceptual study by Das and Teng (1998) and the seminal empirical study by Poppo and Zenger (2002), most governance researchers position contracts and relational governance mechanisms as complements. For example, contracts are often seen as enhancing trust while trust, in turn, can lead to 'learning to contract' effects whereby over time more effective contracts are being designed (e.g., Mayer and Argyres, 2004; Zheng et al., 2008). Contracts can, for instance, support trust development by reducing information asymmetry between contracting parties (Liu et al., 2009; Aben et al., 2021).

The following section considers the various types of contracts that are used in practice.

### *16.2.2 Contract Types*

In practice as well as in prior research, a variety of different contract types can be distinguished. While not seeking to be comprehensive in this chapter (please see further detailed discussions here: Acquisition, 2023), the following offers a brief overview of some key contract types frequently used in practice (other types of contracts, or combinations of characteristics of various contract types are possible too):

- ***Fixed-price contract (lump-sum):*** Contracting parties agree to a fixed price for a specific scope of work. The contractor is responsible for completing the work within the agreed-upon budget, regardless of any cost overruns or unforeseen circumstances. This provides the public buyer with certainty about the final price to be paid as any cost overruns would have to be covered by the contractor. This contract is best used when accurate data are compiled for pricing. Consider a government agency seeking to construct a new government building. They may enter into a fixed-price contract with the contractor that will then complete the project for a predetermined amount, offering budgetary predictability for the public buyer.

- ***Fixed-price incentive fee contract:*** This contract combines a fixed price with an incentive fee based on performance. If the contractor exceeds certain performance targets, they can receive additional compensation. For example, the contractor building a government building is incentivized if they can complete it before the deadline or under budget. The cost savings for delivering such a construction project earlier, or to a lower budget, might then be split between the contractor and the public buyer.
- ***Cost-plus contract:*** The contractor is reimbursed for the actual costs incurred during the procurement process, along with an additional fee or percentage for profit. This type of contract is suitable for public procurement (e.g., a public sector project) with uncertain or variable scopes. There are mainly two key reasons for the inability to accurately estimate costs: (i) lack of knowledge of the work needed to meet contract requirements; and/or (ii) lack of cost experience in performing the work. Imagine a government research project with uncertain requirements and costs. Here, the public buyer/agency agrees to reimburse the research institution for allowable costs incurred during the research, along with an additional fee for their efforts.
- ***Time and materials contract:*** This contract combines elements of fixed-price and cost-plus contracts. The contractor is paid for the actual hours worked (time) and the materials used. This type of contract provides flexibility but can be more challenging to manage for the public buyer as the buyer might, for instance, struggle to monitor how much time was spent and how much materials were used to complete the contracted work. For example, a public agency is undertaking a complex IT system upgrade, and the exact scope and duration of the project are uncertain. In this case, the government may opt for a 'time and materials contract' with a technology-consulting firm. Here, the government pays for the actual hours worked by the technology consultants at an agreed-upon hourly rate. Also, any materials and/or expenses directly related to the project (e.g., software licenses) are reimbursed. Lastly, a negotiated fee (or profit margin) is added to the total cost to compensate the firm for its services.
- ***Unit-price contract:*** In this contract, prices are assigned to specific quantities of work items. The total contract price is calculated based on the quantities of work performed by the contractor. These contracts are quite commonly used in public sector construction and infrastructure projects. For example, a public infrastructure project (e.g., road construction), where the quantity of work can be measured in specific units, can use a 'unit-price contract'. Here, the contact needs to specify unit prices for various items of work (e.g., cost per cubic meter of concrete poured). This type of contract provides flexibility when the exact quantity of work is uncertain at the project outset.
- ***Incentive contracts:*** These contracts seek to align the interests of both parties (i.e., contractor and public buyer) by including incentives for achieving specific performance targets (e.g., time, cost, quality). These contracts often include a variety of agreed bonus payments for early completion or penalties for delays in completing the contractually specified work (please see fixed-price incentive fee contract).
- ***Guaranteed maximum price contract:*** The contractor agrees to complete the public work/project within a set budget, often with an upper limit (the maximum price). If the project is completed under budget, the savings may be shared between the public buyer and the contractor. Please note that this sharing does not necessarily mean a 50/50 split

and should be agreed before contract signature. For example, a public agency wants to build a new public library. Here, the construction company provides a detailed estimate (in terms of the project costs), and then the contract specifies a guaranteed maximum price that the contractor commits not to exceed. If the final project cost is below the guaranteed maximum price, the public buyer pays the actual cost (and the contract earns a profit based on the agreed-upon fee or from the percentage of savings), but if the actual cost exceeds the guaranteed maximum price, the contractor is responsible for covering the additional cost. This type of contract provides cost certainty for the buyer and moves project risks to the contractor.

- ***Framework agreements:*** These are often used for frequent public sector work and services. Contracts are awarded to a single (or multiple) supplier(s) to complete works/deliver services over a set time period. For the public organization, such agreements reduce administration costs and streamline the procurement process (as goods/services can be procured at short notice as details have already been agreed before contract signature). This might be used to buy IT equipment. Multiple suppliers are pre-qualified, and various public agencies can then issue individual purchase orders (as part of the framework).
- ***Joint venture or multi-party agreements:*** A joint venture or multi-party agreement involves two or more parties collaborating on a business venture or specific project. These agreements outline the roles, responsibilities, coordination, and communication mechanisms and channels, as well as financial contributions of each party. This is common in very large projects (worth billions) such as building a new energy station (Taubeneder et al., 2024). In such projects, an individual firm alone might not be able to deliver all relevant work and needs to enter into a joint venture agreement with one or (multiple) other firms.

This list of contract types provides some commonly used examples of contracts used in public procurement. As indicated in the description of individual contract types, the choice of contract type depends on the specific needs, prior experience with a certain type of contract, objectives, and risks of the parties involved in the transaction (Roehrich et al., 2021). For a public buyer, it is important to consider carefully the terms and conditions of the contract to ensure that they align with the desired outcomes (e.g., economic and social value creation) and minimize potential contract management challenges and issues later (e.g., disputes between contracting parties about unclear/imprecise language and terms; coordination failures – Regan et al., 2015; Kalra et al., 2021).

The following section explains the CLM process and key activities to be considered by the public buyer.

### *16.2.3 Contract Lifecycle Management Process*

The CLM process refers to the various stages, processes, and activities involved in effectively managing a contract from its design and negotiation to its eventual closure (e.g., Uher and Davenport, 2009; Roehrich et al., 2021). The process ensures that all parties involved fulfill their obligations and that the terms and conditions of the contract are met. This involves a series of activities aimed at maximizing the value derived from the contract, managing risks, and ensuring that the goals of the contract (and the wider procurement strategy) are achieved. The specific stages and processes (and sometimes the labels of these stages) within the CLM process can vary depending on the organization and the nature of the contract, but the following provides an overview of typical lifecycle stages (Figure 16.1):

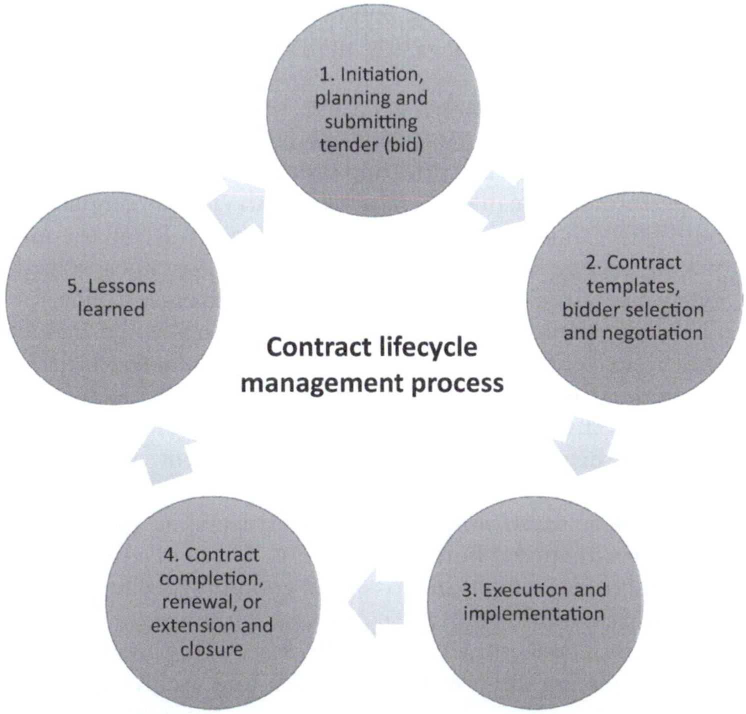


*Figure 16.1* The contract lifecycle management process.
*Source*: Original creation.

1. ***Initiation, planning, and submitting tender (bid):*** Here, the need for public sector work (goods, infrastructure, and/or services) and a contract is identified. A public buyer (possibly in consultation with key stakeholders such as end-users) should determine the scope of the required work to be contracted for, the parties involved and the objectives it seeks to achieve. The work to be contracted should contribute to and fit with the organization's procurement strategy (see Chapter 8). This phase also involves the selection of a contract type (Section 16.2.2), defining the contract's terms, conditions, requirements, and any KPIs. Lastly, the procurer (public buyer) should then publish the tender (bid) documentation (i.e., outlining what is required of the contractor).
2. ***Contract templates, bidder selection, and negotiation:*** During this stage, legal experts and stakeholders work together to customize a standard contract template with boilerplate terms that are accepted as the industry (and country) standard (Roehrich et al., 2021). This document outlines the rights, roles and responsibilities, obligations, and expectations of all parties involved. As public procurement is often subject to complex legal and regulatory frameworks and regulations that vary between different countries, standard contract templates provide a good starting point for negotiations with suppliers. These frameworks and regulations seek to ensure fairness, transparency, and accountability in the procurement process, and the public buyers (and all contracting parties) need to understand and adhere to them to avoid legal issues and unethical practices (*as presented in* Chapter 5). Then, the public organization should review all bids received and create a short list of bidders. This is then followed by the public buyer entering into

negotiations with the preferred bidder(s) to agree on contract terms. Negotiations may involve revisions, additions, or deletions to the contract language (from the contract template). Once all contract terms have been agreed upon, the contract is signed by all parties.

3. ***Execution and implementation:*** After contract signature, the contract becomes legally binding, and the execution (contract management) phase begins, with the public buyer and supplier(s) initiating the agreed-upon activities and tasks. This phase will also include various monitoring and performance management activities to ensure compliance with contract terms (from both buyer and supplier) and to manage risks. Regular communication and progress tracking are essential to ensure that the contractually specified KPIs and targets are met. Sometimes, circumstances or requirements change, calling for contract modifications and renegotiations. These contract modifications could include, for example, adjustments to the scope, timeline, and/or budget. Additionally, any issues or disputes between contracting parties should be addressed promptly and fairly. Effective dispute resolution (not always involving contracts and/or legal courts) helps prevent conflicts from escalating and disrupting the contract management and completion progress.
4. ***Contract completion, renewal or extension, and closure:*** Depending on the contract terms, it might be renewed or extended if both parties agree. Alternatively, the contract could be completed at the end of its term or due to certain conditions being met/broken. Once all obligations and activities outlined in the contract are fulfilled (or parties agree to end the contract pre-maturely), the contract is formally closed. This involves finalizing any remaining payments, completing any outstanding tasks, and archiving all relevant documentation.
5. ***Lessons learned:*** After the contract closure, an evaluation should be conducted to assess whether the contract's objectives were met, and what are possible lessons learned for future contracts. This knowledge is then used to improve future contract management activities across the CLM process, as well as be included in contract training for government officials involved in the procurement process. A clear feedback process that involves key stakeholders will help to achieve continuous improvements across the CLM process.

The CLM process (Figure 16.1) is a dynamic and iterative process that requires ongoing attention, communication, and collaboration between contracting parties (H.M. Government, 2022). It helps organizations achieve the desired outcomes of their contracts while managing risks, ensuring compliance, and maintaining strong relationships with suppliers and other key stakeholders. The outlined activities across the lifecycle are key to ensure appropriate performance management. Thus, contract and performance management are closely related processes that often go hand in hand, especially in the context of public procurement. While they have distinct foci, they intersect in various ways to ensure that contractual obligations are met and desired performance outcomes (for individuals, teams, processes, organizations, contracts, projects, or wider stakeholders) are achieved. Setting contractual KPIs, monitoring progress toward the achievement of these KPIs as well as ensuring clear communications and feedback loops between contracting parties are crucial to enhance overall performance (of the work/services being contracted for) and the successful delivery of the contract. Both contract and performance management should align with the broader goals of the organization and its (procurement) strategy.

This section has briefly reviewed key concepts – contracts and relational governance, contract types, and the CLM process – for the reader. We now delve into emerging contracting themes in practice.

## 16.3 Emerging Contracting Themes in Practice

This section briefly reviews emerging issues and themes of contracting that are vital for governments (and businesses) alike. These themes are then also supported by brief examples from practice. Emerging themes in contracting for (public) organizations reflect the evolving landscape of governance, technology, sustainability, and societal expectations (Caldwell et al., 2017; Roehrich et al., 2021; Patrucco et al., 2023). While not seeking to be comprehensive and all inclusive, the following provides some key emerging contracting themes that may impact contracting for public procurement and organizations. These themes should be considered as a starting point for readers to further explore theses (and related) themes through their own research and exploration.

***Delivering large public sector (infrastructure) projects:*** Public sector organizations often use large inter-organizational projects (worth in the millions or even billions) to deliver vital infrastructure and services (e.g., Roehrich et al., 2023, 2024). These projects deliver a wide range of public infrastructure and services such as roads, bridges, schools, hospitals, public transportation systems, rural development, sports events, IT systems, and energy stations (Flyvberg et al., 2003; Scott et al., 2011). The use of large projects helps governments to manage the complexities and challenges of delivering public infrastructure and services to their communities. Large inter-organizational projects (LIPs) bring together multiple (including, for example, public, private, non-for-profit) organizations that need to work together to deliver unique, or customized, outcomes in uncertain and dynamic environments (Jones and Lichtenstein, 2008). Here, contracts and contract management play a key role of ensuring that activities and stakeholders are coordinated, that roles and responsibilities are clear to all involved parties, and that funds are used in a way it was intended (i.e., as specified in the contract) to deliver the public sector project.

These projects often face significant governance challenges requiring contracts (and relational governance as discussed in Section 16.2.1) and forms of collaboration between diverse actors with often-diverging interests and different goals and levels of capabilities (Zheng et al., 2008; Roehrich and Lewis, 2014; Howard et al., 2019). Here, public organizations seek to specify contracts with detailed control clauses (including, for instance, termination rights and penalties for poor performance) to protect themselves against opportunism (Roehrich and Lewis, 2014; Kapsali et al., 2019), as well as coordination clauses (including, for example, information-sharing routines and partners' resource contributions and responsibilities – Lyons and Mehta, 1997; Van Marrewijk et al., 2016). LIPs, involving a multitude of partners with often no (or limited) prior experience of working together and limited prospect of future collaboration, may need more control clauses to mitigate opportunistic behavior (Roehrich et al., 2020, 2023). Contract clauses may also guide cooperation and coordination in projects (Zheng et al., 2008; Howard et al., 2019) by providing a jointly agreed framework for inter-organizational routines, KPI reviews, and joint problem-solving (Chakkol et al., 2018).

LIPs often include a range of contract types (Section 16.2.2) such as multi-party agreements in which multiple partners (more than two organizations – Taubeneder et al., 2022, 2024) will come together. These multiple private sector suppliers, which are often competitors on other projects and competing for other contracts to deliver public sector work/services, are then asked to cooperate as part of such an agreement for the benefits of the public buyer. Prior studies have investigated the use of contracts in a variety of relationships (such as public–private relationships – Hartmann et al., 2014) and projects delivering a variety of infrastructure and services from energy (e.g., Roehrich et al., 2023), hospitals (e.g., Zheng et al., 2008), transportation (e.g., Aben et al., 2021), to defense projects (e.g., Howard et al., 2019). Studying public–private partnerships (PPPs) in the United Kingdom to delivery two large hospital projects, Zheng et al. (2008) explore the use of contracts (alongside relational governance) to overcome critical incidents (e.g., operational issues with the hospital) during the project lifecycle. They empirically evidence the importance of both contracts and relational governance (arguing for a complementary relationship) and show that contracts 'anchor' the exchange relationship throughout the project lifecycle.

***Beyond economic value creation to consider sustainability and social value:*** Related to the theme of LIPs to deliver public sector infrastructure and services, public buyers seek to not only create economic value by considering a product's whole-lifecycle costing (how much would it cost to not only procure but also manage and recycle a product), but use public procurement to positively impact sustainability and social value creation (Amann et al., 2014; Caldwell et al., 2017). Public organizations are increasingly expected to consider environmental (including Corporate Social Responsibility (CSR)) policies and activities of private firms bidding for public sector contracts – Flammer, 2018), and social value factors in procurement decisions alongside economic decisions (Roehrich and Kivleniece, 2022).

Public procurement and public sector contracting can play a significant role in promoting sustainability by integrating environmental considerations into the procurement process to achieve positive outcomes for people and the planet (Alkadry et al., 2019). Sustainable procurement practices that prioritize eco-friendly products, fair labor practices, and reduced carbon footprints (e.g., NetZero considerations) are gaining importance with a shift toward circular economy principles – where products are designed for durability, reuse, recycling, reducing waste, and environmental impact (Rodriguez-Plesa et al., 2019). Public procurement and especially public sector contracting can ensure to define and incorporate sustainability criteria into contracts to guide suppliers in delivering environmentally friendly and socially responsible products and services. These criteria should then be used throughout the CLM process (Section 2.3), including when evaluating and selecting suppliers, when assessing KPIs, and when considering opportunities for local sourcing. Considering local suppliers may reduce transportation emissions, reduce the risks of non-availability of products (due to shortened supply chains), and support the local economy, especially for goods with a large carbon footprint (e.g., Dimand, 2022; Phillips et al., 2022). While current programs such as 'Set Aside' (in the United States) aim to accomplish equity goals via public procurement contacts for small and disadvantaged businesses, current performance and success of such programs are still often mixed (Brunjes and Rodriguez-Plesa, 2023).

Beyond cost savings and sustainability considerations, contracts are often also expected to deliver social value and positive impact on local communities. The study by Kalra and Roehrich (2019), drawing on rich empirical insights from a large project in the energy sector, outlines key steps for a (private sector) buyer to consider integrating local SMEs into a large network of suppliers and driving skills development in the local community. The study also emphasizes the crucial role that public organizations play in supporting these steps and incentivizing such behavior.

It is vital for public organizations to focus on social value and the positive impact contracts can have on local communities, SMEs, jobs, and skills development by incorporating social responsibility and diversity considerations into key procurement decisions and the wider CLM process (Harris and Brunjes, 2022). For example, this may involve supporting local businesses, promoting diversity and inclusion, and/or ensuring suppliers adhere to ethical practices. Governments can also work closely with large private firms, which were contracted to deliver LIPs, to ensure that some of the money spend on these projects are spend in the region in which the project is taking place (see Kalra and Roehrich, 2019; Karla et al., 2024). This can include community engagement to consider local needs and concerns, increasing local employment and skills development (possibly in collaboration with education providers such as schools, colleges, and universities), and by working with and upskilling local SMEs.

In order to achieve sustainability and social value creation while also aiming for social equity in public procurement (Dimand et al., 2023), public organizations have turned to various forms of partnerships (e.g., PPPs – Roehrich et al., 2014; Wright et al., 2019) and collaborative procurement models (e.g., Abutabenjeh et al., 2023) to, for instance, encourage innovation (Suhonen et al., 2019) and knowledge sharing (Sarafan et al., 2022), tap into private sector funding and resources as well as private management acumen (Barlow et al., 2013). Here, (long-term) contracts and its various functions (e.g., coordination and control – Section 16.2.1) play a key role in information processing and sharing (Aben et al., 2021; Karaba et al., 2023). For example, the study by Sarafan et al. (2022) investigates knowledge sharing in project-based networks (such as the ones that can be found in public sector projects). They find that while both bonus and penalty provisions have previously been shown to have positive effects on knowledge sharing motivation, other governance mechanisms should be considered too. The study shows that bonus provisions are significantly more effective than penalty provisions in motivating knowledge sharing when used in combination with a shared form of network governance (where the buyer delegates authority to multiple suppliers to mutually control and coordinate network-level activities during project execution). However, the study finds no significant differences between the effectiveness of bonus and penalty provisions in lead-governed networks (i.e., where a third-party organization such as a project management organization is appointed by the buyer to coordinate issues and encourage knowledge sharing). Here, the use of various contract functions is depending on other governance factors (such as the network governance form) and public organizations should carefully consider these factors.

***The role of technology and transparency concerns:*** The integration of digital technologies, such as e-procurement platforms, blockchain, and AI, is reshaping public sector contract management and procurement processes (Walker and Brammer, 2012; Pencheva et al., 2020). Digital technology may help to enhance dealing with big data, increase transparency and efficiency, as well as support accountability in public procurement (Moretto et al., 2017). For example, e-procurement platforms such as CLM software are used to streamline processes, enhance transparency, provide access to a wider range of suppliers, and automate routine tasks (Costa et al., 2013). CLM is a centralized platform to manage the entire contract lifecycle. This technology provides visibility to stakeholders in terms of key documentation and decisions that were made (how, why, when, what, by whom). It also offers stakeholders access to the most up-to-date contact information and drives efficiency of contract management by offering automated alerts and notifications to help meet critical deadlines and milestones.

Moreover, AI-powered contract analytics tools can review and extract insights from large volumes of contracts, compliance monitoring, and decision-making (Pencheva et al., 2020). AI can also identify potential risks in contracts by analyzing clauses and terms, helping parties make informed decisions and mitigate risks. Public organizations have started to leverage data analytics to inform procurement decisions, track supplier performance, and optimize procurement processes. This may provide more efficiency as AI can automate routine tasks (e.g., contract review and initial risk assessment), thus saving time and reducing the likelihood of human error. AI can also identify patterns in contract language and provide recommendations for optimizing terms and conditions. Along with the introduction of technology, the shift to more remote work (as an initially response to COVID-19) has implications for contract management and collaboration (Phillips et al., 2023). Thus, tools for virtual contract negotiations, digital signatures, remote contract documentation, monitoring, and management are becoming more important.

While these technologies may bring about positive effects to public organizations, careful consideration is needed before installing and using technologies to support public procurement (*presented in detail in* Chapters 20–22), and the CLM process in particular, in terms of a specific technology's benefits and limitations (e.g., Butijn et al., 2023). For instance, public organizations often handle sensitive data during procurement and contracting processes, and thus ensuring compliance with data protection regulations and safeguarding against cyber threats is becoming more critical (e.g., Wirtz and Weyerer, 2017). Public organizations need robust cybersecurity measures to prevent data breaches and protect the confidentiality of procurement- and contract-related information. Similarly, the use of AI and automation in contract management introduces ethical considerations, transparency concerns, and questions about accountability for decisions made by algorithms. This will raise demands for transparency in contracting decisions, including disclosure of contract details, evaluation criteria, and supplier information, and compliance with data protection laws and various standards (e.g., GDPR, NIST, VPAT), in order to ensure public trust (Beshi and Kaur, 2020).

This section outlined three emerging contracting themes – delivering large public sector (infrastructure) projects, beyond economic value creation to consider sustainability and social value, and the role of technology and transparency concerns – contract management for public organizations.

## 16.4 Conclusions

This chapter offered insights into contract management and its key activities for public buyers. The chapter stressed the importance and crucial role of contracts and contract management, before discussing key contract types. It unpacks the five key stages of the CLM process and associated key activities to ensure effective contract management, before emerging contracting themes are discussed. Further learning and teaching resources as well as teaching tips are provided online for the reader to continue exploring this important topic. I hope that this chapter provides a starting point to encourage readers to conduct their own further research (as part of their work and/or study) into this crucial, but yet often under-explored, area of contract management in public procurement.

## References

Aben, T.A.E.; van der Valk, W.; Roehrich, J.K. and Selviaridis, K. (2021). Managing information asymmetry in public-private relationships undergoing a digital transformation: The role of contractual and relational governance. *International Journal of Operations & Production Management*, 41(7), 1145–1191.

Abutabenjeh, S.; Dimand, A.-M. and Tao, J. (2023). Determinants of the success of cooperative public procurement. *Public Performance & Management Review*, 46(2), 391–417.

Acquisition (2023). Part 16 – Types of Contracts. USA Government website; www.acquisition.gov/far/part-16 (accessed on 29 August 2023).

Alkadry, M.G.; Trammell, E. and Dimand, A.-M. (2019). The power of public procurement: Social equity and sustainability as externalities and as deliberate policy tools. *International Journal of Procurement Management*, 12(3), 336–362.

Amann, M.; Roehrich, J.K.; Essig, M. and Harland, C. (2014). Driving sustainable supply chain management in the public sector: The importance of public procurement in the EU. *Supply Chain Management: An International Journal*, 19(3), 351–366.

Barlow, J.; Roehrich, J.K. and Wright, S. (2013). Europe sees mixed results from public-private partnerships for building and managing health care facilities and services. *Health Affairs*, 32(1), 146–154.

Beshi, T.D. and Kaur, R. (2020). Public trust in local government: Explaining the role of good governance practices. *Public Organization Review*, 20, 337–350.

Brown, T.L. and Potoski, M. (2005). Transaction costs and contracting: The practitioner perspective. *Public Performance and Management Review*, 28(3), 326–351.

Brunjes, B.M. (2020). Competition and federal contractor performance. *Journal of Public Administration Research and Theory*, 30(2), 202–219.

Brunjes, B.M. and Rodriguez-Plesa, E. (2023). Equity in government contracting: Analyzing the performance of small disadvantaged businesses. *Public Administration Review*, 84(3), 484–499.

Butijn, B.-J.; Roehrich, J.K.; Selviaridis, K. and Van der Valk, W. (2023). Beyond the blockchain technology hype: When does it make sense to use smart contracts? *California Management Review (CMR) Insight*, published on 20 February 2023. https://cmr.berkeley.edu/2023/02/beyond-the-blockchain-technology-hype-when-does-it-make-sense-to-use-smart-contracts/

Caldwell, N.; Roehrich, J.K. and George, G. (2017). Social value creation and relational coordination in public-private collaborations. *Journal of Management Studies*, 54(6), 906–928.

Cao, Z. and Lumineau, F. (2015). Revisiting the interplay between contractual and relational governance: A qualitative and meta-analytic investigation. *Journal of Operations Management*, 33, 15–42.

Chakkol, M.; Selviaridis, K. and Finne, M. (2018). The governance of collaboration in complex projects. *International Journal of Operations & Production Management*, 38, 997–1019.

Costa, A.A.; Arantes, A. and Tavares, L.V. (2013). Evidence of the impacts of public e-procurement: The Portuguese experience. *Journal of Purchasing and Supply Management*, 19(4), 238–246.

Das, T.K. and Teng, B.-S. (1998). Between trust and control: Developing confidence in partner cooperation in alliances. *Academy of Management Review*, 23(3), 491–512.

Dimand, A.M. (2022). Determinants of local government innovation: The case of green public procurement in the United States. *International Journal of Public Sector Management*, 35(5), 584–602.

Dimand, A.-M.; Patrucco, A.S.; Rodriguez-Plesa, E. and Hiriscau, A.M. (2023). Social equity in federal contracting during emergencies: A portfolio management perspective. *Public Administration Review*, 83(5), 1319–1338.

Dyer, J.H. and Singh, H. (1998). The relational view: Cooperative strategy and sources of interorganisational competitive advantage. *Academy of Management Review*, 23(4), 660–679.

Flammer, C. (2018). Competing for government procurement contracts: The role of corporate social responsibility. *Strategic Management Journal*, 39(5), 1299–1324.

Flyvbjerg, B.; Bruzelius, N. and Rothengatter, W. (2003). *Megaprojects and Risk: An Anatomy of Ambition*. Cambridge University Press.

Ghoshal, S. and Moran, P. (1996). Bad for practice: A critique of transaction cost theory. *Academy of Management Review*, 21, 13–47.

H.M. Government (2022). *Government Function Commercial: Commercial Continuous Improvement Assessment Framework*. May 2022, version 2.1.

Harland, C.; Telgen, J.; Callender, G.; Grimm, R. and Patrucco, A. (2019). Implementing government policy in supply chains: An international coproduction study of public procurement. *Journal of Supply Chain Management*, 55, 6–25.

Harland, C.M.; Eßig, M.; Lynch, J. and Patrucco, A. (2021). Policy-led public procurement: Does strategic procurement deliver? *Journal of Public Procurement*, 21(3), 221–228.

Harris, A.B. and Brunjes, B.M. (2022). Developing capacity and reducing risk? An analysis of federal international contracting. *International Public Management Journal*, 25(5), 785–808.

Hartmann, A.; Roehrich, J.K.; Frederiksen, L. and Davies, A. (2014). Procuring complex performance: The transition process in public infrastructure. *International Journal of Operations & Production Management*, 32(2), 174–194.

Heide, J.B. and John, G. (1992). Do norms matter in marketing relationships? *Journal of Marketing*, 56, 32–44.

Howard, M.B.; Roehrich, J.K.; Lewis, M.A. and Squire, B. (2019). Converging and diverging governance mechanisms: The role of (dys) function in long-term inter-organizational relationships. *British Journal of Management*, 30(3), 624–644.

Jones, C. and Lichtenstein, B.B. (2008). Temporary inter-organizational projects: How temporal and social embeddedness enhance coordination and manage uncertainty. (pp. 1–27) In: Cropper, S.; Huxham, C.; Ebers, M. and Smith Ring, P. (eds.), *The Oxford Handbook of Inter-Organizational Relations*, 1st edition. Oxford University Press.

Kalra, J. and Roehrich, J.K. (2019). Swimming with the big fish. *APM's 'Project' Journal, Autumn*, 64–67.

Kalra, J.; Lewis, M.A. and Roehrich, J.K. (2021). Manifestation of coordination failures in service triads. *Supply Chain Management: An International Journal*, 26, 341–358.

Kalra, J.; Roehrich, J.K.; Squire, B. and Davies, A. (2024). Orchestrating project networks to deliver local economic and social value. *California Management Review (CMR) Insight* (Frontier – research-based analysis), 13 May 2024. https://cmr.berkeley.edu/2024/05/orchestrating-project-networks-to-deliver-local-economic-and-social-value/

Kapsali, M.; Roehrich, J.K. and Akhtar, P. (2019). Effective contracting for high operational performance in projects. *International Journal of Operations & Production Management*, 39(2), 294–325.

Karaba, F.; Roehrich, J.K.; Conway, S. and Turner, J. (2023). Information sharing in public-private relationships: The role of boundary objects in contracts. *Public Management Review*, 25, 2166–2190.

Liu, Y.; Luo, Y. and Liu, T. (2009). Governing buyer-supplier relationships through transactional and relational mechanisms: Evidence from China. *Journal of Operations Management*, 27, 294–309.

Lyons, B. and Mehta, J. (1997). Contracts, opportunism and trust: Self-interest and social orientation. *Cambridge Journal of Economics*, 21, 239–257.

Macaulay, S. (1963). Non-contractual relations in business: A preliminary study. *American Sociological Review*, 28(1), 55–67.

Mayer, K.J. and Argyres, N.S. (2004). Learning to contract: Evidence from the personal computer industry. *Organization Science*, 15, 394–410.

Moretto, A.; Ronchi, S. and Patrucco, A.S. (2017). Increasing the effectiveness of procurement decisions: The value of big data in the procurement process. *International Journal of RF Technologies*, 8(3), 79–103.

Patrucco, A.S.; Dimand, A.-M.; Neshkova, M.I. and Cevallos, M.M. (2023). How can procurement create (sustainable) public value under the Bipartisan Infrastructure Deal? *Public Administration Review*, 83(4), 960–973.

Patrucco, A.S.; Luzzini, D.; Ronchi, S.; Essig, M.; Amann, A. and Glas, A.H. (2017). Designing a public procurement strategy: Lessons from local governments. *Public Money & Management*, 37(4), 269–276.

Pencheva, I.; Esteve, M. and Mikhaylov, S.J. (2020). Big Data and AI – A transformational shift for government: So, what next for research? *Public Policy and Administration*, 35(1), 24–44.

Petersen, O.H.; Baekkeskov, E.; Potoski, M. and Brown, T.L. (2019). Measuring and managing ex ante transaction costs in public sector contracting. *Public Administration Review*, 79, 641–650.

Phillips, W.; Roehrich, J.K. and Kapletia, D. (2023). Responding to information asymmetry in crisis situations: Innovation in the time of the COVID-19 pandemic. *Public Management Review*, 25(1), 175–198.

Phillips, W.; Roehrich, J.K.; Kapletia, D. and Alexander, E. (2022). Global value chain reconfiguration and COVID-19: Investigating the case for more resilient redistributed models of production. *California Management Review*, 64(2), 71–96.

Poppo, L. and Zenger, T. (2002). Do formal contracts and relational governance function as substitutes or complements? *Strategic Management Journal*, 23, 707–725.

Regan, M.; Love, P.E.D. and Jim, J. (2015). Public infrastructure procurement: A review of adversarial and non-adversarial contracting methods. *Journal of Public Procurement*, 15(4), 405–438.

Reuer, J.J. and Ariño, A. (2002). Contractual renegotiations in strategic alliances. *Journal of Management*, 28(1), 47–68.

Rodriguez-Plesa, E.; Dimand, A.-M. and Alkadry, M.G. (2019). Community social capital, political values, or organizational capacity? Indicators of engagement in sustainable public procurement at the local level. *Journal of Cleaner Production*, 338, 130556.

Roehrich, J.K. and Kivleniece, I. (2022). Creating and distributing sustainable value through public-private collaborative projects. (pp. 473–499) In: George, G.; Hass, M.R.; Joshi, H.; McGahan, A. and Tracey, P. (eds.), *Handbook on the Business of Sustainability: The Organization, Implementation, and Practice of Sustainable Growth*. Edward Elgar Publishing.

Roehrich, J.K. and Lewis, M.A. (2014). Procuring complex performance: Implications for exchange governance complexity. *International Journal of Operations & Production Management*, 32(2), 221–241.

Roehrich, J.K.; Barlow, J. and Wright, S. (2013). Delivering European healthcare infrastructure through public-private partnerships: The theory and practice of contracting and bundling. In: Professor Das, T.K. (Series Editor); series: '*Research in Strategic Alliances*', book: *Managing Public-Private Strategic Alliances*, 1st edition. Information Age Publishing.

Roehrich, J.K.; Davies, A.; Tyler, B.; Mishra, A. and Bendoly, E. (2024). Large interorganizational projects (LIPs): Toward an integrative perspective and research agenda on interorganizational governance. *Journal of Operations Management*, 70(1), 4–21.

Roehrich, J.K.; Kalra, J.; Squire, B. and Davies, A. (2023). Network orchestration in a large interorganizational project. *Journal of Operations Management*, 69(7), 1078–1099.

Roehrich, J.K.; Lewis, M.A. and George, G. (2014). Are public-private partnerships a healthy option? A systematic literature review. *Social Science & Medicine*, 113, 110–119.

Roehrich, J.K.; Sarafan, M.; Squire, B.; Lawson, B. and Bouazzaoui, M. (2025). Conflict and contract use in cross-cultural buyer-supplier relationships: The roles of cultural context. *Production and Operations Management*, 34(5), 974–992.

Roehrich, J.K.; Selviaridis, K.; Kalra, J.; van der Valk, W. and Fang, F. (2020). Inter-organisational governance: A review, conceptualisation and extension. *Production Planning & Control*, 31(6), 453–469.

Roehrich, J.K.; Tyler, B.B.; Kalra, J. and Squire, B. (2021, September). The decision process of contracting in supply chain management. (pp. 563–586) In: Choi, T.; Li, J.; Rogers, D.; Rungtusanatham, J.; Schoenherr, T. and Wagner, S. (eds.), *Handbook of 'Supply Chain Management'*. Oxford University Press.

Sarafan, M.; Lawson, B.; Roehrich, J.K. and Squire, B. (2022). Knowledge sharing within project-based supply networks. *International Journal of Operations & Production Management*, 42(6), 852–874.

Schepker, D.J.; Oh, W.Y.; Martynov, A. and Poppo, L. (2014). The many futures of contracts: Moving beyond structure and safeguarding to coordination and adaptation. *Journal of Management*, 40(1), 193–225.

Scott, W.R.; Levitt, R.E. and Orr, R.J. (2011). *Global Projects: Institutional and Political Challenges*. Cambridge University Press.

Suhonen, N.; Tammi, T.; Saastamoinen, J.; Pesu, J.; Turtiainen, M. and Okkonen, L. (2019). Incentives and risk-sharing in public procurement of innovations: Towards contracting strategy framework. *Journal of Public Procurement*, 19(2), 129–145.

Taubeneder, R.; Roehrich, J.K. and Squire, B. (2022). The legitimation process of a new multipartner alliance. (pp. 1–32) In: Das, T.K. (ed.), *Managing Interpartner Cooperation in Strategic Alliances*. Information Age Publishing.

Taubeneder, R.; Roehrich, J.K.; Tyler, B.; Squire, B. and Gnyawali, D. (2024). Managing coopetition dynamics: A longitudinal study of a multiparty alliance formation in a large utilities project. *Journal of Operations Management*, 70, 875–903.

Uher, T.E. and Davenport, P. (2009). *Fundamentals of Building Contract Management*, 2nd edition. National Library of Australia, UNSW Press Book.

Van Marrewijk, A.H.; Ybema, S.; Smits, K.; Clegg, S. and Pitsis, T.S. (2016). Clash of the titans: Temporal organizing and collaborative dynamics in the Panama Canal megaproject. *Organization Studies*, 37, 1745–1769.

Vandaele, D.; Rangarajan, D.; Gemmel, P. and Lievens, A. (2007). How to govern business services exchanges: Contractual and relational issues. *International Journal of Management Reviews*, 9(3), 237–258.
Walker, H. and Brammer, S. (2012). The relationship between sustainable procurement and e-procurement in the public sector. *International Journal of Production Economics*, 140(1), 256–268.
Wirtz, B.W. and Weyerer, J.C. (2017). Cyberterrorism and cyber attacks in the public sector: How public administration copes with digital threats. *International Journal of Public Administration*, 40(13), 1085–1100.
Wright, S.; Barlow, J. and Roehrich, J.K. (2019). Public-Private Partnerships for health services: Construction, protection and rehabilitation of critical healthcare infrastructure in Europe. (pp. 125–151) In: Clark, R. and Hakim, S. (eds.), *Public Private Partnerships: Construction, Protection, and Rehabilitation of Critical Infrastructure*. Springer.
Zheng, J.; Roehrich, J.K. and Lewis, M.A. (2008). The dynamics of contractual and relational governance: Evidence from long-term public-private procurement arrangements. *Journal of Purchasing and Supply Management*, 14(1), 43–54.

## *Case Study: Transformative Contract Management at Imperial College NHS Trust (London, United Kingdom) (Developed by Jens K. Roehrich together with Duncan Eaton (Non-Executive Director at National Health Service (NHS) London Procurement Partnership (LPP)), Adrian Woodmore (EFPS Director NHS LPP), and Matthew Price (Associate Director at NHS LPP working on the NHS New Hospital Program)*

### Background and Problem Statement

Imperial College NHS Trust (hereafter referred to as 'Trust'), a prominent London acute hospital group, faced challenges with its hard facilities management (FM) contract. Hard FM services focus on the maintenance, operation, and optimization of a building's infrastructure and systems (e.g., regular building inspections and repairs, maintenance of outdoor spaces, mechanical and electrical services). The Trust uses a 'Computer Aided Facilities Management (CAFM) System' for their FM data, however the data points in the system were incomplete as prior contractors did not work with the Trust's systems but with their own databases (very limited collaboration between the Trust and prior contractors). For example, the asset register on the CAFM system did not have any data on the assets on site, details on warranties, last major service, purchase dates, purchase and replacement cost were all absent, and it was a requirement of the new contract to populate the fields in a specific time period. This needed to be changed with the new contractor to work in a more collaborative manner including the sharing of key data points. Moreover, the existing contract, valued at £20 million annually, exhibited several shortcomings, including inadequate KPIs, adversarial relationships with the contractor, lack of visibility into crucial information, reactive responses to repairs, and evidence in some cases of contractor incompetence.

Recognizing the need for a comprehensive overhaul, the Trust commissioned the LPP to support the re-procurement of its FM contract. LPP, an NHS procurement organization serving the English NHS (one of the largest single-payer healthcare system in the world), brought expertise in procurement, project management, and subject matter knowledge.

### Consultation Stage

During the consultation stage, LPP conducted stakeholder engagement meetings with managers from various departments at the Trust, fostering a collaborative approach. Stakeholder groups, including estates, procurement, social value and sustainability, clinical operations, health and safety, decontamination, and fire safety, were actively involved throughout the project including service mapping, service specification design, documentation development, and the tender and evaluation process. For example, the Program Board (one of the key stakeholders) predominantly comprised colleagues from a wide range of disciplines across procurement and estates management. In order to ensure that individual workloads were respected, colleagues from other disciplines were included in communication and permitted to attend Program Board sessions as available but separate 'contract working group sessions' were arranged to draft in support from specialist areas to directly input into elements of the procurement. For instance, colleagues from medicine and care, clinical support, and infection control, all contributed to the specification, both in supporting the drafting of their specialist requirements, but also in providing review of more generic areas of the specifications with an eye on how each element might impact their specialist areas.

Identified weaknesses in the existing contract and its management process needed to be ideally addressed collaboratively (between the Trust and the new contractor), and new clauses (including incentives and penalties), along with critical KPIs, should be incorporated into the new service and contract specifications.

### Tender (bid) and Contract Stage

LPP utilized the newly designed (please see 'consultation stage') FM framework as the basis for tender invitations, inviting 12 suppliers. Two comprehensive and valid supplier bids were received, with a contract value of £20 million per annum for a duration of five years plus an option for two additional years.

Where appropriate, specialisms outside of estates and procurement were asked to support with the evaluation of their specialist areas. The evaluation criteria for the tender were split into key areas:

1. Project method statement – Outlining the bidders' general approach to delivering, and understanding of the service being procured, including each of the individual areas of specialism;
2. Resource proposal – Four scored questions designed to evaluate the quality of the supplier's approach to the management and development of their resource base including their approach to operational staffing and supply chain management;
3. Technical proposal – Eight scored questions assessing the supplier's approach to technical elements of the contract including asset management, data, spares management, and the use of computer-aided FM;
4. Social value – Three questions covering the approach to the delivery of social value and fighting climate change;
5. Contract management – A review of the bidders' approach to contract management over the life of the contract; and
6. Price – Around 40% of the evaluation was allocated to pricing, offering a sliding score with the lowest price receiving full marks.

The winning bidder demonstrated the capability to meet the Trust's core requirements in terms of service provision, contract, and relational management. Also, the winning bidder needed to ensure that 'condition-based monitoring' of high value mechanical and electrical assets was part of the continuous improvement of the contract, adding smart technologies to measure particular failure flags of the asset to enable immediate remedy before the asset failed to prevent clinical downtime which would have a direct impact on patients and emergency call-out costs. This would help to ease pressures on finances and to improve the collaboration between the Trust and the new contractor in working in a more collaborative way including the sharing of vital data points.

### Challenges Encountered during the Re-procurement Process

The following challenges were encountered during the re-procurement process:

- Transmission of documentation – Due to the nature and size of both the technical documents and supplier bid packets, and the fact that the evaluation and program team operated under a hybrid working model, an approach needed to be developed to manage the sharing of documents as email was not fit for purpose. A shared space within the back office architecture was created and provided unique logins to ensure secure access;
- Ensuring momentum – Due to the complex nature and volume of the work required to get to tender stage, there was a need to ensure that momentum was maintained throughout the process. Meetings were arranged ahead of time and the program team membership was consistent throughout the process to ensure accountability in terms of action completion; and
- Timeframe – Due to the complexity of the procurement task, the program team initially underestimated the resource demand that would be placed on bidders in terms of reviewing the information and formulating their bids. Working closely with the bidders helped to agree a four-week extension but in hindsight a focus on bid resourcing in pre-market engagement would have helped.

### Outcomes

Despite the challenges discussed earlier, the re-procurement led to significant positive outcomes for the Trust including, but not limited to, cost savings (a substantial reduction in off-contract spend, resulting in savings of at least £500,000 per annum), and improved reputation to better service delivery. Moreover, the following outcomes were achieved:

- *Robust KPIs:* Delivery of a set of robust and effective KPIs, ranked by criticality, ensuring improved contractor performance;
- *Fit-for-purpose specification:* A specification with the depth required to obtain maximum value and performance, improving the quality of patient care delivery;
- *Incentives for performance:* Incentive and penalty clauses were implemented, driving contractor accountability and performance;
- *Asset management:* An up-to-date, cleansed register of physical assets, with data accessible to both the contractor and Trust managers, promoting transparency and efficiency;

- *Improved relationships:* A shift from adversarial to collaborative relationships between suppliers and the Trust, fostering a positive working environment; and
- *Learning:* As the project was handled by the LPP, this immediately provided a central knowledge point to be shared across other NHS Trusts, members of the LPP network, and 'procurement hubs' nationally for their procurement projects.

In conclusion, the collaborative approach between the Trust and LPP, coupled with comprehensive stakeholder engagement, resulted in a successful re-procurement process. The transformed hard FM contract not only addressed the existing deficiencies but also paved the way for enhanced service quality, cost-effectiveness, and improved relationships between the Trust and its service supplier.

### Discussion Questions

1. What were the key issues identified in the existing Facilities Management (FM) contract at Imperial College NHS Trust? For post-experience students (E/MBAs), this question could include a discussion on students' own experience of contract issues from examples they are familiar with.
2. How did the London Procurement Partnership (LPP) contribute to the re-procurement process, and what specific expertise did they bring to the table? For post-experience students (E/MBAs), this question could include a discussion on students' own experience of the use of consultants (internal or external to the organization) when seeking to improve contract and relationship management for a specific product/service. What issues should be considered?
3. Apart from the challenges faced during the re-procurement process, what other challenges could occur, and how could they be addressed?
4. What do you think is the long-term impact of the transformed FM contract on the Trust's operations and patient care?
5. What lessons can be drawn from this case study that might be applicable to other organizations experiencing similar (or different) contract management challenges?
6. What role could technology play in the re-procurement process, if any, and how could it contribute to the success of the contract management
7. Lastly, what are key activities that public sector organizations should consider as part of the ongoing management of the contract? (Please refer to a more detailed discussion in the accompanying book chapter – Section 16.2.3.)

# 17 Managing Solicitation and Supplier Selection

*Fredo Schotanus and Luitzen de Boer*

## 17.1 Introduction

Supplier selection is a pivotal phase within the formal and regulated landscape of public procurement. In this phase, critical decisions are taken concerning the selection of one or more suppliers to be awarded a contract. As public procurement volumes rise steadily and the focus increasingly shifts from mere pricing to encompass overall value, the significance and complexity of supplier selection are heightened. Moreover, an increasing number of people are engaged and they may possess varying perceptions regarding the relative importance of different aspects of the procurement and who should participate in the award decision-making process (Volker and Schotanus, 2023). Consequently, procurement decisions often evolve into more intricate processes than initially expected, often entailing a growing recognition of the importance of different values. Furthermore, what also makes supplier selection challenging for public organizations is that they often need to have the method of selection largely predetermined during the preparation stage of (larger) tenders. There are multiple reasons for this, such as transparency requirements and preventing supplier selection models from being tailored to favor a particular supplier. Finally, the complexity is further compounded by factors such as heightened policy pressure and pressure from companies to keep supplier selections models simple and fair, and also to incorporate environmental and social criteria, as well as considering a longer-term perspective.

A more comprehensive overview of the factors influencing the growing complexity and importance of supplier selection decisions is depicted in Figure 17.1. In the center of the figure, you can find the main idea, surrounded by various factors contributing to the complexity and importance of supplier selection. For instance, the purchasing function is often distributed across multiple departments (as indicated in the top-left of the figure), involving many individuals with diverse interests in the supplier selection process.

Some factors in the figure are likely to exert a similar impact on supplier selection by every public organization. Research on corruption in public procurement by Hessami (2014), for example, suggests that corruption in supplier selection decisions is an issue across the world, and not limited to low-income countries. There is also a global focus on involving small and medium-sized enterprises (SMEs) in public procurement, for instance, in India, the EU, the United States, Canada, South Korea, Japan, Brazil, and Australia. However, other factors do not universally apply to every country or organization worldwide. For instance, the incorporation of environmental and social criteria is already more common in countries such as the United Kingdom and France, but less so in many others. The emphasis on transparency about supplier selection is increasingly recognized in countries like Ukraine, Chile, and Colombia in contrast to Western European and large Commonwealth countries.

DOI: 10.4324/9781003566670-20

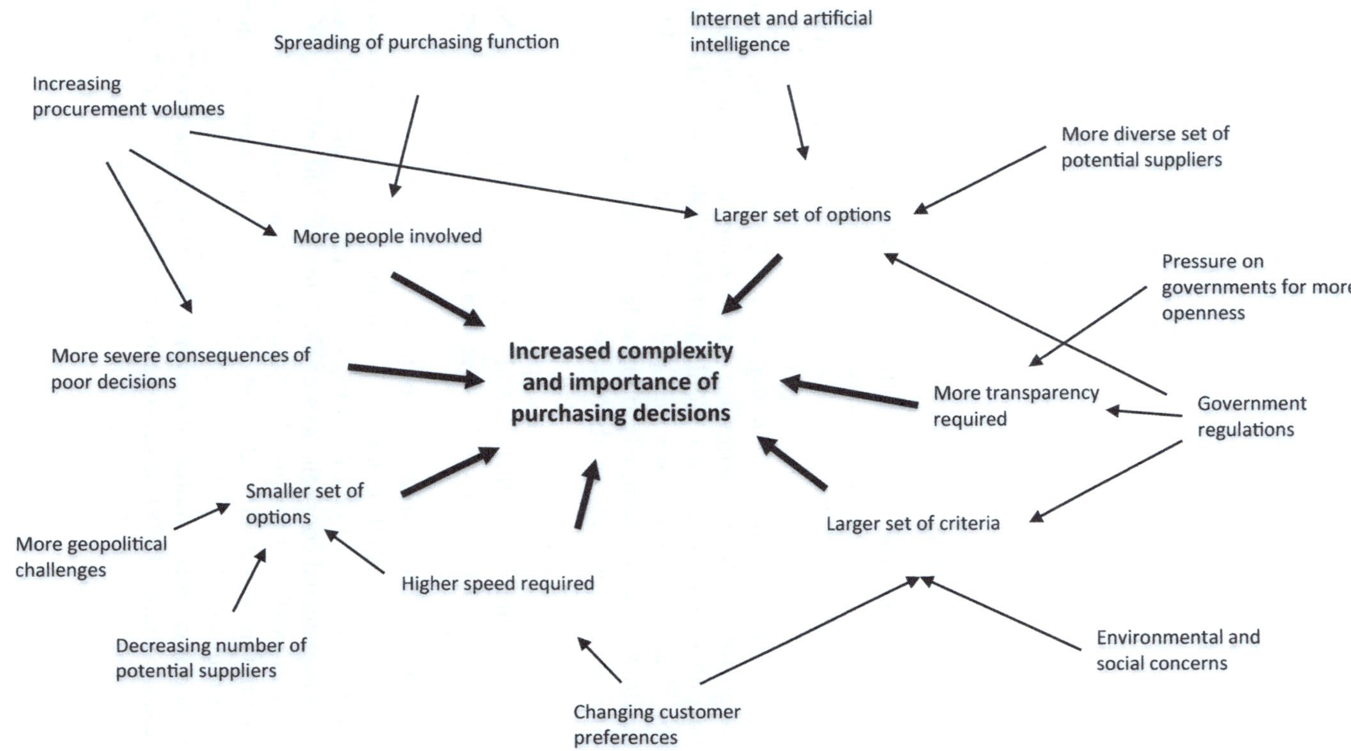


*Figure 17.1* Impact of developments on the complexity and importance of supplier selection decisions.
*Source*: Based on De Boer (1998) and updated to the current time.

Furthermore, in countries like the United States and South Africa, there are specific goals or laws to better involve minority-owned companies in public procurement.

We also observe market-specific differences. In some markets, suppliers merge, acquire each other, or competitors go bankrupt, resulting in fewer choices. In other markets, we see an increase in diversity, with local and (inter)national offerings or social and traditional enterprises. Nevertheless, we anticipate that most factors in the figure are at least of some relevance to every public organization making supplier selection decisions.

The remainder of this chapter elucidates the process of structurally constructing supplier selection models for tenders in nine sequential steps. Alongside theoretical insights, practical application is demonstrated through various examples, showcasing how theory can be effectively applied in practice by public organizations globally. Among other things, we will emphasize the necessity for a methodical approach for supplier selection in the public sector and explain the importance of incorporating true costs, including external costs and benefits, into the tendering process, thereby promoting sustainable and socially responsible procurement practices.[1]

## 17.2 Developing a Supplier Selection Model

Fundamentally, supplier selection in the public sector, when viewed as a cognitive or decision-making process, is no different from selecting suppliers in the private sector. However, certain aspects of the public sector context influence how the process is (or must be) designed or shaped. Examples include the need for transparency and the involvement of a larger number of objectives and stakeholders involved. As a result, many public sector organizations face greater challenges than their private sector counterparts in making and justifying sound supplier selection choices. While artificial intelligence (AI) can help make better decisions by "learning" from past cases, public buyers must still be able to explain their choices. Therefore, understanding selection models remains important.

Furthermore, the integration of sustainable and social criteria adds additional complexity to the selection process. These criteria are often more abstract and harder to measure than monetary values (De Boer et al., 2006), such as price and tangible factors, such as technical strength or specific characteristics, which can already be difficult to assess. Nevertheless, it is important for public buyers to include these aspects in supplier selection models, as demonstrated in Box 17.1.

Like any other individual and organizational decision-making process, supplier selection decisions require cognitive and economic effort, time, and information (Simon, 1978). These are seldom (if ever) free of charge. Still, we want the supplier selection model to accurately capture the expected consequences of choosing one bid over another. However, how close can we realistically get to this ideal? And how much efforts will it required for suppliers to understand the selection model and submit a bid? In essence, we need to strike a balance, weighing the cost of the process against the expected benefits. Furthermore, we need to be aware of our cognitive limitations with fully grasping the "real" totality of the situation and decision (Simon, 1978). It makes sense to consider any tool used in supplier selection as a "heuristic" – a practical approach or rule of thumb that aids in decision-making striving to make the decision as sound as it can be within reasonable efforts. Some heuristics arguably fit better in one situation than another. It is interesting yet challenging at the same time that the prevailing public procurement "doctrine" seems to assume the possibility of one, objective and "right" choice. Using Simon's terminology (Simon, 1978) and its application to supplier selection (De Boer, 2017), it may be appropriate to consider models and directives for supplier selection as ways of achieving procedural rationality (i.e. creating

**Box 17.1 True Costs versus Purchase Costs Only**

This example illustrates the importance of considering the true costs of a tender. The true costs of a tender extend beyond the purchase costs and costs of use, encompassing the *external costs*. External costs are defined as costs created for others or society, not included in the purchase price and the costs of use. Examples of external costs are greenhouse gas emissions, pollution, or staff underpayment. They can be measured quantitatively, but also qualitatively, as will be discussed later in the chapter in more detail.

There can also be *external benefits* associated with a bid from a supplier. These are typically easier to consider when selecting the best supplier. For instance, they can be integrated into the quality part of the bid of a supplier. It is also important to note that a rational supplier has an incentive to "sell" external benefits and "hide" external costs.

Figure 17.2 shows two suppliers with varying purchase prices and external costs. The external costs in this example could be, for instance, $CO_2$ costs created by the supplier for the product to be purchased; the costs could be assumed to be 100 euros per ton of $CO_2$. The emissions could be determined by an independent $CO_2$ footprint measurement. Assuming an equal level of quality for both bids, the more sustainable or social option is the bid of Supplier B. However, if price and quality are the sole criteria, the bid of Supplier A would be selected.

It is worth mentioning that it is often the case that Supplier A can offer a lower purchase price than Supplier B, as B could incur additional expenses to mitigate external costs. Therefore, it is important for buyers to either prequalify only suppliers such as B, excluding suppliers such as A from participating in a public tender. Alternatively, buyers could include requirements and award criteria related to externalities, thereby recognizing and rewarding B's lower external costs compared to A.

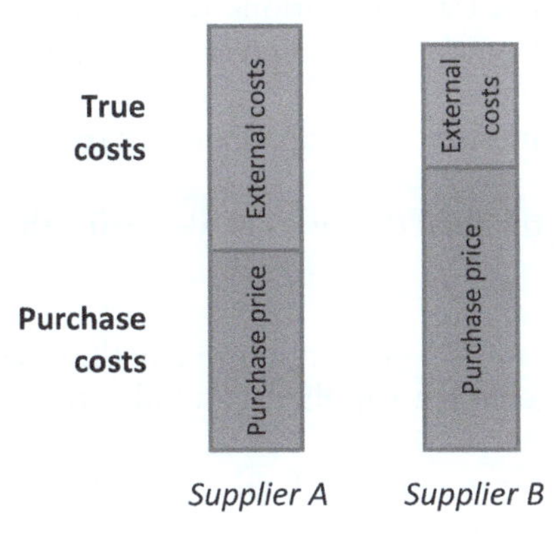


*Figure 17.2* Example of different prices and true costs of suppliers.
*Source*: Original creation.

conditions for finding and choosing a reasonably good supplier or bid) more so than guaranteeing substantive rationality (i.e. finding the very best bid in a universal, absolute sense).

Taking a procedural rationality perspective, we elaborate in the rest of this section on a comprehensive nine-step process for developing a supplier selection model. This process is applicable for awarding contracts to suppliers in one-phase tenders. Moreover, it can be used for both phases of two-phase tenders, serving the purpose of prequalifying suppliers by evaluating requests to participate (phase 1) and subsequently awarding the contract (phase 2). Finally, it can be used for larger tenders, but we recommend caution with using supplier selection models for smaller purchases that are conducted through multiple private tenders. Developing good supplier selection models takes time and effort, which may not always be available for smaller purchases. In such situations, a procurement procedure that relies more on dialogue and less on detailed criteria for evaluation may be more appropriate.

For the rest of this section, we assume that there is sufficient time and capacity to develop a good supplier selection model. As demonstrated throughout this section, each of the following nine steps can significantly influence how suppliers craft their bids and, ultimately, which bid prevails in a tender.

The nine steps are the following:

1. *Understand demand and supply possibilities:* Gain a clear understanding of both demand and the potential supply options available.
2. *Choose on what basis to award contracts*: Determine whether the focus should be on (a) a trade-off between non-cost-related aspects and possibly price, (b) lowest life-cycle costs (LCC), or (c) on the lowest price (LP) only. Steps 3 and onwards are only required if a buyer uses a prequalification phase or uses (b) or (c) to award a contract.
3. *Develop prequalification or award criteria*: Establish the criteria that will guide the prequalification or award process.
4. *Attach weight*: Assign relative importance or weight to each criterion.
5. *Draw scoring methods*: Create scoring methods for each criterion.
6. *Choose a prequalification or award method:* Decide on the method that will be used to calculate the total score, determining which suppliers are prequalified or are awarded the contract.
7. *Simulate and revise the supplier selection model*: Use simulations with fictive requests to participate or fictive bids to assess potential outcomes and revise the supplier selection model.
8. *Assess requests to participate or bids:* Assess requests to participate or bids received from suppliers.
9. *Justify tender decision:* Derive the rationale for the final decisions made during the tender process.

If a formal supplier selection model is used, then steps 2–6 are published in the documents of a public tender. As we will explain later in this chapter, suppliers can tailor their bids to the request based on this information.

While the rest of this chapter primarily concentrates on the final awarding stage, it is essential for the reader to recognize the broader context. For instance, significant impacts on environmental and social performance often stem from market exploration, needs identification, and especially specification definition. Additionally, post-award follow-up stages should not be overlooked or underestimated, as they are crucial for realizing the value derived from selecting a particular bid.

### 17.2.1 *Step 1: Understand Demand and Supply Possibilities*

Before buyers can develop a supplier selection model, they must understand what is needed and what the market has to offer. Buyers have several options to improve their understanding of supply and demand, including analyzing spending from previous years, interviewing users and other stakeholders, conducting a market and buyer consultation (dialogue), and employing or hiring experts. Examples of questions related to supplier selection that are important to answer during this step are the following:

1. What is the substance matter of the purchase and how complex is it?
2. How important is the purchase and what is the estimated value or the size of the budget?
3. What objectives can be realized?
4. Do we or colleagues from other public organizations have experience from earlier, similar purchases?
5. How many interested suppliers can we expect?
6. How can we capture the financial models used by suppliers into the price criterion used for selecting suppliers in that market?[2]
7. How can we assess the price, quality, and societal impact of the bids?

If it is not possible to develop a supplier selection model after using the earlier mentioned tools, then a procurement procedure with negotiation or dialogue options could be explored instead. However, these possibilities might be restricted or limited by the public procurement law and regulations that apply to the country of the reader of this chapter.

### 17.2.2 *Step 2: Choose on What Basis to Award Contracts*

Once the demand and supply possibilities are identified, the buyer needs to decide on what basis the best supplier(s) will be awarded the contract. A buyer can use (1) a trade-off of price and non-cost-related criteria or non-cost-related criteria only (we refer to this as best price-quality ratio (BPQR)), (2) LCC, or (3) LP.

With *BPQR* (also known as *scoring auction* in economic and auction literature) buyers award a contract based on price and quality criteria or on quality criteria only (the price or financial model is then set by the buyer in the procurement documents). There are large differences between countries in how often BPQR is applied. In countries such as the United States, the United Kingdom, France, and the Netherlands, but also for international tenders of the World Bank, BPQR is a popular method or it is becoming a popular method. It is even the default approach in countries such as the Netherlands and for most international tenders of the World Bank. On the other hand, in countries such as Germany and several Eastern European countries, LP is much more popular (Schotanus and Gaaikema, 2020). The popularity of awarding contracts based on the LP may also vary depending on the specific sector and project. For instance, for buying services, BPQR might be more popular while for buying relatively simple works, LP might be more popular.

Note that the word (societal) impact could also be added to BPQR, resulting in the best price–quality–impact ratio. Impact or external costs can be considered as part of the quality criteria, but as there are important differences between the quality of a purchase (such as the performance of a laptop) and the external impact it has on society (such as greenhouse gas emissions created by its production), quality and impact can also be considered as separate topics (Schotanus, 2022). Including impact as a separate category has the added benefit of making societal impact in tenders more visible, rather than it being just an add-on.[3]

Finally, note that in different countries and academic fields, different terms are used for BPQR. Other common terms in the public sector are Best Value and Most Economically Advantageous Tender (MEAT).

With *LCC*, buyers award a contract based on the lowest total costs associated with the purchase during its complete lifetime, ranging from the purchase price, maintenance costs to external costs such as greenhouse emissions and social costs. Essentially, all cost-related elements are aggregated, and the bid with the lowest LCC wins the tender (i.e. the bid with the lowest *true* costs, see Box 17.1 as well). Although several tools are freely available online, LCC can be complex, as it is challenging to quantify all related life-cycle costs to a purchase. The method is therefore rarely used (yet) in its full form in public procurement practice. There are more applications of Total Cost of Ownership (TCO) in which tenders are awarded based on a combination of price and *internal* costs like maintenance costs and energy costs. However, such tenders do not truly calculate the complete life-cycle costs including *external* costs as well.

With *LP*, buyers award a contract based on price only. This can be a single price element or multiple price elements. LP can be a suitable method for commodities, for small purchases, cases where the buyer prescribes all requirements, or for tenders with no expected quality, environmental and social differences between suppliers. The method is straightforward and less prone to corruption and fraud compared to methods involving qualitative award criteria. It can also be appropriate when the buyer possesses or has hired specific knowledge and prescribes the specifications. For instance, it can be prescribed that a new bridge should be build according to a certain design. A prescribed design can limit innovation (unless the buyer has hired or possesses specific expert knowledge), but it also reduces transaction costs and makes it easier for SMEs to participate in public tenders.

Finally, in economic and auction literature, several variants of LP are studied, including so-called first price auctions, second price auctions, and average price auctions. These can all be considered LP tenders, but they differ in the price awarded to the winner. To avoid the winner's curse, in second price auctions and average price auctions, winners do not receive their own bid price, but rather the price of the second-highest bid or the average price (or a variation thereof). It goes beyond the scope of this chapter to delve further into these mechanisms. Interested readers are referred to Chang et al. (2015).

If a buyer does not use a prequalification phase in the tender and uses LCC or LP to award a contract, steps 3 and onwards are not required.

### *17.2.3 Step 3: Develop Prequalification or Award Criteria*

If buyers aim to use a prequalification phase[4] with prequalification criteria or use BPQR in the tender phase, they can start thinking about choosing the prequalification (if applicable) and award criteria that they will apply during the tender. Prequalification criteria and award criteria are quite distinct and are not to be confused. If there is a prequalification phase where a subset of suppliers is selected,[5] the aim is to select those suppliers who are capable to do the job based on general properties of the company, using prequalification criteria. It should be relatively easy for suppliers to submit a "request for participation" for the prequalification phase. Examples of prequalification criteria are prior experience (references), financial health, certificates, and staff qualifications and competency requirements. Price is not allowed as a prequalification criterion in the EU.

The tender phase assesses the best tender received from the (prequalified) suppliers based on award criteria. Criteria can be quantitative (e.g. price) or qualitative (e.g. a plan of approach). Depending on the public procurement law and regulations that apply to the country of the reader, several requirements can apply for qualitative prequalification and award criteria, including (Arrowsmith, 2014) the following:

- Criteria should not be discriminatory.
- Adjustments to criteria during a tender in response to supplier's inquiries are allowed, but significant changes may lead to an extension of the bid submission deadline.
- It is not allowed to modify criteria after the bid submission deadline.
- Criteria should be accountable in the public contract, which could be confirmed by a penalty.

Examples of criteria encompass aspects related to quality (e.g. to what extent is the company's product a fit with what is needed) or societal impact (e.g. to what extent does the company ensure international social conditions in its supply chains?). In some countries, such as the United States, past performance of suppliers can also be an important award criterion. The assumption is that suppliers with positive past performances are likely to perform well again in the future. In other countries, such as for European tenders within the EU, past performance is not permitted as a standalone award criterion.[6] However, bidders can utilize past performance to demonstrate the feasibility of their proposals. Another notable distinction across legal systems is observed in countries like China, where general properties of the firm, such as financial health and certificates, are acceptable as award criteria. Such practice is not permitted in European tenders (Chen, 2024). For European tenders, award criteria need to be directly related to the subject-matter of the contract in question.

In practice, criteria are often replicated from the previous tender or are the result of brainstorming sessions. Replicating criteria from the previous tender can result in outdated tenders, for instance, if what is being asked for has become a standard in the market. It may also lead to overlooking newer developments, such as sustainable procurement. Instead of copying from the previous tender, it is advisable to emulate and contact a contracting authority with a good reputation that has recently conducted a similar tender. Furthermore, in countries such as Norway, Belgium, and the Netherlands, public purchasers can use an open online support system for finding appropriate and up-to-date criteria for evaluating environmental and social performance in various stages of the tender process and for different categories of needs.

Criteria originating from brainstorming sessions often lead to a broad set of (sub)criteria that may lack distinctiveness and potentially overlap. Redundant criteria can lead to confusion and do not contribute meaningfully to the tender. The number of qualitative criteria should thus be restricted to mitigate excessive transaction costs for suppliers and assessors (see also Drake et al., 2024). Aspects that are not distinctive or are overly detailed for the tender could instead be developed by the winning supplier during a verification or implementation phase.

Several techniques are available to prevent having a broad set of (sub)criteria, such as utilizing tree structures or a goal setting technique. The latter involves translating the original (policy) goals associated with a tender into requirements and criteria. For example, the simplified goals of a tender for a public transport contract could be linked to aspects like a fair price, more public transport usage over cars, and reduced $CO_2$-emissions, measurable through a certification process such as the $CO_2$ Performance Ladder (see Box 17.2).

Finally, it is important that criteria are explained in measurable and unambiguous terms within the procurement documents. Award criteria should be assessable both during the bid evaluation and throughout the contract performance stage. Including the contract manager in the procurement team during the development of the award criteria helps prevent the

**Box 17.2 Stimulating Carbon Emission Reduction by Procurement**

The $CO_2$ Performance Ladder is an instrument that helps organizations reduce their carbon emissions in the organization, in projects, and in the business sector.[7] Each organization certified on the ladder is subject to annual audits performed by independent and accredited certifying institutions. Through these audits, a certified organization ensures the implementation of the $CO_2$ Performance Ladder in its management and projects. Furthermore, the certified organizations are evaluated annually on their ambitions and initiatives to reduce carbon emissions, and continuous improvement.

In practice, certified organizations can receive additional points in supplier selection models in several countries, as it is assumed that projects awarded to certified organizations will be more sustainable. The higher the level an organization has on the $CO_2$ Performance Ladder, the higher the award advantage.

submission of proposals from suppliers that are challenging to manage or measure during the contract performance stage. Whenever feasible, articulate criteria using quantifiable metrics or established standards as well. This approach enhances objectivity in assessments and minimizes the potential for subjective interpretations.

To avoid ambiguity and varying interpretations, steer clear of vague language as well. This can be achieved by building on best practices, having a colleague review the documents, and ensuring that the procurement team can envision drafting a bid based on the requirements and criteria. It is also helpful to clearly specify the type of evidence or documentation suppliers should provide to substantiate their claims under each criterion. Additionally, clarifying what is sought and what is *not* sought can prevent misunderstandings. Finally, scrutinize whether all the information requested (the required input) is genuinely necessary for the assessment.

A possible structure for the description of one qualitative goal-oriented criterion is shortly summarized in Box 17.3.

Finally, when it is challenging to formulate award criteria directly tied to the *quality* of the procurement, the buyer may opt to award the contract based on *partner* properties. These properties could include the supplier's ability to collaborate and innovate for the specific project, rather than focusing solely on qualities related to the project itself. By contracting the most suitable partner, there is increased potential for collaboration in the subsequent development of detailed plans and quality-related aspects for the work, supplies, or services.

### *17.2.4 Step 4: Attach Weight*

The buyer must usually specify the relative weighting which it gives to each of the criteria chosen to assess the requests to participate or the bids. Those weightings can be expressed in percentages or as a specific number of points distributed among the criteria. Where weighting is not feasible for demonstrable reasons as determined by the buyer, they usually must indicate the criteria in descending order of importance.

The weights assigned to different aspects (related to price, quality, and/or societal impact) are determined based on the specific context of the work, supply, or service being procured. For instance, in certain situations, quality is more important than costs, and the criteria for

**Box 17.3 Awarding Public Transport Services**

**Objective for One Award Criterion Out of All Award Criteria**

Increase the utilization of public transport services, without attracting those that currently walk or cycle.

**Required Input**

Please provide:

1. A timetable;
2. A network map;
3. An overview and explanation of differences between the new and current timetables;
4. Proof of why the plans are realistic and will contribute to the buyer's objective.

For 3 and 4, a maximum of 5,000 words are allowed.

**Assessment**

Bids will receive higher scores if they demonstrate:

1. Specificity;
2. Realism;
3. Effectiveness (i.e. that they can achieve the stated objective).

Certain combinations of assessments lead to specific scores: a bid that is not specific will be assessed as insufficient. A bid that is specific but lacks proof related to realism and effectiveness will be assessed as satisfactory. A bid that is specific and shows that it is realistic and effective will be assessed as very good.

quality will outweigh cost criteria. Quality-related aspects may allow for more discretion compared to the price, making quality more susceptible to manipulation by corrupt officials who may seek to diminish the weight of price to enhance their control over the outcome. To prevent extreme cases where prices are given negligible weights, China mandates that price weights fall within the range of 30%–60% for supplies procurement and 10%–30% for works and services procurement. In practice, many Chinese tenders often lean toward using the lowest possible price weight (Chen, 2024). In other legal systems, there are less stringent rules for weightings. For instance, in the Netherlands, a EU member state, there is no lower limit for the weight of price, but there is an indication of an upper limit. While there is no exact upper limit, legal precedent suggests that the price weight should not exceed 80%–90%. It is also noteworthy that in countries where LP is a popular method, buyers using BPQR often assign high weights to price.

For individuals not trained as procurement officers, the weight of criteria is usually perceived as the most important indicator of the importance of a criterion. However, as will be shown in steps 5 and 6, this assumption does not always hold true. For instance, a criterion with a high weight that does not distinguish between suppliers ultimately is not important.

Determining weight can be a challenging task for a procurement team, as there is often a trade-off between different policy objectives. In practice, various methods are used for determining weights. They can be the result of business case calculations, where criteria receive higher weight when they add most value beyond the minimum requirements. Alternatively, weights can be determined through developing fictive bids, with the procurement team discussing the extent to which these fictive bids receive the "correct" score under different weighting while considering the minimum requirements. Finally, methods such as Analytic Hierarchy Process (AHP) (Saaty, 1980) can be used to determine initial weighting in case there are three or more criteria. AHP acknowledges that the human brain has difficulties with comparing the importance of several criteria simultaneously. Hence, to make a more reliable decision, AHP compares each criterion pairwise to every other criterion. This can be done at different scales (e.g. a 5-point scale or a 9-point scale) where the procurement team indicates for each pair of criteria whether they are equally important or whether one criterion is slightly to very much more important than the other. Applying AHP may also be useful for detecting inconsistencies in the decision-maker's evaluations. Interested readers can find many AHP tools readily available for free on the web or use an AI to apply AHP.

### *17.2.5 Step 5: Draw Scoring Methods*

Scoring methods (also known as scoring rules) are used to assign a score to supplier bids for each criterion. Scoring methods can be used for qualitative or quantitative assessments, they can be linear or non-linear, and absolute or relative. All types are explained in more detail below.

#### *17.2.5.1 Scoring Methods for Qualitative Assessments*

*Scoring methods for qualitative assessments* are used for assessing plans, designs, interviews, and similar elements. The assessment is done by humans (see step 8). Scores for qualitative criteria can be determined either relatively or absolutely. With a relative method, for instance, one might assert that Supplier A outperforms or is equal to Supplier B on criterion 1. Conversely, with an absolute method, scores for A and B are established based on an absolute scale. An example of an absolute scoring table for assessing quality is presented in Table 17.1.[8] The scoring levels used in Table 17.1 align with earlier research which suggests that people generally use four basic levels of quality assessment: under-performance, basic performance, added value, and excellence (Walden et al., 1993). An additional level is

*Table 17.1* Example of an absolute scoring table for a qualitative assessment

| *Qualitative assessment per criterion* | *Score quality* | *Score impact* |
|---|---|---|
| Contributes very good to realizing the objective (excellence, offering more is not realistic) | 100 | 100 |
| Contributes good to realizing the objective (added value) | 90 | 75 |
| Contributes fairly good to realizing the objective (some added value) | 70 | 50 |
| Contributes satisfactory to realizing the objective (basic performance) | 40 | 25 |
| Does not or barely contribute to realizing the objective (under-performance) | 0 | 0 |

*Source*: Original creation.

introduced ("some added value") to reflect the professional context and importance of supplier selection decisions for public procurement.

The scores for quality in the table are not linear. Successive *quality* increments have diminishing values (Bergman and Lundberg, 2013). In other words, the buyer indicates that "good is good enough": bids of very good quality or excellent quality are rewarded, but only relatively as the difference between good and very good is only 10 points, while the difference between fairly good and good is 20 points, etc. Applying such a technique to tenders can be a simple approach that contributes to either lower prices or higher environmental and social impact. This is because there is little incentive for suppliers to aim for *very* good quality. Instead, they have more financial room to increase positive environmental and social impact or lower their price. This line of reasoning is likely to apply to most public purchases. However, there are exceptions to this. For instance, if bulletproof vests for police officers are bought, the scores in Table 17.1 are more likely to be linear if they represent the utility function of the user. A similar line of reasoning can be applied to environmental and social impact. Here it can be argued that, for instance, each $CO_2$-equivalent molecule reduced or prevented due to public procurement has the same value for society.

In practice, many different types of scoring tables are used. Although there is no academic proof for which scoring table leads to optimal bid quality, it is important that the complete scoring range can potentially be used. For instance, if the scoring range for quality is assigned using Table 17.2 (in contrast to Table 17.1), it is likely that scores of most of the suppliers will rank between 90 points (very good) and 50 points (quite satisfactory). This means that the scoring range for quality is limited (about 40 out of 100 points), what makes it difficult for suppliers to stand out on quality if suppliers can score between 0 and 100 points for price. A reduced scoring range lowers the factual impact of a criterion.

#### 17.2.5.2 Scoring Methods for Quantitative Assessments

*Scoring methods for quantitative assessments* are used for assessing criteria such as price, delivery time, and $CO_2$-reduction. Like qualitative criteria, quantitative criteria can be assessed relatively or absolutely. An example of a popular linear relative scoring method for price is:

$$2 \times max\ points - \frac{price\ supplier\ i}{lowest\ price} \times max\ points$$

*Table 17.2* Poor example of an absolute scoring table for a qualitative assessment

| *Qualitative assessment per criterion* | *Score* |
|---|---|
| Contributes excellent to realizing the objective | 100 |
| Contributes very good to realizing the objective | 90 |
| Contributes good to realizing the objective | 80 |
| Contributes fairly good to realizing the objective | 70 |
| Contributes satisfactory to realizing the objective | 60 |
| Contributes quite satisfactory to realizing the objective | 50 |
| Contributes poorly to realizing the objective | 40 |
| Contributes very poorly to realizing the objective | 30 |
| Contributes extremely poorly to realizing the objective | 20 |
| Does not contribute to realizing the objective | 10 |

*Source*: Original creation.

An example or a popular relative scoring for price with a convex curve is:

$$\frac{lowest\ price}{price\ supplier\ i} \times max\ points$$

The behavior of these methods is shown in the Figure 17.3 below. As evident from the figures, the curved relative scoring method on the right strongly encourages suppliers to offer a very low price, *or* a very high price while compensating with over-the-top quality. The method does not provide clear guidance to suppliers on how to construct their offer but encourages two extremes, both of which can be considered undesirable for public procurement.

In contrast to relative scoring methods, absolute scoring methods are independent of, for instance, the LP. An example of a linear absolute scoring method is depicted in the figure on the left in Figure 17.4 based on the following function:

$$max\ points \times \frac{10{,}000 - price\ supplier\ i}{2{,}000}$$

The Figure 17.4 shows the effects of:

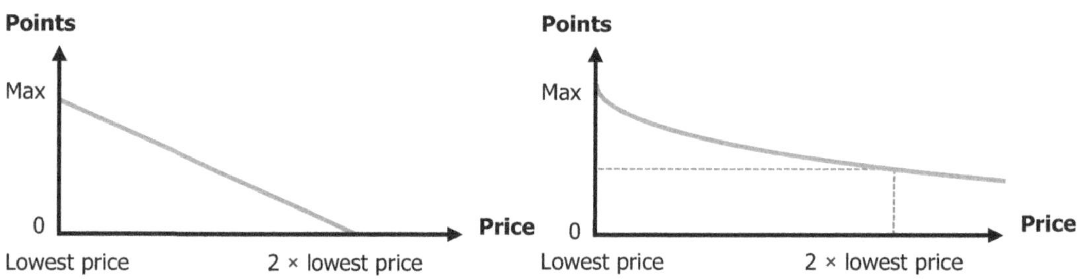


*Figure 17.3* Effects of linear and curved relative price-scoring methods on number of points to be scored by suppliers depending on bid price.

*Source*: Original creation.

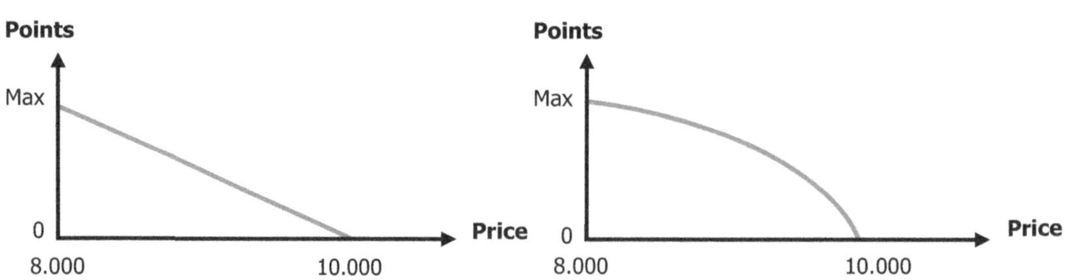


*Figure 17.4* Effects of different absolute price-scoring methods on number of points to be scored by suppliers depending on bid price.

*Source*: Original creation.

$$max\ points - \frac{\left(\max points \times (8{,}000 - price\ supplier\ i)/2{,}000\right)^2}{\max points}$$

The effect of the figure on the right is that suppliers are encouraged to offer a lower price up to the minimum set by the buyer in the procurement documents. However, this incentive decreases which in turn incentivizes suppliers to invest more in quality and impact compared to investing in an even lower (and perhaps unrealistic) price.[9]

It is also noteworthy that absolute scoring methods provide more information to suppliers compared to relative methods, as minimum and maximum prices are now indicated on the horizontal axis. Drawing such figures during the preparation phase of every BPQR tender (and including them in the procurement documents) is useful as it increases insight into the actual behavior of a mathematical function.

In academic and professional literature, there is an intensive debate about the application and effects of relative and absolute (scoring) methods. Relative methods are easy to apply, requiring no market knowledge to establish suitable minimum and maximum prices. However, they lack the guidance for suppliers on an acceptable price range, creating an incentive for them to submit lower prices. Under relative scoring methods, it is always interesting for a supplier to offer a lower price, enhancing their own score and possibly diminishing the scores of competitors. This emphasis on price can have detrimental effects on bid quality and environmental and social impact. It also heightens the risk of a supplier submitting an unrealistically low price, which could lead to performance issues during the execution phase. Furthermore, relative methods allow buyers to make poorly prepared purchases without having to delve into an approximate cost of the purchase. Empirical data and mathematical modeling also show that relative scoring methods may lead to inferior price-quality ratios compared to absolute methods (Albano, 2008; Telgen and Schotanus, 2010).

Another notable concern associated with many relative scoring methods is rank reversal. Rank reversal is a change in the ranking of bids from suppliers leading to a new winner after adding or removing a non-competitive bid[10] (Schotanus et al., 2022). In supplier selection, rank reversal can occur when buyers use a multi-criteria award method in combination with a relative scoring method for price, and when a bidder drops out later in the procurement process. For instance, due to issues uncovered during bidder verification. We will explain what rank reversal is with an example based on De Boer et al. (2006).

Suppose the following relative scoring method is used:

$$\frac{lowest\ price}{price\ supplier\ i} \times 100$$

This can result in the following outcome when the buyer uses the common weighted sum model (WSM) as an award method (this method is explained in more detail in the next step):

In Table 17.3, we see that bid **A** (who finishes third) offers the LP. According to this table, **C** is the winning bid. However, if A's bid is excluded, for instance, because it is later found to be invalid, the result changes as follows:

Now, **B** is the winning bid. The ranking between B and C thus depends on the validity of A's bid, even though A's bid can never be the winning bid.

Rank reversal can also happen if a fictitious bidder is added. While this is not possible in a real tender, it is worth considering the implications if a different bidder would have won had there been an additional fictitious bidder. For suppliers, the possibility of rank

*Table 17.3* Example of a tender with a relative scoring method for price, using the Weighted Sum Model as an award method

| | *Price* | *Score* | | *Total weighted score* | *Ranking* |
|---|---|---|---|---|---|
| | | *Price* | *Quality* | | |
| *Weight* | | 50% | 50% | | |
| Bid A | 40 | 100 | 28 | 64 | 3 |
| Bid B | 80 | 50 | 80 | 65 | 2 |
| Bid C | 100 | 40 | 92 | 66 | 1 |

*Source*: Original creation.

*Table 17.4* Example of a tender with a relative scoring method for price, using the Weighted Sum Model as an award method, excluding bid A

| | *Price* | *Score* | | *Total weighted score* | *Ranking* |
|---|---|---|---|---|---|
| | | *Price* | *Quality* | | |
| *Weight* | | 50% | 50% | | |
| Bid A | - | - | - | - | - |
| Bid B | 80 | 100 | 80 | 90 | 1 |
| Bid C | 100 | 80 | 92 | 86 | 2 |

*Source*: Original creation.

reversal implies that winning a tender can depend on whether a non-competitive supplier participates.

Relative scoring methods permitting rank reversal may also conflict with public procurement principles of transparency and equal treatment (Manunza, 2018). There is also potential for manipulation:

- A supplier offering a high price can have a non-competitive accomplice submit a very low but still realistic price (with correspondingly low quality) to reduce the importance of the price criterion. In other words, the very low bid causes competitive suppliers to score relatively poorly on the price criterion, which decreases the distance between them and the bid with a high price.
- By submitting a very low price themselves, a supplier can lower the scores of other suppliers. Over time, this can lead to a "race to the bottom" in the market. Losing suppliers may try to lower their prices further in future tenders to gain more points. Such incentives in tenders can contribute to an unhealthy market in the long run.

#### *17.2.5.3 Scoring Methods Overview*

Tables 17.5 and 17.6 summarize the most important effects of the various scoring methods examined in this section. It also shows examples of the various methods.

### *17.2.6 Step 6: Choose a Prequalification or Award Method*

A prequalification or award method allows the buyer to calculate the total scores of the bids and make a final supplier selection decision. In practice, numerous methods are

*Table 17.5* Summary of the most important effects of scoring methods for qualitative and quantitative assessments

| *Assessment* | *Measurement* | *Example* | *Key impact* |
|---|---|---|---|
| Qualitative | Relative | *A is better than B, etc.* | Simplifies the evaluation process for assessors. |
| | Absolute | *A contributes good*<br>*B contributes satisfactory, etc.* | Facilitates conveying assessment outcomes more effectively to unsuccessful suppliers. |
| Quantitative | Relative | $2 \times max\ points - \frac{price\ supplier\ i}{lowest\ price} \times max\ points$ | Easy to apply but emphasizes price, risks rank reversal, and lacks guidance for suppliers on what an acceptable price range is. |
| | Absolute | $max\ points \times \frac{10{,}000 - price\ supplier\ i}{2{,}000}$ | Communicates the preferred price range and results in improved price-quality ratios, but may pose challenges in determining the minimum and maximum values. |

*Source*: Original creation.

*Table 17.6* Summary of the most important effects of linear and curved scoring methods

| *Shape* | *Example* | *Key impact* |
|---|---|---|
| Linear | 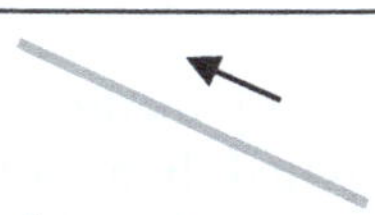 | Guides suppliers incrementally to the highest score for that criterion (e.g. lowest price or most quality). |
| Convex |  | Increasingly guides suppliers toward the highest score for that criterion; or toward a low but not a very low score (e.g. for a very high price). |
| Concave |  | Guides suppliers toward a specific mid-range score. Deviations are decreasingly rewarded or increasingly punished. |

*Source*: Original creation.

used, with commercial procurement systems supporting one or more of these methods. Otherwise, spreadsheets can be used. In this chapter, out of many possible methods, two popular methods are explained: the weighted sum method (WSM)[11] and the monetized method.

In WSM, all suppliers receive scores on each criterion. These scores are multiplied by the respective weights of the criteria. The supplier with the highest total weighted score wins the contract. An example of WSM is shown in Table 17.7. In this example, the buyer has set high quality minimum requirements, leaving little room for quality in the award

*Table 17.7* Example of WSM

| | *Price* | *Score* | | | *Weighted score* | | | | *Ranking* |
|---|---|---|---|---|---|---|---|---|---|
| | | *Price* | *Impact* | *Quality* | *Price* | *Impact* | *Quality* | *Total* | |
| *Weight* | | | | | 60% | 30% | 10% | | |
| Bid A | 1,800 | 100 | 50 | 70 | 60 | 15 | 7 | 82 | 1 |
| Bid B | 2,500 | 50 | 100 | 40 | 30 | 30 | 4 | 64 | 2 |
| Bid C | 2,600 | 43 | 75 | 70 | 26 | 23 | 7 | 56 | 3 |

*Source*: Original creation.

phase. Therefore, the highest weight is allocated to price, next impact (e.g. social return or emission reduction), and finally quality. Each criterion allows a maximum of 100 points. Impact and quality are assessed qualitatively by human assessors using Table 17.1. Price scores are calculated through a linear absolute scoring method with a minimum price of 1,800 and a maximum price of 3,200. As the bid with the highest weighted score wins the tender, supplier A is selected.

The popularity of WSM in practice is probably for a reason, suggesting that it strikes a good balance between conceptual or descriptive quality (i.e. modeling the key features of the perceived problem), customizability (i.e. it can be easily tweaked for different types of tenders), and practical usability (cost of use, data gathering, communication, cognitive effort, etc.) and can be expanded or simplified rather easily depending on the situation. In other words, it often provides a form of procedural rationality as discussed earlier in the chapter.

In addition to WSM, various prequalification and award methods can be applied in public procurement.[12] This wide range of methods can be categorized as follows:

- *Compensatory versus non-compensatory methods (De Boer et al., 2001)*: Compensatory methods, such as WSM, permit suppliers with a low score on one criterion to compensate this with a good score on another criterion. Non-compensatory methods are strict and, for instance, do not allow (very) low scores to be compensated. In addition, semi-compensatory methods such as the family of ELECTRE methods developed by Bernard Roy and his team allow only a limited degree of compensation. See Govindan and Jepsen (2016) for a general overview and De Boer et al. (1998) for an application of ELECTRE in supplier selection.
- *Monetary versus point methods (Bergman and Lundberg, 2013)*: In WSM and many other methods, suppliers receive *points* for all criteria, including price. Another approach is to convert quality and impact assessments to *monetary* values, meaning that better assessments result in higher values. With a monetary method, quality and impact values can be deducted from the price of a supplier. The supplier with the lowest "virtual" price wins the tender. The virtual price is only calculated for the award phase. During the contract performance phase, the supplier is paid according to the price they originally offered.

  An example is shown below in which this version of a monetary method allocates 25 coins to each weighted quality- or impact-related point. The values of quality and impact are deducted from the price. The bid with the lowest virtual price wins the tender, in this case Supplier A (Table 17.8).

*Table 17.8* Example of a monetary method

| *Criteria* | *Price* | *Impact value* | *Quality value* | *Virtual price* | *Rank* |
|---|---|---|---|---|---|
| Bid A | 1,800 | 375 | 175 | 1,250 | 1 |
| Bid B | 2,500 | 750 | 100 | 1,650 | 2 |
| Bid C | 2,600 | 562.5 | 175 | 1,863 | 3 |

*Source*: Original creation.

As far as we know, there is no literature with a strong preference for compensatory or non-compensatory methods. This is different for monetary versus point methods. Among others, Bergman and Lundberg (2013) argue that monetary methods should be preferred. A benefit of a monetary method compared to WSM is that no scoring method is required for price. In addition, the method clearly shows the value of quality and impact.

However, although monetary methods can be valuable when the buyer can accurately determine the value for impact and quality, this is not always the case in public procurement. In addition, monetary models often convey less information to suppliers as the buyer does not have to disclose a preferred price, a price range (such as in Figure 17.4), or a reference price.[13] Another concern is that, in practice, monetary models can be less intuitive to grasp when compared to point-based models. This has led to instances in various tenders where errors have occurred, such as assigning excessively low values to factors like quality and impact, resulting in tenders that closely resemble LP tenders. Conversely, assigning overly high values to these factors has resulted in tenders placing insufficient emphasis on the price component.

Overall, both WSM and monetary methods have seen success and failure in practice. And each method has its own advantages and disadvantages. It is important to understand these and mitigate potential drawbacks as much as possible when using either method.

### *17.2.7 Step 7: Simulate and Revise the Supplier Selection Model*

After completing step 6, all elements of the supplier selection model have been developed. Before finalizing the supplier selection model, a final check needs to be done using simulated requests to participate or bids. This check ensures that the model as a whole functions as intended.

During this step, the buyer can generate various simulated requests to participate or bids and calculate whether the ones considered by the procurement team to have the best scores indeed win the tender. Examples of such simulations are described in Tables 17.3 and 17.4. Typically, the simulated bids for the award phase cover a low-cost bid with low quality and impact scores, a high-cost bid with high quality and impact scores, and one or two intermediate bids. In addition, bids can be simulated that are similar in terms of both price and quality. The bids can be simulated based on experience of the procurement team and AI can also be used for this exercise.

### *17.2.8 Step 8: Assess Requests to Participate or Bids*

When the tender closes, the requests to participate (for prequalifying suppliers) or bids received (for awarding the contract) need to be assessed. Quantitative parts, such as price, are usually straightforward to assess. It often involves filling in the price in the formula, which was published in the procurement documents, unless a price is unrealistically low.

Qualitative parts, such as an implementation plan, a planning, or a conceptual design, often require assessment by human assessors. Assessing these qualitative elements can be challenging for several reasons. It may be difficult to articulate why a particular request or bid is superior to another, without revealing confidential information of a winning supplier. In addition, assessors are often inexperienced, and assessments are conducted in addition to their regular responsibilities. Earlier research indeed suggests that assessors can evaluate the same input quite differently, introducing uncertainty for suppliers (Takahashi, 2018). Moreover, high-cost suppliers tend to benefit more, as increased uncertainty could give them a higher chance of winning the tender (Hortaçsu and Perrigne, 2021). It is therefore important to prepare the assessment process early and provide detailed explanations to all those involved.

A few key factors are essential in the organization of qualitative assessments. First, it is imperative that the procurement documents clearly outline how the requests or bids will be assessed. Any new assessment criteria or elements should not be introduced during the final assessment process. To prevent undue influence, assessments should usually be conducted without knowledge of the prices.

Second, especially when working with assessors who are not well-versed in procurement, an impartial individual, such as a procurement officer, overseeing the assessment process should ensure that no new elements are introduced. The independent person should also confirm that all assessment aspects outlined in the procurement documents are evaluated and included in the feedback provided to the suppliers. Additionally, this independent person should ensure that the order in which the assessors speak alternates. This diminishes the likelihood of an evaluator with a higher hierarchical position or an extroverted individual disproportionately influencing the assessment compared to other evaluators.

Third, at least three assessors should independently assess all bids. The participation of more experts can enhance the quality of decisions, particularly when dealing with purchases that are not part of the daily routine.

Fourth, all assessors should start by individually assessing different requests or bids. The assessment of the first request or bid may differ somewhat from the assessment of the last one, due to the insights gained during the assessment process. This same principle should be applied during plenary group meetings.

Fifth, after discussing any variations in assessments among the assessors, an average score can be calculated based on their individual scores, provided there are no significant disparities in scores between assessors. Some variations between human assessors can be expected and explained, but substantial differences should not exist since all assessors should be using the same assessment guidelines as provided in the procurement documents.

Finally, contracted or in-house AI can serve as an assistant in assessing requests to participate or bids. Early experiments have shown promising results, provided that bid confidentiality is maintained and the AI's output is reviewed by human assessors (Schotanus, 2024).

### *17.2.9 Step 9: Justify the Tender Decision*

The obligation to announce the prequalification and award criteria enable the tender candidates and tenderers to know what to expect during the assessment phase. After a decision has been made, a public organization must justify the decision to their own organization, to the public, to society, and especially to the suppliers that participated in the tender (Volker and Schotanus, 2023).

Offering comprehensive feedback generally enhances the level of trust in the contracting authority and could therefore support the credibility of the supplier selection decision among stakeholders. Merely providing a matrix sheet with scores falls short of meeting this need as it lacks the desired level of transparency sought by suppliers (Volker and Schotanus, 2023). However, providing effective feedback can be challenging because sharing sensitive information about the winner with unsuccessful suppliers is prohibited. When an absolute scoring method for assessing quality is employed, giving feedback becomes more straightforward. In this case, the focus can be on elucidating the absolute score of each unsuccessful supplier. You can highlight strengths and areas that need improvement, explaining why the maximum score was not achieved. Additionally, you can indicate that the winning supplier did not exhibit a specific weakness without disclosing the exact resolution, as it may be sensitive information. For instance, if an unsuccessful supplier failed to provide a convincing rationale for the effectiveness of their solution, you can mention that the winner had a well-substantiated approach, provided this was the case. Finally, you can also elucidate how the decision-makers arrived at their conclusion. The process they followed is not confidential.

Note that the discussion regarding the balance between confidentiality and transparency becomes more manageable when feedback policies are clearly communicated to suppliers at the beginning of the procurement process. It is important to inform them that feedback will be provided in a manner that maintains transparency while ensuring the protection of confidential information.

## 17.3 Conclusion

In this chapter, we have explored the critical topic of supplier selection in public procurement, recognizing its paramount importance. We also discussed the challenges posed by incorporating sustainable and social criteria into supplier selection and stressed the need to consider external costs and benefits in the tender process. Highlighting the true costs of a tender, we elucidated the rationale for adopting a comprehensive approach to supplier selection.

The heart of this chapter is dedicated to a discussion of the nine steps involved in crafting effective supplier selection models. We began by emphasizing the importance of understanding demand and supply possibilities, paving the way for informed decisions. We then explored the choices available when awarding contracts, contrasting BPQR, LCC, and LP methods. We also discussed attaching weight to prequalification or award criteria, considering the limitations of weights in representing true importance and introducing the AHP.

Next, we explained the differences between scoring methods used for qualitative and quantitative assessments and discussed the impact of both non-linear and linear scoring methods, as well as relative and absolute scoring methods. Subsequently, we explored prequalification and award methods, presenting the WSM and a monetized method. We emphasized the importance of simulating requests to participate and bids to fine-tune supplier selection models and elucidated the process for assessing requests to participate and bids.

In the final step, we discussed the critical task of justifying tender decisions, ensuring transparency and accountability in the supplier selection process. With a comprehensive understanding of these steps, the reader should be well-equipped to make supplier selection decisions in public procurement, ultimately leading to more informed and effective decisions.

Finally, we note that the design of supplier selection models not only (partly) determines which requests to participate or bid(s) wins but also significantly influences the nature of the requests and bids themselves when different models are employed. When a buyer attaches a high weight to sustainability, rational suppliers are likely to offer a decent price-quality ratio that aims to maximize positive impact (or minimize negative impact). A very good price-quality ratio is not to be expected. In essence, supplier selection models can guide suppliers to offer solutions aligned with the government's preferences.

## Notes

1 This chapter is based on and builds upon parts of the chapter "Tendering and Supplier Selection" written by Fredo Schotanus from the book *Public Procurement: Theory, Practices, and Tools*, published by Palgrave Macmillan in 2023 and edited by Jolien Grandia and Leentje Volker.
2 For instance, for external labor, hourly rates could be relevant to include in a supplier selection model. For supplies, the purchase price and support rates could be relevant, etc.
3 A further exploration of these choices can be found in Igarashi et al. (2015) reporting on a detailed study of tender documents in Norway and how environmental aspects were included in the supplier selection process.
4 This phase is also known as the selection phase.
5 This is not always the case. The buyer can also prequalify all suppliers that meet the minimum requirements.
6 To ensure the principle of equal treatment is not compromised.
7 See also www.co2-prestatieladder.nl/en
8 The number of points allocated for a maximum score in this example is 100 points, but it could also be, for example, 5 or 10 points. Mathematically, this does not matter as long as all criteria have the same maximum score.
9 Some economists (e.g. Bergman and Lundberg, 2013) assume that the marginal social value of money remains approximately constant. Each reduction of one dollar or euro has a consistent value for the buyer. However, opting for lower prices also introduces additional risk for the buyer. Examples are the winner's curse, subpar performance or suppliers seeking additional compensation after the contract is closed. These are important reasons for contracting authorities to evaluate price in a non-linear manner.
10 A non-competitive bid is a bid from a supplier who participates in a tender but does not win the tender.
11 The method goes by many names. It is also known as the weighted factor method, the weighted point method, the weighted scoring model, the weighted sum model, and so on.
12 Examples of other methods out of scope of this chapter are TOPSIS and Value for Money (quality points divided by price).
13 This can be solved by indicating a minimum and a maximum price in the procurement documents.

## References

Albano, G.L., Dini, F., & Zampino, R. (2008). Suppliers' behavior in competitive tendering: Evidence from the Italian Ministry of Economy and Finance's acquisition of IT services. Paper presented at the 3rd IPCC Conference, Amsterdam, The Netherlands, August 28–30.

Arrowsmith, S. (2014). *The law of public and utilities procurement* (2nd ed.). Sweet & Maxwell.

Bergman, M.A., & Lundberg, S. (2013). Tender evaluation and supplier selection methods in public procurement. *Journal of Purchasing and Supply Management*, 19(2), 73–83.

Chang, W.-S., Chen, B., & Salmon, T.C. (2015). An investigation of the average bid mechanism for procurement auctions. *Management Science*, 61(6), 1237–1254.

Chen, Q.M. (2024). Corruption in public procurement auctions: Evidence from collusion between officers and firms. Retrieved from https://drive.google.com/file/d/1Z_SlTaZe48e7fh1GhXboJo0AZEkGeE3J/view

De Boer, L. (1998). Operations research in support of purchasing: Design of a toolbox for supplier selection (Doctoral dissertation, University of Twente).

De Boer, L. (2017). Procedural rationality in supplier selection: Outlining three heuristics for choosing selection criteria. *Management Decision*, 55(1), 32–56.

De Boer, L., Labro, E., & Morlacchi, P. (2001). A review of methods supporting supplier selection. *European Journal of Purchasing and Supply Management*, 7(2), 75–89.

De Boer, L., Linthorst, M., Schotanus, F., & Telgen, J. (2006). An analysis of some mistakes, miracles, and myths in supplier selection. Paper presented at the 15th IPSERA Conference, San Diego, United States, April 6–8.

De Boer, L., Van der Wegen, L.L.M., & Telgen, J. (1998). Outranking methods in support of supplier selection. *European Journal of Purchasing and Supply Management*, 4(2–3), 109–188.

Drake, S., Lundberg, J., & Lundberg, S. (2024). Market response to environmental policy via public procurement: An empirical analysis of bids and prices. *Journal of Environmental Management*, 365, 121547.

Govindan, K., & Jepsen, M.B. (2016). ELECTRE: A comprehensive literature review on methodologies and applications. *European Journal of Operational Research*, 250, 1–29.

Hessami, Z. (2014). Political corruption, public procurement, and budget composition: Theory and evidence from OECD countries. *European Journal of Political Economy*, 34, 372–389.

Hortaçsu, A., & Perrigne, I. (2021). Empirical perspectives on auctions. In *Handbook of industrial organization* (Vol. 5, pp. 81–175). Elsevier.

Igarashi, M., De Boer, L., & Michelsen, O. (2015). Investigating the anatomy of supplier selection in green public procurement. *Journal of Cleaner Production*, 108, 442–450.

Manunza, E. (2018). Achieving a sustainable and just society through public procurement? On the limits of relative scoring and the principles of equal treatment and transparency. In E. Manunza & F. Schotanus (Eds.), *The art of public procurement: Liber amicorum in honour of Prof. Dr. Jan Telgen* (pp. 139–158). Enschede.

Saaty, T. (1980). *The analytic hierarchy process: Planning, priority setting, resource allocation*. McGraw-Hill.

Schotanus, F. (2022). *A better world starts with public procurement (Inaugural address)*. Utrecht University. Retrieved from www.uu.nl/medewerkers/RestApi/Public/GetFile?Employee=55038&l=EN&id=1225&t=c57c71fc8d0742249feaaf4cee511be6

Schotanus, F. (2024, July). *Offertebeoordeling: AI versus mens*. Deal!.

Schotanus, F., & Gaaikema, K. (2020, December). *De status van circulair en duurzaam inkopen: Van best practice naar common practice*. Tijdschrift Aanbestedingsrecht & Staatssteun.

Schotanus, F., van den Engh, G., Nijenhuis, Y., & Telgen, J. (2022). Supplier selection with rank reversal in public tenders. *Journal of Purchasing & Supply Management*, 28, 100744.

Simon, H.A. (1978). Rationality as process and as a product of thought. *The American Economic Review*, 68(2), 1–16.

Takahashi, H. (2018). Strategic design under uncertain evaluations: Structural analysis of design-build auctions. *RAND Journal of Economics*, 49, 594–618.

Telgen, J., & Schotanus, F. (2010). Supplier selection requires full transparency. Paper presented at the 19th Annual IPSERA Conference, Lapeenranta, Finland.

Volker, L., & Schotanus, F. (2023). Tendering and supplier selection. In J. Grandia & L. Volker (Eds.), *Public procurement* (pp. xx–xx). Palgrave Macmillan. https://doi.org/10.1007/978-3-031-18490-1_6

Walden, D., Berger, C., Blauth, R., Boger, D., Bolster, C., Burchill, G., ..., & Walden, D. (1993). Kano's methods for understanding customer-defined quality. *Center for Quality Management Journal*, 4(2), 1–37.

### *Case Study: Developing a Supplier Selection Model (Developed by Fredo Schotanus)*

**The university plans to buy new coffee and tea vending machines. Your first challenge related to this (and the learning objective) is to obtain some practical experience in using different supplier selection/awarding methods for a tender and to demonstrate how the university could benefit from your analytics skills.**

You are working as a procurement officer at the university. Right now, you are responsible for inviting several potential suppliers and finding the best one for coffee and tea vending machines.

You've decided that you will use two phases to find the best supplier. In the first phase (preselection or prequalification phase), you will preselect five suppliers out of a total of ten. You will select these suppliers using *prequalification* criteria.

In the second phase (tender or award phase), only the five selected suppliers will be asked to submit an actual bid based on your *award* criteria. In that bid, suppliers can quote a price and describe the quality and sustainability of their bid.

#### General Remarks and Recommendations

- Try to make yourself part of the university. If information is not given and you think you have to add information, then point it out in your answers.
- It is allowed to use AI tools, but realize that it might give you wrong answer suggestions.
- Use (and refer to) relevant background information by different sources:
  - Lectures materials
  - Other literature
- Prepare a Word document with your answers (about two pages).

#### Phase 1: Prequalification

You invited ten suppliers for the prequalification phase (also known as the preselection phase). You already composed several knock-out criteria. Knock-out criteria are criteria that *must* be satisfied. In this case, the knock-out criteria are defined as:

a. Information received on time
b. Information received in twofold
c. Information received digitally
d. Audit-certificate received
e. Bank-certificate received
f. Insurance policy received
g. Compliant with safety guidelines
h. Compliant with ethical guidelines
i. Office in the country
j. Profit overview over the last three years received
k. Balance sheet over the last three years received

You also developed one prequalification criterion. It is *defined* as "relevant experience". This criterion is *measured* by "number of vending machines the supplier has delivered in the past 3 years". Other prequalification criteria have not been defined yet and it is not clear yet how they will be measured during the assessment of the bids.

1. Make suggestions for *defining* and *measuring three* other prequalification criteria (maximum 6 points out of 30).

**Phase 2: Award**

After the preselection phase, you must develop a supplier selection model for finding the best supplier (as part of the request for proposal). The award criterion "price" will be measured in euros. The annual prices of suppliers are expected to range between €200,000 and €300,000. You pay about €270,000 per year to your current supplier.

2. Provide a *scoring method* that will evaluate the award criterion "price".
   Also, shortly explain what makes this a good/suitable method based on the lecture materials (maximum 6 points).

An example of an award criterion could be the level of circularity of the vending machines. You want to include circularity as a criterion for your award decision, but you are concerned that the transaction costs (such as the time and money it takes for the supplier to prepare a bid, as well as the costs for you as a buyer to verify and evaluate it) might become too high.

3. Suggest a measure for the award criterion circularity that avoids disproportional transaction costs. What is the main downside of such a measure? (maximum 6 points).
4. Make suggestions for *defining* and *measuring three other award* criteria (maximum 6 points).
5. Which *supplier selection method* (e.g. weighted sum method; monetary method, etc.) would you use to award the contract to the best supplier? Make sure you clearly explain *why* you would use *this* method for awarding the contract to the *best supplier*, over other methods (maximum 6 points).

# 18 Managing Contract Performance

*Lachezar G. Anguelov, Benjamin M. Brunjes and Josh Klika*

## 18.1 Introduction

Government contracting and public procurement rose to prominence with the New Public Management (NPM) movement of the 1980s and are still of great importance today. NPM reforms sought to improve government by embracing and adopting private sector management practices, including the use of competitive markets to lower production costs (Osborne and Gaebler 1992; Savas 1987; Warner 2023; Anguelov and Brunjes 2023). Proponents expected this shift would improve the efficiency of government service provision, resulting in lower costs and higher service quality (Osborne and Gaebler 1992; Savas 1987). At the most basic level, NPM reforms were an effort to maximize the use of scarce government revenues and improve the performance of public programs (Lane 2002).

Performance is notoriously difficult to define and measure in the context of public services. At a government- or organization-wide level, performance regimes are policies designed to encourage public organizations to build and implement accountable programs. Performance regimes include complex combinations of incentives, measures, and accountability mechanisms (Kristiansen et al. 2019). Studies of performance regimes assess the extent to which more micro-level performance management initiatives, such as defining measures and tracking performance in particular programs, create a "cumulative effect" that leads to a "fundamental change in the way we govern" (Moynihan et al. 2011, p. i141). For public procurement, big picture questions on governmental costs and service quality are about performance regimes – the overall impact of performance management. While there is some mixed evidence that NPM reforms may reduce the cost of government programs, there is little support for the idea that contracting is improving the technical quality (or performance) of public services (Boyne 1998; Petersen et al. 2018).

For the day-to-day management of services that are increasingly contracted, studies of performance regimes offer little insight into the micro-level role of and strategies for public managers. Indeed, public managers oversee contracts for nearly all types of public services, suggesting that, despite questionable macro-level impacts, performance and contracting are of the utmost importance (Anguelov and Brunjes 2023). More work is needed to help practitioners identify specific tactics to influence contractor performance.

In this chapter, we explore the performance management levers that government employees can use to influence contractor performance. Moving away from performance regimes, this chapter focuses on micro-level performance management. In this chapter, performance refers to the extent to which a contractor fulfills the government's expectations, which are often (but not always) clearly specified in the contract. Linking to a burgeoning literature on implementing government contracts, this chapter investigates how public

DOI: 10.4324/9781003566670-21

employees can manage markets, develop performance measures, build relationships, and apply incentives to influence their vendors' performance. Along the way, we identify key empirical results from academic research and important takeaways for public managers interested in improving the performance of government contracts.

## 18.2 Summary of Literature

Much of the early literature on government contracting and public procurement focused on the make-or-buy decision. Many studies investigated which types of goods and services are appropriate for privatization, while others attempted to assess which types of vendors might be viable contracting partners (Auger 1999; Dunleavy 1986; Ferris and Graddy 1986; Seidman 1990). These studies suggest that performance potential may be largely dependent on market competitiveness, the complexity of the good or service required, and the institutional characteristics surrounding the contract (Brown et al. 2006). These studies find that contracting out is more likely to be successful if:

1. The public organization contracting out has sufficient political support and administrative capacity to manage the procurement
2. There is a competitive marketplace where many firms vie to provide the government with the required good or service
3. The good or service required is easy to describe and has a clear set of desired outputs and outcomes

Under these conditions, scholars would expect contracts to perform relatively well, perhaps lowering costs and improving the quality of public services. In general, these remain important considerations for public employees attempting to determine what to procure from the marketplace and what to produce internally.

However, two problems have arisen when attempting to apply these criteria. First, governments are contracting out for nearly every type of good and service, regardless of whether these conditions are met. Though some have suggested this is the result of political preferences (Lerusse and Van de Walle 2022; Obinger et al. 2016), it is clear that public managers are less concerned with the make or buy decision than scholars. Instead, they are tasked with managing a diverse set of contracts spanning a wide range of goods and services. Rather than determining which aspects of government work to contract out, public administrators are already responsible for a broad portfolio of contracts that rarely meet all (or any) of these criteria.

Second, scholarship on the make or buy decision has few insights for practitioners interested in how to manage contracts during their period of performance. The literature offers plenty of advice for things to consider before contracting out: seek political support, build agency capacity, research market competitiveness, encourage firms to submit proposals, consider required investments for firms, and try to specify requirements and outcomes carefully. But once the work has started, these criteria are much less insightful. How should public organizations plan for and respond to any performance-related problems that might arise? Firms may deliver low-quality products, take too long to complete their work, or simply fail to meet the expectations of the contract.

In response to these concerns, recent scholarship has started exploring how contracts are managed to identify a combination of tools and oversight strategies procurement officials can use to motivate contractors and hold them accountable for the delivery of goods and services.

### *18.2.1 Measuring Contractor Performance: Implications for Managers*

Governments often contract out to improve the performance of public organizations and public programs. Yet, contracting out creates a new performance dynamic, with the government tasking a third party to perform some required work. Instead of directly managing organizational or program performance, governments are responsible for overseeing the work of an increasingly complex web of vendors and partner organizations (Cordella and Willcocks 2010). As Amirkhanyan (2011) states, "designing and implementing performance measurement systems in public contracts is not easy." Difficulties arise because contract performance is multidimensional and complex (Fernandez 2009; Amirkhanyan et al. 2014). As a result, there is no one best way to assess contract performance. The literature[1] has used many measures to analyze contractor performance, including:

- Cost
- Service quality
- Responsiveness to contract requirements
- Compliance with specifications
- Regulatory violations
- Timeliness of delivery
- Service continuity
- Compliance with laws
- Customer (client/citizen) satisfaction
- Fair or equitable access
- Concluding status

In practice, governments often use some combination of cost control, quality, management, scheduling, and regulatory compliance measures (U.S. Department of Defense, 2025). Alternative ways of conceptualizing performance include assessing the evaluation capacity and use of monitoring by public agencies (Yang et al. 2009; Amirkhanyan 2010), analyzing the use of performance information (Hall 2017), or estimating direct impact by measuring outcomes for service recipients (Lu 2016).

This myriad of ways to define and operationalize performance has important implications for the management of government contracts. First, it suggests that there is no real agreement on which organizational or environmental factors improve overall results (Amirkhanyan et al. 2018). Public contract managers must wield their discretion to design an appropriate set of performance measures and metrics. While there may be some common elements of most performance approaches, such as reporting expenditures and delivering interim and final products, much of the design of the performance management strategy is left up to the procurement officer, particularly the specifics of incentives and informal oversight mechanisms (Girth 2016).

Second, the diversity of (and lack of agreement on) generalizable performance measures suggests that performance management approaches for public procurement are highly dependent on the context of each contract. Service recipients, politicians, and public managers all care about contract performance. However, the specific dimensions they value, the ways they process different types of performance information, how they evaluate tradeoffs between performance dimensions, and how their prior beliefs and biases impact their assessments can vary substantially (Baekgaard and Serritzlew 2016; Brogaard et al. 2024; Lerusse and Van de Walle 2022; Amirkhanyan et al. 2014). As a result, contract performance is often in the eye of the beholder.

Public procurement officers, like many other street-level bureaucrats, must balance top-down and bottom-up pressures to determine the correct way to implement government contracts. There are three phases of the contracting cycle where procurement officers make critical choices that are likely to influence performance: the solicitation of proposals, selecting winning vendors, and overseeing partners during their work. In the next sections, we discuss lessons from the literature in each of these phases of contract management, offering practical insights into how public officials might work to enhance the possibility of good performance.

### *18.2.2 Soliciting Proposals: Design and Market Competition*

Public procurement begins with contract design. During this phase, contract managers define many of the key levers that will be used to influence contractor performance. Contract design is similar to strategic planning for organizations as it offers the chance to devise an intentional approach to help parties to a contract achieve their shared goals (Frydlinger et al. 2019). Key design elements include crafting work requirements, determining the financial structure of the contract, creating a package of incentives, and developing an approach to finding bidders (Shetterly 2000; Brunjes 2020). Recent scholarship suggests that each of these decisions can influence vendor performance in important ways.

#### *18.2.2.1 Requirements and Performance-Based Contracts*

Before any procurement can begin, public officials must develop requirements, or a description of the work that needs to be done. Requirements specify the what, when, and how of a procurement, covering both interim steps and the final state. Government officials have discretion over the extent to which they specify requirements (Schooner 2002). More specificity can clarify work objectives but may also constrain contractors as they attempt to meet all formalized requirements.

Since the real world is inherently unpredictable, it is almost always impossible to fully define all work requirements (Hart and Moore 1988). As a result, most contracts will begin with a set of incomplete requirements that need to be revisited occasionally to ensure the fulfillment of government and contractor expectations. Since requirements are likely to be incomplete, there may be diminishing returns associated with the exhaustive development of requirements – resources and effort expended on requirements generation may, at some point, be more effectively applied to other aspects of contract management, such as relationship-building and inter-organizational communication.

Acknowledging incomplete contracting problems, performance-based contracting (PBC) initiatives often reduce the specificity of requirements in favor of prioritizing desired outputs and impacts. Where traditional contracts provide payments based on the delivery of products or services, PBCs tie at least a portion of payments to assessed impact (Selviaridis and Wynstra 2015). PBCs tend to specify a desired end state, leaving much of the interim details up to the contractor. For example, consider a contract for childcare services. A traditional contract might specify many details about meals, naptimes, educational content, recreation, and safety, requiring vendors to submit comprehensive proposals that demonstrate their ability to deliver in all areas. A performance-based contract might instead specify generally that the childcare center should be safe, healthy, and educational and establish some performance measures for each area to be assessed regularly (say, every six months). The contractor would be responsible for developing the details of the day-to-day management of the facility and would receive performance-based bonuses if they were able to create and maintain a safe, healthy, and educational childcare center.

PBCs are appealing as they acknowledge problems of incomplete contracting and use incentives to overcome these issues. While some studies suggest that PBCs can lead to improved outcomes (Selviaridis and Wynstra 2015), others show that governments can struggle to establish effective performance measures and may lack the capacity to oversee PBCs (Heinrich and Choi 2007; Lu 2016). Potential contractors also worry about PBCs, particularly when governments fail to pay on time and when contractors perceive the performance objectives as difficult to reach (Brown and Potoski 2003; Ogden and Brady 2015).

#### *18.2.2.2 Financial Structure and Incentives*

Government contract managers also face another important design decision that can influence contractor performance: how to pay and reward vendors. Though it might seem that there is little difference between types of payment, both the overall financial structure and financial incentives can influence contract outputs and outcomes. Contract managers must carefully choose the financial structure and incentives most appropriate for the context of the procurement.

Financial structure refers to the way that payments are allocated to vendors. There are two primary ways used to pay government contractors: cost-reimbursement contracts and fixed-price contracts, each of which motivates different contractor behaviors.

For cost-reimbursement contracts, governments remit payments to vendors based on billed activities. At pre-determined intervals, contractors submit summaries of their work, including the total time of all labor hours and receipts for any services or materials purchased to complete the work. Government officials review these summaries and remit payment. Contractors interested in earning the most money possible will charge as much work to the contract as possible. Though these contracts may have price caps, contractors often charge up to these caps without completing the work, forcing the government to pay above the initially agreed-upon price to finish projects (Kim and Brown 2017).

Fixed-price contracts establish a maximum, or fixed, price the government will pay for a good or service. The government may still require progress reports and status updates, but any expenses incurred under the contract (including materials and labor) are taken out of the fixed amount. To make a profit, contractors must complete the work for less than the maximum price. To maximize profits, a fixed price contract encourages vendors to be as efficient as possible, as any leftover money (after deducting the cost of their work) below the cap becomes their profit.

As shown in Figure 18.1, the basic financial structure of a contract has important ramifications for performance. You might think of a contract as a bucket into which resources are poured. On a fixed price contract, governments offer a full bucket to their contractor, allowing them to keep what remains after the work is done. Cost-reimbursement contracts require the vendor to slowly fill the bucket by charging the contract. The only way to make more money is to charge for the contract, meaning that there is no incentive to stop until the bucket begins to overflow (or even after that point – overflows are just more profit!). Studies indicate that cost-reimbursement contracts are more likely than fixed-price contracts to experience performance problems, including termination and cost overruns (Brunjes 2018; Girth and Lopez 2019). In general, government agencies should use fixed-price contracts when possible, as they incentivize better performance and require less active oversight (lowering administrative costs).

Despite these known performance ties, there is evidence that many government agencies continue to use cost-reimbursement contracts (Kim and Brown 2017). In some cases, this

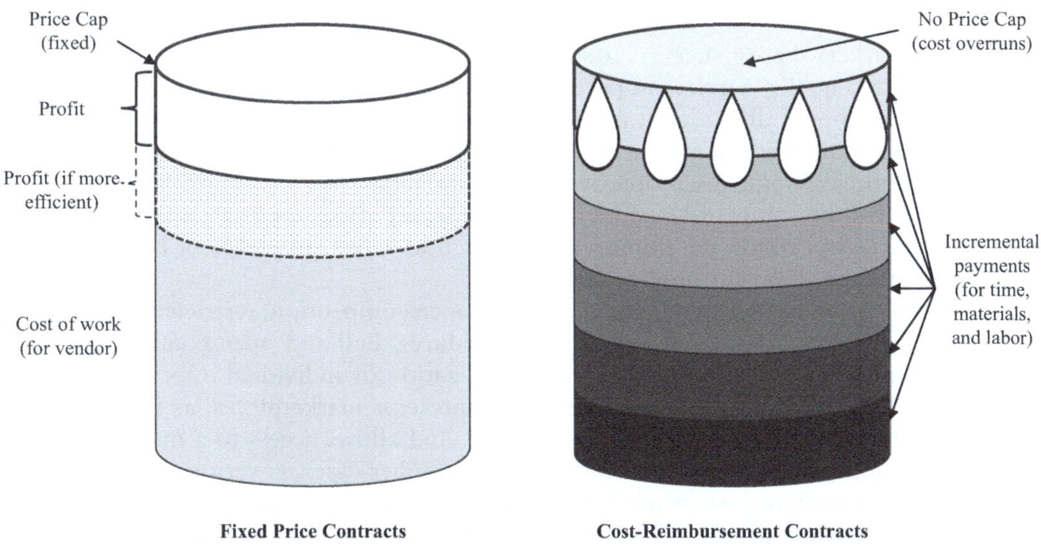


*Figure 18.1* Comparison of financial structures.
*Source*: Original creation.

may be due to path dependence, as contract administrators simply do what has been in the past, while in other cases, it may be a strategic choice to attract firms to bid on a complex contract where a fixed price might be seen as a risk rather than an opportunity (Brunjes 2018).[2] In some cases, fixed-price contracts may be modified to adjust for changes in expectations, but this reduces the effectiveness of the price cap in inspiring efficient performance (Kim and Brown 2012).

In addition to the basic financial structure of a contract, public managers must decide whether to employ financial incentives. There are three primary types of incentives:

- *Fixed Fees*: a payment at the inception of a contract, often appended to cost-reimbursement contracts, to incentivize contractors to bid on risky (potentially less profitable) projects.
- *Award Fees*: a payment at the conclusion of a contract, made if the contract manager assesses the quality of the work provided to meet agreed-upon standards. This type of incentive allows for subjective assessment of performance at the discretion of the government contracting official.
- *Incentive Fees*: a payment at the conclusion of a contract, made if the contractor achieves the standards established in a pre-determined performance formula (often based on the total cost). This type of incentive removes administrative discretion, instead relying on pre-determined measures of cost-efficiency.

Though the use of financial incentives is relatively rare (Girth 2016), contract managers should consider applying incentives if appropriate for their procurement. Generally, incentives are useful if the government expects to receive very few bids (fixed fees) or if the government is very worried about motivating efficient performance (award and/or incentive fees). A careful design of a contract's financial structure and incentives can have important implications for the long-term performance of a contractor.

*18.2.2.3 Solicitation and Competition*

Economic (market) theory suggests a strong link between competition and performance (cost savings and quality services in particular). The conventional wisdom suggests a competitive market should drive down prices, improve accountability, and perhaps even promote innovation, all of which are likely important for performance (Brunjes 2020). Contract managers often have some discretion over how contracts are marketed, including whether a solicitation will be competitive and where information about the contract will be shared (Cooper 2002). As a result, developing an approach to solicit proposals or bids is another critical performance lever for public managers.

Contracts tend to be solicited through full and open competition, restricted competition, or through sole sourcing (non-competitive) procedures. Full and open competition refers to soliciting proposals from any interested organization or individual. Open competition is generally the preferred way to interact with contractor marketplaces, as it achieves the benefits of market theory, promotes transparency, and allows access to a more diverse set of potential suppliers (Johnston and Girth 2012). In other cases, governments may choose to restrict competition to certain subsets of firms. These contracts are still solicited competitively, but only certain kinds of firms can bid. The most common examples are set asides for small firms, woman-owned firms, and minority-owned firms, which can struggle to win contracts when competing against larger, better-resourced businesses. Recent evidence suggests that small and small, disadvantaged firms perform well in comparison to larger businesses (Brunjes and Rodriguez-Plesa 2024; Polyviou et al. 2024).

In some instances, governments may choose not to compete a contract. Instead, public managers will select a sole source as the contractor. Though generally discouraged, sole sourcing can happen if there is not a competitive marketplace in which to locate contractors, if there is a contractor with unique qualifications (particularly if those unique qualities will lead to cost savings), or if a contract is required urgently or in response to an emergency. Sole sourcing is more common when the work outputs from a contract are uncertain or complex (Resh and Marvel 2012; Van Slyke 2003), or when a relationship with a contractor is important to preserve (Brunjes 2020).

And therein lies the rub: competition, while desirable, is often a hindrance to the development of lasting and trusting relationships between partners. As governments increasingly think of and treat vendors more like partners in a collaborative effort to jointly produce public services (Van Slyke 2009), competition may do more harm than good (Hartley et al. 2013). The challenge for public managers is to determine how competition will influence a relationship with a vendor.

Scholars have long been interested in the role of markets and competition in government contracting. In recent years, literature has begun to assess how competitive sourcing influences contractor performance (Brunjes 2020; Lamothe and Lamothe 2010). Competition remains popular among contract managers, as in many service areas and across a range of national contexts, procurement officials report being satisfied with the market-centered model (Lindholst 2017). But does competition improve performance? In a few cases, competitive tendering has been found to reduce costs without sacrificing quality (DeHoog 1990; Savas 1977; Verhoest 2005), but these competitive procedures may be subject to declining marginal returns – that is, frequent re-competition is costly and will not necessarily lower prices (Lindholst et al. 2018). Some studies also show that market competition can improve regulatory compliance, but the impact varies across public and private sectors (Song 2023).

Other studies note that, while competition is often found to be a significant predictor of performance, it pales in comparison to the importance of other factors (Lindholst 2017). As

Figure 18.2 shows, when compared with collaboration, capacity, and formalization, competition is the least important performance indicator. Counter to the conventional wisdom, recent studies show that in "the most successful contractual relationships, public managers can improve performance by limiting the number of bidders on the contract rather than by increasing the pool of bidders," as this strategy can help "weed out unqualified service providers who may try to 'lowball the government' in order to win the contract" (Fernandez 2007, p. 1134). Other studies find either no link between competition and performance or note that competition is associated with poorer performance (Brunjes 2020, 2022; Fernandez 2007, 2009; Romzek and Johnston 2005; Lamothe and Lamothe 2009, 2010).

There are many possible reasons for that competition may have limited effects in public procurement, including the high costs associated with bidding on government contracts (Brown et al. 2006), dominance of a subset of preferred firms even in competitive marketplaces (Atkinson 2020), the capacity of government officials to accurately assess contractor performance potential (Joaquin and Greitens 2012), and the damaging effect of competition on the relationship between the buyer and seller (Brunjes 2022).

If competition is not going to improve performance, what should managers do? Build strong relationships.

As Figure 18.2 shows, the factor that best explains contractor performance may be the quality of the relationship between the government and its contractor. Particularly when

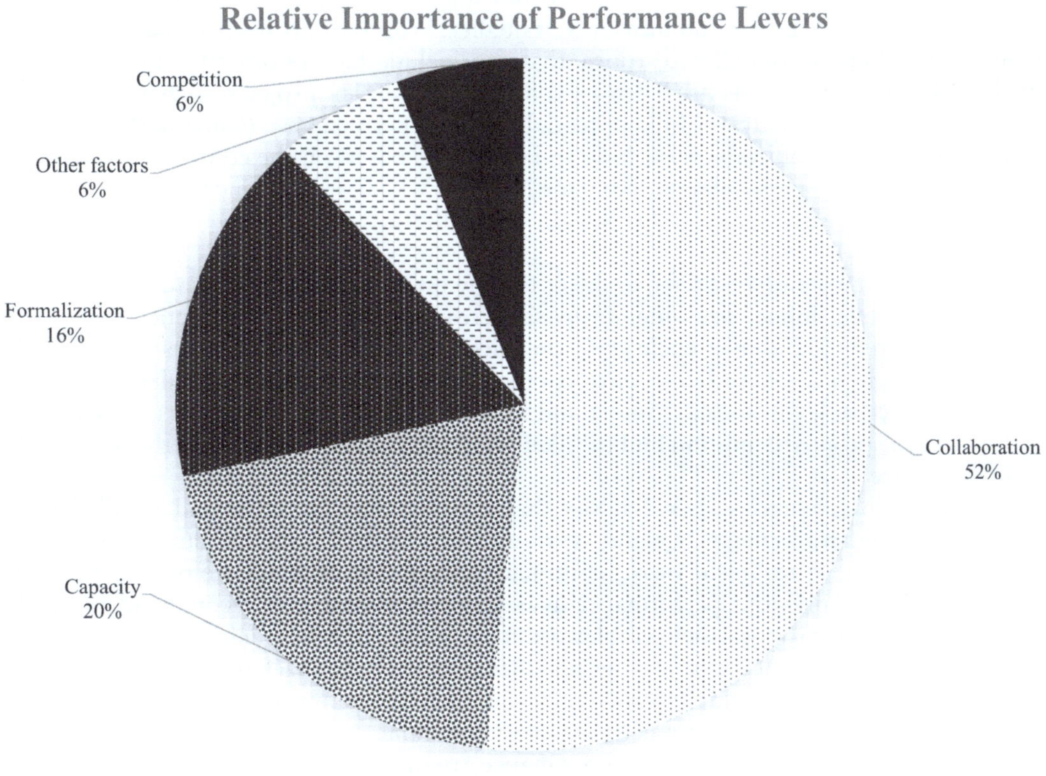


*Figure 18.2* Relative importance of performance levers.
*Source*: Adapted from Lindholst (2017).

managing more complex contracts like management services, information technology suites, or defense systems, relationships seem to matter a great deal. Studies find that relationships, prior experience, learning, goal alignment, trust, and monitoring capacity all lead to better contract performance, and as a result, improved vendor accountability (Romzek and Johnston 2005; Amirkhanyan 2009, 2011; Brunjes 2020, 2022; Vos and Voets 2023; Baekgaard and Serritzlew 2016; Potoski et al. 2023; Fernandez 2009; Amirkhanyan et al. 2010; Lamothe and Lamothe 2010). Together, there is a wealth of evidence to suggest that administrative effort is better spent developing a relationship rather than perfecting a marketing and competition strategy.

### *18.2.3 Evaluating Proposals: Assessing Performance Potential*

Choosing the right vendor is also important. Good vendors can lead to mutually beneficial relationships, while unreliable ones can increase costs and reduce the benefits of contracting out. Governments tend to receive either bids or proposals, which must be reviewed. Bids are usually price quotations received in response to a call for relatively simple services. Public agencies often request sealed bids, which are then opened in a public forum where the lowest responsive bidder is declared the winner. Sealed bids tend to be used for goods and services where there are competitive marketplaces, where the deliverables are clear and easily understood, and where there is little uncertainty about what good performance looks like (Curry 2016).

For other contracts, governments ask firms to submit detailed proposals that describe things like the timeline, the firm's management capacity, a proposed project approach, and information on deliverables and measures of quality. Proposals are assessed based on a previously agreed-upon (and shared) rubric that can include factors other than cost (such as quality). Detailed proposals are often used for more complex projects as they allow for a more comprehensive analysis of the potential for good performance (Curry 2016).

In general, public officials assess bids and proposals based on the contractor's perceived ability to meet key performance indicators (KPIs), which usually include the following (Adotévi 2004; Patrucco et al. 2016; Boykin et al. 2024):

- *Cost*: governments often prefer to select the lowest cost bid or proposal. Spending less frees up public dollars for other purposes, creating efficiency. In practice, sealed bid decisions are based almost exclusively on price (assuming all bids are responsive to the contracting initiative), and cost remains one of the most important considerations when evaluating complex proposals (Snider and Rendon 2012). Cost assessments must account for both the proposed amount and the likelihood of the vendor delivering the work at the quoted price.
- *Quality*: public agencies seek vendors that can demonstrate clear and detailed plans that meet the requirements. Quality attributes vary across contracts but are frequently assessed based on technical merit, contractor qualifications, evidence of past performance (including previous performance assessments and letters of recommendation), the extent to which proposal deliverables are measurable and well defined, and the possibility for innovative or exciting solutions (Rönnbäck 2012; Fazekas and Czibik 2021).
- *Timeliness*: though difficult to predict, public officials attempt to ascertain whether the potential contractor can complete the work on time. Contract managers review the proposed schedule, examine past performance, assess the current capacity of the organization, seek to identify any risk mitigation strategies included in the proposal, and consider the clarity and scalability of the project (Curry 2016).

- *Compliance/Internal Processes*: it is also necessary to ensure the proposal accounts for regulations (such as permits or certifications). These are especially important for construction projects or contracts in environmentally sensitive areas. In addition, government officials investigate whether the vendor has sufficient capacity (financial, technical, and managerial) to complete the work as presented, assess the potential for successful communication and reporting between the organizations, and note any plans for subcontracting that could complicate management (Atkinson 2020; Joaquin and Greitens 2012).
- *Innovation*: evaluation teams may also assess the creativity of a proposal, a firm's track record for innovation, its research and development (R&D) capacity, the proposed uses of technology, and the flexibility and adaptability of the proposed approach (Knutsson and Thomasson 2017).
- *Sustainability*: governments increasingly consider sustainability a critical contract performance indicator (Dimand 2022; Halonen 2021). Adopting a lifecycle perspective to public procurement, governments might consider the environmental impact of a contract (resource efficiency, waste reduction, carbon footprint), the extent to which sustainable materials and production practices are used, and whether the proposal aligns with sustainability standards.

Ultimately, evaluating proposals requires a careful balance of many factors. By rigorously assessing each proposal's potential to fulfill KPIs, public agencies can award contracts to the vendors best positioned to deliver value and meet expectations. This approach fosters transparency and accountability and can lead to long-term benefits for both the government and the contractor.

### *18.2.4 Overseeing Partnerships: Monitoring and Evaluation*

After selecting a bidder, the contract's "period of performance" begins. During the period of performance, contracting officials oversee the day-to-day management of the contract. Management is difficult due to information asymmetries between the government and the contractor, as neither has a complete picture of the expectations and actions of the other. Known as an "agency problem" (see Chapter 2), most of the steps taken during the period of performance are designed to reduce information asymmetries, ensure transparency, and limit shirking (Johnston and Romzek 1999).

Though many performance levers can be manipulated before a contract is signed, public procurement rarely leads to self-executing relationships (Joaquin and Greitens 2012; Brown and Potoski 2003). Instead, contract managers must work closely with their vendors to build relationships that encourage openness and communication. While vendors work toward delivering on a contract's requirements, government officials implement a complex combination of patrols and alarms to ensure that performance is high.

#### *18.2.4.1 Implementing Performance Patrols (Active Monitoring)*

During the period of performance, government officials often develop a series of regularly scheduled check-ins to assess the work the contractor is doing. These patrols are largely formal processes that are scheduled or at least acknowledged by both parties. Patrols require active engagement on behalf of contract administrators, who must adhere to the schedule and activities they have identified as being the most useful. Performance patrols include:

- *Site Visits*: Conducting routine inspections to observe work processes and verify progress toward performance objectives.
- *Performance Audits*: Regularly reviewing contractor deliverables to ensure that they meet KPI benchmarks and any other requirements.
- *Document Reviews*: Examining reports, invoices, or other submitted documentation for accuracy, completeness, and compliance.

##### *18.2.4.2 Monitoring Performance Alarms (Reactive Monitoring)*

Contracting officials must also create systems that will alert them to potential problems. These are more passive methods used to ensure that progress is being made or to identify the possibility of serious problems. Alarms require monitoring, but this may be automated (see the chapter on artificial intelligence (AI) in procurement) or assessed only if an alarm arises. Common alarms include:

- *Performance Dashboards*: Developing tracking systems or dashboards to flag deviations from timelines, budgets, or quality standards.
- *Complaint Mechanisms*: Providing channels (e.g., feedback forms or hotlines) for stakeholders or end-users to report issues or concerns about contractor performance.
- *Contractual Penalties and Incentives*: Implementing contract design provisions for sanctions if deadlines or quality standards are missed (and rewards for exceeding expectations).

##### *18.2.4.3 Building Relationships: What Really Motivates Performance*

While performing these more routine (and important) tasks, contracting officials must also work to create effective relationships with contractors. After all, contract management is relationship management, particularly for complex and repeat projects. The academic literature consistently links good relationships to fewer problems and better contract performance (Brunjes 2020, 2022; Amirkhanyan et al. 2010). Others are more direct, holding that "developing an authentic collaborative relationship with the contractor is the best way to achieve long-term performance benefits" (Yang et al. 2009, p. 693).

There are many ways to build successful relationships, which almost always depend on the context of the interaction. Literature on collaborative governance, which worries extensively about building relationships, notes that relationships is more likely to succeed if there is principled engagement, shared motivation, and the capacity for joint action (Emerson et al. 2012), which require some mixture of autonomy and mutuality undergirded by norms of trust and reciprocity (Thomson and Perry 2006; Scott and Thomas 2017).

Luckily, the procurement process provides a starting point for principled engagement, offering both parties the chance to discover things about one another, defining key terms and expectations, and offering mechanisms for deliberation should problems arise. Shared motivation is harder to achieve, particularly due to the differing priorities and values between governments and their vendors (Cordella and Willcocks 2010) and the power imbalances that a contract creates (Malatesta and Smith 2014). Shared motivations do not need to be the same – rather, each party needs to understand the motivations of the others and believe that they will work in a relatively predictable (and agreeable) manner toward achieving some shared objective or end goal (Krogh 2022). This requires transparency in motivations and objectives and a shared commitment to building a successful relationship (Emerson et al. 2012).

The capacity for joint action also requires a sufficient and well-trained staff of contract managers. Contracting officials are primarily of two types: (1) technical representatives who are issue experts responsible for managing the day-to-day details of the contract and (2) procurement process officials who are responsible for overseeing the minutiae of the rules and regulations that government contracts must adhere to (Cooper 1980). Public organizations require both types of expertise to successfully manage procurements. As Figure 18.2 indicates, capacity is the second most important contributor to contract performance (Lindholst 2017). However, the relationship between contract management capacity and improved performance may not be linear and "contracting capacities … also have costs which … . may depend on the passage of time or the stage of the contracting process" (Yang et al. 2009, p. 693). Underscoring the relative importance of the capacity of the contracting process, Fernandez' (2007) asserts that:

> experts on contracting have overestimated the impact of contract management practices aimed at controlling and programming the contractual relationship, and, conversely, that greater attention must be given to factors that build trust between the parties and facilitate problem solving and mutual adjustment to meet unforeseen circumstances.
>
> (p. 1136)

That is, building successful relationships seems to hinge on trust (Negoita 2018; Poocharoen and Wong 2016; Lamothe and Lamothe 2012), a fundamental building block of effective and high-functioning relationships. Trust has been shown to have a positive effect on contracting performance (Fernandez 2007, 2009). Contracting governments tend to find their peers (other governments) more trustworthy than private firms. Nonprofits are seen as more trustworthy than for-profit firms, as their goals may align more closely with those of public organizations (Witesman and Fernandez 2013). Trust is also more easily extended to vendors with well-established reputations, firms that have strong community ties, and contractors who have demonstrated their ability to perform the tasks well (Lamothe and Lamothe 2011).

Trust between organizations develops through the learning that comes from repeated interactions. For vendors, learning and experience can help lower the costs of selling to public agencies, as they develop knowledge of the processes and expectations of public agencies (Potoski et al. 2023). For governments, repeated interactions give administrators the chance to build familiarity with contractor work and communication styles, while also offering the chance to observe professionalism and performance first-hand (Scott and Thomas 2017; Van Slyke 2007). Informal relationships that develop between people over time add to these more technical aspects, as social pressures arise to build a sense of mutuality and reciprocity across organizations and individuals (Thomson and Perry 2006; Girth 2016).

Thus, a combination of careful contract design, the cultivation of shared motivations and objectives, sufficient capacity for successful contract administration, and the development of relationships based on learning can create familiarity and trusting relationships over time. Ultimately, these kinds of relationships can improve performance, particularly for complex contracts or those with uncertain objectives (Bertelli and Smith 2010; Brown et al. 2016; Brunjes 2020, 2022; Lamothe and Lamothe 2010; Lee and Kingsley 2009).

## 18.3 Emerging Issues

### *18.3.1 Increasing Uncertainty in an Era of Complex Contracts*

Uncertainty is pervasive in public procurement. There are many potential sources of uncertainty when managing contracts, including the characteristics of services to be outsourced, the competitiveness of markets, the characteristics of vendors, the extent of information asymmetry, and political and economic conditions. Greater awareness of the context and the use of multiple contingencies can be vital for our understanding of contract performance management and legitimacy (Lee and Kim 2024; Lindholst 2023).

Selecting appropriate governance mechanisms that are aligned with specific transactions can reduce uncertainty and mitigate potential opportunism (Maurya and Srivastava 2020; Blomqvist and Winblad 2022). One strategy is to only outsource services with lower transaction costs (see Chapter 3), because simpler contracts might increase the chances of good performance (Helby Petersen et al. 2022; Zhao and LeRoux 2021; Casady et al. 2022). But governments are increasingly contracting out for complex services with high transaction costs (Brown et al. 2018).

Where uncertainty is high, contract management capacity is particularly important, requiring human capital investments on behalf of governments (Brown and Potoski 2004; Brown and Potoski 2003). To successfully manage contracts, procurement officials should use a mixture of formal and relational accountability mechanisms in a complementary rather than a substitution fashion (Poppo and Zenger 2002; Frydlinger et al. 2019). Formal–relational contracts that "specify mutual goals and establish governance structures to keep the parties' expectations and interests aligned over the long term" are one possible solution (Frydlinger et al. 2019, p. 116). A formal–relational contract focuses on formalizing mechanisms for aligning expectations as new information emerges through the identification of governance structures, such as communication pathways, dispute resolution techniques, and modification procedures. This is a promising new area of scholarship that many practitioners will want to follow closely.

In the coming years, AI is also likely to be integrated into many public procurement systems. AI will undoubtedly be used to help monitor performance – it is well-suited to things like evaluating the compliance of proposals, identifying fraud, monitoring reactive alarm systems, and reviewing interim deliverables (Siciliani et al. 2023). AI will also help with some of the capacity challenges that governments face, as it can step in to perform some of the roles that governments are currently struggling to fill (Joaquin and Greitens 2012). However, AI will also come with its own challenges, including the reinforcement of social inequalities (as AI learns from what has been done and is not yet creative), worrisome security and data-sharing protocols, and limited knowledge of end users (Bose 2025; Kushwaha et al. 2023; Zajko 2021).

To reduce uncertainty on increasingly complex contracts, governments will need to build upon the principal-agent models that have long dominated contract management tactics. As contracted work becomes more uncertain, procurement officials should incorporate ideas from relational contracting and adopt new management technologies. While these will help reduce uncertainty, it will remain pervasive, serving as the most important challenge to effective contract performance management.

### *18.3.2 Performance and the Pursuit of Social Equity*

Public procurement and government contracting are important ways to promote social equity, because "decisions about contracting out or privatization are among the best places to go to tease out the meaning of public values" (Jørgensen and Bozeman 2002, p. 70). Small businesses, woman-owned firms, and minority owned firms struggle to win government contracts, and "while many jurisdictions have performed disparity studies over the last few years, few governments, if any, are spending proportionately to the availability of firms led by people of colour."[3]

Small, disadvantaged businesses perform on par with or better than other vendors, which indicates mutual benefits from public procurement with such firms (Brunjes and Rodriguez-Plesa 2024). Using small, disadvantaged business enterprises (SDBEs) has been shown to positively moderate the relationship between use of contracting and agency performance (Choi 2024). During the COVID-19 pandemic, SDBE suppliers were more likely than larger firms to provide contracts for strategic and important supplies (Dimand et al. 2023).

Some jurisdictions have taken steps to increase the participation of disadvantaged businesses and are focusing on the equity impact of their public procurement processes. For example, the "Equity in Contracting" initiative in the city of Seattle (Washington, USA) is engaged in "purchasing and contracting through a lens of equity and social responsibility."[4] The strategy requires prime contractors to voluntarily submit an inclusion plan that is then enforced if they win the contract. Similar initiatives are underway in other nations as well. In the UK, the guidance for contractors regarding diversity and equality from the Department for Work and Pensions mandates that vendors:

> monitor and report the makeup of their workforce in terms of gender, disability and ethnicity...demonstrate what actions have been taken/are planned to try and improve the workforce figures in these areas.
>
> (Schedule section – 2 (2.3), Compliance, Diversity and Equality Delivery Plan, DWP)[5]

SDBEs offer the opportunity for governments to make socially impactful investments while also receiving high-quality goods and services. Over the coming years, finding ways to attract SDBEs and manage their performance will be among the most important work contracting officials engage in around the world. This type of work is hard, as it requires active marketing, handholding through administrative processes, and ongoing education and relationship building, particularly when working with new government contractors (Woldesenbet and Worthington 2019).

## 18.4 Practical Applications

In this chapter, we have highlighted the importance of relationships for improved contract performance. We begin the concluding section with a list of requirements for successful contracting relationships, and present applications using the analogy of well ... relationships. We focus on two issues procurement officials must overcome in their contracting relationships and conclude the chapter with thoughts on how structured opportunities for learning might be beneficial ways to supplement other performance management approaches.

Contract management is a relationship that requires principled engagement, shared motivation, the capacity for joint action, and norms of mutuality and reciprocity. We argue that, in practice, public organizations and their contractors should strive to:

1. Foster authentic and open communication.
2. Build and maintain mutual trust.
3. Acknowledge and address past triggers that may affect interactions.
4. Collaborate to allocate resources equitably.

5. Regularly reassess and adapt to evolving needs.
6. Cultivate positive relationships by enjoying time spent together.
7. Encourage and support one another in achieving shared objectives.
8. Maintain strong and consistent communication channels.
9. Support and nurture each other's aspirations and goals.

#### *18.4.1 Why Would Someone Want to Enter into a Relationship with You?*

Building successful relationships with vendors and partners requires intentional effort and strategic outreach. Just as in personal connections, your professional reputation and approach play a pivotal role in how others perceive you.

Consider this: what is your reputation, and what value do you bring to the table? To what extent do potential partners view an exchange with you as risky or beneficial? Have you tried to introduce yourself, build visibility, and make connections? If the answer to these questions is "no," it's worth reflecting on where and how you're seeking to establish relationships.

Have you participated in social events to meet vendors or engaged in meaningful outreach? Are you taking steps to make yourself approachable and compelling, so others see value in building a partnership with you? Tools like Requests for Information (RFIs) and early notice solicitations can be effective for initiating connections, but if you're not leveraging them into real connections, you may be missing opportunities to attract potential partners.

Additionally, consider whether vendors can easily find and engage with you online. Are you reaching out to those who may lack strong digital skills or capacity? If this feels reminiscent of setting up a dating profile, that comparison isn't far off. The principles of building strong professional relationships – being visible, approachable, and intentional – are like those used in personal relationship-building, especially in today's digital-first landscape.

#### *18.4.2 Once You Are in a Relationship, What if You Are Both Unfulfilled?*

Addressing performance concerns in vendor relationships requires open dialogue and a shared commitment to finding solutions. Key questions to consider include: How are performance issues identified and resolved? Are both partners equally invested in resolving challenges? What are the terms and expectations of the relationship, and are past experiences or assumptions influencing current dynamics? These are critical considerations for procurement officials and vendors as they navigate performance challenges.

The answers to these questions often lie in fostering improved communication and clarity. Strategies such as onboarding meetings can set the stage for strong partnerships, while regular meetings can provide opportunities to review direct performance measures and align on priorities. Specific tools, such as monitoring stockouts or setting minimum order levels, can help maintain mutual accountability. Finding ways to interact informally is also important, as it can promote relationship building.

Equally important is evaluating whether the expectations on either side are realistic and manageable. For instance, are price increase requests reasonable given the longevity of the agreement? Or are other demands putting unnecessary strain on the relationship? By ensuring expectations are balanced and clearly defined, procurement officials and vendors can build stronger, more resilient partnerships.

#### *18.4.3 Making Space for Learning: A Formal–Relational Approach*

We have established that relationships are central to managing performance in public procurement. We have also noted the inherent tension between relationship-building and the traditional means of motivating and assessing performance, such as market competition, financial sanctions, police patrols, and fire alarms. In closing, we offer one way to create contract formal–relational contract governance: the use of options.

Traditional contract designs tend to require procurement officials to negotiate performance measures early, maintain regular evaluations, and adapt as necessary. To make contracts more collaborative, early engagement with vendors is crucial. Marvel and Marvel (2009) emphasize that performance assessment spans the entire contract lifecycle, from setting requirements and performance targets during design to evaluating and rewarding progress once the period of performance begins. In more collaborative procurement, contract monitoring is a spectrum where procurement officials may adopt a top-down approach or actively engage vendors in defining, refining, and negotiating performance measures (Amirkhanyan 2009). Options offer a formal–relational way to continue to learn and negotiate after the period of performance begins, building in a governance structure for both the vendor and the government to revisit the contract, the relationship, and contract performance.

By incorporating options into contracts, government agencies can avoid the high transaction costs of rebidding or renegotiating while simultaneously limiting risks. If vendor performance is unsatisfactory, the contract can expire with minimal loss. For vendors, options offer a way out if the government is hard to work with or the expectations are unclear. Conversely, satisfactory performance allows agencies and vendors to extend agreements and maximize future benefits. Including options on a contract provides a structured yet adaptable framework for agencies and vendors to learn about what works, attempt to build a relationship, and proceed into the future with a better understanding of contract performance.

## Notes

1 The following studies have assessed contractor performance using one or more of these measures: Amirkhanyan (2011), Amirkhanyan et al. (2010, 2014, 2018), Brunjes (2022), Brunjes and Rodriguez-Plesa (2024), Domberger and Hensher (1993), Fernandez (2007, 2009), Girth and Lopez (2019), and Poppo and Zenger (2002).

2 If the work required on a contract is uncertain (that is, the government and contractor have trouble approximating what it might take to perform the work or what the completed project will look like), then contractors may find fixed-price contracts restrictive and decline to bid.

3 Using Government Procurement to Advance Racial Equity, 2022, Government Performance Lab – Harvard Kennedy School, p.3.

4 https://performance.seattle.gov/stories/s/Equity-in-City-Contracting/irn2-dbmh/

5 www.gov.uk/government/publications/guide-for-dwp-contractors-diversity-and-equality-requirements/guide-for-dwp-contractors-diversity-and-equality-requirements#schedule-section--2-compliance

## References

Adotévi, S. (2004). Public procurement performance. In International Public Procurement Conference Proceedings (Vol. 3, pp. 243–261).

Amirkhanyan, A. A. (2009). Collaborative performance measurement: Examining and explaining the prevalence of collaboration in state and local government contracts. *Journal of Public Administration Research and Theory*, 19(3), 523–554.

Amirkhanyan, A. A. (2010). Monitoring across sectors: Examining the effect of nonprofit and for-profit contractor ownership on performance monitoring in state and local contracts. *Public Administration Review*, 70(5), 742–755.

Amirkhanyan, A. A. (2011). What is the effect of performance measurement on perceived accountability effectiveness in state and local government contracts? *Public Performance & Management Review*, 35(2), 303–339.

Amirkhanyan, A. A., Kim, H. J., & Lambright, K. T. (2010). Do relationships matter? Assessing the association between relationship design and contractor performance. *Public Performance & Management Review*, 34(2), 189–220.

Amirkhanyan, A. A., Kim, H. J., & Lambright, K. T. (2014). The performance puzzle: Understanding the factors influencing alternative dimensions and views of performance. *Journal of Public Administration Research and Theory*, 24(1), 1–34.

Amirkhanyan, A. A., Meier, K. J., O'Toole Jr, L. J., Dakhwe, M. A., & Janzen, S. (2018). Management and performance in US nursing homes. *Journal of Public Administration Research and Theory*, 28(1), 33–49.

Anguelov, L. G., & Brunjes, B. M. (2023). A replication of "contracting out: for what? With whom?". *Public Administration*, 101(3), 1163–1197.

Atkinson, C. L. (2020). Full and open competition in public procurement: Values and ethics in contracting opportunity. *International Journal of Public Administration*, 43(13), 1169–1182.

Auger, D. A. (1999). Privatization, contracting, and the states: Lessons from state government experience. *Public Productivity & Management Review*, 22(4), 435–454.

Baekgaard, M., & Serritzlew, S. (2016). Interpreting performance information: Motivated reasoning or unbiased comprehension. *Public Administration Review*, 76(1), 73–82.

Bertelli, A. M., & Smith, C. R. (2010). Relational contracting and network management. *Journal of Public Administration Research and Theory*, 20(suppl_1), i21–i40.

Blomqvist, P., & Winblad, U. (2022). Contracting out welfare services: How are private contractors held accountable? *Public Management Review*, 24(2), 233–254.

Bose, M. (2025). Bias in AI: A societal threat: A look beyond the tech. In *Open AI and computational intelligence for society 5.0* (pp. 197–224). IGI Global Scientific Publishing.

Boykin, E., Lofaro, R. J., McCue, C., & Prier, E. (2024). Advancing the practice of public procurement performance measurement: A framework for conceptualizing efficiency and effectiveness. *Public Money & Management*, 45(4), 1–11.

Boyne, G. A. (1998). Bureaucratic theory meets reality: Public choice and service contracting in US local government. *Public Administration Review*, 58(6), 474–484.

Brogaard, L., Madsen, J. K., & Petersen, O. H. (2024). Interpreting performance information: Motivated reasoning or unbiased comprehension? A replication and extension. *Public Administration*, 102(1), 318–340.

Brown, T. L., & Potoski, M. (2003). Contract – Management capacity in municipal and county governments. *Public Administration Review*, 63(2), 153–164.

Brown, T. L., & Potoski, M. (2004). Managing the public service market. *Public Administration Review*, 64(6), 656–668.

Brown, T. L., Potoski, M., & Van Slyke, D. (2016). Managing complex contracts: A theoretical approach. *Journal of Public Administration Research and Theory*, 26(2), 294–308.

Brown, T. L., Potoski, M., & Van Slyke, D. M. (2006). Managing public service contracts: Aligning values, institutions, and markets. *Public Administration Review*, 66(3), 323–331.

Brown, T. L., Potoski, M., & Van Slyke, D. M. (2018). Complex contracting: Management challenges and solutions. *Public Administration Review*, 78(5), 739–747.

Brunjes, B. M. (2018). Reducing risk and leveraging markets: The impact of financial structure on federal contractor performance. *Journal of Strategic Contracting and Negotiation*, 4(1–2), 6–29.

Brunjes, B. M. (2020). Competition and federal contractor performance. *Journal of Public Administration Research and Theory*, 30(2), 202–219.

Brunjes, B. M. (2022). Your competitive side is calling: An analysis of Florida contract performance. *Public Administration Review*, 82(1), 83–101.

Brunjes, B. M., & Rodriguez-Plesa, E. (2024). Equity in government contracting: Analyzing the performance of small disadvantaged businesses. *Public Administration* Review, 84(3), 484–499.

Casady, C. B., Petersen, O. H., & Brogaard, L. (2022, November). Cancel culture: The role of transaction costs and government capacity in failed public procurements. In APPAM 2022 Fall Conference, November (pp. 17–19).

Choi, I. (2024). Justice delayed is justice denied: Managing contracting performance for equal employment opportunity discrimination complaints. *Review of Public Personnel Administration*. https://doi.org/10.1177/0734371X241253018.

Cooper, P. J. (1980). Government contracts in public administration: The role and environment of the contracting officer. *Public Administration Review*, 40, 459–468.

Cooper, P. J. (2002). *Governing by contract: Challenges and opportunities for public managers*. CQ Press.

Cordella, A., & Willcocks, L. (2010). Outsourcing, bureaucracy and public value: Reappraising the notion of the "contract state". *Government Information Quarterly*, 27(1), 82–88.

Curry, W. S. (2016). *Government contracting: Promises and perils*. Routledge.

DeHoog, R. H. (1990). Competition, negotiation, or cooperation: Three models for service contracting. *Administration & Society*, 22(3), 317–340.

Dimand, A. M. (2022). Determinants of local government innovation: The case of green public procurement in the United States. *International Journal of Public Sector Management*, 35(5), 584–602.

Dimand, A. M., Patrucco, A. S., Rodriguez-Plesa, E., & Hiriscau, A. M. (2023). Social equity in federal contracting during emergencies: A portfolio management perspective. *Public Administration Review*, 83(5), 1319–1338.

Domberger, S., & Hensher, D. (1993). On the performance of competitively tendered, public sector cleaning contracts. *Public Administration*, 71(3), 441–454.

Dunleavy, P. (1986). Explaining the privatization boom: Public choice versus radical approaches. *Public Administration*, 64(1), 13–34.

Emerson, K., Nabatchi, T., & Balogh, S. (2012). An integrative framework for collaborative governance. *Journal of Public Administration Research and Theory*, 22(1), 1–29.

Ernita Joaquin, M., & Greitens, T. J. (2012). Contract management capacity breakdown? An analysis of US local governments. *Public Administration Review*, 72(6), 807–816.

Fazekas, M., & Czibik, Á. (2021). Measuring regional quality of government: The public spending quality index based on government contracting data. *Regional Studies*, 55(8), 1459–1472.

Fernandez, S. (2007). What works best when contracting for services? An analysis of contracting performance at the local level in the US. *Public Administration*, 85(4), 1119–1141.

Fernandez, S. (2009). Understanding contracting performance: An empirical analysis. *Administration & Society*, 41(1), 67–100.

Ferris, J., & Graddy, E. (1986). Contracting out: For what? With whom? *Public Administration Review*, 46(4), 332–344.

Frydlinger, D., Hart, O., & Vitasek, K. (2019). A new approach to contracts. *Harvard Business Review*, 97(5), 116–125.

Girth, A. M. (2016). Incentives in third-party governance: Management practices and accountability implications. *Public Administration Review*, 77(3), 433–444.

Girth, A. M., & Lopez, L. E. (2019). Contract design, complexity, and incentives: Evidence from US federal agencies. *The American Review of Public Administration*, 49(3), 325–337.

Hall, J. L. (2017). Performance management: Confronting the challenges for local government. *Public Administration Quarterly*, 41(1), 43–66.

Halonen, K. M. (2021). Is public procurement fit for reaching sustainability goals? A law and economics approach to green public procurement. *Maastricht Journal of European and Comparative Law*, 28(4), 535–555.

Hart, O., & Moore, J. (1988). Incomplete contracts and renegotiation. *Econometrica: Journal of the Econometric Society*, 56(4), 755–785. https://doi.org/10.2307/1912698

Hartley, J., Sørensen, E., & Torfing, J. (2013). Collaborative innovation: A viable alternative to market competition and organizational entrepreneurship. *Public Administration Review*, 73(6), 821–830.

Heinrich, C. J., & Choi, Y. (2007). Performance-based contracting in social welfare programs. *The American Review of Public Administration*, 37(4), 409–435.

Helby Petersen, O., Potoski, M., & Brown, T. L. (2022). Businesses' transaction costs when contracting with governments: the impact of product complexity and public contract management experience. *International Public Management Journal*, 25(5), 741–766.

Johnston, J. M., & Girth, A. M. (2012). Government contracts and "managing the market" exploring the costs of strategic management responses to weak vendor competition. *Administration & Society*, 44(1), 3–29.

Johnston, J. M., & Romzek, B. S. (1999). Contracting and accountability in state Medicaid reform: Rhetoric, theories, and reality. *Public Administration Review*, 59, 383–399.

Jørgensen, T. B., & Bozeman, B. (2002). Public values lost? Comparing cases on contracting out from Denmark and the United States. *Public Management Review*, 4(1), 63–81.

Kim, Y. W., & Brown, T. (2017). Autonomy versus control in procurement and contracting: The use of cost-reimbursement contracts in three US federal departments. *International Review of Administrative Sciences*, 83(1_suppl), 41–58.

Kim, Y. W., & Brown, T. L. (2012). The importance of contract design. *Public Administration Review*, 72(5), 687–696.

Knutsson, H., & Thomasson, A. (2017). Exploring organisational hybridity from a learning perspective. *Qualitative Research in Accounting & Management*, 14(4), 430–447.

Kristiansen, M. B., Dahler-Larsen, P., & Ghin, E. M. (2019). On the dynamic nature of performance management regimes. *Administration & Society*, 51(6), 991–1013.

Krogh, A. H. (2022). Facilitating collaboration in publicly mandated governance networks. *Public Management Review*, 24(4), 631–653.

Kushwaha, A. K., Pharswan, R., Kumar, P., & Kar, A. K. (2023). How do users feel when they use artificial intelligence for decision making? A framework for assessing users' perception. *Information Systems Frontiers*, 25(3), 1241–1260.

Lamothe, M., & Lamothe, S. (2009). Beyond the search for competition in social service contracting: Procurement, consolidation, and accountability. *The American Review of Public Administration*, 39(2), 164–188.

Lamothe, M., & Lamothe, S. (2010). Competing for what? Linking competition to performance in social service contracting. *The American Review of Public Administration*, 40(3), 326–350.

Lamothe, M., & Lamothe, S. (2012). What determines the formal versus relational nature of local government contracting?. *Urban Affairs Review*, 48(3), 322–353.

Lane, J. E. (2002). *New public management: an introduction*. Routledge.

Lee, S., & Kim, S. (2024). Where do citizens place blame for service delivery failure? A closer look at public-private partnerships. *Public Performance & Management Review*, 47(6), 1482–1511.

Lee, S., & Kingsley, G. (2009). The impact of relational factors on contracting management in public organizations. *Review of Public Personnel Administration*, 29(3), 270–292.

Lerusse, A., & Van de Walle, S. (2022). Buying from local providers: the role of governance preferences in assessing performance information. *Public Administration Review*, 82(5), 835–849.

Lindholst, A. C. (2017). Comparing contracting performance: Culture, competition, contracts, capabilities and collaboration in UK and Scandinavia. In Paper presented at 21th Annual International Research Society for Public Management (IRSPM) Conference, Budapest, Hungary.

Lindholst, A. C. (2023). Long live marketization for local public spaces: A study of Scandinavian managers' satisfaction with private provider performance. *Urban Affairs Review*, 59(1), 200–237.

Lindholst, A. C., Helby Petersen, O., & Houlberg, K. (2018). Contracting out local road and park services: Economic effects and their strategic, contractual and competitive conditions. *Local Government Studies*, 44(1), 64–85.

Lu, J. (2016). The performance of performance-based contracting in human services: A quasi-experiment. *Journal of Public Administration Research and Theory*, 26(2), 277–293.

Malatesta, D., & Smith, C. R. (2014). Lessons from resource dependence theory for contemporary public and nonprofit management. *Public Administration Review*, 74(1), 14–25.

Marvel, M. K., & Marvel, H. P. (2009). Shaping the provision of outsourced public services: Incentive efficacy and service delivery. *Public Performance & Management Review*, 33(2), 183–213.

Maurya, D., & Srivastava, A. K. (2020). Controlling opportunism in partnerships: A process view. *International Journal of Public Sector Management*, 33(6/7), 751–769.

Moynihan, D. P., Fernandez, S., Kim, S., LeRoux, K. M., Piotrowski, S. J., Wright, B. E., & Yang, K. (2011). Performance regimes amidst governance complexity. *Journal of Public Administration Research and Theory*, 21(suppl_1), i141–i155.

Negoita, M. (2018). Beyond performance management: A networked production model of public service delivery. *Public Performance & Management Review*, 41(2), 253–276.

Obinger, H., Schmitt, C., & Traub, S. (2016). *The political economy of privatization in rich democracies*. Oxford University Press.

Ogden, J. A., & Brady, S. (2015). Balancing incentives and risks in performance-based contracts. *Defense AR Journal*, 22(4), 472.

Osborne, D., & Gaebler, T. (1992). *Reinventing government: How the entrepreneurial spirit is transforming the public sector*. Penguin.

Patrucco, A. S., Luzzini, D., & Ronchi, S. (2016). Evaluating the effectiveness of public procurement performance management systems in local governments. *Local Government Studies*, 42(5), 739–761.

Petersen, O. H., Hjelmar, U., & Vrangbæk, K. (2018). Is contracting out of public services still the great panacea? A systematic review of studies on economic and quality effects from 2000 to 2014. *Social Policy & Administration*, 52(1), 130–157.

Polyviou, M., Ried, L., & Wiedmer, R. (2024). Selection of small and diverse suppliers and contractual performance: Do set-asides pay off? *Production and Operations Management*, 34(3), 475–492. https://doi.org/10.1177/10591478241265646.

Poocharoen, O. O., & Wong, N. H. L. (2016). Performance management of collaborative projects: The stronger the collaboration, the less is measured. *Public Performance & Management Review*, 39(3), 607–629.

Poppo, L., & Zenger, T. (2002). Do formal contracts and relational governance function as substitutes or complements? *Strategic Management Journal*, 23(8), 707–725.

Potoski, M., Petersen, O. H., & Brown, T. L. (2023). Same product, different price: Experimental evidence on the transaction cost expenditures of selling to governments and firms. *Public Administration Review*, 83(3), 623–638.

Resh, W. G., & Marvel, J. D. (2012). Loopholes to load-shed: Contract management capacity, representative bureaucracy, and goal displacement in federal procurement decisions. *International Public Management Journal*, 15(4), 525–547.

Romzek, B. S., & Johnston, J. M. (2005). State social services contracting: Exploring the determinants of effective contract accountability. *Public Administration Review*, 65(4), 436–449.

Rönnbäck, Å. (2012). Quality in the public procurement process. *The TQM Journal*, 24(5), 447–460.

Savas, E. (1987). *Privatization: The key to better government*. Chatham House

Savas, E. S. (1977). An empirical study of competition in municipal service delivery. *Public Administration Review*, 37(6), 717–724.

Scott, T. A., & Thomas, C. W. (2017). Unpacking the collaborative toolbox: Why and when do public managers choose collaborative governance strategies? *Policy Studies Journal*, 45(1), 191–214.

Schooner, S. L. (2002). Desiderata: Objectives for a system of government contract law. *Public Procurement Law Review*, 11, 103.

Seidman, H. (1990). Public enterprise versus privatization in the United States. *International Review of Administrative Sciences*, 56(1), 15–28.

Selviaridis, K., & Wynstra, F. (2015). Performance-based contracting: A literature review and future research directions. *International Journal of Production Research*, 53(12), 3505–3540.

Shetterly, D. R. (2000). The influence of contract design on contractor performance: The case of residential refuse collection. *Public Performance & Management Review*, 24(1), 53–68. https://doi.org/10.2307/3381076

Siciliani, L., Taccardi, V., Basile, P., Di Ciano, M., & Lops, P. (2023). AI-based decision support system for public procurement. *Information Systems*, 119, 102284.

Snider, K. F., & Rendon, R. G. (2012). Public procurement: Public administration and public service perspectives. *Journal of Public Affairs Education*, 18(2), 327–348.

Song, M. (2023). Market competition and regulatory compliance in public, non-profit, and for-profit organizations. *Public Management Review*, 25(10), 1982–2002.

Thomson, A. M., & Perry, J. L. (2006). Collaboration processes: Inside the black box. *Public Administration Review*, 66, 20–32.

U.S. Department of Defense. (2025, July 7). *Guidance for the Contractor Performance Assessment Reporting System (CPARS)*. www.cpars.gov/cparsweb/assets/documents/CPARS-Guidance.pdf

Van Slyke, D. M. (2003). The mythology of privatization in contracting for social services. *Public Administration Review*, 63(3), 296–315.

Van Slyke, D. M. (2007). Agents or stewards: Using theory to understand the government-nonprofit social service contracting relationship. *Journal of Public Administration Research and Theory*, 17(2), 157–187.

Van Slyke, D. M. (2009). Collaboration and relational contracting. In R. O'Leary & L. B. Bingham (Eds.), *The Collaborative Public Manager* (pp. 137–156). Georgetown University Press.

Verhoest, K. (2005). Effects of autonomy, performance contracting, and competition on the performance of a public agency: A case study. *Policy Studies Journal*, 33(2), 235–258.

Vos, D., & Voets, J. (2023). Examining municipalities' choices of service delivery modes through the lens of historical institutionalism. *Public Management Review*, 26(7), 1892–1914.

Warner, M. E. (2023). Pragmatic municipalism: Privatization and remunicipalisation in the US. *Local Government Studies*, 50(4), 677–695.

Witesman, E. M., & Fernandez, S. (2013). Government contracts with private organizations: Are there differences between nonprofits and for-profits? *Nonprofit and Voluntary Sector Quarterly*, 42(4), 689–715.

Woldesenbet, K., & Worthington, I. (2019). Public procurement and small businesses: Estranged or engaged? *Journal of Small Business Management*, 57(4), 1661–1675.

Yang, K., Hsieh, J. Y., & Li, T. S. (2009). Contracting capacity and perceived contracting performance: Nonlinear effects and the role of time. *Public Administration Review*, 69(4), 681–696.

Zajko, M. (2021). Conservative AI and social inequality: Conceptualizing alternatives to bias through social theory. *AI & Society*, 36(3), 1047–1056.

Zhao, T., & LeRoux, K. (2021). Are outsourced public health services linked to better health outcomes? Findings from a national study of service contracting by local health departments. In *Performance and public value in the 'Hollow State'* (pp. 43–63). Edward Elgar Publishing.

### *Case Study: Janitorial Services (Developed by Lachezar G. Anguelov, Benjamin M. Brunjes and Josh Klika)*

#### Background

As a contract manager for a mid-sized city, you oversee a newly awarded three-year janitorial services contract valued at $1.2 million annually. The contract has been awarded to a provider with no prior experience working with the city. This provider will be responsible for maintaining 14 buildings, ranging from small administrative offices to large, high-traffic facilities such as city hall and the central library.

The contract includes a 120-day transition period to allow the incoming contractor to establish operations, familiarize staff with the buildings, and address any logistical or operational concerns. However, despite the preparation window, stakeholders from the finance and site management departments have already raised concerns, citing past frustrations with janitorial services.

#### Stakeholder Concerns

1. **Billing Confusion**
    - **Current Issue**: Invoices from the outgoing contractor are often unclear, lacking details about which services were provided at specific locations.
    - **Impact**: This has led to delays in processing payments and frustration among accounting staff managing multiple budgets for the 14 serviced buildings.
2. **Low-Quality Supplies**
    - **Perception**: Site managers at various locations report dissatisfaction with the quality of soap, paper towels, and toilet paper, believing that this reflects poorly on the contractor.
    - **Clarification**: According to the contract's Scope of Work, the city is responsible for providing cleaning supplies, but this distinction is often misunderstood by stakeholders.
3. **Inconsistent Cleaning Standards**
    - **Complaint**: Managers report frequent lapses in daily cleaning routines, with some areas overlooked while others receive unnecessary attention.
    - **Past Challenge**: These inconsistencies have contributed to a lack of trust in the contractor's ability to meet the city's expectations for cleanliness.

#### Pre-Contract Considerations

Recognizing the high visibility and importance of this contract, you organize a series of onboarding meetings during the transition period. These meetings aim to build a strong working relationship with the contractor while addressing the specific concerns raised by stakeholders.

Key onboarding activities include:

- **Invoice Standardization**: Working with finance representatives and the contractor to create a standardized invoicing template that includes detailed line items for each

location. This template will feature unique building codes linked to the city's facilities database.
- **Stakeholder Orientation**: Coordinating building tours for the contractor's supervisory staff to familiarize them with the unique needs of each site. During these visits, site managers will provide input on high-priority areas and expectations for cleanliness.
- **Clarifying Roles**: Addressing the supply quality issue by clearly communicating to site managers that the city provides cleaning supplies. Exploring whether an adjustment in procurement practices for supplies is warranted to improve stakeholder satisfaction.

### Contract Management Strategies

Given the scale and complexity of this contract, active and relationship-focused management will be critical. Specific strategies include:

- **Performance Metrics**: Establishing measurable Key Performance Indicators (KPIs) such as timeliness of service, adherence to the cleaning schedule, and responsiveness to stakeholder concerns.
- **Regular Check-Ins**: Scheduling monthly check-ins with the contractor to discuss performance metrics and resolve emerging issues.
- **Differentiated Service Levels**: Tailoring cleaning schedules and service intensity to the specific needs of different buildings. For example, high-traffic locations like city hall may require daily deep cleaning, while smaller administrative offices may need less frequent services.

### Scenario Development

Two months into the transition period, you begin receiving reports of challenges:

- **Communication Breakdown**: Site managers report that some contractor employees appear unfamiliar with building layouts, leading to inefficiencies in cleaning operations.
- **Invoice Errors**: The contractor's initial invoices lack clarity and do not align with the agreed-upon template, causing delays in payment processing.
- **Perception of Poor Quality**: Despite clarifications, stakeholders continue to express dissatisfaction with the quality of cleaning supplies, incorrectly attributing this to the contractor.

### Questions for Discussion

1. How can you address communication breakdowns between the contractor's staff and site managers to ensure smooth operations?
2. What steps can you take to build trust with the contractor and stakeholders while addressing persistent misconceptions about supply quality?
3. How can you leverage relationship-building techniques to ensure contractor performance improves over the life of the agreement?
4. If these challenges persist, how would you evaluate whether the contract should be renewed or terminated at the end of the initial term?

# 19 Public Procurement and Logistics Management in Federal and State Systems

*Robert Handfield, Zhaohui Wu and Daniel Finkenstadt*

## 19.1 Public Procurement at the Federal, State, and Local Levels: What Is It?

Public procurement is an essential component of government and provides an essential cog in meeting government policies and objectives.

Efficiency in public procurement is essential to the nation's functioning. No one understood this more than President Dwight D. Eisenhower, who, in his farewell address in 1961, noted that:

> A vital element in keeping the peace is our military establishment. Our arms must be mighty, ready for instant action, so that no potential aggressor may be tempted to risk his own destruction. . . . American makers of plowshares could, with time and as required, make swords as well. But now we can no longer risk emergency improvisation of national defense; we have been compelled to create a permanent armaments industry of vast proportions. . . . This conjunction of an immense military establishment and a large arms industry is new in the American experience. . . .Yet we must not fail to comprehend its grave implications. . . . In the councils of government, we must guard against the acquisition of unwarranted influence, whether sought or unsought, by the military-industrial complex. The potential for the disastrous rise of misplaced power exists and will persist.[1]

Perhaps the single most important objective for public procurement (also called "acquisition") is not simply to leverage spending to drive down cost but to support organizational goals and objectives. Although this sounds easy, purchasing goals do not always align well with organizational goals. However, this has become an important caveat for the adoption of strategic supply management in the public sector and certainly applies to the acquisition of logistics services as well. This objective implies that acquisition can directly (positively or negatively) affect the performance outcomes and mission of government agencies and the American taxpayer.

Public procurement and logistics apply at three levels in the U.S. Government: federal, state, and local. This chapter will primarily deal with federal and state government acquisition, but we will touch briefly on local government procurement.

Federal procurement involves all third-party purchases of products and services for federal agencies, which include the Department of State, the Department of Transportation (DOT), the Department of Commerce, the Department of Homeland Security, the Federal Bureau of Investigation, and other federal agencies. Each agency generally has its own

DOI: 10.4324/9781003566670-22

procurement department. However, many purchases are coordinated through the General Services Administration (GSA), which is often responsible for common indirect purchases, such as computer technology, information technology, travel expenses, and other types of purchases that benefit from group purchasing leverage. The Department of Defense (DoD) also has its own purchasing group, the Defense Logistics Agency (DLA), but also has pockets of procurement activity within each of the armed forces (Army, Navy, Air Force, Marines).

State procurement is primarily involved with contracting products and services for state government agencies, including Health and Human Services, Transportation, Commerce, and others. One of the primary functions of a State Procurement Office (SPO henceforth) is contract management. This activity involves identifying and vetting suppliers, who are then approved for other agencies to buy from, using agreed-upon prices, terms, and conditions. In such cases, SPOs do not take physical ownership of goods and services but are involved in negotiating contracts for state agencies and establishing purchasing policies to guide state personnel in obtaining third-party products and services. (The degree to which procurement has sole authority over contracting decisions varies by state and is often influenced by the governor's policies and historical precedent as well as state laws.) Other typical supply chain management activities (e.g., supply network management, logistics risk assessment, warehouse management, distribution to end users, transportation management, and supplier development), which are common practices for a buying firm in the private sector, are generally not part of purchasing's mandate in the public sector. Often, SPOs purchase through formal bidding procedures. In the case of some products like personal protection equipment (PPE) during COVID, states typically sourced these items through contracts with distributors, such as Grainger, Cardinal Health, or McKesson, rather than directly from manufacturers. In the United States, the collective spending of the 50 states on procurement contracts is roughly equivalent to that of the federal government, amounting to approximately $600 billion in 2023.

Local procurement is primarily involved with purchasing products and services for a city, county, or local community. Many large cities require a DOT, waste management, prisons, courts, water, power, road maintenance, police force, fire department, social services, and other critical services that enable the city to function efficiently. These functions typically report to the mayor's office and/or city council, depending on the local requirements. County-level purchasing offices may also function as the primary contractors in rural communities for road maintenance, the local department of health, social services, jails, police force, fire department, etc. Local procurement offices are typically staffed by a small group of individuals, who may have limited authority to award business depending on the situation.

Federal, state, and local government procurement manages and relies on several business processes that mirror those of commercial business. Examples of the types of elements outsourced include the following:

- Logistics
- Facilities management
- Accounting operations
- Resource management
- Talent management and training
- Performance management
- Business systems (IT)
- Shared service delivery
- Communications
- Security

- Medical services
- Travel

This chapter will focus on procurement and logistics, which is generally in the form of "logistics outsourcing". As we will see, procurement agencies have not historically been involved in operating their own logistics operations, except for the Strategic National Stockpile (SNS). In most cases, procurement has outsourced logistics to third parties, often called "third-party logistics providers" or 3PLs. As we shall see in this chapter, several exceptions occurred during COVID, which suggests that logistics is evolving to become a more important component of federal and state acquisition strategies.

### 19.2 Federal Acquisition

The mandate to pursue a strategic approach to supply management was recently expressed by the OMB in a December 14, 2014, memo[2] that explicitly identifies the need for a new approach that applies to GSA, all federal agencies, the DoD, and, by implication, the intelligence community. The Office of Management and Budget (OMB) memo calls for the following actions:

- Recognition of a need for an enhanced approach to procurement and Strategic Sourcing Leadership Council (SSLC) and agencies commitment to category management as that new approach.
- Use of category management to move from managing through thousands of business and procurement units to coordinated management of entire categories of common spend and total cost.
- GSA's lead role in developing guidance and standards for category management development and execution.
- Sharing of data, reports, and best practices.
- Development of talent and tools.
- Building stronger vendor relationships.

Not surprisingly, organizational resistance to change is strong and growing stronger when making changes to government acquisition. One of the primary reasons for the resistance to change is the Federal Acquisition Regulations (FAR). The FAR is one of the most prominent complexities facing changes to federal acquisition. This is a book of acquisition regulations that is several inches thick – and contains multiple criteria and regulations that federal buyers must use to develop requirements, communicate with industry, make sourcing decisions, and manage contracts. Many of the pages contain terms and conditions to be levied on firms themselves. Given the nearly 2,000 pages of FAR governance policies, defense contracting and procurement activities are highly controlled, if not onerous, relative to commercial practices. This has led to calls to "improve efficiency, reduce red tape, and provide greater benefit for taxpayer dollars".[3] No less than eight major acquisition reform initiatives have been undertaken since the 1980s.[4] The most recent initiative, dubbed the Section 809 Panel,[5] was created in 2016 with a charge "to deliver recommendations that could transform the defense acquisition system to meet the threats and demands of the 21st century". This panel provided 98 recommendations for improving the U.S. federal defense acquisition system alone.

Another criticism is that federal evaluation criteria, which are seen as generic and too rigid, preclude innovative companies from fully demonstrating the value they can bring to supporting public agency missions. The rigidity of requirements also further prevents suppliers from proposing innovative and potentially more cost-effective solutions. What makes it worse is when an investment is made on an Request for Proposals (RFP), and it is suddenly canceled. Volume uncertainty is a transaction cost incurred from the firms' inability to forecast volume requirements in a relationship (contract, etc.). For example, the uncertainty the firm has regarding options being exercised on current contracts or the probability of winning new government contracts in the future. Nontraditional defense firms have more to lose from unsuccessful offerings and from using capital to support the government at the expense of competition in the commercial market due to finite resources.

A multitude of studies have called for policymakers and acquisition professionals to reform government acquisition policies and approaches, citing the importance of creating an efficient and viable procurement process that not only meets the demands of parties but also encourages the right level of dialogue and collaboration between private industry and government. Although the DoD and GSA are pursuing some form of procurement reform, there is significant room for improvement. In this chapter, we review some of the key elements of federal procurement.

Contracting officers spend a large amount of time working through business processes and standard operating procedures (SOP), yet often do not have the appropriate tools, techniques, and documentation for contracting logistics effectively. As a result, time and energy are spent on routine tactical activities rather than operational or strategic activities. In many cases, few controls or standard business processes are utilized in contracting with third parties, and opportunities for leveraging spending across agencies or even within an agency are often overlooked or not explored at all.[6]

In such cases, contracting agents may have little exposure to emerging trends in the logistics outsourcing discipline, including strategic sourcing, category analysis, spend analysis, demand management, and other management processes for managing third-party contracts. These processes have emerged in the private sector over the last 20 years, have enjoyed significant success, and are well documented in management curricula and professional associations.[7] However, there also exist special caveats to acquisition in the federal community that may limit the application of these approaches. To our knowledge, federal acquisition is beginning to explore best practices in procure-to-pay management, category management, strategic sourcing, or other defined methodologies that are driven by procurement analytics and process management in the field of public procurement.

### *19.2.1 Logistics in the Federal Government*

Within the U.S. Federal Government, there is no one agency responsible for all federal logistics. As one might imagine, that would be an intractable problem to solve. There are various departments that have responsibilities for various aspects of public logistics support, and there are agencies within departments that are responsible for supporting the direct needs of a specific department.

This section of the textbook covers the diverse and complex landscape of federal-level public logistics in the United States. It highlights the decentralized nature of logistics management across various federal departments and agencies, each with distinct responsibilities. Key entities include the GSA, responsible for a wide range of services, including property management and fleet services; the U.S. Postal Service (USPS), delivering mail and essential supplies nationwide; the DOT, with its multiple administrations overseeing different transport sectors; and the Department of State's Office of Logistics Management, which supports diplomatic missions. Additionally, the chapter touches on strategic stockpiles like the SNS and the roles of military logistics entities such as the DLA and the U.S. Transportation Command (TRANSCOM). Collectively, these organizations ensure the efficient and effective management of logistics and supply chains critical to national security, emergency preparedness, and day-to-day governmental operations.

### *19.2.2 General Services Administration*

Harry Truman established the GSA in 1949. Its original purpose was to consolidate federal administrative actions. They were charged to manage the disposal of surplus goods from military operations, oversee the storage and management of government records, coordinate emergency preparedness strategies, and maintain stockpiles of essential supplies for use during wartime until these responsibilities were transferred to FEMA in 1979.[8] Only a small portion of their budget is appropriated by Congress. The majority of their funds are generated by gathering service fees from the agencies and departments that they support.

The GSA is primarily known for its acquisition support to nine major federal categories. Those categories include the following:

1. Facilities and Construction;
2. Human capital;
3. Industrial products and services;
4. Information technology;
5. Office management;
6. Professional services;
7. Security and protection;
8. Transportation and logistics services;
9. Travel and lodging.

In addition to its acquisition support, the GSA also provides central shared services for the federal government in the areas of acquisition support, payment, and payroll. They also issue government-wide policies and assist in presidential transitions. Specifically, within transportation and logistics, they handle fleet management, fleet management education services, freight management, package delivery, and air and ground transportation services.

### *19.2.3 U.S. Postal Service*

The GSA and the USPS are distinct federal entities that support some similar objectives. The USPS is charged with providing reliable, affordable, universal mail services to the American public. The USPS was first established in 1775 with the appointment of the first Postmaster General. In 2006, the USPS was broken into two distinct operational categories:

1. Market Dominant: The traditional mailing services offered by USPS are capped for price growth by the CPI.
2. Competitive: Shipping services are allowed to shift as necessary to cover all attributable costs.

During times of extreme federal challenge, the USPS may be called upon to offer logistics support over and above the norm. For instance, during the COVID-19 epidemic, the USPS was used to deliver essential medical supplies and prescriptions. To date, the United States still delivers free COVID tests to citizens through the USPS.

### *19.2.4 Department of Transportation*

The U.S. federal DOT is charged with delivering a world-leading transportation system for "safe, efficient, sustainable and equitable movement of people and goods".[9] The federal DOT is responsible for managing the nine operating administrations (OAs). These consist of the following:

1. Federal Aviation Administration (FAA):
   The FAA is responsible for regulating and overseeing civil aviation in the United States. Its duties include ensuring the safety and efficiency of the national airspace system, certifying aircraft and pilots, and managing air traffic control. A historical example of its responsibilities in action is the investigation and implementation of safety regulations following aviation accidents, such as the investigation into the crashes of Boeing 737 Max aircraft, leading to the grounding of these planes until safety concerns were addressed.
2. Federal Highway Administration (FHA):
   The FHA is tasked with planning, developing, and maintaining the nation's highway infrastructure. It provides funding to states for highway construction and maintenance projects, ensures highway safety standards are met, and promotes sustainable transportation practices. An example of its responsibilities in action is the funding and oversight of the construction and maintenance of the Interstate Highway System, a massive infrastructure project initiated in the 1950s to connect major cities and regions.
3. Federal Motor Carrier Safety Administration (FMCSA):
   The FMCSA focuses on regulating and improving the safety of commercial motor vehicles, including trucks and buses. It sets and enforces safety standards for vehicles and drivers, conducts inspections, and oversees compliance with regulations. An example of its responsibilities in action is the implementation of the Electronic Logging Device (ELD) mandate, which requires commercial drivers to use electronic devices to track their hours of service accurately, reducing the risk of driver fatigue and related accidents.
4. Federal Railroad Administration (FRA):
   The FRA is responsible for regulating and promoting the safety and efficiency of the nation's railroad systems. It oversees railroad infrastructure, equipment, and operations. A historical example of its responsibilities in action is the enforcement of safety standards following major train derailments, such as the investigation into the Amtrak derailment in Philadelphia in 2015, which resulted in safety improvements and recommendations for the industry.
5. Federal Transit Administration (FTA):
   The FTA supports and regulates public transit systems across the country, providing funding, technical assistance, and oversight. It works to improve public transportation options and ensure the safety and reliability of transit services. An example of its responsibilities in action is the funding and support provided for the development of new urban transit systems, like light rail or bus rapid transit, in various cities.
6. Marine Administration (MARAD):
   MARAD is responsible for promoting and maintaining a strong U.S. maritime industry. It oversees the nation's merchant marine, administers shipping-related programs, and supports the development of a modern fleet. An example of its responsibilities in action is the promotion of shipbuilding and the Maritime Security Program, which ensures a fleet of U.S.-flagged commercial vessels available for national defense and emergency response.

7. National Highway Traffic Safety Administration (NHTSA):
   NHTSA is dedicated to improving road safety by regulating and enforcing vehicle performance standards, promoting vehicle and road safety technologies, and conducting research on traffic safety issues. A historical example of its responsibilities in action is the recall and safety investigation of defective vehicle parts or systems, like the recall of millions of vehicles due to faulty airbags produced by Takata Corporation.
8. Pipeline and Hazardous Materials Safety Administration (PHMSA):
   PHMSA is responsible for the safety of the nation's pipelines and the transportation of hazardous materials. It sets and enforces safety regulations for pipelines, gas and oil transportation, and hazardous materials shipping. An example of its responsibilities in action is the regulation and inspection of pipelines, ensuring their integrity and preventing leaks or accidents, such as the oversight of the Keystone XL pipeline project.
9. Great Lakes St. Lawrence Seaway Development Corporation (GLS):
   GLS oversees and operates the U.S. portion of the Great Lakes St. Lawrence Seaway System, which connects the Great Lakes to the Atlantic Ocean. Its responsibilities include navigation, maintenance, and infrastructure improvements along this vital waterway. An example of its responsibilities in action is the ongoing maintenance and dredging of the seaway to ensure safe and efficient maritime transportation of goods between the Great Lakes and international markets.

### *19.2.5 Department of State*

The Office of Logistics Management within the U.S. Department of State provides logistical support for diplomatic mission needs. The Office of Logistics is split into two main mission areas:

1. Logistics Operations:
   Logistics Operations (OPS) is responsible for coordinating and executing various logistical functions to support the Department of State and its employees. OPS arranges travel, transportation, and warehousing services for employees and their families. This includes packing and shipping household effects, including personally owned vehicles. OPS also manages the storage of household effects in Hagerstown and at commercial facilities nationwide. They have despatch agents in key locations, such as Baltimore, Brownsville, Dulles, Miami, New York, and Seattle. Additionally, the European Logistics Support Office (ELSO) in Antwerp, Belgium, assists in the storage and transshipment of posts in Europe, Africa, and the Middle East. OPS oversees the forward-deployed supply system through the Expedited Logistics Program in collaboration with the Regional Procurement Support Office (RPSO). Annually, OPS handles a substantial workload, including 30,000 shipments, 26 million pounds of household effects in storage, 50,000 travel transactions through the American Express Travel Management Center, and 5,500 receipts with 4,000 lines of inventory in secure warehouses. They also manage the purchase and inventory of overseas motor vehicles, with 6,300 vehicles in overseas inventory.
2. Program Management and Policy (PMP):
   PMP focuses on developing and implementing logistics systems, policies, and management strategies. PMP is responsible for managing the diplomatic pouch and mail systems, facilitating the movement of 184,000 pouches and 8 million pounds of materials annually between Washington and posts overseas, with an average transit time of less than three days. PMP also provides domestic mail services for the department's Washington offices. They develop and maintain logistics policies and provide professional development and

training opportunities for Acquisition, Logistics, and Management (A/LM) staff and the worldwide logistics and General Services Officer (GSO) community. PMP offers operational support to over 1,100 purchase-card holders worldwide and manages the department's property management program, overseeing worldwide property management, training, and support for posts and domestic bureaus, as well as domestic excess property management. Additionally, PMP coordinates strategic planning and performance management for A/LM. These two sections work together to ensure the efficient management of logistics and supply chain operations within the Department of State, supporting its mission and employees around the world.

### *19.2.6 Defense Production Act*

The Defense Production Act (DPA) of 1950, as amended, is a significant piece of legislation in the United States that confers upon the President a broad set of authorities to influence domestic industry in the interest of national defense. During the COVID-19 pandemic, the DPA played a critical role in addressing shortages of essential medical supplies and equipment.

*Table 19.1* DPA titles and description

| *Title* | *Description* | *Use Cases* |
|---|---|---|
| **DPA Title I – Priorities and Allocations** | Authorizes the President to require acceptance and priority performance of contracts or orders and to allocate materials, services, and facilities to promote national defense or to maximize domestic energy supplies. | - Ensuring timely performance of military and space contracts. Supporting homeland security programs like counter-terrorism, emergency preparedness, critical infrastructure protection, and continuity of government. Limited use in homeland security to procure resources for emergency conditions, infrastructure protection, and counter-terrorism. |
| **DPA Title III – Expansion of Productive Capacity and Supply** | Provides financial measures, such as loans, loan guarantees, purchases, and purchase commitments to improve, expand, and maintain domestic production capabilities for national defense and homeland security procurement requirements. | - Increasing production capacity and reducing costs for new technologies needed for military and homeland security. Focuses on state-of-the-art technologies and involves cooperation between DOD and other agencies. |
| **DPA Title VII – General Provisions (Including Voluntary Agreements)** | Authorizes the President to develop voluntary agreements and plans of action for national defense. Provides relief from antitrust laws for participants in these agreements. | - Facilitating cooperation among business competitors to increase the supply of materials and services for military and homeland security. Enabling emergency preparedness, response, and recovery activities through industry cooperation. Oversight and reporting responsibilities such as CFIUS, DPAC, and annual reports on offsets. |

*Source*: Original creation.

*Notes*: The use of the DPA is overseen by the President and is delegated to various federal departments and agencies, including the Department of Defense, Department of Energy, Department of Homeland Security, etc. The act plays a crucial role in national security and emergency preparedness by ensuring the timely availability of necessary resources and capabilities.

### *19.2.7 Military Logistics and the U.S. Department of Defense*

Outside of the DOT, when one thinks about public logistics support at the federal level, one thinks of the DoD. The DoD plays a vital, complex, and comprehensive role in delivering federal-wide logistics support to the United States. From transportation to material production and delivery to acquisition, maintenance, and oversight, the DoD's responsibilities run the gamut.

#### *19.2.7.1 Military Logistics – History and Future Projections:*

Serrano et al. (2023) provide a detailed analysis of military logistics over time and its future projections. They show that the origins of military logistics, as outlined in the literature, are marked by three key aspects. First, the earliest documentation of military logistics thought dates back to the Ancient Egyptian Middle Empire, around 1991–1785 B.C. This period marks the initial framework for understanding military logistics. Second, the formal definitions of military logistics began to take shape in 1792, starting with the roles of the "Officier de Logis", an officer responsible for tasks such as lodging troops, directing columns, and placing them on the battlefield. This period marks the beginning of a structured approach to military logistics.[10]

Third, there is a significant relationship between military logistics and military revolutions, particularly evident in the 16th–17th centuries. This relationship shows that advancements in military logistics often coincided with significant changes in military strategy and technology. The evolution of military logistics is not just a chronological progression but also an expansion in its scope and complexity, reflecting changes in military needs and capabilities. Additionally, the study incorporates insights from prominent academics, contributing to a richer understanding of the evolution of military logistics thinking.

The future trajectory of military logistics is anticipated to be increasingly shaped by the integration of technology and focused logistics (FL) strategies. Military logistics is evolving into a science that not only plans and manages the supply process but also systematically executes it in a timely manner, using available technologies to dynamically support military operations and enhance the maneuverability of units. A key observation is that every military revolution has been accompanied by a corresponding revolution in military logistics, driven by technological advancements. This interdependence signifies that as technology progresses, military logistics must adapt to meet the changing needs of armed forces.

The concept of FL is emerging as a pivotal trend. FL is about providing the armed forces with the right personnel, equipment, and supplies at the right place and time across various military operations. This approach necessitates further exploration to understand its benefits, contribution to strengthening army capabilities, and relationship with technological advancements.

A significant challenge for future military logistics is to support new war strategies characterized by dynamic organization, changing needs, and diffuse force structures. This involves providing real-time support without disrupting ongoing operations, adopting concepts like just-in-time logistics, and leveraging networked command-and-control systems. Additionally, there's a need to develop smaller, more agile logistics platforms for global deployment and sustainment, addressing the demands of multi-domain battles and mosaic warfare.

Furthermore, the concept of contested logistics is being recognized by advanced military organizations. This approach focuses on ensuring agile and resilient logistics by integrating resilient logistics command and control, projection, and assured joint energy sustaining for distributed operations. Finally, the literature highlights the importance of distinguishing between business and military logistics, suggesting that the principles guiding military logistics are increasingly drawing from business logistics practices yet remain distinct due to the unique challenges and objectives of military operations.

#### *19.2.7.2 DLA and TRANSCOM*[1112]

1. DLA: DLA was officially established in 1961.
   DLA is a combat support agency (CSA) within the U.S. DoD. Its primary mission is to provide logistics, sustainment, and materiel support to the military services (Army, Navy, Air Force, Marine Corps), combatant commands, and other federal agencies. DLA is responsible for procuring and distributing a wide range of supplies, including food, fuel, medical supplies, spare parts, and more. It also manages storage and distribution networks to ensure timely and efficient support to the armed forces.
2. TRANSCOM: It was established in 1987.
   TRANSCOM is one of the 11 unified combatant commands of the U.S. DoD. Its primary mission is to provide strategic mobility and transportation support to the entire U.S. military. TRANSCOM coordinates the movement of troops, equipment, and supplies by air, sea, and land, ensuring the rapid deployment and sustainment of forces during military operations. It also manages aerial refueling and airlift capabilities and oversees the Military Sealift Command for sea transportation.

Both DLA and TRANSCOM play crucial roles in the logistics and operational readiness of the U.S. military, and their establishment dates reflect their importance in supporting the nation's defense and security efforts.

DLA and TRANSCOM provide a host of logistical support and services. It can be hard to discern their individual responsibilities at any given time. However, they do interoperate in the following fashion:

Logistics and supply chain coordination: DLA is responsible for managing the logistics and supply chain for the DoD. This includes procuring, storing, and distributing a wide range of supplies, including food, fuel, spare parts, and medical supplies. DLA maintains a vast inventory and distribution network. When military units require these supplies, DLA provides them. TRANSCOM plays a critical role in moving these supplies to where they are needed, whether it's within the United States or to overseas theaters of operation.

Strategic mobility and transportation: TRANSCOM's primary mission is to provide strategic mobility, which includes the rapid deployment and movement of troops and equipment. When DLA needs to transport large quantities of supplies or equipment to support military operations, TRANSCOM facilitates the transportation aspect. This involves coordinating the use of military aircraft, ships, and ground transportation to move supplies to the right location at the right time.

Aerial refueling and airlift: TRANSCOM's Air Mobility Command operates aircraft for airlift and aerial refueling. DLA relies on these capabilities when it needs to move supplies, including oversized or urgently needed cargo, to remote or critical locations. Airlift and aerial refueling extend the reach and capabilities of military logistics.

Joint planning and coordination: Both DLA and TRANSCOM work together in the joint planning and coordination of logistics for military operations. They collaborate to ensure that logistics support aligns with the overall military strategy and operational plans. This involves regular communication and cooperation to meet the needs of combatant commands and military units.

Contingency and crisis response: During contingency operations or crises, such as natural disasters or military conflicts, DLA and TRANSCOM collaborate closely to respond rapidly to emerging logistical requirements. DLA may need to expedite the delivery of critical supplies, and TRANSCOM ensures the transportation assets are available to meet those needs.

### *19.2.8 Joint Logistics*

Guidance on joint defense logistics is covered by the joint doctrine. Most notably, the military outlines its logistical doctrine in Joint Publication 4.0, *Joint Logistics*, as well as additional doctrine related to defense transportation, joint health services, bulk petroleum and water, contingency basing, joint mobilization planning, and operational contract support (OCS).[13] These are extensive documents. Some of the key takeaways include the following:

1. **Joint logistics**: Joint logistics refers to the globally integrated logistics operations conducted in a complicated, interconnected transregional environment involving various military forces, governmental organizations, NGOs, and multinational forces. It encompasses the coordination, synchronization, planning, execution, and assessment of logistics support to joint forces during all operation phases, with a focus on integrating capabilities with operations and maximizing effectiveness and responsiveness.
2. **Joint logistics environment**: The joint logistics environment is characterized by globalization, technology advancements, anti-access/area denial challenges, and flexible threats, creating a complex and ever-changing operational environment (OE). It requires supporting unified action by meeting increasingly demanding logistics requirements with constrained resources, particularly in potentially contested environments. This environment necessitates a capability to allocate and adjudicate joint logistics support on a global scale based on strategic priorities.
3. **Core logistics functions**: Core logistics functions provide a framework for integrated decision-making, effective synchronization, resource allocation, and optimization of joint logistics processes. These functions include deployment and distribution, supply, maintenance, logistics services, OCS, engineering, and joint health services. Deployment and distribution capability are vital for rapid deployment, execution, and sustainment of operations worldwide.
4. **OCS**: OCS involves the integration, coordination, and synchronization of service component and CSA logistics capabilities to support the joint force. It includes planning and executing requirements for joint reception, staging, onward movement, integration process, contingency base planning, and sustainment utilizing outsourced support. OCS ensures that logistics capabilities from various service agencies and providers are effectively utilized to support the changing needs of the joint force.
5. **Technology in joint logistics**: Technology plays a crucial role in joint logistics by enabling globally integrated logistics operations. It facilitates the allocation and adjudication of joint logistics support on a global scale, allowing for the reconciliation of competing demands for limited logistics resources. Technology is essential for planning, executing, synchronizing, assessing, and coordinating logistics operations, especially in a complex and rapidly changing OE.

### *19.2.9 Rapid International Logistical Capabilities*

The Army Logistics Civil Augmentation Program (LOGCAP) is a component of the civil augmentation programs (CAPs) utilized by the U.S. military services. Designed specifically for the U.S. Army, LOGCAP's objective is to extend the Army's logistical capabilities through contracted support. This program encompasses a variety of services that align with DoD policies. It also includes a workforce of U.S. citizens, third-country nationals (TCNs), and local national (LN) contractor employees. The services provided under LOGCAP are diverse, catering to different operational needs such as staff augmentation, catering, housing support, and collecting trash.[14]

LOGCAP has been deployed in various operational contexts, including in countries like Iraq. In these scenarios, LOGCAP has provided essential support services, which include but are not limited to food, laundry, and firefighting capabilities. This deployment was particularly notable during the shift from military operations to diplomatic missions in Iraq, reflecting the program's ability to adapt to different operational phases and requirements. The implementation process of LOGCAP in such environments involves significant planning and coordination, with procurement phases often spanning multiple months, to meet the specific needs of each mission context.

### 19.3 State Procurement and Logistics

During COVID-19, states were suddenly confronted with the need to manage an end-to-end supply chain! As COVID-19 cases surged, state-approved distributors experienced PPE shortages that were sudden in nature, and inventory stockpiles rapidly disappeared as they were overwhelmed with orders. Most states did not have warehouses or modern logistics capabilities to manage stockpiles, as many states have eliminated warehouse capacity over the years. Facing acute shortages, SPOs were compelled to initiate sourcing with brokers and overseas suppliers. Most of the state procurement agents we spoke with noted that they had never worked with suppliers outside of their state, let alone a supplier located across the globe in China.[15] Most procurement agents working at a state level had never worked with international bills of lading and had never established a warehouse and distribution capability to enable the storage and distribution of PPE across the state through third-party transportation providers. Overnight, many of these managers were suddenly faced with the need to develop new suppliers, coordinate international logistics shipments, deal with import tariffs, fees, and customs brokers, and sign warehouse leases to enable storage of inbound materials!

There was a single positive outcome that represents somewhat of a silver lining coming out of the pandemic: the **status** of state procurement was elevated, and state agencies recognized the critical role of logistics management in an emergency response. This recognition unfolded in two ways. First, PPE shortages and supply chain disruption shed light on the importance of SPOs and the value of relying on the expertise of procurement professionals in supplier vetting, contract negotiation, compliance management, and, more importantly, the ability to secure PPE using existing contracts and establishing new sources, and the transportation and distribution of these supplies. Second, the pandemic led to supply disruptions of other products that state procurement buys, such as IT hardware and new products and services, including such critical response services as nursing, temporary hospitals, homeless shelters, quarantining space for infected citizens, and unemployment services. During this time of crisis, procurement played a critical role in developing statements of work and service level agreements and negotiating prices and payment terms. In some cases, it was instrumental in influencing the type of PPE product used by healthcare providers. Purchasing became a hub of market intelligence on supply conditions and thus served as a key source of information for emergency management agencies during relief operations. Due to the heroic and reliable actions of state procurement personnel, stakeholders quickly learned to appreciate the expertise and value of their skill set in the agile response to the pandemic.

As SPOs became recognized as a resource that extends beyond simple contract and transaction managers, they emerged as a hub between emergency operation centers and the PPE brokers and suppliers. During COVID, procurement agencies demonstrated their capability as an enabler of **end-to-end supply chain coordination**. Due to its vantage point as the central hub bringing together supply market intelligence and demand management, we observed acquisition professionals in different states making integrated procurement decisions in logistics that optimized delivery lot size, exploited idled production capacity in the supply base, and acted to render agile decisions under extreme pressure to perform. State agencies acted quickly to adjust to rapid market capacity shifts and price fluctuations to ensure contract adjustments took place to get materials to healthcare workers, first responders, and patients in need.

### *19.3.1 Challenges and Solutions in Logistics at the State and Local Levels*

COVID certainly elevated state procurement to a position of increased recognition, but there are gaps that remain. According to a 2023 survey by the National Association of State Procurement Officers (NASPO), state purchasing managers identified ten priorities in the coming year – modernizing the procurement process, continuous process improvement, talent management and succession planning, customer service to agency stakeholders, eProcurement, establishing a central procurement office as a strategic leader, analytics for data-driven decision-making, effective contract administration, training and certification, and innovative solution-based solicitation methods.[16]

These priorities boil down to three aspects of interrelated challenges and opportunities: people, processes, and technology. First, the government needs to recruit and retain supply chain talents and elevate the procurement profession to a strategic position. Following the pandemic and supply chain disruptions, leaders in the government and the public have become more aware of the role of public procurement to ensure not only the basic functioning of government agencies but also the safety and security of citizens. Less competitive salaries and the retirement of the baby boomer generation can limit the pool of supply chain professionals in the public sector. Second, broad economic change and the need for data analytics, cyber and supply chain security, digitization, and supply chain transparency mandate the state and federal governments to implement technology and upskill supply chain management capabilities. Last, improve the efficiency of procurement processes and elevate public procurement to strategic supply management.

### *19.3.2 The Impact of COVID on Federal and State Logistics*

The COVID-19 pandemic brought disruption and new challenges to all sectors, from public services to manufacturing. Organizations were forced to reimagine how they do business – state and federal governments were no exception. During the onset of the COVID-19 pandemic, public procurement offices grappled with how to secure adequate supplies of PPE for public employees and their constituents. The outbreak reportedly first occurred in the Wuhan region of China, which further exacerbated the shortage of critical PPE supplies due to China's role as a major global producer. The race to secure PPE was on, and this started a bidding war between nation-states, the federal government, and state governments.

Many U.S. states' public procurement officers played an increasingly critical role in each region's successful emergency response. In a report released by NASPO,[17] increased centralized governance of state procurement led to a more effective response in tackling large-scale supply chain disruptions. Centralized procurement enabled increased coordination, improved leveraging of the volume of the state's purchasing power, and provided for a more efficient application of contracting expertise in a difficult market situation. A centralized approach also led to better coordination among disaster relief entities, PPE suppliers, hospitals, counties, and agencies requiring PPE to operate.

## 19.4 Strategic Stockpiles

Strategic stockpiles are used throughout the world. The most notable, after the COVID-19 pandemic, is the U.S. SNS, which received a lot of criticism for its state of readiness during the early days of the pandemic. There are, however, a host of international stockpiles and additional U.S. stockpiles that are not normally discussed in the media.

The more common international stockpiles are shown in Table 19.2.

The U.S. federal government has multiple strategic stockpiles (Table 19.3).

The SNS began as the National Pharmaceutical Stockpile in 1999 and was renamed the SNS in 2001 following the September 11th attacks on the United States.

The SNS has had challenges over its history, none more glaring than responding to the unprecedented demand and uncertainty of the COVID-19 crisis.[18][19] We can analyze these challenges through the lens of supply chain immunity principles. These principles include traceability, persistent response, global independence, equity, and flexibility. Here's how these issues align with these principles:

*Table 19.2* Types of stockpiles at the international level

| *Stockpile Name* | *Organization* | *Purpose* |
|---|---|---|
| IEA Emergency Oil Stockpiles | International Energy Agency | Emergency oil stocks for global supply disruptions. |
| WFP Emergency Food Stockpiles | World Food Programme | Rapid response to global food crises. |
| Global Seed Vault | Various International Contributors | Preserving agricultural diversity. |
| Nuclear Fuel Banks | International Atomic Energy Agency | Guaranteed nuclear fuel supply, minimizing proliferation risks. |
| Pandemic Influenza Preparedness (PIP) Framework Stockpile | World Health Organization | Resources for pandemic influenza outbreaks. |
| European Medical Corps and Stockpiles | European Union | Medical assistance for emergencies within and outside the EU. |

*Table 19.3* Types of stockpiles held by the U.S. federal government

| *Stockpile Name/Types* | *Purpose* |
|---|---|
| Strategic Petroleum Reserve (SPR) | Emergency crude oil supply to mitigate supply disruptions. |
| National Defense Stockpile (NDS) | Critical materials for national defense. |
| Strategic National Stockpile (SNS) within HHS/ASPR | Medical supplies for public health emergencies. |
| Food Stockpiles | Food assistance during disasters or emergencies. |
| Rare Earth Elements Stockpile | Securing rare earth elements for technology and defense. |
| Strategic Uranium Reserve | Domestic uranium supply for energy security and defense. |

Insufficient stockpiles (flexibility and persistent response): The lack of sufficient medical supplies in the SNS, such as PPE and ventilators, is a clear indicator of a lack of flexibility and persistent response in the supply chain. Flexibility in this context would mean the ability of the supply chain to adapt quickly to unexpected demands and requirements, such as those posed by a pandemic. Persistent response would refer to the supply chain's preparedness and ongoing capacity to address long-term crises.

Distribution challenges (traceability and equity): The difficulties in efficiently distributing supplies from the SNS highlight issues with traceability and equity. Effective traceability systems would allow for clear tracking of supplies from the SNS to end-users, ensuring timely and accurate delivery. Equity is crucial in ensuring that all regions, particularly those most in need, have fair access to the supplies.

Demand exceeding supply (persistent response and flexibility): The overwhelming demand exceeding the SNS's supply reflects a lack of persistent response and flexibility. This speaks to the need for a more robust, responsive, and adaptable supply chain that can scale up rapidly in response to surging demands.

Lack of preparedness (persistent response): The unpreparedness for a pandemic of COVID-19's magnitude points to a shortfall in persistent response. There was a clear need for better planning and readiness for such large-scale health emergencies.

Coordination and communication issues (traceability): The coordination and communication breakdowns between federal, state, and local entities indicate a lack of effective traceability mechanisms, which are crucial for clear and efficient communication channels in the supply chain.

Dependency on overseas manufacturing (global independence): The pandemic exposed the SNS's reliance on international supply chains, which is contrary to the principle of global independence. This principle emphasizes the importance of reducing dependency on external sources, especially in critical sectors like healthcare.

Equity in distribution (equity): The disparities in the distribution of supplies from the SNS highlight issues with equity. Ensuring equitable access to essential medical supplies is fundamental to an effective and ethical supply chain response in a crisis.

## 19.5 Sustainable Practice in Logistics Management

Integration of sustainability with government and agency strategies is a dynamic, two-way process that relies on several information sources, including government objectives, agency and functional capabilities, market conditions, competitive pressures, and customer requirements. Linking sustainability to each government objective has the added advantage of linking all the functional strategies to one another, which helps to remove many of the barriers to environmental integration.

### *19.5.1 Social Responsibility*

Another way of thinking about sustainable procurement in logistics is the idea of social responsibility. **Social responsibility** is the idea that organizations and institutions have an obligation to society that extends beyond compliance with regulations in considering the broader effects of their actions. Social responsibility is becoming more accepted in 21st-century corporations. The Institute of Supply Management (ISM) has developed a guide to assist supply managers in developing their socially responsible practices. The areas covered in the policy are (1) community, (2) diversity, (3) environment, (4) ethics, (5) financial responsibility, (6) human rights, and (7) safety. These elements are essential in sourcing logistics.

### 19.5.2 ISM Principles of Sustainability and Social Responsibility

*Sustainability* is the ability to meet current needs without hindering the ability to meet the needs of future generations in terms of economic, environmental, and social challenges. *Social responsibility* is defined as a framework of measurable corporate policies and procedures and resulting behavior designed to benefit the workplace and, by extension, the individual, the organization, and the community. Listed below are the 11 ISM principles of sustainability and social responsibility (in alphabetical order)[20]:

1. Anti-corruption. Do not tolerate corruption in any form.
2. Diversity and inclusion. Promote diversity and inclusion throughout the organization and the supply chain.
3. The environment supports environmental precaution, promotes environmental responsibility, and encourages environmentally friendly technologies and processes.
4. Ethics and business conduct. Behave ethically always and demand ethical conduct within the organization and throughout the supply chain.
5. Financial integrity. Conduct all financial business dealings and decision-making with integrity.
6. Global citizenship. Act (in person and virtually) for the benefit of all global citizens, locally and elsewhere, fulfilling ethical and moral obligations.
7. Health and safety. Protect persons in the supply chain from the risk of injury, danger, failure, error, harm, and/or loss of life.
8. Human rights. Recognize and acknowledge that human beings have universal and natural rights and status regardless of legal jurisdiction and local factors.
9. Labor rights. Respect, promote, and protect an individual's labor rights as defined by applicable international conventions.
10. Supply chain sustainability. Support supplier development of more sustainable business practices, products, and services and the embedding of sustainability throughout supply chains.
11. Transparency. Make available full and complete information necessary for collaboration, cooperation, and collective decision-making. Require a corresponding level of transparency from suppliers and throughout the supply chain.

Sustainable logistics, also known as green logistics, is defined as "supply chain management practices and strategies that reduce the ecological and energy footprints of the distribution of goods which focuses on material handling, waste management, packaging and. transport" (Seroka-Stolka & Ociepa-Kubicka, 2019, p. 472). Logistics sector companies are initiating sustainable practices as they cause environmental pollution, such as carbon emission, noise pollution, and resource depletion.

Logistics plays an important role in the whole supply chain, and it contributes to air pollution: transportation, one of the key operations in logistics, accounts for 24% of the world's $CO_2$ emissions (Ritchie, 2020), so green logistics may focus on reducing emissions and conserving resources. However, there are many different examples of ways that logistics can have sustainable impacts (for example, see Table 1 in the article from Jayarathna et al., 2023 [21]).

### 19.5.3 Types of Unethical Purchasing Behavior in Public Acquisition

Ethics have their basis in the field of philosophy and identify common principles associated with appropriate versus inappropriate actions, moral duty, and obligation. Ethics are the set of moral principles or values guiding our behavior. In a business setting, ethical behavior is the use of recognized social principles involving justice and fairness throughout a business relationship. When interacting with suppliers, an ethical buyer treats them in a just, decent, fair, honest, and fitting manner. Being ethical means following a code viewed as fair by those within the profession as well as the community.[22]

Suppose a buyer at a state or federal agency has the highest moral and ethical values – the buyer has strong beliefs about what is proper behavior within the purchasing profession. Conflict can occur if a supervisor asks the buyer to do something the buyer feels is unethical. For example, a supervisor may ask a buyer to award a contract because of a personal friendship with a supplier. The buyer may feel this is unethical.

Does the buyer simply award the contract in compliance with the manager's instruction and ignore his or her own personal and moral values? Or does the buyer refuse to award the contract, thereby challenging the authority of a manager and jeopardizing his or her career? While a professional buyer should know the difference between right and wrong, organizational pressures can force a buyer to behave in ways that conflict with personal values, which creates a difficult situation for the individual. How should a person respond in this situation?

The definition of ethical behavior can differ from buyer to buyer or from firm to firm. Despite these possible differences, most professionals recognize certain behaviors or actions as unethical. Most companies have established guidelines that reinforce that these behaviors are unethical and, therefore, unacceptable. Some of these behaviors are listed below.

*Reciprocity*. This action involves giving preferential treatment to suppliers who are also customers of the buying organization. In simple terms, it refers to a purchasing arrangement that dictates, "*I'll buy from you if you buy from me*". The Federal Trade Commission (FTC) has taken an aggressive stance against reciprocal buying arrangements, ruling that it is illegal "to abusively use large buying power to restrict competitive market opportunities". In the early 1970s, many larger firms entered into agreements with the FTC forbidding reciprocal purchasing. These firms also eliminated their internal trade departments established to coordinate these arrangements.[23]

FTC rulings have convinced most firms to prohibit reciprocal purchasing. Most firms do recognize a customer's right for consideration as a potential supplier. A buyer, however, must rely only on legitimate performance criteria to evaluate supplier capability.

*Personal buying*. This occurs when a purchasing department purchases material for the personal needs of its employees. Some states have outlawed such practices with statutes called trade diversion laws. These laws prohibit purchasing from engaging in personal buying for items not required during the normal course of business.

Some exceptions to these laws do exist. For example, an agency can purchase safety shoes, hats, gloves, or even special tools required by the employee. A purchasing department can use its knowledge to purchase products conforming to specific quality standards. Personal buying is a gray area for some purchasing departments. Some firms view personal buying as a fringe benefit and service to the employee. Other firms flatly prohibit the practice. A buyer confronted with a request for personal buying should determine the legal status of the practice and then discuss the subject with management.

*Accepting supplier favors*. Accepting gifts and favors from a supplier is the most common ethical infraction involving buyers. These gifts and favors can affect a buyer's judgment in evaluating and selecting the most capable suppliers. The policy on supplier offerings is often a confusing issue. At what point does a supplier's gift or favor depart from a friendly showing of appreciation for a firm's business to an attempt to influence a buyer's purchase decisions? Accepting free items from potential suppliers is especially questionable. Here, a supplier does not even have a purchase contract. Firms can address this issue in their ethics policy by specifying exactly what a buyer may accept from a supplier.

*Sharp practices.* A sharp practice is any misrepresentation by a buyer that falls just short of actual fraud. Sharp practice occurs whenever a buyer "plays games" with a supplier and operates in an underhanded manner. The practice includes many different behaviors:

- Willful use of misinformation is when a buyer knowingly deceives a supplier to realize some advantage. For example, requesting quotes on inflated volumes and then placing smaller orders at the reduced price is a willful use of misinformation.
- Exaggerating problems. A buyer who exaggerates the size of a supplier-caused problem to extract a larger penalty or concession from a supplier is using a sharp practice.
- Requesting bids from unqualified suppliers for the sole purpose of driving a qualified supplier's price lower. A buyer should request bids from qualified suppliers only.
- Gaining information unfairly through deception.
- Sharing information on competitive quotations. The integrity of the competitive bid process requires confidentiality. Buyers who share supplier-quoted information violate the ethics of the bid process.
- Not compensating a supplier for design or other work. Buyers often request design and cost-saving assistance from suppliers. A supplier who helps a buyer should receive fair compensation for their efforts.
- Taking unfair advantage of a supplier's financial situation. A buyer who knowingly pressures a financially troubled supplier into providing a lower-than-normal price places the supplier in further financial jeopardy. Taking advantage of a financially susceptible supplier is an unethical business practice.
- Lying or misleading. Any instance of lying to or misleading a seller is a sharp practice.

*Financial conflicts of interest.* When a buyer awards business to a supplier because the buyer, the buyer's family, or relatives of the buyer have a direct financial interest in a supplier, this is considered a major unethical practice. This behavior is one reason many companies require employees to detail any investments in outside companies.

Awarding a purchase contract to a company in which a buyer has a significant personal financial interest (versus owning a mutual fund that owns a small amount of stock in the company) is a serious breach of ethics. This action is similar to an executive buying or selling stock because of inside knowledge, which is an illegal act.

## 19.6 Best Practices in Procurement Logistics

In most cases, logistics acquisition by government agencies involves forming contracts with third-party logistics providers, known as "3PLs". Most government agencies do not "operate" a logistics network but utilize 3PLs. A third-party company is responsible for managing all inbound and outbound transportation, as well as distribution and warehousing in many cases. Companies that fall into this category include DHL, XPO, FedEx, UPS, and others. The use of these types of third parties is increasingly becoming an option for smaller shippers and shipments. They are convenient, relatively inexpensive, and extremely reliable. They also offer linked information systems that provide a substantial advantage over their competitors. For this reason, many distributors and mail-order companies use FedEx and UPS as their primary providers of transportation services.

### *19.6.1 Selection of Providers*

Purchasing managers should be very careful in selecting 3PLs providers, who often bill themselves as "Integrated Global Logistics Service Providers" and offer their services as providing complete end-to-end supply chain services. Especially in a global environment, there are many different elements of transportation and logistics that have to be managed, including:

- Customs brokers;
- Freight (Air and surface);
- Warehousing operations;
- Packaging/Export Doc's;
- Delivery services;
- Local sourcing/purchasing;
- International trade management;
- Global transportation optimization;
- Supply chain planning.

It is very rare to be able to find a 3PLs provider who is capable of providing world-class services in all of these areas simultaneously. In particular, purchasing should be leery of companies who claim that they are world-class providers in all of these areas. To avoid selecting a 3PLs provider that cannot meet the requirements, purchasers should adopt the following approach:

1. PLAN
    - Define logistics service requirements and confirm the selection process.
    - Involve key players to ensure buy-in and remove barriers to success.
2. SELECT
    - Target best in class logistics service providers (3PLs/contractors).
    - Select 3PL/contractor and establish a Win/Win agreement.
3. IMPLEMENT
    - Share supply chain management information to deliver superior value.
    - Build relationships and work jointly to resolve start-up issues.
4. IMPROVE
    - Exchange performance measures to identify improvement opportunities.
    - Encourage cross-organization training and project activities.
5. PARTNER
    - Develop supply chain alliances to agree on trade-offs and share risks.
    - Involve partners in strategic planning and decision-making (win/win).

When selecting 3PLs providers, purchasers should consider the following elements of performance and whether the provider can execute in each of these areas.

### 19.6.2 Gain Access to Critical and Timely Data

Accurate and timely information is the power of a decision-maker. It is difficult to manage material shipments without the ability to collect and analyze critical transportation data. Ideally, the following transportation-related information should be available and can be reported by the third-party provider to the buying company. An inability to provide this information may mean that the 3PL is not effectively managing the supply network.

- Number of carriers providing inbound, intraorganizational, and outbound transportation services;
- Total transportation expenditures by specific carrier and form of transportation;
- Number of suppliers shipping material (the number of shipping points) to a purchaser;
- Volume and transportation costs associated with shipments from each supplier;
- Breakdown of volumes by commodity type (type of purchased material);
- Performance ratings of individual carriers;
- Percentage of shipments arranged by suppliers versus buyers.

### 19.6.3 Develop System Visibility to Material Shipments

Up-to-the-minute data about the location of shipments can provide, at least partially, the visibility required for total material control. The need to achieve this control supports the development of electronic data systems between carrier and buyer. 3PLs companies should be able to provide access to information on the status of shipments, whether it is on a motor carrier linked electronically with transportation buyers through global positioning systems or the location on a ship, plane, or customs location. Many 3PLs offer detailed tracking systems to provide current updates on shipment locations. Several levels of complexity exist in these systems. One-way information systems allow a buyer to gain information about the location of a shipment on a real-time basis. A buyer simply requests data directly from a carrier's information system. However, many 3PLs are moving toward the use of "event-based" systems – which provide alerts via email, fax, pager, etc., to a buyer or salesperson that a shipment has been delayed and that this may affect other participants in the supply chain (manufacturing locations, customers, etc.). Even though these types of problematic events cannot always be prevented, early warning signals via event-management systems can help purchasing companies deal with the problem more effectively.

### 19.6.4 Develop Closer Relationships with Fewer Providers

A common theme throughout this chapter is that buyers and sellers can often benefit from closer relationships. This logic also applies to 3PLs. Transportation buyers are increasingly reducing the number of 3PLs they do business with on a company-wide basis with the intention of working closer with the remaining ones in a collaborative manner. This allows a buyer to realize additional services and benefits that otherwise might not be available through a traditional business relationship. For example, a transportation buyer may receive a guarantee that equipment will always be available to service the buyer's needs. Controlling and managing the movement of goods is easier and more efficient when a buyer selects only the best 3PLs available and then develops a closer working relationship with them.

### *19.6.5 Establish Company-Wide Contracts*

The real cost and service benefits are possible when transportation volumes between locations, divisions, or business units are combined for increased purchasing leverage and put under the jurisdiction of a limited number of 3PLs. An example of such a relationship is discussed in the sourcing snapshot on General Motors.

One clear trend is that many carriers will no longer market themselves simply as providers of physical transportation. For complex movements of freight (movements requiring multiple parties or multiple handling), many carriers will perform duties previously requiring the use of in-house personnel or third parties. Full-service providers, in addition to picking up and delivering goods, may consolidate shipments, provide simplified billing, ship just-in-time from local storage points, handle complex overseas shipments, coordinate shipments with other carriers or transportation modes, or configure final products for shipment directly to end customers. This allows a transportation buyer to focus on strategy development, while the full-service carrier manages the routine and clerical details of the transportation network.

There are many examples of using transportation suppliers for more than just transportation. UPS handles all the worldwide after-market spare part business for Allison Engine. Burlington Air Express has reduced a computer company's order-cycle time by warehousing inventory, configuring PCs with correct software, and delivering directly to customers. Internet services provided by carriers are expanding as well. UPS and FedEx provide full tracking of packages via the Internet, and FedEx has created software that allows users to complete entire shipping transactions via the Internet.

## 19.7 Technological Innovations in Procurement Logistics

One critical mission in recent years in state procurement is the adoption of Enterprise Resource Planning (ERP) Systems and eProcurement. The procurement officer is expected to take charge of streamlining the procurement process and eliminate inefficiencies associated with duplication, review, and approvals. This requires information integrity and integration.

States that have adopted eProcurement systems have made a quick transition to remote work during the pandemic. Prospective vendors and state purchasing managers are able to interact using eProcurement systems without physical interactions and, consequently, minimal disruption of contract creation and fulfillment.

ERP adoption of eProcurement is part of a broad initiative to digitize government services (eGovernment). Like it is in private sectors, digital transformation brings different types of procurement and capabilities to state agencies. This also leads to more service-oriented government procurement, including cloud-based computing, cyber-security services, and exploration of new capabilities in areas of more blockchain and artificial intelligence (AI).

Digital transformation brings different types of procurement and capabilities to state agencies. This also leads to more service-oriented government procurement, including cloud-based computing, cyber-security services, and exploration of new capabilities in areas of more blockchain and AI.

Like it has been in the private sector over the past three decades, the state government overtime outsourced a significant part of transportation and logistics services to third-party private logistics providers. With the just-in-time model, the suppliers hold and manage inventory. As a result, state governments also reduced warehouse ownership. COVID-19 taught the state an important lesson – state governments not only need to hold inventory of emergency goods (e.g., respirators, PPE) and medicals but also maintain warehouse and transportation capacity at times of a pandemic or other natural disasters. We see more states taking ownership of warehouses or at least establishing long-term leasing contracts and working closely with logistics providers. States are re-building the logistics muscle, so to speak, as a stranger to mitigate supply chain risks.

More specifically, AI applications are being developed to provide decision support in order management, forecasting and predictive analysis, and negotiation. Over time, AI tools developed by companies such as Microsoft, Amazon, and Oracle will be seamlessly incorporated into their enterprise's IT service offerings. Similarly, blockchain providers promise to offer chain of custody certifications to ensure product traceability and transparency.

State procurement typically is not involved in the procurement of highway construction projects. Such procurement is handled by a state's DOT. DOT has a lot of autonomy, and a significant part of its financial resources comes from the federal government. In recent years, state procurement has been getting more involved in transportation and logistics procurement. There are several reasons. First, smart transportation systems and vehicles require new technology (e.g., Internet of Things, IoT) and hardware, and the state DOT seeks expertise from the state (central) procurement office concerning supplier development and compliance. One such successful collaboration was between Minnesota DOT (MDOT) and the SPO. MDOT is tasked with purchasing automatic shuttle vehicles used by hospitals to transfer patients within large hospital compounds. This is a challenging project because it is a new product. The specifications and requirements need to be defined. Getting procurement involved early in the process, open communication, and clear articulation of rules in contracting turned out to be the crucial factors of the eventual success of the partnership.

### *19.7.1 Examples of Technology Implementation at Different Levels of Public Procurement*

#### *19.7.1.1 A Public Procurement Debacle – Cover Oregon*

One of the instances of large-scale government procurement programs ending in spectacular failures is the Cover Oregon project, which aimed to build a health insurance marketplace for the state of Oregon in the United States. It ended up in a "racketeering" lawsuit filed by the state against the IT contractor Oracle and a countersuit by Oracle against the state for breach of contract. This ultimately cost the state (and federal government) more than $200 million before the state dissolved Cover Oregon, including litigation fees. Third-party investigations suggested that Oracle took advantage of the state's ignorance of project management and administrative hubris.[24]

#### *19.7.1.2 The Commonwealth of Virginia Leads the Way in eProcurement*

Before the state of Virginia implemented eProcurement, it had a decentralized procurement model like it is in many other states. The buyers do not have accurate information about the suppliers and prices. There are many errors in paper-based contracts and catalogs. Suppliers experienced similar inefficiency – they did not have real-time information on business opportunities and had to travel to the purchasing office to conduct business.

The state is the early adopter of eProcurement systems. Its eVA system has over 26,000 government users and in excess of 800 state and local government agencies and institutions of higher education (eva.virginia.gov). It has achieved savings and cost avoidance from administrative efficiency and a high level of transparency and data integrity.

## 19.8 Conclusion: Future Trends in Public Procurement and Logistics

Unlike procurement in the private sector, in state and public procurement, the CPO and buyers purchase sourcing on behalf of state agencies. Their mission-critical task is contract management. We often think the products and services of state procurement are readily available commodities. The suppliers handle supply chain risks. However, recent supply disruptions due to the pandemic and trade war and ongoing uncertainties associated with supply chain de-risking expose state governments to supply shortages that affect every citizen. Now, state CPOs are embracing supply chain management like private firms. Supply risk assessment and deeper engagement with upstream supply chains.

The importance of public procurement is also gaining awareness among supply chain professionals and policymakers. While state procurement does deal with seemingly easy-to-source off-the-shelf "commodities" instead of cutting-edge high-tech or complex products, procurement policy on such commodities can be used by policymakers to influence meaningful changes in those sectors. For example, mandates for miles-per-gallon, green electronics, products free from slave labor, and conflict minerals are shaping operations changes and innovation across supply chains. Because of the impact of COVID and the subsequent reliance on federal and state procurement, we are likely to continue to witness the evolution and improvement of this function.

## Notes

1 Farewell address by President Dwight D. Eisenhower, January 17, 1961; available at www.archives.gov/milestone-documents/president-dwight-d-eisenhowers-farewell-address
2 December 4, 2014 Memo: "Transforming the Marketplace: Simplifying Federal Procurement to Improve Performance, Drive Innovation, and Increase Savings" by Anne Rung.
3 December 4, 2014 Memo: "Transforming the Marketplace: Simplifying Federal Procurement to Improve Performance, Drive Innovation, and Increase Savings" by Anne Rung.
4 "Critical Issues for Intelligence Acquisition Reform", Industry's Assessment of the Intelligence Community Acquisition Process, October 2008, *Intelligence and National Security Alliance Acquisition Reform Task Force.*
5 Defense Technical Information Center. Section 809 Panel. https://discover.dtic.mil/section-809-panel/
6 Handfield, R., and Finkenstadt, D. (2023) *Supply Chain Immunity: Overcoming our Nation's Sourcing Sickness in a Post-COVID World.* New York: Springer.
7 Examples of management textbooks documenting these approaches include Chick, G., and Handfield, R. (2014). *Procurement's Value Proposition.* London: Kogan-Page; Monczka, R., Handfield, R., Giunipero, L., and Patterson, J. (2014). *Purchasing and Supply Chain Management.* Cincinnati, OH: Southwestern Publishing, College Division, 6th edition. Handfield, R. (2010, July). *Planning for the Inevitable: The Role of the Federal Supply Chain in Preparing for National Emergencies*, IBM Center for Government, Published Report. Examples of professional organizations include the Institute for Supply Management (www.instituteforsupplymanagement.org/) and the International Association for Commecial and Contract Management (http://iaccm.com).
8 General Services Administration. Our Mission's Evolution. www.gsa.gov/about-us/mission-and-background/our-missions-evolution
9 U.S. Department of Transportation. Home Page. www.transportation.gov/about
10 Serrano, A., Kalenatic, D., López, C., and Montoya-Torres, J. R. (2023). "Evolution of Military Logistics," *Logistics*, 7: 22. https:// doi.org/10.3390/logistics7020022
11 U.S. Transportation Command (USTRANSCOM). Doing Business With USTRANSCOM — Home. www.ustranscom.mil/dbw/index.cfm
12 Defense Logistics Agency. About DLA. www.dla.mil/About-DLA/

13 Joint Chiefs of Staff. Joint Publications — 4-0 Logistics Series. www.jcs.mil/Doctrine/Joint-Doctrine-Pubs/4-0-Logistics-Series/
14 Congressional Research Service. Defense Logistical Support Contracts in Iraq and Afghanistan. https://sgp.fas.org/crs/natsec/RL33834.pdf
15 Patrucco, A., Wu, Z., Handfield, R., Yukins, C., and Slaughter, T. (2023, May 9). "A New Acquisition Model for the Next Disaster: Overcoming Disaster Federalism Issues with a Strategic Application of the National Stockpile," *Public Administration Review*, https://doi.org/10.1111/puar.13656
16 National Association of State Procurement Officials (NASPO). Modernization tops state procurement priorities for 2024. www.naspo.org/news/modernization-tops-state-procurement-priorities-for-2024/
17 Handfield, R., Wu, Z., Patrucco, A., Yukins, C., and Kull, T. (2021). *Assessing State PPE Procurement during COVID-19: A Research Report*. National Association of State Procurement Officers.
18 Handfield, R., Finkenstadt. D. J., Schneller, E. S., Godfrey, A. B., and Guinto, P. (2020). "A Commons for a Supply Chain in the Post-COVID-19 Era: The Case for a Reformed Strategic National Stockpile," *Milbank Quarterly*, 98(4): 1058–1090. https://doi.org/10.1111/1468-0009.12485
19 Finkenstadt, D. J., Handfield, R., and Guinto, P. (2020). "Why the U.S. Still Has a Severe Shortage of Medical Supplies," *Harvard Business Review*. https://hbr.org/2020/09/why-the-u-s-still-has-a-severe-shortage-of-medical-supplies
20 Institute for Supply Management (ISM). ISM Principles of Sustainability and Social Responsibility with a Guide to Adoption and Implementation. www.ismworld.org/globalassets/pub/docs/526-prinsussocres_5_20.pdf
21 Jayarathna, C. P., Agdas, D., and Dawes, L. (2023). "Exploring Sustainable Logistics Practices toward a Circular Economy: A Value Creation Perspective," *Business Strategy and the Environment*, 32(1): 704–720.
22 Haynes, P. J., and Helms, M. M. (1991). "An Ethical Framework for Purchasing Decisions," *Management Decision (UK)*, 29(1): 35; Page, H. (1986, December). "More on Ethics—Helping Your Buyers," *Purchasing World*, 30(12): 60.
23 Parker, R. C., Fordyce, G. C., and Graham, K. P. (1982). "Ethics in Purchasing," in *Purchasing Handbook*, L. G. Farrell and L. A. Alijian, ed. New York: McGraw-Hill, 7–16.
24 Wikipedia. Cover Oregon. https://en.wikipedia.org/wiki/Cover_Oregon

## References

Ciscel, D. H., & Smith, B. E. (2005). The Impact of Supply Chain Management on Labor Standards: The Transition to Incessant Work. *Journal of Economic Issues*, *39*(2), 429–437. https://doi.org/10.1080/00213624.2005.11506820

Mohun, B. (1913). The Effect of the Uniform Warehouse Receipts Act. *Columbia Law Review*, *13*(3), 202–212. https://doi.org/10.2307/1110356

NIGP. (2024). *Dictionary of procurement terms*. www.nigp.org/dictionary-of-terms

Rider, G. W. (1970). Evolution of the Concept of Logistics. *Naval War College Review*, *23*(4), 24–33. www.jstor.org/stable/44641172

Ritchie, H. (2020). Where do greenhouse gases come from? Available at https://ourworldindata.org/ghg-emissions-by-sector/

Scmedu. (2022, April 21). *What is a public warehouse receipt in Logistics? – SCM edu*. SCM EDU – Supply Chain Management Education. https://scmedu.org/publicwarehousereceipt/

Seroka-Stolka, O. & Ociepa-Kubicka, A. (2019). Green logistics and circular economy. *Transportation Research Procedia*, *39*(2019), 471–479.

Warehousemen. Warehouse Receipts. Liability for Fraudulent Issuance by Agent: Effect of Uniform Warehouse Receipts Act. (1915). *Harvard Law Review*, *28*(3), 336–336. https://doi.org/10.2307/1325725

### *Case Study: A Case Study on Operational Challenges in the Central Warehouse (Developed by Tamara Harden, Department of Defense(War), Department of the Navy at Naval Air Station Pensacola)*

#### Introduction

Managing the logistics cycle involves much more than inventory management and organizing shelves. It requires a comprehensive, 360-degree approach to operations, encompassing the stages of planning, sourcing, transportation, warehousing, and distribution on every small to globalized operation. Logistics, a term historically rooted in Latin, Greek, and French, has evolved since the 1500s to refer to lodging, mathematical reasoning, and the commonly known supply chain's definition as the supplying and transporting of goods (Rider, 1970).

The infrastructure of labor operating within the logistical cycles is vast between production workers, storekeepers (warehousemen), financial administrators, transportation workers, procurement professionals, plant, logistic, and warehouse managers (Ciscel & Smith, 2005). Managerial personnel do carry the burden of overseeing the varying operations in the logistics cycle. However, logistical operations are often supported by labor workers in each stage.

In the 1900s, the classification of a warehousemen title and position is one who conducts the business of renting spaces and storing items (Mohun, 1913). The legislative policies that were active in multiple states under the Uniform Warehouse Receipts Act (UWRA) were designed to provide simple protections for warehousemen-governing them liable for the receipts written and protect warehouse depositors from fraudulent or erroneous transactions. The UWRA was also designed to govern regulations concerning public warehousing operations (Scmedu, 2022).

The Uniform Commercial Code (UCC) was introduced in 1892 and would later expand to include necessary articles to govern various commercial laws, including Article 7, Documents of Title, which covers warehouse receipts, bills of lading, and other commercial complexities enacted by the Uniform Law Commission (ULC).

#### Executive Summary

Effective management of the logistics cycle requires not only operational oversight but also a collaborative effort among all contributors to ensure efficiency and accuracy.

This case study examines a real-world scenario within the Central Warehouse of a Florida School District, highlighting the complexities and challenges of managing a logistics operation serving over 38,000 students across 50 locations. A discrepancy in detergent shipments revealed failures in inventory management, supplier communication, and operational processes, ultimately resulting in financial and procedural consequences.

Through detailed analysis, this case study explores how these challenges were addressed, focusing on corrective actions and the critical role of regulatory frameworks like the UCC in governing logistics operations. The findings emphasize the importance of proactive management and the integration of modern inventory practices to prevent and mitigate logistical disruptions.

#### Keywords/Terms

- **Caveat emptor** | Latin meaning for "Let the buyer beware".

- **Caveat venditor** | Latin meaning for "Let the Seller beware".
- **Disbursement** | The process is distributing goods or tender based on an order or requisition.
- **ERP | inventory management system** | Business software designed to manage multiple financial operations that strategically work together relating to accounting, human resources, inventory management, purchasing, and other financial disciplines.
- **Logistics cycle** | The sequence of processes involved in the movement and storage of goods from point of origin to point of consumption.
- **Procurement** | The functionality of acquiring goods and services for various commodities from the solicitation process through disposal operations, including contract management, inventory control, purchasing, logistics, warehousing, and transportation.
- **Receiving** | The process of accepting goods for processing or storing.
- **3PLs** | A 3PLs company is contracted to provide inventory management, transportation, processing, warehousing, and other supply chain-related activities on behalf of another company.

### Problem Statement

The Central Warehouse oversees the operation of multiple divisions within a Florida school district. The warehouse boasts over 120,000 square feet of storage and operation space. The main commodity holder of the Central Warehouse is the Food Service Department. The warehouse is responsible for receiving, storing, managing, and disbursing the main food and cafeteria assets that are required to feed over 38,000 students throughout each school year. On a scheduled receiving day, the Central Warehouse received a shipment of soap powder detergent. The Lead Receiving Warehouse Technician noticed that something was unusual regarding the shipment as he began to verify the quantity offloaded from the tractor trailer. According to the purchase order, 780 total cases were ordered. The warehouse receiver shows that 320 cases were expected to be delivered, with 383 cases still showing as outstanding from the supplier.

However, the supplier's packing slip and bill of lading showed that the order is now complete with zero remaining quantities to fill for the detergent. It is customary for the technicians to investigate discrepancies before the courier or 3PLs driver leaves the premises. This is standard practice in the receiving process should products need to be returned to the supplier due to damage or extra quantities refused at the time of delivery. The technician signed the bill of lading in acceptance of the delivery, and the driver left. After speaking with the supplier's agent, the technician realized multiple receiving failures had occurred posing as *caveat emptor* (NIGP, 2024).

The first failure was that the previous shipment was received incorrectly. The first shipment included 462 cases, but according to the inventory management system, only 67 cases were on hand due to disbursements since the last shipment. The supplier changed the pack size and how the product was shipped, which concealed the contents on each pallet. Due to the pack size change, the shipment was also increased by six cases. The supplier never informed the Central Warehouse or the Procurement Department of the intent for a critical change to the awarded item. The storekeepers that normally picked the detergent on their picklist failed to mention or inquire about the variation in the product. The storekeepers picked the cartons as case packs without regard to the true inner cases that should have been picked. Each carton now contained six cases. All the disbursements for soap powder detergent equaled a total of ten cases, which means that each time a storekeeper picked the detergent, they gave the end-user five extra cases. When the Lead Warehouse Technician went to verify and perform a physical inventory of the detergent, the actual quantity on hand was 402 cases in its location. The Central Warehouse was now short of 50 cases of detergent.

The technician was required to report all inventory discrepancies to the management team. The escalation of errors posed a greater problem. The inventory management system needs to be updated with the correct receiving quantity, but unfortunately the disbursements only accounted for the cost of each case and not the cost of a carton. A cost correction in the inventory management systems had to be performed to balance the inventory cost.

Due to the timing of the disbursements, most of the extra product could not be recovered and placed back into the physical inventory. The Central Warehouse must recover the cost from the facilities for the extra product, which caused much confusion regarding their usage practices. The cost of the product disbursement was based on the initial proposed amount by the supplier for case volume. The detergent provides a recommended use for each application, and in turn, the Food Service Department orders inventory volumes based on facilities' needs annually or semiannually.

The supplier is now in violation of the contract requirements for the awarded product. The supplier offered no apology and refused to offer any concessions to minimize the errors that were made, defying *caveat venditor* (NIGP, 2024; Warehousemen, 1915). The Procurement department must become involved at this point because the supplier was awarded the item in a competitive bid. The Central Warehouse and the Procurement Department must now plan and proceed with a formal process to procure the product from another bidding supplier or choose another method to procure detergent. These efforts were further complicated as the United States and other global areas had received orders to self-quarantine during the onset of the pandemic, interrupting normal business operations and making supplier communication difficult.

### Discussion Questions

1. What are the key operational failures identified in the Central Warehouse's handling of the detergent shipment? How could they have been prevented?
2. How does the mismanagement of one stage in the logistics cycle (e.g., receiving) create a ripple effect across the entire supply chain?
3. Considering the supplier's violation of bid requirements, what steps should the Procurement Department take to address this issue effectively?
4. How did the lack of communication about the supplier's pack size changes impact the warehouse's inventory system and disbursement process?
5. What strategies can be implemented to improve accuracy in receiving, storing, and distributing inventory to avoid such discrepancies in the future?

Section 4

# Technologies and Skills in Government Contracting and Public Procurement

# 20 E-Procurement

## The Hope and the Hype

*Barbara Allen*

### 20.1 Introduction

This chapter summarizes the evolution of electronic procurement (e-procurement) in the context of public procurement. It defines e-procurement, situates it with respect to public procurement more generally, reviews key literature, examines emerging issues, and then describes practical applications for further learning.

Procurement itself is defined in this text in a number of places; see, for example, Chapter 1 or Chapter 15. For a brief reminder, and for our purposes here, public procurement involves expenditure by the state on obtaining goods, services, and works, usually from the private sector but not exclusively, and the extent to which the state has planned, executed and monitored procurement has varied depending on the ideological frame and context of the time (Allen, 2021).

E-procurement refers to the use of electronic methods, typically web-based applications, in any or every stage of the procurement process (Allen et al., 2001). This ranges from requisition to payment and aims to streamline the traditional methods of procurement to create efficiencies and reduce costs. McCue and Roman (2012), based on a number of other definitions, defined it as 'the use of ICT to automate and make more responsive and dynamic the purchasing process' (p. 225). Vaidya et al. (2006) describe e-procurement as an end-to-end solution meant to integrate and streamline procurement processes in an organization. More recently, from the construction industry, Yevu et al. (2023) suggest it refers to activity using online portals and platforms to perform construction procurement processes.

There is some question as to when 'electronic procurement' – e-procurement – became 'digital procurement'. For the purposes of this chapter, the terms e-procurement and digital procurement will be used interchangeably.

E-procurement was the 'hoped-for' solution to problems of cost, transparency, and efficiency in public procurement. This translated into 'hype' – huge interest in and the promotion of a set of tools that had the potential to fundamentally change many of the most onerous tasks embedded in procurement activities. It attracted much attention; the excitement of using new technology to solve some of the public administration's greatest challenges drew scholars, public officials, and consultants to its study.

E-procurement emerged out of the efficiency and effectiveness drive of the 1990s and 2000s, alongside and an integral part of the wave of New Public Management (NPM). The drive to reduce the size of the public sector and adapt it to a rapidly changing environment (note the influence of the 'Reinventing Government' movement[1] ) had a significant impact on politicians and public officials searching for innovative and cost-effective ways to restructure public administration. The environment was now open to how the internet

DOI: 10.4324/9781003566670-24

and advances in information and communication technology (ICT) could significantly influence how governments and public sector organizations conducted procurement activities (MacManus, 2002; Margetts, 2008).

Reducing costs was, of course, an attractive proposition. Procurement was believed to be a function where significant costs could be saved despite the lack of evidence. Automating and streamlining procurement processes were thought to reduce administrative burdens and save money by reducing the number of human-enabled transactions (Walker and Brammer, 2012). NPM reforms also included a demand for greater transparency and accountability, and by using more computer-enabled and then internet-enabled procurement platforms, an organization could gather visibility into its procurement activities and have some 'quick wins' through the reduction of red-tape, potentially helping to combat corruption and fraud.

The shift to the 'contracting state' (Greve, 2007) – the widely expanding use of contracts to obtain and deliver public services – meant widening competition and improving supplier management. Digitizing the procurement process provided an opportunity to better manage this growing activity area. With the need to adhere to the public sector procurement rules and regulations, e-procurement functions, such as the seemingly simple, more comprehensive, and easier access to information, meant these requirements could be organized online for potential suppliers (Costa et al., 2013). E-procurement platforms could facilitate a more transparent, competitive environment and integrate with other business systems for a seamless operational workflow (Croom and Brandon-Jones, 2017). As technology advanced and the benefits became more apparent, public sector organizations started implementing more sophisticated and comprehensive electronic procurement solutions embedded in the sourcing, tendering, and auction functions (Khalfan et al., 2022). These advancements were expected to enhance transparency, competition, and stakeholder collaboration.

E-procurement is now also contributing to enabling environmental and social sustainability. Studies have found that public sector organizations with higher utilization of e-procurement and more frequent supplier communication are more actively engaged in various dimensions of sustainable procurement. These dimensions include environmental considerations, labor practices, health and safety measures, community and philanthropic initiatives, and purchasing from minority-owned and local small to medium-sized enterprises (Walker and Brammer, 2012; Yevu et al., 2021).

The impact of e-procurement remains an interesting research area and an important part of the evolution of public administration. Scholars continue to look at whether technology has improved public procurement, whether e-procurement plays a significant role in improving efficiency, and whether it actually enhances transparency and accountability and reduces corruption risks.

## 20.2 Summary of the Literature

The e-procurement literature is partially a story of how technology has impacted the public sector. During the technology boom of the 1990s, there was much excitement about how e-procurement would revolutionize business-to-business practices, that efficiencies would be obtained, procurement costs reduced, the flow of information in the supply chain upgraded, and the strategic partnerships between networks of firms deepened (Johnson and Klassen, 2005). The public sector was just behind; with NPM taking root, the necessity of working increasingly closer with the private sector meant embedding new technologies would be crucial. Both developing and industrial nations launched a variety of initiatives on procurement reform. The signing of the World Trade Organisation (WTO) Agreement on Government Procurement (GPA) in 1994, and the OECD and EU, NAFTA, and Asia-Pacific Economic

Cooperation (APEC) all were making moves to include procurement reform – there was a mix of market access and good government objectives (Evenett and Hoekman, 2003). The chapter presents an overview of the relevant literature in a vast field under four themes: the potential and opportunity of e-procurement in a public sector context, questions of performance and impact, e-procurement as it relates to e-governance, and e-procurement in the international trade context.

### *20.2.1 Early Days – The Potential and the Challenges of E-Procurement in the Public Sector*

In the early 2000s, governments and public sector organizations began exploring the capabilities of e-procurement systems while scholars reflected on what was driving the uptake of e-procurement tools and practices (Allen et al., 2001; MacManus, 2002; Moon, 2002, 2005; Neef, 2001). Technological advancement promised the automation of rudimentary tasks and the streamlining of procurement processes.

Yet the early challenge was technological infrastructure, or more precisely, the lack thereof (Vaidya et al., 2006). During the infancy of digital procurement initiatives, many public sector organizations found themselves constrained by inadequate technological resources (Bulut and Yen, 2013). Basic requirements such as high-speed internet connectivity and compatible hardware and software systems were often lacking.

The technology infrastructure was a problem as was organizational inertia, marked by a resistance to change (Croom and Brandon-Jones, 2017). Procurement operations in the public sector were manual and repetitive but certain, and as a result, staff members accustomed to these processes were often skeptical and even resistant to the technological innovations presented by digital procurement (Henriksen and Mahnke, 2005). This internal inertia necessitated technological adaptation and a cultural shift within organizations.

Croom and Brandon-Jones (2007) published a small but significant study in which they created a model of the e-procurement effect. Drawing from the literature, they drew out key themes to test, including changes to total acquisition costs due to e-procurement, organizational characteristics, governance structures, system specification, and implementation management. E-procurement implementation was found to reduce search costs, leading to increased supply availability and, subsequently, greater leverage in negotiation. Concerning total cost, the cost of processing purchase requisitions was reduced through improvements to the procurement system. There was a reduction in maverick purchasing, and price reductions accrued from increased visibility, compliance, management information, demand aggregation, and increased leverage in negotiations. The authors found a vital effect – the reputation of the procurement function and the general disposition of an organization toward e-procurement were strongly influenced by users' perceptions of internal service. They also found that users needed support, which may affect maverick spending.

Many aspects of the human element were recognized, such as a lack of necessary digital skills and expertise among public sector procurement professionals (MacManus, 2002; Vaidya et al., 2006). While the technology was advancing rapidly, there was often a skills gap among those responsible for its implementation. Procurement officers and other professionals had to quickly adapt to new tools and methods, a challenge that was only easily overcome with targeted training and development programs (Williams and Hardy, 2007).

Concerns around data security and privacy were evident even at this point in time. E-procurement systems were not well developed in terms of protecting sensitive data, raising concerns about unauthorized access and data breaches. Initial digital procurement systems were sometimes not sufficiently robust in protecting sensitive data, thus impacting the perceived benefits of digital procurement (Moon, 2002; Vaidyanathan *et al.*, 2012).

### *20.2.2 Questions of Performance and Impact*

While the main challenges with e-procurement and some benefts had been discovered, studies into e-procurement's potential for transformative change continued. Empirical research questioning the performance of e-procurement and its impact emerged. The technology continued to be of interest, especially that enabling e-auctions.[2] E-auctions first appeared in private-sector procurement in the late 1990s. However, as technology uptake increased in the public sector so too did interest in the potential for technology-based tendering and bidding. Much work was done on looking at procurement auctions (Dimitri et al., 2006; Johnson, 2011; Tassabehji, 2010) and the extent to which e-auctions could improve the efficiency of public procurement (Pavel and Sičáková-Beblavá, 2013).

McCue and Roman (2012) found that significant transformative changes were still *not* occurring. A study in the United States and Canada found the unsuitability of software platforms, organizational resistance, lack of strategic systems integration, and failure to involve public procurement professionals in the design of e-procurement systems. However, they found that adopting an e-procurement system played a significant role in promoting accountability and transparency in the procurement process.

Gardenal (2013) used a measurement framework based on five impact dimensions, each with a set of indicators. The dimensions included efficiency, effectiveness, competitiveness, dematerialization, and transparency. Gardenal (2013) found efficiency benefits in the early and final phases of a procurement process, concluding through a test of procurement in the Lombardia region of Italy that e-procurement is an effective means to optimize procurement activities.

Implementation and performance continued to be in question in terms of efficiency – by 2015, in a study on e-procurement implementation in 191 of the largest U.S. cities, Bromberg and Manoharan (2015) concluded that professional city management and IT quality and capacity were critical for the uptake and growth of e-procurement.

Questions regarding the connection of e-procurement to institutional form appeared in some studies – Patrucco et al. (2021) point out that from their literature search, the design configuration of public procurement influences its performance. Digitalization forms one of the structural variables in their study, and digital tools seem to influence procurement – the authors were looking at how these tools interact with centralization and standardization. Mélon et al. (2020) set out to verify a hypothesis that the implementation of e-procurement implies better institutions in terms of public purchasing, analyzing Denmark, the Netherlands, and Portugal. Ofori-Amanfo et al. (2023) undertook a performance and content review using bibliometric analysis, showing that 'measuring the contribution of e-procurement in optimizing public expenditure can break the resistance to the adoption of a digitalized procurement system' (p. 314).

Mohungoo et al. (2020) identified three themed areas for e-procurement implementation challenges: (1) technological challenges of acceptance and usage, e-procurement as a disruptive innovation, and technical issues with e-procurement (2) organizational challenges of stakeholders' issues, leadership, inadequate training, and skilled personnel, resistance to change and value-driven outcomes, and (3) key environmental factors of the procurement regulatory framework, the country context, and the problems faced by SMEs. Specific regional research is exemplified by Gasco et al. (2018), who looked at two innovative European regions and identified how different variables affect e-procurement adoption, diffusion, and upscaling.

### *20.2.3 E-Procurement and E-Governance*

E-procurement has been seen as a way to improve the governance of public expenditure through public procurement (Neupane et al., 2012). ICTs and e-procurement continued to be considered important mechanisms for dealing with issues of transparency, accountability, and corruption. However, e-procurement alone cannot improve governance. Akpan-Obong et al. (2023) found through an analysis of the 2016 and 2018 Worldwide Governance Indicators and E-government Development Index that ICTs achieve better outcomes when integrated with established institutions and structures of governance.

E-procurement as a strategic tool in health s ervices delivery was studied by Mahuwi and Israel (2024) where they found that accountability and transparency are complementary principles that 'mutually strengthen the fight against corruption in the pharmaceutical procurement system' (2024, p. 13) and emphasized the significant role played by e-procurement in moderating the relationship between transparency and anti-corruption. Mackey and Cuomo (2020) set out to better understand how digital technologies are used to combat corruption, increase transparency, and detect fraud in pharmaceutical procurement systems to improve population health outcomes; they recommended that more research was required on tying cost-savings measurements with anti-corruption indicators and increasing the use of anti-corruption technologies in procurement processes.

Puspita et al. (2024) found that using e-procurement significantly decreases the amount of government procurement corruption in Indonesian provinces with relatively high government procurement spending or capital expenditure. In an extensive bibliometric analysis, Ofori-Amanfo et al. (2023) found that public e-procurement can reduce the power of government officers in procurement processes, thus strengthening the argument that e-procurement has the potential to reduce corruption. Another less-studied hypothesis is that e-procurement may actually expand corruption-related and rent-seeking opportunities for technology-literate public officials (Anthony, 2018; Heeks, 1999).

Hardy and Williams (2008) looked at how high-level governmental e-procurement policies were translated into public procurement practices – they raise interesting questions about how government agencies evaluate their e-procurement sourcing performance given their fragmented systems and information, ambiguity that can surround the procurement organization, the interests and politics that are embedded in the information, and the unintended consequences that arise as an implementation process unfolds (p. 23). Walker and Harland (2008) indicated that e-procurement should be considered in the context of other procurement policy objectives. For example, sustainability has increasingly become part of the policy objectives pursued through procurement. In another study, Walker and Brammer (2012) looked at 280 public procurement practitioners from 20 countries. They showed that e-procurement and communication with suppliers might support some types of sustainable procurement, including environmental, labor, health, and safety aspects.

### *20.2.4 E-Procurement in the International Trade Context*

Governance is related to the international context in which countries' procurement profiles emerge. The integration of frameworks for digital procurement in the international trade context has led to trade successes in government contracts, which most often build on well-functioning, open, and efficient public procurement tenders (Yukins and Fazekas, 2021).

International frameworks for digital procurement have become an integral part of the global public procurement landscape. Initiatives led by organizations such as the WTO and the United Nations Commission on International Trade Law (UNCITRAL) aimed to standardize and harmonize procurement processes across different jurisdictions (Anderson and Müller, 2017). For instance, the WTO's Agreement on Government Procurement (GPA) outlines best practices and policies that promote fair, transparent, and competitive procurement activities (Khorana et al., 2015).

The *UNCITRAL Model Law on Public Procurement* has been pivotal in offering a legal framework that countries can adapt to meet their specific needs, facilitating easier cross-border procurement activities (Nicholas, 2020). The Model Law aims to promote key principles such as transparency, efficiency, competition, participation, and integrity in procurement systems. Although these objectives universally apply to most systems, their emphasis can differ. The Model Law implicitly incorporates additional goals such as accountability and non-discrimination. E-procurement has been highlighted as a tool to achieve these objectives, particularly in enhancing transparency and integrity.

The technology, in theory, minimizes the scope for corruption by reducing human contact and, thereby, the opportunity for bribery. The opportunity to standardize procurement processes, which technology does, makes it most effective for recurring purchases of common items. Given the growing reliance on e-procurement, UNCITRAL included it in the Model Law. Three core principles guide this inclusion: encouraging e-procurement where feasible, maintaining technological neutrality due to varying levels of technical sophistication among member states, and providing additional guidance on the controls needed for e-procurement.

The European Union Commission advocated for e-procurement to become standard practice across member states, guided by various strategies and action plans (Khorana et al., 2015). These plans aimed to connect e-procurement capabilities throughout the EU to maintain the fluidity of the single market and not hinder e-commerce (Arrowsmith, 2017).

The directives offer comprehensive guidelines on electronic communication between suppliers and public authorities, as well as protocols for electronic tendering. They emphasize the importance of adopting secure and advanced electronic signatures, thereby ensuring the integrity and confidentiality of data. These directives aim to streamline digital procurement processes across member states, thus creating a more unified and efficient market for public procurement in Europe. Regional frameworks in other parts of the world, such as the African Union's guidelines and the APEC Non-Binding Principles on Government Procurement, offer complementary approaches (Thai, 2017). These frameworks are often more tailored to address the unique challenges and opportunities presented by the respective regions. For example, the African Union's procurement framework focuses on issues related to capacity building and inclusivity, aiming to ensure that smaller suppliers are not left behind in the transition to digital procurement. On the other hand, APEC's principles stress the importance of transparency and good governance, aiming to reduce corruption and improve public trust in digital procurement systems.

The proliferation of international frameworks has generated both opportunities and challenges. While they provide a foundation for best practices and legal compliance, the need to align with multiple frameworks can pose operational difficulties for public sector entities. Understanding and adhering to these frameworks requires a deep knowledge base and skilled personnel, especially for countries involved in several regional and international agreements.

## 20.3 Emerging Issues

E-procurement continues to be an important area of research and practice with respect to public procurement. The changing policy and technological environment make e-procurement more possible than ever. However, the issues of privacy, security, integrity, and transparency also make it more risky than ever. The open data and open government context seem to push procurement officials toward more competitive bidding but will lead to poorer actual contract performance (Duguay et al., 2023). The opportunities for scrutiny grow with greater access to procurement data; however, this also opens many possibilities for rigidity in selecting suppliers as officials need to gain more discretion based on their knowledge and private information. We explore some of the impacts of this new environment in the following section.

### *20.3.1 AI and E-Procurement*

While relatively new in its adoption by public procurers, artificial intelligence (AI) has rapidly found various applications, both in quantitative terms for enhancing performance metrics and in qualitative aspects such as decision-making and human interactions. Various operations can be improved, such as the scrutiny of spending across purchasers, suppliers, internal clients, networks, projects, and partnerships. As with earlier, simpler forms of e-procurement, the facilitation of real-time monitoring and control through automation has the potential to result in more efficient and effective purchasing processes (Allal-Chérif et al., 2021). AI can process volumes of data far exceeding human capabilities, accomplishing this with a high level of reliability and at a reduced cost (Salminen *et al.*, 2017).

The introduction of AI and machine learning technologies in digital procurement has also ushered in significant advancements in decision-making and analytics (Schulze-Horn et al., 2020). Traditional decision-making mechanisms often involve cumbersome processes and rely heavily on human judgment. AI technologies are adept at sifting through large sets of data to provide actionable insights, potentially enabling procurement professionals to make well-informed decisions swiftly. These insights can range from supplier reliability scores to predictive analytics on price fluctuations, all of which significantly augment the human capability to make data-driven decisions. Siciliani et al. (2023) developed an AI-based decision support system for public procurement that is an example of the efforts to see tenders as a strategic development resource – and a way to improve public investment and spending.

Machine learning algorithms, a subset of AI, further enhance this decision-making process by continuously learning from data trends and patterns (García Rodríguez et al., 2022; Mulligan and Bamberger, 2019). For example, machine learning models can forecast demand based on historical data, thereby assisting procurement professionals in making timely orders or renegotiating contracts. Such capabilities make machine learning not just a tool but potentially a strategic asset in procurement decision-making.

Automated supplier risk assessment is an emerging application of AI in digital procurement (Falco et al., 2021). The traditional means of assessing supplier risk often involve manual methods, such as document reviews or site audits, which are time-consuming and sometimes unreliable. AI enables a systematic approach by gathering and analyzing a multitude of data points, including financial records, compliance certificates, and market trends, thereby generating a more comprehensive risk profile of the suppliers in real time.

Machine learning algorithms significantly enhance this risk management strategy by learning from ongoing transactions, compliance reports, and market fluctuations. As more data is ingested into these algorithms, they evolve to identify subtle trends and anomalies that might be overlooked by human analysts. For example, an algorithm could flag a supplier who consistently delivers slightly behind schedule or whose materials show a trend of declining quality. Such capabilities enable proactive management of risks, thus averting potential crises before they escalate.

AI tools can scrutinize large volumes of data to forecast supplier performance against a multiplicity of criteria, including, but not limited to, costs, quality, and timeframes. For example, criteria such as sustainable development and relationship quality are now being weighted more significantly in evaluations. With the use of AI, these performance metrics can be gauged not just retrospectively but also in real time or even in a predictive matter, giving an agile and dynamic view of supplier satisfaction levels (Batran et al., 2017). This allows procurement departments to not only monitor high-volume clients but also to build quality relationships with suppliers, ensuring preferential treatment in emergencies or for innovative projects.

Despite all of these opportunities and these advancements, the use of and support for e-procurement by AI is not yet widespread (Konnerth, 2023). No matter how much AI is used and embedded in the public procurement system, the role of human judgment remains critical in leveraging the benefits of AI and machine learning for decision-making and analytics in procurement. Ethical considerations, stakeholder relationships, and other intangible factors still require human evaluation.

### *20.3.2 New Challenges Vis-á-Vis Integrity and Anti-Corruption*

Digital procurement platforms have introduced new challenges around integrity and anti-corruption measures (Attaran, 2020; Mattsson and Andersson, 2019). While these platforms add layers of transparency and accountability, they are not immune to fraudulent activities. The digital nature of the systems can make them susceptible to cyber threats such as hacking, data manipulation, or unauthorized access. A breach of integrity can lead to significant financial losses and erode public trust. To address this, robust cybersecurity measures, constant monitoring, and periodic auditing are essential, which require additional resources and specialized skills.

In addition, the transparency features of digital procurement systems often rest on the assumption that all activities logged are legitimate and free from corruption. This issue could go unnoticed if corruption is embedded within the selection criteria or decision-making algorithms, primarily if the system operates without significant human oversight. The ease and speed of digital processes could, paradoxically, make it easier to execute corrupt practices on a large scale. Thus, integrating anti-corruption measures, such as checks and balances, third-party audits, and secure encryption, is vital for preserving integrity.

Another pertinent challenge relates to the balance between efficiency and inclusiveness. Digital procurement systems can inadvertently create barriers to entry for smaller suppliers or those lacking technological sophistication. The efficiencies gained by automation and real-time analytics may privilege more prominent vendors with the resources to engage effectively with digital platforms. Consequently, public procurement could become less inclusive, limiting the pool of suppliers and potentially undermining social procurement objectives such as promoting local businesses or social enterprises.

Organizations may need to implement transitional measures or support mechanisms to achieve a balance. For example, offering training sessions or user-friendly interfaces can lower barriers to entry for less tech-savvy suppliers. Creating different tracks within the digital procurement platform, one for highly complex contracts and another for less complex or lower-value agreements may also foster inclusiveness. This enables a more diverse supplier base while still leveraging the advantages of digitalization. Therefore, careful planning and ongoing evaluation are crucial to ensure that the drive for efficiency does not compromise inclusiveness or integrity.

Regardless of the sophistication of AI and the opportunities through enhanced e-procurement and in the various stages of the procurement process itself, public officials need to have an active role in both the design of the systems and their implementation, with ongoing scrutiny and monitoring.

### *20.3.3 Practical Application*

This section presents key issues that any organization should consider when the decision has been made to create a digital procurement system, or, the organization intends to upgrade a system that currently has minimal functionality. These elements will involve a network of people that need to collaborate in order to successfully create or upgrade their procurement technology.

1. Most organizations will already have some procurement systems and processes in place. So with regard to digital procurement, it will be a a complex endeavor involving a wide range of existing systems, roles, and organizational areas. Older systems may require significant modification or complete overhauls.

   One of the challenging aspects will be *data migration*. A thorough audit of existing data will be needed in order to identify which datasets are essential and need to be migrated, what data has quality issues, and what datasets are compatible. The new digital procurement system must be able to deal with the organization's data formats or data conversion processes will have to be undertaken increasing the complexity and cost. It is likely that both new and old systems will need to run in parallel initially to compare performance and ensure that business can continue.
2. Changes to existing systems will impact *workflow* and those in their current roles. Change management strategies will be crucial to ensure a smooth transition along with focused training. Undertaking a needs analysis to identify gaps in skills is a crucial step to ensure effective training and learning takes place. Training should involve both the technical aspect and procedural changes that are occurring in the form of workshops, online courses, practical sessions, and individual support where needed.

   *Change management* processes are crucial that organizational leaders will need to guide. This must involve articulation of the benefits of a new system, with achievable milestones and identification of what success will look like. Communication updates through multiple channels will be needed over the period of the transition to ensure key messages are articulated and understood. Incentivizing change through rewards and acknowledgments may support the process.

   Technical issues or organizational problems are likely to occur in any major transformation, so contingency plans will be important to have in place. Troubleshooting processes, escalation processes and feedback frameworks all need to be developed. Continuous improvement arises from these elements, and real-time training changes may be needed.
3. Robust *frameworks* for monitoring and evaluation should include key performance and metrics. Quantifiable measures are benchmarks for success that can be translated into insights for cost-efficiency and supplier performance. Key Performance Indicators (KPIs) need to be focused on specific goals and operational context; specifically, public sector organizations may require greater emphasis on transparency and stakeholder engagement. Both short-term and long-term metrics have important uses and should evolve over time dynamically; immediate insights can be gained quickly but also long-term metrics may help demonstrate performance on sustainability and any transformative change of digital procurement strategies.
4. Continuous *improvement* aligned with broader organizational goals and integrated into strategy is critical in the digital procurement context. Iterative, systematic evaluation will pick up issues and ideally signal where innovation can next occur – especially as AI takes an increasingly important role in any digital procurement strategy.

## Notes

1 The new lexicon around change in government emerged from the Osborne and Gaebler work in the early 1990s. Osborne, David, and Ted Baebler, 1992. *Reinventing Government: How the Entrepreneurial Spirit Is Transforming the Public Sector from Schoolhouse to Statehouse, City Hall to Pentagon*. Reading, MA: Addison Wesley.
2 Electronic reverse auctions or e-auctions are dynamic downward bidding events linking procuring entities and tenderers in real time (Eyo, 2012).
3 Ada County expressly authorizes the use of the County's name in this case study.
4 "2023 Cronin Submission Booklet," NASPO, last modified December 2023, https://cms.naspo.org/wp-content/uploads/2023/12/2023-Cronin-Committee-Booklet-All-Submissions_KSUpdatesB.pdf
5 "eVA Virginia's Market Place," Commonwealth of Virginia, accessed January 17, 2024, https://eva.virginia.gov/
6 "2023 Cronin Submission Booklet," NASPO.
7 "2023 Cronin Submission Booklet," NASPO.

## References

Akpan-Obong, P.I., Trinh, M.P., Ayo, C.K. and Oni, A. (2023), "E-Governance as good governance? Evidence from 15 West African countries", *Information Technology for Development*, Routledge, Vol. 29 No. 2–3, pp. 256–275.

Allal-Chérif, O., Simón-Moya, V. and Ballester, A.C.C. (2021), "Intelligent purchasing: How artificial intelligence can redefine the purchasing function", *Journal of Business Research*, Vol. 124, pp. 69–76.

Allen, B. (2021), "Broader outcomes in procurement policy – A case of New Zealand pragmatism", *Journal of Public Procurement*, Emerald, Vol. 21 No. 3, pp. 318–341.

Allen, B.A., Juillet, L., Paquet, G. and Roy, J. (2001), "E-Governance & government on-line in Canada: Partnerships, people & prospects", *Government Information Quarterly*, Vol. 18 No. 2, pp. 93–104.

Anderson, R.D. and Müller, A.C. (2017), "The revised WTO Agreement on Government Procurement (GPA): Key design features and significance for global trade and development", *Georgetown Journal of International Law*, doi: 10.30875/188535E1-EN.

Anthony, A. (2018), "The use of e-procurement in south African public procurement law: Challenges and prospects", *Law Democracy & Development*, Academy of Science of South Africa, Vol. 22 No. 1, pp. 39–47.

Arrowsmith, S. (2017), "EC Regime on Public Procurement*", in *International Handbook of Public Procurement*, doi: 10.4324/9781315092539-14.

Attaran, M. (2020), "Digital technology enablers and their implications for supply chain management", *Supply Chain Forum: An International Journal*, Taylor & Francis, Vol. 21 No. 3, pp. 158–172.

Batran, A., Erben, A., Schulz, R. and Sperl, F. (2017), *Procurement 4.0: A Survival Guide in a Digital, Disruptive World*, Campus Verlag.

Bromberg, D. and Manoharan, A. (2015), "E-procurement implementation in the United States: Understanding progress in local government", *Public Administration Quarterly*, SAGE Publications, Vol. 39 No. 3, pp. 360–392.

Bulut, C. and Yen, B.P.-C. (2013), "E-procurement in public sector: A global overview", *Electronic Government, an International Journal*, Inderscience Publishers, Vol. 10 No. 2, pp. 189–210.

Costa, A.A., Arantes, A. and Valadares Tavares, L. (2013), "Evidence of the impacts of public e-procurement: The Portuguese experience", *Journal of Purchasing and Supply Management*, Elsevier, Vol. 19 No. 4, pp. 238–246.

Croom, S. and Brandon-Jones, A. (2007), "Impact of e-procurement: Experiences from implementation in the UK public sector", *Journal of Purchasing and Supply Management*, Vol. 13 No. 4, pp. 294–303.

Croom, S. and Brandon-Jones, A. (2017), "Key Issues in E-Procurement: Procurement Implementation and Operation in the Public Sector", in *International Handbook of Public Procurement*, doi: 10.4324/9781315092539-24.

Dimitri, N., Piga, G., Spagnolo, G., Carpineti, L., Zanza, M., Dini, F., Albano, G.L., *et al.* (2006), *Handbook of Procurement*, Cambridge University Press.

Duguay, R., Rauter, T. and Samuels, D. (2023), "The impact of open data on public procurement", *Journal of Accounting Research*, Wiley, Vol. 61 No. 4, pp. 1159–1224.

Eppel, E. and Allen, B. (2020), "Digital government Leadership, innovation and integration", in Berman, E. and Karacaoglu, G. (Eds.), *Public Policy and Governance Frontiers in New Zealand*, Emerald Publishing Limited, pp. 233–255.

Evenett, S.J. and Hoekman, B.M. (2003), "Transparency in government procurement: What can we expect from international trade agreements?", alexandria.unisg.ch, available at: www.alexandria.unisg.ch/server/api/core/bitstreams/b9720006-1d3d-4c39-84ef-dbb5b3a5bc0b/content (accessed 29 August 2023).

Eyo, A. (2012), "Regulation of e-auctions in the us federal procurement system: Lessons from the e-auction rules in the United Kingdom", ippa.org, available at: https://ippa.org/images/PROCEEDINGS/IPPC5/Part11/PAPER11-2.pdf (accessed 14 July 2024).

Falco, G., Shneiderman, B., Badger, J., Carrier, R., Dahbura, A., Danks, D., Eling, M., *et al.* (2021), "Governing AI safety through independent audits", *Nature Machine Intelligence*, Nature Publishing Group, Vol. 3 No. 7, pp. 566–571.

García Rodríguez, M.J., Rodríguez-Montequín, V., Ballesteros-Pérez, P., Love, P.E.D. and Signor, R. (2022), "Collusion detection in public procurement auctions with machine learning algorithms", *Automation in Construction*, Vol. 133, p. 104047.

Gardenal, F. (2013), "A model to measure e-procurement impacts on organizational performance", *Journal of Public Procurement*, Emerald Publishing Limited, Vol. 13 No. 2, pp. 215–242.

Gasco, M., Cucciniello, M., Nasi, G. and Yuan, Q. (2018), "Determinants and Barriers of E-Procurement: A European Comparison of Public Sector Experiences", *Hawaii International Conference on System Sciences 2018 (HICSS-51)*, aisel.aisnet.org.

Greve, C. (2007), *Contracting for Public Services*, Routledge.

Hardy, C.A. and Williams, S.P. (2008), "E-government policy and practice: A theoretical and empirical exploration of public e-procurement", *Government Information Quarterly*, Elsevier, Vol. 25 No. 2, pp. 155–180.

Heeks, R. (1999), "Information and Communication Technologies, Poverty and Development", 5, The University of Manchester, 30 October.

Henriksen, H. and Mahnke, V. (2005), "E-procurement adoption in the Danish public sector: The influence of economic and political rationality", *Scandinavian Journal of Information Systems*, Vol. 17, p. 2.

Johnson, M. (2011), "Public sector e-procurement: A study of benefits from e-markets in the local government sector", *International Journal of Services, Technology and Management*, Vol. 16 No. 1, p. 1.

Johnson, P.F. and Klassen, R.D. (2005), "E-procurement", *MIT Sloan Management Review*, Vol. 46 No. 2, pp. 7–10.

Khalfan, M., Azizi, N., Haass, O., Maqsood, T. and Ahmed, I. (2022), "Blockchain technology: Potential applications for public sector e-procurement and project management", *Sustainability: Science Practice and Policy*, Vol. 14 No. 10, p. 5791.

Khorana, S., Ferguson-Boucher, K. and Kerr, W.A. (2015), "Governance issues in the EU's E-procurement framework", *Journal of Common Market Studies*, Wiley, Vol. 53 No. 2, pp. 292–310.

Konnerth, H. (2023), "Artificial Intelligence (AI) In E-procurement: A literature review", *Economy & Business Journal*, International Scientific Publications, Bulgaria, Vol. 17 No. 1, pp. 98–113.

Mackey, T.K. and Cuomo, R.E. (2020), "An interdisciplinary review of digital technologies to facilitate anti-corruption, transparency and accountability in medicines procurement", *Global Health Action*, Taylor & Francis, Vol. 13 No. sup1, p. 1695241.

MacManus, S.A. (2002), "Understanding the incremental nature of e-procurement implementation at the state and local levels", *Journal of Public Procurement*, Vol. 2 No. 1, pp. 5–28.

Mahuwi, L. and Israel, B. (2024), "Promoting transparency and accountability towards anti-corruption in pharmaceutical procurement system: Does E-procurement play a significant role?", *Management Matters*, Vol. 21, No. 1, pp. 20–37.

Margetts, H. (2008), "European political organizations and the internet: Mobilization, participation, and change", in Chadwick, E.A. and Howard, P.N. (Eds.), *Routledge Handbook of Internet Politics*, Routledge, pp. 41–55.

Mattsson, L.-G. and Andersson, P. (2019), "Private-public interaction in public service innovation processes- business model challenges for a start-up EdTech firm", *Journal of Business & Industrial Marketing*, Emerald Publishing Limited, Vol. 34 No. 5, pp. 1106–1118.

McCue, C. and Roman, A.V. (2012), "E-procurement: Myth or reality", *Journal of Public Procurement*, Emerald Publishing Limited, Vol. 12 No. 2, pp. 221–248.

Mélon, L. and Spruk, R. (2020), "The impact of e-procurement on institutional quality", *Journal of Public Procurement*, Emerald Publishing Limited, Vol. 20 No. 4, pp. 333–375.

Mohungoo, I., Brown, I. and Kabanda, S. (2020), "A systematic review of implementation challenges in public E-procurement", in *19th IFIP WG 6.11 Conference on e-business, e-Services, and e-Society*, I3E2020 Skukuza, South Africa, April 6–8, 2020 Proceedings Part II, pp. 46–58. https://doi.org/10.1007/978-3-030-45002-1_5

Moon, M.J. (2002), "The evolution of E-government among municipalities: Rhetoric or reality?", *Public Administration Review*, Wiley, Vol. 62 No. 4, pp. 424–433.

Moon, M.J. (2005), "E-procurement management in state governments: Diffusion of e-procurement practices and its determinants", *Journal of Public Procurement*, Emerald Publishing Limited, Vol. 5 No. 1, pp. 54–72.

Mulligan, D. and Bamberger, K. (2019), "Procurement as policy: Administrative process for machine learning", *SSRN Electronic Journal*, doi: 10.2139/SSRN.3464203.

Neef, D. (2001), *E-Procurement: From Strategy to Implementation*, FT Press.

Neupane, A., Soar, J., Vaidya, K. and Yong, J. (2012), "Role of Public E-Procurement Technology to Reduce Corruption in Government Procurement", *Proceedings of the 5th International Public Procurement Conference (IPPC5)*, presented at the 5th International Public Procurement Conference (IPPC5), research.usq.edu.au, United States, p. 31.

Nicholas, C. (2020), "Policy Choices in the Implementation of Electronic Procurement: The Approach of the Uncitral Model Law on Procurement to Electronic Communications", *Proceedings of 4th International Public Procurement.*

Ofori-Amanfo, J., Owusu, G.M.Y. and Arku, F.K. (2023), "Twenty-one years of the Journal of Public Procurement: A performance and content review using bibliometric analysis", *Journal of Public Procurement*, Emerald Publishing Limited, Vol. 23 No. 3/4, pp. 297–320.

Patrucco, A.S., Agasisti, T. and Glas, A.H. (2021), "Structuring public procurement in local governments: The effect of centralization, standardization and digitalization on performance", *Public Performance & Management Review*, Routledge, Vol. 44 No. 3, pp. 630–656.

Pavel, J. and Sičáková-beblavá, E. (2013), "Do e-auctions realy improve the efficiency of public procurement? The case of the Slovak municipalities", *Prague Economic Papers*, pep.vse.cz, Vol. 2013, pp. 111–124.

Puspita, A.C. and Gultom, Y.M.L. (2024), "The effect of e-procurement policy on corruption in government procurement: Evidence from Indonesia", *International Journal of Public Administration*, Routledge, Vol. 47 No. 2, pp. 117–129.

Salminen, V., Ruohomaa, H. and Kantola, J. (2017), "Digitalization and big data supporting responsible business co-evolution", in Kantola, J.L, Barath, T., Nazir, S., and Andre, T. (Eds.), *Advances in Human Factors, Business Management, Training and Education*, Springer, pp. 1055–1067.

Schulze-Horn, I., Hueren, S., Scheffler, P. and Schiele, H. (2020), "Artificial intelligence in purchasing: Facilitating mechanism design-based negotiations", *Applied Artificial Intelligence: AAI*, Taylor & Francis, Vol. 34 No. 8, pp. 618–642.

Siciliani, L., Taccardi, V., Basile, P., Di Ciano, M. and Lops, P. (2023), "AI-based decision support system for public procurement", *Information Systems*, Elsevier, Vol. 119, p. 102284.

Tassabehji, R. (2010), "Understanding e-auction use by procurement professionals: Motivation, attitudes and perceptions", *Supply Chain Management: An International Journal*, Emerald Group Publishing Limited, Vol. 15 No. 6, pp. 425–437.

Thai, K.V. (2017), *International Handbook of Public Procurement*, Routledge.

Vaidya, K., Sajeev, A.S. and Callender, G. (2006), "Critical factors that influence e-procurement implementation success in the public sector", *Journal of Public Procurement*, Emerald Publishing Limited, Vol. 6 No. 1/2, pp. 70–99.

Vaidyanathan, G., Devaraj, S. and D'Arcy, J. (2012), "Does security impact e-procurement performance? Testing a model of direct and moderated effects", *Decision Sciences*, Wiley, Vol. 43 No. 3, pp. 437–458.

Walker, H. and Brammer, S. (2012), "The relationship between sustainable procurement and e-procurement in the public sector", *International Journal of Production Economics*, Vol. 140 No. 1, pp. 256–268.

Walker, H. and Harland, C. (2008), "E-procurement in the United Nations: Influences, issues and impact", *International Journal of Operations & Production Management*, Emerald Group Publishing Limited, Vol. 28 No. 9, pp. 831–857.

Williams, S.P. and Hardy, C.A. (2007), "E-Procurement: Current Issues & Future Challenges", *European Conference on Information Systems*, aisel.aisnet.org, pp. 131–142.

Yevu, S.K., Yu, A.T.W. and Darko, A. (2021), "Digitalization of construction supply chain and procurement in the built environment: Emerging technologies and opportunities for sustainable processes", *Journal of Cleaner Production*, Elsevier, Vol. 322, p. 129093.

Yevu, S.K., Yu, A.T.W. and Darko, A. (2023), "Barriers to electronic procurement adoption in the construction industry: A systematic review and interrelationships", *International Journal of Construction Management*, Taylor & Francis, Vol. 23 No. 6, pp. 964–978.

Yukins, C. and Fazekas, M. (2021), "Public Procurement and International Trade Agreements – CETA, TTIP and beyond", in Castelli, A., Piga, G., Saussier, S. and Tatrai, T. (Eds.), *The Challenges of Public Procurement Reforms*, Routledge, pp. 167–183.

### *Case Study: The Uptake of Digital Procurement and the Creation of a 'Marketplace': The Case of New Zealand (Developed by Barbara Allen)*

New Zealand is a small country known for its innovation and agility in digitalization and institutional change. It can be compared to other jurisdictions with ambitions in the digital space.

The Government ICT Strategy and Action Plan from 2013 to 2017 recognized that procurement time scales needed to be shorter and less costly; public procurement often squeezed out all but the most prominent suppliers. Streamlining procurement became a key priority, and efforts to adapt processes and innovate through procurement gained momentum. Syndicated agreements – a type of approved collaborative contract whereby a group of agencies aggregate their respective needs and collectively go to market for goods, services, or works – became available with some information available online with a contracts register.

The development of the New Zealand 'Marketplace' was a key element of digitization of procurement, an alternate mode for buying and supplying, making it 'easier, quicker and more cost-effective for government to access a full range of digital capabilities and for suppliers to deliver them' (Eppel and Allen, 2020). The marketplace process involves a pre-qualification stage where the main assurances are put in place, allowing suppliers to become suppliers to the government straightforwardly. The first channel involved public cloud services, analytics, collaborative working, creative design, publishing, marketing, and project management and planning. Other channels have evolved, including consultancy, professional services, and enterprise software. These new kinds of systems create new intersections between the private sector and government.

One problematic area has been that technology investment planning has considered 'information' as technology infrastructure tied down by highly specified contracts, often ending up as legacy systems that continue to be used past their lifespan. Patching old systems and adding functionality created elements of out-of-date infrastructure unable to respond to agency requirements and growing demands for internet/cloud-based services.

Procurement processes are often criticized as barriers to innovation. However, over time, jurisdictions' uptake of digital technology has shown substantial innovation that both drives and is driven by change.

#### Discussion Questions

How can governments use digital procurement to promote innovation while maintaining transparency and fairness in supplier selection?

What organizational or cultural barriers typically hinder the successful adoption of digital procurement systems?

How can public institutions balance efficiency gains from digital tools with the need for long-term strategic planning and system sustainability?

### *Case Study: E-Procurement and the Electronic Office – The Ada County Experience[3] (Developed by Bob Perkins, CPPO, CPPB, NIGP-CPP)*

#### Background

Ada County in Boise, Idaho is the largest county in Idaho by population with 558,000 residents. In terms of land size, it is roughly the size of the state of Rhode Island. Ada County government is in the heart of downtown Boise and is often referred to as the "Great State of Ada" by various other Idaho counties due to the political pull and influence that the county has across Idaho. In Ada County government there are 9 elected officials and 12 department heads that help to guide the county's strategic direction. The 12 departments all report directly to the Ada County Board of Commissioners. Ada County Procurement is one of these departments.

Prior to 2019 Ada County Procurement utilized tried and true paper-based methods of solicitation delivery. Everything was paper including solicitations, bid summaries, Request For Proposal (RFP) evaluation scoring, and award letters. Additionally, since the Procurement Department was paper-based, it meant the department also had to retain the paper records which required file folders, file cabinets, and banker boxes to store multiple years' worth of records. While paper-based procurements are very reliable and widely emulated across the United States with many local governments, the transition to e-procurement was a priority for the department. So why part ways with a delivery methodology that has worked so well in the past? The answer points to efficiency and access.

Paper-based solicitations are not efficient. For example, a sealed bid would need to be dropped off at the Ada County Courthouse and Administration building where the Procurement Department is located and/or mailed to our office. To get through our doors at the Courthouse, the public needs to go through a security check point that checks for all metal objects and subjects the individual to a search of all bags and items. This is the first hurdle. The second hurdle is then finding where our office is in the Courthouse to drop off the bid, and by the way, we are only open Monday to Friday – 8 a.m. to 5 p.m. and not in the office during lunch hours. The other option is to mail in the sealed bid, hoping that the United States Postal Service or another package delivery company like UPS or FedEx delivers your bid in time before the due date. I have seen multiple examples of lost bids in the mail system. It is not infallible.

Then there is the issue of access with paper-based solicitations. Typically, with paper-based solicitations, they are not widely distributed to vendors. There is usually a "vendor list" to send the solicitation to by email or the vendors are invited to pick up the solicitation on a website. So, if a vendor is not actively searching websites or is not lucky enough to be listed on a vendor list, the vendor will miss out on the opportunity to participate. This is not good for the vendor, but equally bad for the department as the pool of competitive bidders dwindles.

In 2014 the Idaho Legislature added Idaho Code § 31-871A allowing the retention of digital records to take the place of paper records. This statute helped to shape the digital transformation for our department and helped to lead the charge for an all-electronic department.

#### The Journey

With Idaho Code § 31-871A in place, the Procurement Department in 2016 set out to achieve two objectives: (1) migrate to a digital format for all paper records and

(2) transition to an e-procurement system. These two objectives would lead us down the path of being fully electronic in our department which at the time was geared toward saving paper and providing for the efficiencies and access mentioned earlier. The migration to a digital format was fairly simple. With the help of our Information Technology Department, we were able to set up shared network drives as our repository for digital records and there was a structured naming schema for all files and folders that all staff utilized for continuity and compatibility.

The second objective was not as easy. The Procurement Department did not have funding for an e-procurement solution. So a business plan of how to make this work needed to be developed. In October of 2017 a Request for Information (RFI) was issued from Ada County Procurement to canvas the marketplace for e-procurement solutions and costing for budgetary purposes. In response to the solicitation, Ada County received 11 proposals to help identify useful functionality and costs that the county might consider. With this information summarized, the Director of Procurement took to making a case for funding e-procurement to the FY2018 Budget Presentations before the Ada County Commissioners. The Commissioners unanimously agreed this was a great project to get our solicitations in front of more competition and to help our vendors with submitting their solicitations. They fully funded the project.

At the start of the county's new fiscal year in October of 2019, the Procurement Department issued an RFP for an e-procurement system. We decided early on in the scope of work development that we didn't want to put the financial burden on the bidders to "pay to play" so we were only interested in e-procurement systems that didn't charge the bidders for winning solicitations. RFP19032 was released for consideration and nine vendors responded. After careful consideration and evaluation, the selection team recommended the award of the contract to Bonfire Interactive.

The Procurement Department was ecstatic at the prospects of implementing a new e-procurement system to take the place of our archaic web/paper delivery. It only took two months to get Bonfire fully implemented and to start issuing our first e-procurement solicitations. E-procurement significantly changed our process for the better. It was efficient, accurate, and promoted a level of fairness for our vendors we didn't have before. What we didn't know at this time was that we had a six month head start to what would be a world-altering event, COVID.

COVID reared its head in Idaho in February of 2020. On March 16, 2020, the state of Idaho shut down businesses and non-essential work. Staff assigned to the Ada County Courthouse were forced out the doors, with very little notice and no plan in place, to the new norm – "Work from Home."

It was serendipitous for the Procurement Department as the electronic office was already put in motion, which was particularly suited for work from home. An internet connection was the lifeline of our work from home plan. From home we were able access our electronic shared network files, our Bonfire e-procurement platform, and we held meetings via WebEx. Procurement thrived in this environment. Ada County Procurement's continuity of operations was unfazed which allowed us to respond quickly to the call for COVID mitigation and the purchase of personal protective supplies for our employees. Procurement helped tremendously in the ongoing operations for all Ada County departments and offices. It felt good to be the department that others turned to for help to solve problems.

A major advantage to having an e-procurement system is the data that is readily available for analytics. Reports can be generated for various areas of interest such as spend, project savings, time to process solicitations, workload for procurement staff, and vendor information to name a few. These reports proved to be valuable in telling Procurement's story for budget setting. In justifying more staff, more dollars, and more resources to our Board of County Commissioners, these analytics were presented to showcase Procurement's workload and the volume of dollars that were being processed through our department. These analytics were compared to past analytics to illustrate the upward trend in procurement activity. This information helped to make the case for an additional buyer, more training dollars, and updated technology in our 2023 Budget Presentation.

One of the benefits of having an e-procurement system and an electronic office is that these are elements of a high functioning Procurement Department. The National Procurement Institute (NPI) recognizes exceptional procurement departments with their annual award the "Achievement of Excellence in Procurement", also known as the AEP Award. One of the benchmarks for this award is for the utilization of e-procurement systems in departments to improve efficiency. Having an e-procurement system puts the department in the upper echelon of procurement programs and was a factor in our successful application for the AEP Award. Ada County Procurement has been successful in being recognized for this award each year since 2021.

## Conclusion

E-procurement and the electronic office has been a monumental shift in our efficiency as a Procurement Department. As a Procurement Director for Idaho's largest county and a 30-year practitioner of government procurement, I have seen a lot of changes in the world of procurement. None is more impactful than e-procurement. Where paper solicitations, file cabinets, and banker boxes once adorned the procurement office space, it is now quickly becoming a bygone memory of the "good ole' days" – in its place stands e-procurement and the electronic office. Memories of the good ole days are fond, but I for one do not miss the paper cuts.

## Discussion Questions

What organizational, technological, and cultural factors contributed to Ada County's successful transition from a paper-based to an electronic procurement system, and how did leadership secure buy-in and funding for this digital transformation?

How did the implementation of e-procurement and digital recordkeeping enhance Ada County's resilience and continuity of operations during the COVID-19 pandemic, and what lessons does this provide for future emergency preparedness in public procurement?

In what ways can the use of data analytics generated through e-procurement systems strengthen accountability, performance management, and strategic decision-making in local government procurement operations?

### *Case Study: E-Procurement in the Commonwealth of Virginia (Developed by NASPO)*

The Commonwealth of Virginia is an experienced leader in the use of e-procurement systems and recently implemented a second iteration platform. The Commonwealth's legacy e-procurement platform was competitively solicited and awarded in 2000 and launched in 2001. For over 20 years, the platform has followed a carefully crafted project and program management plan to meet the Commonwealth's commitment to transparency and enhancing opportunities for suppliers. Savings achieved through administrative efficiencies and enhanced sourcing capabilities are approximately $25 million annually, with more than an 80% adoption rate by agencies and entities across the Commonwealth.[4]

On November 1, 2022, a new eVA software platform was launched. The robust online electronic procurement solution, branded by the Commonwealth and known as "eVA." eVA provides a single, centralized electronic portal for:

- all Commonwealth entities, including all local political subdivisions and higher education institutions, enabling them to source and acquire any goods and services required for their operations and mission;
- businesses to facilitate open competition and to provide tools to receive notifications, track and respond to business opportunities, and access order, contract, and billing information; and
- citizens by providing the Commonwealth's purchase and spending data that ensures that procurements are fair, open, and transparent.[5]

eVA's functionality, technical solutions, and multi-jurisdictional business model provide the Commonwealth with a comprehensive government-to-business and government-to-government electronic procurement solution that has contributed significantly to the Commonwealth's procurement process by providing consistent standards and modernizing procurement. eVA provides a fully integrated set of comprehensive electronic procurement and data analytics tools, which include the following:

- Supplier self-registration and portal
- Requisitioning, ordering, and receiving
- Unsealed/informal sourcing
- Sealed/formal sourcing
- Public posting and supplier notifications
- Contract management
- User, data, and entity management setup and maintenance
- Reporting (transparency), business intelligence analytics, and spend management
- Integration-interface to ERP financial systems
- Procurement data warehouse and data retention.

Additionally, eVA continues to be a data warehouse for the Commonwealth, including all historical and current data. When launching the new platform, a data conversion process was implemented that converted reference data (addresses, users, suppliers, custom workflow) and recent transactional data (requisitions, purchase orders, receipts, sourcing, contracts) into the new system that allowed staff to seamlessly continue workflows on the new eVA platform when it went live.

eVA integrates with multiple applications and interfaces to allow agencies to implement end-to-end information streams exchanging:

- requisition,
- purchase order,
- receipt,
- solicitation,
- supplier response/bid tabulation, and
- supplier account/profile data.

The eVA BizTalk server facilitates the exchange of 64 unique integrations that process transactions between eVA and external information systems.[6] The BizTalk server messaging engine supports an assortment of batch and real-time transactions. These systems implement the "hub-and-spoke" model such that eVA can accept integrations from many external systems and agencies without developing new or custom code. This allows for the easy assimilation of new entities into the Commonwealth's procurement practices.

As of 2023, eVA provides support to 245 Commonwealth entities, over 900 local public entities, and over 125,000 suppliers.[7] The eVA solution is a fully self-supporting service ("software-as-a-service" or "cloud solution") funded solely through nominal purchase order transaction fees collected by the Commonwealth from supplier and Commonwealth entities when an order is delivered for fulfillment. The Commonwealth continues to explore ways to improve its e-procurement platform to help align suppliers with business opportunities and improve workflows.

**Discussion Questions**

How has Virginia's eVA system transformed procurement transparency, efficiency, and supplier engagement across state and local entities, and what lessons can other states learn from its long-term implementation and modernization?

What are the potential benefits and risks of funding an e-procurement system through transaction-based fees from vendors and entities, and how might this model affect participation and equity among suppliers?

In what ways does eVA's integrated data and analytics capability enhance strategic sourcing, accountability, and policy decision-making within the Commonwealth's public procurement framework?

# 21 Unlocking Procurement's Potential Using Robotic Process Automation, Artificial Intelligence, Machine Learning, and Blockchain Technologies

*Godfrey Mugurusi, Marius Langseth, Sarah Eyaa and Moutaz Haddara*

## 21.1 Introduction

Imagine a future where efficient, innovative public procurement spurs societal progress. This chapter introduces the digital revolution currently happening within the public sector; it focuses on the impact of emerging technologies such as bots, artificial intelligence (AI), machine learning (ML), big data and data analytics, and blockchain in public procurement systems. The chapter aims to demonstrate that these technologies do not just enhance process efficiency; they reshape the public procurement landscape, making processes more transparent, accountable, and effective.

As we explore the transformative potential of these technologies, we invite you to envision how digital tools can turn conventional procurement into a strategic asset that propels economic and social advancements. It is precisely for this reason that digitalization and digital transformation have been advanced as a solution for clogged public procurement systems to improve procurement decision-making, lower administrative costs, and increase process transparency (OECD, 2019). In addition, the pressure to do more with less and the growing public demand for high-quality public services amidst shrinking public sector budgets have placed a spotlight on leveraging emerging technologies toward a more efficient public procurement system through the digital transformation of the end-to-end procurement cycle. Empirical evidence shows that digital transformation in public procurement will enable substantially faster procurement processes, better risk management, and provide higher-quality, less-expensive goods and services for the public (Pappianou & Spencer, 2019).

There is evidence that emerging technologies are already being used extensively in public procurement, including:

- AI and ML are being used in demand forecasting and spend categorization (Guida et al., 2023)
- big data and data analytics are used in business intelligence, data aggregation, and price analysis (Deloitte-EU report, 2020)
- robotic process automation (RPA) is used for automating repetitive procurement administrative tasks such as purchase order administration and inventory monitoring (Flechsig et al., 2022)
- distributed ledger technologies (blockchain) for end-to-end visibility and supplier onboarding (Sánchez, 2019).

DOI: 10.4324/9781003566670-25

Therefore, to promote a deeper understanding of digital transformation in public procurement, this chapter attempts to:

- Define digital transformation in the public procurement context.
- Explain how public procurement can leverage technology to eliminate opportunities for inefficiency and corruption and encourage fair, transparent, and efficient public spending practices.
- Locate and present some examples of digital transformation across the entire public procurement cycle – and describe the adoption strategies in each of those examples.
- Identify some of the challenges associated with digital transformation projects in public procurement.

In the following sections, we introduce and explain each of the emerging technologies and offer projections of how they will influence public procurement. We conclude with some practical case-based examples to emphasize certain areas of technology adoption in public procurement, offering insights for education and practice.

## 21.2 Digital Transformation in the Public Procurement

First and foremost, it is important to unpack the concept of "digital transformation," which is often tangled with digitization and digitalization (McKinsey, 2023). "*Digitization*" refers to the conversion of analog processes into digital ones, while "*digitalization*" refers to the use of digital and data-based technologies to improve work processes and change how customers and companies engage and interact with each other (Mugurusi et al., 2021). "*Digital transformation*" is a much broader concept than digitization and digitalization, as shown in Table 21.1. It involves entirely rethinking how an organization uses technology, people, and processes in pursuit of new business models and mechanisms of value capture driven by changes in customer expectations around its products or services (Morakanyane et al., 2017).

*Table 21.1* Digitization vs. digitalization vs. digital transformation

| | *Digitization* | *Digitalization* | *Digital transformation* |
|---|---|---|---|
| **Goal** | Change analog to digital | Automate existing business processes | Changing how the company's routines and its processes work |
| **Focus** | Data conversion | Information processing and process adaptation | Leveraging knowledge and business model rethinking |
| **Activity** | Digitizing physical resources | Creating full digital workflow process | Creating a new digital company |
| **Capabilities** | Systems management | Service management | Digital leadership |
| **Tools** | Computers and conversion equipment | IT systems and computer applications | New (disruptive) digital technologies |
| **Challenges** | Material | Financial | Resistance to change. |
| **Outputs** | Sporadic automation and innovation | Efficiency and effectiveness | New types of value |
| **Example** | Scanning paper-based registration forms | A complete electronic registration process | Everything electronic, from registration to content delivery |

*Source*: https://quixy.com/blog/digitization-digitalization-and-digital-transformation/

Digital transformation means organizations change their value creation model through new digital products or service models built around technology. A more nuanced understanding of digital transformation is described by Khanna et al. (2020) using the concept of a "digital factory" where:

> *Top executives from a North American bank entered a converted warehouse run by a European telecom giant; they couldn't believe what they were seeing. Engineers were live coding in small teams with designers and business people and reviewing the results right away with customers. They were making adjustments to feedback on the fly. They were launching products and marketing campaigns at record speed, and data were available quickly for rapid adjustments—and everyone was clear on their priorities, which were displayed in simple metrics on their team boards. The CEO of the bank team turned to his colleagues and said, this is what we need.*

We have elected to define "digital transformation in the public procurement" *as a holistic, often gradual, development of public procurement capacity and resources using digital tools and technologies to meet the growing complexity of public sector needs in a more economically, socially, and environmentally efficient way.*

Our definition underscores a deeper and more specific understanding of how public procurement has evolved and integrated legacy e-procurement systems with new disruptive technologies to improve procurement efficiency, increase participation in public tenders, enhance transparency and accountability, and eliminate corruption blind spots.

Within the public procurement context, digital transformation is based on system-wide, often nationwide, digitalization models. Such models include legacy e-government initiatives that target national development objectives such as enhancing public service delivery, human capital, private sector development, gender empowerment, and the green transition. It was from such models that the 1st-generation e-procurement platforms were built to address mundane elements of the procure-to-pay cycle (Basheka et al., 2012). "E-procurement" involves the integration of digital technologies to replace or redesign paper-based procedures throughout the procurement cycle (OECD, 2019). The goal of e-procurement was similar to that of digitization described in Table 21.1. These 1st-generation e-procurement platforms are well-established in most countries around the world.

The current 2nd generation of digital procurement systems tapped into the 1st-generation platforms, which generated huge amounts of unsystematized data. Today's 2nd-generation systems focus on end-to-end process automation to ensure all procurement workflows are fully integrated. These additional functionalities integrate public procurement's financial systems with external factors such as business registries, banks, insurance companies, and tax/custom systems into a seamless ecosystem to provide a highly efficient and one-stop interface between suppliers and the government (OECD, 2016).

South Korea's KONEPS is one good example of a 2nd-generation e-procurement system. According to Dener (2019), KONEPS, which stands for "Korea ON-line E-Procurement System," is an electronically integrated end-to-end procurement system allowing about 140 external systems to share and retrieve information in real-time, providing a one-stop service for the automatic collection of bidders' qualification data, delivery reporting, e-invoicing, and e-payment. In 2017, about 88% of all public procurement transactions in Korea were conducted through KONEPs. In 2012, 45,000 public entities interacted with 244,000 registered suppliers, showing huge potential for big data to digitally transform the entire public procurement system (OECD, 2016).

The Deloitte-EU report (2020) presented several examples of technology applications within public procurement involving the use of AI, ML, big data, data analytics, blockchain, RPA, augmented and virtual reality, the Internet of Things, and drones. This chapter will focus specifically on AI/ML, blockchain, and RPA technologies. We shall demonstrate how these could be the game-changer for innovative and efficient public services. From healthcare, welfare and housing, education, and transport to water utilities, digital transformation in public procurement will ease the availability, quality, and usability of public sector services. Most importantly, digital transformation has been hailed as an important cost-saver for many public sector programs due to improvements in public procurement spending management.

## 21.3 Opportunities in Leveraging Digital Tools and Technology within Public Procurement

Digital transformation extends beyond mere automation of tasks, including revolutionary procurement execution and management. For example, the use of big data and data analytics in public procurement provides valuable insights for decision-making, risk management, and performance evaluation. Data analytics promotes transparency, efficiency, and fairness in public procurement (Radu, 2020). This section examines specific technologies and how technology-driven interventions can support transparency, curb corruption, and facilitate efficient spending practices within public procurement. The benefits of leveraging technology across the procurement process include:

a. *Enhanced transparency:* Technology empowers public procurement actors with real-time visibility into procurement activities. E-procurement platforms, for instance, facilitate digital documentation and traceability of each stage in the procurement lifecycle. This enables stakeholders and the public to monitor and scrutinize the process, curbing the potential for hidden or non-competitive dealings (Mynenko & Lyulyov, 2022). Currently, blockchain technology, with its immutable and decentralized data features, has the potential to further reinforce transparency by ensuring that procurement records remain tamper-proof and auditable (Čeke et al., 2022).
b. *Mitigates the risk of corruption:* The integration of technology into procurement minimizes corruption risks by reducing discretionary decision-making. Automated procurement systems streamline processes, reducing opportunities for favoritism, bribery, and embezzlement. Data analytics and AI-powered tools can detect irregular patterns, anomalies, or collusion, thus flagging potential instances of corruption for investigation. Moreover, electronic marketplaces and e-tendering platforms promote open competition, discouraging corrupt practices such as bid rigging.
c. *Promotes fair competition:* Technology-driven procurement pulls down barriers to entry and fosters broader participation, thereby promoting fair competition among vendors. E-marketplaces, in particular, provide a level playing field for suppliers, allowing small and medium-sized enterprises (SMEs) to compete alongside larger firms. Reverse auctions and dynamic pricing mechanisms further drive efficiency and fairness by optimizing costs while avoiding favoritism.
d. *Driving efficiency and value for money (VfM):* Automation expedites the procurement process, reducing administrative bottlenecks and delays. Electronic catalogs and online vendor databases facilitate efficient supplier management and procurement planning. Data-driven insights from spend analytics enable informed decision-making and strategic

sourcing, leading to optimal allocation of resources and cost savings that contribute to VfM objectives.

e. *Enhanced accountability:* Technology-enabled procurement fosters accountability by establishing clear audit trails and an accountability chain. Electronic signatures, digital records, and time-stamped documentation assure accountability in each step of the procurement process. Moreover, e-procurement systems enable seamless access to historical procurement data, aiding in retrospective audits and performance assessments.

The fusion of emerging technologies within public procurement has high transformative potential, eliminating corruption, promoting fairness, and driving efficient spending practices. However, there are also concerns about cybersecurity and low digital literacy in the public sector, which may counter the benefits of technology-driven procurement (Langseth & Haddara, 2024). In this section, we discuss the unique characteristics and applications of RPA, AI/ML, and blockchain technologies.

### *21.3.1 Robotic Process Automation (RPA)*

Briefly, RPA systems involve different software types that automate repetitive, rule-based tasks traditionally performed by humans. They use software robots ("bots") to execute predefined sequences of actions across various applications, just as a human would do (Lacity & Willcocks, 2016).

There is evidence that bots have been used in procure-to-pay processes in public organizations, significantly increasing process efficiency and accuracy. Flechsig et al. (2022) cite cases where bots have been used to streamline administrative tasks such as the creation of requests for quotation and purchase orders, communication, and supplier categorization, which are classified as either high-volume tasks (i.e., many transactions) or with low complexity levels (i.e., little human interaction).

Lintukangas (2017) suggests that high-volume, standardized, and mature procurement processes such as supplier selection, order approvals, invoicing, order tracking, and supplier performance management are the best candidates for RPA because they are well-documented, stable, and predictable.

Hidayanti et al. (2022, 665), who define RPA as "virtual people that are infinitely scalable and can be programmed to conduct operational tasks at machine speed," argue that RPA tools are most relevant for procurement audits as they can web scrap, clean, and process all types of data on tenders, making it easy to monitor fraud and irregular procurement behavior and enhance transparency.

By automating these processes, Lintukangas (2017) shows that RPA can reduce human error, eliminate duplicative tasks, reduce human capital costs, and allow procurement officials to focus on more strategic tasks. RPA also reduces the risk of corruption by limiting human intervention in rule-based procurement processes, thus reducing the opportunities for manipulation and fraudulent activities (Hidayanti et al., 2023). Beyond operational tasks, Engel et al. (2022) introduce something described as "robotic cognitive automation" (RCA), where RCA combines the efficiency of RPA with the decision-making capabilities of cognitive computing, enabling more sophisticated automation of procurement tasks. RCA targets high-level procurement tasks that require understanding and interpretation of specific data points, such as supplier evaluation and contract negotiation, for the bot to propose an accurate decision. This way, purchasers can make complex decisions based on accurate evidence, further enhancing procurement's strategic role in public organizations (Langseth, 2024). In addition, RPA frees purchasers to focus on high-impact tasks, which increases their legitimacy (Viale & Zouari, 2020).

However, there are downsides to RPA in procurement. Lintukangas (2017) cites the tedious training and staff retraining, the increase in workloads around the quality of base data, and the organizational pressure to keep up with automation speed. Among the 25 barriers to RPA adoption, Flechsig et al. (2022) identified some specific technical and organizational risks, such as the increased complexity and error susceptibility due to the multiplicity of data formats, interfaces, and IT systems involved; employee resistance and capital costs; and limited supplier collaboration in automation projects.

### *21.3.2 Artificial Intelligence and Machine Learning (AI and ML)*

AI refers to various types of systems that can emulate human thought and take adaptive actions in a real-world environment; ML refers to the methods and algorithms that enable AI systems to identify patterns, make decisions, and improve themselves through all sources of input data (Sun et al., 2024).

ML is among various subfields of AI that include, among others, natural language processing, large language models, and computer vision. Unlike RPA, AI/ML tools learn from experience, making decisions and solving complex problems with almost human-like intelligence (Russell & Norvig, 2010).

AI and ML applications offer numerous possibilities for procurement by automating repetitive tasks and analyzing vast amounts of data to identify patterns, predict trends, and optimize procurement strategies. Guida et al. (2023) cite examples where AI/ML applications are used for demand forecasting and spend categorization, facilitating efficient allocation of resources and strategic procurement decisions. AI tools analyze historical data and market trends to determine the optimal timing and pricing for procurement. Additionally, AI/ML algorithms detect anomalies in procurement data that might indicate fraudulent activities, thereby enhancing the accountability and integrity of the procurement process. Woschank et al. (2020) explore AI/ML applications in smart manufacturing, where these technologies significantly improve the efficiency and effectiveness of procurement processes by enabling real-time tracking of goods, predictive maintenance of equipment, and optimized inventory management. This reduces operational costs and improves procurement performance. Moreover, AI and ML have shown high levels of risk classification accuracy (>90%), which translates into reliable prediction of potential risks and challenges, such as supplier defaults or price fluctuations, thus enabling procurement professionals to take proactive measures to mitigate these risks (Aldana et al., 2022). AI/ML can identify specific patterns of decision-making and reduce human error, enhancing procurement efficiency (Aran et al., 2020).

However, recent literature suggests using AI/ML applications in procurement may also have downsides. Mugurusi and Oluka (2021) note that AI can make procurement decisions harder to verify and validate, contradicting procurement principles of integrity, transparency, and fairness.

To address issues of algorithmic opacity, new research on explainable artificial intelligence (XAI) has emerged. These studies advance techniques, processes, and strategies that provide explanations for predictions, recommendations, and decisions made by opaque and complex AI/ML systems.

### *21.3.3 Blockchain and Distributed Digital Ledger Technologies*

Distributed ledger technology (DLT) refers to a system where users spread across several computing devices (i.e., nodes) store and access information in a shared database (i.e., the ledger) without a central validation system (Kakavand et al., 2017). Blockchain is a form of distributed DLT that's been defined as "a distributed, shared, encrypted database that serves as an irreversible and incorruptible repository of information" (Kakavand et al., 2017, 4). The purpose of DLTs is to ensure transparency, security, and immutability of data in a shared database, making them particularly useful in distributed decision-making domains such as finance and supply chain management (Tapscott & Tapscott, 2016). Blockchains ensure that every action taken by different procurement actors is recorded and cannot be altered retrospectively. This feature enhances accountability and makes it difficult for corrupt practices to go unnoticed (Sánchez, 2019). Blockchains can serve as a powerful tool to combat corruption and promote transparency. According to Tapscott and Tapscott (2016), blockchain's decentralized nature makes it inherently resistant to data manipulation, thereby reducing the risk of fraudulent activities. Furthermore, the study argues that blockchain's transparency can deter corruption by making it easier to detect irregularities in procurement processes. Moreover, blockchains facilitate secure, transparent, and efficient supplier onboarding, contract management, and payment processes. This eliminates potential loopholes for corruption and ensures fair competition. Mougayar and Buterin (2016) find that blockchains streamline procurement processes by automating contract execution and ensuring the integrity of financial transactions. For public procurement, where open solicitation and tendering are critical, blockchain technology can help promote fair market competition where more suppliers may participate. Treiblmaier (2018) notes that blockchains can enhance competition in procurement by providing a transparent and tamper-proof record of all bids, preventing favoritism, and ensuring that contracts are awarded based on merit. However, the implementation of blockchain technology in public procurement is not without challenges. According to Mistry and Tan (2019), technical issues, lack of understanding, and regulatory barriers are among the main obstacles to the adoption of blockchain in public procurement.

While blockchain technology has many potential benefits, such as creating immutable and accountable transactions and facilitating secure, open, competitive, and efficient processes, policymakers must create an environment where public managers understand and trust blockchains across the procurement system.

Whilst the three technologies in Sections 21.3.1, 21.3.2, and 21.3.3 are discussed separately, they can also be integrated across an entire public procurement value chain. For instance, RPA and AI can be combined to create an intelligent, automated solution across the entire purchase-to-pay process (Davenport & Ronanki, 2018). Similarly, blockchains can be integrated with AI to create transparent and secure AI-based procurement platforms (Ferrag et al., 2021).

Table 21.2 summarizes the possible benefits and use cases for RPA, AI/ML, and blockchain in public procurement. We have also shown that leveraging these technologies in public procurement also poses challenges. These include data security and privacy concerns, the need for significant investments in technology and skills development, and resistance to change among procurement officials and stakeholders. Moreover, implementing these technologies requires rethinking procurement policies, processes, and systems to accommodate new digital tools and capabilities. Very few governments have a comprehensive approach to digital transformation in public procurement, which requires policy reform, capacity building, and change management. As Firouzi et al. (2021) noted, these technologies can be harnessed to tackle global challenges and create a better world, including transforming public procurement for the better.

*Table 21.2* A summary of the benefits and challenges of different technologies in public procurement

| *Technology* | *Characteristics and benefits* | *Challenges* | *Use cases in public procurement* |
|---|---|---|---|
| Robotic process automation | Automates repetitive, rule-based operational tasks using software robots.<br>Reduces costs and human error, increases efficiency and accuracy; frees procurement resources. | – Ambiguity in rules, IT interfaces, and data formats<br>– Tedious and continuous staff training<br>– High initial investment costs.<br>– Employee resistance<br>– Difficulty in establishing stable data environments. | – Streamline high volume, standardized, and mature tasks like inventory monitoring, order approvals, and supplier performance management.<br>– Procurement auditing and monitoring errors and irregular procurement decisions.<br>– Web scraping, processing and cleaning tender data using Root Cause Analysis (RCA) allowing for efficient cognitive interpretation. |
| Artificial intelligence and machine learning | Machines or software that mimic human intelligence.<br>Capable of learning, decision-making, and problem-solving. | – Low digital maturity in public procurement<br>– Limited AI capabilities and technical expertise<br>– Low quality and quantity of data<br>– Incompatible organization cultures<br>– Concerns on security and confidentiality<br>– Data governance issues | – Enhance demand forecasting and spend categorization.<br>– Detect anomalies and fraudulent activities in procurement processes.<br>– Implement explainable AI for intricate procurement decisions.<br>– Real-time tracking of market prices.<br>– Predict potential risks such as supplier defaults or price fluctuations. |
| Blockchains | Decentralized digital ledger that securely records transactions.<br>Ensures transparency, security, and immutability: deter corruption. | – Demand significant computational power to maintain.<br>– Few validated blockchain pilots in public procurement<br>– Incompatibility with existing e-procurement legacy systems<br>– Organizational reluctance to use the blockchain.<br>– Absence of unified governance and regulatory standards | – Create an immutable record of each procurement transaction for record keeping,<br>– Automate and secure supplier onboarding, contract management, and payment processes.<br>– Transparent and tamper-proof recording of all bids to prevent favoritism.<br>– Use in supplier verification processes<br>– Track procurement spend vs. organizational budgets |

*Source*: Original creation.

## 21.4 Challenges and Risks of Digital Transformation Projects in Public Procurement

Digital transformation projects in public procurement can bring about numerous benefits, but they also come with a range of challenges that can hinder their successful implementation.

This is often compounded by the public sector context, whose features make it structurally different from the private sector. According to Mikalsen and Farshchian (2020), public sector digital transformation projects must take into account several crucial factors and stakeholders, such as users, citizens, a wide range of systems, institutional cultures, and broader societal goals. These factors, together with their competing demands, further complicate the process.

In the next subsections, we discuss some institutional and technical challenges that organizations may face during digital transformation projects in public procurement. In one area, we highlight how the public procurement context further exacerbates the potential challenges of digital transformation.

### *21.4.1 Institutional Challenges*

- *The complexity of processes and systems:* Digital transformation in public procurement requires translating various legacy processes into new systems, which presents significant challenges due to interoperability problems, regulatory demands, and the need for alignment between processes and IT systems (Mugurusi et al., 2022). This complexity, heightened by the intricate nature of procurement workflows and multiple stakeholders, often makes technology-enabled implementations very burdensome (Mikalsen & Farshchian, 2020).
- *Resistance to change:* Shifting to digital requires changes in technology, processes, roles, and culture, often met with resistance from employees used to traditional methods. Successful digital adoption requires a comprehensive change management program, which includes clear communication, training, and proactive stakeholder engagement, to address concerns, build ownership, and highlight the benefits of digitalization. Public sector digital efforts must reflect the organization's mission and values to ensure buy-in from users (Moser-Plautz & Schmidthuber, 2023).
- *Cultural and competency shifts:* Beyond technological adoption, digital transformation in public organizations requires a cultural shift toward the development of new IT competencies. Investment in new tools means a change in the work sub-culture. This involves changing mindsets, adopting innovative work practices, and navigating the complexities of professional development and talent management to support transformation initiatives (Leal-Rodríguez et al., 2023).
- *Legacy systems and integration:* Legacy systems and integration challenges significantly obstruct digitalization efforts in the public sector, mainly due to outdated, monolithic systems (Irani et al., 2023). We discuss interoperability in the next subsection, but these challenges stem from incompatibilities in data formats, protocols, and architectures, which can block data flow and impede the benefits of digitalization. Additionally, the inflexibility of legacy systems complicates adapting to the rapidly changing digital landscape, making integration both complex and costly. Overcoming these obstacles is crucial for governments to fully leverage digital transformation and ensure the seamless transition and continuity of critical services (Irani et al., 2023).
- *Lack of skilled workforce:* Public organizations embracing digital transformation often face a critical shortage of professionals with the digital skills necessary for its implementation and management, such as data analytics and cybersecurity. This gap hinders the effectiveness of digital initiatives in the public sector. Addressing this issue requires investments in training, partnerships with educational institutions, and fostering a culture of continuous learning to equip employees with next-generation digital competencies. Without overcoming this challenge, the full benefits of digitalization may remain unattainable (Van Veldhoven & Vanthienen, 2022).

- *Regulatory compliance:* The shift to digital technologies (e.g., AI) in the public sector brings complex legal and regulatory challenges, especially in data privacy, protection, and security, as entities adopt digital data management (Gabryelczyk, 2020). Balancing digital advancement against the need to protect sensitive data and comply with changing laws is a significant hurdle. The variability of regulations across different regions also adds to the difficulty of creating consistent digital strategies. However, with effective governance, strong data protection, and proactive risk management, public sector organizations can navigate these challenges, align digital initiatives with legal requirements, and build public trust in their digital transformation efforts (Reier Forradellas & Garay Gallastegui, 2021).

### 21.4.2 *Technical Challenges*

- *Data security and privacy:* As governments adopt digital technologies to improve operations and services, managing and securing the vast, sensitive amounts of data they collect, store, and share becomes crucial. The rise in digital activity heightens the risk of data breaches and cyberattacks. Balancing data accessibility with strong security measures is critical to protect against these risks (Sestino et al., 2023). As the cyber threats landscape evolves, public entities must both harden security measures and embrace new and innovative digital approaches. Effectively addressing these security and privacy challenges is essential for maintaining public trust and advancing digital government initiatives.
- *Vendor lock-in and interoperability:* Adopting digital solutions, in particular cloud infrastructures, often leads to reliance on third-party vendors, which has risks of vendor lock-in and limiting flexibility for public sector organizations (Øverdal et al., 2022). Interoperability challenges compound lock-in problems as providers gain unique knowledge across multiple systems and processes (Mugurusi et al., 2022). The lack of standardization impedes information flow and collaboration, which is crucial for effective decision-making. Addressing these issues through open standards, sharing application programming interfaces (APIs), and modular designs can enhance flexibility and efficiency in digitalization efforts in the public sector (Bousdekis & Kardaras, 2020).

## 21.5 Challenges Unique to the Public Procurement Context

While the organizational and technical challenges presented are arguably universal, highlighting the challenges of digital transformation projects in the public sector, the uniqueness of the public procurement context may frame different types of challenges and even risks that affect the success of digitalization projects at the procurement level. By public procurement context, we refer to the environment within which public procurement activities and events occur. It is characterized by three overarching factors, that is: (a) a stringent regulatory framework that dictates the process, spend thresholds, the scope of contract awards, and how the market must respond to the needs of the buyers (Mikalsen & Farshchian, 2020). (b) Multiple stakeholders with high and diverse expectations. From government agencies, employees, suppliers, and taxpayers to the public, each with its unique demands (Leal-Rodríguez et al., 2023). And (c) a highly dynamic market in which the public sector has to compete for prices and technology with other private actors (Van Veldhoven & Vanthienen, 2022).

As a result, the following challenges and risks can be attributed to that procurement context alone.

- *Data fragmentation*: Procurement-related information often exists in disparate systems, ontologies, and formats, making data integration and management across the entire procurement ecosystem extremely difficult. This fragmentation has been cited as one major barrier to data-driven decision-making in public procurement (Langseth, 2024).
- *Complex vendor management*: Managing relationships with multiple technology vendors presents vendor lock-in, interoperability, and technological alignment problems. Effective vendor management strategies are necessary to mitigate these risks and ensure successful digital transformation (Øverdal et al., 2022).
- *Trust and ethical concerns*: There is a general anxiety among procurement practitioners that digitalization will directly translate into job losses, diminished value of their work, and loss of acquired skills. Other stakeholders have deep-seated concerns, such as data privacy and surveillance. According to Craglia et al. (2020), building and maintaining trust with all stakeholders, including suppliers and the public, is critical for the success of digital initiatives.

The procurement context involves unique challenges distinct from broader technical and institutional issues. By understanding these challenges, public sector organizations can effectively navigate the complexities of digital transformation in public procurement.

## 21.6 Strategies to Address the Challenges in Public Procurements' Digital Transformation Projects

In navigating the complex landscape of digital transformation, public procurement actors encounter a myriad of challenges that span technological, organizational, and procedural dimensions. To effectively mitigate these challenges, we found some strategies in the literature that have been categorized across three main areas: technology-oriented, organization-oriented, and process-oriented strategies. Each area addresses specific aspects of the digital transformation journey, offering a roadmap for public entities to achieve procurement digitalization objectives while minimizing the associated risks and obstacles presented in Section 21.3. The proposed strategies are not intended as a recipe for digital transformation projects but rather as examples and an overview of the main strategies and actions that can be relevant for successful digital transitions in public procurement.

### *21.6.1 Technology-Oriented Strategies*

The heart of digital transformation lies in the adoption and integration of advanced and complex technologies, most often alongside people and existing processes and systems. The technology-oriented strategies we discuss here emphasize the selection, implementation, and management of digital tools and platforms that align and fit with the organization's goals and user needs. This approach not only focuses on deploying cutting-edge solutions but also ensures that the technology infrastructure is robust, secure, and scalable. By prioritizing technological readiness and innovation, public organizations can overcome technical barriers, enhance service delivery, and foster a culture of continuous improvement. Below are examples of the technology-related strategies that organizations can implement.

- *Ensuring IT-organization alignment:* In digital transformation projects, aligning IT and organizational requirements and strategies is crucial for success. According to Daidj (2022), digital transformation influences the alignment between business and IT, which supports operational efficiency and facilitates strategic innovation. From a procurement perspective, a seamless IT–procurement alignment means it is easier to monitor compliance and simplify third-party integration processes, such as supplier identification and onboarding. These are important measures for public procurement in the digital era. IT governance mechanisms and frameworks can aid in successful transformations (Mulyana et al., 2021).
- *Adoption of open, interoperable, and scalable solutions:* Emphasizing the need for open technologies that follow international standards and ensure compatibility and scalability is paramount for addressing future growth and integration challenges (Fernández-Rovira et al., 2021). The basic principles of public procurement are transparency and competition. Open and interoperable solutions enable high-quality data for better data-driven decision-making, increasing overall competition and transparency in the public sector supply chains. These factors are fundamental for effective risk management in procurement.
- *Risk management and cybersecurity measures:* As digital processes increase, so do potential cybersecurity threats. Public procurement holds critical assets such as vendor contracts and supplier master data. In the event of a data breach, entire public sector supply chains and service utilities can be disrupted. Public organizations must prioritize risk management strategies and invest in robust cybersecurity measures to protect sensitive information, as they are the basis for maintaining public trust (Stewart, 2023).
- *Integration of advanced analytics and AI:* Utilizing analytics and AI on all levels can enhance operations and decision-making processes. The use of analytics can help refine procurement processes, enable more informed decisions, improve resource optimization, and improve efficiency (Sousa & Rocha, 2019). Employing data-driven insights for strategic decision-making can optimize procurement outcomes and tailor procurement strategies to meet organizational needs more effectively (Parviainen et al., 2017).

### *21.6.2 Organization-Oriented Strategies*

Organization-oriented strategies concentrate on building internal capabilities, culture, and structures needed to support digital initiatives. For procurement, this includes nurturing digital literacy among employees, fostering leadership commitment, and promoting a culture of agility and innovation. By focusing on the human and structural aspects, the following strategies can reduce resistance to change, enhance collaboration, and ensure that digital transformation efforts are closely aligned with organizational values and objectives:

- *Develop a strategic digital transformation framework:* A strategic digital transformation framework defines an organization's roadmap toward digital transformation, ensuring a cohesive transformation across all organizational dimensions (Zaoui & Souissi, 2021). In public procurement, such a framework mirrors a national digital transformation framework, defining what kind of people, capabilities, and technologies are required for procurement to function effectively in the near or long term. Such a framework supports digital processes and establishes dedicated digital roles or teams (Pedersen, 2018).
- *Top management support and leadership:* The organization's top management must provide clear leadership and a vision for digital transformation, outlining the strategic importance and expected outcomes of digitalization projects (Bresciani et al., 2021).

Good leadership creates an optimal working environment for procurement to function effectively. Top management support is essential for defining resource needs and orchestrating the transmission of knowledge between top leadership members and procurement people. Studies suggest this factor alone minimizes resistance to change.

- *Develop digital skills and promote a digital culture:* Building a digitally adept workforce through training and continuous learning enhances digital literacy across the organization and reduces the lack of skills challenge (Parviainen et al., 2017). Procurement flourishes in a culture that supports digital innovation backed by leadership and effective communication (Trenerry et al., 2021).
- *Foster collaboration and stakeholder engagement:* Promoting active collaboration, communication, and engagement among stakeholders, including suppliers, regulators, and procurement professionals, can enhance the adoption of digital strategies and ensure a more inclusive digital transformation process (Mariani & Bianchi, 2023). In addition, providing training programs, continuous communication, and engaging employees at all levels of the organization ensures buy-in and support for digitalization projects, mitigating resistance and facilitating smoother transitions (Datta, 2020).
- *Ensure legal compliance and ethical standards:* Adopting legal and regulatory frameworks that align with digital procurement activities is critical to ensure compliance and uphold ethical standards. Regular audits and compliance checks can safeguard against legal breaches and maintain integrity (Ghobakhloo & Iranmanesh, 2021).

### *21.6.3 Process-Oriented Strategies*

Until now, the emphasis has generally been on the efficiencies of process automation, data analytics, and technology organization. But do public procurement processes have the capacity and maturity to withstand the density and complexity of emerging technologies? Digital transformation demands a rethinking of traditional processes and workflows to fully leverage digital efficiencies. Process-oriented strategies involve the re-engineering of business processes to optimize performance, improve user experience, and eliminate inefficiencies. By adopting the process-oriented strategies below, public procurement can achieve greater operational agility, responsiveness, and resilience in the face of changing digital landscapes.

- *Process mapping, optimization, and then automation:* Before implementing new digital tools, public procurement organizations should undertake comprehensive process mapping. This involves identifying all existing processes, evaluating their efficiency gaps, and pinpointing areas for improvement before considering automation. Process optimization can lead to significant improvements in service delivery and operational efficiency (Kane, 2019).
- *Enhance user experience:* Digital transformation is expected to improve customer experiences in public organizations by blending technology with customer service functions. It plays a crucial role in attracting and retaining customers by meeting their evolving needs through new technologies and restructured organizational processes (Shojaei, 2022). These strategies not only enhance operational efficiency and innovation in value creation but also boost sales and customer engagement, giving organizations a competitive advantage (Masoud & Basahel, 2023).
- *Iterative improvement and feedback loops:* Implementing a culture of continuous improvement, where feedback is actively sought and used to make iterative improvements to digital processes, can significantly enhance the effectiveness of digital transformation

*Table 21.3* Summary of strategies to address the challenges and risks in public procurement's digital transformation projects

| *Technology-oriented strategies* | *Organization-oriented strategies* | *Process-oriented strategies* |
|---|---|---|
| – IT-organization alignment<br>– Open standards and systems<br>– Security and privacy measures<br>– Comprehensive e-procurement platforms<br>– Data analytics and AI | – Top-management support<br>– Strategic digital transformation framework<br>– Promoting digital culture<br>– Stakeholder engagement and collaboration<br>– Legal and ethical compliance | – Process management and optimization<br>– Agile and lean methodologies<br>– Design thinking<br>– Enhancing user experience<br>– Feedback loops and KPIs |

*Source*: Original creation.

efforts (Bharadwaj et al., 2013). Key performance indicators (KPIs) also play a crucial role in the digital transformation of public organizations, guiding the transition and measuring its success. For example, Behrens et al. (2023) highlight the importance of automation, efficiency gains, and financial metrics as KPIs in assessing the success of digital transformation efforts, indicating a broad applicability of these measures across various sectors (Table 21.3).

## 21.7 Emerging Issues

In this chapter, we have outlined the benefits and challenges of digital transformation in public procurement using three examples: RPA, AI, and blockchain. We also touched on some consequences of digital transformation, including cybersecurity risks such as hacking, data breaches, and cyber espionage, which could disrupt procurement activities.

There are various answered questions about the digitalization of public procurement processes, which we will outline below as emerging issues, namely:

- How might public procurement digitalization projects interact with the various degrees of digital maturity found in public institutions and, maybe, in different nations? There are suggestions that this will become an even more problematic issue in the future due to fragmented digital strategies at the macro level, low digital skills, and limited interoperability, which in turn reduce the ability to leverage shared data, resulting in a more complex environment for suppliers.
- How will public procurement ensure effective data quality and data governance? This is going to be important given that AI and ML algorithms are data hogs that require enormous amounts of data and data sets from which to learn. Already, public procurement systems face issues with data accuracy and consistency, which lead to algorithmic biases and errors, hence, poor-quality decisions. Suggestions show that poor data governance practices will be a big problem, resulting in reduced trust in the procurement process. The other concern is that the race to implement stringent data governance frameworks in order to ensure high data quality may relegate procurement roles to more operational work and procurement to a check-box function.
- How will digital transformation projects affect the professional development of the procurement function and the public procurement skill set of the future? The projected

job losses aside, there are already emerging suggestions (e.g., Pappianou & Spencer, 2019) that new technologies will change the future skills and knowledge of procurement officials, and yet today's procurement professionals appear little prepared for such leaps.

- How will the public procurement digitalization projects be funded? Already, public procurement budgets have been shrinking gradually. Digitalization suggests a complete overhaul of outdated procurement infrastructure that may not easily be compatible with advanced technology solutions on the market today. This may mean high initial costs and a burden to the taxpayer.
- How will the public sector integrate and onboard its disparate suppliers onto its digital procurement platforms? Onboarding a very diverse group of suppliers with varying levels of technological proficiency will definitely become a major problem. There are already calls to use a government service bus and open APIs, but these also require that internal procurement processes be well-standardized to simplify digital supplier onboarding. Dener (2019) argues that most public sector processes are not yet there because of the disjointed nature of e-government systems, let alone e-public procurement systems.
- Are private-sector targeted tools and software suitable and robust enough for the public sector? Most initial tools and software on the market today are often developed for industry and other small private actors. Yet public procurement requirements can differ significantly from those in the private sector by scale and complexity, necessitating tailored solutions that address specific public sector needs and regulations. Adapting industry-developed software to meet these unique requirements will be costly. A new market of developers will emerge to specifically customize and test these tools to meet the specific demands of public procurement processes.
- How ready is public procurement to deal with the ethical issues associated with new technologies, especially AI/ML technologies? There are suggestions (e.g., in Nagitta et al., 2022) that a few public procurement agencies have started using AI/ML, but they lack the right data science competencies and legislation to help deploy these AI/ML models ethically and transparently. So, there will be a need to address issues of access to clean data for AL/ML systems, data privacy, and data ownership. In particular, the integration of generative AI into public procurement must be approached with caution to ensure robust ethical guidelines and oversight to mitigate risks related to bias, transparency, and accountability.

## References


Aldana, A., Falcón-Cortés, A., & Larralde, H. 2022. A machine learning model to identify corruption in Mexico's public procurement contracts. arXiv preprint arXiv:2211.01478.

Arán, M. I., Carabetta, J., Wen, J., Julià-Verdaguer, A., Rosado, P. J., Sidgwick, J., Vollmer, S. J., & Ghani, R. 2020. Reducing corruption in public procurement using machine learning. https://doi.org/10.5281/zenodo.3967837.

Basheka, B. C., Oluka, P. N., & Mugurusi, G. 2012. Adopting new approaches for public procurement efficiency: critical success factors (CSFs) for the implementation of e-procurement in Uganda's public sector. *International Journal of Procurement Management*, 5(6), 712–732.

Behrens, V. J., Pjero, E., Krause, S., & Hangl, J. 2023. What are the essential elements of a digital transformation process to develop an efficient digitization strategy for management? *Journal of Management Development*, 42(5), 399–419.

Bharadwaj, A., El Sawy, O. A., Pavlou, P. A., & Venkatraman, N. 2013. Digital business strategy: toward a next generation of insights. *MIS Quarterly*, 37(2), 471–482. www.jstor.org/stable/43825919

Bousdekis, A., & Kardaras, D. 2020. *Digital transformation of local government: A case study from Greece*. In *Paper presented at the 2020 IEEE 22nd Conference on Business Informatics (CBI)*, Vol. 2, pp. 131–140.

Bresciani, S., Ferraris, A., Romano, M., & Santoro, G. 2021. Building a digital transformation strategy. In *Digital Transformation Management for Agile Organizations: A Compass to Sail the Digital World* (pp. 5–27). Emerald Publishing Limited.

Čeke, D., Buzadija, N., & Kunosić, S. 2022. Enhancing transparency and fairness in public procurement process with the support of blockchain technology: A smart contract-based approach. In *21st International Symposium Infoteh-Jahorina (INFOTEH, 2022)*, East Sarajevo, Bosnia and Herzegovina, 2022, pp. 1–6. 10.1109/INFOTEH53737.2022.9751322

Craglia, M., de Nigris, S., Gomez-Gonzalez, E., Gomez, E., Martens, B., Portela, M. I., ..., & Kotzev, A. 2020. *Artificial Intelligence and Digital Transformation: Early Lessons from the COVID-19 Crisis*. Publications Office of the European Union Luxemburg.

Daidj, N. 2022. Towards renewed Business-IT alignment models in the digital era: the impact of data inclusion. *Information Resources Management Journal (IRMJ)*, 35(1), 1–13.

Datta, P. 2020. Digital transformation of the Italian public administration: a case study. *Communications of the Association for Information Systems*, 46(1), 11.

Davenport, T. H., & Ronanki, R. 2018. Artificial intelligence for the real world. *Harvard Business Review*, 96(1), 108–116.

Deloite-EU Report, 2020. Study on up-take of emerging technologies in public procurement. DG GROW G.4, Req. No 146. Framework Contract DI/07624 – ABC IV Lot 3. D01.06: Final Report.

Dener, C. 2019. How to connect e-procurement and financial management systems. *PEMPAL Treasury CoP Thematic Group Workshop*, Hungary, June 2019.

Engel, C., Ebel, P., & Leimeister, J. M. 2022. Cognitive automation. *Electronic Markets*, 32(1), 339–350.

Fernández-Rovira, C., Valdés, J. Á., Molleví, G., & Nicolas-Sans, R. 2021. The digital transformation of business. Towards the datafication of the relationship with customers. *Technological Forecasting and Social Change*, 162, 120339.

Ferrag, M. A., Shu, L., & Choo, K. K. R. 2021. Fighting COVID-19 and future pandemics with the Internet of Things: security and privacy perspectives. *IEEE/CAA Journal of Automatica Sinica*, 8(9), 1477–1499.

Firouzi, F., Farahani, B., Daneshmand, M., Grise, K., Song, J., Saracco, R., ..., & Luo, A. 2021. Harnessing the power of smart and connected health to tackle COVID-19: IoT, AI, robotics, and blockchain for a better world. *IEEE Internet of Things Journal*, 8(16), 12826–12846.

Flechsig, C., Anslinger, F., & Lasch, R. 2022. Robotic process automation in purchasing and supply management: a multiple case study on potentials, barriers, and implementation. *Journal of Purchasing and Supply Management*, 28(1), 100718.

Gabryelczyk, R. 2020. Has COVID-19 accelerated digital transformation? Initial lessons learned for public administrations. *Information Systems Management*, 37(4), 303–309.

Ghobakhloo, M., & Iranmanesh, M. 2021. Digital transformation success under Industry 4.0: a strategic guideline for manufacturing SMEs. *Journal of Manufacturing Technology Management*, 32(8), 1533–1556.

Guida, M., Caniato, F., Moretto, A., & Ronchi, S., 2023. The role of artificial intelligence in the procurement process: state of the art and research agenda. *Journal of Purchasing and Supply Management*, 29(2), 100823.

Hidayanti, E., Kunrat, K. A., & Ikram, S. 2023. Implementation of robotic process automation in public sector goods and services e-procurement audit. *Khazanah Sosial*, 4(4), 662–677.

Irani, Z., Abril, R. M., Weerakkody, V., Omar, A., & Sivarajah, U. 2023. The impact of legacy systems on digital transformation in European public administration: lesson learned from a multi case analysis. *Government Information Quarterly*, 40(1), 101784.

Kakavand, H., Kost De Sevres, N., & Chilton, B. 2017. The blockchain revolution: An analysis of regulation and technology related to distributed ledger technologies. Available at SSRN 2849251.

Kane, G. 2019. The technology fallacy: people are the real key to digital transformation. *Research-Technology Management*, 62(6), 44–49.

Khanna, S., Konstantynova, N., Lamarre, E., & Sohoni, V. 2020. *Welcome to the Digital Factory: The Answer to How to Scale Your Digital Transformation.* McKinsey & Company.

Lacity, M. C., & Willcocks, L. P. 2016, September. A new approach to automating services. *MIT Sloan Management Review.*

Langseth, M. 2024. *Data-Driven Decision-Making in the Public Procurement System: The Case of Norway.* Doctoral thesis at Norwegian University of Science and Technology (NTNU), 2024:70.

Langseth, M., & Haddara, M. 2024. Spend analytics in Norwegian public procurement: adoption status and influencing factors. *International Journal of Information Systems and Project Management*, 12(2), 5–27.

Leal-Rodríguez, A. L., Sanchís-Pedregosa, C., Moreno-Moreno, A. M., & Leal-Millán, A. G. 2023. Digitalization beyond technology: proposing an explanatory and predictive model for digital culture in organizations. *Journal of Innovation & Knowledge*, 8(3), 100409.

Lintukangas, A. 2017. *Improving Indirect Procurement Process by Utilizing Robotic Process Automation.* Master's Degree thesis from Lappeenranta University of Technology https://lutpub.lut.fi/handle/10024/143385

Mariani, I., & Bianchi, I. 2023. Conceptualizing digital transformation in cities: a multi-dimensional framework for the analysis of public sector innovation. *Sustainability*, 15(11), 8741.

Masoud, R., & Basahel, S. 2023. The effects of digital transformation on firm performance: the role of customer experience and IT innovation. *Digital*, 3(2), 109–126.

McKinsey. 2023. *What Is Digital Transformation?* McKinsey & Company. www.mckinsey.com/featured-insights/mckinsey-explainers/what-is-digital-transformation

Mikalsen, M., & Farshchian, B. A. 2020. Can the public sector and vendors digitally transform? A case from innovative public procurement. In *Proceedings of the 28th European Conference on Information Systems (ECIS)*, Marrakech, Morocco/Online, 15–17 June 2020.

Mistry, S., & Tan, G. 2019. Challenges in the implementation of blockchain technology in the public sector: an exploratory study. *Government Information Quarterly*, 36(4), 801–811.

Morakanyane, R., Grace, A. A. & O'reilly, P. 2017. Conceptualizing digital transformation in business organizations: A systematic review of literature. In *30th Bled Conference* (June 18–21, 2017, Bled, Slovenia).

Moser-Plautz, B., & Schmidthuber, L. 2023. Digital government transformation as an organizational response to the COVID-19 pandemic. *Government Information Quarterly*, 40(3), 101815.

Mougayar, W., & Buterin, V. 2016. *The Business Blockchain: Promise, Practice, and Application of the Next Internet Technology.* John Wiley & Sons.

Mugurusi, G., Korsen, E.B.H., & Eshaghzadeh, A., 2021. Defining and measuring supply chain digitalization: A systematic literature review. In *2021 IEEE Technology & Engineering Management Conference-Europe (TEMSCON-EUR)* (pp. 1–6). IEEE.

Mugurusi, G., & Oluka, P. N. 2021. Towards explainable artificial intelligence (xai) in supply chain management: a typology and research agenda. In *IFIP International Conference on Advances in Production Management Systems* (pp. 32–38). Cham: Springer International Publishing.

Mugurusi, G., Vestertė, J., Asamoah, D., Khatiwada, P., Mitcheltree, C. M., Holtskog, H., & Underbekken, S. 2022. The significance and barriers to organizational interoperability in smart service ecosystems: a socio-technical systems approach. In Kim, D.Y., von Cieminski, G., Romero, D. (eds) *Advances in Production Management Systems. Smart Manufacturing and Logistics Systems: Turning Ideas into Action* (vol. 664, pp. 253–261). IFIP Advances in Information and Communication Technology.

Mulyana, R., Rusu, L., & Perjons, E. 2021. *IT governance mechanisms influence on digital transformation: A systematic literature review.* In *Paper presented at the Twenty-Seventh Americas' Conference on Information Systems (AMCIS)*, Digital Innovation and Entrepreneurship, Virtual Conference, August 9–13, 2021.

Mynenko, S., & Lyulyov, O. 2022. The impact of digitalization on the transparency of public authorities. *Business Ethics and Leadership*, 6(2), 103–115.

Nagitta, P. O., Mugurusi, G., Obicci, P. A., & Awuor, E. 2022. Human-centered artificial intelligence for the public sector: the gate keeping role of the public procurement professional. *Procedia Computer Science*, 200, 1084–1092.

OECD. 2016. Country case: Integrated e-procurement system KONEPS in Korea. www.oecd.org/governance/procurement/toolbox/search/integrated-e-procurement-system-koneps.pdf

OECD. 2019. "Digital transformation of public procurement", in *Government at a Glance 2019*, OECD Publishing, Paris.

Øverdal, M., Haddara, M., & Langseth, M. 2022. Exploring Public Cloud-ERP Systems' Impact on Organizational Performance. Paper presented at the Proceedings of the Future Technologies Conference.

Pappianou, G., & Spencer, A. 2019. A path to successful state procurement transformation. www.mckinsey.com/~/media/McKinsey/Industries/Public%20Sector/Our%20Insights/A%20path%20to%20successful%20state%20procurement%20transformation/A-path-to-successful-state-procurement-transformation-vF.pdf

Parviainen, P., Tihinen, M., Kääriäinen, J., & Teppola, S. 2017. Tackling the digitalization challenge: how to benefit from digitalization in practice. *International Journal of Information Systems and Project Management*, 5(1), 63–77.

Pedersen, K. 2018. E-government transformations: challenges and strategies. *Transforming Government: People, Process and Policy*, 12(1), 84–109.

Radu, L. D. 2020. Disruptive technologies in smart cities: a survey on current trends and challenges. *Smart Cities*, 3(3), 1022–1038.

Reier Forradellas, R. F., & Garay Gallastegui, L. M. 2021. Digital transformation and artificial intelligence applied to business: legal regulations, economic impact and perspective. *Laws*, 10(3), 70.

Russell, S. J., & Norvig, P. 2010. *Artificial intelligence – A modern approach* (3rd ed.). Prentice Hall.

Sánchez, A. 2019. Blockchain in public procurement: enhancing transparency and reducing corruption. *Journal of Public Procurement*, 19(3), 275–289.

Sestino, A., Kahlawi, A., & De Mauro, A. 2023. Decoding the data economy: a literature review of its impact on business, society and digital transformation. *European Journal of Innovation Management*, 28(2), 298–323.

Shojaei, A. 2022. Does digital transformation impact customer experience? In B. Barbosa, S. Filipe, & C. A. Santos (Eds.), *Handbook of Research on Smart Management for Digital Transformation* (pp. 210–232). Hershey, PA: IGI Global.

Sousa, M. J., & Rocha, Á. 2019. Digital learning: developing skills for digital transformation of organizations. *Future Generation Computer Systems*, 91, 327–334.

Stewart, H. 2023. Digital transformation security challenges. *Journal of Computer Information Systems*, 63(4), 919–936.

Sun, K., Roy, A., & Tobin, J. M. 2024. Artificial intelligence and machine learning: definition of terms and current concepts in critical care research. *Journal of Critical Care*, 82, 154792.

Tapscott, D., & Tapscott, A. 2016. *Blockchain Revolution: How the Technology behind Bitcoin Is Changing Money, Business, and the World*. Penguin.

Treiblmaier, H. 2018. The impact of the blockchain on the supply chain: a theory-based research framework and a call for action. *Supply Chain Management*, 23(6), 545–559.

Trenerry, B., Chng, S., Wang, Y., Suhaila, Z. S., Lim, S. S., Lu, H. Y., & Oh, P. H. 2021. Preparing workplaces for digital transformation: an integrative review and framework of multi-level factors. *Frontiers in Psychology*, 12, 620766.

Van Veldhoven, Z., & Vanthienen, J. 2022. Digital transformation as an interaction-driven perspective between business, society, and technology. *Electronic Markets*, 32(2), 629–644.

Viale, L., & Zouari, D. 2020. Impact of digitalization on procurement: the case of robotic process automation. *Supply Chain Forum: An International Journal*, 21(3), 185–195. Taylor & Francis.

Woschank, M., Rauch, E., & Zsifkovits, H. E. 2020. A review of further directions for artificial intelligence, machine learning, and deep learning in smart logistics. *Sustainability*, 12(9), 3760.

Zaoui, F., & Souissi, N. 2021. *A Framework for a Strategic Digital Transformation*. Paper presented at the 2020 6th IEEE Congress on Information Science and Technology (CiSt).

### *Case Study: Digital Transformation in Public Procurement at Granite Ridge (Developed by Brooke Smith, Recorder, City of Murray)*

#### Background and Problem Statement

Granite Ridge, a mid-sized municipality serving a population of 50,000, operates with a general budget of approximately $65 million. It has a workforce of 500 employees, including a small procurement team with two dedicated purchasing agents. Like many public procurement agencies, Granite Ridge faces several operational challenges, including overwhelming caseloads, outdated processes, and bureaucratic inefficiencies. The procurement team is responsible for managing high volumes of purchase orders, request for proposals (RFPs), bids, contracts, and compliance reviews—all while adhering to local, state, and federal regulations. This high workload and need for transparency have placed considerable strain on the small team.

To address these challenges, Granite Ridge made a strategic decision to pursue digital transformation, specifically leveraging artificial intelligence (AI) to increase efficiency within procurement operations. The city aimed to automate routine tasks, enhance data analytics capabilities, and streamline processes. However, adopting AI required significant change management, including re-evaluating long-standing procedures and updating legacy systems to align with modern procurement needs.

#### Consultation Stage

Granite Ridge began its transformation journey by consulting with key stakeholders to evaluate the need for modernization. Stakeholders, including the city attorney, department heads, and IT specialists, participated in a series of discussions to identify specific pain points within procurement. These consultations highlighted issues such as lengthy approval times, inconsistencies in bid evaluations, and limited access to data-driven insights, all of which hindered procurement efficiency. There was a broad consensus that AI could alleviate many of these challenges by automating repetitive tasks, providing real-time analytics, and enabling procurement staff to focus on strategic planning and relationship-building with suppliers.

#### Process Review and Standardization

With stakeholder input in hand, the procurement team conducted a thorough review of its existing procedures. They mapped workflows to identify bottlenecks, looking to integrate AI solutions for high-volume, low-complexity tasks. For instance, they envisioned using AI-powered bots to automate purchase orders, invoice processing, and compliance checks based on a specific set of rules that followed their agency's procurement code. By reducing the manual workload associated with these routine tasks, the team aimed to allocate more time toward activities like market analysis and strategic sourcing, which have a greater impact on procurement value.

#### Capacity Building and Training

Granite Ridge recognized that for AI adoption to succeed, procurement staff would need to develop a digital mindset. The city invested in training programs focused on AI fundamentals, data literacy, and digital procurement techniques to equip staff to use AI as a supportive tool. Training also aimed at shifting perspectives, encouraging staff to view AI as a partner that could reduce their administrative burden and support more effective decision-making in procurement.

### Implementation Stage

Granite Ridge rolled out its digital transformation in phases to ensure a smooth transition:

1. **AI-Enabled Automation:** In the initial phase, the focus was on automating repetitive tasks. AI algorithms were deployed for bid evaluation, where they scanned documents for compliance, allowing procurement staff to concentrate on qualitative analysis. AI tools also monitored contract terms to flag compliance issues, reducing potential risks.
2. **Advanced Analytics and Strategic Insights:** The second phase introduced AI tools that provided insights into procurement metrics. By analyzing spending patterns, optimizing supplier selection, and predicting potential risks, the procurement team was able to enhance planning processes and achieve cost savings.
3. **Standard Forms and Procedure Updates:** With routine tasks automated, staff now have time to update outdated forms and procedures. A new AI-enhanced Request for Proposals (RFPs) template, for example, allowed procurement officers to draft, customize, and distribute RFPs more efficiently, improving the scope and quality of procurement projects.

### Challenges Encountered

Granite Ridge's transformation was not without obstacles. Initially, some staff resisted AI, fearing it might replace their roles or reduce the value of their expertise. To address these concerns, the city's leadership implemented change management initiatives that emphasized AI as a tool to streamline repetitive tasks and support, rather than replace, human expertise. A key element of this approach was the principle of *keeping a human-in-the-loop*, which proved essential in fostering trust in the new technology and ensuring that AI-driven decisions aligned with Granite Ridge's values and regulations. AI tools could automate initial reviews or flag issues in procurement documents, but final decisions were left to experienced procurement professionals. This allowed AI to handle quantitative tasks, while procurement staff focused on qualitative factors such as supplier reputation and potential economic impacts.

The human-in-the-loop model also proved essential for risk management. AI could identify patterns or anomalies, but the complex nature of procurement decisions—especially in interpreting vague contract terms or assessing risks—required human oversight. By maintaining human judgment in critical areas, Granite Ridge ensured that technology complemented rather than replaced professional expertise, reducing the risk of automation errors or unchecked biases.

Another significant challenge was integrating AI into the city's existing systems, which required substantial IT investment and a commitment to data governance to protect privacy and confidentiality. The city implemented a robust data governance framework, ensuring that AI tools access only anonymized or restricted data when necessary. Regular audits and data protection measures were established to comply with privacy laws and maintain public trust. Human oversight added an extra layer of security, with staff reviewing and flagging sensitive information before processing it through AI tools.

### Outcomes

Despite these challenges, Granite Ridge's digital transformation yielded notable improvements in both operational efficiency and employee satisfaction. By automating repetitive tasks and keeping humans-in-the-loop for strategic decisions, the city reduced its average procurement cycle time by 35 percent. This streamlined process allowed the procurement team to handle 25 percent more cases without additional staff, easing the burden of overwhelming caseloads that previously contributed to stress and burnout.

With AI managing tasks like compliance checks, data entry, and contract monitoring, employees now had more time to focus on complex, value-added activities, such as supplier management, strategic sourcing, and risk analysis. This shift allowed staff to engage more deeply in their work, making use of their expertise and judgment. Employee satisfaction increased significantly as staff no longer felt bogged down by outdated processes and bureaucratic inefficiencies. The reduction in administrative tasks gave employees a greater sense of purpose in their roles, and they felt reassured that their expertise was still essential to the team's success. AI was viewed not as a replacement, but as a collaborative tool that enabled them to make better, data-informed decisions.

### Reflection and Discussion Points

1. **How does keeping a human-in-the-loop enhance trust and job satisfaction in digital transformation efforts?**
   - Discuss how Granite Ridge's approach to involving humans in critical decisions helped alleviate concerns over job replacement and foster a collaborative environment.
   - What other strategies might procurement teams use to integrate AI while maintaining or improving employee satisfaction?
2. **In what ways does AI integration redefine the roles and responsibilities of procurement professionals?**
   - Explore how Granite Ridge's employees shifted from handling routine tasks to focusing on strategic activities. How might this shift impact professional development, required skill sets, and future hiring in procurement?
   - What additional support or training might be necessary to maximize these new roles?
3. **What are the ethical and operational considerations of balancing AI automation with human oversight in public procurement?**
   - Reflect on the importance of AI transparency, especially when it comes to compliance and risk assessment. How does a human-in-the-loop model contribute to ethical decision-making?

What are the potential risks if too much or too little reliance is placed on AI in public procurement processes?

# 22 Application of Digital Twin and 3D-Printing

## Creating Capabilities for Resilient Public Procurement

*Andreas H. Glas and Michael Essig*

### 22.1 Introduction

In an era defined by rapid technological advancements, the traditional landscape of public procurement is undergoing a profound transformation. Citizens expect a much higher degree of performance in public services; at the same time, the public sector faces multidimensional challenges, e.g., in health care (global pandemic) or security (war in Europe). Therefore, governments worldwide strive to enhance the resilience of their public services. Resilience in this chapter refers to research that aims to discuss how public procurement organizations adapt in the face of turbulent change (following Fiksel et al., 2015). One means to achieve resilience is the integration of a digital twin (DT) and additive manufacturing (AM). Both technologies promise to not only streamline and speed up the procurement process but also fortify public services against unforeseen challenges, ushering in a new era of efficiency and adaptability.

This is necessary, as the fragility of global supply chains has been severely highlighted by a series of unprecedented disruptions in recent times. From the ripple effects of the COVID-19 pandemic to natural disasters and geopolitical tensions to ship accidents in the Suez Canal, governments have found themselves grappling with unforeseen challenges. Supply disruptions have effects on very heterogenous public services, such as missing equipment in Health Care (WHO, 2020), delays and cost overruns in public construction (McKinsey, 2020), and problems in food distribution in social services impacting vulnerable populations (Swinnen and McDermott, 2020), or missing spares, staff or repair services to hold a specific technology and infrastructure level in times of crisis (Deloitte, 2022).

Generally, procurement and supply management must be capable of coping with different supply risks (Glas et al., 2021a). The emergence of new and unexpected supply bottlenecks is a severe issue for every organization, but is even more critical for the public sector. Public sector organizations such as hospitals, schools, social care, police, military, and other public institutions are of systemic importance (Meyer et al., 2022b). Ensuring a level of continuity or at least the avoidance of a breakdown of public service delivery is mandatory for societies in case of severe supply disruption (United Nations, 2020).

Public procurement, historically marked by paperwork and bureaucratic hurdles, is now evolving. On the one hand, public procurement is moving into a more strategic role with a clearly formulated procurement strategy that aims to better achieve specific government objectives like sustainability and innovativeness (Patrucco et al., 2016). On the other hand, public procurement has developed into a digital frontier where information flows seamlessly, and decisions are data-driven and evidence-based. Public procurement strategies, often formulated in the form of portfolio strategies (Nellore and Söderquist,

DOI: 10.4324/9781003566670-26

2000; Gelderman and van Weele, 2005; Jonen, 2023), are required to also provide decision support on how to make use of data and information flows in procurement.

Not only does the procurement function have to adapt to digitalized innovations. At the same time, manufacturing technology developed AM, also widely named 3D-Printing, which provides a solution that enables rapid and decentralized production of almost any demand object. Recent research combined both aspects in order to increase public sector resilience (Meyer et al., 2022a, 2022b). This fits very well with the identified factors that influence public sector resilience (Glas and Eßig, 2023). Following Pettit et al. (2010), important supply chain capabilities are collaboration, capacity, efficiency, recovery, dispersion, adaptability, anticipation, and flexibility.

The solution idea is quite simple: Demand (necessity of public service production) shall be identified in quantity and quality as early as possible by the use of DT technology. This allows the planning and organization of public sector supply to meet demand. In case of urgent demands, i.e., the time between demand identification and supply from traditional sources is not sufficient, (local) AM is used to further reduce production and logistics time. Together, DT-enabled AM shall be able to supply a public organization very quickly. As such, DT-enabled AM to be in a "risk hedge position" in comparison to traditional supply relations.

What will be outlined below is that the application of DT-enabled AM is not without challenges and implementation alternatives. Therefore, DT-enabled AM necessitates the formulation of a supply strategy. Public sector practitioners shall be prepared to use DT-enabled AM. In the face of potential supply disruption risks, public procurement professionals shall be capable of formulating an appropriate procurement strategy integrating the transformative power of DT-enabled AM.

To further explain the idea of DT-enabled AM for public sector resilience, the remainder of this chapter is as follows: The next section will provide a summary of the research literature on the topic. This is followed by a section on emerging issues. This is followed by practical applications, briefly presenting examples from public procurement practice. A conclusion section summarizes this chapter.

## 22.2 Insights into the Research Discussion on the Topic

### *22.2.1 Digital Twin and Ultimate Demand Transparency*

The concept of a DT can be described as the ultimate virtual representation of an object for advanced analytics (Bhandal et al., 2022; Oehlschlaeger et al., 2024). The Building Information Modelling (BIM) that then results in a DT allows integrated planning and execution of the production and procurement of complex assets/products and lays the foundation for data-sensor-enabled surveillance of the whole asset during its long-term operation, including later optimization of maintenance, repair, overhaul, and spare-parts management.

As an object for the virtual representation of a DT, one might consider products, infrastructure, processes, systems, humans, and more or less everything that can be captured in a digital model. Briefly, DT may have different content dimensions depending on the context of the application (Dietz and Pernul, 2020). For this chapter, several application layers are distinguished for a DT: processes and systems DT, assets DT, and individual part DT (see also Singh et al., 2021). At the part level, a piece of equipment is virtually represented by the DT by means of its geometric, functional, and operational model. At the asset level, the overarching machine, vehicle, building, or general asset is represented, in which single parts are embedded. Finally, at the process or system level, different workflows and aggregated data on the system level are represented by the DT. This helps, on the one hand, to have interdependent assets like traffic control systems or energy grids under control; on the other hand, process DT supports management decision-making and monitoring of key business metrics (Parks, 2020).

Furthermore, different DT levels are distinguished according to their sophistication (Singh et al., 2021). Several authors follow the distinction of three different levels of DT, depending on how the real object and its digital counterpart are interacting (following Juarez et al. (2021):

Digital Model: the virtual representation of a physical subject with no automated flow of information from physical to virtual worlds (e.g., CAD plan of a building).

Digital Shadow: Virtual representation where there is a unidirectional flow of information, usually from the physical to the virtual world (e.g., sensors in the building deliver real-time information into the BIM model during operations).

DT in the Narrower Sense: Uses a bidirectional flow of information scheme to enable the management and monitoring of the object's life cycle (e.g., BIM is not only able to monitor the building but also steers heating, cooling, and maintenance directly).

Generally, a DT is a concept that is based on technologies and architectures that allow big data analytics (Aheleroff, 2021) and the application of even higher-level analytical methods, including artificial intelligence (AI) (Rathore et al., 2021). There is only a few DT research literature focusing on its application in the public sector, mainly to support strategic goals like green public procurement (Meschini et al., 2022). However, it is expected that DT will be able to improve demand management significantly, as enhanced AI analytics considers data in a very timely and comprehensive manner, including all information from supply disruption risks. By having the opportunity to analyze comprehensive data with DT technology, forecast accuracy or event transparency of supply disruptions will be very high. With the use of DT, public procurement shall have ultimate transparency, which contributes to improved procurement planning and decision-making.

### *22.2.2 Additive Manufacturing and Its Effects on Supply Chain Design*

AM is an umbrella term for a number of different manufacturing procedures for a relatively wide range of materials, ranging from alloy, steel, porcelain, plaster, and concrete to polymer. All these procedures have in common that a "printer" machine manufactures a product following its digital model, usually joining materials layer upon layer, in contrast to subtractive manufacturing procedures (Durach et al., 2017; Rogers et al., 2016). Briefly, a DT of an individual part is the starting point for AM to produce it.

AM is not a new technology, but it has received increased attention in research and practice in the last few years (Meyer et al., 2021). AM has some specific characteristics that are mentioned very briefly following Waller and Fawcett (2014): AM economizes inventory and materials management, as it uses less material and raw materials only. As AM follows the DT of products, changes in production can happen as fast as the data can be altered. Furthermore, AM can be located close to supply recipients, as the machines are standardized and need a simplified view – besides raw materials management – only energy and data, there is no "tooling" necessary. This economizes logistics and, foremost, transport time. AM is able to produce very individual and customized products. AM is able to print different items at the same time, depending on the available space in the printer. Finally, supply chains are expected to become shorter, as AM only needs raw materials to make the final product instead of multiple tiers from raw materials to the final product.

As such, the implementation design of AM can differ. Glas et al. (2021b) have identified four different scenarios. In the first one, the public organization operates AM itself and buys raw materials as well as printers from markets. In the second one, the public organization buys only printing services/AM-manufactured products from AM service provider companies. The third alternative is a hybrid model, combining the first and second ones. The fourth AM implementation design focuses on (open source) platforms for getting the data and open platforms for sharing printing capacity along the supply chain. Other literature explicitly addresses the possibility of using AM in a decentralized or local manner with the aim of economizing transport and decreasing lead times (e.g., Montero et al., 2020; Kleer and Piller, 2019).

In summary, two decisions must be made regarding AM usage. The first decision addresses whether AM or a traditional manufacturing supply source is used. The second decision focuses on implementation design aspects. The alternatives are, on the one hand, in-house AM operation vs. outsourcing (buying AM products and services) and, on the other, a central or more decentralized layout (Braziotis et al., 2019).

### *22.2.3 DT-enabled AM*

Both technologies are integrated with each other. The AM process relies heavily on the DT of a product part. Without a digital representation of that part, AM is not able to reproduce it layer by layer. On the other hand, a DT on an asset level allows for improved forecast demand and planning as well as disposition in a way that the investment in an AM process (printer machinery, capabilities, etc.) is justified by getting the right products at the right time. Embedded in a DT on the systems and process level, the AM source can be planned and scheduled, in contrast to traditional manufacturing, where AM increases resilience and enhances supply security.

From an overarching perspective, both technologies are interlinked. DT and its data and process analytics allow fast detection and evaluation of potential supply risks and disruptions. Improved and fast planning and scheduling on the DT process/system level can be merged with DT data from the assets. If a potential supply risk emerges, AM can be activated, as AM has the potential to produce almost any part very fast without losing time in logistics and transport. Therefore, AM production is activated according to a product/part DT. This is why this chapter not only addresses DT or AM separately but also merges both topics into a DT-enabled AM.

## 22.3 Public Procurement Strategy for DT-enabled AM

Generally, a procurement strategy is embedded in the overarching organization (business) strategy and linked to it by strategic alignment, while the procurement strategy itself formulates strategic objectives and gives priorities to guide purchasing decisions (Gonzáles-Benito, 2007). Portfolios are a tool for formulating a procurement strategy as they try to differentiate alternative options. Their origin is in the portfolio theory for investment strategies (e.g., Markowitz, 1952), but portfolios have also been applied to procurement for a long time (e.g., Nellore and Söderquist, 2000; Gelderman and Van Weele, 2005). A very prominent example is the Kraljic matrix on supply risk and profit impact axes, differentiating noncritical, leverage, bottleneck, and strategic items (Kraljic, 1983). Another portfolio uses the axes of forecast reliability and supply lead times in order to differentiate lean, agile, or leagile setups of supply chains (Christopher et al., 2006).

In case a public procurement organization aims to increase resilience, several response strategies can be undertaken. Prominent examples are switching from global to local sourcing, increasing the number of supply sources from single to multiple, or using supplier support strategies like financial incentives or regulation (Dube et al., 2022). Generally, the aim is to reduce risks by choosing better supply sources with a lower risk exposure, to distribute the risk to more and different sources of supply, or to strengthen the risk resilience of a supply source. AM can be implemented as a new local source instead of a traditional global source. AM can be implemented in addition to an existing other source of supply. Finally, AM can be supported by resources in order to make that source of supply particularly resilient to specific threats. In that sense, it is required to consciously make a decision in which case and under which circumstances DT-enabled AM is applied.

A procurement strategy for DT-enabled AM shall achieve this decision support: Differentiate alternative options on how public organizations can make use of DT-enabled AM. As a result, the portfolio must be able to give strategic recommendations based on an analysis of central dimensions influencing the procurement situation. In the DT-enabled AM portfolio in Figure 22.1, this can be done considering the accuracy of the DT (forecast reliability; supply disruption risks) and the agility of traditional supply sources (see also Meyer et al., 2020) following the approach of Christopher et al. (2006). Dimension 1 deals with the analysis of lead times in "traditional" supply chains: If changes in demand need

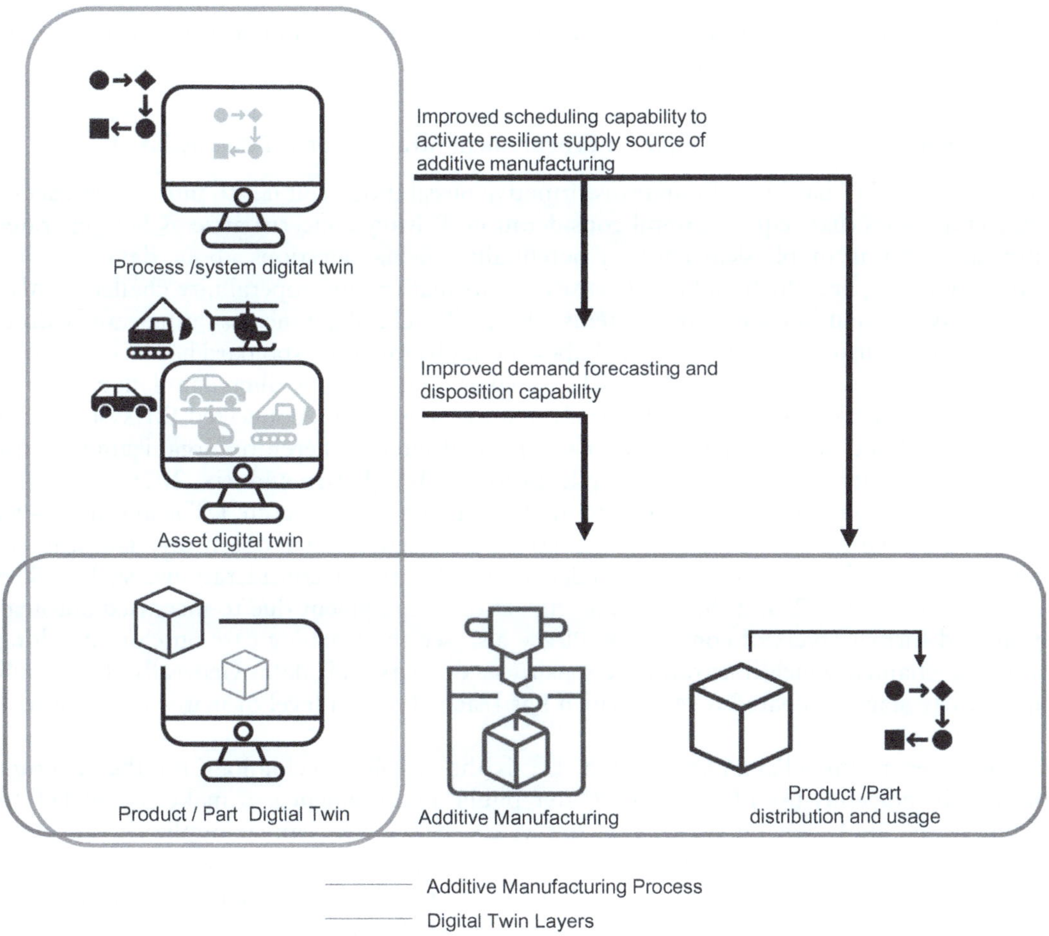


*Figure 22.1* Integrated view on DT layers and the AM process.
*Source: Original creation.*

a long-term forecast to be reflected in changes in the supply chain, the result is long lead times. Dimension 2 analyses the capabilities of the DT application – it answers the question of whether DT improves forecast accuracy. It is acknowledged that DT enhances transparency, but disruptions will still disturb initial planning.

If AM is either not necessary because disruption risks are low (and DT, therefore, cannot really improve the situation with its forecast accuracy), and/or traditional manufacturing is flexible enough because of relatively low lead times, there is no real necessity for a DT-enabled AM strategy (grey fields in the portfolio in Figure 22.1). However, if forecast accuracy is not sufficient or supply disruption risks are expected in severe ways, and resilience cannot be provided by traditional supply sources, then DT-enabled AM is recommended (white field in the portfolio in Figure 22.1).

Zooming into that application field, the next decisions have to be made concerning the implementation design. The presented AM business models imply deciding along the axes of in-/outsourcing and central-decentralized design. Following that implementation design (see right side of Figure 22.2), public procurement could use specific instruments to build up AM capacities. For example, long-term contracts may suit central outsourcing, while lot-wise public procurement can be used in the case of local outsourcing (see, e.g., Glas et al., 2018). Central AM in-house may be suitable for creating its own administrative organization, while decentralized AM in-house is a capability that could be attached to existing public organizations in order to economize administrative overhead.

## 22.4 Emerging Issues in Developing a Procurement Strategy for DT-enabled AM

The advent of DT has brought up transformative possibilities, but it also introduces a set of emerging issues that require careful consideration. Privacy concerns arise as DT generates intricate replicas of physical entities, potentially raising questions about data security, property rights, and the handling of sensitive information. Interoperability challenges also emerge as different industries and systems adopt DT technology, necessitating standardization efforts to ensure seamless (data) collaboration. Overall, each standard has its own goals, focuses, and representations for DTs, which makes it necessary to align data languages and system frameworks. (Schmidt et al., 2023). On the other hand, connected DT systems can be exploited and attacked (sometimes easily) for ill intent. Therefore, organizations must seriously consider the cybersecurity implications of a DT (Hearn and Rix, 2019).

The resource-intensive nature of creating and maintaining accurate DT is another issue, especially for large-scale applications. The complexity management of sensors, data storage, and data compilation shall not be underestimated. Ethical considerations, such as the responsible use of DT and the potential impact on employment due to increased automation, add further layers of complexity. Please also see the teaching case on clothing along with the chapter, which illustrates the sensitivity of (personal) data. Generally, DT is still in an early stage compared to AM, which has reached a high level of maturity in the past decades.

However, in this chapter's approach, DT is the enabling technology for the economically advantageous use of AM. The better public procurement can make use of DT to improve risk and demand forecast accuracy; the better AM can be applied to produce urgent demand, which, in effect, helps to achieve resilience and agility goals. However, AM also has some emerging issues that require consideration. Intellectual property concerns are significant, as the ease of digital reproduction challenges traditional notions of ownership and control. Quality assurance remains a pressing issue, particularly as industries increasingly rely on AM for critical and even healthcare products. Material limitations

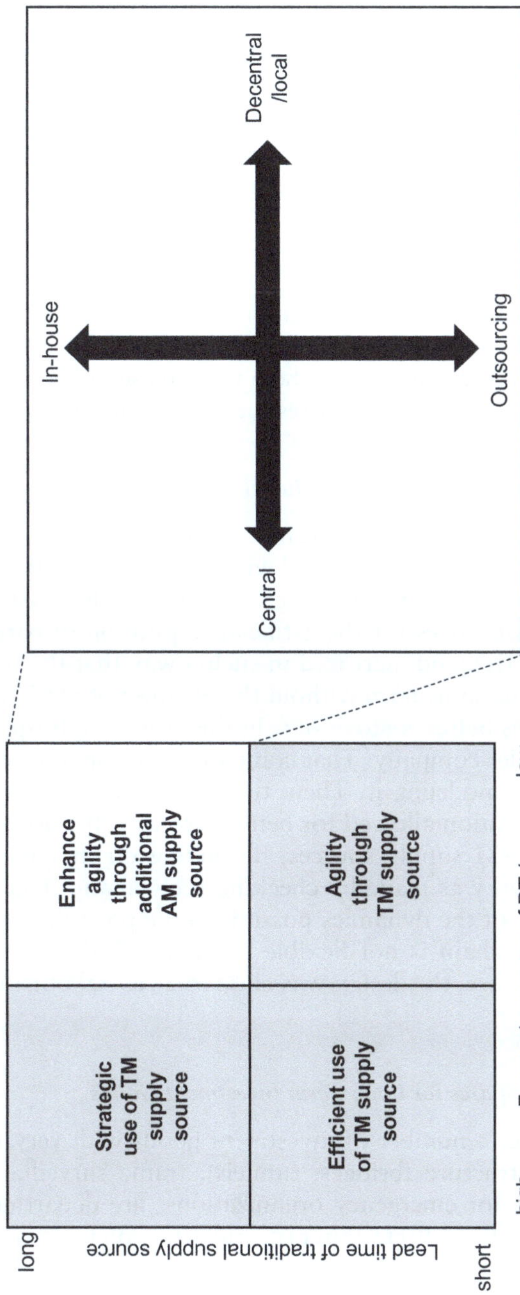


*Figure* 22.2 A portfolio perspective on DT-enabled AM.

*Source*: Original creation.

and sustainability considerations also come to the forefront, with the increasing call for eco-friendly alternatives and addressing the environmental impact of certain materials. Regulatory frameworks are evolving to keep pace with the rapidly advancing technology, posing challenges in standardization and certification. Furthermore, the workforce requires upskilling and training to harness the full potential of AM, which is of particular interest if AM is implemented in-house.

Overall, public procurement should be aware of these issues when formulating the strategy to adopt these technologies. However, the next section, with examples from practical applications, will show that in times of crisis or in case of urgent demands, a DT-enabled AM significantly increases public sector resilience. As such, usage decisions should consider not only emerging issues but also the potential of technology.

## 22.5 Practical Applications

The examples presented below are selected to show DT-enabled AM in heterogeneous application scenarios. The application content and risk causes are very different. This shall illustrate and teach how these technologies help to increase public procurement and public sector security of supply. This all underscores the wide applicability of DT-enabled AM.

### *22.5.1 Medical Supplies for Hospitals through Local AM*

This example refers to four reported healthcare cases described in Meyer et al. (2022a). Due to COVID-19, hospitals in Europe were faced with demand quantities and demand qualities (new or changed products) that were completely out of initial forecasts. Medical masks, face visors, and even ventilator valves for the artificial respiration of patients were in demand and created bottlenecks. Demand increased in such a way that the remaining stock would be entirely consumed in the short term without the prospect of receiving new products from established supply sources before a stock-out. In this situation, hospitals got in touch with a local AM service provider company. That company was able to rapidly make a DT of the product by scanning and modeling it. Then, the ventilator valves were reproduced using AM. As the pandemic situation allowed for better forecasts, the hospital switched between the traditional and the AM supply sources, depending on the stock level and expected supply dates. The decision was made by checking the demand data (process/system DT). This is a typical example of the dynamics possible in the portfolio of Figure 22.1: As long as the traditional supply chain is not flexible enough, a DT-enabled AM strategy offers additional agility. In this case, the design was close to a central outsourcing to a single AM service provider.

### *22.5.2 Supply of Obsolete Spares for Long-Term Investment Goods*

The public sector operates a number of investment goods with very long life cycles. Some examples refer to infrastructure (bridges, tunnels), traffic surveillance systems (air, rail, ground), or vehicle fleets for emergency organizations (fire department, police, military). The life cycles of such vehicle fleets (aircraft and helicopters) can last from 30 to over 50 years. It is a standard problem in spare parts management to solve the obsolescence of specific parts (Heinen and Hoberg, 2019). Aside from the reasons for the obsolescence (i.e., the supply source is not available any longer), it is essential that the part is printable with AM (material, design) and that there is a DT of the product available. Modern scanners can be used to get a DT model of the spare. However, it is also possible to use elder documentation to create such a DT model. Then, the public organization can produce the part with its own AM capacities or can contract an AM service provider company, which is then in charge of producing the item. In contrast to the first example above, there are no dynamics in switching between a DT-enabled AM strategy and a traditional manufacturing supply chain strategy (and back); instead, the AM replacement of traditional manufacturing is part of a long-term planning of the product life cycle. Depending on the forecast accuracy that can be improved by an asset DT of the related investment goods and the opportunity for last-time buy/final-order and its quantity, AM can be used to address the risk of over-underestimation of demand quantities or delays if the investment good shall be replaced by newer ones. Often, the new investment good, e.g., a new helicopter fleet, is ramped up with a delay, so the older fleet must be kept in service longer than expected. AM then could step in to satisfy demand. The design, in this case, can vary, but it is expected that different parts have their own AM source. As such, this case can be implemented as a decentralized AM design with its own internal or outsourced AM capacities.

### *22.5.3 Supply of Public Emergency Entities during Operations*

In this case, a public emergency organization reacts to a global crisis and deploys in a foreign country (one might consider an earthquake emergency response). Then, supply lines are overstretched, and the transport of spares limits the already scarce capacities. Meyer et al. (2020) provide insights into such a case in which a supply relation is established by means of AM in a foreign country. Very urgent demands can be printed on a local site, even if the quality is below the original part. The printer is operated by the public emergency organization itself in order to ensure availability and operability. Through the internet, the part DT data of spares is exchanged in a spare parts library (digital stock). While AM is used to supply the organization with unpredictable demands, the analysis of operations data in a DT is also used to establish a traditional supply line. This example stands for a decentralized, local, and in-house AM design, referring back to the procurement strategy above.

### *22.5.4 Procurement of AM-Licenses Instead of Spare Parts for Public Transport Buses*

The next example addresses public transport. In a recent business model, transportation service organizations with certified 3D printers have new supply options. Since June 2022, they can order spare parts for transportation buses, or they can procure licenses to produce the spares using AM by themselves (Daimlertruck, 2022). In a digital library, the data on printable spare parts is made available. For the buses, around 40,000 different spare parts are defined as printable, of which a smaller number of 1,500 parts are the nucleus to build up the full digital stock. The product data with licenses is available in digital stock. The license data of the spare is encrypted. After the print job is finished successfully and in the procured quantity, the license expires automatically. With a sufficient implementation of a DT on the bus fleet, a public service provider is able to execute equipment and operations condition monitoring in order to forecast spare parts demand (Wang et al., 2022). Depending on the supply risk situation, the most economically advantageous supply source is either to procure the part in the traditional way or to buy the license and print it with AM. The implementation design is locally outsourced AM at the central bus manufacturer site in this specific case.

### *22.5.5 Showcase of the Digital Twin in Public Railway Operation*

The state railway operation is a very complex task. Investment goods, spares, operator personnel, repairs, and maintenance services, do not forget infrastructure, and last but not least, the passengers have to be synchronized for a stable operation. This showcase exemplifies the system size a DT can get. In the railway organization, a DT is used to receive a virtual image of all activities with all relevant components, actors, influencing factors, and relationships. Based on this comprehensive knowledge and the ability to simulate scenarios, the railway organization aims to identify weak points in the system, evaluate optimizations, and thus develop significant performance improvements (Härdi, 2021). A DT is an appropriate instrument, as it is very flexible and can describe objects, products, and persons, as well as processes, algorithms, and simulations in a digital model. The aim of the public railway organization is to fully mirror the "rail ecosystem" in a DT. Repair sites, trains with their wagons, traffic monitoring, infrastructure data, passenger booking, and seating data, train station data, stocks, and storage data, and system analytics data are seen as one ultimate DT (Härdi, 2021). One mentioned aim is to use real-time DT data to further improve diagnostics and forecasts so that repair and overhaul are planned in a predictive and accurate manner (Härdi, 2021). To achieve this, data is collected for specific purposes, but it shall be exchanged and combined for joint DT analytics. Interoperability of systems is challenging in this showcase, so the vision is realized in steps, starting from smaller DT applications, e.g., for trains. AM can then be linked to that data and provide products for urgent demand. An in-house and decentralized design of AM can be seen in this case, as the operation of a railway is sufficient to operate AM at full capacity, which decreases unit costs.

### *22.5.6 "America Makes"-Initiative and the role of the Data Ecosystem*

The final example addresses the issue that in the United States, it is also acknowledged that AM increases the resiliency and competitiveness of supply chains, but there are a number of implementation barriers (The White House, 2022). This is generally in line with the above-mentioned challenges and performance prospects of DT-enabled AM.

Government support is necessary to support the implementation and usage of AM (The White House, 2022). A number of programs and institutions have been created, e.g., the National Additive Manufacturing Innovation Institute (NAMII) of the Department of Defence or the Office of Advanced Manufacturing of the Department of Commerce (Manufacturing.gov, 2023). These initiatives aim to accelerate the adoption of AM not only in public procurement but also in the manufacturing industry in general. One peculiar initiative is the public-private partnership organization of "America Makes." This example is highlighted because it aims not only to train the AM workforce but also to increase AM application maturity by developing standards. One main aspect is to establish an ecosystem for its application (Americamakes.us, 2024). In that sense, America Makes does foster collaboration but also works on providing a digital platform and system to enable AM usage. One pillar of America Makes is a secure online platform (named CORE) that enables access and exchange of DT data of products. It is an advanced AI engine that provides very quick product and project data in a secure information technology environment (Americamakes.us, 2024). Therefore, the initiative America Makes can be perceived as one example of an enabling organization that, on the one hand, informs a public procurement official with the required DT data and, on the other hand, provides contact with appropriate AM providers. All this can "[...] increase the effectiveness of government programs [...]" (The White House, 2022). That case stands for linking public procurement with the decentralized outsourcing design of AM implementation.

## 22.6 Summary

This chapter informs about the transformative impact of DTs on increased demand prognosis accuracy and its consequential role in reshaping procurement and supply strategies. Using DT technology, public organizations can gain far better insights into the conditions of public service operations, allowing for more accurate and far-seeing prognostic analyses. By integrating this enhanced prognosis into decision-making processes, organizations can strategically decide on AM or traditional supply lines depending on supply disruption risk. A shift toward AM can affect quicker and more customized demand satisfaction, but foremost, it increases resilience against supply disruptions. On the other hand, AM is not always the preferred sourcing strategy. Instead, there are dynamics that have to be anticipated in a kind of life cycle AM assessment.

This chapter also mentioned that DT and AM are already implemented and are productive applications, not a science-fiction vision. As such, it is the management responsibility of public professionals to develop a strategy to best integrate and make use of these technologies for their public services. This chapter outlined a number of emerging issues and some relevant cornerstones of such a strategy. Cases from the past were used to illustrate how this can be implemented. As a managerial implication, it is recommended that public organizations have a strategy for DT-enabled AM readiness before the next supply disruption happens.

## References

Aheleroff, S., Xu, X., Zhong, R. Y., and Lu, Y. (2021), Digital twin as a service (DTaaS) in industry 4.0: An architecture reference model. *Advanced Engineering Informatics*, Vol. 47, p. 101225.

Americamakes.us (2024), When America makes, America works, available at: www.americamakes.us/membership/america-makes-core/ (accessed 15 October 2024).

Bhandal, R., Meriton, R., Kavanagh, R. E., and Brown, A. (2022), The application of digital twin technology in operations and supply chain management: A bibliometric review. *Supply Chain Management: An International Journal*, Vol. 27, No. 2, pp. 182–206.

Braziotis, C., Rogers, H., and Jimo, A. (2019), 3D printing strategic deployment: The supply chain perspective. *Supply Chain Management*, Vol. 24, No. 3, pp. 397–404.

Christopher, M., Peck, H., and Towill, D. (2006), A taxonomy for selecting global supply chain strategies. *The International Journal of Logistics Management*, Vol. 17, No. 2, pp. 277–287.

Daimlertruck (2022), Daimler Buses revolutioniert den Teileservice, available at: www.daimlertruck.com/newsroom/pressemitteilung/daimler-buses-revolutioniert-den-teileservice-zukuenftig-koennen-busunternehmen-und-servicepartner-ersatzteile-per-3d-druck-selbst-anfertigen-51941003 (accessed 12 February 2022).

Deloitte (2022), Reimagining resilience for government and the public sector, available at: www.deloitte.com/global/en/services/risk-advisory/blogs/reimagining-resilience-for-government-and-the-public-sector.html (accessed 12 February 2024).

Dietz, M., and Pernul, G. (2020). Digital twin: Empowering enterprises towards a system-of-systems approach. *Business & Information Systems Engineering*, Vol. 62, pp. 179–184.

Dube, N., Li, Q., Selviaridis, K., and Jahre, M. (2022). One crisis, different paths to supply resilience: The case of ventilator procurement for the COVID-19 pandemic. *Journal of Purchasing and Supply Management*, Vol. 28, No. 5, p. 100773.

Durach, C. F., Kurpjuweit, S., and Wagner, S. M. (2017), The impact of additive manufacturing on supply chains. *International Journal of Physical Distribution and Logistics Management*, Vol. 47, No. 10, pp. 954–971.

Fiksel, J., Polyviou, M., Croxton, K., and Pettit, T. (2015), From risk to resilience: Learning to deal with disruption. *MIT Sloan Management Review*, Vol. 56, pp. 79–86.

Gelderman, C. J., and Van Weele, A. J. (2005), Purchasing portfolio models: A critique and update. *Journal of Supply Chain Management*, Vol. 41, No. 3, pp. 19–28.

Glas, A. H., and Eßig, M. (2018), Factors that influence the success of small and medium-sized suppliers in public procurement: Evidence from a centralized agency in Germany. *Supply Chain Management: An International Journal*, Vol. 23, No. 1, pp. 65–78.

Glas, A. H., and Eßig, M. (2023), Additive Manufacturing Application for Resilience in Defence Supply Chains: Pooled Capacity Hedging as an Hybrid Instrument, in: European Defence Agency: Research Technology and Innovation Awards 2023, S. 62–70. https://eda.europa.eu/docs/default-source/brochures/eda-rti-papers-award-2023_web.pdf

Glas, A. H., Meyer, M. M., and Eßig, M. (2021a), Covid-19 attacks the body of purchasing and supply management: A medical check of the immune system. *Journal of Purchasing and Supply Management*, Vol. 27, No. 4, p. 100716.

Glas, A. H., Meyer, M. M., and Eßig, M. (2021b), Business models for additive manufacturing: A strategic view from a procurement perspective. In *Industrializing Additive Manufacturing: Proceedings of AMPA2020* (pp. 483–499). Springer International Publishing.

González-Benito, J. (2007), A theory of purchasing's contribution to business performance. *Journal of Operations Management*, Vol. 25, No. 4, pp. 901–917.

Härdi, R. (2021), Digital Twin: Ein Fundament für die Zukunft der Bahn. *Deine Bahn*, Vol. 4, No. April, available at: www.system-bahn.net/aktuell/digital-twin-ein-fundament-fuer-die-zukunft-der-bahn/ (accessed 12 February 2024).

Hearn, M., and Rix, S. (2019), Cybersecurity considerations for digital twin implementations. *IIC Journal of Innovation*, Vol. 10, pp. 107–113.

Heinen, J. J., and Hoberg, K. (2019), Assessing the potential of additive manufacturing for the provision of spare parts. *Journal of Operations Management*, Vol. 65, No. 8, pp. 810–826.

Jonen, A. (2023), *Beschaffungsportfolios*. Springer Books, Wiesbaden.

Juarez, M. G., Botti, V. J., and Giret, A. S. (2021), Digital twins: Review and challenges. *Journal of Computing and Information Science in Engineering*, Vol. 21, No. 3, p. 030802.

Kleer, R., and Piller, F. T. (2019), Local manufacturing and structural shifts in competition: Market dynamics of additive manufacturing. *International Journal of Production Economics*, Vol. 216, pp. 23–34.

Kraljic, P. (1983), Purchasing must become supply management. *Harvard Business Review*, Vol. 61, No. 5, pp. 109–117.

Manufacturing.gov (2023), Additive manufacturing, available at: www.manufacturing.gov/topic/additive-manufacturing (accessed 15 October 2024).

Markowitz, H. (1952), Portfolio selection. *Journal of Finance*, Vol. 7, No. 3 (March), pp. 77–91.

McKinsey (2020), How construction can emerge stronger after Coronavirus, available at: www.mckinsey.com/capabilities/operations/our-insights/how-construction-can-emerge-stronger-after-coronavirus (accessed 12 February 2024).

Meschini, S., Tagliabue, L. C., Di Giuda, G. M., Campi, S., and Paleari, F. (2022), An innovative digital twin prototypes system to enhance tender evaluation in green public procurement. In EC3 Conference 2022 (Vol. 3). University of Turin.

Meyer, M. M., Glas, A. H., and Eßig, M. (2020), Der Einfluss additiver Fertigung auf Operational Performance: Lieferkettenmodellierung am Fallbeispiel einer globalen Einsatzorganisation. *Controlling, Zeitschrift für erfolgsorientierte Unternehmenssteuerung*, Vol. 32, No. 3, pp. 14–21.

Meyer, M. M., Glas, A. H., and Eßig, M. (2021), Systematic review of sourcing and 3D printing: Make-or-buy decisions in industrial buyer–supplier relationships. *Management Review Quarterly*, Vol. 71, No. 4, pp. 723–752.

Meyer, M. M., Glas, A. H., and Eßig, M. (2022a), Learning from supply disruptions caused by SARS-CoV-2: Use of additive manufacturing as a resilient response for public procurement. *Journal of Public Procurement*, Vol. 22, No. 1, pp. 17–42.

Meyer, M. M., Glas, A. H., and Eßig, M. (2022b), Achieving Supply Chain Resilience through Additive Manufacturing. In: Kummer, S., Wakolbinger, T., Novoszel, L., Geske, A. M. (eds) *Supply Chain Resilience*. Springer Series in Supply Chain Management, Vol. 17. Springer, Cham, pp. 223–245.

Montero, J., Weber, S., Bleckmann, M., and Paetzold, K. (2020), A methodology for the decentralised design and production of additive manufactured spare parts. *Production & Manufacturing Research*, Vol. 8, No. 1, pp. 313–334.

Nellore, R., and Söderquist, K. (2000), Portfolio approaches to procurement: Analysing the missing link to specifications. *Long Range Planning*, Vol. 33, No. 2, pp. 245–267.

Oehlschläger, D., Glas, A. H., and Eßig, M. (2023), Customization vs. Ultimate Customer Transparency: Experiment Indications for Digital Customer Twin, in: EUROMA-2023 annual conference, Leuven, 03.–05. July 2023.

Oehlschläger, D., Glas, A. H., and Eßig, M. (2024), Acceptance of digital twins of customer demands for supply chain optimisation: An analysis of three hierarchical digital twin levels. *Industrial Management & Data Systems*, Vol. 124, No. 3, pp. 1050–1075..

Parks, M. (2020), Digital twinning: Types of digital twins. *Method: Mouser's Technology & Solutions Journal*. 2018, available at: https://eu.mouser.com/applications/digital-twinning-types/ (accessed on 12 October 2020).

Patrucco, A., Luzzini, D., Ronchi, S., Eßig, M., Amann, M., and Glas, A. H. (2016), Designing a public procurement strategy: Lessons from local governments. *Public Money & Management*, Vol. 37, No. 4, pp. 269–276, DOI: 10.1080/09540962.2017.1295727

Pettit, T., Fiksel, J., and Croxton, K. (2010), Ensuring supply chain resilience: Development of a conceptual framework. *Journal of Business Logistics*, Vol. 31, pp. 1–21.

Rathore, M. M., Shah, S. A., Shukla, D., Bentafat, E., and Bakiras, S. (2021). The role of AI, machine learning, and big data in digital twinning: A systematic literature review, challenges, and opportunities. *IEEE Access*, Vol. 9, pp. 32030–32052.

Rogers, H., Baricz, N., and Pawar, K. S. (2016), 3D printing services: Classification, supply chain implications and research agenda. *International Journal of Physical Distribution and Logistics Management*, Vol. 46, No. 10, pp. 886–907.

Schmidt, C., Volz, F., Stojanovic, L., and Sutschet, G. (2023), Increasing interoperability between digital twin standards and specifications: Transformation of DTDL to AAS. *Sensors*, Vol. 23, No. 18, p. 7742.

Singh, M., Fuenmayor, E., Hinchy, E. P., Qiao, Y., Murray, N., and Devine, D. (2021), Digital twin: Origin to future. *Applied System Innovation*, Vol. 4, No. 2, p. 36.

Swinnen, J., and McDermott, J. (2020), Covid-19 and global food security. *EuroChoices*, Vol. 19, No. 3, pp. 26–33.

The White House (2022), Using additive manufacturing to improve supply chain resilience and bolster small and mid-size firms, available at: https://bidenwhitehouse.archives.gov/cea/written-materials/2022/05/09/using-additive-manufacturing-to-improve-supply-chain-resilience-and-bolster-small-and-mid-size-firms/ (accessed 15 October 2024).

United Nations (2020), The role of public services and servants during the COVID-19 pandemic, available at: www.un.org/development/desa/dpad/publication/un-desa-policy-brief-79-the-roleof-public-service-and-public-servants-during-the-covid-19-pandemic/ (accessed 22 October 2020).

Waller, M. A., and Fawcett, S. E. (2014), Click here to print a maker movement supply chain: How invention and entrepreneurship will disrupt supply chain design. *Journal of Business Logistics*, Vol. 35, No. 2, pp. 99–102.

Wang, S., Wang, Y., and Wang, J. (2022), Spare parts demand forecasting method of modern enterprises based on digital twin model. *International Journal of Modeling, Simulation, and Scientific Computing*, Vol. 13, No. 06, p. 2250045.

WHO (2020), Shortage of personal protective equipment endangering health workers worldwide, available at: www.who.int/news/item/03-03-2020-shortage-of-personal-protective-equipment-endangering-health-workers-worldwide (accessed 12 February 2024).

### *Case Study: Protection Vests for "Giants" or "Dwarfs" (Developed by Andreas H. Glas and Michael Essig)*

In this section, we present a project of a Defence Agency, which is responsible for uniforms and personnel equipment to emergency organizations (police, special fire departments, and the military) (loosely following Oehlschlaeger et al., 2023).

#### Situation

The Defence Agency supplies a very high number of persons with uniforms and personnel equipment. Around 150,000 people receive their clothing from that agency from a number of around 80 decentralized distribution centers. Clothing and equipment include a wide range of several hundred different items, such as socks, trousers, shirts, sweaters, jackets, and so on. Besides quite common clothing items, the clients of the Agency also receive some very specific items, such as clothing for specific environments (tropics, polar) and specific situations (fire protection, safety jackets). This case addresses the issue of a bulletproof protection vest.

All items are designed and produced on the basis of clothing size charts. The size charts are quite old. The original data originated in the 1960s. Since then, the sizes of clients have changed. Most specifically, the share of women increased significantly. Data on size charts for women is hardly available, and if data is available, it does not necessarily match the population average. But also, the size charts for men do not fit any longer, as the share of taller men increased, but also the share of smaller men increased, as size restrictions on employment were eliminated. Overall, the sizes became far more heterogeneous, and slimmer or fuller-body sizes increased in the sample of clients.

This is generally a problem for the agency, as it is hardly possible to supply all distribution centers with every item in every size. Even worse, the data system is old, and monitoring of stock data is not possible for every site. Thus, it happens more and more often that clients appear at a distribution center and do not get the right item. Often, a client then receives a size that is a second-best solution, for example, a too loose size. This results in either dissatisfied customers and/or redistribution and replacement processes, forcing the internal customer to come in for a second fitting procedure. Often, suppliers have long lead times, so waiting time for the right item is significant. Most severe is that the client, when swapping clothing, is not able to fulfill the duty in the public organization (opportunity cost).

In the case of the protection vest, the problem is even more severe. A vest that does not fit properly on the person does not provide the right level of protection. To hand over a second-best vest is not a good option, because it is not about style and appearance, but about personal protection. Officials of the agency are convinced that, due to outdated size charts, the problem cannot be fixed without getting new data about the real and current sample of clients. For calculating new size charts, a minimum sample of several thousand clients must be measured by a tailor.

At this point, Jens Zimmer steps in. He is the responsible director for a research center on personnel equipment and mentions:

> "This is far too costly. But I have an idea: I have heard a speech of an international colleague at a Body-Tech-Conference. He mentioned the existence of stationary or mobile scanners to measure sizes. Then we have individual body

data. If we could use that data to produce individual items, e.g. with additive manufacturing, then the problem is solved. Let´s change the whole system and make a new clothing procurement strategy – in peculiar for the vests!" **Please help Jens Zimmer!**

1. What are the core challenges in the supply of the vests?
2. How would you use scanners to get the data (Digital Twin of Sizes)?
3. Develop a procurement strategy in which cases you use AM for the vests.

# 23 Competencies for Effective Public Procurement

*Klaas Stek*

Editors' Note: Readers, the previous chapters in this book have been largely about the theories and processes of procurement, offering essential knowledge for academics, students, and practitioners. However, procurement is, at its core, an interaction between people and between organisations. Interpersonal and interorganisational exchanges involve building relationships, communicating effectively, and embracing the humanity of interaction. This chapter introduces and explores these softer skills directly, delving into the practical considerations of working together and offering specific strategies exploring the softer side of public procurement.

## 23.1 Introduction

Public procurement is transforming towards strategic significance, spurred by evolving public policy and governmental directives, exemplified by a focus on sustainability (Grandia & Kruyen, 2020; Minoja & Romano, 2021), the creation of societal value for money (Callens, Verhoest, & Boon, 2021; Meehan, Ludbrook, & Mason, 2016), digitalisation (Nicoletti, 2018), the promotion of human-centricity, diversity, and inclusion (Benjamin, 2020) and stimulating innovation within private enterprises (Amann & Essig, 2015; Nijboer, Senden, & Telgen, 2017; Yeow & Edler, 2016), often supported by economic development incentives at local, regional, and national levels (Preuss, 2011; Sánchez-Carreira, Peñate-Valentín, & Varela-Vázquez, 2019). Moreover, public procurement expenditures substantially influence supplier markets, causing a notable economic impact (Alvarez & Rubio, 2015; Obwegeser & Müller, 2018; Yeow & Edler, 2016).

Within this context, specialised competencies embedded in the daily practices of individual practitioners emerge as pivotal (Lau, 2010; Ogden, Rossetti, & Hendrick, 2007; Orlikowski, 2002). Organisations need to prioritise creating, disseminating, and applying knowledge, recognising that the value lies in managing these processes to enhance organisational performance (Jasimuddin, Klein, & Connell, 2005; Nonaka & Takeuchi, 1995; Smith, 2001). Therefore, defining specific competency sets is essential for organisations since individual competencies are considered significant resources (Grant, 1996).

Traditionally, public procurement practices required operational and transactional competencies (Grandia & Meehan, 2017; Patrucco, Walker, Luzzini, & Ronchi, 2019). However, public procurers increasingly need to combine a profound understanding of the internal business partners' requirements and the dynamic possibilities in the market to connect both (Amann & Essig, 2015; Patrucco et al., 2017). This paradigmatic shift from traditional to strategic public procurement necessitates re-evaluating the essential competencies, particularly for professionals in public procurement, now tasked with increasingly

DOI: 10.4324/9781003566670-27

strategic responsibilities associated with sourcing innovation (Delke, Schiele, & Buchholz, 2023; Yeow & Edler, 2012).

Despite the growing recognition of the importance of competencies, a widening gap persists between the competencies currently possessed by public procurement professionals and those demanded for their new roles in strategic public procurement. This gap is particularly pronounced as public procurement efforts shift towards sourcing innovative products, services, and works, necessitating inventiveness, creativity, and out-of-the-box thinking (Yeow & Edler, 2016). This emphasis aligns with the findings of Von der Gracht, Giunipero, and Schueller (2016), who advise recruiting industrial purchasing and supply management (PSM) professionals with creative and innovative competencies to ensure future adaptability for complex problem-solving.

This chapter aims to deepen the understanding of the competencies essential for strategic public procurement, explicitly focusing on sourcing innovations and exploring effective didactical approaches. The first section examines the interpersonal competencies, intrapersonal attitudes, or *soft skills* crucial for public procurement professionals involved in innovative sourcing. The second section introduces guidelines on implementing up-to-date, real-life case studies as a practical method for developing these soft skills in higher education and professional training settings. Key questions include identifying the most effective pedagogical approaches and assessing their impact on competency development.

To clarify the required competencies for strategic public procurement, especially sourcing innovation, the subsequent sections present overviews of (1) skills classifications, (2) competency frameworks for public procurement practitioners, (3) the context of public procurement competencies for fostering innovation, (4) crucial interpersonal skills and intrapersonal attitudes for public procurement for innovation, (5) public procurement competencies in the context of the digital revolution, and (6) public procurement for innovation competencies in developing countries. The second part, clarifying effective didactical methods, concentrates on how interpersonal skills and intrapersonal attitudes can be taught. It describes (1) student-centred teaching methods, (2) practical applications to include soft skills learning objectives, with the use of practical case studies to facilitate soft skills learning objectives in higher education, and (3) the implementation of soft skills learning into public procurement practices. Eventually, the chapter presents conclusions on the required soft skills, and its teaching methods in public procurement education. In a comprehensible figure displaying the competence triangle or *KSA triangle* of theory and knowledge (K), professional and interpersonal skills (S), and intrapersonal attitudes (A) for each of the KSA elements, specific didactics and assessment methods are suggested.

## 23.2 Personal Competencies or Soft Skills in Public Procurement

### *23.2.1 Classifications to Define Competency*

The literature concerning organisational knowledge and skills encompasses various classifications and taxonomies. One prevalent categorisation distinguishes hard and soft skills (Andrews & Higson, 2008; Bailly & Léné, 2013; Heckman & Kautz, 2012; Laker & Powell, 2011). Soft skills are defined by Heckman and Kautz (2012, p. 451) as encompassing "personality traits, goals, motivations, and preferences", while Laker and Powell (2011, p. 113) differentiate between "hard skills or technical training (working with equipment and software) and soft-skills training (interpersonal or intrapersonal focus)", whereas the term *interpersonal* regards the skills required for human-to-human interaction and *intrapersonal* the personal attitudes of an individual.

Professionals need to develop soft skills further during their careers. Soft skills are crucial for effectively applying professional expertise or hard skills (Ahmed, Fernando Capretz, Bouktif, & Campbell, 2012; Socha, Razmov, & Davis, 2003). Research showed that soft skills are equally crucial as hard skills for professionals and that the absence of soft skills is more likely to lead to employment termination than knowledge deficiencies (Ahmed et al., 2012; Stek & Schiele, 2021). Employers express that they highly value soft skills (Bals, Schulze, Kelly, & Stek, 2019); research showed that half of the requirements in PSM job advertisements are soft skills (Stek, Zunk, Koch, & Schiele, 2022). Moreover, soft skills are vital for articulating a vision, rallying others, and communicating values and expectations (Muir, 2004).

Another classification includes "Business Specific Issues (Hard business-related knowledge and skills); Interpersonal Competences (Soft business-related skills)" along with an unspecified category, "Work Experience and Work-Based Learning" (Andrews & Higson, 2008, p. 414). Here, the differentiation between hard and soft skills may not comprehensively cover all facets. The definitions of explicit and tacit knowledge are applied to clarify the undefined "Work Experience and Work-Based Learning" category.

Various approaches to managing, classifying, and sharing knowledge hinge on the fundamental dichotomy between explicit *know-what* and tacit *know-how* (Nonaka & Takeuchi, 1995; Smith, 2001) and particularly on the ease of knowledge transfer and aggregation (Grant, 1996). Polanyi (1966, p. 4) introduced the notion of tacit knowledge, positing that "we can know more than we can tell". This concept is exemplified by the recognition that individuals can, for instance, recognise a familiar face yet often struggle to articulate how they do so, demonstrating that specific knowledge cannot be easily verbalised (Polanyi, 1966, p. 4):

> I shall reconsider human knowledge by starting from the fact that we can know more than we can tell. This fact seems obvious enough, but it is not easy to say exactly what it means. Take an example. We know a person's face and can recognise it among a thousand, indeed among a million. Yet, we usually cannot tell how we recognise a face we know. So most of this knowledge cannot be put into words.
>
> (Polanyi, 1966, p. 4)

Tacit knowledge is characterised by its multidimensionality, context specificity, and frequent embedding within organisational routines (Kothari et al., 2012). Its acquisition depends on practical application and can only be transferred through its utilisation (Grant, 1996; Kogut & Zander, 1992). Conversely, explicit knowledge is expressible in a formal language, such as texts, manuals, graphs, tables, mathematical expressions, copyrights, and patents (Smith, 2001). Explicit knowledge, therefore, possesses characteristics of freely available public goods since it can be shared more easily among individuals and organisations (Grant, 1996; Tamer Cavusgil, Calantone, & Zhao, 2003).

In contrast, the transfer of tacit knowledge is comparatively slower, costlier, and less specific (Grant, 1996; Kogut & Zander, 1992). Consequently, the significance of tacit knowledge is profound, constituting approximately 90% of organisational knowledge (Smith, 2001). Jasimuddin et al. (2005, p. 109) summarise this dichotomy: "Tacit knowledge is less vulnerable but less accessible by legitimate organisational users, whilst explicit knowledge is more accessible but also more vulnerable to illegitimate exploitation".

While the division between explicit and tacit knowledge may seem distinct, there is evidence that knowledge exists on a continuum between these two extremes (Jasimuddin et al.,

2005; Nonaka & Von Krogh, 2009). Through codification, tacit knowledge can transition to explicit knowledge (Nonaka & Takeuchi, 1995). Shared experiences are the predominant means of transferring tacit knowledge among individuals, as without such shared experiences, projecting oneself into another individual's thought process becomes exceedingly challenging (Nonaka & Takeuchi, 1995).

The classification of skills and knowledge into hard, soft, explicit, and tacit, though widely employed, does not comprehensively encapsulate the entirety of an individual's competence. Boyatzis (1982) introduced a more comprehensive definition of competence as an underlying characteristic contributing to effective job performance, which may encompass motives, traits, skills, self-image, social roles, or knowledge and may be known or unknown to the individual. It partly aligns with Polanyi's notion of tacit knowledge, where individuals can know more than they can tell.

More nuanced definitions of competence incorporate conceptual and operational elements, encapsulating cognitive, knowledge, understanding, functional, psycho-motoric, applied skills, meta-competence, and social competence (Campion et al., 2011). Delamare-Le Deist and Winterton (2005) provided a comprehensive definition:

> The competences required of an occupation include both conceptual (cognitive, knowledge and understanding) and operational (functional, psycho-motoric and applied skill) competences. The competences more associated with individual effectiveness are also both conceptual (meta-competence, including learning to learn) and operational (social competence, including behaviours and attitudes.
>
> (Delamare-Le Deist & Winterton, 2005, p. 39)

In conclusion, this section revealed the evolution of competencies, emphasising the significance of interpersonal skills and intrapersonal attitudes for practitioners in general.

## 23.3 General Competency Frameworks for Public Procurement Practice

Several general competency frameworks for public procurement are developed by notable organisations such as the National Institute of Governmental Purchasing (NIGP), the European Commission, the International Federation of Purchasing and Supply Management (IFPSM), and the World Bank. These organisations advocate for professionalisation, recognising that public procurement is a complex and strategic function. They achieve this by offering training, certification, networking opportunities, and supporting procurement reform and innovation.

This overview highlights these entities' significant role in shaping frameworks for public procurement competencies. The NIGP identifies seven critical focus areas, while the European Commission categorises competencies into six key groups. The IFPSM presents a Global Standard, and the World Bank provides contemporary tools for competency development. Collectively, these frameworks emphasise the comprehensive nature of the competencies required in public procurement.

### *23.3.1 National Institute of Governmental Purchasing (NIGP)*

*NIGP: The Institute for Public Procurement* is a US-based provider of educational and research programmes for public procurement to support practitioners. Its Public Procurement Competency Framework (PPCF) outlines vital skills across seven focus areas NIGP (2015):

- **Strategy**: Procurement strategies are developed, alignment with organisational goals is ensured, and legal and ethical compliance is overseen.
- **Policy and legislation**: Procurement policies and legislation are understood and interpreted, and procurement policies and procedures are developed and implemented.
- **Planning and analysis**: Market research is conducted, procurement data is analysed, and procurement plans are developed.
- **Sourcing and solicitation**: Supplier relationships are developed and managed, competitive solicitations are conducted, and contracts are negotiated.
- **Contract administration**: Contracts are managed, supplier performance is monitored, and contract disputes are resolved.
- **Leadership**: Procurement teams are led, professionals are developed, and excellence is promoted.
- **Business principles**: Business principles are understood, financial management is executed, and risk management is undertaken (NIGP, 2015).

### *23.3.2 European Commission*

The European Commission has developed the *ProcurComp$^{EU}$* competency framework for public procurement professionals in the European Union and beyond (European Commission, 2020). This framework defines key competencies, providing a standard reference for public procurement professionals.

ProcurComp$^{EU}$ is structured around two main categories of competencies: *Procurement-Specific Competencies*, which encompass the technical and procedural aspects of procurement throughout the *Pre-Award*, *Horizontal*, and *Post-Award* phases, and *Soft Competencies*, which emphasise personal, interpersonal, and performance skills vital for effective collaboration, leadership, and strategic decision-making. The various competencies per cluster are detailed in Table 23.1. The framework articulates these competencies across four proficiency levels: *Basic, Intermediate, Advanced,* and *Expert*, thereby offering a tailored growth pathway suitable for various roles and contexts.

Further analysis divided the *ProcurComp$^{EU}$* competencies into six categories:

- **Strategy and policy**: Competencies related to developing and implementing procurement strategies and policies, such as developing procurement strategies and monitoring and evaluating procurement performance,
- **Procurement process**: Competencies for conducting market research and managing procurement risks,
- **Contract management**: Managing contract performance and contract disputes,
- **Supplier management**: Developing supplier relationships and managing supplier performance,
- **Legal and regulatory**: Interpreting and applying procurement law and managing conflicts of interest,
- **Personal effectiveness**: Communicating effectively and working collaboratively (European Commission, 2020).

### *23.3.3 International Federation of Purchasing and Supply Management (IFPSM)*

IFPSM is a global organisation uniting 44 national and regional purchasing associations, representing around 250,000 procurement and supply chain management professionals. IFPSM aims to enhance the profession by developing and sharing knowledge, thereby

*Table 23.1* Overview of the 30 competencies contained in the ProcurComp[EU] Competency Matrix

| *Category of competence* | *Cluster of competences* | *Competence* |
|---|---|---|
| Procurement specific competences | Horizontal | 1. Planning; 2. Life-cycle; 3. Legislation; 4. e-Procurement and other IT tools; 5. Sustainable procurement; 6. Innovation procurement; 7. Category specific; 8. Supplier management; 9. Negotiations |
| | Pre-award | 10. Needs assessment; 11. Market analysis and engagement; 12. Procurement strategy; 13. Technical specifications; 14. Tender documentation; 15. Tender evaluation |
| | Post-award | 16. Contract management; 17. Certification and payment; 18. Reporting and evaluation; 19. Conflict resolution and mediation |
| Soft competences | Personal | 20. Adaptability and modernisation; 21. Analytical and critical thinking; 22. Communication; 23. Ethics and compliance |
| | People | 24. Collaboration; 25. Stakeholder relationship management; 26. Team management and Leadership |
| | Performance | 27. Organisational awareness; 28. Project management; 29. Business and performance orientation; 30. Risk management and internal control |

*Source:* European Commission (2020, p. 29).

improving global business practices and living standards. It covers purchasing, materials management, logistics, supply chain management, and strategic sourcing. IFPSM, contributing to *ProcurComp[EU]* as an advisor to the European Commission, established a Global Standard for Professional Competence for industrial PSM and public procurement. Essential skills are categorised as follows:

- **PSM-specific competencies**: Specialist PSM knowledge, appreciation of the role of IT systems; identifying, analysing, formulating, and solving PSM problems; analytical skills using PSM models, processes, and theories.
- **General management skills**: Business case analysis, commercial writing, decision-making, proficiency in basic IT, research and enquiry, and time management.
- **Personal skills and attitudes**: Critical analysis, cross-functional and interdisciplinary skills, interpretative skills exercising judgement, global awareness, initiative, integrative skills, personal responsibility, prioritisation, problem-solving, engaging in reflection/reflective learning, problem identification and analysis, social and ethical responsibility (Brennan & Crowe, 2012).

### *23.3.4 World Bank*

Whereas IFPSM proposed a Global Standard, in 2016, the World Bank launched a new Procurement Framework that provides a modern set of tools and techniques that ensure faster delivery with value for money (World Bank, 2020). These include the following:

- **Project Procurement Strategy for Development (PPSD)**: PPSD helps develop procurement strategies tailored to their project's specific needs and considers the risks associated with different procurement approaches.

- **Hands-on Expanded Implementation Support (HEIS)**: HEIS provides hands-on support when implementing procurement plans.
- **Alternative Procurement Arrangements (APA)**: APA guides alternative procurement arrangements, such as framework agreements, electronic reverse auctions, and public–private partnerships (PPPs).
- **Systematic Tracking of Exchanges in Procurement (STEP)**: STEP tracks exchanges between borrowers and the World Bank during procurement, providing a record of all communications and ensuring transparency and accountability (World Bank, 2020).

In conclusion, these frameworks underscore a broad spectrum of skills crucial for successful public procurement. From strategic planning to legal compliance and effective communication, practitioners can leverage these models to enhance their proficiency and navigate the dynamic landscape of public procurement. Examining prominent competence models, including those by NIGP, the European Commission, IFPSM, and the World Bank, reveals common grounds crucial for public procurement professionals. Core competencies span strategic planning, legal compliance, and effective communication. Table 23.2 summarises the overview of the essential competencies in the public procurement frameworks above. This unified synthesis highlights a holistic set of competencies crucial for successfully navigating the multifaceted landscape of public procurement.

## 23.4 Context of Public Procurement Competencies for Fostering Innovation

Recent research has identified the organisational circumstances that allow for the flourishing of particular personal skills and competencies required for effective performance in public-sector procurement. For instance, McKevitt et al. (2012) studied procurement professionals' competencies in public sector contexts in Ireland and Wales. They identified four typologies of competency profiles: the *Commercial, Pragmatic, Political*, and *Person-Centred* types.

In the *Commercial* category, individuals were primarily recruited from the private sector and tasked with introducing a commercial mindset into public-sector departments previously dominated by procurement compliance. Procurement, where formal structures were in place, exhibited a resigned acceptance of hierarchical culture and formal communication norms among budget holders. This group leveraged procurement concepts, principles, and

*Table 23.2* Unified overview: Synthesising essential competencies in public procurement frameworks

| | |
|---|---|
| **Strategic competence** | All models prioritise developing and aligning procurement strategies with organisational goals, ensuring legal and ethical compliance. |
| **Operational competence** | Skills in policy interpretation, planning and analysis, sourcing and solicitation, and contract administration are universally essential for effective procurement. |
| **Leadership and relationship management** | The significance of leadership, supplier relationship development, and effective contract management resonates across all models. |
| **Personal effectiveness** | A common thread involves personal effectiveness, emphasising communication, collaboration, critical analysis, and ethical responsibility. |
| **Global awareness and adaptability** | Acknowledgement of global awareness, adaptability, and integrative skills is evident, catering to the dynamic nature of procurement. |

*Source*: Brennan and Crowe (2012); European Commission (2020); NIGP (2015); World Bank (2020).

models to enhance cost-effectiveness, albeit with a reluctance to engage suppliers due to compliance concerns (McKevitt et al., 2012).

The *Pragmatic* group emphasised employing a structured procurement process that had proven beneficial for buyers and managers. Unlike the *Commercial* group, they placed less emphasis on conceptual thinking and valued professional and technical knowledge more. Their collective experience encompassed providing guidance and interacting with stakeholders when necessary. In some instances, procurers were not involved in the requirements identification stage, limiting the influence of procurement. Suppliers were engaged for specific, complex projects (McKevitt et al., 2012).

The distinctive characteristic of the *Political* group was their emphasis on the human element. Unlike the *Commercial* and *Pragmatic* groups, these individuals saw themselves as adept at navigating obstacles and influencing stakeholders. For instance, coaching stakeholders in defining their requirements allowed participants to advance the broader organisational agenda, prioritising standardisation over optimising individual functional needs. Outcomes were driven by reputation considerations and a defensive stance (McKevitt et al., 2012).

The core philosophy of the *Person-Centred* group revolved around customising support to individual stakeholders. Participants in this subgroup strongly believed in fair treatment and utilised interpersonal skills to understand stakeholder needs. Unlike the other three competency subgroups, emotions guide behaviour and decision-making. The needs of stakeholders were given precedence over broader organisational considerations. However, participants acknowledged the need to improve networking skills to engage with external stakeholders effectively (McKevitt et al., 2012).

Hence, competencies play a fundamental role in public administration, particularly in enhancing government bureaucracy's efficiency. Initially, the term referred to technical expertise, encompassing subject knowledge and skills of individual civil servants (Osborne, 2006). This approach aimed to streamline government operations by selecting and promoting civil servants based on their technical competence (Hood & Lodge, 2004). Over time, the concept of competencies in public administration evolved to encompass behavioural attitudes associated with excellence. Utilising Boyatzis' (1982) notion that competencies differentiate outstanding performers, this approach has been instrumental in distinguishing superior collaborators in the public sector (Getha-Taylor, 2008; Kruyen & Van Genugten, 2020).

The public sector has a significant influence in stimulating and catalysing private-sector investments in research and innovation (Mazzucato, 2018). As a demand-side innovation policy instrument, strategic public procurement leverages its purchasing power to position itself as a frontrunner in innovative solutions not readily available to commercial entities (Edler & Georghiou, 2007; Geroski, 1990). These interventions aim to bolster innovation demand, streamline introduction conditions, and enhance demand identification (Edler, 2007). Furthermore, public authorities can significantly contribute to policy targets by promoting the development of sustainable innovations in businesses (Bals, Laine, & Mugurusi, 2018; Ghisellini, Cialani, & Ulgiati, 2016).

Thus, public procurement missions are powerful instruments for driving innovation within the market (Mazzucato, 2018). Drawing on insights from programmes focused on innovation policy and investment-driven growth, Mazzucato (2018) emphasises the need for these missions to encompass market correction, market co-creation, and market shaping. Mazzucato (2018) underscores the significance of fostering a culture of experimentation and risk-taking, asserting that incentivising creative thinking is pivotal in generating novel solutions aligned with mission objectives. Mazzucato's (2018) perspective emphasises that successful missions must go beyond rectifying market issues, actively engaging in collaborative innovation and cultivating an environment encouraging bold, out-of-the-box ideas.

Overcoming risk aversion, establishing risk-reward structures, and integrating procurement decisions with other departments' strategies are crucial for enhancing procurement performance. Recognising public organisations' unique needs and expectations is vital in fostering innovation (Knutsson & Thomasson, 2014; Obwegeser & Müller, 2018; Thai, 2008). Within this context, it is essential to develop risk management approaches and implement organisational procedures, routines, and capacities to facilitate innovation and change (Kiers, Seinhorst, Zwanenburg, & Stek, 2022; Yeow & Edler, 2016). The procurement function should act as a value-adding department, which can be attributed to various factors, including recognition from other departments, its position in the organisational hierarchy, and involvement in strategic planning (Patrucco, Luzzini, & Ronchi, 2016).

The evolution of competency literature in public management, spurred by the *new public management* paradigm, underscores the significance of leadership and management competencies. This literature extends to specific policy areas and general leadership competencies in the public sector (Kruyen & Van Genugten, 2020). Recent studies have explored particular competencies civil servants require to navigate the challenges of the 21st century. These initiatives seek to identify the competencies needed for adequate public service provision (van der Wal, 2020). Initiatives by Patrucco et al. (2016) and Brogaard (2017) have delved into the effects of innovation training and the effectiveness of public procurement as part of performance management systems, respectively.

In conclusion, as fostering innovations reshapes procurement processes, the value of human skills and competencies in the public sector becomes apparent. Nurturing these competencies is essential for driving sustainable and innovative solutions. A comprehensive overview of the evolving landscape of competencies in public procurement has been provided, emphasising their pivotal role in enhancing organisational performance and stimulating innovation. Exploring future directions in competency research highlights the imperative of adapting to the contemporary demands for adequate public service provision.

## 23.5 Crucial Interpersonal Skills and Intrapersonal Attitudes for Public Procurement for Innovation

Despite its critical importance, research on public procurement competencies has received limited attention (Mogre, Lindgreen, & Hingley, 2017), highlighting the urgency to bridge this gap and delineate the specific competencies required for this domain. Whereas other chapters focus on essential knowledge and professional competencies, this chapter outlines the soft skills or interpersonal skills and intrapersonal attitudes critical for future strategic public procurement experts and guides effective training methodologies (Loader & Norton, 2015).

Stek (2022b) performed a systematic literature review to find procurement competencies. About 30 studies on purchasing competencies were published between 1987 and 2020. Remarkably, despite the assumed urgency, the studies almost exclusively refer to private-sector purchasing and have overlooked those needed for public procurement and the required competencies for more strategic public procurement of ecologically sustainable innovations. Mogre et al. (2017) confirm this literature gap.

In a mixed-method study, Stek (2021) identified the essential current and future competencies for public procurement of innovations (PPIs), presenting the skill set needed for professionals transitioning from an operational buyer to a strategic business partner role. Notably, the literature emphasises the divergence between public procurement and private purchasing, particularly regarding legal frameworks and regulations (Harland, Telgen, & Callender, 2013; Telgen, Harland, & Knight, 2007). However, as will be demonstrated, this demarcation appears less applicable to interpersonal behavioural aptitudes. Intrapersonal attributes are elucidated in this study's competencies profile for PPIs, showing parallels with those observed in industrial purchasing (Stek, 2021).

The subsequent requisites for an innovation buyer in public procurement encompass interpersonal skills (e.g. human-to-human skills such as persuasion, communication, challenging, and listening), intrapersonal attributes that serve out-of-the-box thinking (e.g. creativity, curiosity, sensitivity, persistence), professional capabilities (e.g. teamwork, contract development, data analysis, interviewing, category strategy development), and knowledge or cognitive skills (e.g. understanding of the organisation and market, legal and technical proficiency, familiarity with circularity, and digitisation) (Stek, 2021).

The emphasis on interpersonal competencies and intrapersonal attitudes is crucial for the evolving public procurement function. Essential interpersonal competencies to strategic public procurement, integral to effective human-to-human communication, encompass sharing information, empathy, multilingual proficiency, and presentation skills. Intrapersonal attitudes, such as creativity combined with result-driven efficiency, are essential for out-of-the-box thinking, complex problem-solving, and driving innovative solutions (Kruyen & Van Genugten, 2020; Stek, 2022b).

Creativity is an example of an individual attitude associated with an interpersonal dimension. Creative ideas emerge in individual minds. Cultivating a fundamental intrapersonal attitude, such as creativity, requires recognising its presence in the subconscious mind (Kaufman, Kaufman, & Plucker, 2013; Sawyer & Henriksen, 2024). The subconscious mind plays a critical role in producing innovative ideas and solutions, demystifying the misconception that creativity is a conscious or inherent trait (Csikszentmihalyi, 1997).

However, creativity is also seen as a collaborative endeavour within innovation-sourcing teams (Kiratli, Rozemeijer, Hilken, de Ruyter, & de Jong, 2016). Kiratli et al. (2016) emphasise the critical role of creativity within procurement by introducing the notion of a "team creativity climate" as a crucial mechanism for addressing the distinctive challenges associated with collaborative, cross-functional efforts to develop value-enhancing sourcing strategies.

Team creative climate pertains to the organisational environment that facilitates the collective sensemaking process that precedes the generation of innovative and successful sourcing strategies (Kiratli et al., 2016). To foster creativity, Kiratli et al. (2016) recommend that organisations establish sourcing teams capable of leveraging their employees' specialised knowledge and expertise across the organisation, positioning individuals as boundary spanners to navigate a complex terrain of conflicting transparency, accountability, and economic efficiency demands.

Stek (2021) distinguishes three roles for the PPIs and combines the roles with competencies sets, displayed in Figure 23.1 (adapted from Stek, 2021, p. 108). The initial role involves establishing connections within the internal organisation and potential suppliers of innovative solutions in the market. The second challenge public procurers face in the innovation sphere is to act as intermediaries, aligning the internal partners' requirements with the external partners' innovative capabilities (Stek, 2021).

The third role entails the proactive stimulation and encouragement of suppliers to innovate. This necessitates an entrepreneurial mindset, which may appear inconsistent with traditional public procurement practices. The set of competencies labelled entrepreneurial closely aligns with the literature on capabilities needed for PPI. It can be deduced that individuals involved in sourcing innovation in public procurement should ideally

*Figure 23.1* Competences of public procurers of innovation.
*Source*: Derived from Stek (2021, p.108).

possess attributes such as risk-taking, courage, and confidence in innovation (Stek, 2021). The literature addresses these attitudes as *intrapreneurial* behaviour (e.g. Steward, Wu, & Hartley, 2010).

While divergent laws and regulations often distinguish public procurement from private purchasing (Harland et al., 2013), the competencies required for success in these domains appear to share more similarities than anticipated. Therefore, this research profile does not hold the presumed significant distinction between the public and private sectors, particularly concerning interpersonal, behavioural, and intrapersonal attitudes (Telgen et al., 2007).

## 23.6 Public Procurement, the Digital Revolution, and Soft Skills

As the digital revolution reshapes public procurement, nurturing human skills and attitudes is vital for sustainable and innovative solutions. Public procurement is increasingly associated with a significant transformation, primarily accelerated by the digital revolution in which AI has been detected as the most promising technology in procurement (Dubey et al., 2020; Schulze & Bals, 2020). With AI tools, procurement professionals can analyse larger data volumes to identify patterns. AI tools reduce the workload in operational tasks, like forecasting the demand, supporting activities in the strategic sourcing process, and optimisation of procurement processes (Allal-Chérif, Simón-Moya, & Ballester, 2021; Spreitzenbarth, Bode, & Stuckenschmidt, 2024).

Moreover, AI can support supplier identification, communication, and selection with data analytics, text mining, and interactive communication bots (Choi, Wallace, & Wang, 2018; Delke, Schiele, Buchholz, & Kelly, 2023; Schiele & Torn, 2020). Whereas with AI support, algorithms execute procurement processes, procurement professionals focus on the more strategic role of preparing these processes (Delke, Schiele, & Buchholz, 2023; Lorentz, Aminoff, Kaipia, & Srai, 2021). Due to AI implementation, e-procurement systems support the procurement process, altering procurement professionals' tasks and required competencies (Spreitzenbarth et al., 2024). Therefore, AI is one of the central future technologies that need to be educated to support procurement practices (Delke, Schiele, & Buchholz, 2023; Meyer & Henke, 2023).

The concern accompanying AI is which tasks will remain for human beings. AI can adopt many tasks regarding explicit knowledge, such as cognitive, analytical, and hard skills. However, tacit knowledge elements like soft skills, higher-order thinking, interpersonal skills, and intrapersonal attitudes are less suitable for AI adoption (Von der Gracht et al., 2016). It underscores the significance of re-evaluating the competencies in procurement essential for effective task execution, particularly interpersonal skills and intrapersonal attitudes such as imagination, curiosity, creativity, out-of-the-box thinking, higher-order thinking modes like strategic thinking or ethical judgements, which are crucial for humans and cannot easily be automated or taken over by AI (e.g. Bals et al., 2019; Glas & Kleemann, 2016; Schulze & Bals, 2020; Stek, 2022a). These intrapersonal abilities are essential in fostering sustainable and innovative solutions (Bals et al., 2019; Kiers et al., 2022; Stek & Schiele, 2021).

The development of creativity for procurement practitioners is essential (e.g. Bals et al., 2019; Kiratli et al., 2016; Stek & Schiele, 2021). This is in line with Von der Gracht et al. (2016), who presented future procurement skills and predicted a "*talent war*" for "*creative and innovative minds*" (Von der Gracht et al., 2016, p. 30). Similarly, Von der Gracht et al. (2018, p. 9) warned that procurement personnel need to be "*creative, productive and innovative*" due to further digitalisation.

Hence, AI will potentially take over multiple procurement tasks and change procurement tasks for data analytics, allowing systems to make more profound assessments and decision support (Meyer & Henke, 2023). Therefore, the right interpersonal skills and intrapersonal attitudes will be crucial in the upcoming era in which the "*digital transformation is also transforming our society into a knowledge society*" (Von der Gracht et al., 2016, p. 10). The economy will convert into "*a knowledge economy, or even a 'human economy', where not only intellect but especially creativity, passion, character and team spirit will make the difference*" (Von der Gracht et al., 2016, p. 10).

In conclusion, interpersonal skills and intrapersonal attitudes are indispensable in the era of the Internet-of-things, machine-to-machine communication, and AI. These digital tools will likely serve and accelerate human creativity.

## 23.7 Public Procurement for Innovation Competencies in Developing Countries

Kundu, James, and Rigby (2020) shed light on the existing research landscape, highlighting a notable gap in public procurement and innovation studies in non-OECD, non-EU countries. The current literature predominantly originates from a Western, liberal-democracy-specific standpoint, leading to an incomplete understanding of the dynamics in diverse global contexts. Nonetheless, some scholars have explored the opportunities and challenges of employing public procurement as a demand-side innovation policy tool in these countries.

Public procurement is a powerful catalyst for innovation, offering substantial benefits compared to traditional public investments. Governments must strategically utilise procurement contracts to stimulate innovative activities, encouraging businesses to develop solutions that address pressing regional challenges. Despite its potential, this approach confronts obstacles such as the absence of a clear innovation strategy, limited resources, weak procurement instruments, and a deficiency in fostering a cultural mindset that embraces innovation. However, navigating these challenges is crucial as PPI remains pivotal for promoting regional progress, necessitating a strategic and comprehensive approach to address existing issues and optimise potential (Rullan, Saucedo, & Bacaria, 2012).

In the context of developing economies, particularly in Latin America, PPI emerges as a critical strategy. Governments in this region face common challenges such as natural disasters, poverty, and climate change. While innovation is recognised as a solution, these governments encounter hurdles when competing with global leaders like Japan and the USA in research and development (Rullan et al., 2012).

The Eastern African study of Matunga, Ngugi, and Odhiambo (2021) recommended that local Kenyan governments invest in procurement staff capacity building to improve the implementation of public procurement regulations. They emphasised the importance of procurement staff competency and identified monitoring and evaluation as crucial complements to staff competency. They concluded that most regional governments in Kenya have invested in procurement staff capacity building, recognising that competent officials enhance regulatory implementation and staff performance. County governments should invest heavily in capacity building to improve regulatory compliance.

The recommendations included adopting procurement staff competency to improve regulatory implementation, noting a significant positive relationship between staff competency and implementation levels. The study also highlighted the need for in-service training to address gaps in technical skills among procurement staff, recommending that county governments support and organise such training initiatives (Matunga et al., 2021).

In the Western-African context of Ghana and Nigeria, Asiedu et al. (2023) recognise soft skills essential for effective public procurement in developing countries. They clustered the construct soft skills into four variables (creative thinking, problem-solving, entrepreneurship, and decision-making) and underlined that soft skills, combined with traditional technical skills, lead to a more balanced skillset affecting the relationships with external and internal business partners (Asiedu et al., 2023).

For Nigerian public infrastructure procurement, the survey-based study of Mahamadu et al. (2018) revealed the need for further development of procurement skill areas operationalised, including ICT computing, problem-solving, communication, decision making, health and safety management, quality management, relationship management, team building, time management, procurement planning, project monitoring, and evaluation. This indicates a skills gap among procurement personnel in Nigeria's public sector.

Li and Georghiou (2016) delved into China's specific case, offering insights into the role of PPI as a tool for innovation policy. The study evaluates the effectiveness of PPI tools, highlighting the emergence of successful products through complex and often incidental paths unrelated to the initial objectives of the procurement. Concerns arise about using accreditation as a protectionist tool, posing challenges to international relations. Regional protectionism within China is also underscored, emphasising the need for a unified and adaptive approach.

Li and Georghiou (2016) recommend that China address implementation difficulties, coordinate horizontally, and negotiate PPI policies with international trade partners. Despite acknowledging risks, the study advocates for retaining the best elements of PPI, focusing on capacity building, cultural change, and a nuanced policy mix for innovation. It emphasises the importance of considering the industry's clock speed, potential pitfalls in accreditation, and the need for a unified procurement regulatory system.

Guarnieri and Gomes (2019) highlight the significance of procurement-related topics in developing countries, particularly in light of the prevalent fraud and corruption issues. They propose focusing on PPPs in developing countries and advocating the adoption of best practices observed in developed countries. The authors recommend that developing nations embrace PPPs and other partnering practices. It represents a pathway for small- and medium-sized enterprises to access and secure public procurement tenders within consortiums. Furthermore, they underscore the importance of observing and studying best practices in developed countries and comparing them to those in developing nations to understand the feasibility of PPPs in different contexts.

This section examined the global, non-Western landscape of public procurement for innovation, shedding light on the diverse challenges and opportunities countries face in various economic and cultural contexts. Also, in a non-Western context, elevating competency levels becomes crucial in crafting and implementing effective policies and strategies that foster regional progress and enhance international competitiveness. Whether navigating the hurdles present in Latin America, Africa, or China, it becomes evident that a comprehensive understanding of the global perspectives on public procurement for innovation is imperative. To effectively address these challenges and capitalise on opportunities, it is essential to emphasise the need for high competency levels among professionals involved in public procurement. The emphasis on competency development serves as a cornerstone for achieving innovation-driven success in the evolving landscape of public procurement across the globe. In conclusion, public procurement professionals in non-Western countries require specific technical skills related to situations that might differ from the Western context. However, soft skills in public procurement appear similar to those in Western countries, especially interpersonal skills and intrapersonal attitudes like creative thinking, problem-solving, entrepreneurship, or decision-making.

## 23.8 Teaching Methods of Interpersonal Skills and Intrapersonal Attitudes in Public Procurement

### *23.8.1 Student-Centred Teaching Methods*

In general, lecturers should design a *KSA triangle* to equip their students with a balanced mix of necessary knowledge (K), professional and interpersonal skills (S), and intrapersonal attitudes (A) for addressing the discipline's challenges (Bakarman, 2005). Each triangle corner can be extended with elements depicting the constructive alignment of intended learning outcomes, didactics, and assessments (Biggs, 1996).

Developing interpersonal skills and intrapersonal attitudes is essential for effective public procurement. However, higher education procurement programmes often prioritise hard skills such as theory, knowledge, and professional skills over soft skills. To address this gap, lecturers should shift from traditional teacher-centred towards student-centred learning approaches to effectively teach interpersonal skills and intrapersonal attitudes. It encourages active student engagement and reflection to create a dynamic learning environment where students practice and refine their skills in realistic contexts.

Therefore, lecturers are encouraged to implement challenge-based or project-based learning techniques, where students work collaboratively to solve real-world procurement problems. Integrating real-life practical case studies into a course can significantly enhance the teaching of interpersonal skills. Lecturers should select cases that require students to analyse stakeholder interactions, negotiate effectively, and make decisions under uncertainty.

Using cases enhances critical thinking and problem-solving abilities, allowing students to develop interpersonal skills through teamwork and effective communication. Engaging in projects that simulate actual procurement scenarios helps students navigate complexities while fostering creativity and strategic thinking. This approach enables students to apply theoretical knowledge in practice, reinforcing the relevance of interpersonal skills in professional settings.

Assessing the development of interpersonal skills and intrapersonal attitudes can be challenging but essential for ensuring students achieve the desired learning outcomes. Lecturers could employ diverse assessment methods, such as peer evaluations, self-reflections, group reporting, presentations, or practical demonstrations, to increase students' proficiency in these areas. Providing constructive feedback on these assessments will help students identify strengths and areas for improvement.

Distinguishing the intended learning outcomes, didactics, and assessments for knowledge, skills, and attitudes is essential. For instance, intrapersonal attitudes like creativity should not be assessed as knowledge items. An illustrative example is obtaining a driving license, where understanding traffic rules is assessed through a multiple-choice test, and practical driving skills are evaluated through driving lessons and practical exams.

Lecturers could utilise challenge-based case studies from practice to cultivate competencies such as analytical, change management, communication, and stakeholder relationship skills. Collaborating with public procurement professionals to present real-life cases can enrich this learning experience. Students should be prepared to engage with these professionals, further contextualising their learning. Higher education should prioritise integrating interpersonal skills and intrapersonal attitudes into the curriculum to prepare students for the demands of public procurement effectively. By adopting student-centred teaching methods, incorporating real-world applications, and assessing soft skills development, lecturers can play a pivotal role in cultivating the competencies necessary for success in today's complex procurement landscape.

#### *23.8.2 Practical Case Study Examples to Facilitate Soft Skills Learning Objectives in Higher Education*

Case studies can serve as effective methods for achieving learning objectives, particularly in developing interpersonal skills and intrapersonal attitudes. The lecturer or a team of lecturers can design case studies. However, the design of case studies is complex and time-consuming. Moreover, designed case studies are fictitious, whereas practical examples resonate with students, especially when the issues presented are unresolved. The students can interact with the practitioners who "own" the practical, real-life case problems (Stek, 2022b; Stek, Picaud-Bello, Koch, & Johnsen, 2025).

Although practical, real-life case problems are suitable in courses, they can be challenging, mainly due to dependence on external practitioners. By introducing these practical, real-life case problems, the lecturer and the course depend on the external practitioners' input. Therefore, ideally, each case is represented by two or more practitioners. The lecturer should engage with strategic public procurement professionals early, communicate crucial dates for the student interviews and presentations, and clarify the course objectives and case study aims (Stek, 2022b; Stek et al., 2024).

Moreover, the case studies must be simple but wicked, meaning the problems should be easy to explain but challenging to solve. Students are encouraged to propose creative solutions, receiving context and case issues from practitioners in a brief description (200–400 words) to prepare for their interviews with the practitioners early in the course. The goal is for the students to combine practitioners' insights with the course's theoretical lessons. Therefore, it is recommended that the case owners present case issues that they have not yet solved (Stek, 2022b; Stek et al., 2024).

Before the students interview the practical case problem owners, they need to be instructed about the aim of the assignment to propose an inventive solution, on how to interview and about inventive and creative techniques like De Bono's (1995) divergent and convergent thinking techniques for defining the problem, the problem solution, and improvement. Eventually, the students present their solutions to the lecturer and practitioners at the end of the course. During the creative process, each student case group meets at least once with the lecturer or tutor and, if possible, visits the case owner's organisation to discuss the progress of solving the case (Stek, 2022b; Stek et al., 2024).

Table 23.3 guides educators in instructing practitioners on how public procurement cases could be designed to emphasise aligning procurement with long-term goals, particularly sustainability, innovation, and user satisfaction. Sustainability is a recurrent theme in energy-efficient server procurement, green building designs, and eco-friendly hot drink vending machines. The procurement approach prioritises creativity and innovation, aiming to optimise processes while maintaining high-quality standards. Strategic planning, collaborative relationships, and legal compliance are vital considerations across cases, ensuring procurement activities contribute to immediate needs and the public organisation's responsible development and efficiency objectives.

Table 23.4 displays examples of practical case study topics, learning objectives and procurement foci. As an example of a possible case study to be introduced in a course, the "hot drinks vending machine tender" case from Table 23.4 is explained. The objective of this case study is to tender the purchase of hot drinks that will provide personnel and guests of a public organisation with various coffee options, hot cocoa, and tea via vending machines. Therefore, students are tasked with developing a creative procurement plan that prioritises quality, speed of service, and sustainability, ensuring alignment with the public organisation's sustainability policy. In doing so, they will explore critical factors, including supplier selection, service delivery timelines, and compliance with sustainability criteria. For instance, regarding the sustainability policy of the public organisation, the students are encouraged to explore sustainability issues in supply chains, like energy use and modern slavery on cocoa and coffee plants, or to consider social return and apply these criteria in the supplier selection process.

This case study directly connects to several key competencies in public procurement. Students will engage in strategic thinking as they assess how their procurement plan aligns with the organisation's long-term sustainability goals while also considering user

*Table 23.3* Practical case study requirements

| | |
|---|---|
| **Strategic alignment** | The case emphasises the importance of aligning procurement activities with the long-term strategic objectives of the public organisation. This includes considerations for sustainability, innovation, and user-centric approaches. |
| **Sustainability focus** | Sustainability is a recurring theme, reflecting the public organisation's commitment to environmental responsibility. This is evident in the criteria for energy efficiency, green building designs, and sustainable practices. |
| **User-centric approach** | The user experience is a central consideration in several cases, particularly in the hot drinks vending machine tender that will be explained below. Emphasising user preferences and satisfaction underscores the organisation's commitment to meeting the needs of employees and stakeholders. |
| **Innovation and creativity** | The cases encourage innovation and creativity in procurement processes. This is seen in the emphasis on finding novel solutions for sustainable options, utilising new (software) models, and promoting innovative problem-solving in the tendering process. |
| **Efficiency and optimisation** | There is a common theme of optimising procurement processes for efficiency. This includes strategies to increase the number of tenders, reduce tenderer costs, and streamline the tendering process while maintaining high-quality assessments. |
| **Strategic procurement planning** | The cases highlight the importance of thorough planning in procurement. This involves strategic thinking, for instance, in real estate development, focusing on the next three decades, carefully selecting suppliers and design team tenders, and planning for tenders. |
| **Collaborative relationships** | Collaboration is emphasised in cases where a mutual relationship between the public organisation and first- and second-tier suppliers is crucial. Establishing and maintaining collaborative relationships between parties is essential for successful procurement outcomes. |
| **Compliance and legal considerations** | The cases acknowledge the legal obligations and compliance requirements associated with public procurement. This includes adherence to tender thresholds, compliance with procurement laws, and addressing potential legal issues in contracts. |

*Source*: Original creation.

satisfaction. The complexity of selecting suitable suppliers and negotiating contracts will foster their problem-solving skills, encouraging critical thinking and innovation. Additionally, by engaging with practitioners and presenting their proposed solutions to stakeholders, students will develop essential communication skills necessary for effective collaboration in procurement contexts.

Hence, professional and interpersonal skills can be developed through workshop-style lectures and case studies in collaboration with practitioners, with assessments based on case reports and presentations. Before the start of the course, the students and case owners are provided with a rubric to calculate the case scoring. The case owners share their scores with the lecturer responsible for grading the case groups. Possible scoring items could be the extent to which the group understood the case problem, demonstrated in their ability to fully grasp and integrate the client's challenge-based assignment into their consultancy report. The quality of the report itself is another criterion, assessing whether it is well-written, logically structured, and easy to understand (Stek, 2022b; Stek et al., 2024).

Additionally, the soundness of the advice provided is important, reflecting the team's consideration of all relevant stakeholders, such as the client, executors, and end-users and ensuring alignment with the organisation's strategy. Creativity and inventiveness are also valued, as the advice should offer the case owner fresh insights while showcasing the team's originality and problem-solving skills. Effective cooperation within the team is essential, with all members contributing equitably and addressing free-riding issues. Lastly, the quality of the presentation of the consultancy report outcomes is assessed, emphasising clarity and coherence. Learning objectives related to intrapersonal attitudes are fostered through workshops and evaluated using a self-reflection report and a personal development plan (Stek, 2022b; Stek et al., 2024).

The hot drinks vending machine tender case is one example that can inspire lecturers and public procurement professionals to develop a tailored, up-to-date case study applicable to the course's objectives. Table 23.4 presents additional case studies that serve as examples of strategic objectives and targeted procurement strategies. Each case highlights distinct organisational needs, ranging from civic integration programmes to a waste management tender. This table consolidates critical information, showcasing the objectives and procurement focuses across various domains. It underscores the public organisation's commitment to effective procurement processes and strategic excellence.

When developing case studies for developing countries, particular attention should be given to the challenges and opportunities associated with PPPs and PPI. These regions face unique dynamics influenced by their economic, social, and regulatory contexts. In Table 23.5, some suggestions for case studies are displayed.

By concentrating on these issues, the practical case studies can provide a nuanced understanding of the complexities inherent in emerging economies. They would emphasise the pivotal role of PPPs and PPI in driving innovation, addressing infrastructure gaps, and promoting sustainable development in developing countries. These practical case studies would serve as valuable educational tools and contribute to the ongoing discourse on effective procurement strategies in diverse global contexts. These cases focus on strategic public procurement activities and align best with graduate education. Nevertheless, the cases can, when simplified, serve undergraduates in their development.

The practical case studies highlight the diverse challenges and strategic considerations in procurement across various sectors. Each case, from civic integration programmes to hot drinks vending machines, underscores the importance of aligning procurement strategies with organisational goals and societal needs. Whether optimising the tendering process, fostering sustainability in IT infrastructure, or addressing food insecurity, a common thread emerges the significance of stakeholder engagement, legal compliance, and strategic planning. These cases emphasise the pivotal role of procurement in achieving efficiency, sustainability, and social impact, showcasing how well-crafted strategies can drive positive outcomes and innovation. As organisations navigate complex procurement landscapes, these lessons provide valuable insights into creating effective and impactful procurement strategies for the future.

This chapter focuses on providing training guidelines for undergraduate and mainly graduate learners. However, the guidelines are also valid for educating experienced public procurement practitioners. Organisations can bridge the gap between theoretical competencies and their practical application, fostering a skilled and adaptable workforce in public procurement as is demonstrated by the Horizon Europe project PROCEDIN on their website *Building Procurement Capability for Embedding and Driving Innovation* (PROCEDIN, 2024). The guidelines aim to enhance the learners' knowledge of strategic public procurement by identifying barriers and enablers and analysing recent developments and future trends.

PROCEDIN's guidelines to effectively train practitioners in strategic public procurement are to adjust the learning materials to the practitioners' experience level. The proposed training programme introduces core concepts, covering basic definitions, distinctions

*Table 23.4* Examples of practical case study topics, learning objectives, and procurement foci

| | |
|---|---|
| **Integration programme for recognised refugees** – for a municipality | **Learning objective:** Implement a new civic integration system to facilitate social participation, particularly for recognised refugees facing language barriers.<br>**Procurement focus:** Selection of a leading contractor for the integration programme for recognised refugees, considering legal requirements, integration obligations, and partnerships with educational and participation organisations. |
| **Food Bank shortages** (providing groceries to low-income persons and families) – for a local Food Bank at a municipality | **Learning objective:** Fill shortages of shelf-stable food products for the Food Bank, addressing the challenge of engaging large wholesalers and local market players.<br>**Procurement focus:** Developing a procurement strategy to reach and engage local market players, ensuring their participation in tender management systems, and defining eligibility requirements and award criteria. |
| **Renewal of Microsoft software** – for a public organisation | **Learning objective:** Renew Microsoft software for a healthcare institution, considering compliance, cost-effectiveness, and alternatives to purchasing new licenses.<br>**Procurement focus:** Assess alternatives, obtain at least three quotations, and navigate the complexity of the vendor's licensing model to provide the best advice. |
| **Tackling barriers to innovation procurement** – for a ministry | **Learning objective:** Remove limiting factors to realise innovation in the sector's procurement processes.<br>**Procurement focus:** Addressing limitations in the current innovation-oriented procurement approach, particularly in scaling up successful innovations after the proof of concept. |
| **Simplifying the tendering process in road construction** – for a province | **Learning objective:** Align legality and efficiency in government tenders, considering the scarcity of resources and the need for streamlined processes.<br>**Procurement focus:** Investigate whether the bulkiness of tenders is due to technical knowledge, skills, attitude, or habit, and explore ways to enhance information selection and organisation. |
| **Tender waste management** – for a public organisation | **Learning objective:** Reduce and prevent waste at the public organisation by finding a partner for waste management solutions.<br>**Procurement focus:** Developing a strategy for the tender, including the tendering procedure, market analysis, eligibility requirements, and award criteria, and incorporating sustainability and social return considerations. |
| **Hot drinks vending machines tender** – for a public organisation | **Learning objective:** Tendering the purchase of hot drinks vending machines to provide personnel and guests with coffee variants, hot cocoa, and tea.<br>**Procurement focus:** Develop a creative plan that considers the quality, speed of service, and sustainability of hot beverage supply, aligning with the public organisation's sustainability policy. |
| **Software broker tender** – for a municipality | **Learning objective:** Select a software broker for the municipality to handle office automation software licensing, transition to cloud solutions, and address legal issues.<br>**Procurement focus:** Define the scope, establish mutual relationships between the municipality, software broker, and vendors, and market the tender effectively, considering the expanded scope and sustainability. |
| **Improving the software tendering process** for a public organisation | **Learning objective:** Improve the tendering process to attract more suppliers and increase competition. Optimise the tender process to reduce costs for tenderers while maintaining high assessment quality. Enhance the public organisation's negotiating position by optimising the tendering process.<br>**Procurement focus:** Implementing framework agreements, dividing tenders into smaller lots, clear communication, standardised requirements, pre-qualification processes, centralised information hubs, longer contract durations, and performance-based contracts. |

*Table 23.4* (Continued)

| | |
|---|---|
| **Server and storage award criteria for sustainability** for a public organisation | **Learning objective**: Align the server and storage tender with the public organisation's strategy, mainly focusing on sustainability.<br>**Procurement focus**: Define award criteria aligned with sustainability goals, including energy efficiency, renewable energy usage, lifecycle assessment, resource efficiency, scalability, carbon footprint, and supplier sustainability practices. |
| **Optimising supplier management in balancing costs and resources** for a hospital | **Learning objective:** Understand the challenges hospitals face in managing supplier relationships, particularly in balancing cost control with the administrative burden, and explore strategies for managing smaller suppliers without increasing staffing levels.<br>**Procurement focus:** The focus is on developing efficient procurement strategies for managing most suppliers (80%) but contributing minimally to overall purchasing turnover (20%). Emphasis will be placed on how hospitals can streamline processes and leverage existing resources to manage these relationships without additional personnel. |

*Source*: Original creation

*Table 23.5* Suggestions for case study topics, learning objectives and procurement foci in developing countries

| | |
|---|---|
| **Enhancing civic infrastructure through PPPs** – for a lower-governmental | **Learning objective**: Implement a civic infrastructure improvement programme in a municipality through a Public Procurement for Innovation (PPP), aiming to address challenges such as rapid urbanisation, environmental concerns, and the need for sustainable development.<br>**Procurement focus**: Implement a civic infrastructure improvement programme in a Chinese local government through a PPP, aiming to address challenges such as rapid urbanisation, environmental concerns, and sustainable development. |
| **Fostering technological innovation healthcare** – for a public healthcare organisation or ministry | **Learning objective**: Enhance healthcare services by incorporating technological innovations through PPI, focusing on improving patient care, accessibility, and overall healthcare system efficiency.<br>**Procurement focus**: Designing a PPI strategy that encourages collaboration with innovative technology providers, navigates regulatory frameworks in healthcare procurement, and addresses challenges unique to the country's context. This case study would highlight the role of PPI in driving advancements in critical sectors, fostering economic development and meeting societal needs. |
| **Navigating procurement challenges in managing supplier relations** for public organisations in developing countries | **Learning objective:** Exploring the procurement challenges public organisations face in developing countries, particularly in managing a diverse supplier base with limited resources and complex bureaucratic systems. The aim is to identify strategies that can help streamline procurement processes, improve supplier relationships, and ensure a consistent supply of essential goods and services.<br>**Procurement focus:** The focus is on addressing the inefficiencies in supplier management within the public sector of developing countries. Strategies will be explored to improve procurement processes, enhance supplier reliability, and ensure that even smaller local suppliers can meet the organisation's needs without compromising quality or timeliness. Special attention will be given to overcoming bureaucratic hurdles and optimising resource allocation to improve overall procurement effectiveness. |

*Source*: Original creation.

between public and private procurement, tendering processes, and organisational structures. Preparatory materials should support this foundational module, including training videos, book chapters, and scientific papers (PROCEDIN, 2024).

Following this, practitioners will explore the barriers and enablers in strategic procurement, which involves discussing real-world challenges presented by public contracting authorities. Practitioners should review specific case-related materials to prepare for this segment. Practical assignments, such as an advice report or a case-study presentation, are recommended. Practitioners are encouraged to introduce real-life cases from their daily practice. For the assignments, practitioners have to assess how their organisation integrates strategic procurement objectives. They should then produce an advice report, proposing ways to enhance these objectives. This report should be informed by the course literature and practical case studies. Through this streamlined approach, practitioners will acquire practical and applicable skills tailored to their experience level, focusing on future-oriented procurement strategies (PROCEDIN, 2024).

## 23.9 Conclusion

### *23.9.1 Soft Skills in Public Procurement*

The first part of this chapter delved into public procurement personal competencies, aiming to address which soft skills are required for public procurement professionals when sourcing innovations. The interpersonal skills and intrapersonal attitudes critical for public-sector procurement professionals to carry out their roles effectively and efficiently are displayed in Table 23.6 *(effective human-to-human communication; being challenging and experimental towards suppliers; creativity, inventiveness, out-of-the-box thinking for complex problem-solving; and critical analysing and ethical responsibility).*

Effective communication with internal business partners and suppliers is crucial. Public procurement practitioners should question internal business partners about the requirements and challenge suppliers to be inventive. Creativity is the cornerstone for higher-order thinking, complex problem-solving, critical analysis, and ethical responsibility. The specific soft skills may vary among countries, organisations, procurement targets, and contexts (Stek & Schiele, 2021; Stek et al., 2022). Moreover, training these soft skills is significantly more complex than training knowledge, theory, and professional skills, as will be shown in the second part of this chapter (Laker & Powell, 2011).

### *23.9.2 Teaching Methods of Soft Skills in Public Procurement*

The second section of this chapter addresses the didactical methods employed for competency development in public procurement in higher education. Key questions included unravelling the most effective pedagogical approaches, evaluating their impact on competency enhancement, providing insights, and offering a roadmap for academic enquiry and practical strategies to fortify the competency development of public procurement professionals in innovation sourcing.

Learners in public procurement courses should be offered a balanced mix of theory, knowledge (K), professional and interpersonal skills (S), and intrapersonal attitudes (A) to become *competent* in addressing the challenges of acquiring, for instance, sustainable innovations from the supply market. Therefore, lecturers need to rethink their courses' "KSA triangle" (Bakarman, 2005). When drawing this triangle, each of the three ends is extended with specific constructive alignments of intended learning outcomes, didactics, and assessments for theory and knowledge, professional and interpersonal skills, and intrapersonal attitudes, as is shown in Figure 23.2 (Biggs, 1996).

*Table 23.6* Interpersonal skills and intrapersonal attitudes essential for strategic public procurement

| *Interpersonal skills* | | *Intrapersonal attitudes* | |
|---|---|---|---|
| *Effective human-to-human communication* | Sharing information, empathy, multilingual proficiency, and presentation skills (Kruyen & Van Genugten, 2020; Stek, 2022b).<br>Persuasion, communication, presentation and networking abilities, listening, asking critical questions, distinguishing the 'real need' behind the demand of the internal partner, multidisciplinary teamwork, being connective, being visible to the internal partner and having organisational sensitivity (Stek, 2021).<br>Personal effectiveness attributes like communication and collaboration (Brennan & Crowe, 2012; European Commission, 2020; NIGP, 2015; World Bank, 2020). | *Creativity, inventiveness, and out-of-the-box thinking for complex problem-solving* | Creativity combined with result-driven efficiency is essential for out-of-the-box thinking, complex problem-solving, and driving innovative solutions (Kruyen & Van Genugten, 2020; Stek, 2022b).<br>Attributes of out-of-the-box thinking include courageousness, curiosity, creativity and inventiveness, persistence, sensitivity and confidence to innovate, being proactive, being able to think 'out-of-the-box' and holistic thinking (Stek, 2021).<br>Imagination, curiosity, creativity, and out-of-the-box thinking (Bals et al., 2019; Glas & Kleemann, 2016; Schulze & Bals, 2020; Stek, 2022a).<br>Creative thinking, problem-solving, entrepreneurship, and decision-making (Asiedu et al., 2023). |
| *Being challenging and experimental* | Being challenging and experimental towards suppliers (Stek, 2021). | *Critical analysis and ethical responsibility* | Critical analysis and ethical responsibility (Brennan & Crowe, 2012; European Commission, 2020; NIGP, 2015; World Bank, 2020).<br>Higher-order thinking modes like strategic thinking for ethical judgements (Bals et al., 2019; Glas & Kleemann, 2016; Schulze & Bals, 2020; Stek, 2022a). |

*Source*: Original creation.

The model in Figure 23.2 provides lecturers with tools to effectively integrate competencies outlined by various frameworks into training and development programmes for procurement professionals by adopting a holistic approach. Identifying commonalities among frameworks, customising training modules based on specific organisational needs and utilising a mix of methods, such as workshops, simulations, and mentorship programmes, it is crucial to develop experienced public procurement practitioners in lifelong learning programmes. Emphasising continuous learning and adapting training content to evolving industry standards ensures a dynamic and comprehensive development strategy.

The didactics for theory and knowledge could be frontal interactive lectures, paper assignments, and tutoring, and to assess these learning objectives, written exams and assessing the paper and the paper presentations are advised. Professional and interpersonal

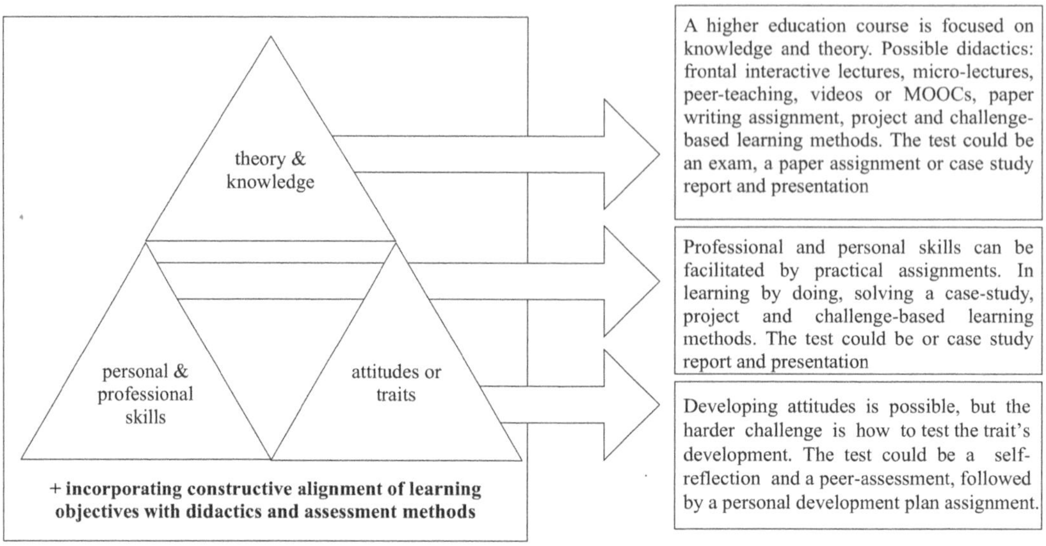


*Figure 23.2* Constructive alignment of various learning objectives, didactics and assessment methods.
*Source*: Adapted from Bakarman (2005), Biggs (1996).

skills can be developed with workshop lectures and offering case studies with practitioners. The case reports and presentations are part of the assessment. Learning objectives regarding intrapersonal attitudes are promoted via workshops and assessed with a self-reflection report and a personal development plan (Stek, 2022b).

Public procurement professionals can balance innovation and compliance by fostering a culture of adaptability within their organisations. This involves staying up-to-date on emerging technologies and innovative practices while maintaining a keen awareness of legal and regulatory frameworks. Establishing cross-functional teams that include legal experts can facilitate collaborative decision-making, ensuring innovative approaches align with compliance requirements.

Professionals need a strategic integration plan to transition seamlessly to digital tools in procurement, including investing in training programmes that enhance digital literacy, promoting a user-friendly interface for procurement tools, and ensuring clear communication about the benefits of automation. Maintaining a human touch involves recognising the irreplaceable value of interpersonal skills such as negotiation or relationship-building and intrapersonal attitudes as creativity and result-driven. Professionals should view automation as a complement to human capabilities, fostering a synergy that optimises efficiency while preserving the essential human elements in procurement processes.

## References

Ahmed, F., Fernando Capretz, L., Bouktif, S., & Campbell, P. (2012). Soft skills requirements in software development jobs: a cross-cultural empirical study. *Journal of Systems and Information Technology, 14*(1), 58–81.

Allal-Chérif, O., Simón-Moya, V., & Ballester, A. C. C. (2021). Intelligent purchasing: how artificial intelligence can redefine the purchasing function. *Journal of Business Research, 124*, 69–76. https://doi.org/10.1016/j.jbusres.2020.11.050

Alvarez, S., & Rubio, A. (2015). Carbon footprint in Green Public Procurement: a case study in the services sector. *Journal of Cleaner Production, 93*, 159–166.

Amann, M., & Essig, M. (2015). Public procurement of innovation: empirical evidence from EU public authorities on barriers for the promotion of innovation. *Innovation: The European Journal of Social Science Research, 28*(3), 282–292. Retrieved from https://doi.org/10.1080/13511610.2014.998641

Andrews, J., & Higson, H. (2008). Graduate employability, 'soft skills' versus 'hard' business knowledge: a European study. *Higher Education in Europe, 33*(4), 411–422.

Asiedu, R. O., Manu, P., Mahamadu, A.-M., Booth, C. A., Olomolaiye, P., Agyekum, K., & Abadi, M. (2023). Critical skills for infrastructure procurement: insights from developing country contexts. *Journal of Engineering, Design and Technology, 21*(6), 1948–1974. https://doi.org/10.1108/JEDT-08-2021-0437

Bailly, F., & Léné, A. (2013). The personification of the service labour process and the rise of soft skills: a French case study. *Employee Relations: The International Journal, 35*(1), 79–97. https://doi.org/10.1108/01425451311279429

Bakarman, A. A. (2005). Attitude, skill, and knowledge: (ASK) a new model for design education. *Proceedings of the Canadian Engineering Education Association (CEEA)*.

Bals, L., Laine, J., & Mugurusi, G. (2018). Evolving purchasing and supply organizations: a contingency model for structural alternatives. *Journal of Purchasing and Supply Management, 24*(1), 41–58.

Bals, L., Schulze, H., Kelly, S., & Stek, K. (2019). Purchasing and supply management (PSM) competencies: current and future requirements. *Journal of Purchasing and Supply Management, 25*(5), 100572.

Benjamin, O. (2020). Diversity as job quality: toward the inclusion of trade unions in public procurement of social services. *Equality, Diversity and Inclusion: An International Journal, 41*(7), 1014–1028.

Biggs, J. B. (1996). Enhancing teaching through constructive alignment. *Higher Education, 32*(3), 347–364.

Boyatzis, R. E. (1982). *The Competent Manager: A Model for Effective Performance*. New York: John Wiley & Sons, Ltd.

Brennan, L., & Crowe, D. (2012). IFPSM – Global Standard in Purchasing & Supply Management (GSPSM) – Assessors' Guide. Retrieved from www.ifpsm.org

Brogaard, L. (2017). The impact of innovation training on successful outcomes in public–private partnerships. *Public Management Review, 19*(8), 1184–1205.

Callens, C., Verhoest, K., & Boon, J. (2021). Combined effects of procurement and collaboration on innovation in public-private-partnerships: a qualitative comparative analysis of 24 infrastructure projects. *Public Management Review, 24*(6), 860–881.

Campion, M. A., Fink, A. A., Ruggeberg, B. J., Carr, L., Phillips, G. M., & Odman, R. B. (2011). Doing competencies well: best practices in competency modeling. *Personnel Psychology, 64*(1), 225–262.

Choi, T. M., Wallace, S. W., & Wang, Y. (2018). Big data analytics in operations management. *Production and Operations Management, 27*(10), 1868–1883. https://doi.org/10.1111/poms.12838

Csikszentmihalyi, M. (1997). *Flow and the Psychology of Discovery and Invention* (Vol. 39, pp. 1–16). New York: Harper Perennial.

Davis, B.D, &. Muir, C. (2004). Learning soft skills at work: An interview with Annalee Luhman. *Business Communication Quarterly, 67*(1), 95–101. https://doi.org/10.1177/1080569903261973

De Bono, E. (1995). Serious creativity. *The Journal for Quality and Participation, 18*(5), 12.

Delamare-Le Deist, F., & Winterton, J. (2005). What is competence? *Human Resource Development International, 8*(1), 27–46.

Delke, V. F., Schiele, H., & Buchholz, W. (2023). Differentiating between direct and indirect procurement: roles, skills, and Industry 4.0. *International Journal of Procurement Management, 16*(1), 1–30.

Delke, V. F., Schiele, H., Buchholz, W., & Kelly, S. (2023). Implementing Industry 4.0 technologies: future roles in purchasing and supply management. *Technological Forecasting and Social Change, 196*, 122847.

Dubey, R., Gunasekaran, A., Childe, S. J., Bryde, D. J., Giannakis, M., Foropon, C., …, & Hazen, B. T. (2020). Big data analytics and artificial intelligence pathway to operational performance under the effects of entrepreneurial orientation and environmental dynamism: a study of manufacturing organisations. *International Journal of Production Economics, 226*(1), 107599. https://doi.org/10.1016/j.ijpe.2019.107599

Edler, J. (2007). *Demand Based Innovation Policy* (p. 9). Manchester Institute of Innovation Research.

Edler, J., & Georghiou, L. (2007). Public procurement and innovation—resurrecting the demand side. *Research Policy, 36*(7), 949–963.

European Commission. (2020). *ProcurComp[EU]: The European competency framework for public procurement professionals.* Retrieved from Brussels: https://ec.europa.eu/info/publications/procurcompeu-european-competency-framework-public-procurement-professionals_en

Geroski, P. A. (1990). Innovation, technological opportunity, and market structure. *Oxford Economic Papers, 42*(3), 586–602.

Getha-Taylor, H. (2008). Identifying collaborative competencies. *Review of Public Personnel Administration, 28*(2), 103–119.

Ghisellini, P., Cialani, C., & Ulgiati, S. (2016). A review on circular economy: the expected transition to a balanced interplay of environmental and economic systems. *Journal of Cleaner Production, 114*, 11–32. https://doi.org/10.1016/j.jclepro.2015.09.007

Glas, A. H., & Kleemann, F. C. (2016). The impact of Industry 4.0 on procurement and supply management: a conceptual and qualitative analysis. *International Journal of Business and Management Invention, 5*(6), 55–66.

Grandia, J., & Kruyen, P. P. (2020). Assessing the implementation of sustainable public procurement using quantitative text-analysis tools: a large-scale analysis of Belgian public procurement notices. *Journal of Purchasing and Supply Management*, 26(4), 100627.

Grandia, J., & Meehan, J. (2017). Public procurement as a policy tool: using procurement to reach desired outcomes in society. *International Journal of Public Sector Management, 30*(4), 302–309.

Grant, R. M. (1996). Toward a knowledge-based theory of the firm. *Strategic Management Journal, 17*(S2), 109–122.

Guarnieri, P., & Gomes, R. C. (2019). Can public procurement be strategic? A future agenda proposition. *Journal of Public Procurement, 19*(4), 295–321.

Harland, C., Telgen, J., & Callender, G. (2013). International research study of public procurement. In C. Harland, G. Nassimbeni, & E. Schneller (Eds.), *The SAGE Handbook of Strategic Supply Management* (pp. 374–401). London: Sage.

Heckman, J. J., & Kautz, T. (2012). Hard evidence on soft skills. *Labour Economics, 19*(4), 451–464.

Hood, C., & Lodge, M. (2004). Competency, bureaucracy, and public management reform: a comparative analysis. *Governance, 17*(3), 313–333.

Jasimuddin, S. M., Klein, J. H., & Connell, C. (2005). The paradox of using tacit and explicit knowledge: strategies to face dilemmas. *Management Decision, 43*(1), 102–112.

Kaufman, J. C., Kaufman, S. B., & Plucker, J. A. (2013). Contemporary theories of intelligence. In D. Reisberg (Ed.), *Oxford Handbook of Cognitive Psychology* (pp. 811–822) Oxford: Oxford University Press.

Kiers, J., Seinhorst, J., Zwanenburg, M., & Stek, K. (2022). Which strategies and corresponding competences are needed to improve supply chain resilience: a COVID-19 based review. *Logistics, 6*(1), 12. Retrieved from www.mdpi.com/2305-6290/6/1/12

Kiratli, N., Rozemeijer, F., Hilken, T., de Ruyter, K., & de Jong, A. (2016). Climate setting in sourcing teams: developing a measurement scale for team creativity climate. *Journal of Purchasing and Supply Management, 22*(3), 196–204.

Knutsson, H., & Thomasson, A. (2014). Innovation in the public procurement process: a study of the creation of innovation-friendly public procurement. *Public Management Review, 16*(2), 242–255. https://doi.org/10.1080/14719037.2013.806574

Kogut, B., & Zander, U. (1992). Knowledge of the firm, combinative capabilities, and the replication of technology. *Organization Science, 3*(3), 383–397.

Kothari, A., Rudman, D., Dobbins, M., Rouse, M., Sibbald, S., & Edwards, N. (2012). The use of tacit and explicit knowledge in public health: a qualitative study. *Implementation Science, 7*(1), 1–12.

Kruyen, P. M., & Van Genugten, M. (2020). Opening up the black box of civil servants' competencies. *Public Management Review, 22*(1), 118–140.

Kundu, O., James, A. D., & Rigby, J. (2020). Public procurement and innovation: a systematic literature review. *Science and Public Policy, 47*(4), 490–502.

Laker, D. R., & Powell, J. L. (2011). The differences between hard and soft skills and their relative impact on training transfer. *Human Resource Development Quarterly, 22*(1), 111–122.

Lau, A. K. (2010). Training needs of purchasing and supply management personnel in Hong Kong. *Journal of European Industrial Training, 34*(5), 400–415.

Li, Y., & Georghiou, L. (2016). Signaling and accrediting new technology: use of procurement for innovation in China. *Science and Public Policy, 43*(3), 338–351.

Loader, K., & Norton, S. (2015). SME access to public procurement: an analysis of the experiences of SMEs supplying the publicly funded UK heritage sector. *Journal of Purchasing and Supply Management, 21*(4), 241–250.

Lorentz, H., Aminoff, A., Kaipia, R., & Srai, J. S. (2021). Structuring the phenomenon of procurement digitalisation: contexts, interventions and mechanisms. *International Journal of Operations & Production Management, 41*(2), 157–192. https://doi.org/10.1108/IJOPM-03-2020-0150

Mahamadu, A.-M., Manu, P., Booth, C., Olomolaiye, P., Coker, A., Ibrahim, A., & Lamond, J. (2018). Infrastructure procurement skills gap amongst procurement personnel in Nigeria's public sector. *Journal of Engineering, Design and Technology, 16*(1), 2–24.

Matunga, D. A., Ngugi, P. K., & Odhiambo, R. (2021). Relationship between staff competency and implementation level of public procurement regulatory framework in the devolved governments in Kenya. *International Journal of Supply Chain Management, 6*(1), 13–23.

Mazzucato, M. (2018). Mission-oriented innovation policies: challenges and opportunities. *Industrial and Corporate Change, 27*(5), 803–815.

McKevitt, D. M., Davis, P., Woldring, R., Smith, K., Flynn, A., & McEvoy, E. (2012). An exploration of management competencies in public sector procurement. *Journal of Public Procurement, 12*(3), 333–355.

Meehan, J., Ludbrook, M. N., & Mason, C. J. (2016). Collaborative public procurement: institutional explanations of legitimised resistance. *Journal of Purchasing and Supply Management, 22*(3), 160–170.

Meyer, D., & Henke, M. (2023). Developing design principles for the implementation of AI in PSM: an investigation with expert interviews. *Journal of Purchasing and Supply Management, 29*(3), 100846. https://doi.org/10.1016/j.pursup.2023.100846

Minoja, M., & Romano, G. (2021). Managing intellectual capital for sustainability: evidence from a Re-municipalized, publicly owned waste management firm. *Journal of Cleaner Production, 279*, 123213. https://doi.org/10.1016/j.jclepro.2020.123213

Mogre, R., Lindgreen, A., & Hingley, M. (2017). Tracing the evolution of purchasing research: future trends and directions for purchasing practices. *Journal of Business & Industrial Marketing, 32*(2), 251–257. https://doi.org/doi:10.1108/JBIM-01-2016-0004

Nicoletti, B. (2018). The future: Procurement 4.0. In *Agile Procurement: Volume II: Designing and Implementing a Digital Transformation* (pp. 189–230). Cham: Springer. https://doi.org/10.1007/978-3-319-61085-6_8

NIGP. (2015). Public Procurement Competency Framework. Retrieved from www.nigp.org

Nijboer, K., Senden, S., & Telgen, J. (2017). Cross-country learning in public procurement: an exploratory study. *Journal of Public Procurement, 17*(4), 449–482.

Nonaka, I., & Takeuchi, H. (1995). *The Knowledge-Creating Company: How Japanese Companies Create the Dynamics of Innovation*. New York: Oxford University Press.

Nonaka, I., & Von Krogh, G. (2009). Perspective-tacit knowledge and knowledge conversion: controversy and advancement in organizational knowledge creation theory. *Organization Science, 20*(3), 635–652.

Obwegeser, N., & Müller, S. D. (2018). Innovation and public procurement: terminology, concepts, and applications. *Technovation*. https://doi.org/10.1016/j.technovation.2018.02.015

Ogden, J. A., Rossetti, C. L., & Hendrick, T. E. (2007). An exploratory cross-country comparison of strategic purchasing. *Journal of Purchasing and Supply Management, 13*(1), 2–16.

Orlikowski, W. J. (2002). Knowing in practice: enacting a collective capability in distributed organizing. *Organization Science, 13*(3), 249–273.

Osborne, S. P. (2006). The new public governance? *Public Management Review, 8*(3), 377–387. https://doi.org/10.1080/14719030600853022

Patrucco, A. S., Luzzini, D., & Ronchi, S. (2016). Evaluating the effectiveness of public procurement performance management systems in local governments. *Local Government Studies, 42*(5), 739–761. https://doi.org/10.1080/03003930.2016.1181059

Patrucco, A. S., Luzzini, D., Ronchi, S., Essig, M., Amann, M., & Glas, A. H. (2017). Designing a public procurement strategy: lessons from local governments. *Public Money & Management, 37*(4), 269–276. https://doi.org/10.1080/09540962.2017.1295727

Patrucco, A. S., Walker, H., Luzzini, D., & Ronchi, S. (2019). Which shape fits best? Designing the organizational form of local government procurement. *Journal of Purchasing and Supply Management, 25*(3), 100504.

Polanyi, M. (1966). *The Tacit Dimension.* Garden City, NY: Doubleday & Company, Inc.

Preuss, L. (2011). On the contribution of public procurement to entrepreneurship and small business policy. *Entrepreneurship & Regional Development, 23*(9–10), 787–814.

PROCEDIN. (2024). Building Procurement Capability for Embedding and Driving Innovation. Retrieved from https://procedin.eu

Rullan, S., Saucedo, E., & Bacaria, J. (2012). *Public procurement for innovation: Challenges and prospects for Latin America.* Paper presented at the 2012 International Symposium on Management of Technology (ISMOT).

Sánchez-Carreira, M. d. C., Peñate-Valentín, M. C., & Varela-Vázquez, P. (2019). Public procurement of innovation and regional development in peripheral areas. *Innovation: The European Journal of Social Science Research, 32*(1), 119–147.

Sawyer, R. K., & Henriksen, D. (2024). *Explaining Creativity: The Science of Human Innovation*: Oxford University Press.

Schiele, H., & Torn, I. A. R.-J. (2020). Cyber-physical systems with autonomous machine-to-machine communication: Industry 4.0 and its particular potential for purchasing and supply management. *International Journal of Procurement Management, 13*(4), 507–530. https://doi.org/10.1504/IJPM.2020.108617

Schulze, H., & Bals, L. (2020). Implementing sustainable purchasing and supply management (SPSM): a Delphi study on competences needed by purchasing and supply management (PSM) professionals. *Journal of Purchasing and Supply Management, 26*(4), 100625.

Smith, E. (2001). The role of tacit and explicit knowledge in the workplace. *Journal of Knowledge Management, 5*(4), 311–321.

Socha, D., Razmov, V., & Davis, E. (2003). Teaching reflective skills in an engineering course. *AGE, 8*, 2.

Spreitzenbarth, J. M., Bode, C., & Stuckenschmidt, H. (2024). Artificial intelligence and machine learning in purchasing and supply management: a mixed-methods review of the state-of-the-art in literature and practice. *Journal of Purchasing and Supply Management*, 100896. https://doi.org/10.1016/j.pursup.2023.100846

Stek, K. (2021). *Purchasing Skills Leading to Success: How to Succeed in Innovation Sourcing* (PhD). University of Twente, Enschede.

Stek, K. (2022a). Personality development in higher education in the era of Industry 4.0 – Comparing educational practices and philosophies in Industry 1.0 and Industry 4.0. In M. Olivas-Lujan & T. Bondarouk (Eds.), *Smart Industry – Better Management* (pp. 35–50). Bingley: Emerald Publishing.

Stek, K. (2022b). A soft skills experiment in an Industrial Engineering and Management academic course – A demonstration of how to develop soft skills. In A. Alves & N. van Hattum (Eds.), *Training Engineering Students for Modern Technological Advancement* (pp. 20–49). Hershey, PA: IGI Global.

Stek, K., Picaud-Bello, K., Koch, V., & Johnsen, T. (2025). Rethinking purchasing and supply management education for sustainability and innovation challenges: Crafting a future-ready competency-based curriculum design. *Journal of Purchasing and Supply Management, 31*, 100974. https://doi.org/10.1016/j.pursup.2024.100974

Stek, K., & Schiele, H. (2021). How to train supply managers –necessary and sufficient purchasing skills leading to success. *Journal of Purchasing and Supply Management, 27*, 100700. https://doi.org/10.1016/j.pursup.2021.100700

Stek, K., Zunk, B. M., Koch, V., & Schiele, H. (2022). Culture's consequences for purchasing: comparing purchasing job ad requirements from different European countries with cultural models. *International Journal of Procurement Management, 15*(3), 305–339.

Steward, M. D., Wu, Z., & Hartley, J. L. (2010). Exploring supply managers' intrapreneurial ability and relationship quality. *Journal of Business-to-Business Marketing, 17*(2), 127–148.

Tamer Cavusgil, S., Calantone, R. J., & Zhao, Y. (2003). Tacit knowledge transfer and firm innovation capability. *Journal of Business & Industrial Marketing, 18*(1), 6–21.

Telgen, J., Harland, C., & Knight, L. (2007). Public procurement in perspective. In L. Knight, C. Harland, J. Telgen, K. V. Thai, G. Callender, & K. McKen (Eds.), *Public Procurement: International Cases and Commentary* (pp. 16–24). New York: Routledge.

Thai, K. V. (Ed.) (2008). International public procurement: Concepts and practices. *International Handbook of Public Procurement* (pp. 2–22). New York: Routledge.

van der Wal, Z. (2020). The public servant of the future: An introduction. In Sullivan, H., Dickinson, H., Henderson, H. (Eds.), *The Palgrave Handbook of the Public Servant* (pp. 1–18). Cham: Palgrave Macmillan. https://doi.org/10.1007/978-3-030-29980-4_112

Von der Gracht, H., Giunipero, L. C., & Schueller, M. (2016). Future-proof procurement; now or never: The big procurement transformation. Retrieved from https://advisory.kpmg.us/articles/2017/future-proof-procurement.html

Von der Gracht, H., Huber-Straßer, A., Schueller, M., Müller, N., Lichtenau, P. E., & Zühlke, H. (2018). Rethinking the value chain. A study on AI, humanoids and robots – Artificial Intelligence: Possible business application and development scenarios to 2040. Retrieved from https://assets.kpmg/content/dam/kpmg/xx/pdf/2018/09/rethinking-the-value-chain.pdf

World Bank. (2020). Procurement for Development. Retrieved from www.worldbank.org/en/topic/procurement-for-development

Yeow, J., & Edler, J. (2012). Innovation procurement as projects. *Journal of Public Procurement, 12*(4), 472–504. https://doi.org/10.1108/JOPP-12-04-2012-B002

Yeow, J., & Edler, J. (2016). Connecting demand and supply: the role of intermediation in public procurement of innovation. *Research Policy, 45*(2), 414–426. https://doi.org/10.1016/j.respol.2015.10.010

# Subject Index

*Note*: Page numbers in **bold** refer to tables and those in *italics* refer to figures. Also, references to the page numbers followed by b refer to box.

# Author Index

*Note*: Endnotes are indicated by the page number followed by "n" and the note number e.g., 111n5 refers to note 5 on page 111.

For Product Safety Concerns and Information please contact our
EU representative GPSR@taylorandfrancis.com Taylor & Francis
Verlag GmbH, Kaufingerstraße 24, 80331 München, Germany